ENSIGN TO THE NATIONS

The Saints Enter Salt Lake Valley. *Painting by C.C.A. Christensen, used by permission of Brigham Young University art collection.*

Ensign to the Nations

A HISTORY OF THE CHURCH
FROM 1846 TO THE PRESENT

Russell R. Rich

Complete in One Volume
Illustrated

Brigham Young University Publications
Provo, Utah

Library of Congress Catalog Card Number: 72-91730
International Standard Book Number: 0-8425-1540-2 (cloth)
0-8425-0671-3 (paper)
Brigham Young University Publications, Provo, Utah 84602
Third printing 1976
Printed in the United States of America
76 5Mp 15560

And it shall come to pass in the last days, that the mountain of the Lord's house shall be established in the top of the mountains, and shall be exalted above the hills; and all nations shall flow unto it.

. . . For out of Zion shall go forth the law. . . .

(*Isaiah 2:3, 4.*)

And he will lift up an ensign to the nations from far, and will hiss unto them from the end of the earth: and, behold, they shall come with speed swiftly.

(*Isaiah 5:26.*)

And it shall come to pass in that day, that the Lord shall set his hand again the second time to recover the remnant of his people, which shall be left, from Assyria, and from Egypt, and from Pathros, and from Cush, and from Elain, and from Shivar, and from Hamath, and from the islands of the sea.

And he shall set up an ensign for the nations, and shall assemble the outcasts of Israel, and gather together the dispersed of Judah from the four corners of the earth.

(*Isaiah 11:11-12.*)

All ye inhabitants of the world, and dwellers on the earth, see ye, when he lifteth up an ensign on the mountains; when he bloweth a trumpet, hear ye.

(*Isaiah 18:3.*)

Contents

Illustrations

MAPS, LETTERS, AND CHARTS

Abbreviations

CHC B. H. Roberts, *A Comprehensive History of The Church of Jesus Christ of Latter-day Saints*

CR *Conference Reports of The Church of Jesus Christ of Latter-day Saints*

HC Joseph Smith, *History of The Church of Jesus Christ of Latter-day Saints*

HU Orson F. Whitney, *History of Utah*

JD *Journal of Discourses*

JH Journal History of The Church of Jesus Christ of Latter-day Saints

Note: Errors in original direct quotations are retained without the use of *sic*.

Acknowledgments

This book was prepared by assignment from the Department of Church History and Doctrine of the College of Religious Instruction at Brigham Young University as a text for a survey course in Church history.

Grateful acknowledgment is given to the secretaries and to my colleagues in the department for their many helpful suggestions; to my graduate students in Church History 543 for their criticisms; to the personnel of the Historical Department of the Church; to the Brigham Young University Library staff; to my wife, Margaret; to my daughter, Merilynne Rich Smith; and to the editors, Darold Marlowe and Mrs. Louise Hanson, for their careful editing.

I alone, however, am responsible for any errors that may have persisted in the manuscript.

Russell R. Rich

Introduction

Ensign to the Nations is a text prepared at the request of the College of Religious Instruction at Brigham Young University. The book does not purport to be an in-depth study of the history of the Church from 1846 to the present (1972), but it does deal with many of the vital experiences of the Saints as they attempted to establish The Church of Jesus Christ of Latter-day Saints in the "top of the mountains" to fulfill the commandment to "take the gospel to every nation, kindred, tongue, and people." Of course, such a wide range of history would in no way fit into one concise volume. And since the text is intended for use in a survey course in Latter-day Saint Church history, it must be reasonably comprehensive yet logically applicable to a student-oriented time element.

As the author, I recognize that to bring about the demands of the course and to gratify the earnest historian constitute impossible goals. Wherever necessary I have attempted to direct the reader to further sources of study. The scope of the text begins with the Saints preparing for their exit from Nauvoo, Illinois, during the fall and winter of 1845 and 1846. The death of our latest president, Joseph Fielding Smith, and the appointment of our newest, Harold B. Lee, bring the volume to its conclusion. Perhaps I might be permitted to make the following observations, hoping they will assist the reader in his appreciation of the history and purpose of The Church of Jesus Christ of Latter-day Saints.

The restoration of the gospel of Jesus Christ in the dispensation of the fulness of times was a struggle between the forces of good and the forces of evil. The people with whom the Lord had to work were not perfect, but neither were they expected to be, for the gospel of Jesus Christ is for the perfection of the Saints and if they had reached perfection, the guidance provided by the gospel plan would not have been needed. Some of them failed under pressure and did not "endure to the end." Nevertheless sufficient numbers were loyal, faithful, and righteous enough that with God's help, Christ's Church was restored and began to grow in preparation for his second coming.

Latter-day Saints have been faithful in carrying out certain responsibilities of the Church: to take Christ's message to the world and to seek out their dead so that those who live may hear the gospel, and those who have died without having heard it may have the earthly ordinances performed for them when, in the spirit world, they are ready to accept it. (1 Peter 3:18-20, 4:6.)

Much work is yet to be done. Members of the Church have a long way to go toward becoming perfect. Many people in the world still have not heard the gospel, and a great deal more genealogical information must be searched out in order that the Saints may continue providing the ordinances for the salvation of their dead. The three million members of the Church in the world are small in number compared with the more than three billion children of God who still need the plan of salvation as authorized by God and his son Jesus Christ. Nevertheless the Church has a solid foundation, and Lucifer can no longer make it appear "as a reed shaken with the wind" because of small digressions from righteousness on the part of a few of its members or because of persecution which may still come occasionally from the "outside."

The Church has a bright future and will continue to expand throughout the world in preparation for the second advent of Christ. Only the unrighteousness of the Saints could stop the expansion, but the Lord has decreed that his work will not be thwarted. Righteousness abounds within his fold sufficient to keep the plans of God moving forward, his realm continuing to grow so that the kingdom of Heaven may soon be ushered in with Christ's coming, though no man knows the day and the hour. (Matthew 24:36.)

ENSIGN
TO THE
NATIONS

1

A Driven People

LEAVING NAUVOO

Nauvoo, Illinois, was a busy place during the winter of 1845-46. There was approximately one blacksmith shop for every one hundred Latter-day Saint families in the area, and every shop was buzzing.

Companies were organized so that each one had cabinet-makers, wheelwrights, carpenters, and wagonmakers; and all were kept constantly at work. People were making tents and wagon covers out of anything.

> Green timber was prepared for spokes and felloes, some kiln-dried, and some boiled in salt and water. . . . Iron was brought from different parts of the country, and blacksmiths were at work night and day.[1]

Instead of using the large, heavy conestoga wagons generally known as prairie schooners, the Saints were building their own wagons to specifications that would more nearly fit their needs, except for some wagons that were purchased from Louis Epenschield. Also, the money saved from making their own would help to provide the supplies that every person was to have with him when he left. Parley P. Pratt had reckoned that a family of five persons should take the following:

1

1 good wagon, 3 yoke cattle, 2 cows, 2 beef cattle, 3 sheep, 1,000 lbs flour, 20 lbs sugar, 1 rifle and ammunition, a tent and tent-poles, from 10 to 20 lbs seed to a family, from 25 to 100 lbs tools for farming, and a few other items. . . . [2]

As early as Saturday, October 11, 1845, President Young announced that captains for twenty-five companies had been chosen. Each of these companies was to consist of one hundred families. The captains met from time to time to discuss the business of the migration. On Sunday, November 23, 1845, Brigham Young stated:

I met with the captains of the Emigrating Companies and gave them appropriate counsel.
Families organized, 3285.
Wagons on hand, 1508.
Wagons commenced, 1892. [3]

On January 18, 1846, Brigham Young recorded:

A meeting of the captains of Emigrating Companies was held in the attic story of the Temple, to ascertain the number ready and willing to start should necessity compel our instant removal, being aware that evil is intended towards us, and that our safety alone will depend upon our departure from this place, before our enemies shall intercept and prevent our going. [4]

Brigham Young's statement, "being aware of evil that is intended towards us," refers to rumors that were in circulation that the federal government intended to prevent the Mormons from going west. Governor Thomas Ford of Illinois was at least one of the parties who started such rumors. He stated it this way in his *History of Illinois*:

But with a view to hasten their removal they were made to believe that the President would order the regular army to Nauvoo as soon as the navigation opened in the spring. This had its intended effect; the twelve, with about two thousand of their followers, immediately crossed the Mississippi before the breaking up of the ice. [5]

At this meeting a committee was appointed to officially represent the Church as well as any individuals who might desire to dispose of property. This committee consisted of Almon W. Babbitt, Joseph L. Heywood, John S. Fullmer, Henry W. Miller, and John M. Bernhisel. They were to receive power of attorney so that they could legally act. They were also instructed to enclose the Nauvoo House and complete the first floor of the temple. The attic story of the temple had been the first story to be completed, as that was where the endowment work was being done.

On Monday, February 2, 1846, at 10:00 a.m., the Twelve Apostles, the trustees (Bishops Newel K. Whitney and George Miller), and a few others met to determine the feelings of those who were about to start westward. An agreement was reached that it was necessary to start as soon as possible. Brigham Young told the brethren to

> procure boats and hold them in readiness to convey our wagons and teams over the river, and let everything for the journey be in readiness, that when a family is called to go, everything necessary may be put into the wagon within four hours, at least, for if we are here many days, our way will be hedged up. Our enemies have resolved to intercept us whenever we start. I should like to push on as far as possible before they are aware of our movements.[6]

At 4:00 p.m. the same day Brigham Young met with the captains of hundreds and fifties to give them the same advice. They approved of it and dispersed to carry it out.

In the meantime the Nauvoo Temple continued to be used for endowment work, which had begun for the general membership of the Church on December 10, 1845. By February 7, 1846, at least 5,615 endowments had been given.[7] Apparently, Brigham Young did not want to administer the endowment in the temple on Tuesday, February 3. Instead, he wanted to go home to begin loading his wagons for the trek westward. He reminded the Saints gathered at the temple that they would build more temples and there would be further opportunities to perform temple ordinances. He left the temple but soon returned and found the crowd still gathered, hoping for their endowments. He recorded in his journal:

> Looking upon the multitude and knowing their anxiety, as they were thirsting and hungering for the word, we continued at work diligently in the House of the Lord.[8]

4   That day 295 ordinances were administered. Gustive O. Larson, in *Prelude to the Kingdom,* has described the Mormons as having "labored under two major obsessions during the fall and winter of 1846. The first was the completion of the Temple, the second, preparations for leaving it." [9]

X   On February 4, 1846, the first wagons (which belonged to Charles Shumway) pulled out of Nauvoo, crossing the Mississippi River on the ferries and landing on the Iowa side of the river, where they broke a trail westward that thousands of Saints would soon follow. They traveled nine miles to the banks of Sugar Creek, where they camped to await the arrival of Brigham Young and other Church leaders. [10]

On February 6, Bishop George Miller and his family crossed the Mississippi River with their six wagons. On February 8, John Smith (the Prophet's uncle and president of the Nauvoo Stake) and his family, along with his clerk, Albert Carrington, and his family crossed the river. On Monday, February 9, Elder George A. Smith (one of the Twelve Apostles and son of John Smith) sent his family on ahead across the river.

It was 3:00 p.m. on this same day that the fire on the roof of the temple was discovered. Brigham Young said:

> I saw the flames from a distance, but it was out of my power to get there in time to do any good towards putting out the fire, and I said if it is the will of the Lord that the Temple be burned, instead of being defiled by the Gentiles, Amen to it. [11]

President Young went to the temple as soon as he could; but by the time he arrived, the fire had already been extinguished, for Willard Richards had organized the people into a bucket brigade between the basement floor and the attic. The fire, lasting about one-half hour, burned a hole about sixteen feet long and ten feet wide up the northern slope of the roof.

At the same time that the temple was on fire, more people were attempting to cross the Mississippi River. There was at least one accident, however; some members in a flatboat had to go to the rescue of a man and two boys who were in a skiff behind them and were sinking because they were overloaded and inexperienced. Brigham Young said:

> As soon as they got the three on board the flatboat, a filthy wicked man squirted some tobacco juice into the

The ox bolted forward, dragging his teammate and the wagon
with him into the river. One of the sideboards of the flatboat
was torn off so that the water flowed in and the boat sank as
they approached the shore. Many of the men were rescued from
the water in an exhausted condition, and two oxen were
drowned. A few things floated out of the wagon and were lost,
and when the wagon was finally drawn out of the river, the rest
of its contents were damaged. This was an awful price to pay
for a mean trick, yet the saddest part was that the man who did
the "filthy" deed was not the one who suffered the loss.

For the most part, the river crossing

> was superintended by the [Nauvoo] police, under the
> direction of Hosea Stout. They gathered several flatboats,
> some old lighters, and a number of skiffs, forming alto-
> gether quite a fleet, and were at work night and day,
> crossing the saints.[13]

Apparently, from the beginning of the crossing of the
Mississippi the flatboats were busy every day until the Mississippi River froze over, which stopped the exodus from Nauvoo
for a few days until the ice became sufficiently solid for teams
pulling wagons to cross.

Brigham Young was loading his wagons all day on February
4, but he did not cross until February 15, which was also the
day when most of the rest of the Twelve Apostles crossed.
Parley P. Pratt had crossed on the evening of February 13.
From Brigham Young's history for February 15, 1846, we read:

> I crossed the river with my family accompanied by
> W. Richards and family and George A. Smith. We traveled on
> four miles, when we came to the bluff. I would not go on
> until I saw all the teams up. I helped them up the hill with
> my own hands. At dusk started on, and reached Sugar
> Creek about 8 p.m., having traveled nine miles. The roads
> were very bad.[14]

The weather became extremely cold. On February 25 Charles
C. Rich walked across the river on the ice near Montrose. For
the next number of days long caravans of covered wagons could

6

Crossing the River on Ice. *A painting by C. C. A. Christensen used by permission of Brigham Young University art collection.*

be seen crossing the river on a solid floor of ice. But soon the ice broke up, and there was a halt until the great blocks of ice that choked the passage were cleared away and the ferryboats began again to ply the river. The Mormon exodus from Illinois was well under way; it was to continue throughout the coming summer.

CAMP ON SUGAR CREEK *9 babies born first night.*

The banks of Sugar Creek were selected as the first temporary gathering place of the Saints on their westward journey. This rendezvous, about nine miles from Nauvoo, was far enough away so that the Saints would be definitely on their way, yet near enough so that they could easily cross the Mississippi River and continue the journey as far as Sugar Creek without having to make an overnight camp. Sugar Creek would also supply them with much-needed water so necessary for life of both man and beast.

This early exodus from Nauvoo had not come of the Saints' own free will but had instead been forced on them. They had hoped to be able to stay in Nauvoo until spring had come and grass was growing; but the rumors about the federal government's plans to interfere with their leaving, the constant stream

of warrants for the arrest of Church leaders, the pressures from
their enemies, and the fact that nearly all worthy adults had
already been able to receive their temple endowments caused
the leaders to start the westward trek early.

Advice had been given for every family to have eighteen
months of supplies on hand, but when loyal Church members
saw their leaders leaving, many of them did not wait until they
could comply with this requirement. Instead, they hurried on to
be with the heads of the Church.

Brigham Young went into more detail than did Parley P.
Pratt and listed the necessities to outfit five people for the
Rocky Mountain journey as

> One good strong wagon well covered with a light box;
> two or three good yoke of oxen between the age of four
> and ten years; two or more milch cows; one or more good
> beefs; three sheep if they can be obtained; one thousand
> pounds of flour or other bread stuffs in good sacks; one
> good musket or rifle to each male over the age of twelve
> years; one pound powder; four pounds lead; one pound
> tea; five pounds coffee; one hundred pounds sugar; one
> pound cayenne pepper; two pounds black pepper; one-half
> pound mustard; ten pounds rice for each family; one
> pound cinnamon; one-half pound cloves; one dozen nut-
> megs; twenty-five pounds salt; five pounds saleratus; ten
> pounds dried apples; one bushel of beans; a few pounds of
> dried beef or bacon; five pounds dried peaches; twenty
> pounds dried pumpkin; twenty-five pounds of seed grain;
> one gallon alcohol; twenty pounds of soap for each family;
> four or five fish hooks and lines; fifteen pounds of iron
> and steel; a few pounds of wrought nails; one or more sets
> of saw or grist mill irons to a company of one hundred
> families; one good seine and hook for each company; two
> sets of pulley blocks and ropes to each company for cross-
> ing rivers; from twenty-five to one hundred pounds of
> farming and mechanical tools; cooking utensils to consist
> of bake kettle, frying pan . . . plates, knives, forks, spoons
> and pans as [few] as will do; a good tent and furniture to
> each two families; clothing and bedding to each family,
> not to exceed five hundred pounds; ten extra teams for
> each company of one hundred families.[15]

Although the drop in temperature had added to the suffering
of the Saints, many of them felt that the freezing over of the

8   Mississippi River was the help of Divine Providence in hastening them away from their enemies. And with the river frozen solid for a time after February 25, people made haste to leave while it was unnecessary to await their turn for ferry service.

In fact, they hastened so fast that by the end of February about five thousand people had crossed the river on their way west, including eight hundred leaders of families who reported at Sugar Creek with not more than two weeks' provisions for themselves and their teams.[16] The lead camp had moved approximately only 150 miles from Nauvoo when the supplies of Brigham Young and the other apostles ran out because of their sharing with those in need. Yet we find only one statement from the leaders that might be termed a complaint, and this appears to be more of an explanation. It was made by Brigham Young to the camp at Garden Grove.

When the removal westward was in contemplation at Nauvoo, had the brethren submitted to our [the Twelve Apostles'] counsel, and brought their teams and means and authorized me to do with them as the Spirit and wisdom of the Lord directed, then we could have fitted out a company of men, who were not encumbered with large families, and sent them over the mountains to put in crops and build houses, and the residue could have gathered, beginning with the priesthood, and the gathering continued from year to year, building and planting at the same time. Were matters to be so conducted, none would be found crying for bread, or destitute of clothing; but all would be provided for as designed by the Almighty. But instead of taking this course the saints have crowded on us all the while, and have completely tied our hands by importuning and saying, 'Do not leave us behind. Wherever you go we want to go, and be with you'; and thus our hands and feet have been bound, which has caused our delay to the present time; and now hundreds at Nauvoo are continually praying and importuning with the Lord that they may overtake us, and be with us. And just so it is with the saints here. They are afraid to let us go on and leave them behind; forgetting that they have covenanted to help the poor away at the sacrifice of all their property.[17]

From this statement it is evident that Brigham Young and the leaders of the Church had wanted a more orderly exodus from

Nauvoo westward, which would have taken longer and would have been done with much less suffering, but the leaders also realized that it was because of the loyalty and faithfulness of the people that they were so anxious to be with the Apostles and were so willing to endure the hardships of pioneer life. Therefore when Brigham Young reproved the people, "it was never for their being there and in destitute circumstances."[18]

There was a great deal of suffering in Sugar Creek during the latter half of February as temperatures dropped and snow fell, but by March 1 the weather had moderated. As early as Wednesday, February 25, Bishop George Miller, with sixteen wagons and thirty or forty pioneers, left the Sugar Creek camp for the Des Moines River.[19] On this day at 7:00 p.m. the thermometer stood at 10° Fahrenheit. On Saturday, February 28, the thermometer was 20°F when the second company of pioneers left Sugar Creek.

Poor —

math. 25 - 35
Jacob 2 - 17 - 22
Mosiah 4 : 26
Alma 34 : 28 *Alma 8:*
Alma 9:

Petition to Governor James Clark

This same day Brigham Young met in council with the Twelve, where they approved a letter written to Governor James Clark of the Iowa Territory explaining why the Mormons were in Iowa, asking for protection while passing through the territory, and requesting his influence and power in behalf of any Latter-day Saints who might find it necessary to stop in settled or unsettled parts of Iowa for the purpose of raising crops to preserve them from suffering, starvation, and death.[20]

No reply to this letter was ever received by the Saints, but perhaps Governor Clark had a reason for not answering. The land within the territory of Iowa had been purchased by the United States from the confederated tribes of Sac and Fox Indians as a result of four successive treaties. The first of these was made at the conclusion of the Black Hawk War in 1832 and resulted in the Black Hawk Purchase. The second was in 1836 and resulted in the purchase of the Keokuk Reserve which lay along both sides of the Iowa River. The third purchase was made as the result of a treaty in Washington, D.C., in 1837. The fourth purchase was made in 1842, after Iowa had become a territory in 1838, and resulted in the United States' receiving title to approximately 15,000,000 acres.[21] In 1844 the citizens of Iowa made an attempt to become a state; but the boundaries specified in the proposed constitution did not meet the requirements, and the United States Congress refused her statehood. .

one child first Primary was organized by her —

X

The Poor Saints on the Banks of the Mississippi. *A painting by C. C. A. Christensen used by permission of Brigham Young University art collection.*

Nevertheless, feeling this could easily be corrected, the people met again and drew up a new constitution, which was completed May 18, 1846. This time it was satisfactory to the United States Congress, and Iowa was granted statehood to be effective on December 28, 1846. It appears that Governor James Clark, realizing that statehood was near, did not feel it would be appropriate to make a decision that would affect Iowa beyond the days of her territorial status, and yet he did not wish to deny the Saints the privilege of growing crops on the public domain during the summer of 1846; he therefore chose not to answer the Saints' request. They, having received no refusal to their request, proceeded to camp on public lands and to plant crops.

On February 28, 1846, Brigham Young recorded:

Our encampment on Sugar Creek has had a tendency to check the movements of the mob, as they were generally of the opinion that our outfit was so insufficient that in a short time we would break to pieces and scatter.

The great severity of the weather, and not being able to sell any of our property, the difficulty of crossing the river during many days of running ice, all combined to delay our departure, though for several days the bridge of ice

across the Mississippi greatly facilitated the crossing, and
compensated, in part for the delay caused by the running
ice. [22]

WESTWARD FROM SUGAR CREEK

About noon on March 1, 1846, wagons began to pull out
from the Sugar Creek camp; but Brigham Young's wagons did
not leave until almost an hour before sundown because he had
to wait for certain men and horses to return from Nauvoo
where he had sent them on errands.[23] They traveled about five
miles to where they found Brother Bent and his group at work
on a job. When they pitched their tents there for the night,
nearly five hundred wagons had arrived from Sugar Creek.
Orson Pratt recorded in his journal:

> After scraping away the snow we pitched our tents and,
> building large fires, we soon found ourselves as com-
> fortable as circumstances would permit; . . . and after
> bowing before our Great Creator and offering up praise
> and thanksgiving to him and imploring his protection, we
> resigned ourselves to the slumbers of the night.[24]

The next morning, March 2, the camp moved to the east
bank of the Des Moines River, which was four miles below the
Iowa village of Farmington. After camp was made and the day's
work done, several fires were made in the camp enclosure. Bon-
fires were lighted and the Saints spent the evening singing,
dancing, and enjoying the music of Captain William Pitt's brass
band which was traveling with the pioneer camp. A number of
people from Farmington came into the camp and seemed
astonished to see a homeless people making the most of a bad
situation by shedding their sorrows with song and dance.

On March 3 the Saints traveled only until 2:00 p.m., then
made camp. They had passed through Farmington and camped
about four miles beyond, having moved eight miles since
morning. Here they joined Bishop George Miller who, with his
encamped group, had cleared a field and fenced it. They and the
pioneer company had also secured some much-needed corn.[25]

Bancroft states:

> Without attempting long distances in a single day, they
> made camp rather early, and after the usual manner of
> emigrants, the wagons in a circle or semi-circle round the

camp-fire, placed so as best to shield them from the wind and wild beasts and Indians, with the animals at a convenient distance, some staked, and some running loose, but all carefully guarded. The country through which they passed was much of it well wooded; the land was fertile and afforded abundant pastures, the grass in summer being from one to ten feet high. Provisions were cheap: corn twelve cents and wheat twenty-five to thirty cents a bushel, beef two cents a pound, and all payable in labor at what was then considered good wages, say forty or fifty cents a day. [26]

After dark a council was held, and they decided to lay over the next day to make repairs. That evening the band played again.

On Wednesday, March 4, a number of people from Farmington came into camp and gave "a very pressing invitation for the band to go to Farmington and play some." They accepted and left camp about 3:00 p.m., arriving in Farmington at 4:30 p.m. They first played at the "principal hotel" and then went to the schoolhouse and played until "nearly dark," when they returned to the hotel and were provided with a good supper and were also given five dollars "in money." At 8:00 p.m. they started for camp; upon arriving, they found that thirty members of the guard were just starting out to meet them. William Clayton later wrote, "The President felt uneasy at our staying so long and was sending the men to protect us." [27] From this statement it is evident that the leaders of the Church were not sure how the people would receive them as they moved west. They were apparently not going to take any chance that the federal government or someone else might try to prevent them from leaving the United States, for they had a few hundred men in a well-organized guard that moved along with the camp.

While the camp was halted on March 4, Hosea Stout spoke to the members of the guard about a policy of finding work when the camp was stopped so that it would relieve the Church from the expense of supporting them when they were not traveling. [28]

On Thursday, March 5, the wagons moved on again. They reached the little town of Bonaparte, Iowa, about noon, where there was a very good flour mill on the banks of the Des Moines River. Upon leaving Bonaparte they found that the weather had moderated and the frost was leaving the ground. As a result

they encountered difficult roads, and it was late in the afternoon before they reached the next campground. Travel for the
day was a good twelve miles, which was their biggest day of
travel to date. They spent the next day, March 6, recuperating
and putting everything in good order again. On Saturday President Young moved forward about sixteen miles to a place called
Richardson's Point, which was between the Fox and the
Chequest Rivers. This put them fifty-five miles from Nauvoo;
during the first week of travel the lead wagons had averaged
nearly eight miles per day. Members of Captain Pitt's band
traveled only eight miles on March 7 and stopped "near to Dr.
Elbert's." They accepted employment splitting rails in exchange
for corn for their teams. By dark they had made 130 rails. [29]

Richardson's Point became the second rest camp (Sugar
Creek was the first). The Saints stayed here much longer than
they had intended because of the rain that began on Tuesday,
March 10, the day they had intended to begin moving on. While
camped at Richardson's Point the band accepted three different
invitations to play in the town of Keosauqua (a distance of 10
miles). They played on March 10, 11, and 17 and made twenty-
five, twenty, and seven dollars over and above expenses.
Attendance was small the third time because the priests persuaded most of the "sectarians" not to attend. [30]

The leaders decided to lighten the loads of the artillery by
burying the ball and shot in the ground and getting them some
other time. [31] It also appears that the leaders concluded the
danger of being detained by federal troops or attacked by mob
forces was no longer of great concern, and those members of
the guard who had families back in Nauvoo or along the way
could be released to return to them. [32] About thirty out of one
hundred eighty were honorably released for this purpose. Later,
seven men of the artillery under Captain Scott and nineteen
men of the "pioneers" under Captain Markham were similarly
released.

On Tuesday, March 17, the camp was ready to move on again
but was prevented from doing so by the death of Edwin Little,
a nephew of Brigham Young, who was said to have "died from
being over done on the road." [33]

On March 19, after a twelve-day stop, the teams took up the
line of march again. During the next four days of travel they
covered a distance of forty-five miles. At about noon on March
22 they arrived on the east bank of the Chariton River where they
found the crossing so steep they had to use ropes attached to

14 the backs of the wagons to slow them down going into the river
and use them on the front to help the teams pull the wagons up
the west bank when leaving the river. [34] Wagons were crossing
all afternoon.

While they were crossing the river, Henry B. Jacobs' wife,
Zina D. Huntington Jacobs, gave birth to a baby boy and "no
harm happened to her not withstanding the inclement
weather." [35] Mrs. Jacobs named her son Chariton in honor of
the occasion.

Reorganization of Leadership

The Saints were about one hundred miles from Nauvoo,
when they decided to stop for a few days in order to purchase
corn for the horses and to properly organize the company.
Although twenty-five captains of one hundred had been appointed in Nauvoo, the members of each hundred had usually
found it impossible to leave together, thereby making it impossible for most captains to preside over their groups. As a
result, up to this point the various wagons on the road had not
been traveling according to the organized plan for the whole
group. Word had been sent to the leaders of the various groups
to meet and organize. The companies of Charles C. Rich,
Charles Shumway, and John Taylor (who had crossed the
Chariton River ahead of Brigham Young's group and the guard)
were waiting; but Bishop George Miller had taken his camp
farther on. On March 23 Brigham Young had William Clayton
write a letter to Bishop Miller telling him that if he did not
return to organize, the camp would be organized without them
and they would be disfellowshipped.[36] They came back on
horseback on March 26; on March 27 they proceeded to
organize at a point on Shoal Creek which was between Bishop
Miller's camp and Brigham Young's camp. Again their organization was divided into families of hundreds, fifties, and tens,
with a captain over each segment. Brigham Young was general
superintendent of the whole camp with William Clayton as
general clerk. The guard and pioneers were distributed equally
among the different fifties. [37]

The leaders also gave the following orders to be observed by
the whole camp:

No man to set fire to prairies. No man to shoot off a
gun in camp without orders. No man to go hunting unless

he is sent and all to keep guns, swords and pistols out of
sight.[38]

One important reason for organizing was to avoid having so many people out buying corn, bidding against one another, and thereby pushing the price of corn from fifteen cents per bushel up to twenty and twenty-five cents and even higher.

It was decided to send a company of men to the Platte country to take jobs and also to store grain for the camp while it was moving west. Other jobs were to be taken when they could be obtained.[39]

The Chariton camp became the third temporary camping place to be established. The pioneer group remained here from March 22 until April 1. The inclement weather had much to do with their long stay. Only the first fifty and the band moved forward on April 1, and they occasionally found the road still soft and muddy. By April 3 the lead wagon arrived at Locust Creek in a downpour of rain. A fourth temporary camp was established here, perhaps more because of the weather than for any other reason, for April 4, 5, and 6 were very rainy days, making it impossible to move forward. Brigham Young's wagons arrived at Locust Creek on April 6. Many of the camps still to the east of Locust Creek tried to move forward on April 9; however, wagons became stuck all along the trail. Most of three days were needed to go back and help those who were stuck. John Taylor's fifty managed to move across Locust Creek on April 9 to a point about one and one-half miles west.

On April 12 a council was held at Heber C. Kimball's camp, which was still three miles east of Locust Creek. This council was attended by Brigham Young, the other members of the Twelve, Bishops Whitney and Miller, Charles C. Rich, William Clayton, Captain Howard Egan, and about thirty other brethren. Hosea Stout, head of the police who were also the camp guards, was too sick to attend.

Brigham Young told them he was satisfied they were taking a course that would lead to the salvation of the Saints. He did not believe there had been a people since the days of Enoch, placed under such undesirable circumstances, who had done so little grumbling. He felt the Lord was pleased with the majority of the camp. Nevertheless there had been some stealing and some passing of counterfeit money. Some tried to justify stealing from enemies because they had stolen from the Saints. He said "such a course tends to destroy the kingdom of God."

16　　　He proposed fencing in a field two miles square on the Grand River where they could plant crops and build cabins and recommended that those who were coming behind could stop there for the winter and come on another year. He also suggested sending men ahead to find a good location on the river and proposed that he, Heber C. Kimball, other members of the Twelve present, and a number of other men should proceed directly to Council Bluffs, Iowa, on the banks of the Missouri River.[40]

"Come, Come, Ye Saints"

After they left Locust Creek the traveling was again slow and tedious because of the wet weather. The next two or three days saw only about six miles of travel covered by most of the wagons. On Wednesday, April 15, Heber C. Kimball's wife Ellen walked over to William Clayton's wagon to congratulate him, telling him that news had arrived that his wife Diantha, who was still back in Nauvoo, had given birth to a son on March 30, but she was very sick with the ague and mumps. Although Clayton felt uneasy about his wife's illness, he was happy to know that the child had arrived in safety and that, although the mother was ill with other sickness, she had survived the childbirth. In honor of the occasion he composed a new song which he called "All Is Well," known today as "Come, Come, Ye Saints." In the evening he invited a few friends, most of whom were members of the band, into his tent to have "a social christening," naming his new son William Adriel Benoni Clayton.[41]

CAMP AT GARDEN GROVE

The advance companies, headed by Colonel Stephen Markham and his one hundred pioneers—whose duty it had been from the beginning to travel in advance of the companies for the purpose of building and repairing roads, making bridges, picking out campsites, and establishing temporary places of shelter—arrived on April 19 at a place on the east fork of the Grand River, approximately 145 miles from Nauvoo. Within two more days there were 359 laboring men, in addition to those guarding the stock, who had reported in the camp. This was the spot chosen as a more permanent camping place where crops could be planted and a number of people who were not prepared to move on could stop until they were better prepared to do so. Also, the Saints still back in Nauvoo or on the road who were too poor to properly equip themselves could be encouraged to move this far to the west where they would be out of the hands of the enemy and could stop long enough to acquire the necessary goods to move on to the new permanent home of the Saints.

The soil was rich and the timber was plentiful. The Saints named their settlement Garden Grove.[42] The 359 laboring men were divided into groups: 100 were selected to cut trees and make rails under the direction of Charles C. Rich, Stephen Markham, L. C. Wilson, and James Pace; 10 were to build fences under the direction of James Allred; 49 were to build houses under the direction of father John Smith, the Prophet's uncle; 12 were to dig wells supervised by Jacob Peart; 10 were to build bridges under A. P. Rockwood; 180 under Daniel Spencer were to clear land, plow, and plant.[43]

John R. Young recorded in his memoirs:

> All were thus employed, and the camp became presently like a hive of bees. There being no room for idlers, all seemed happy. . . . Samuel Bent, Aaron Johnson, and David Fullmer were chosen to preside over those that should remain. They were instructed to divide the lands among the poor without charge; but to give to no man more than he could thoroughly cultivate. There must be no waste and no speculation. Moreover, the settlement was not regarded as more than temporary; for as soon as our leaders should find the "place," all energies were to be centered in gathering to that place. As yet, however, no one, not even Brigham Young, knew where the "place" would be; but it was talked at the campfires that President Young had seen, in vision, a wonderful valley, so large that all our people could be gathered into it, and yet so far from civilization, that mobs could not come at night to burn and whip and kidnap. Strange as it may seem, this vision formed the most entrancing theme of our conversations, and the national song of Switzerland became our favorite hymn: "For the strength of the hills we bless thee, Our God, our fathers' God."[44]

Seven hundred and fifteen acres of grain and other crops were eventually planted at Garden Grove. They were enclosed by a neat rail fence. "Log houses were built along hastily laid out streets in orderly fashion."[45]

Present-day marker at Garden Grove, Iowa.

CAMP AT MOUNT PISGAH

On May 13, Brigham Young and the pioneers moved on, having sent Parley P. Pratt with a few men in advance to choose another location for a semipermanent camp. They found a beautiful area about twenty-seven miles west and a little north of Garden Grove. Parley P. Pratt stated:

> ... I came suddenly to some round and sloping hills, grassy and crowned with beautiful groves of timber; while alternate open groves and forests seemed blended in all the beauty and harmony of an English park. While beneath and beyond, on the west, rolled a main branch of [the] Grand River, with its rich bottoms of alternate forest and prairie. As I approached this lovely scenery several deer and wolves, being startled at the sight of me, abandoned the place and bounded away till lost from my sight amid the groves.
>
> Being pleased and excited at the varied beauty before me, I cried out, "this is *Mount Pisgah*." [46]

It was on the middle fork of the Grand River and was reached by President Young and a number of the Apostles on

Monument to those who died at Mt. Pisgah. *Courtesy of LaMar C. Berrett.*

Mt. Pisgah. *Courtesy of Church Historical Department.*

May 18, being 172 miles from Nauvoo.[47] It was on the land of the Potawatomie Indians. Again, similar to the procedure at Garden Grove, the laboring force was divided up, streets were laid out, houses were built, rails were split, fences were built, and several thousand acres of farmland were enclosed by a fence. Most of it was planted into grain. William Huntington was made president of the settlement with Ezra T. Benson and Charles C. Rich as counselors.

While here, Elder Noah Rogers—he had returned from a three-year mission to the Society Islands just before the Saints left Nauvoo—who was a captain of ten in the guard under Hosea Stout, was the first to die at Mt. Pisgah, Iowa.

CAMP ON THE MISSOURI RIVER

As others poured into Mt. Pisgah, Brigham Young and the pioneers left on June 2 for the Missouri River on the western border of Iowa. Brigham Young, Heber C. Kimball, Parley P. Pratt, and Bishop George Miller arrived at Council Bluffs on the east bank of the river on June 14, having made the distance of about 125 miles in twelve days, which was a far greater average than was obtained for the earlier part of the journey across Iowa. Brigham Young and a few other apostles had crossed the Mississippi River from February 13 to 15, 1846; the lead

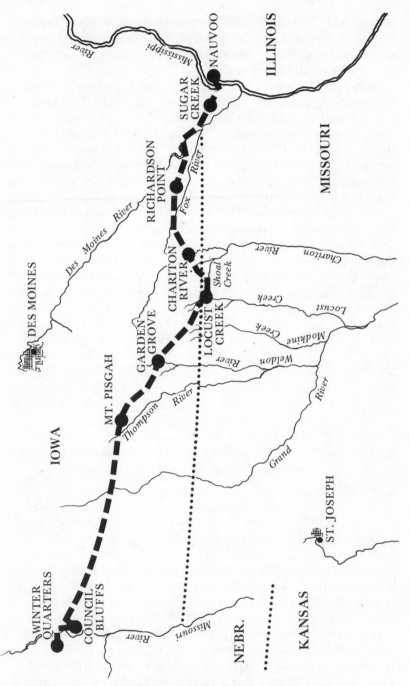

Fig. 1. The trek across Iowa. *Courtesy of LaMar C. Berrett.*

wagons had taken a full four months to cross the Iowa Territory and reach the banks of the Missouri River, a distance of approximately 300 miles in about 120 days, making an average of two and one-half miles per day.

Although the season was late for planting, preparations began for enclosing land. By Monday, June 22, about five hundred wagons had arrived on the Missouri River, and nine of the Apostles were there—Brigham Young, Heber C. Kimball, Orson Hyde, Parley P. Pratt, Orson Pratt, John Taylor, George A. Smith, Willard Richards, and Amasa Lyman.[48] Wilford Woodruff was at Mt. Pisgah and John E. Page had not come west. Page was officially excommunicated from the Church five days later on Saturday, June 27, on grounds of apostasy. On July 16 Ezra T. Benson was ordained in his place.

Plans still called for a vanguard of men to push forward to the Great Basin beyond the Rocky Mountains where they could establish a settlement and, if possible, plant fall wheat.[49] On June 21 Hosea Stout was still perhaps fifty or sixty miles east of Council Bluffs and traveling west when he met Thomas Williams, who was on his way from Council Bluffs to Mt. Pisgah with a message to General Rich to raise men to send over the mountains. Plans for the vanguard called for four hundred men, a number deemed sufficient for protection against the depredations of the Indians. They could not raise the requisite number at the Bluffs because a sufficient number had not arrived there; hence the message requesting people from Mt. Pisgah.

Nine days later, on June 30, Hosea Stout was camped on the bank of the Nishnabotna River helping to build a bridge over it when other messengers from Council Bluffs came by. Stout recorded:

This morning Elder Parley P. Pratt came here accompanied by Solomon Hancock on their way to Pisgah to try and forward the expedition to the Mountains and instructed us to push on with all possible speed that if we did not get to the Bluffs by the time that he returned it would be needful for us to go on and leave our families such was the necessity to push forward this expedition. The reason of which we could not imagine. Neither did he as the sequel will soon prove.

As Elders Pratt & Hancock came here this morning they came to creek about one mile the other side of the Indian village the bridge of which was also gone & our hand[s]

Entrance to Kanesville, 1846. From *Route from Liverpool to Salt Lake City* by Fred Piercy, 1855.

now building it as well as this one. In an attempt to cross it by swimming his mule Br Pratt & the mule came very near being drownd. He floted to shore and was so much exhausted that he could not get out. After resting awhile he attempted it again and came near being drowned the second time. I believe he was finally assisted over by some indian boys, not however untill they were satisfied that they were "Good Mormonee" as they call us. He left Br Hancock & went on but he came on and followed as soon as he could. Br Pratt was in such a hurry that he could not wait an hour or so for Br Hancock such was the emergency of his mission.[50]

But these plans to send four hundred men to the mountains were soon canceled because of the call of the Mormon Battalion.

Parley P. Pratt stated in his autobiography:

The lateness of the season, the poverty of the people, and, above all, the taking away of five hundred of our best men, finally compelled us to abandon any further progress westward till the return of another spring. The camps, therefore, began to prepare for winter.[51]

[1]Hubert Howe Bancroft, *History of Utah* (1890; reprint ed., Salt Lake City: Bookcraft, 1964), p. 214.

[2]Bancroft, p. 214, footnote.

[3]Joseph Smith, *History of the Church of Jesus Christ of Latter-day Saints*, ed. B. H. Roberts, 7 vols. (Salt Lake City: Deseret News Press, 1964), 7:532. Hereafter cited as *HC.*

[4]*HC*, 7:569.

[5]Thomas Ford, *A History of Illinois* (Chicago: S. C. Griggs and Co., 1854), p. 413.

[6]*HC*, 7:578.

[7]*HC*, 7:542-81, passim. The endowment is a sacred ordinance, performed in a house of the Lord, wherein certain blessings are bestowed upon the individual, who in return makes certain promises of obedience to righteous living.

[8]*HC*. 7:579.

[9]Gustive O. Larson, *Prelude to the Kingdom* (Francestown, N. H.: Marshall Jones Co., 1947), p. 58.

[10]Journal History of The Church of Jesus Christ of Latter-day Saints, 4 February 1846, located in the Church Historical Department; hereafter referred to as JH. *See also* Andrew Jenson, *Latter-day Saint Biographical Encyclopedia*, 4 vols. (Salt Lake City: Deseret News Press, 1936), 4:718.

[11]*HC*, 7:581.

[12]*HC*, 7:582.

[13]*HC*, 7:582. The Nauvoo police, consisting of approximately one hundred men under the direction of Colonel Hosea Stout, were given the responsibility of not only keeping law and order during the westward trek in 1846 but of being the Saints' first line of protection. They were reinforced by the military where necessary as part of the guard.

[14]*HC*, 7:585.

[15]Carter E. Grant, *The Kingdom of God Restored* (Salt Lake City: Deseret Book Co., 1960), pp. 339, 341. *See also* B. H. Roberts, *A Comprehensive History of the Church of Jesus Christ of Latter-day Saints*, 6 vols. (Salt Lake City: Deseret News Press, 1930), 2:539. Hereafter cited as *CHC.*

[16]*CHC*, 3:41.

[17]*CHC*, 3:58-59.

[18]*CHC*, 3:41.

[19]*HC*, 7:598.

[20]*HC*, 7:601. See Appendix 1 for full text of the letter.

[21]John B. Newhall, *A Glimpse of Iowa in 1846* (1846; reprint ed., Iowa City: State Historical Society of Iowa, 1957), pp. 11-12.

[22]William E. Berrett and Alma P. Burton, *Readings in L.D.S. Church History*, 3 vols. (Salt Lake City: Deseret Book Co., 1955), 2:140.

[23]Juanita Brooks, ed., *On the Mormon Frontier: The Diary of Hosea Stout*, 2 vols. (Salt Lake City: University of Utah Press, 1964), 1:128.

[24]*CHC*, 3:46.

[25]Brooks, 1:130.

[26]Bancroft, pp. 220-21.

[27]William Clayton, *William Clayton's Journal* (Salt Lake City: Deseret

News, 1921), p. 3.

[28] Brooks, 1:130.

[29] Clayton, p. 4.

[30] Clayton, p. 7.

[31] Brooks, 1:136.

[32] Brooks, 1:138.

[33] Brooks, 1:139.

[34] Clayton, p. 8. *See also* Brooks, 1:141.

[35] Brooks, 1:141.

[36] Clayton, p. 9.

[37] Brooks, 1:145.

[38] Clayton, p. 10.

[39] Brooks, 1:143.

[40] *HC*, 7:608.

[41] Clayton, p. 19.

[42] Called a permanent camping place because the Saints built houses and planted crops here.

[43] John R. Young, *Memoirs of John R. Young, Utah Pioneer, 1847* (Salt Lake City: Deseret News Press, 1920), p. 19.

[44] Young, p. 19. The leaders of the Church had fairly well settled on the Great Basin long before this time, but nevertheless their minds were still flexible, and if they could find a more suitable location in the meantime, they were amenable to a change.

[45] William E. Berrett, *The Restored Church* (Salt Lake City: Deseret News Press, 1965), p. 223.

[46] Parley P. Pratt, *Autobiography of Parley Parker Pratt* (Salt Lake City: Deseret Book Co., 1964), p. 342.

[47] Andrew Jenson, *Church Chronology* (Salt Lake City: Deseret News Press, 1914), p. 29.

[48] Jenson, *Church Chronology*, p. 30.

[49] Brooks, 1:69.

[50] Brooks, 1:172-73.

[51] Pratt, p. 344.

2

Sailing of the Brooklyn

PREPARATIONS TO SAIL TO CALIFORNIA

While the people in Nauvoo were making plans to leave, Samuel Brannan in New York was commissioned to charter a ship and take a load of Saints with farming tools, a printing press, and some other useful items around Cape Horn to California. At this time Orson Pratt, of the Council of the Twelve Apostles, was in the East. Hearing that the Saints would be leaving Nauvoo in the spring of 1846—as early as "grass would grow or water run"—Elder Pratt, on November 8, 1845, issued a message to the members in the eastern and middle states urging every member of the Church to go west—"flee out of Babylon"—either by land or by sea. He announced that Samuel Brannan was appointed to take charge of the company that would go by sea.[1]

On November 12, four days after Orson Pratt's message had been given at a conference in New York over which he had presided, further plans were revealed for this exodus to the West by sea. Samuel Brannan presented his credentials to the conference and requested the names of all those who desired to go with him.

By December 29 Elder Brannan announced through the *New York Messenger*[2] that he had chartered the *Brooklyn,* a ship of 450 tons, for $1,200 per month. Port charges were to be paid

27

by the lessee. Sailing was planned for January 24, 1846. Cost of passage was $50 per adult person, with an additional cost of $25 for provisions. Children between the ages of six and fourteen were to go for half fare, while those five years old and under were given free passage.

Soon there were 300 applications for the journey; of these, 238 people finally sailed. As nearly as can be ascertained, there were 70 men, 68 women and 100 children on board.

A. G. Benson and Co. Intrigue

The day of sailing seems to have been set several times before the ship finally embarked. The biggest interference with the sailing was due to Brannan's dealings with a group of men from Washington, D.C., who were known to him as A. G. Benson and Co. This is an interesting story of intrigue that goes back to the first rumors that the United States government would intervene if the Saints tried to leave the United States. Such news first came to the attention of the Church leaders in a letter from Governor Thomas Ford to Sheriff Backenstos of Illinois dated December 29, 1845, in which he said:

> I also think that it is very likely that the government at Washington will interfere to prevent the Mormons from going west of the Rocky Mountains. Many intelligent persons sincerely believe that they will join the British if they go there, and be more trouble than ever, and I think that this consideration is likely to influence the government.[3]

Robert Bruce Flanders explains that the implication that the government in Washington would interfere was "without basis in fact, but was intended as a spur to the Mormon removal. In this it succeeded."[4]

The idea of preventing the Mormons from going west because they might become enemies of the country was later discussed by some of the newspapers in the country including the *New York Sun* and the *Washington* (D.C.) *Union*.[5] Whether Samuel Brannan was secretly a partner in the resulting scheme will perhaps never be known, but through Amos Kendall, a former United States postmaster general, a contract was drawn up between A. G. Benson and Co. and the Latter-day Saints in which they were to promise to give to Benson and Co. "the odd numbers of all the lands and town lots they may acquire in the country where they may settle" in return for the influence of A. G. Benson and Co. in persuading the federal government not to interfere with the Saints' going west.[6]

The contract had been signed in the presence of Elder W. I. Appleby by A. G. Benson, representing A. G. Benson and Co. (the company included Amos Kendall and approximately twenty-five other influential and prominent men who claimed that even President Polk was a "silent partner"), and Samuel Brannan representing the Latter-day Saints until it could be approved by Brigham Young and the rest of the Twelve Apostles to whom it was mailed. They received it, along with a letter from Samuel Brannan which was dated at New York, January 26, 1846, while they were on the banks of Sugar Creek in Iowa.

A council was called to consider the matter. Those present were: Brigham Young, Heber C. Kimball, Orson Hyde, Orson Pratt, John Taylor, George A. Smith, and Willard Richards.[7] The contract was read and, as summarized by Brigham Young, the brethren

> concluded that as our trust was in God and that we looked to him for protection, we would not sign any such unjust and oppressive agreement.
>
> This was a plan of political demagogues to rob the Latter-day Saints of millions and compel them to submit to it, by threats of federal bayonets.[8]

They ignored the matter and did not send an answer to Brannan. The historian Bancroft states:

> Brigham Young and his council declined to approve the contract, and no very serious result to the Mormons ensued; but the war with Mexico may have interfered with the plans of the speculators, of which nothing more is known.[9]

VOYAGE OF THE *BROOKLYN*

The *Brooklyn* finally set sail on February 4, 1846, which was the same day the first wagons pulled out of Nauvoo for the westward trek. This was only a happenstance; no such plans had been made to begin the westward movement "by land and by sea" on the same day.

30   The ship *Brooklyn* was not fast but was apparently strong. Opinions differ as to whether she was an old ship or a new one,[10] but all writers seem to feel that she was a sturdy vessel. She encountered two severe storms, the first one in the Atlantic and the second in the Pacific. Two babies were born on the trip, and each was named after the ocean upon which it was born.

Altogether there were ten deaths during the voyage, four adults and six children.[11] Most of the deaths were due to scurvy caused by lack of proper vegetables and fruit in the diet.

After rounding Cape Horn the ship began to sail north with a number of passengers sick with scurvy. Captain Richardson was heading north in the Pacific for Valparaiso on the west coast of South America, where he intended to put into port in order to take on fresh water and purchase the proper foods to cure and prevent scurvy, when the second major storm arose. The ship was driven nearly five hundred miles to the west where it lay near the island of Juan Fernandez (the island upon which Alexander Selkirk [Robinson Crusoe] lived from 1704 to 1709). It was fifteen miles long and four miles wide. They went ashore on the island on May 4, 1846, just three months from the day they had set sail. Here they were permitted to load up with thousands of gallons of fresh water and all of the different fruits and vegetables the island had to offer; all was free of charge, graciously given to them by the two families who were living there. These supplies would have been very expensive at Valparaiso.[12]

The second day on the island they buried Mrs. Isaac Goodwin who had died of scurvy shortly before the ship arrived at the island. Those who were suffering with scurvy showed rapid improvement with the fresh food of Juan Fernandez.

After five days of exploring the island, eating good food, and loading the ship, the passengers went aboard and set sail for the Hawaiian Islands (then the Sandwich Islands), where they arrived at Honolulu on June 20. Here they unloaded freight they had taken on before leaving New York. They also met Commodore Stockton, who was about to set sail for Monterey, California. He informed the Saints of the likelihood that California would soon be taken over by the United States. He left in their minds the possibility that they might have to help fight against Mexico upon their arrival. At his suggestion they purchased a number of arms in Honolulu and during the remainder of the voyage spent many hours in military drill.[13] After ten days in Hawaii, the *Brooklyn* set sail for the west

The U.S.S. *Brooklyn*

coast of America, leaving the Orrin Smith family behind because of illness, and possibly Mrs. Mercy Narrimore and son, whose husband and father Edwin Narrimore had died at sea.[14]

Accounts differ as to the date of the arrival of the *Brooklyn* in Yerba Buena Harbor (San Francisco Bay); some claim arrival on July 29, 1846, while others claim July 31, 1846. If the last date is correct, it had taken them five months and twenty-seven days to make the journey from New York.

ARRIVAL OF THE *BROOKLYN*

When the ship first pulled into the bay, fog shrouded everything; but as it drew nearer to shore and the fog shifted somewhat, the passengers saw the Stars and Stripes waving in the breeze, and the story is that Brannan said, "There is that damned flag again."[15] It is possible that this is true, as Brannan was anxious to be the first man to raise the American flag on California soil. In fact he was anxious that the Mormons be the first United States citizens in California so that other citizens could not consider the Mormons interlopers and attempt to drive them out. Nevertheless, it was to their advantage that they were on United States soil, as they did not have to pay a heavy import duty on their large shipment of machinery, which included a printing press and sufficient agricultural machinery "for eight hundred men," consisting of plows, hoes, forks, shovels, spades, plow irons, scythes, sickles, nails, glass, blacksmith, carpenter, and millwright tools, materials for three grain mills, turning lathes, and sawmill irons. There were also dry goods, twine, brass, copper, iron, tin and crockery ware, two new milk cows, about forty pigs, and a number of fowls.[16] They also had brought with them slates and a large quantity of school books, among which were spelling books, histories, books on arithmetic, astronomy, grammar, geography, Hebrew grammar, and 179 volumes of Harpers' *Family Library*.[17]

As Brannan and company still owed about one thousand dollars upon arrival, the captain agreed to take pay in lumber. Many of the men went logging in order to pay the debt.

Samuel Brannan had high hopes that the Saints with Brigham Young would come to California. He established a colony about eighty miles northeast of San Francisco on the north bank of the Stanislaus River and about one and a half miles from the San Joaquin River in the San Joaquin Valley. This settlement was named New Hope.

On April 4, 1847, Sam Brannan took two men with him, followed the California trail across the rugged Sierra Nevada, braved the desert and Indians, and met Brigham Young and the pioneer company on the banks of the Green River in present-day Wyoming about July 2, 1847, after having traveled eight hundred miles. When he was unable to persuade Brigham Young to take the Saints to California, he became a disappointed man. He went into the Salt Lake valley with them; and then in August of 1847, in company with Captain James Brown and a few other men from the sick detachment of the Mormon Battalion, who went to California to collect the back pay for the men, he returned to San Francisco.

Brannan's Subsequent Years

Sam Brannan showed his disappointment by shirking his Church obligations (except that of his leadership as branch president until forced to do so) and spending his time becoming California's most wealthy man and first millionaire. He became famous as a merchant, as the man who advertised the discovery of gold in California thereby starting the Gold Rush, as the man who published the first Anglo-Saxon newspaper in California, and is given credit by some people as the man who brought law and order to San Francisco.

At one time when the missionaries were in California trying to raise funds to go to the Sandwich Islands (Hawaii)—it was in 1852 when Sam was wealthy—he refused to give them anything. Parley P. Pratt prophesied that he would live to see the day when he would want for money enough to buy a loaf of bread.[18] When Sam heard this he laughed, but it nevertheless happened. In his later years he actually sold pencils from door to door and on the street in Nogales, Arizona, to get a little money.[19]

Footnotes

[1]*CHC*, 3:25. *See also Millennial Star*, 7:35-36.

[2]The *New York Messenger* was a paper that was being published by Parley P. Pratt. It had replaced the *Prophet*, which had formerly been published in New York for the Church by Samuel Brannan. *See CHC*, 3:27.

[3]*CHC*, 2:534.

[4]Robert   Bruce   Flanders,   *Nauvoo: Kingdom   on   the   Mississippi* (Urbana: University of Illinois Press, 1965), pp. 336-37.

[5]*CHC*, 2:535.

[6]Hubert Howe Bancroft, *History of California*, 7 vols. (San Francisco: History Co., Publishers, 1886), 5:547. A list of passengers is in the footnote of that volume on pages 546-47. Appendix 2 in this present volume gives the contract in full together with Brannan's letter that accompanied the contract.

[7]*HC*, 7:586.

[8]*HC*, 7:591.

[9]Bancroft, 5:548.

[10]*CHC*, 3:28,36, footnote 1.

[11]Those who died were Isaac Aldrich, Elias Ensign, Eliza Ensign, (sister of Elias), Mrs. Isaac Goodwin, Edwin Narrimore, a child of Jerusha Fowler, a child of Mr. and Mrs. Joseph Nichols, two children of Mr. and Mrs. John R. Robbins, and a child of Mr. and Mrs. George K. Winner.

[12]Bancroft, 5:549.

[13]Bancroft, 5:549-50.

[14]Bancroft, 5:549, footnote 39.

[15]Bancroft, 5:550.

[16]*CHC*, 3:27.

[17]*CHC*, 3:27-28.

[18]Reva Scott, *Samuel Brannan and the Golden Fleece* (New York: Macmillan Co., 1944), p. 316. *See also* Paul Bailey, *Sam Brannan and the California Mormons* (Los Angeles: Westernlore Press, 1959), p. 192.

[19]Bailey, p. 238. *See also* Scott, p. 438.

3

Mob Pressure at Nauvoo

THE MOB VERSUS AUTHORITY OF THE STATE

In the fall of 1845 the leaders of the Saints had concluded they would have to leave Nauvoo. They reached this decision because of the relentless pressure of the mob forces against them. The Quincy Committee had inquired of the Saints as to whether they were willing to leave. They had answered on September 24, 1845, that they were willing to leave; but they asked that the people in Hancock and surrounding counties use their influence to help them sell their properties at a fair market value so they could get the necessary means to take the widowed and fatherless with them, that the people would not file vexatious law suits against them (for they had broken no law), and that the people would assist them in getting the necessary items and animals to accomplish their removal without suffering to an extent beyond "the endurance of human nature."

The Saints said they would use all lawful means to preserve the public peace and would expect to have no house burnings or other depredations to waste their property while preparing to leave. They also said that it was a mistaken idea that they could leave within six months as that would be too early for water to run or for grass to grow, but that after gathering their present crops they intended to have no more seed time and harvest among their people.

36   The Quincy Committee presented the proposition of the Saints to the people of Quincy, who replied that they would accept it as an unconditional proposition to remove, but they would in no wise obligate themselves to help the Mormons.[1]

Josiah B. Conyers, author of *A Brief History of the Leading Causes of the Hancock Mob, in the Year 1846,* wrote:

> They accepted and recommended to the people of the surrounding counties, to accept an unconditional proposition to remove. But understand, Mr. Mormons', though we accept this, and recommend the surrounding counties to do so, likewise, (reprobate you, unconditionally), we do not intend to bring ourselves under any obligations to purchase your property, or to furnish purchasers; but we will be *very kind* and *obliging,* and will, in no way, hinder or obstruct **you in your efforts to sell,** *Provided,* nevertheless, this shall not be so construed, as to prevent us from running off the purchasers. But we expect this small favor of you, viz: that you must dispose of your property, and leave at the appointed time.[2]

As we have seen, the Saints spent the winter in feverish preparation for an early departure in the spring; and when their wagons began to roll out of Nauvoo in early February of 1846,

> ... the non-Mormons were surprised to learn that the Mormons at Nauvoo had begun crossing the river as a beginning of their departure for the far West. "We scarcely know what to make of this movement," said the *Warsaw Signal,* the general belief being that the Mormons would be slow in carrying out their agreement to leave "so soon as grass would grow and water run." [3]

They continued to leave Nauvoo throughout the spring of 1846 from the ferries at Nauvoo, Ft. Madison, and Keokuk, keeping them busy day and night.

General John J. Hardin (who originally took over control of Hancock County in the fall of 1845 with four hundred men), under orders from Governor Ford, had declared martial law and had taken away from Sheriff Jacob Backenstos the power to arrest house burners. He soon left the county, leaving Major William B. Warren with one hundred men to keep the peace. During the winter Major Warren's command was reduced to fifty men and later to ten.[4] Major Warren's men were from Quincy in Adams County. He stationed his men at Carthage, the county seat of Hancock County.

As a steady stream of Mormon wagons left Nauvoo each week throughout the latter part of March and the forepart of April, Governor Ford issued an order to Major Warren to dismiss his men on May 1, which he did; but when it was obvious that not all of the Saints would be out of Hancock County by that time, Governor Ford notified him on May 2 to muster his men into service again.

Major Warren was having a difficult time holding off the mob forces. Although they were surprised that the Mormons began leaving so early in the spring, when it was discovered that some of them would probably stay throughout the summer in order to sell their property, it caused a furor among the anti-Mormons. After mustering his men into service again, Major Warren moved into Nauvoo and made the Mansion House his headquarters. He issued a weekly bulletin to the *Warsaw Signal* showing how many Mormons had left Nauvoo during the past week.

On May 11 he wrote a proclamation which appeared in the *Qunicy Whig* on May 20, telling the people of the recall of his men to service, saying that he had been in Nauvoo a week and the Mormons were leaving and preparing to leave "with every means that God and nature has placed in their hands." Five ferry boats were running at Nauvoo night and day, and many Mormons were also crossing at Nashville and Fort Madison. He exhorted all people to stay at home and said that he would keep them notified of events.

He told of a sixty-year-old man living seven miles from Nauvoo who was stripped of his clothing and whose back was cut to pieces just because he was a Mormon and too old to resist. "Conduct of this kind would disgrace a horde of savages." He said some of the mob leaders had given orders to rendezvous the following Friday, but no more than four armed men were to assemble together except state troops; although the force under his command was small, he was confident it would be able to meet successfully any mob which might assemble. He told the Mormons to go on with their preparations and leave the fighting to him.[5]

The warning to those mob leaders who were trying to raise a military force had its effect but only for a short time. Major Warren's bulletin for May 14 described the exodus:

... the Mormons were leaving with all possible speed: that
the ferry was crossing them over the river as fast as
possible; that an estimate of 450 teams and 1,350 souls
had left within the week. . . . [6]

His bulletin for May 22 said:

The Mormons still continue to leave the city in large
numbers. The ferry at this place averages about 32 teams
per day, and at Fort Madison, 45. Thus it will be seen that
539 teams have left during the week, which average about
three persons to each, making in all, 1,617 souls. [7]

Governor Thomas Ford stated:

By the middle of May it was estimated that sixteen
thousand Mormons had crossed the Mississippi and taken
up their line of march with their personal property, their
wives and little ones, westward across the continent to
Oregon or California; leaving behind them in Nauvoo a
small remnant of a thousand souls, being those who were
unable to sell their property, or who having no property to
sell were unable to get away. [8]

A meeting was held at Carthage on June 6 to make preparations for celebrating the Fourth of July, but someone suggested
that inasmuch as all Mormons had not yet left the state,
Hancock County could not be considered free and therefore
they ought not to celebrate the Fourth in the usual way. [9] The
meeting was then adjourned to reconvene on June 12 to take
into consideration why it was that all the Mormons had not left
Nauvoo. This happened to be the day the governor of Illinois
had designated for raising volunteers for the Mexican War,
which had broken out. This caused quite a little excitement
among the militia, and quite a large number of men were found
who wanted to march into Nauvoo.
It was soon discovered, however, that the Mormons had sold
property to quite a number of what were called *new citizens*
(not natives or previous citizens of Hancock County), and these
people were not willing to let the mob forces enter the city. It
appears that this mob force then retired to Golden's Point
about six miles south of Nauvoo in order to plan their strategy.
While they were there, Stephen Markham, whom many of the

mobbers feared, returned to Nauvoo from the pioneer camp in Iowa in order to obtain some Church property. It was rumored that he had a large body of men with him, and "the mob took to flight, though no one was in pursuit. It was a case of the wicked fleeing when no man pursued." [10]

This disorganized the mob forces for a time, but they agreed to assemble again at the call of their leaders; and they issued an ultimatum to the Mormons in Nauvoo not to go outside of the city limits, except in making their way westward. [11]

As things remained quiet for a time, Sheriff Jacob Backenstos accepted a captaincy in the U.S. Army to fight in the war with Mexico. He therefore resigned as sheriff of Hancock County. General Hardin and Major Warren also joined the federal army.

On July 11 a few Mormons disregarded the orders of the mob forces not to leave the Nauvoo city limits and went about eight miles northeast of the city near Pontoosuc to harvest a field of grain along with some of the new citizens of Nauvoo. This field had been purchased by one of the new citizens. [12] While busy at their work they were surrounded by a mob and captured. Their arms were taken from them and they were stripped of clothing and beaten. [13] When they reported in Nauvoo what had happened, both the Mormons and new citizens were aroused to action, and they rounded up a posse and arrested the offenders. [14] While they were awaiting trial, another Mormon party, consisting of Phineas H. Young, his son Brigham Young, Richard Ballantyne, and a Mr. Herring, were kidnapped and held as hostages to insure the safety of those arrested from the mob forces. They were held for a period of fourteen days and were "constantly threatened with death" until their escape. The mob forces who were arrested secured a change of venue to Quincy, Illinois, but for some reason they were never brought to trial.

Among those of the mob who were arrested was Major M'Calla (spelled *McAuley* by Gregg and some others), who was in possession of a gun that had been taken from the party of harvesters. Several persons recognized the gun; and William Pickett, owner of the gun, who was one of the non-Mormon new citizens, took it from him. The mobbers then made out a warrant for arrest of Pickett, Furness, and Clifford, charging them with stealing. [15] The warrant was put into the hands of a "special constable" from Carthage by the name of John Carlin, who arrested Furness and Clifford but was resisted by Pickett, who had been warned by a friend that the warrant was a "sub-

40 terfuge to get him into the hands of his enemies."[16] Pickett asked Constable Carlin if he would guarantee his safety and Carlin replied that he would not. It is claimed that afterwards Pickett went before the magistrate at Green Plains.[17] This magistrate was supposed to have issued the writ, but inasmuch as he had no record of it, he would not put Pickett under arrest. Furness and Clifford were acquitted upon examination.

Special Constable Carlin now saw an opportunity, or rather an excuse, to attack Nauvoo. On August 24 he assembled a posse at Carthage, ostensibly for the purpose of arresting William Pickett, but in reality to drive the Mormons out of Nauvoo.

In discussing the controversy Governor Ford states:

But to create a necessity for a great force to make the arrests, it was freely admitted by John Carlin, the constable sent in with the writs, that the prisoners would be murdered if arrested and carried out of the city. This John Carlin, under a promise to be elected recorder in the place of a Jack Mormon recorder to be driven away, was appointed a special constable to make the arrests. And now the individuals sought to be arrested were openly threatened to be murdered. The special constable went to Nauvoo with the writs in his hands, the accused declined to surrender. And now having failed to make the arrests, the constable began to call out the *posse comitatus*. This was about the 1st of September, 1846. The posse soon amounted to several hundred men.[18]

Governor Ford goes on to say that the trustees of Nauvoo, being new citizens (non-Mormons), applied to the governor for a militia officer and ten men, whom they thought would restore confidence and order. On August 21 Governor Ford ordered Major James R. Parker of Fullton County, who was a member of the 32nd regiment of the Illinois Militia, to go to Nauvoo with ten men, and also "to take command of such forces as might volunteer to defend the city. . . ."

Major Parker went to Nauvoo where he issued a proclamation "in the name of the people of Illinois, and by virtue of the authority vested in him by the governor of the State to disperse." The issue then was no longer between the mob forces and the Mormons, but was between the recognized authority of the state and the lawless banditti. Major Parker also announced

he was prepared to assist proper officers in serving writs in their
hands.[19]

Carlin issued a proclamation of his own, stating that if he were resisted he would treat Major Parker and his force as a mob.[20]

In the meantime, on August 25 Constable Carlin placed Colonel John B. Chittendon of Adams County in charge of his "posse" with the understanding that when Colonel James W. Singleton of Brown County arrived, he should be in charge. Colonel Singleton arrived on August 28 and took command. The camp was fixed about five miles from Carthage on the Nauvoo Road.[21] Major Parker wrote to Colonel Singleton expressing a desire to settle the difficulty without the shedding of blood. About this time the committee of one hundred from Quincy also stepped in and urged a peaceful settlement. In some ways it seemed to be an effort to help the mob force and gain control of Nauvoo without risk of life on their part.

An agreement was eventually reached between Major Parker and Colonel Singleton in which the Mormons were given sixty days to get out of the city. In the meantime, a force of twenty-five men from the mob forces was to be stationed in the city with half the expense of maintaining them being paid by the citizens of Nauvoo, for which amount they were to give bond; the Mormons were to surrender their arms which were to be returned to them when they left the state; as soon as their arms were surrendered, the forces under Singleton were to disperse; all hostilities were to cease as soon as the terms were accepted. [22]

This agreement, which was concluded and signed by Colonels Singleton and Chittendon on the part of the mob and by Major Parker "and others" on the part of the Nauvoo citizens, was "unanimously rejected" by the other officers and men of the mob forces. [23]

One must notice that, although the so-called posse was supposedly assembled by Constable Carlin for the ostensible purpose of arresting William Pickett for resisting him, there was not one word in the agreement mentioned about giving up Pickett.

Colonel Singleton resigned in disgust and Constable Carlin appointed Thomas Brockman of Brown County to replace him.[24] Brockman, who immediately took upon himself the title of general, rejected another offer of compromise made by the Mormons, and on September 10 led his force of seven hundred men toward Nauvoo, where they camped about three miles from the temple. [25]

Linn states that

> Governor Ford had authorized Major Flood, commanding the militia of Adams County, to raise a force to preserve order in Hancock; but the major, knowing that such action would only incense the force of the Antis, disregarded the governor's request. [26]

About this time Major Parker withdrew from service, and Major Benjamin Clifford, Jr., of the 33rd regiment of Illinois volunteers was put in command in Nauvoo. [27] The defenders of the city took a position on high ground about one mile east of the temple, placing themselves between the mob camp and the city.

BATTLE OF NAUVOO

On September 10, 11, and 12 there was desultory firing on the part of both sides without much advantage being gained by either. Governor Ford says that they were more than half a mile apart and were therefore "not near enough to do each other material injury." Ford says the forces under Brockman numbered eight hundred armed men and six or seven hundred unarmed men; by the time the fighting started, the Mormons and their allies numbered about 150 fighting men. [28] Actually there were three groups of men defending the city. These consisted of Major Clifford and his ten men of the Illinois State Militia, the few Mormons still in the town, and the new citizens who had bought property from the Mormons.

The anti-Mormon forces had five six-pound cannons which belonged to the state, and were also armed with state arms that had been given to them by independent militia companies in adjacent counties. The Mormons and their allies had five cannons that had been crudely made out of steamboat shafts, sixteen shooting rifles, and some muskets.

On September 13 Brockman's force made a general advance and a battle ensued with the cannons as well as small arms exchanging shots. The battle lasted about an hour and a quarter, after which the mob retreated to the house of a Mr. Carmichael, where they waited for wagons and returned to their camp. Gregg and Linn claim that when General Brockman discovered his cannon balls had been used up, he did not have the courage to move forward without the use of his cannon.[29]

Captain Anderson and his fifteen-year-old son were killed on the side of the defenders, along with a Mr. Morris who was killed by a cannon ball while crossing a field. About ten others were wounded. The anti-Mormons reported eight wounded, one of whom later died.

Terms of Peace

It appears that the mob was short of ammunition and sent to Quincy, Illinois, for more. During the next three days they reinforced their positions, generally preparing for another assault upon the Mormon positions. Four more men were wounded on the part of the mob during the exchange of shots fired on Sunday and Monday, September 13 and 14. On Tuesday morning, September 15, a deputation from Quincy arrived in camp with proposals for mediation "on the basis of a removal of the Mormons."[30] Andrew Johnson of Quincy was chairman of a subcommittee which carried on negotiations between the two camps; negotiations lasted from Tuesday until Wednesday evening, when terms for peace were finally agreed upon.

B. H. Roberts states:

... the citizens of Nauvoo, seeing that the State authorities rendered them no assistance, but permitted even their own authority to be braved by a lawless mob, and knowing that they would eventually be overpowered, accepted the following terms of settlement, in order to stop the further effusion of blood:—

1. The city of Nauvoo will surrender. The force of Colonel Brockman to enter and take possession of the city tomorrow, the seventeenth of September, at three o'clock p.m.

2. The arms to be delivered to the Quincy committee, to be returned on the crossing of the river.

3. The Quincy committee pledge themselves to use their influence for the protection of persons and property from all violence, and the officers of the camp and the men pledge themselves to protect all persons and property from violence.

4. The sick and the helpless to be protected and treated with humanity.

5. The Mormon population of the city to leave the State or disperse as soon as they can cross the river.

6. Five men, including the Trustees of The Church, and five clerks, with their families (Wm. Pickett not one of the number) to be permitted to remain in the city, for the disposition of property, free from all molestation and personal violence.

7. Hostilities to cease immediately, and ten men of the Quincy committee to enter the city, in the execution of their duty as soon as they think proper.[31]

These terms were signed by Almon W. Babbit, Joseph L. Heywood, and John S. Fullmer on the part of the citizens of Nauvoo; on the part of the mob, by John Carlin and Thomas S. Brockman; and by Andrew Johnson in behalf of the Quincy committee.

Again we notice that not a word was said about the arrests of the persons "named in the writs held by Carlin, and for the service of which the expedition was undertaken."[32] Still another anti-Mormon writer, William A. Linn, states:

The noticeable features of these terms are the omission of any reference to the execution of Carlin's writs, and the engagement that the Mormons should depart immediately. The latter was the real object of the "posse's" campaign.[33]

Shortly after the agreement was signed, Major Clifford gave orders for the withdrawal of the troops (ten men) under his command. One would think that the militia troops of the state should have stayed on in order to assure obedience to the agreement on the part of both sides. The agreement was not actually signed until the morning of Thursday, September 17; but the Mormons, knowing that it would be, were busy throughout the night preparing to leave. As many as could possibly go left before 3:00 p.m. that afternoon when Brockman's forces marched into the city with eight hundred armed men and six or seven hundred unarmed men.[34]

Governor Ford had sent Mason Brayman (sometimes spelled Braman) from Springfield to Nauvoo so that he could have first-hand reports from an observer he could trust.[35] He had used Brayman for similar reports about the Mormons and their enemies ever since 1843; Brayman, as a general rule, had a fair sense of judgment in giving these reports, which he did in an honest and conscientious manner. He had been in Nauvoo off and on during the winter and spring of 1846, and was now there observing the battle for its possession.

His second report to Governor Ford describing the activities of the Saints on the day of September 17 prior to Brockman's forces entering the city mentioned that, although the terms of surrender were not signed until the morning of September 17, the Mormons were so convinced their lives and property would fall a sacrifice to the vengeance of their enemies, they had been busy throughout the night in removing, in order to be beyond their reach. "In every part of the city scenes of destitution, misery and woe met the eye." Families were leaving their homes without a shelter or means of conveyance, without tents, money, or a day's provision, with as much "household stuff" as they could carry in their hands. The sick were carried in their beds, all fleeing from their enemies whom they feared more than hunger or death on the prairies. [36]

Brayman sent another report to the governor after Brockman's forces had entered Nauvoo in which he said the Quincy committee had closed its labors at sunrise "leaving a subcommittee to complete the reception and delivery of the arms of those Mormons who had not yet departed." He said Brockman had not only assumed the duty of superintending the removal of the Mormons but had also ordered the expulsion from the state of all non-Mormon new citizens who had borne arms in defense of Nauvoo. Brayman said he could scarcely believe that such an order had been given in violation of the agreement of the Quincy committee, but when he inquired of Brockman he discovered that it had been and would be executed. The order was enforced throughout the day, under circumstances of cruelty and injustice, for sympathizing with the Mormons or worse still for fighting in defense of the city *"under command of officers commissioned by* **you**" (Governor Ford), until one-half of the new citizens were forced from their homes.

46   Mr. Brayman went on to say that it was disgraceful to the character of the state, "and a humiliation not to be borne," to permit a military leader without a shadow of lawful authority to thwart the will of the executive and banish citizens for acting under it. [37]

Thus not even the new citizens of Nauvoo who aided the Mormons in the city's defense escaped the wrath of the mob.

Daniel H. Wells

One of the chief defenders of Nauvoo was Daniel H. Wells, from whom the Church purchased the ground upon which the temple was later constructed. All during the Nauvoo period he had lived in the community as a non-Mormon and had been treated with respect and dignity by the Mormon leaders. Now, in one of the darkest periods, with the Saints on their way to a home in the wilderness, Daniel H. Wells was baptized into the Church on August 9, 1846, just slightly over one month before the Battle of Nauvoo began. At one point in the battle he rallied the men to charge instead of retreat. After he arrived in Utah, he not only became the commanding officer of the Nauvoo Legion (the Utah territorial militia) but also a counselor to Brigham Young in the First Presidency. Later, one of his sons became the first governor of the state of Utah.

FINAL DEPARTURE FROM NAUVOO

The Saints from Nauvoo gathered on the Iowa side of the Mississippi River as they had no place else to go and no transportation to take them elsewhere. Word was soon taken to Brigham Young and the other Church leaders, who sent back wagons from Council Bluffs and elsewhere along the westward trail for relief of the refugees. Perhaps seven hundred men, women, and children had been on the banks of the Mississippi for three weeks before the wagons arrived. But on October 9, before starting the trek westward, these refugees were to witness what to many of them was just as much a gift from God as his feeding the Israelites in the wilderness: flocks of quail suddenly alighted in the camp, and the Saints were able to capture many of them alive as well as to kill many more. These birds provided much-needed nourishment for the Poor Camp, as it was called, when they began their journey westward.

Before the arrival of the wagons and the quail, those in the

Poor Camp were visited by Colonel Thomas L. Kane, who had lately arrived from visiting the Mormons at Council Bluffs. He painted a vivid description of the city of Nauvoo after it was taken over by the mob and also of the Poor Camp on the Iowa side of the river. [38] This description is to be found in Appendix 3.

Nauvoo after the Departure of the Saints

Although the agreement with the mob never said anything about forcing the new citizens to leave, we have seen that more than half of them were driven out by Brockman and his men. Because of their complaints and Brayman's reports to Governor Ford, he finally marched into Nauvoo with a posse of over two hundred men for the purpose of restoring these new citizens to their property—Governor Ford said about sixty families. [39] A part of the militia remained there until December 12, when it was withdrawn by Governor French who had become Governor of Illinois on December 8.

But Nauvoo never really prospered after the Mormons were driven out. B. H. Roberts tells about a visit there in 1885 when the population of the town was seventeen hundred people. M. M. Morrill, who was one of the new citizens who had helped the Mormons defend Nauvoo, was the mayor of the city at the time. The principal occupation was grape growing. The Nauvoo Temple had been burned by an arsonist—Joseph Agnew, assisted by Squire M'Calla, the Major M'Calla of the mobbers, on November 10, 1848. This caused visitors to drop to one-fourth of the previous number.

Although the Mormons sold their property at a tremendous sacrifice, values dropped still lower. T. Edgar Lyon of Nauvoo Restoration, Inc., tells of one perfectly liveable brick house in Nauvoo that sold at a tax sale for $1.60.

In 1935 the population of Nauvoo was 980 and had been decreasing at an average of two people per year for the previous eighty years. Today, however, Nauvoo Restoration, Inc., has moved into Nauvoo and is endeavoring to restore some of it as it was in the days of the Saints.

Footnotes

[1] B. H. Roberts, *The Rise and Fall of Nauvoo* (Salt Lake City: Book-craft, 1965), pp. 351-53.

48   [2]Josiah B. Conyers, *A Brief History of the Leading Causes of the Hancock Mob, in the Year 1846* (St. Louis: Cathcart and Prescott, 1846), pp. 13-14.

[3]William A. Linn, *The Story of the Mormons* (New York: Macmillan Co., 1902), p. 344.

[4]Linn, p. 343. *See also* Thomas Ford, *A History of Illinois* (Chicago: S. C. Griggs and Co., 1854), p. 411.

[5]*CHC*, 3:3-4.

[6]*CHC*, 3:3. *See also* Thomas Gregg, *History of Hancock County, Illinois* (Chicago: Charles C. Chapman and Co., 1880), p. 345.

[7]Gregg, pp. 345-46.

[8]Ford, p. 412.

[9]Roberts, p. 358.

[10]Roberts, p. 358.

[11]Roberts, pp. 358-59.

[12]Linn, p. 347, footnote.

[13]Gregg, p. 347, reports it this way: "It is stated that they behaved in a very unruly manner, when some of the neighbors collecting, seized and whipped them, and sent them away." *See also* Linn, p. 347.

[14]*CHC*, 3:6-7.

[15]Roberts, p. 359.

[16]Roberts, pp. 359-60.

[17]Green Plains was a small settlement about four or five miles out of Carthage toward Nauvoo.

[18]Ford, p. 415.

[19]Roberts, pp. 360-61.

[20]Roberts, p. 361.

[21]Gregg, p. 348.

[22]Gregg, p. 348. *See also* Ford, p. 417; and Roberts, pp. 361-62.

[23]Gregg, p. 348. Ford, p. 417, says it was rejected by a small majority.

[24]Linn, p. 348. Governor Ford said of Thomas Brockman: "This Brockman was a Campbellite preacher, nominally belonging to the democratic party. He was a large, awkward, uncouth, ignorant, semi-barbarian, ambitious of office and bent upon acquiring notoriety. He had been county commissioner of Brown county, and in that capacity had let out a contract for building the court-house, and it was afterwards ascertained had let the contract to himself. He managed to get paid in advance and then built such an inferior building, that the county had not received it up to December 1846. He had also been a collector of taxes, for which he was a defaulter, and his lands were sold whilst I was governor, to pay a judgment obtained against him for moneys collected by him." (Ford, pp. 417-18.).

[25]Linn, p. 348.

[26]Linn, p. 348. *See also* Ford, p. 419.

[27]Linn, p. 348.

[28]Ford, pp. 421-22, 424.

[29]Gregg, p. 350. *See also* Linn, p. 349.

[30]Linn, p. 349.

[31]Roberts, p. 365. *See also* Linn, pp. 349-50.

[32]Gregg, p. 353.

[33]Linn, p. 350.

[34]Ford, p. 424.

[35]Mason Brayman became a general during the Civil War and was later a governor of Idaho Territory.

[36]*Warsaw Signal*, 20 October 1846; as cited in Linn, p. 350.

[37]Conyers, pp. 73-74.

[38]John R. Young, *Memoirs of John R. Young, Utah Pioneer, 1847* (Salt Lake City: Deseret News Press, 1920), pp. 31-38.

[39]Ford, p. 429.

4

Mormon Battalion

EVENTS LEADING TO THE FORMATION OF THE MORMON BATTALION

An Appeal to the Government

When the Latter-day Saints realized they would have to migrate to the West, they began making various plans for such a move. They had heard that President James K. Polk had proposed to the United States Congress that a series of forts and blockhouses be built along the trail to Oregon for the purpose of giving comfort and protection to American citizens as they pioneered the West. On January 20, 1846, an article appeared in the *Times and Seasons* under the signatures of the members of the Nauvoo high council in which they stated that they intended to send a company of young, hardy men with some families into the western country in early March, 1846 so that they could put in a spring crop and build houses in preparation for the coming of other families who would start in the spring as soon as grass had grown sufficiently to sustain teams and stock. The pioneer company were instructed to proceed west until they found a good valley in the neighborhood of the Rocky Mountains where they would infringe upon no one and would not likely be infringed upon, where the Saints could rest until they found a permanent location.

51

52   The article further mentioned that if the president of the United States recommended the building of blockhouses and stockade forts along the route to Oregon, the Saints had reason to believe they would receive the work to do, as under their circumstances they could do it at less expense to the government than anyone else. Some people had concluded that persecution, although not from the federal government, had nevertheless alienated the Mormons from their country, but this was not so. If hostilities between the United States and any other power should arise over the territory of Oregon, the Saints would be on hand to sustain the claim of the United States government to that country, as "it is geographically ours; and of right, no foreign power should hold dominion there." [1]

The Saints did not intend the federal government to give them a handout, as they expected to work for what they received.

On January 26, 1846, just six days after the article appeared in the *Times and Seasons,* President Brigham Young wrote to Jesse C. Little, appointing him president of the mission in the eastern and middle United States. In the letter he also instructed him to go to Washington, D.C., to see the nation's leaders in an effort to get aid for the Saints:

> If our government shall offer any facilities for emigrating to the western coast, embrace those facilities, if possible. As a wise and faithful man, take every honorable advantage of the times you can. Be thou a savior and a deliverer of that people, and let *virtue, integrity,* and *truth,* be your motto—salvation and glory the prize for which you contend. [2]

Elder Little in a later report to Brigham Young said:

> In consonance with my instructions, I felt an anxious desire for the deliverance of the saints, and resolved upon visiting James K. Polk, president of the United States, to lay the situation of my persecuted brethren before him, and ask him, as the representative of our country, to stretch forth the federal arm in their behalf. [3]

In preparing for this trip Elder Little obtained a number of letters of introduction to take with him. One was from his friend, Governor John H. Steel of New Hampshire, who said

Nauvoo (Ill.) Dec. 17. 1845

Sir

As there is a recommend to Congress in the President Message for a suitable number of stockades and block houses to be erected between our Western frontiers, and the Rocky Mountains. If some one of our people could be favored with the Agency, for that purpose we would build them cheaper, then in any otherwise could be done, as we expect to emigrate West of the mountains next season. If we should eventually settle on Vancouver's Island, according to our calculation we shall greatly desire to have a Mail route, established between here, and Oregon we would like to contract for the same through the summer months. When we arrive at the place of our destination we fondly anticipate, we shall have no old settlers to find fault with us and if Oregon should be annexed to the United States, which in all probability will be, and Vancouver's Island incorporated in the same, by our promptly paying the national revenue, and taxes, we can live in peace with all men.

Yours &c
Most Obediently
Brigham Young
President of the Church
of Jesus Christ of
Latter day

[W. L. marcy]
Hon W. L. Marcy
Secy of War
Washington D. C

Fig. 2. Letter of Brigham Young to the United States secretary of war seeking government employment for the Saints to aid them in moving west.

that he had known Jesse Little since childhood and believed him to be honest in his intentions. He then added:

> Mr. Little visits Washington, if I understand him correctly, for the purpose of procuring, or endeavoring to procure, the freight of any provisions or naval stores which the government may be desirous of sending to Oregon, or to any portion of the Pacific. He is thus desirous of obtaining freight for the purpose of lessening the expense of chartering vessels to convey him and his followers to California, where they intend going and making a permanent settlement the present summer.[4]

While in New York previous to going to Washington, D.C., Elder Little also obtained a letter of introduction from A. G. Benson to ex-Postmaster General Amos Kendall of Washington, D.C., in which Benson requested Kendall to "aid Mr. Little in the object of his visit to Washington."[5] One will remember Benson and Kendall as parties to a nefarious scheme of wresting title to half the property where the Saints were to settle, as mentioned in chapter 2.

While holding a conference of the Church in Philadelphia on May 13, before proceeding on his way to Washington, D.C., President Little met Colonel Thomas L. Kane, a young man of twenty-four years from a prominent Pennsylvania family, who had become very much interested in the Latter-day Saints. He gave Elder Little a letter of introduction to George M. Dallas, vice-president of the United States. Colonel Kane spoke of the excellent character of Elder Little and said:

> He visits Washington, too, I believe, with no other object than the laudable one of desiring aid of government for his people, who forced by persecution to found a new commonwealth in the Sacramento valley, still retain American hearts, and would not willingly sell themselves to the foreigner, or forget the old commonwealth they leave behind them.[6]

War with Mexico

Elder Little arrived in Washington on May 21, 1846, eight days after Congress had officially declared war on Mexico. A message received during the early part of May stated that an

American troop of dragoons (cavalrymen) under Captain
Thornton had been captured by Mexican soldiers, sixteen
having been killed in the battle, which was fought on the east
side of the Rio Grande. This news made it possible for President
Polk to say to Congress that "Mexico had invaded our territory
and shed the blood of our citizens on our own soil."[7] The
report greatly excited the people, and Congress declared war
two days later. By the time Elder Little arrived in Washington,
D.C., news that General Taylor's army had been victorious in
two battles against the armies of Mexico on May 8 and 9 had
caused even greater excitement in Washington.

Aid in the Form of Enlistment

Elder Little called upon Amos Kendall but found that he was
ill. In the evening he called upon President Polk in company
with Mr. Dame and Mr. King, both from Massachusetts. Sam
Houston of Texas and "other distinguished gentlemen" were
present. Apparently there were too many present for Elder
Little to get down to the basic reasons for his call, but the next
day he called on Amos Kendall and submitted to him his letters
of introduction. Elder Little stated, "We talked upon the subject of emigration, and he thought arrangements could be made
to assist our emigration by enlisting one thousand of our men,
arming, equipping and establishing them in California to defend
the country; he said he would be able to inform me on Tuesday
morning, what could be done."[8]

From this statement it appears that the original idea of
having a Mormon battalion came from Amos Kendall. Elder
Little met with him again on three successive days, May 25, 26,
27, when Kendall said that the president had laid the case before his cabinet, but that they had not fully decided. The
president was determined to take California and had in mind to
employ the Mormons in doing it; the plan was that one thousand men should be fitted out, with their pay to start when
Little contacted them. They were to be officered by their own
men except that the commanding officer was to be appointed
by President Polk. In addition, another thousand men were to
go by sea around Cape Horn; their pay was to begin on
September 1.[9]

As three days had elapsed and Elder Little had heard no
further word, he wrote a long letter on June 1 directly to President Polk. On June 2 Kendall called on Elder Little and told

56   him the president had received his message and desired him to call on June 3; on that day Kendall and Elder Little visited the President together. The president expressed confidence in the Saints and told the men he would do something for them; but as he had not decided what, he wished to talk with Kendall and the secretary of the navy the next day. When Elder Little next visited President Polk on June 5, he was informed that five hundred or a thousand men would be taken into the service and that Elder Little should have letters to the "squadron" from him and from the secretary of the navy.[10] That evening Elder Little wrote to the president, on behalf of the Latter-day Saints, a letter of acceptance of the offer.

It appears that through the influence of Senator Thomas H. Benton, a bitterly anti-Mormon senator from Missouri, the number of two thousand soldiers to be furnished by the Saints—one thousand by land and another thousand Saints in the East who were to go by sea to California—was cut down to about five hundred to go by land. Apparently Senator Benton was not sure of Mormon loyalty to the United States and convinced the president that not more than one-third of the soldiers of General Kearny's "Army of the West" should be made up of Mormons. Thus, if the call of the Mormon Battalion is looked upon as a hardship, we can at least thank Senator Benton for reducing the numbers called. It does appear from some sources, including Brigham Young, that Senator Benton doubted the Mormons would respond at all and therefore wanted the privilege of having sufficient soldiers to "pursue, cut off their route, and disperse them" for disloyalty in case they did not respond.[11] Whatever the attitude of Senator Benton may have been toward the Mormons, we must give credit to President Polk's sincerity in his efforts to help them.

One point we must keep in mind is that the government was not short of volunteers for the war, for nearly every call in the western states was oversubscribed, although young men in the East were not so enthusiastic.[12]

Instead of one thousand Mormons in the East to go by ship, President Polk called for one thousand gentile volunteers from New York, from which 955 eventually sailed on September 26, 1846. They arrived in the early part of March 1847, which was a little more than a month after the arrival of the Mormon Battalion in California.

Amos Kendall's participation in negotiations, along with the suggestion that two thousand Mormons be sent, gives color to

the idea that he was probably still hopeful that the Church
leaders would sign the secret agreement with A. G. Benson &
Co.

News of the Call

Elder Little saw President Polk for the last time on June 8,
when he left Washington in company with Colonel Thomas L.
Kane and his father, Judge John K. Kane, who left them at
Harris, Pennsylvania. The other two traveled together as far as
St. Louis, Missouri, where they separated. Elder Little was to go
to the camps of Israel by way of Nauvoo, and Colonel Kane was
to carry messages to Colonel Stephen W. Kearny at Fort Leavenworth, Kansas, who was to be commander of the Army of the
West during the Mexican War. The messages to Kearny contained many items, among which was his promotion to brevet
brigadier general and an order to raise volunteers among the
Mormons.[13] Colonel Kearny (later general) in turn designated
Captain James Allen to proceed to the Mormon camps and raise
such as would volunteer up to five companies.

In his orders to Captain Allen he stated that these companies
should consist of 73 to 109 in each company and that the
privates of each company could elect their commissioned
officers, subject to Captain Allen's approval, which officers
would appoint the noncommissioned officers, also subject to his
approval.

When the companies were organized Captain Allen was
authorized to muster them into the service and begin their pay,
rations, and so forth. As soon as the fourth company was
mustered in, Captain Allen was to receive the rank and pay of a
lieutenant colonel and was authorized to appoint appropriate
officers for the battalion.

The companies were to be marched to Fort Leavenworth to
be armed and prepared for the field, after which they were to
follow the trail of General Kearny to Santa Fe, New Mexico,
where they were to receive further orders from the general.

The Mormons were to be enlisted for twelve months,
marched to California, and at the time of their discharge were
to be allowed to retain as their private property the guns and
accoutrements furnished them at Fort Leavenworth. Each
company was to be allowed four women as laundresses, who
would travel with the company and receive pay and rations the
same as given to other laundresses in the army.

58   General Kearny pledged to the Mormons to abide faithfully by the conditions mentioned in Captain Allen's instructions.[14]

Captain Allen first contacted the Saints at Mt. Pisgah on June 26, 1846, where he passed out a circular explaining the purpose of his coming and giving the particulars of the call for volunteers. Those who were desirous of serving their country were requested to meet him without delay at the Mormons' principal camp at Council Bluffs, 138 miles west, where Captain Allen hoped to complete the organization of the battalion six days after his arrival there or nine days from the time of his announcement at Mt. Pisgah. All healthy able-bodied men between the ages of eighteen and forty-five were eligible to enlist.[15]

A meeting of the stake presidency and high council was called at Mt. Pisgah, but all they felt they could do was to treat Captain Allen courteously and give him a letter to Brigham Young. Wilford Woodruff, who was at Mt. Pisgah, sent a special messenger to Brigham Young to inform him about Captain Allen.[16]

It seems that many of the brethren regarded Captain Allen with suspicion, as we read in Hosea Stout's journal from June 28:

> Br Phinehas R. Wright came on to day from Pisgah. He informed me that there were some officers of the United States Army at Pisgah with a requisition from the President of the United States, on us for 500 soldiers to march to Santa Fe against Mexico & from thence to California & there to be discharged. . . .
>
> We were all very indignant at this requisition and only looked on it as a plot laid to bring trouble on us as a people. For in the event that we did not comply with the requisition we supposed they would now make a protest to denounce us as enemies to our country and if we did comply that they would then have 500 of our men in their power to be destroyed as they had done our leaders at Carthage. I confess that my feelings was [sic] uncommonly wrought up against them This was the universal feelings at Pisgah and Genl Rich sent me word by Br Wright to keep a sharp look out for him as he passed and see that he did not get any knowledge of the public arms which I had. For he supposed that he might be looking after them. Such was our feelings towards the President &c

This officer passed here today but I did not get to see   59
him as I was encamped some distance from the road.[17]

The Call Accepted

Five days later, on July 3, Hosea Stout recorded in his
journal that they saw Brigham Young, Heber C. Kimball, and
Willard Richards coming with others from Council Bluffs:

> They were on their way to Pisgah & Garden Grove. I
> had a few minutes interview with President Young who
> briefly told me that they were going to comply with the
> requisitions of the President of the United States and
> furnish the 500 men demanded and that there was a good
> feeling existing between us and him [Captain James Allen]
> & all was right & that they were going to Pisgah & Garden
> Grove to raise the men &c. Their presence seemed to give
> new life to all the camp who flocked around them. . . .[18]

Captain Allen's manner and personal attitude towards the
Mormons had a lot to do with allaying their feelings and suspicion towards the federal government in calling for soldiers. On
Sunday, July 5, when Hosea Stout had reached the camp at
Council Bluffs, he personally went to see Captain Allen. He said
Captain Allen "was a plain non assuming man without that
proud over bearing strut and self conceited dignaty [*sic*] which
some call an officer-like appearance." He was pleased with
Captain Allen's manner as a gentleman—in his words, "notwithstanding my prejudice against, not only him but also the government which he was sent here to represent."[19]

Captain Allen arrived at Council Bluffs on June 29. On July 1
he and the two dragoons which had accompanied him held a
council meeting with Brigham Young, Heber C. Kimball, Willard
Richards, Orson Pratt, George A. Smith, John Taylor, John
Smith, and Levi Richards. One of the problems discussed concerned permission for the Saints to camp on the lands there-
abouts, as they now would be especially shorthanded of
capable young men. Captain Allen, as the representative of
President Polk, assumed the responsibility of permitting them
to camp wherever it was necessary until he could notify the
president and have him ratify the decision or specify otherwise.[20]

Following the council meeting, a public meeting was held in

60 which Captain Allen explained to the people the purpose of his being among them. Brigham Young next addressed the people. He recorded:

> I addressed the assembly; wished them to make a distinction between this action of the general government and our former oppressions in Missouri and Illinois. I said, the question might be asked, "Is it prudent for us to enlist to defend our country?" If we answer in the affirmative, all are ready to go.
>
> Suppose we were admitted into the union as a state and the government did not call on us, we would feel ourselves neglected. Let the "Mormons" be the first to set their feet on the soil of California. Captain Allen has assumed the responsibility of saying that we may locate on Grand Island, until we can prosecute our journey. This is the first offer we have ever had from the government to benefit us.
>
> I proposed that the five hundred volunteers be mustered and I would do my best to see all their families brought forward, as far as my influence extended, and feed them when I had anything to eat myself.[21]

After the public meeting another council meeting was held and the specific questions of the Saints remaining on Indian lands and camping on them all along the route were discussed. They decided that Brigham Young and Heber C. Kimball should go back as far as Mt. Pisgah to raise volunteers, while John Taylor, Parley P. Pratt, and George A. Smith would do so at Council Bluffs.

When they were within eleven miles of Mt. Pisgah, Elders Young, Kimball, and Richards met Elder Jesse C. Little, who gave them a firsthand report of his labors in Washington, D.C. From Pisgah, Brigham Young sent word back to Garden Grove telling of Jesse Little's experiences in Washington and then said:

> The United States want our friendship, the president wants to do us good and secure our confidence. The outfit of this five hundred men costs us nothing and their pay will be sufficient to take their families over the mountains. There is war between Mexico and the United States, to whom California must fall a prey, and if we are the first settlers, the old citizens cannot have a Hancock or Missouri pretext to mob the saints.[22]

Church at Nauvoo, in which he said:

Now, brethren, it is time for action; and if you succeed in selling our property in Hancock county, and as unitedly succeed in removing all the poor saints this fall, we will soon be where we can rejoice in each other's society, and by early spring we can move a portion of the camp over the mountains and next spring plant our corn in yonder valley. This is the first time the government has stretched forth its arm to our assistance, and we receive their proffers with joy and thankfulness. We feel confident they [the battalion] will have little or no fighting. The pay of the five hundred men will take their families to them. The "Mormons" will then be the old settlers and have a chance to choose the best locations.[23]

On July 11, Colonel Thomas L. Kane arrived in Council Bluffs and met with members of the Twelve. He had also brought some papers from Washington, D.C., for the brethren. On Sunday, July 12, a meeting was held near John Taylor's camp. Among the speakers was Parley P. Pratt, who spoke against "the abominable practice of swearing" and then spoke at length "in favor of sending off the 500 troops to Santa Fe and explained it to the satisfaction of most of the Saints." "Indeed it needed considerable explaining for every one was about as much prejudiced as I was at first," declared Hosea Stout.[24]

The Battalion Enlisted

The next day, when Brigham and those who had gone to Mt. Pisgah returned to Council Bluffs, a meeting was held in which many of the brethren spoke about enlisting in the army. It seems that President Young spoke a number of times. During one address he mentioned that he would have rather undertaken to raise two thousand a year ago in twenty-four hours than to raise one hundred in a week now; but he still felt that they could raise the number.[25] In another speech he said, "The president of the United States has now stretched out his hand to help us, and I thank God and him too."[26]

Daniel Tyler leaves with us the impression that it was only through the recommendation and influence of the Church authorities that the men had enlisted:

Assistance in emigrating with their families westward, would have been hailed with joy. Work of any kind and at any price, on the route of their proposed journey, by which they could earn a subsistence, would have been considered a God-send. But joining the army and leaving their families in such a condition was repugnant to their feelings. Such a thing had never been thought of, much less asked for, by the Saints. The assertion which has been made by their enemies: that they desired and solicited the privilege of joining the army to go against Mexico, leaving their wives and children homeless and destitute wanderers on the banks of the Missouri, is a base libel on the character of the Saints. They were loyal citizens, but they never expected such a sacrifice would be required of them to prove their loyalty to the government. Though Captain Allen represented the call as an act of benevolence on the part of the government, and assured the Saints that there were hundreds of thousands of volunteers in the States ready to enlist, it is doubtful whether he would have got one of the Saints to join him if it had been left to his own influence. Indeed, it is said that he admitted afterwards that he could not have blamed the people if they had refused to respond. [27]

Tyler said there was much to prove that the leaders did not regard the call simply as an invitation that they could "accept or decline with impunity." President Young said, "We want to conform to the *requisition* made upon us, and we will do nothing else till we have accomplished this thing. If we want the privilege of going where we can worship God according to the dictates of our consciences, we must raise the Battalion." [28]

Four companies of soldiers enlisted on July 13. By July 16 a fifth company had enlisted. At the request of the privates (whom the government had given the right to choose their commissioned officers), the commissioned officers were named by Brigham Young. The commissioned officers then chose the non-commissioned officers.

Although the age limit was set at 18-45 years, there were a few younger and a few older who were permitted to enroll. David Pettigrew at age fifty-five was the oldest man enrolled, and D. W. Hendricks at the age of sixteen years, eight months, and ten days was probably the youngest.

On July 16 Captain Allen took the battalion under his command and before leaving Council Bluffs gave a grand ball in the

soldiers' honor. Colonel Kane, in a pamphlet called *The*
Mormons (published in Philadelphia in 1850), described it as a
lively affair.[29]

MARCH OF THE BATTALION

Sergeant William Hyde said that on Saturday, July 18, six of
the Apostles met in private council with the officers, both commissioned and noncommissioned, and gave them their last
charge and blessing:

They instructed the officers to be as fathers to the
privates, to remember their prayers, to see that the name
of the Deity was revered, and that virtue and cleanliness
were strictly observed. They also instructed us to treat all
men with kindness and never take that which did not
belong to us, even from our worst enemies, not even in
time of war if we could possibly prevent it; and in case we
should come in contact with our enemies and be successful, we should treat prisoners with kindness and never
take life when it could be avoided. [30]

The soldiers left Council Bluffs on July 20 for Fort Leavenworth, Kansas, but they were not entirely alone. Four laundresses enrolled in each company, making 20 in all, and some of
the officers' wives were permitted to go along; so there were at
least 33 women and 51 children who accompanied them. In
addition the officers hired a few young men as private teamsters
tc drive some of the wagons that took their families along. A
number of boys too young to enlist as soldiers were also hired
as servants by certain of the officers. When the battalion left
Council Bluffs, there were nearly one hundred others in
addition to the 549 soldiers. Daniel Tyler in his "Concise
History of the Mormon Battalion in the Mexican War," pages
118-26, lists the members of the battalion and those who
accompanied it; however the list is not complete.

It took the battalion from July 20 to August 1 to march to
Fort Leavenworth, Kansas, a distance of 200 miles. They lost
their first soldier just after midnight on the morning of July 23
when Samuel Boley died. It became evident that a few others
were not physically prepared for the journey. There is no
evidence that any physical examination was given or that any
physical standards had to be met. And inasmuch as the Saints
were in the midst of trying difficulties, it is obvious that many

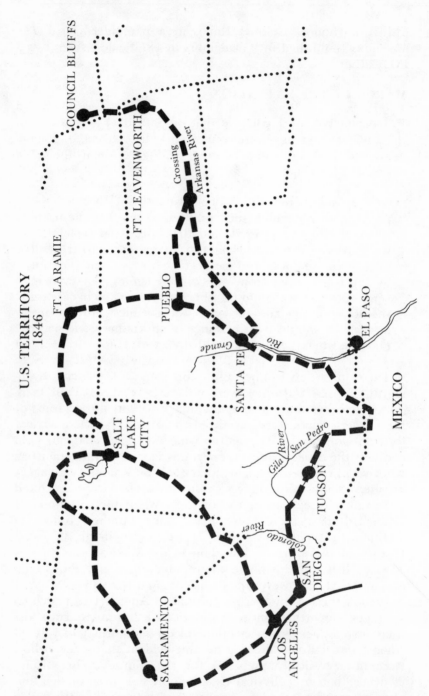

Fig. 3. Route of the Mormon Battalion. *Courtesy of LaMar C. Berrett.*

who enrolled were not physically prepared for such a journey as was coming, although they may have thought they were.

Outfitted at Fort Leavenworth

On August 3, Companies A, B, and C drew their arms and accoutrements; Companies D and E drew them the next day. On August 5 each man drew $42 as clothing money for the year, as the men were permitted to take money instead of being outfitted with uniforms. This meant that only the commanding officer was wearing a military uniform, except for one soldier who had "a peculiar kind of hat belonging to an officer's uniform of the Nauvoo Legion." [32] One can imagine that the Mormon Battalion showed little resemblance to a regular military outfit, with no uniforms and nearly one hundred women and children following along.

Sergeant Tyler said that the paymaster was much surprised to see every man able to sign his own name to the payroll because only one out of three of the Missouri volunteers, who were also at Fort Leavenworth at this time, could sign his name. One report states that Colonel Allen turned to his fellow officers and said, "That is the only battalion in the United States army in which every man can sign his own name." [33] Much of the money was given to Parley P. Pratt to take back to Winter Quarters to aid the soldiers' families who had stayed behind. A donation was also made to help P. P. Pratt, Orson Hyde, and John Taylor, who went with the battalion to Fort Leavenworth but were on their way to Great Britain on a mission, and also to aid Jesse C. Little, who was also with them but on his way back to his mission in the eastern states.

Leaving Fort Leavenworth

On August 12 the first three companies left Fort Leavenworth for Santa Fe, New Mexico; and the last two left on August 14. Colonel Allen, who was taken seriously ill after the battalion's arrival, was not with them. He had instructed Captain Jefferson Hunt to take charge and move out. By the evening of the 15th, Companies D and E caught up with the other three companies that had moved ahead rather slowly.

A Question of Command

The battalion was hardly two weeks out of Fort Leavenworth and was only 40 to 45 miles away when what probably turned out to be their greatest tragedy occurred. On August 27 Sergeant Shelton reported that Colonel Allen had died on August 23. Sergeant Tyler said of Colonel Allen, "He was universally beloved by the command." The question now arose as to who should take command. Captain Jefferson Hunt asserted that it was his right to do so, and there appears to be some basis for this, as it is claimed that Colonel Allen had said that in the event he could not be their commanding officer, he would recommend that it be one of the members of the battalion.[34]

The march of the battalion was continued under the direction of Captain Hunt as far as Council Grove, where they heard that Lieutenant A. J. Smith of the regular army was on the way to take command.

At the time of the death of Colonel Allen, Lieutenant James Pace had returned from the battalion to Fort Leavenworth to learn of the condition of Colonel Allen. Lieutenant Samuel Gully, quartermaster of the battalion, was also at the fort. Major Horton, commander at Fort Leavenworth, asked to see Lieutenants Gully and Pace. He told them that the battalion now had a perfect right to elect their own colonel, and that no one had any right to assume command. He said he had written a letter to Captain Hunt and would inform General Kearny of the situation. Lieutenant Pace said, "He also added that we were a separate corps, from all other soldiers in the service."[35] He suggested that one of them go to inform President Brigham Young of their situation and then return to the command as soon as possible. It was decided that Lieutenant Pace would go. Lieutenant Smith and Dr. Sanderson, who had previously been very belligerent, now changed their tone and asked Lieutenant Pace to take a letter from each of them to Brigham Young. In his letter Lieutenant Smith said, "If it is the wish of your people that I should take charge of the Battalion, and conduct it to General Kearney, I will do it with pleasure and feel proud of the command."[36]

Brigham Young answered:

You kindly offered to take the charge of the Battalion and conduct it safely to Gen. Kearney. We have not the pleasure of a personal acquaintance, and consequently can have no personal objection to you; but, sir, on the subject of command we can only say, Col. Allen settled that matter at the organization of the Battalion; therefore, we must leave that point to the proper authorities, be the

result what it may. Any assistance you may render the
Battalion while moving will be duly acknowledged by a
grateful people. [37]

To Lieutenant Samuel Gulley, quartermaster, and the
Mormon Battalion Brigham Young wrote:

> You will all doubtless recollect that Colonel Allen re-
> peatedly stated to us and the Battalion that there would be
> no officer in the Battalion, except himself, only from
> among our people; that if he fell in battle, or was sick, or
> disabled by any means, the command would devolve on
> the ranking officer, which would be the Captain of
> Company A, and B, and so on, according to *letter*. Con-
> sequently the command must devolve on Captain Jefferson
> Hunt, whose duty we suppose to be to take the Battalion
> to Bent's Fort, or wherever he has received marching
> orders for, and there wait further orders from General
> Kearney, notifying him by express of Colonel Allen's
> decease at the earliest date. [38]

When the battalion officers first heard of the death of
Colonel Allen, they met in council and agreed that Captain
Hunt should assume command. Later, when they heard Lieutenant Smith was on the way intending to assume command,
they appointed a committee of two—Captain Jesse Hunter of
Company B and George P. Dykes, battalion adjutant—to
"examine the law and ascertain to whom the right of command
belonged and report accordingly to the council." Captain
Hunter reported in favor of Captain Hunt, and Lieutenant
Dykes was of the opinion that because the battalion was enlisted by a United States officer, the right of command belonged to an officer of the regular army. [39] It was at this point
that Lieutenant A. J. Smith, accompanied by Major Walker, Dr.
George B. Sanderson, and others, arrived. They brought with
them a letter from Major Horton, who had previously informed
Lieutenants Gully and Pace that the battalion had the right to
appoint whomever they wanted; but in this letter he did suggest
that the government property in possession of the battalion had
not been receipted for and that it might save them considerable
trouble if they submitted to the command of Lieutenant Smith.
This caused another council of the officers to be held, and they
were addressed by Major Walker and Lieutenant Smith, who
advised them to submit to Major Horton's suggestion. Captain

Hunt stated his right to assume command and then left it to the council to decide.

Lieutenant A. J. Smith Chosen

Brigham Young's letter had not arrived yet, and Captains Nelson Higgins and Daniel L. Davis moved and seconded that Smith be given the command. The vote was taken, and all but three of the officers, Lieutenants Lorenzo Clark, Samuel Gully, and Wesley W. Willis, voted in favor. Sergeant Tyler later wrote:

A little postponement by the officers until Lieutenant Pace's return [from seeing Brigham Young], which was daily looked for, would have been satisfactory to all, and Captain Hunt, who had been duly elected would have continued in command with the rank of Lieutenant Colonel. [40]

Sergeant Tyler also stated:

When the command was given to Lieutenant Smith, the soldiers were not consulted. This caused an ill-feeling between them and the officers that many hold to this day. The appointment of Smith, even before his character was known, caused a greater gloom throughout the command than the death of Colonel Allen had. [41]

Ordinarily one might say that the privates never have a say in the choice of their officers, but this was not an ordinary case, since from the beginning the president of the United States had given the privates the privilege of choosing all of their commissioned officers except the commanding officer. Also, Colonel Allen had assured them that if he did not lead them it would be one of their own officers. Thus the privates felt that their own officers should have consulted them about a new commander.

One other point is also obvious, and that is that it was not the United States or the army who thrust Lieutenant Smith upon them; it was perhaps the shrewdness of Lieutenant Smith plus the vote of the officers themselves. Lieutenant Smith did not come to them with an appointment as their commanding officer from anyone. Of course, the officers of the battalion were not acquainted with his character; nevertheless the choice for him to lead them was of their own doing. It was the privates, however, who suffered the most under his rather tyrannical command.

As it turned out, Lieutenant A. J. Smith and Dr. George
Sanderson became the heaviest burdens the battalion had to
bear, for they were completely unsympathetic with the men
and their problems. On the other hand, Lieutenant Smith did
make many decisions that were for the best good of the battalion, some of which the men would have readily accepted if
they had been made by Colonel Allen. For example, when they
came to the Arkansas River crossing for the last time, Lieutenant Smith insisted that all women and children who were not
directly connected with the battalion (the women would be
those who were neither wives of officers nor laundresses) must
go under the command of Captain Nelson Higgins to Pueblo,
Colorado, for the winter. Although many of the men who were
to be separated from their wives and children objected to this, it
was a wise move. Colonel Allen could have made such a decision
and, with the proper examination, the men would have readily
accepted it.

Lieutenant Smith sometimes pushed on relentlessly, considering the condition of both men and animals, and he forced
the men to be treated against their own will with Dr. Sanderson's medicine when they were sick. Sanderson's medicine for
nearly everything was a dose of calomel or arsenic, which the
men felt was poisoning them. Alvin Smith, the Prophet Joseph's
oldest brother, had been killed by an overdose of calomel given
by a young doctor as treatment for a stomach disorder. Some of
the men may have been aware of this. Alva Phelps, who became
ill when they had been out about two months, pleaded with Dr.
Sanderson not to force him to take his calomel, but Sanderson
insisted and Private Phelps died. The battalion members were
convinced the doctor's medicine had killed him.

Dr. McIntyre (a Church member), who had been appointed
assistant surgeon by Colonel Allen on the day of enlistment,
was not permitted to administer any herbs to the men without
the specific permission of Sanderson.

Sergeant Tyler stated:

> It would have been difficult to select the same number
> of American citizens from any other community who
> would have submitted to the tyranny and abuse that the
> Battalion did from Smith and Sanderson. Nor would we
> have done so on any consideration other than as servants
> to our God and patriots to our country. [42]

Of course, there were many hardships of the journey that were not the fault of the lieutenant and the doctor. These were due to the excessive heat, the lack of sufficient food, and the occasional long distances between drinking water.

On October 3 the battalion was divided by selecting the able-bodied men and animals to push on ahead while the weaker men and teams were to follow as best they could. The first division arrived at Santa Fe on October 9. Upon their approach, General Alexander Doniphan, the commander and friend of the Mormons, ordered a salute of one hundred guns to be fired from the roofs of the houses in honor of the battalion. Colonel Sterling Price, a bitter anti-Mormon from Missouri, and his Missouri volunteers had been accorded no such honor when they had arrived earlier. The second division of the battalion arrived on October 12.

Change of Command at Santa Fe

At Santa Fe the battalion members were disappointed because Captain Jefferson Hunt was not appointed the commanding officer of the battalion; but at least they were pleased that Lieutenant A. J. Smith was relieved of the command. General Kearny had left word that Philip St. George Cooke should take command at Santa Fe and march the men to California.

Colonel Cooke knew that the trip from Santa Fe would be a rugged one that only the healthiest of men could accomplish, so he ordered the rest of the women and children—except for five officer's wives—and all soldiers who were declared incapable of making the journey to go to Pueblo for the winter. One notable change was that Dr. McIntyre, the assistant surgeon, rather than Dr. Sanderson, was given the privilege of deciding which soldiers were unable to proceed west. This party, made up of two officers with Captain James Brown in command, about eighty-six enlisted men, and many women and children, left Santa Fe on October 18, replenished their supplies from Bent's Fort, and arrived in Pueblo on November 17.

Colonel Cooke recognized that even among the rest of the battalion the men had really been worn down by marching from Nauvoo, Illinois, before the start of the battalion trek. Sergeant Tyler remarked that they were "much worse 'worn' by the foolish and unnecessary forced marches of Lieutenants Smith and Dykes, which utterly broke down both men and beasts, and

Monument to the Mormon Battalion on the Utah capitol grounds. Utah's sister state, Arizona, graciously made a donation for its erection.

was the prime cause of the greater part of the sickness and probably of many deaths." Tyler goes on to say, "I am satisfied that any other set of men but Latter-day Saints would have mutinied rather than submit to the oppressions and abuse thus heaped upon them."[43]

Lieutenant Dykes was George P. Dykes, a Mormon who was appointed to be adjutant of the battalion by Colonel James Allen. It seems that even under Colonel Allen he urged longer marches for the men than was good for their best health; for example, on July 24, four days after leaving Council Bluffs for Fort Leavenworth, Sergeant Tyler commented: "The weather being excessively warm, Colonel Allen was in favor of moderate marches; but Adjutant Dykes, being himself a great walker, and having the advantage of a horse to ride, urged long marches."[44] Later, under Lieutenant A. J. Smith, Adjutant Dykes sided with him against the men in enforcing many long marches; so the entire blame cannot be laid to Commander Smith.

As Captain Nelson Higgins of Company D had been sent with ten soldiers to guard the first group of women and children who left the battalion for Pueblo on September 16, Colonel Cooke made use of this opportunity on November 1 to release Lieutenant Dykes as adjutant of the battalion and put him in command of Company D. Second Lieutenant Philemon C. Merrill of

Company B was appointed adjutant in his place. Later on, because of Lieutenant Dykes' officious acts the soldiers gave him the unofficial title of "accuser of the brethren."

While at Santa Fe the men were paid their wages in checks which could not be cashed there, but John D. Lee and Howard Egan had come as messengers from the camps of Israel and were given the men's checks to carry back.

From Santa Fe to San Diego

On October 19 the main body of the battalion left Santa Fe with orders from General Kearny to take wagons through to California. With few exceptions, said Tyler, the mule and ox teams that pulled their baggage wagons "were the same worn-out and broken down animals that we had driven all the way from Council Bluffs and Fort Leavenworth; indeed, some of them had been driven all the way from Nauvoo the same season." [45] As the men passed through a number of small settlements, they endeavored to purchase fresh draft animals, but they found the people were so prejudiced against the United States government they would not help them except to sell them a little feed and a few fresh vegetables; but on October 23 they managed to pick up ten yoke of oxen and twenty or more fresh mules.

The Men Help the Teams

By October 26 travel was down the Rio Grande del Norte, where the country was so sandy the men had to help the teams pull the wagons, although they were on reduced rations. The men saw canals for irrigating purposes all along the banks of the river, "some of them several miles in length." On October 30, when they left the banks of the Rio Grande del Norte for a time, it was necessary for twenty men with long ropes to help the teams pull the wagons over the sand hills. Traveling, however, was much better than it had been under Lieutenant Smith. On November 2 the battalion met the guides who had been engaged by General Kearny and sent out to explore the country ahead of the soldiers. They reported it would take at least ninety days more to reach the Pacific Coast.

On November 6 the battalion reached the point where General Kearny had left his wagons and proceeded with pack animals. This was 288 miles southwest of Santa Fe. General Kearny had heard while in Santa Fe that the Mexicans in California had surrendered to Commodore Stockton; so he disbanded most of his soldiers and hurried on with a hundred selected men in order to reach the coast as rapidly as possible, where he was to assume control of the country as governor and commander-in-chief of California. But his orders to Colonel Cooke and the battalion were to open a road to California; and inasmuch as wagons could no longer be taken by following General Kearny's trail, it was necessary to go much farther to the south.

A Third Detachment to Pueblo *(in Colorado)*

On November 10, because of the arduous task, many men were weakened and sick and fifty-five more were detached to return to Santa Fe and then on to Pueblo for the winter. Colonel Cooke ordered twenty-six days of reduced rations to be given to them, but they were only given five days rations with which to travel 300 miles back to Santa Fe. They finally reached there about November 25, having had three deaths on the way. Here they recuperated for a few days, were given some teams and provisions, and left on December 5 on another 300 mile trip to Pueblo. All but a few of the sickest arrived on December 20, having lost one more soldier after departing from Santa Fe. Not counting those who had died, there were about 150 soldiers now at Pueblo, along with perhaps 80 women and children. In addition, there were about 47 Latter-day Saints from Mississippi who had arrived at Fort Laramie in the summer of 1846 and were waiting for the lead company of pioneers when they received word that the pioneers would not be going further west until 1847. As Fort Laramie did not have sufficient supplies to take care of them for the winter, it was recommended that they go south to Pueblo, where they could get food from the Mexican settlement. A total of about 273 Mormons wintered at Pueblo in 1846-47. Here the first Anglo-Saxon children born in Colorado were born to some of the Latter-day Saint women that winter.

On December 23 two of the soldiers, John H. Tippets and Thomas Woolsey, left Pueblo to take back money to their families at Winter Quarters and other camps. They were fifty-two days making the journey. They arrived February 15, going the last three days without eating.

"Blow the Right"

Back on the Rio Grande on November 10, Colonel Cooke found it necessary to leave two wagons and some equipment.

started Mar 30 July 46" — San Diego Jan 1847 = 6 mo

They put what they could on thirty-six pack mules and some oxen, which made quite a fuss since they had not been previously broken for such labor. It amused the soldiers and even Colonel Cooke to watch their antics. The battalion continued on down to the southwest, as it was still impossible to take wagons directly west. Each day as they traveled farther south, the men became more fearful of falling in with General John E. Wool, who was the commander of what was called the Army of the Center in the Mexican War. If this happened they were likely not to get to California at all before their enlistment ran out; so during the evening of November 20 Brother Levi Hancock, one of the seven presidents of the First Council of the Seventy and the only General Authority in the battalion, and father David Pettigrew, the oldest man, went from tent to tent asking the men to "pray to the Lord to change the Colonel's mind."

The next day as they continued on, they soon discovered that the road began to bear southeast instead of southwest. The colonel looked over the situation, rose in his saddle, ordered a halt, and said, "This is not my course. I was ordered to California; and . . . I will go there or die in the attempt." Turning to the bugler he said, "Blow the right."

At this point father Pettigrew exclaimed, "God bless the Colonel!" The colonel looked around to see who had spoken and a look of satisfaction came on his face.[46]

The Continental Divide

On November 28, the battalion passed over the continental divide, after which they noticed that all streams ran westward instead of eastward. By December 2 they arrived at San Bernardino, a deserted ranch in New Mexico, where they encountered wild cattle for the first time.

Battle with Wild Bulls

On December 11, while on the banks of the San Pedro River, the battalion was actually attacked by a herd of wild cattle. In the battle that followed, two mules were gored to death, two men were wounded, one having been thrown about ten feet in the air, and thirty to sixty bulls were killed. From the wild bulls they made jerked beef.[47] By now the battalion was heading north.

On December 13 the guides brought word that two hundred Mexican soldiers were stationed at Tucson. The guides said that to go around Tucson would be an extra hundred miles to march; so Colonel Cooke ordered the battalion to march straight through. But he reminded the men that the people of Sonora (this was the name of the whole surrounding area) were not their enemies and that the American soldier always showed justice and kindness to the "unarmed and unresisting." He stated, "The property of individuals you will hold sacred."

Captain Comaduran, the Mexican commander, had been given orders not to allow an armed force to pass through the town; so he declined a proposition to surrender, although from reports he was led to believe the United States armed force approaching was much larger than it really was. On December 16, as the battalion marched toward Tucson with their guns loaded, two Mexicans met them and told them the soldiers had fled and had forced most of the citizens to flee with them. About a dozen well-armed men in citizens' dress later met the battalion and conducted it into town. They marched through town, "where a few aged men and women, as well as some children, brought [them] water and other little tokens of respect." About one hundred citizens out of four or five hundred were all that had remained in the town. The soldiers marched on through and camped on the stream about one half mile below the village. Later some of the officers and men returned to the village. Some of the women were at first frightened, but when all were treated with kindness, they showed "strong signs of gratitude." Nothing was taken, except some wheat from the public storehouse with which to feed the animals.

Before moving on, Colonel Cooke left a note to Captain Comaduran containing a conciliatory letter for Don Manuel Gandra, governor of Sonora, explaining that the soldiers were not the enemies of the people and that the making of a wagon road from the Atlantic to the Pacific should be beneficial "to the citizens of either republic."

Kearny's Route

On December 18 the command continued their journey, during which they suffered immensely for the next few days

76   because of the scarcity of water. They arrived on the Gila River
on December 21, and joined up again with General Kearny's
route, having traveled a distance of 474 miles since they had left
Kearny's route on the banks of the Rio Grande.[48] This route
later became the location of the Southern Pacific Railroad
across the desert to San Diego (just as the Mormon pioneer
route became the location of the Union Pacific Railroad) and
showed the necessity of owning this land, which was purchased
from Mexico on December 30, 1853, and became known as the
Gadsden Purchase.

Honest and Peace-Loving Indians

On December 22 the command arrived at the Pima Indian
village, where there was a population of about two to four
thousand Indians. Both Sergeant Tyler and Colonel Cooke commented upon the cleanliness, happiness, and general honesty of
these Indians.[49]

On December 23 they left the Pima village and shortly thereafter met three guides who had helped take General Kearny
through to San Diego. They informed the battalion they were at
least one month ahead of the general's expectations; General
Kearny had taken twelve days on pack mules from the Pima
village to San Diego, and he had expected it would take the
battalion from forty to sixty days with wagons.

The nights of December 23 and 24 were spent near the villages of the Maricopa Indians, who were found to be equally as
honest and peace-loving as the Pima Indians. The number of
Maricopa Indians was estimated at ten thousand.

California   (6 months).

The battalion crossed the Colorado River into California
January 9 and 10. Much suffering was endured until they
reached Warner's ranch on January 21 where they saw their first
house in California. Tyler says it was here at Warner's ranch that
they had their first full meal, except for those at Tucson and in
the wild bull country, since they had left the Rio Grande del
Norte. The meal consisted of fresh fat beef without salt. Cattle
and horses were very cheap since the country was overrun with
them and there was very little market.

On the day prior to arrival at Warner's ranch, orders were
received to march to San Diego rather than Los Angeles, as a

previous order had directed that they do. They arrived within sight of San Diego on January 29, 1847, and camped about five miles below the town where General Kearny was quartered. In ·the evening Colonel Cooke rode down to report to Kearny. The next day Colonel Cooke issued order one, highly complimentary to the achievements of the battalion, found in Appendix 4. [50]

Termination of the Mexican War

The American forces under Commodore Stockton, Lieutenant Colonel John C. Fremont, and General Kearny met at Los Angeles on January 14, 1847, after some of them had had severe altercations with the Californians. General Kearny and Commodore Stockton had fought the last decisive battle with the Californians at Los Angeles on January 8 and 9, 1847. The enemy in retreat had met Lieutenant Colonel Fremont on January 12, to whom they surrendered and signed articles of capitulation. This treaty was ratified by Commodore Stockton and General Kearny; so the war was actually over when the Mormon Battalion arrived on the scene. Brigham Young's prediction before the expedition began that they would have no fighting to do except with "wild beasts" had been literally fulfilled. [51]

Stationed at San Diego, San Luis Rey, and Los Angeles

On February 1 the battalion was ordered to march to San Luis Rey, fifty-three miles to the north, and occupy the post, just in case of future difficulties. On February 15 Company B of the battalion was ordered to San Diego to garrison that post.

On March 19 a small number of men from Companies A, C, D and E were left at San Luis Rey and the majority of the companies were transferred to Los Angeles. Later, on April 6, the San Luis Rey garrison was closed, and the soldiers were transferred to Los Angeles.

The battalion was later called on to perform certain duties in protecting the Californians from the Indians, inasmuch as the Californians were not permitted to bear arms.

On about May 10 fifteen men of the battalion were detailed to return to Fort Leavenworth with General Kearny, but when he left Monterey on May 31 only twelve battalion men accompanied him. While in Los Angeles the Mormon Battalion built a military fort, which became famous as Fort Moore, being so named on July 4, 1847.

When the Mormon Battalion men were off duty, they were permitted to take jobs from the local citizens of San Diego and Los Angeles such as "making adobies, burning brick, building houses, digging wells," and other various jobs. The men were conscientious workers and lived as moral, upright citizens to the extent that on July 6 the San Diego people sent a written request to the commander of the southern military district "that another company of Mormons be immediately sent to take the place of Company B, stating that they did not wish any other soldiers quartered there."[52]

Efforts to Reenlist

On June 29 at Los Angeles Colonel Stephenson gave a talk to the battalion members similar to one he had given Company B at San Diego, encouraging the men to reenlist, stating that if they would reenlist, they could be discharged in February, 1848, with twelve months' pay. But after paying them many fine compliments, he ended by telling them that another year's service would place them on a level with other communities. Sergeant Tyler stated:

> The Colonel, in this last remark might be compared to the heifer that gave a good bucketful of milk and then kicked it over. It was looked upon as an insult added to the injuries we had received without cause.[53]

On July 16, Company B having arrived the day before, the five companies of the battalion were formed at 3:00 p.m. at Fort Moore and were discharged. On July 20 eighty men reenlisted for six months along with Captain Daniel C. Davis as their commanding officer. They were sent to San Diego where the people had requested them.

Scattering of the Battalion

The men of the battalion now became scattered in many directions: twelve had left for Fort Leavenworth with General Kearny; 81 reenlisted; of about 150 who started out by the northern route for the Salt Lake valley, about half stopped to work at Sutter's Fort and elsewhere in California for the winter, and the rest arrived in Salt Lake valley on October 16 almost destitute of clothing. Thirty-two of those from California were so anxious to see their families who had not yet arrived in the Salt Lake valley that they continued their journey east even though the season was late, leaving on October 18 and arriving at Winter Quarters on December 18, 1847.

Captain Hunt also came to Salt Lake valley by way of the northern route with another group of the battalion members, arriving in October of 1847. In the spring of 1848 about twenty-five members among those who had reenlisted came to Utah by the southern route and were the first people ever to take wagons over the Cajon Pass. While this group was making the first wagon road over the southern route to Utah in 1848, the battalion members who had spent the winter working for Captain Sutter, building the first flour mill and the first sawmill in that part of the country, were making a new wagon road over the Sierra Nevada along the northern route east of Sacramento, "the Truckee route being impracticable at that season of the year."

A few battalion members, such as Captain Jesse Hunter, stayed in California and never did make their way to Utah, although most of them remained loyal to the Church.

ADVANTAGES AND DISADVANTAGES OF THE ENLISTMENT OF THE MORMON BATTALION

Looking at the situation from today's perspective, it is evident that the federal government officials did not suggest the call of the Mormon Battalion as a way of destroying the Mormons, or of even working to their disadvantage, as was later thought and occasionally suggested by a Church official, although Senator Benton of Missouri and one or two other anti-Mormons may have uttered idle threats or boasts. The officials who were connected with the call meant it only for the good of the Mormons and of the country. We must keep in mind that getting plenty of volunteers for the war was no problem as many volunteers were turned away.

The call of the battalion came as a result of Jesse C. Little's attempts to seek aid from the government in the emigration of the Saints to the West.

At the time, the government had only recently entered into a war with Mexico and it was only natural that this war was uppermost in the minds of the government officials. Although such a call to arms had not been thought of by Church leaders, it was readily accepted, even though it could hardly have come

80   at a more inopportune time, as the young men of the Church who could have gone most conveniently were widely scattered. Thus much recruiting was done among family men. It also meant that nearly five hundred wagons were left without teamsters and many families were left without a protector or a provider. Many of them, having already been driven from their homes a number of times, could not be expected to enlist merely from an appeal to their patriotism. The encouragement of Church leaders helped sway the balance to the side of patriotism, however, and there were a number of distinct advantages to the Church:

1. It was evident to all that the Mormons were loyal American citizens.

2. It gave the Mormons a justifiable reason to camp temporarily on Indian lands and government lands.

3. The Saints were short of money, and the soldiers' pay and clothing-allowance money was a great aid to them.

4. Upon release the soldiers received their guns and other accoutrements.

5. It probably gave the Saints some influence in preventing former Governor Boggs of Missouri from being appointed governor of California if President Polk had really had it under consideration as was rumored.

On the side of the government it was quite obvious to the officials that there were certain advantages to having Mormon soldiers in the federal army:

1. The Mormons would not be likely to join with Canada or Mexico while their men were fighting against these countries in the United States army. (This thought, of course, had never entered the minds of the Mormons.)

2. The Mormons would realize that the federal government held no prejudice against them.

3. It was an opportunity for the Mormons and the government to be mutually helpful to each other.

4. Having Mormon soldiers in government service would be less costly, for they were already near Fort Leavenworth and would not need to be transported back to the States.

Footnotes

[1] *Times and Seasons* (Nauvoo) 6:1096. *See also HC*, 7:570.
[2] *CHC*, 3:67.
[3] *CHC*, 3:67-68.
[4] *CHC*, 3:68.

[5]*CHC*, 3:68.

[6]*CHC*, 3:69.

[7]*CHC*, 3:70. Mexico recognized the Nueces River and not the Rio Grande as the border between Mexico and Texas.

[8]*CHC*, 3:70-71.

[9]*CHC*, 3:71.

[10]*CHC*, 3:73.

[11]Edward W. Tullidge, *Life of Brigham Young* (New York: n.p., 1876), pp. 45-52. *See also CHC*, 3:75, including footnotes 37 and 38.

[12]*CHC*, 3:82-83, footnote 55.

[13]*CHC*, 3:77, including footnote 40.

[14]Daniel Tyler, "A Concise History of the Mormon Battalion in the Mexican War" (n.p., 1881), pp. 113-14. Copies are available in Brigham Young University Library, Provo, Utah.

[15]Tyler, pp. 114-15.

[16]Tyler, p. 115.

[17]Juanita Brooks, ed., *On the Mormon Frontier: The Diary of Hosea Stout*, 2 vols. (Salt Lake City: University of Utah Press, 1964), 1:172.

[18]Brooks, 1:174.

[19]Brooks, 1:175.

[20]*CHC*, 3:77-78.

[21]*CHC*, 3:79.

[22]*CHC*, 3:81. (Italics deleted.) When we think of California as here referred to, we must keep in mind that everything south of the 42nd parallel and west of the Rockies was considered California. This included the Great Basin area.

[23]*CHC*, 3:81-82. (Italics deleted.)

[24]Brooks, 1:177.

[25]*CHC*, 3:82.

[26]*CHC*, 3:83. (Italics deleted.)

[27]Tyler, p. 116.

[28]Tyler, p. 117.

[29]*CHC*, 3:84, including footnote 61.

[30]Tyler, pp. 128-29.

[31]Tyler, p. 125.

[32]This statement is found in Sergeant Daniel Tyler's book, p. 134, which is one of the most informative books available on the Mormon Battalion. The writer will take a number of ideas and statements from this work from this point on to the end of the chapter without always footnoting them.

[33]*The Mormon Battalion and Its Monument* (Salt Lake City: State of Utah Mormon Battalion Committee, 1916), p. 19.

[34]*CHC*, 3:105, 109. *See also* Tyler, pp. 155-56.

[35]Tyler, p. 151.

[36]Tyler, p. 154.

[37]Tyler, p. 155.

[38]Tyler, pp. 155-56.

[39]Tyler, p. 143.

[40]Tyler, p. 156.

[41]Tyler, p. 144.

[42]Tyler, p. 147.

[43]Tyler, p. 174.

In honor of Battalion monuments

San Diego

Utah

Los Angeles

82   [44]Tyler, p. 132.
[45]Tyler, p. 175.
[46]Tyler, p. 207.
[47]Tyler, pp. 218-23; Phillip St. George Cooke, *Conquest of New Mexico and California* (Chicago: Rio Grande Press, 1964), pp. 145-46.
[48]Cooke, p. 158.
[49]Tyler, p. 235; Cooke, pp. 161-64.
[50]Tyler, pp. 254-55.
[51]Tyler, p. 118.
[52]Tyler, pp. 289-90.
[53]Tyler, p. 294.

5

Winter of 1846-47

CAMPS FARTHEST WEST

With the Mormon Battalion off on its trek West, Brigham
Young and the leaders of the Church turned to other tasks. The
hope of sending a vanguard on to Oregon or California in 1846
was, as yet, not entirely gone. Brigham Young and other leaders
still wanted a group to find a location somewhere in the Great
Basin where they would be on hand at an early date in the
spring of 1847 to plant crops. On Monday, July 20, 1846—the
day the Mormon Battalion left Council Bluffs—Brigham Young
and Heber C. Kimball, whose pioneer companies had already
crossed the Missouri River and were camped about four miles
west near some springs, later called Cutler's Park, called for
volunteers from their respective companies to leave for the West
the next morning.[1] On Tuesday, July 21, approximately
seventy-five men with their families from each of the two
companies responded to the call. By the evening of July 22 they
had arrived on the banks of the Elkhorn River and that night
they crossed fourteen wagons over. Brigham Young, Heber C.
Kimball, and Willard Richards came into their camp that evening. Joseph Holbrook states that the next morning, July 23,
they organized the company with "John Maxwell, Newel
Knight, and Joseph Holbrook as captains of fifties of the first
company on their way over the mountains," after which Young,

Kimball, and Richards returned to the main camp. "They told us to go ahead and they thought they should be on our heels in a few days. If not, [they] would send us word in due season."[2]

On Friday, July 24, the first company was organized with captains over each ten. There were seven captains of ten: Anson Call, Jerome Kempton, David Lewis, Solomon Hancock, William Matthew, Erastus Bingham, and a Brother Dana. They took inventory and found there were 130 persons, 71 wagons, 268 oxen, 142 cows, 35 calves, 132 sheep, 34 young cattle, 22 horses, 2 mules, and 3 pigs. Presumably Heber C. Kimball's company of volunteers had nearly the same number of wagons and people.

After traveling another twenty-five miles west, Brigham Young's advance company met with some teams of Brother George Miller's camp on Saturday, July 25. By Sunday afternoon, July 26, they had traveled another ten miles and arrived on a branch of the Platte River, by Thursday, July 28, another twenty-seven miles to the main Platte River. This put them nearly one hundred miles west and a little north of where the main camp was located at what became known as Winter Quarters. On Friday, July 31, having traveled another thirty miles, they met Bishop George Miller, whose main camp was still ahead of them. All the way west Bishop Miller had been a restless spirit, out ahead of all the others except during one period when Brigham Young had chastised him for not cooperating with the other leaders. Miller wanted Brigham's company to move forward immediately to join his company at the Pawnee village. This village had been mostly burned by the Sioux Indians about two months previously.

On August 1 Brigham Young's volunteer company traveled three miles and reached the Loup Fork of the Platte River, where they met in council at Bishop Miller's camp. There they resolved that Bishop Miller visit Brigham Young as soon as possible, presumably for counsel as to what to do next. On August 4 Brother Heber C. Kimball's company caught up with them, and the companies prepared the banks of the Platte River and crossed it. On August 5 leaders of the three companies totaling approximately 200 wagons, decided to form an encampment on the south side of Loup Fork.

On August 7 Newel Knight and John Hay, returning from the main camp, brought a letter from the Council of the Twelve suggesting that they not "cross the mountains this fall." The letter also suggested that as many of the Saints who could be sustained should winter at the Pawnee village and the remainder at Grand Island, or some nearby locality. In the spring the authorities would overtake them, and they could all cross the mountains together.[3]

The letter also contained a suggested organization for the camp for the winter, advising as president George Miller; as high councilors Newel Knight, Joseph Holbrook, Anson Call, Erastus Bingham, John Maxwell, Thomas Gates, Charles Crismon, Titus Billings, David Lewis, Hyrum Clark, and a Brother Bartholomew; as clerk Jacob Houtz.

On Saturday, August 8, the camp met together and effected the suggested organization. They also discussed whether they should themselves camp on the Missouri River. On Sunday evening, August 9, the Saints held a council with a number of Ponca Indians for the purpose of helping the Poncas make peace with the Pawnees, with whom the Poncas had been at war and whom they expected to find there. The Ponca chief invited the Saints to winter with them in their country which they said was only "three sleeps" away; there they would find timber for their houses and fuel and pasture for their cattle.[4] Through the influence of Bishop Miller and James Emmett, the council accepted the invitation of the Poncas rather than camp at the Pawnee Mission or at Grand Island. Grand Island had been spoken of as a good place for the advance camp to spend the winter, but the leaders had apparently decided to stay on the Missouri River where they could more readily obtain supplies from the settlements in northern Missouri.

CAMP AT PONCA

On Monday, August 10, the council decided that about twenty-nine families would winter at the Pawnee Mission—only a few miles away—under the presidency of Jacob Gates. On August 11 Brother Gates and the families who were to stay with him left the camp.

On about August 14 the rest of the camp, consisting of over 160 wagons, started for the Ponca country, about ninety miles north; but instead of three days and nights—the length of time required to travel with ponies—the journey took eleven days for the wagons to cover the hard, rough, rocky country. The trip to Ponca country turned out to be a major mistake, since it put the camp far away from provisions that could be procured no nearer than the settlements in northern Missouri. They built a fort at a settlement they called Ponca on the Running Water River, today the Niobrara River, about three miles from its confluence with the Missouri.

On December 15 Joseph Holbrook, a member of the Ponca settlement, wrote in his journal that his wagon had returned from the state of Missouri where it had gone for grain: "It has been absent for two months and traveled over 700 miles, there and back again." On Sunday, December 20, he wrote:

> We divided our grain into three equal parts with my brother Chandler and Dwight Harding. I had 14½ bushels of corn and meal, with the loss of one yoke of oxen. $14.00 in property which made my corn cost me $5.00 per bushel besides my own team to haul it. We are now living on bread and water and that on short allowance. One half or two thirds of the camp are no better.[5]

Death of Newel Knight and Others

At evening on Christmas day the people at Ponca sighted the prairies afire about ten or twelve miles northwest of them on the south side of the Missouri River. The fire swept down upon them like swift horses, and soon more than 200 men and women were carrying water from the river in an attempt to protect their property. That the fort had been built of green logs saved it, but five stacks of hay were burned, Brother Bartholomew's wagon was completely destroyed, many others were damaged, and all of the grass thirty miles to the west and south was burned.[6] A number of deaths later resulted from exposure and overwork in the camp. Newel Knight's death was one of these. He died on January 11, 1847. His complaint was said to have been cold and inflammation of the lungs. He had no doubt contracted pneumonia from perspiration and exposure to the cold weather on the evening of the fire. He was forty-six at his death and had been one of the first to embrace the gospel, the one for whom the first miracle in the last days had been performed—when the Prophet Joseph Smith cast an evil spirit out of him. His mother, Polly Knight, had been the first Church member to die in Missouri when the first Saints had moved there in July of 1831, and his father had died at Mt. Pisgah only a few months before Newel's death; it is possible Newel had not even heard of it. At Ponca Newel left his wife Lydia with seven children of her own and one stepson Samuel,

the son of his first wife Sally Coburn Knight, who had died in
Clay County, Missouri, in 1834 following the expulsion of the
Saints from Jackson County, Missouri.

Reorganization and Abandonment of the Ponca Settlement

On February 6 Ezra T. Benson—ordained an apostle on July
16, 1846, replacing John E. Page—and Erastus Snow came into
camp. They requested that Bishop George Miller return to
Council Bluffs with them. Bishop Miller had tried to persuade
the camp at Ponca that he, instead of the Twelve Apostles,
should be their leader. The camp had overruled him, however.
On February 8 the camp was reorganized, and Titus Billings
became president with Erastus Bingham and Joseph Holbrook
as counselors. The next day Bishop Miller returned to the main
settlements with the Apostles.

At the end of March the Apostles requested the people at
Ponca to return to the settlements on the Missouri and plant
crops along the banks of the river. They left twenty-three of
their number buried at Ponca.

WINTER QUARTERS

When Brigham Young and the Council of the Twelve wrote
to Bishop Miller on August 1, 1846, they were camped four
miles west of the Missouri River at a place called Cutler's Park
in honor of Alpheus Cutler. They eventually retraced their steps
three miles east to the west bank of the Missouri River, about
twelve miles north of Council Bluffs on the opposite side of the
river. Here they laid out a city and built a large stockade. It
became known as Winter Quarters. At the beginning the town
was divided into thirteen wards, which were later divided into
twenty-two wards. A high council was chosen and authorized to
perform the dual functions of both an ecclesiastical high council
and a municipal council. B. H. Roberts describes their self-
imposed government:

The community had no laws save such as were self-
imposed; no officers save those provided in the church
organization, and their special appointees to exercise
functions of a semicivic nature such as a marshal of a camp
and his aids to enforce order and prevent people from
trespassing upon each other in regard to stock running at

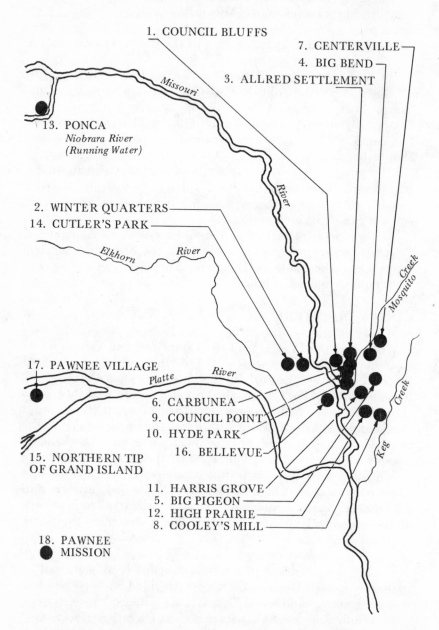

1. COUNCIL BLUFFS

7. CENTERVILLE
4. BIG BEND
3. ALLRED SETTLEMENT

Missouri

River

13. PONCA
Niobrara River
(Running Water)

Creek

Mosquito

2. WINTER QUARTERS
14. CUTLER'S PARK

Elkhorn   *River*

17. PAWNEE VILLAGE
Platte   *River*

Creek

6. CARBUNEA
9. COUNCIL POINT
10. HYDE PARK
16. BELLEVUE

15. NORTHERN TIP
OF GRAND ISLAND

Keg   *Creek*

11. HARRIS GROVE
5. BIG PIGEON
12. HIGH PRAIRIE
8. COOLEY'S MILL

18. PAWNEE
● MISSION

Fig. 4. The Saints' communities in the area of Council Bluffs and Winter Quarters during the winter of 1846-47.

large, destroying gardens, or intruding into camp grounds; also to hold in check the thoughtless buoyancy of youth which had not yet learned the lessons of self-restraint, and ever grows somewhat impatient of discipline; also to guard the camps from the intrusion of strangers who would spy out their liberties and impose upon the unwary, and likewise to check by punishing promptly, the thieving propensities of the Indians by whom they were surrounded. Their laws were edicts or regulations issued from the councils of their wisest men. It was literally the rule of Carlyle's "*can*-ning, or able-men,' voluntarily submitted to by the people with right willing loyalty and nothing doubting, because they recognized in the edicts promulgated 'precisely the wisest, fittest' thing which in all ways it behooved them to do.[7]

In addition to Ponca and Winter Quarters, other Mormon settlements for the winter of 1846-47 which had a sufficient population to warrant a high council of twelve men were Kanesville (Council Bluffs), Mt. Pisgah, Garden Grove, and Council Point. That these high councils had a wide range of duties can be ascertained from the instructions of Isaac Morley when he was installed as president of the high council at Kanesville:

The council was instructed to oversee and guard the conduct of the saints, and counsel them that the laws of God and good order are not infringed. . . . It will be wisdom and necessary to establish schools for the education of children during the coming winter in this region, and we wish you to see that this is done.[8]

Samuel Bent had been appointed president of the high council at Garden Grove and William Huntington at Mt. Pisgah, but by August 28, 1846, word came to Winter Quarters that both men were dead.

The winter of 1846-47 found approximately 15,000 Saints and perhaps 30,000 head of livestock scattered across an area of over 500 miles. In addition to their principal points of settlement, many had scattered up and down the Missouri River for over forty miles and inward on the Iowa side for fifteen or twenty miles, where they settled on good farmland. Others had scattered out on farms all across southern Iowa and into northern Missouri.

The site that became Winter Quarters was not selected until September 11, 1846, when the surveying of it began. On Thursday, September 17, the council made the official decision to move from Cutler's Park back to the newly selected site on the banks of the Missouri River. President Young and many others moved back to the new site on September 23; and because more people were continually coming across the river from the east, Winter Quarters became the most populated of all the Mormon settlements. Hosea Stout later gave the population on December 24 as 3,483, including 75 widows, 502 well men, 117 sick men, and 138 absent men who had gone with the battalion—a total of 757 men and 2,726 women and children.[9]

Property Tax

In order to protect the herds and the city, a property tax of ¾ of 1% was levied so that an organized police force could be financed. Hosea Stout was still the head of the police force. Each policeman was paid seventy-five cents for each shift— usually half the night—and Hosea, as the head of the police, received $1.25 per day.[10]

Indian Agreement and Troubles

Although a formal agreement was made with the Omaha Indians, the Saints had to be constantly on guard because the poverty of the Omahas almost compelled them to steal. Brigham Young said that during the winter the Omahas lived by gift or by theft.[11]

But another tribe of Indians, the Otoes, also claimed the land. They, too, gave the Saints permission to stay on the land. The Saints endeavored to stay clear of the quarrel between the Otoes and the Omahas, whose difficulties seemed to be confined to quarreling; whereas the Iowas and the Sioux were aggressive warriors.

On the night of December 9, 1846, the Iowas attacked a small band of Omahas who were camped near Winter Quarters. Big Head, the Omaha second chief, was severely wounded, and a squaw's arm was shattered. The Omahas fled to the home of Brigham Young, who sent for Hosea Stout and other policemen to come and assist him. The policemen took some of the Indians and went to investigate their lodges to find those still missing. Hosea Stout said "their lodges were in a gore of

blood." The Iowas had attacked in the dead of night, shooting
at random into the lodges, and then had fled back across the
Missouri River. President Young had the wounded Indians
moved into a sod hut nearby, and the other Indians moved all
of their lodges beside President Young's house.

Most of the Omaha warriors were away on a hunt at the time
of the attack. On December 12 the Saints learned that the
Sioux had attacked the Omaha hunting party sixty miles to the
north and had killed seventy-three of them. Only a small
number escaped. The Indians stayed near President Young's
home until another group of their people came, at which time
they all went south of Winter Quarters near the settlement of
Bellevue on the west side of the Missouri River.[12]

Sickness at Winter Quarters

Because of a shortage of food—especially fresh vegetables—
and the already run-down condition of many of the Saints,
there was a great deal of sickness at Winter Quarters. The
Missouri bottoms, sometimes called "Misery Bottom" by the
Saints, with its marshy waters collecting sewage from streams
flowing into it, added to the unhealthful conditions. Scurvy
seemed to be the most prevalent disease and was brought on
through a dietary deficiency. Potatoes from northern Missouri
and horseradish found growing at an old abandoned government
fort not far from Winter Quarters did much to check the
disease. Wagons were rolling constantly to and from the
northern Missouri settlements where, on the whole, the Saints
found most of the Missourians friendly and sympathetic, as
attested to in Hosea Stout's journal on January 2, 1847:

> The most opposition we have in Missouri is in con-
> sequence of the Stories of the dissenters otherwise the
> Missourians are very friendly. Pork can be bought from
> two to four cents a pound. Corn from 40 to 50 cents a
> bushel. Wheat from 31 to 40 or 50 cents a bushel. and
> other things in proportion. I have seen potatoes sell at a
> dollar per bushel here. Had not the Saints been here the
> Missourians could not have sold anything for previous to
> our coming they had no market for their produce.[13]

John R. Young also tells of some of the discomfiting circumstances of Winter Quarters and an instance of relief:

Winter Quarters was the Valley Forge of Mormondom. Our home was near the burying ground; and I can remember the small mournful-looking trains that so often passed our door. I also remember how poor and same-like our habitual diet was: corn bread, salt bacon, and a little milk. Mush and bacon became so nauseating that it was like taking medicine to swallow it; and the scurvy was making such inroad amongst us that it looked as if we should all be 'sleeping on the hill' before spring, unless fresh food could be obtained. [14]

While we were in this condition there happened one of these singular events which so often flit across the life of a Mormon. President Young called one day at the door of our cabin, and said to my father:

'Lorenzo, if you will hitch up your horses and go down into Missouri, the Lord will open the way, so that you can bring up a drove of hogs, and give the people fresh meat, and be a blessing to you.'

As I remember, the next day father took me in the wagon, and . . . started on that mission. . . .

Upon arriving at St. Joseph we put up at Polk's Tavern. A Mormon family by the name of Lake had left Winter Quarters in search of work. One of the daughters had found employment at Mr. Polk's. Being frequently questioned, she had told much about the sufferings and the present conditions of our people. She knew my father well, and joyfully recognized him.

In the evening the bar room was full of gentlemen, all eager to learn the news and for two hours they listened almost breathless to father's talk. The next day parties approached father and offered to load him with merchandise. This he declined; but he secured the loan of one thousand dollars—I believe from a Jewish merchant—and wasted no time in getting down to business.

The first move was to buy a forty-acre field of unharvested corn. He paid four dollars an acre for the corn as it stood in the field. It was estimated to average sixty bushels to the acre. The best corn was gathered and put in bins. Heavy logs were then drawn crosswise over the field to mash down the stalks. Then a notice was posted for hogs. As a rule, they came in droves of about thirty and were bought in the bunch, at seventy-five cents a head. They would weigh from 150 to 400 pounds each. Father returned to Winter Quarters with a thousand head of hogs, and in this way President Young's promise to him had been realized.

We read in the good old Bible of an angel giving water to Hagar and Ishmael in the desert, when the patriarch Abraham had sent them away; and when Moses led two million Hebrew bondsmen from slavery to freedom, we read of how God rained manna down from heaven for their sustenance, and so wrought upon the elements, that for forty years their garments did not wax old. And I understand that the Hebrew children to this day remember with grateful hearts those special acts of providence.

Now, while I do not claim for the Latter-day Saints manifestations so marked as these, yet was there many a providential help given to us.[15]

Many other journalists mention the shortage of food at Winter Quarters, but for some reason a number of others do not. Hosea Stout had talked of the shortage of food in his family many times while crossing Iowa. But he did not say anything of a like manner during the winter of 1846-47 although as chief of police he should have been in a position to observe the poverty or prosperity of the people.

Employment during Fall and Winter

On January 2, 1847, Hosea Stout, commenting that their stay at Winter Quarters was about half over, gave a brief synopsis of affairs there. A portion of his report follows:

> The brethren have mostly got into their houses.
> The city is divided into 22 wards & has a Bishop over each ward. They seem to be doing their duty better than I ever knew the Bishops to do before. The poor are uncommonly well seen & attended to. . . .
> The [flour] mill will be in operation next month.
> There are now arraingements being made to send off three hundred pioneers before winter breaks who will proceed to the head of running watter and sustain their teams on the rushes as they will travail up the river. and wait there till grass rises & then proceed to the foot of the mountains near the head of the Yellow Stone where they will put in a crop. [This plan and route of travel was not used.]

The Twelve contemplate & are now raising companies that is each is raising a company who will follow after the pioneers when grass rises here with as many persons as can subsist on the crop put on by the pioneers [By "the pioneers" he of course is referring to the advance company of 300 which they intended to send.] . . .

Our herds and flocks are wintering well on the rushes & are thriving well The weather has been thus far uncommonly favorable but the wind often changing had no snow to interfear with any business yet & every body seem to be industerously & usefully employed

The Council decided to have this place stockaded or Picketed in to keep out the Omahas. . . .

The place hase the appearance of a log, town some dirt ruffs and a number of caves or "dug outs" made in the banks sometimes called "Dens". . . .

The town would be hard to set on fire & burnt down for there are so many "dirt toped & dirt houses [16]

Wintering the Cattle

Most of the cattle that were not in use for milking or for work were kept in a large herd approximately six miles north of Winter Quarters where they were fed on rushes along the Missouri River bottoms. John Tanner and his family—except two of his sons who were with the Mormon Battalion—took over the responsibility of herding the cattle for the camp. [17] The cattle seemed to do well on the rushes.

The Cost in Suffering

Although life on the Missouri was made as comfortable as possible, exposure to weather and the shortage of nourishing food, combined with unhealthy surroundings and the already low resistance of the people caused many to succumb to the ravages of nature. According to Colonel Thomas L. Kane, 600 Saints died during the year at Winter Quarters. [18] A massive bronze plaque at Winter Quarters cemetery today bears the names of 600 Saints buried there. And a large statue by Avard Fairbanks, depicting a mother and father looking upon the body of their infant child in his grave, has been erected in honor of those who died at Winter Quarters. Many, upon visiting the spot, experience a feeling of reverence and appreciation for those who gave their lives for their religious beliefs.

Mormon pioneer cemetery monument at Winter Quarters, by Avard Fairbanks. Names of six hundred dead are shown on a bronze plaque at the foot of the monument. *Courtesy of Church Historical Department.*

Garden Grove and Mt. Pisgah also suffered heavy losses by death for similar reasons, both President Bent of Garden Grove and President Huntington of Mt. Pisgah being among those who died.

And of those who successfully lived through the winter, a small number who had made it this far but now found the price too high, gave up the westward journey and returned to the East—some of them to disappear from the records of the Church and blend into the gentile civilization. But the great majority of the survivors were steadfastly loyal to the Church, suffering many hardships but continuing their rugged journey westward where they assisted in building a spiritual empire, destined to become too sturdy for its enemies to destroy.

Footnotes

[1]The Life of Joseph Holbrook, p. 79. Typewritten copy available in Brigham Young University Library, Provo, Utah. Most of the material concerning these lead companies has been drawn from this journal where more detail can be found pertaining to them.

[2]Holbrook, pp. 79-80.

[3]William E. Berrett and Alma P. Burton, *Readings in L.D.S. Church History,* 3 vols. (Salt Lake City: Deseret Book Co., 1955), 2:165; quoting JH 1 August 1846.

[4]Orson F. Whitney, *History of Utah,* 4 vols. (Salt Lake City: George Q. Cannon and Sons Co., 1904), 4:118. Hereafter cited as *HU.*

[5]Holbrook, pp. 93-94.

[6]Holbrook, p. 95.

[7]*CHC,* 3:130.

[8]*CHC,* 3:150. (Italics deleted.)

[9]Juanita Brooks, ed., *On the Mormon Frontier: The Diary of Hosea Stout,* 2 vols. (Salt Lake City: University of Utah Press, 1964), 1:219-20, including footnote 15.

[10]Brooks, 1:215, 220.

[11]*CHC,* 3:151.

[12]Brooks, 1:216-17, 219.

[13]Brooks, 1:222.

[14]This hill is now known in Florence, Nebraska, as the Mormon Pioneer Memorial Cemetery.

[15]John R. Young, *Memoirs of John R. Young, Utah Pioneer, 1847* (Salt Lake City: Deseret News Press, 1920), pp. 41-44.

[16]Brooks, 1:222-23.

[17]Brooks, 1:183, including footnote 53.

[18]Daniel Tyler, "A Concise History of the Mormon Battalion in the Mexican War" (n.p., 1881), p. 94, footnote. *See also CHC,* 3:151.

6

From the Plains
To the Mountains:
Part 1

A REVELATION PRECEDING DEPARTURE

On January 14, 1847, Brigham Young wrote a revelation from the Lord pertaining mostly to the organization and mode of travel for the westward trek. This is the only revelation written and presented by him in a formal way to the Latter-day Saint people although he often spoke about his revelations, usually referring to them as "the Light." This one is recorded today as Section 136 in the Doctrine and Covenants. It contained many instructions pertaining to the westward trek that would begin in the spring: (1) all of the Latter-day Saints "and those who journey with them" were to organize into companies with captains of hundreds, fifties, and tens, with a president and two counselors over each company; (2) each company was to make a covenant and promise to keep all of the laws of God; (3) after preparing for the trek westward, those in each company were to "prepare for those who are to tarry," referring to those who were to stay to raise crops; (4) each company was to bear its portion of the poor and of those families whose men were in the army; (5) preparations were to be made without fear of enemies who did not have power to stop the Lord's work; (6) every person was to refrain from evil, i.e., from evil speaking, from drunkenness, from possessing that which did not belong to him; (7) every person should praise the Lord with singing, music, dancing, prayer, and thanksgiving; (8) the Lord's people were to be tried in all things so that they would be prepared to receive the glory that was theirs; (9) the prophet should seal his testimony with his blood.

Final Plans Begun

On March 22, 1847, at a meeting of the officers of the two emigrating companies, Brigham Young announced that it was the intention of the Twelve to travel to the Great Basin without stopping, taking only two pioneers to a wagon.[1] They would locate "a stake of Zion" and then return for their families. He further said that only small families should migrate during the summer.[2]

This appears to be the beginning of the final plan, a plan to take only 144 men and 72 wagons so that the company would not be too cumbersome.

Bishop Miller's Defection

Bishop George Miller who, along with Bishop Newel K. Whitney, was trustee-in-trust for the Church, had been somewhat prone to disregard instructions from the Twelve and had merited the displeasure of Brigham Young on more than one occasion while traveling across Iowa. Although he would cooperate with other Church leaders in an organized plan, he continued to go off on his own, usually ahead of everyone except those for whom he was group leader. It was mostly his influence that caused the three leading companies to go up to the Ponca country for the winter. This extra traveling was a needless burden, as they could have wintered better on Grand Island—directly in the line of march to the West—or, more easily, they could have returned to Winter Quarters where supplies were much nearer.

Miller had made a trip or two from Ponca to Winter Quarters during the winter of 1846-47; and in February 1847, Elders Ezra T. Benson and Erastus Snow were sent to Miller's camp on the Running Water River to request Bishop Miller to move immediately to Winter Quarters with his family. Bishop Miller felt this was an intrusion by the Twelve Apostles upon his authority, claiming he had the right to lead the camp himself "by virtue of a special appointment from the Prophet Joseph Smith."[3] The members of the camp, however, accepted the authority of the Twelve and therefore reorganized their camp

along the lines suggested by them; Bishop Miller reluctantly
returned to Winter Quarters with Ezra T. Benson and Erastus
Snow. He remained rather disgruntled, however; and finally, on
April 2, a few days before the pioneer company left for the
Great Basin, he came out in open opposition to the Twelve
Apostles, declaring that he was convinced they should move to
the southern area of Texas between the Nueces River and the
Rio Grande.[4] Hosea Stout spoke of this area as "in dispute now
between the United States and Mexico and [as] the great
thoroughfare for both armies."[5] When Miller's views were not
accepted, he withdrew from the camp, taking his family and a
few followers to Texas where he joined with Lyman Wight who
had gone there in 1845. He soon left Wight and joined James J.
Strang on Beaver Island in Lake Michigan.

THE PIONEER COMPANY MOVES FORWARD

For almost a year the Saints had been singing:

> In upper California, O that's the land for me—
> It lies between the mountains and the Great Pacific sea,
> The Saints can be protected there, and enjoy their
> liberty
> In upper California, O that's the land for me.[6]

John R. Young said they also remembered the prophecy of
Joseph Smith given on August 6, 1842, stating that the Saints
would be driven to the Rocky Mountains.[7]

The Church leaders selected wisely the 144 men who were to
make up the pioneer company. Builders, mechanics, masons,
and men of various professions were chosen "with a view of
making roads, building bridges or erecting temporary quarters
and . . .preparing for a summer of genuine mountaineering."[8]

On Monday, April 5, 1847, the first wagons of the pioneer
company left Winter Quarters for the West. Heber C. Kimball
moved with six wagons to a spot three or four miles west where
they stopped for the night at Cutler's Park, the first camp
grounds established west of the Missouri River. Other wagons
joined Kimball as soon as they could get ready and together
they moved forward to the Elkhorn River. Brigham Young
stayed behind to conduct the general conference of the Church
on April 6, where the people voted unanimously to sustain
eleven of the Twelve Apostles with Brigham Young at their
head. Lyman Wight, who was in Texas, was not accepted unan-

imously and his case was held over. The other members of the Twelve were Brigham Young, Heber C. Kimball, Orson Hyde, Parley P. Pratt, Orson Pratt, Willard Richards, John Taylor, Wilford Woodruff, George A. Smith, Amasa M. Lyman, and Ezra T. Benson.

The meeting was held only in the forenoon because there was so much work to be done in order to get underway. On April 7 President Young left, and by evening he had traveled ten miles to the spot where about twenty-five wagons camped for the night. On April 8 Brigham Young received word that Parley P. Pratt had returned from his mission to Great Britain. President Young and the other apostles were anxious to hear his report; therefore they decided that the main company should rendezvous on the banks of the Elkhorn River and then move on across, while the apostles returned to Winter Quarters. Elder Pratt, along with John Taylor and Orson Hyde, had been sent to Great Britain at the time the Mormon Battalion had left on July 20, 1846, because of an uneasiness the apostles had felt pertaining to conditions in the British Mission.

At Winter Quarters Elder Pratt gave a complete report of conditions and told them that John Taylor would arrive within a few days with the scientific instruments the Twelve had sent for from Council Bluffs. Thus for the next few days the apostles were busy shuttling back and forth from Winter Quarters to the banks of the Elkhorn River thirty-five miles west, where the pioneer company had rendezvoused. Elder Taylor arrived on the evening of April 13, bringing with him "two sextants, one circle of reflection, two artificial horizons, two barometers, several thermometers, telescopes, etc."

The pioneers also had with them a map of John C. Fremont's, sent to them by David R. Atchison, then United States senator from Missouri.[9]

On Wednesday, April 14, the other apostles left the two newly arrived apostles, Parley P. Pratt and John Taylor, in charge at Winter Quarters and returned to the pioneer camp, where they found that the camp had crossed the Elkhorn River and was now—April 15, 1847—camped on the banks of the Platte River twelve miles beyond the Elkhorn and forty-seven miles from Winter Quarters. At 7:40 p.m. President Young called the camp members together and gave them a short talk. Among other things he admonished them to be prayerful and faithful and stated that the traders and Protestant missionaries were stirring up the Indians to plunder the Mormons of their horses

Pioneers Circle Wagons for the Night. *A Painting by C. C. A. Christensen used by permission of Brigham Young University art collection.*

and goods. But if the brethren would be faithful and obey council, "the Lord would bless them and they would pass through the country in safety."[10]

Personnel of the Camp

By April 16 the personnel of the camp was complete. It consisted of 144 men, 3 women, and 2 children. The original plans did not call for any women or children, but Harriet Page Wheeler Young, wife of Lorenzo Young, whose life was in danger from malaria fever, pleaded to be taken along because it might save her life. The leaders finally permitted her and her two sons Isaac Perry Decker—by a former husband—and Lorenzo Zabriskie Young to go. This opened the way for including two other women: Clara Decker Young, wife of Brigham Young (and daughter of Harriet Young), and Ellen Sanders Kimball, wife of Heber C. Kimball.

There were 73 wagons, 93 horses, 52 mules, 66 oxen, 19 cows, 17 dogs, and some chickens in the camp.[11]

At 8 a.m. of April 16 the pioneer camp was called together for the purpose of effecting an organization. There were two divisions with Brigham Young over division one and Heber C. Kimball over division two. Stephen Markham and Albert P.

Rockwood were appointed captains of hundreds, with Addison Everett, Tarlton Lewis, James Case, John Pack, and Shadrach Roundy captains of fifties. Obviously the captains of fifties did not have a full fifty in each group. Next, fourteen captains of tens were chosen and the camp members divided into tens accordingly, except that each group did not necessarily have an even ten members. See Appendix 5 for organization of the camp.

Stephen Markham was selected as captain of the guard for the camp and forty-eight men were chosen as a standing guard. Each night twelve men were to be on guard duty for half the night, and another twelve were to stand guard for the last half of the night. The standing guard was to protect the area where the wagons were, and if more men were needed to protect the animals, which might be tied some distance from the camp, "an extra guard taken from the balance of the company" was "to be selected."[12]

THE JOURNEY CONTINUES

At 2:00 p.m. on April 16, the pioneer company moved on for a distance of three miles where they camped for the night. They were now fifty miles from Winter Quarters, near a cottonwood grove where the men cut down trees that their horses might browse upon the twigs and bark.

After a cold night the camp moved on at 9:05 a.m. on Saturday, April 17, in companies of ten with Heber C. Kimball's division leading the way. They traveled for seven or eight miles and stopped at 12:00 m. "to prepare for the Sabbath," camping near a cottonwood grove where they again felled hundreds of trees to feed their teams. At 5:00 p.m. a meeting was called for the purpose of establishing a military organization which would take charge in case of danger from Indians. The camp was to be one regiment with Brigham Young as lieutenant general, Stephen Markham as colonel, John Pack and Shadrach Roundy as majors, and Albert P. Rockwood as aide. The captains of tens previously chosen were also to be captains of tens in the military organization, except that Appleton M. Harmon replaced John Pack, who had been selected as a major. Thomas Tanner was selected to be captain of the cannon—they had only one cannon with them—and was given the privilege of selecting a crew of nine men to manage it in case of necessity. He chose Rufus Allen, Charles D. Barnum, Sylvester H. Earl, Stephen H.

Thornton, and Thomas Woolsey.

President Young next gave the following instructions:

> After we start from here, every man must carry his
> loaded gun or keep it in the wagon where he can put his
> hand on it at a moment's warning. If the gun is a cap
> locker, take off the cap and put on a little leather to keep
> wet, etc., out, but if it is a flint lock, take out the priming
> and fill the pan with twine or cotton. The wagons must
> keep together when traveling and not separate as they have
> hitherto done, and every man must walk beside his own
> wagon, and only leave it by permission.[13]

During the organization Thomas Bullock was selected as the
clerk of the camp.

Sunday, April 18, was spent as a day of rest. At about 10:00
a.m. seven teams loaded with pelts belonging to Peter A. Sarpy
passed the pioneer camp, having come from the Pawnee village
in two days. Ellis Eames, one of the men in the pioneer camp,
returned to Winter Quarters because of ill health in company
with Sarpy's teams. This left the pioneers with 143 men. At
about 6:30 p.m. Brigham Young and Ezra T. Benson met in the
cottonwood grove with the captains of the companies and gave
further instructions in regard to the method of traveling. At
5:00 a.m. each morning a bugle would sound as the signal for
every man to arise and attend to prayers before leaving his
wagon. This was to be followed first by feeding the cattle then
by cooking and eating. At 7:00 a.m. the bugle sounded as the
signal for the camp to move on. Each extra man was to travel
on the

> off [right] side of his team with his loaded gun over his
> shoulder, and each driver should carry his gun with caps
> and powder flasks ready for use in such a way that he
> could lay his hand upon it at a moment's warning, in case
> of attack by hostile Indians, or when there were signs of
> danger.[14]

If danger appeared to be present, the wagons were to travel in
double file. They were to stop one hour for dinner. The camp
was to be set up each time with the wagons in a circle and the
mouth of the wagon facing the outside, "after the custom of

the plains." The livestock were to be kept inside the circle. Gateways were to be left on two opposite sides of the circle and were to be always carefully guarded. At 8:30 p.m. the bugle would sound, at which time every man would retire to his wagon and pray, and all except the night guard were to be in bed by 9:00 p.m.

Most of the pioneers slept in their wagons, but tents were set up near the wagons on the outside of the circle. Sometimes when camps were later made by a lake or stream, the camp would be set up in a half circle with the bank and the water forming protection on one side. With experience, the camp members became quite proficient in setting up camp, so that it could be done in a minimum of time.

The pioneer camp now traveled up the north bank of the Platte River and would continue to do so until they reached Fort Laramie in present-day Wyoming. Through the area they were now traveling they found "the roads very good, the country being level, and the soil somewhat dry and sandy."[15] Orson Pratt took "observations daily for the latitude and longitude, and also barometric and thermometric observations."[16]

On Monday, April 19, the camp moved on, covering a distance of twenty miles over the level prairie. They stopped for the night at about 6:00 p.m., forming a half circle on the north bank of the Platte River. The animals were placed inside the semicircle to keep them safe from the Indians. The grass along the Platte River was at this time about four inches high but was scattered and not very good. The Platte River, which varied from one to three miles wide, was only about one mile wide at this point and "flowed deep and rapid."

Up to this time William Clayton had been keeping a record of the distance traveled by measuring the circumference of a wagon wheel on one of the wagons, tying a red rag around one of the spokes near the tire, marching by the wheel constantly, and counting the revolutions; but during the afternoon of this day, he suggested to Orson Pratt the idea of fixing a set of wooden cog wheels to the hub of one of the wagon wheels in such a way as to measure the distance each day. Orson Pratt agreed with him that it could be "easily done."

After the encampment William Clayton went to Luke Johnson to ask him to pull a tooth that had been paining him. While they were talking, Stephen Markham asked Luke to take the leather boat which was known to the pioneers as the Revenue Cutter and go back up the road two miles to one of

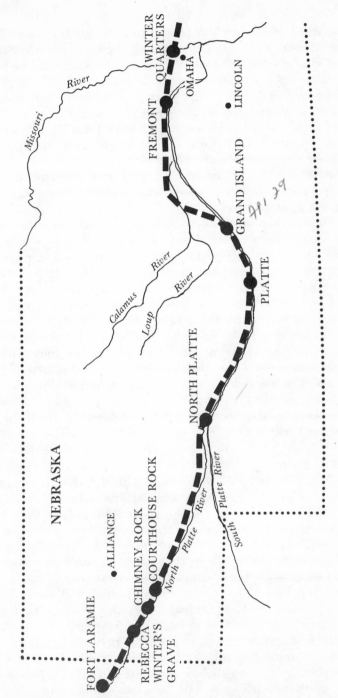

Fig. 5. The pioneer trek across Nebraska in 1847.

the small lakes they had passed to seine for fish. Luke Johnson was the driver of the team hauling the boat and while traveling rode in the boat as he would have in a wagon box. The boat was constructed of leather and had previously belonged to Ira Eldredge. Traveling items were packed in it, but it was also useful in many other ways.[17] Keeping company with those who had gone for fish, Clayton suggested to John Higbee the idea he had discussed with Orson Pratt concerning the cog wheels. Higbee also agreed that it could be done.

After arriving at the lake, they made three hauls but caught only "a snapping turtle, four small turtles, one duck, two small catfish and two creek suckers."[18]

On Tuesday, April 20, soon after the bugle blew at 5:00 a.m., the animals were turned out to graze until 6:30 a.m. at which time they were gathered up. At 7:30 a.m. the camp got underway, traveling along the north bank of the Platte River, now running in a southwesterly direction. The camp traveled eighteen miles that day. About noon John S. Higbee, Luke Johnson, and Stephen Markham struck out ahead of the camp to a lake about two miles beyond where the pioneers stopped for the night. This time their luck was better; they caught over 200 fish, mostly buffalo fish and carp. They arrived back in camp as it was being set up for the night and distributed their fish throughout the camp so that everyone had a good meal.

Cottonwood trees were again cut down "to feed the horses on the bark; the animals would seemingly gnaw off the bark from limbs and sticks ten inches through as readily as they would eat corn."[19]

On the morning of Wednesday, April 21, the oxteams started at 7:00 a.m. and the horse teams at 8:00 a.m. Before long they reached the Loup Fork of the Platte River, where they decided to travel up the fork before crossing. By 1:00 p.m. when they stopped near the river for lunch, they had passed a small Indian village on the north side of the river and could see a much larger Pawnee village—one of about 100 lodges—on the south side of the Loup Fork. About seventy-five Indians followed them into camp, some of them wading across the Loup Fork from the south side at a shallow point. Some of them presented certificates from white travelers who had previously passed or had been to their village, showing that their grand chief, Shefmolan, was friendly toward the white people and that the white people had given him presents. The company gathered together a few items such as powder, lead, tobacco, salt, flour, and a number of fish hooks to give the Indians; but the chief was angry because the quantity was insufficient, and he complained about the Mormons passing through the country and killing off the buffalo. He refused to shake hands with Brigham Young although most of the other Indians seemed friendly enough and shook hands with many of the men. The chief seemed to feel that the white men were rich and that such a large company should produce more gifts. He wanted some tea, coffee, and sugar.

This incident convinced the brethren that the "traders, Missourians, and others had used their influence with the Indians against the Mormons; so it put them on their guard."[20] After traveling twenty miles for the day Brigham Young called for volunteers to stand night guard, and nearly the whole camp volunteered. Fifty were selected to stand guard the fore part of the night and fifty more for the latter part of the night. Brigham Young and Heber C. Kimball were among those on guard. A picket guard of ten men with each watch was stationed outside and mules were stationed with the pickets to help them note the approach of Indians if any happened to be prowling about; mules were noted for their ability to sound an alert when Indians were near. The cannon was also prepared for action. Through the night Indian fires could be seen burning in all directions, and the members of the camp felt it was wise to shoot off a few guns in the night to let the Indians know that they were alert.[21] The night was cold, windy, and rainy. No Indians appeared.

On Thursday, April 22, the pioneers started to travel at 7:30 a.m. They traveled two miles and crossed Looking Glass Creek, "a small stream about one rod wide." After another eight miles they crossed Beaver Creek, a stream about two feet deep and twenty-five feet wide with banks so steep that the men had to help the animals pull the wagons up them. At 5:30 p.m. the pioneers arrived at the Pawnee missionary station, seven miles west of Beaver Creek, formerly occupied by the Reverend J. Dunbar but deserted in the summer of 1846. The Pawnee missionary station was located at a point about three-fourths of a mile north of where Plum Creek emptied into the Loup Fork. Plum Creek ran through the missionary station. The government station where father James Case had lived as a government farmer was one-fourth mile south of the missionary station. Case became converted to the Church, and when Major Thomas H. Harvey learned of it in November, 1846, he dismissed him from government service. Since that time the Sioux Indians had swooped down and burned the government station houses, the blacksmith shop, and almost everything else, but they had not bothered the missionary station. There were considerable amounts of old and new iron around the government station that could be used to good advantage, particularly the plows; but at first Brigham Young told the brethren not to carry away anything although they might use some of the hay that was stacked there for their livestock. The next morning, however, recalling that the government still owed back wages to father Case, President Young proposed that father Case take the hay as part payment from the government, then write the government and tell them how much credit he had taken.

While camped at the mission, William Clayton again mentioned the feasibility of making a set of cog wheels to measure the distance traveled. He estimated that their present campsite was 134 miles from Winter Quarters.

On April 23, the camp traveled four miles west where they tried to cross to the south side of the Loup Fork but found because of quicksand it was difficult to take even empty wagons across; it was 4:00 p.m. of April 24 before the last wagon crossed over. They traveled four more miles and stopped to set up camp.

April 25 was Sunday, and the pioneers rested. "The order of the camp was that there should not be fishing, hunting, or unnecessary labor on the Sabbath."[22] Apparently some of the men of the camp had formed a choir, for President Young called on its members to begin the 5:00 p.m. worship service with the song "This Earth Was Once a Garden Place." Several of the brethren spoke. While George A. Smith was recounting the Prophet Joseph Smith's instructions not to kill any of the animals or birds or anything created by Almighty God merely for the sake of killing, a large wolf appeared on the right side of the camp and walked within fifty rods of the wagons. Later in the evening some of the leaders met near Brigham Young's wagon and selected eight men to hunt buffalo on horseback. Only eight men could hunt because only eight horses in the company were not attached to teams. These men were Thomas Woolsey, Thomas Brown, John Brown, Orrin Porter Rockwell, John S. Higbee, Joseph Matthews, and two others. Eleven other men were selected to hunt on foot. These were John Pack, Phineas H. Young, Tarlton Lewis, Joseph Hancock, Edmund Ellsworth, Roswell Stevens, Edson Whipple, Barnabas L.

Adams, Benjamin F. Stewart, Jackson Redding, and Eric Glines.
The leaders also decided that the Twelve should have the privilege of hunting if they so desired. The reason the number of hunters was limited was that game was becoming plentiful and the brethren did not want to have more game killed than could be profitably used.

On Monday, April 26, just before daylight, the guard fired at what they thought were wolves in the grass. They found them instead to be Indians who had crept within a few rods to steal horses. The camp moved on in a southwesterly direction along the south side of the Loup River. Until crossing the Loup Fork, the pioneers had had a fairly good road to follow, but now there was no road and they had to make their own. President Young, George A. Smith, Amasa Lyman, Heber C. Kimball, and others went out ahead on horses to pick a path for the road. The horse teams then followed, breaking a path through the coarse grass "so it would not hurt the feet of the oxen which followed." [23] After traveling fifteen miles, they made camp on Sand Creek. At dusk they discovered that Indians had crawled up to the encampment and stolen two horses belonging to Willard Richards and Jesse C. Little. A party including Heber C. Kimball, Brigham Young, and about ten others went in pursuit, with no luck, and did not return to camp until after 10:30 p.m.

On April 27 the camp traveled sixteen miles almost due south in order to reach the Platte River. After camp had been made, at about 6:30 p.m., Porter Rockwell, Thomas Brown, John Eldredge and Joseph Matthews returned to camp. They had found the horses' tracks and had seen where they had been tied up, but approximately fifteen fully armed Indians had tried to lure them into an ambush; they had given up the chase and returned to camp. One of Stephen Markham's horses was shot by a gun that accidentally went off in John Brown's wagon. Counting a horse of Brigham Young's that had suffocated on April 24, the pioneers had now lost four horses in four days.

After traveling south another seven miles, on Wednesday, April 28, the pioneers were within a mile of the Platte River. They now turned southwest and began again to follow along the north bank of the Platte River.

On Thursday, April 29, they began moving their wagons at 5:00 a.m.; after traveling three miles, they reached the eastern end of Grand Island, where there were plenty of rushes and cottonwood trees to feed the animals. They stopped here for breakfast. Grand Island, in the middle of the Platte River, was

110 three to four miles wide and nearly fifty miles long. At noon they stopped on the banks of the Wood River, not far from the Platte River on the north and parallel with Grand Island. During the afternoon some of the men set fire to the dry grass so that the green grass would grow faster and those who came later would have better feed for their animals.[24] That night camp was made 204 miles from Winter Quarters; fifteen days had elapsed since the departure of the last brethren from there.

On Friday, April 30, the camp moved forward seventeen miles. The weather was extremely cold and windy, and every man needed his overcoat and a buffalo robe to keep warm.[25] In the evening they had no wood, but they discovered that dried buffalo dung made a good substitute. Heber C. Kimball invented a new way of building a fire for cooking that was well adapted to this type of fuel.

> He dug a hole in the ground about eight inches deep, fifteen inches long and eight inches wide; at each end of the hole he dug another about the same dimensions as the first, leaving about three inches of earth standing between the middle and two end holes. Through these partitions he made a hole about three inches in diameter to serve as a draft. In the bottom of the middle hole the fire and fuel were placed and across the top were set two wagon hammers, upon which pots and pans were placed so that the fire could have free circulation underneath. By this method much cooking was done with very little fuel.[26]

First Buffalo Hunt

On Saturday, May 1, the pioneers saw buffalo for the first time and engaged in a three-hour buffalo hunt from 1:00 p.m. to 4:00 p.m. Altogether they killed 12 head: 3 cows, 3 bulls, and 6 calves. The meat was distributed equally among the tens, and it saved considerably on their breadstuffs, in addition to increasing the tastiness of their diet. The buffalo hunt had been partially in view from the trudging pioneer train, and the train stopped often to observe the hunt. In spite of this, however, they covered eighteen miles during the day.

On Sunday, May 2, they moved westward two miles to a better camping location near the head of Grand Island where water, wood, and feed were available. Orson Pratt had taken an observation, as he had done each day of the journey, and found that the camp was in latitude 40 degrees, 41 minutes, 42 seconds near the head of Grand Island. This agreed with John C. Fremont's observations, or within two miles of his deductions; Fremont's camp had been on the south side of the river, two miles south of the pioneer encampment.[27]

The pioneers observed that the Indians had set the prairie on fire to the west of them, and upon later investigation they found it had come within a mile of their camp. Because the camp was in a desirable location, the pioneers decided on Sunday afternoon to lay over on Monday to set wagon wheels, make other repairs, and hunt. The next day the camp hummed with activity. When the hunters saw an Indian war party of two to three hundred, they reported to camp, where appropriate preparations were made; the cannon was removed from the wagon bed and from thenceforth "hauled in the rear of the company ready for immediate use."

On Tuesday, May 4, the wagons traveled five abreast in order to be more compact in case of an attack from the Indians. During the day they saw three wagons traveling east on the south bank of the Platte River about two miles away. Soon a man from these wagons crossed over in order to ascertain the pioneers' identity. The man was Charles Beaumont, who said he had been at Fort Laramie for three years and had not tasted bread for two. [28] He and his party were the first white men the Saints had encountered since leaving Winter Quarters. He cheerfully agreed to carry letters to Winter Quarters; accordingly, a number of letters were quickly written, with Willard Richards writing one for President Young addressed to John Smith or Alpheus Cutler. When Beaumont left, he took with him fifty-four letters. His own destination was Sarpy's Point, a few miles south of Winter Quarters on the east bank of the river.

The noon camp was made seven miles west beyond Grand Island. Because all of the grass except a few patches here and there had been burned by the Indians, at a meeting that evening the pioneers considered crossing to the south side of the Platte River. Mr. Beaumont had reported it was a good road and that they had seen no Indians during the sixteen days of their journey from Fort Laramie.[29] Wilford Woodruff records the incident.

> We were convinced that it would be better for us to cross the river on the old traveled road to Laramie [Ft. Laramie] as there was good grass on that side, while the

Indians were burning it off on the north side where we were traveling.

When, however, we took into consideration the fact that other companies would soon follow and that we were the pioneers, and had not our wives and children with us, we thought it best to keep on the north banks and face the difficulties of burning prairies. A road would thus be made which would serve as a permanent route, independent of the old immigrant trail. There was the further consideration that the river would separate us from other immigrant companies that might be disposed to quarrel with us over the grass or water. Besides, by the time the next company came along, the grass would be much better than on the south side of the river.[30]

Thus the pioneer company endured the "scant feed, burning prairies, and troublesome Indians" on the north side of the river. It was not difficult to make a new road, for the country was flat and the streams between the Loup Fork and Fort Laramie were not very difficult to cross.

From the time they passed the western end of Grand Island on May 4 until they reached Fort Laramie, the pioneers saw very few trees and usually had to rely upon driftwood along the banks of the Platte River or buffalo chips for fuel. Occasionally they would see a few trees on an island in the Platte River.

The pioneers had entered buffalo country on May 1, and by May 6 they were having difficulty keeping their own animals from mingling with the buffalo that were now much closer. A guard had to be placed over the cattle. By May 7 and 8, they saw thousands of buffalo on both sides of the Platte River, and Brigham Young once more gave orders to the hunting party not to kill more than the camp could use for food. For the next few weeks the hunters kept the camp supplied with fresh buffalo meat as well as deer, antelope, geese, and ducks. Next to buffalo meat, the most often-killed animal was the antelope, quite numerous throughout this country, although not nearly so numerous as the buffalo, of which the brethren claimed to have "seen more than 50,000 in a day." On May 8 Orson Pratt said, "we have seen near 100,000 since morning."[31]

That day William Clayton placed a cedar post in the ground with the words written on it in pencil: "From Winter Quarters 295 [miles], May 8, 1847. Camp all well. William Clayton."[32] This was for the benefit of other companies they expected

up such guide posts every few days after that until they reached
Fort Laramie. Sometimes letters were left in these posts in
ingenious ways. One prepared by Willard Richards on May 10
was left in a slit made by sawing into a post. A note in red chalk
was written on its outside: "Open this and you will find a
letter." On the other side of the post it said: "Look in this, 316
miles from Winter Quarters, bound westward. Pioneer's Latitude 41 degrees." The letter was directed to Charles C. Rich
and contained an account of the journey up to that point.[33]

The Roadometer Invented

Also on May 10 the pioneers passed the confluence of the
South and North Platte rivers, following hereafter along the
north bank of the North Platte River. On this day, also,
Brigham Young told Orson Pratt to give some thought to
William Clayton's proposal of making an instrument to attach
to a wagon wheel to measure the miles traveled. Orson Pratt
recounts the incident:

Accordingly, this afternoon I proposed the following
method: Let a wagon wheel be of such a circumference,
that 360 revolutions make one mile. (It happens that one
of the requisite dimensons is now in camp). [The wheel of
one of Heber C. Kimball's wagons in which William
Clayton rode was this size.] Let this wheel act upon a
screw in such a manner that six revolutions of the wagon
wheel shall give the screw one revolution. Let the threads
of this screw act upon a wheel of sixty cogs, which will
evidently perform one revolution per mile. Let this wheel
of sixty cogs be the head of another screw, acting upon
another wheel of thirty cogs. It is evident that in the movements of this second wheel, each cog will represent one
mile. Now, if the cogs were numbered from 0 to 30, the
number of miles traveled would be indicated during every
part of the day. Let every sixth cog of the first wheel be
numbered from 0 to 10, and this division will indicate the
fractional parts of a mile or tenths; while if anyone shall be
desirous to ascertain still smaller divisional fractions, each
cog between this division will give five and one-third rods.
This machinery (which may be called the double endless
screw) will be simple in its construction, and of very small
bulk, requiring scarcely any sensible additional power, and

The odometer, (or roadometer) planned by William Clayton and Orson Pratt. *Courtesy of Church Historical Department.*

the knowledge obtained respecting distances in travelling will certainly be very satisfactory to every traveller, especially in a country but little known. The weight of this machinery need not exceed three pounds.[34]

On May 11 Appleton Harmon was busy all evening under William Clayton's direction making the odometer according to the plan given by Orson Pratt. They called it a "roadometer." William Clayton was anxious to get it completed, as he was becoming weary of counting the revolutions of a wagon wheel to measure the distance which he had done up to this time.[35] On the morning of May 12 the roadometer was completed and was attached to a wagon wheel. Clayton ceased counting. Four days later, May 16, Appleton Harmon again "completed" the roadometer by adding a wheel to revolve once in ten miles showing "each mile and also each quarter-mile" traveled. He then encased it to protect it from the weather. William Clayton then put up another guide post stating that the distance from Winter Quarters was 356¾ miles and that the last seventy miles were measured.[36] On May 10 the pioneer camp had passed over the Sioux hunting ground. "Acres of land were found covered with buffalo wool, where the Indians had dressed their skins." Also scattered around were dressed buffalo, moccasins, wolf skins, and the carcasses of many buffalo. The pioneers estimated that from 500 to 1,000 Sioux had been camped here as few as ten days ago. They found a saddle tied to a buffalo chip "which was to show the way the buffalo had gone."[37]

Because in some places the Indians had burned off most of last year's grass and the herds of buffalo had eaten off both the new grass which had come up and most of the remaining old grass, it was often difficult during much of the month of May to locate campgrounds where sufficient feed for their animals could be obtained. As a result, their animals became weaker, and they could not travel as far each day as they otherwise would have done. This Sioux hunting ground was located about twenty miles west of the confluence of the South Platte and North Platte rivers, forming the Platte River.

Often, when stopping for the night, if the camp was more than a half mile from fresh water, the pioneers would dig one or two wells, perhaps four feet deep, into which cold water would seep, sometimes at the rate of a "pail a minute."

Rattlesnake Bite Changes Attitude

Sunday, May 23, at 11:00 a.m. Nathaniel Fairbanks was bitten on the leg by a rattlesnake. He said that within two minutes "his tongue began to prick and feel numb." His leg was treated with tobacco leaves and turpentine, and Luke Johnson gave him a strong drink of alcohol and water after which he gave him "a dose of lobelia," which caused him to vomit. His leg swelled and he became nauseous and complained of "dimness in his eyes." This experience seemed to change the attitude of the pioneers toward rattlesnakes. They had started out the trek by following Joseph Smith's policy of never needlessly taking any life, even that of "brute creation," including rattlesnakes, and they had run into many of them on the westward trek. But on May 18 as Brigham Young rode his horse up to a creek he came close to a large rattlesnake and "turned his horse away without harming it." As Thomas Woolsey came up on foot the snake "immediately coiled and sprang at him, but he jumped to one side." At this point John S. Higbee shot at Brigham Young's request. These two experiences encouraged the pioneers to kill rattlesnakes more often rather than risk danger from them.[38]

The Pioneers Commended and Chastised

At the religious services on Sunday, May 23, President Brigham Young expressed himself as being pleased to see so

116 much union among the camp members and their willingness to obey counsel. He told the brethren to "seek after knowledge and be willing to acknowledge God in all things, but never take His name in vain, or use profane language."

The following Friday, however, it appears that both Heber C. Kimball and Brigham Young saw things that displeased them. On that evening William Clayton recorded in his journal:

> I went to writing in Heber's journal and wrote till nearly eleven o'clock. Elder Kimball came to the next wagon where some of the boys were playing cards. He told them his views and disapprobation of their spending time gaming and dancing and mock trying, etc., and especially the profane language frequently uttered by some. He reasoned with them on the subject and showed them that it would lead from bad to worse if persisted in until the consequences would become serious. He exhorted them to be more sober and wise.[39]

From Wilford Woodruff's journal we read:

> During the evening, President Young called at my fire, and seeing several brethren playing dominoes in a wagon nearby, he began to teach, saying that the devil was getting power over the camp which had for several days given way to cards and dominoes, etc. and that if they did not speedily repent, their works, labors, and journey would be in vain. He said that to be sure the camp did not quarrel, for the devil would not set them at that as long as he could draw them gradually away from their duty and fill them with nonsense and folly, for the devil was very cunning in winning away the people of God.[40]

That evening President Young, Heber C. Kimball, Willard Richards, and Wilford Woodruff met in council in "Brother Brigham's tent." The next morning, May 29, President Young called the camp together and had each captain take a separate roll call. Two men, Andrew Gibbons and Joseph Hancock, had gone hunting. Elijah Newman and Nathaniel Fairbanks were confined to their wagons but answered to roll call. All of the other camp members were present. President Young then said that he felt like preaching a little and would take for his text "that as far as to pursuing our journey with this company with the spirit they possess, I am about to revolt against it." He then proceeded to chastise the men for playing cards, dominoes, dice and checkers; for quarreling; for using profane language; and for dancing—"all for recreation." "Joking, nonsense, profane language, trifling conversation and loud laughter do not belong to us." [41] In general he chastised them for not spending their time in a more humble manner. It was perhaps one of the longest sermons he delivered on the trek. He reminded the pioneers that their purpose was to seek out a home for the people of God, after which they would be going out to preach the gospel. After speaking for some time he called for a roll of the priesthood and found there were in the camp eight of the Twelve Apostles, four bishops, fifteen high priests, eighty Seventies, and eight elders. To each separate group he put forth the question, "If you are willing to humble yourselves before the Lord and consent to the right, and walk humbly before Him, make it manifest by raising the right hand." In each case the vote was unanimous. After this he addressed himself to the non-members of the Church, as there were some present.[42] He told them they would be protected in their rights but they must reverence God and the priesthood and must not introduce wickedness into the camp. He spoke highly of the conduct of Benjamin Rolfe who was not a member of the Church.

Brigham Young was followed in speaking by Heber C. Kimball, Orson Pratt, Wilford Woodruff and Col. Markham. Orson Pratt reminded the men there were many good books in the camp they could read in their spare time and recommended besides prayer and obedience the pursuit of knowledge. He summed up the long talk of Brigham Young and those talks of the other authorities into one rather short sentence in his journal:

> About noon the people were called together and addressed by several of the Twelve upon the necessity of a prayerful, faithful, and upright course before the Lord; and instead of spending time in idleness and vanity, to lay up a store of useful knowledge from everything that was seen and heard.[44]

Brigham Young suggested that the next day, the Sabbath, should be devoted to prayer and fasting. On Sunday a prayer and testimony meeting was held early in the morning and a sacrament meeting was convened a little before twelve.

The President's talk on Saturday had brought a stop to jesting, laughing, and nonsense, and William Clayton said he had

118 never noticed the brethren so still and sober on a Sunday since they had started.[44]

A Meeting with Sioux Indians

After leaving the Pawnee country and coming into Sioux territory, the pioneers only occasionally saw one or two Indians at a time; but on May 21, an Indian and his squaw came quite near camp, and several others were seen peeping over the edge of a hill. They indicated that they were Sioux Indians and that a larger party of them was farther away on the bluffs. With the aid of a spyglass the brethren could see several of them with their ponies on the bluffs. The Indian nearest them wore a good cloth coat and was dressed in white man's clothes. This was somewhat different from Pawnees, who often wore only a breechcloth and seemed to be rather unkempt.

About noon on Monday, May 24, two Indians came into the pioneer camp. They were evidently after a large dog which had followed the pioneers into the noon camping grounds. After staying a short time, they took the dog and left. As the pioneers began to prepare their evening camp, they saw a party of Indians on the south side of the North Platte River. About thirty-five Indians—half of them women and children—crossed the river, and some of the pioneers went to meet them at the water's edge, carrying a white flag as a symbol of peace. When the Indians saw the flag, they began to sing, and their chief held up a United States flag. They had with them two letters of recommendation certifying their friendship. The pioneers gave them some food and showed them "a six and fifteen shooter and also the cannon. The gunners went through military maneuvers a number of times, which seemed to please the Indians much."[45]

These Indians were clean and well dressed, having "good clean blankets and nice robes." They wore moccasins which were clean and beautifully made. William Clayton said that for cleanness and neatness, they would vie with the most tasteful whites.[46] Soon after dark Owastotecha, the chief, sent his men to a camp about a quarter of a mile away while he and his squaw asked for the privilege of staying with the pioneer camp overnight. A tent was put up for them. In the evening the chief amused himself by looking at the moon through a telescope.

Although the Indians were shown through the camp, they did not try to steal anything. They were Sioux Indians of the

The pioneers pass Chimney Rock, a sentinel of the desert and the most prominent landmark along the pioneer trail. *Courtesy of Church Historical Department.*

Dacotah (also spelled Dakota, Dacota, Dakcota) tribe and were much different from the thieving Pawnee Indians. Some trading was done with them the next morning; they were given breakfast before they left.

Chimney Rock

During the morning of May 26 the pioneer company arrived at the meridian of Chimney Rock, a most prominent sentinel which they had seen for the past 41½ miles of travel. Taking observations, Orson Pratt discovered that it was 260 feet high from its base to its summit and was on the south side of the river exactly three miles due south of the pioneer camp. Because of its height and distance, it became the most prominent landmark along the pioneer trail. It had been 470 miles from Winter Quarters to the meridian of Chimney Rock.

Footnotes

[1]The emigrants had been divided into two companies, one under Brigham Young and one under Heber C. Kimball. Each of these groups became divided into smaller groups.

120   [2]Juanita Brooks, ed., *On the Mormon Frontier: The Diary of Hosea Stout*, 2 vols. (Salt Lake City: University of Utah Press, 1964), 1:242.

[3]*CHC*, 3:158.

[4]*CHC*, 3:159.

[5]Brooks, 1:245.

[6]John R. Young, *Memoirs of John R. Young, Utah Pioneer, 1847* (Salt Lake City: Deseret News Press, 1920), p. 52.

[7]Young, p. 53.

[8]Andrew Jenson, "Day by Day with the Utah Pioneers" *Salt Lake Tribune*, 7 April 1947.

[9]David R. Atchison was a friend of the Mormons and was a member of the law firm of Atchison, Wood, Doniphan, and Reese whom the Mormons often hired as their lawyers during their Missouri difficulties. He was also a Major General in the Missouri Militia during the Mormon difficulties in northern Missouri but was "dismounted" by Governor Boggs because of being "too friendly" toward the Mormons.

[10]Jenson, 15 April 1947.

[11]One of these wagons was a boat mounted on a wagon frame and another was a cannon; but since the boat was used as a wagon bed and the cannon was also mounted, they were counted as wagons. In some journals, however, the boat was counted as a wagon but not the cannon. *See CHC*, 3:164, including footnote 13.

[12]William Clayton, *William Clayton's Journal* (Salt Lake City: Deseret News, 1921), p. 77.

[13]Jenson, 17 April 1947. *See also* Clayton, p. 79.

[14]Jenson, 18 April 1947.

[15]N. B. Lundwall, comp., *Exodus of Modern Israel* (Salt Lake City: N. B. Lundwall, n.d.), p. 30.

[16]Lundwall, p. 31.

[17]Jenson, 19 April 1947.

[18]Clayton, p. 83.

[19]Jenson, 20 April 1947.

[20]For a fuller account of this incident, see *CHC*, 3:170-71; Clayton, pp. 86-88; Jenson, 21 April 1947; Matthias F. Cowley, *Wilford Woodruff* (Salt Lake City: Deseret News Press, 1909), p. 267.

[21]*CHC*, 3:170-71.

[22]Jenson, 25 April 1947.

[23]Jenson, 26 April 1947.

[24]Jenson, 29 April 1947.

[25]Clayton, p. 115.

[26]Jenson, 30 April 1947. *See also* Clayton, pp. 115-16.

[27]Jenson, 2 May 1947.

[28]Jenson, 4 May 1947.

[29]*CHC*, 3:168.

[30]Cowley, p. 277.

[31]Lundwall, p. 34.

[32]Jenson, 8 May 1947.

[33]Jenson, 10 May 1947.

[34]Lundwall, p. 36.

[35]Clayton, p. 143. *See also* Jenson, 11 May 1947.

[36]This roadometer, or at least most of the cogs, can be seen today in the museum on Temple Square.

[37]Jenson, 12 May 1947.

[38]Jenson, 23 May 1947.

[39]Clayton, p. 187.

[40]Cowley, p. 289.

[41]Jenson, 29 May 1947.

[42]These were Ozro Eastman, Benjamin Rolfe and, up to this time, the Negro members of the camp had not yet been baptized. They were Green Flake, Hark Lay and Oscar Crosby.

[43]Lundwall, p. 49.

[44]Clayton, pp. 189-203. *See also* Cowley, pp. 290-93.

[45]Jenson, 24 May 1947.

[46]Clayton, p. 181.

7

From the Plains
to the Mountains:
Part 2

FORT LARAMIE

By 3:00 p.m. on June 1, Brigham Young's 46th birthday, the pioneers could plainly see Fort Laramie on the opposite side of the North Platte River; this created a great deal of interest, for they were anxious to see some semblance of civilization again. At 5:40 p.m., after traveling twelve miles for the day, they made camp on the east bank of the North Platte about forty rods south of Fort Platte.[1] The pioneers formed a V-shaped camp, which was 543¼ miles from Winter Quarters and 227½ miles above the junction of the North and South Platte rivers. The distance from Winter Quarters had been made in seven weeks lacking one-half a day. Fort Platte was now vacated and crumbling in ruins. It was 144 feet long, 103 feet wide, 11 feet high, 2½ feet thick, and was built of clay and unburnt brick. Fort Platte was on the opposite bank of the North Platte River from the pioneers, about two miles east of Fort Laramie and one-half mile below the confluence of the Laramie and North Platte rivers. The Oregon Trail ran one rod from the southwest corner of Fort Platte.[2]

Fort Laramie was situated on the southeastern bank of the Laramie River and was about 1½ miles from its confluence with the North Platte River. The walls of Fort Laramie were

   . . . built of clay or unburnt brick, being about 15 feet

123

high, and of rectangular construction, measuring on the exterior 116 feet by 168 feet. Ranges of houses are built in the interior adjoining the walls, leaving a central yard of above 100 feet square. This post belongs to the American Fur Company and is now occupied by about eighteen men with their families under the charge of Mr. Budeau.[3]

When the first men arrived on the campground near Fort Platte, they saw two men on the opposite side. They soon had the Revenue Cutter in the water, rowed over, and discovered that the men were Robert Crow and his son-in-law George W. Therlkill, a part of the Mississippi company of Saints who had wintered at Pueblo, Colorado. They had been at Fort Laramie for two weeks awaiting the arrival of the pioneer company. John Brown of the pioneers who had led the Mississippi Saints to Fort Laramie the previous year was especially happy to see some of his old friends.[4]

Brother Crow reported that the rest of the Mississippi company—about thirty more—were at Pueblo and would leave for Fort Laramie with the sick detachment of the Mormon Battalion about June 1, expecting to take two weeks for the journey.

On June 2 the members of the Twelve Apostles and a few others crossed over the river to visit Fort Laramie and learn all they could in regard to their journey west. Orson Pratt measured the width of the river where they crossed and found that it was 108 yards. After visiting the ruins of Fort Platte—the walls were standing but the inside had been destroyed by fire—they walked west two miles to Fort Laramie, first built of wood thirteen years previously and called Fort William; but it had burned down, had been re-built of adobe, and had been named Fort John. Shortly afterwards the name was changed to Fort Laramie because it was on the Laramie River, forty-one yards wide near the fort. The brethren went inside, where they were kindly welcomed by Bordeaux, the superintendent of the fort, who invited them to comfortable chairs. He gave them all the information he could in regard to the route west, telling them they could not travel more than four miles farther on the other side of the North Platte without running into great difficulty because they would come to bluffs which they could not cross with loaded wagons. During the sociable chat, Bordeaux offered to rent to the pioneers his flatboat that would haul two wagons at once across the river for fifteen dollars, or he himself would take them across for eighteen dollars or twenty-five cents per

wagon. He also informed them that ex-Governor Lilburn W.
Boggs of Missouri and his men, who had passed through only a
few days earlier, had had a great deal to say against the
Mormons and had cautioned Bordeaux to take care of his horses
and cattle or the Mormons would steal them. The Missourians
had tried hard to prejudice him against them. He said that
Boggs's men were quarreling all the time and most of them had
left him. Bordeaux had finally told Boggs that no matter how
bad the Mormons were they could not be any worse than he
and his men were.[5] Before leaving, the pioneers visited the
trading post on the north side of the square.[6] Brigham Young
struck up a conversation with a trader who informed them that
the owners of the fort traded only with the Sioux Indians because the Crow Indians came only to steal. A few weeks before
the arrival of the pioneers, they had stolen all of the horses and
mules at the fort, numbering twenty-four or twenty-five.

The Sioux, he said, would not steal on their own land (Fort
Laramie was on land claimed by the Sioux). The people at the
fort sent their furs to Fort Pierre on the Missouri River, a distance of 400 miles by land; and they received all of their stores
and provisions by the same teams, except their meat, since they
could locate buffaloes within a two-day drive. They had recently sent 600 bales of buffalo robes with ten robes to the
bale. Their wagons had been gone for forty-five days.

The people at the fort had tried raising a garden which did
well the first year, but they had not been able to raise anything
since then because of lack of rain.

The pioneers were informed that the distance from Fort
Laramie to Fort Bridger was 350 miles.

After their visit at the fort, the brethren went down to
Laramie River where about twenty of them climbed into
Bordeaux's flatboat. They traveled to the Laramie's confluence
with the North Platte; there they went down the North Platte
one-half mile to the pioneer camp, arriving at 2:15 p.m.

During the day, three portable blacksmith shops were put
into operation in the pioneer camp; the smiths were kept busy
shoeing horses, repairing wagons, and making repairs in general.
The Twelve held a council meeting and decided to send Elder
Amasa M. Lyman in company with Thomas Woolsey, John H.
Tippets, and Roswell Stevens to meet the sick detachment of
the Mormon Battalion and the rest of the Mississippi Saints who
had wintered at Pueblo, Colorado. The Twelve told the men to
hurry the sick detachment on to Fort Laramie, about 210 miles
north of Pueblo, and from there along the trail of the pioneer

company. The escorts left on three horses and one mule at 11:15 a.m. on June 3.

They took with them a number of letters. Elder Lyman took a letter addressed to Captain James Brown of the battalion and one to Elder Thomas Dowdle, the presiding elder at Pueblo. Thomas Woolsey carried with him 349 letters to the members of the battalion, with instructions from Dr. Willard Richards to bring back all the letters that he could not deliver to them.

At 5:00 a.m. on the morning of June 3, the first division, led by Brigham Young, began ferrying the wagons across the North Platte River, a wagon every 15 minutes. Soon after the first wagons had crossed, the blacksmiths set up their forges in the ruins of old Fort Platte and continued to make repairs. Because of a storm, the ferrying was temporarily halted but was resumed again after 3:00 p.m.; by 5:00 p.m. the wagons of the first division were over. Bordeaux called at the pioneer camp to watch them cross on his flatboat. The second division then began to ferry their wagons over, with John S. Higbee as captain. They averaged a crossing every eleven minutes. Friendly competition between the divisions helped to create interest and give diversion to the men from their tedious tasks. At 7:00 p.m. it commenced to rain again and ferrying was halted until 4:40 a.m. on June 4. By 8:00 a.m. all of the wagons had crossed over.

Orson Pratt visited Fort Laramie again where he went up into the tower over the entrance to the fort with his instruments and determined the longitude of the fort to be 104 degrees, 11 minutes and 53 seconds, the latitude to be 42 degrees 12 minutes and 13 seconds, and the altitude to be 4,090 feet. The latitude presumably differed from John C. Fremont's calculations by 18 rods, or 3 seconds.

William Clayton put up a sign on the northeast side of the North Platte River: "Winter Quarters 543½ miles; Junction of the Forks 227¼ miles; Ash Hollow 142½ miles; Chimney Rock 70¼ miles; Scotts Bluffs 50½ miles. William Clayton June 4, 1847."

About 9:00 a.m. President Young, Heber C. Kimball, Willard Richards, Albert P. Rockwood, and Thomas Bullock walked to Fort Laramie where Brigham Young paid Bordeaux fifteen dollars for the use of the flatboat and Bordeaux told him that this was the most civil and the best behaved company that had ever passed the fort, for the pioneers would not go anywhere without first asking permission.[7] Dr. Luke S. Johnson took care

of some of the inhabitants of the fort in his capacity as a doctor
"and they paid him in moccasins, skins, etc." [8]

About 11:30 a.m. Robert Crow's company from Mississippi—part of them were from Illinois—joined the second division of the pioneer company.

William Clayton told of the diminished number of animals since they had left Winter Quarters: 2 horses had been stolen by Pawnee Indians, 2 others had been killed by accidents; 1 mule had been traded for a pony by Stephen Markham; 3 horses and 1 mule had been ridden by the brethren toward Pueblo; 1 horse had been traded by Porter Rockwell for 3 cows and 2 calves; 1 horse had been traded by John Pack for 3 buffalo robes; 1 horse had been traded by Nathanial Brown for a pony at Fort Laramie, and a pony was traded by John S. Higbee to the Sioux for another pony; with the addition of the Crow company, the pioneers left Fort Laramie with 95 horses, 51 mules, 100 head of oxen, 41 cows, 3 bulls, 7 calves, dogs and chickens, 77 wagons, and 1 cart.[9] There were now 161 people in the company.

On June 3 the pioneers heard from three white men who had arrived on horseback from St. Joseph, Missouri that there were approximately 2,000 wagons on the road to Oregon in detached companies mostly of twenty to fifty wagons each; they were principally from Missouri, Illinois, and Iowa. The pioneers felt the estimate was too high, although emigration westward was greatly on the increase.

WESTWARD FROM FORT LARAMIE

At noon on June 4 the pioneers pulled out of Fort Laramie on the Oregon Trail on the southwest side of the North Platte River. They traveled seven and one-half miles before coming to a steep hill where they had to lock all of the wagon wheels and attach ropes to the rear of the wagons so that a number of men could hold back on the wagons in order to descend without accident. This was the first time in six weeks these precautions had been necessary. They drove on another half mile and camped for the night.

The next day William Clayton began putting up markers or mileposts along the road, continuing to do so every ten miles throughout the remainder of the journey for the benefit of oncoming parties. Each marker stated the distance between that point and Fort John; for some reason Elder Clayton used the

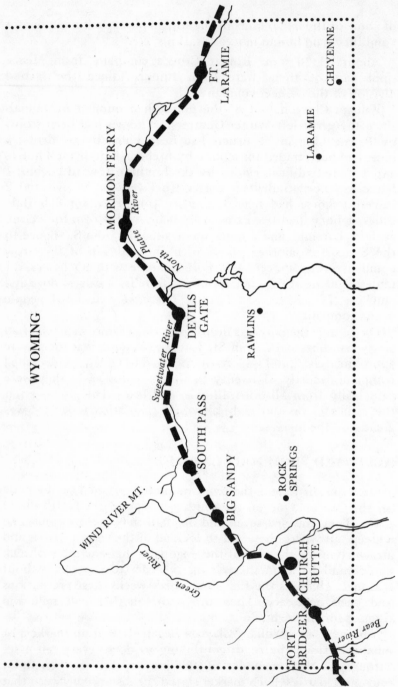

Fig. 6. The pioneer trek across Wyoming. *Courtesy of LaMar C. Berrett.*

older name of Fort John rather than the new name of Fort
Laramie.

As the pioneers traveled onward, they either met or were overtaken by three different companies of Missourians having from three to five yoke of oxen to each wagon, many more than the Saints had. On June 5 they met the first Missouri company about fifteen miles from Fort Laramie. These people had come on a different road which they said was only ten miles from Fort Laramie; whereas the one the pioneers had taken was nearly fifteen miles to the same point. This company had eleven wagons and was on its way to Oregon.

Shortly before reaching the fifteen-mile point from Fort Laramie, the main road of travel left the proximity of the North Platte River and was usually about four miles from it until it came to a river crossing which the main body of pioneers reached on June 12. This crossing was 124 miles from Fort Laramie. On June 6, while the pioneers were stopped for the Sabbath day, a second company from Missouri passed them. They had 19 wagons, 2 carriages, from 3 to 5 yoke of oxen for each wagon, and many cows, horses and young cattle; their guide was a man from the west who lived on the St. Mary's River near the Columbia River in Oregon. Because the guide told them water was ahead six miles and then no more for fifteen miles, they decided to move to the water that afternoon; they felt that twenty-one miles might be too much for the next day's travel. They passed the other Missouri company, and that evening Burr Frost, a blacksmith, welded a spring to the carriage of one of the Missourians in the nineteen-wagon party. Willard Richards wrote a letter to be taken by one of the Missourians to Samuel Brannan, giving him the details of the situation with the Saints.

On Monday, June 7, while the pioneers were stopped at noon, a third company of Missourians passed them, having 13 wagons, 14 horses, 43 yoke of oxen (for the most part 4 yoke to each wagon), and 64 cows.

It appears that the Crow party, the Mississippi Saints, did not have any food except a little flour which their guide Lewis Myers had obtained for them, and they depended entirely on Myers not only as their guide but also as their hunter to supply them with food.

Inasmuch as there were many cobble rocks in the road, creating a problem for the teams, a number of the pioneers spent a few days going ahead with pickaxes, bars and shovels improving the road. This was a great help to the teams and to all companies that would follow. On June 8 the pioneers did not see any of the Missouri groups who were ahead, but John S. Higbee had gone ahead to see them start. He found there was so much strife among them as to which group should start first that they did not stop to milk their cows; while hurrying to clear up after breakfast they spilled malt, salt, bacon, shortcake, johnnycake, beans, and other items on the ground. When the pioneers arrived at the spot, there were three wolves feeding upon the leavings.

While the Saints camped in the evening, a party of traders from Fort Bridger arrived. The pioneers had been expecting them and had letters written for them to take to Fort Laramie. The traders said the crossing of the North Platte was about seventy miles ahead and Fort Bridger was about 300 miles. They also told the pioneers about the beautiful valley around Utah Lake. The next morning the pioneers traded with these trappers for robes, moccasins, skin shirts, and pants. The traders said they had left a kind of ferry boat made out of three buffalo skins hanging in a tree on the North Platte, and they wanted Myers and the Crow party to have it. The pioneers therefore decided to send a company on ahead in order to get there before the Missouri companies did, to build a raft the pioneers could use to cross the river, and to hunt. The Crow party, along with nineteen wagons and about forty men, were sent on ahead with the Revenue Cutter. The main company started about thirty minutes later. Someone remarked they had worked off their road tax in full because they usually had ten or twelve men out with implements to work on the road.

On Thursday, June 10, the pioneers found themselves on the banks of the North Platte, again having traveled seventy-seven miles from the proximity of the river, and slightly over ninety miles from Fort Laramie. On Friday evening, June 11, the Saints had traveled about 106 miles from Fort Laramie, camping within one-half mile of two of the Missouri companies, who informed them that a crossing of the North Platte was ten or twelve miles ahead. The advance company of pioneers and the other company of Missourians had gone there, they said. Thomas Bullock wrote that in the evening the Missourians made ten times more noise than the whole pioneer camp, and the brethren could clearly hear their bawling and profanity.[10]

During the entire day of June 11 the pioneers had been probing for a crossing over the North Platte, swollen because of melting snows.

The advance company of pioneers reached the crossing of the North Platte about noon on June 11. They were four hours ahead of the first party of Missourians. While they were building a raft and waiting for the pioneer company, the Missourians made a contract with them for the pioneers to carry their goods across the stream in the Revenue Cutter for $1.50 each wagon load; they could take it out in provisions at $2.50 per hundred for flour, 50¢ per bushel for meal and 6¢ per pound for bacon. They finished their work in the evening of June 12, having ferried over twenty-four wagon loads. They had also done some blacksmithing for these emigrants, who were mainly from Jackson, Clay, Lafayette and Daviess counties in Missouri where so many enemies of the Saints were. When the pioneers first began ferrying for them, the Missourians were armed with bowie knives and pistols; before the work was finished, they had put away their weapons and their fears and treated the brethren kindly. After the job was finished, the Missourians prepared a fine meal for them. During the day the pioneers, with the help of the Revenue Cutter, had saved the life of one of the Missourians who had tried to swim over the stream fully clothed. This incident helped considerably in alleviating the fears of the Missourians toward the Mormons.

A few miles from the ferry the hunters in the advance company had been busy. They had killed five fat buffaloes, two antelope, and four bears. In the meantime, the main company reached the point where the Oregon Trail crossed the North Platte at about 4:30 p.m. on Saturday, June 12, having traveled 124 miles from Fort Laramie since June 4. Ordinarily the North Platte was forded at this place, but at this time of the year the melting of the snow had made the stream both swift and deep, swollen 100 yards wide. Upon thorough investigation, they found that the stream was from four to six feet deep at the crossing.

The brethren began ferrying their own wagons over on Monday, June 14. At first they tried taking the empty wagons over on a light raft they had built, but it proved to be so slow they tried to lash two wagons together and ford the river; the depth of the stream and swiftness of the current caused them to roll over, and some damage was done. They attempted then to lash together four wagons; when this proved unsatisfactory, they tried fording one wagon alone. But when it entered the current, it rolled over and over. Finally, they returned to the slow process of ferrying over one wagon at a time. By the end of the first day they had crossed over only twenty-three wagons, but because ferrying one wagon at a time proved to be the safest, they continued with this method until the last wagons were over on Thursday, June 17.

There was no difficulty getting the freight over because one man could carry it in the Revenue Cutter faster than all the others could cross the wagons over.

In the meantime, the pioneers had been experimenting with rafts and canoes and had finally made two large canoes 2½ feet in diameter and 23 feet long, "which when coupled about five feet apart with cross timber covered with puncheons and manned with oars, made a boat with which three men could cross a wagon with its load." [11]

The pioneers decided to leave nine men at the ferry in order to earn supplies from other emigrant companies and to help a large company of Saints which they had heard were coming. The nine men appointed to stay were Thomas Grover, Captain John S. Higbee, Luke S. Johnson, Appleton M. Harmon, Edmund Ellsworth, Francis M. Pomeroy, William Empey, James Davenport, and Benjamin F. Stewart. Eric Glines also decided to stay. These ten were instructed to come on with the next pioneer company which would arrive in a month or six weeks.

While the pioneer company was at the North Platte crossing, other companies of Saints were holding a rendezvous on the Elkhorn; by June 15, 300 wagons were there. On June 18, the first of the companies to form moved off the ground under the leadership of Daniel Spencer. Approximately ten other companies would follow.

Before the pioneer company left the North Platte, enough provisions had been received as pay for ferrying to last the pioneers for twenty-three days, and other Missouri companies had arrived and requested to be ferried over.

THE SWEETWATER COUNTRY

On Saturday, June 19, the pioneers left the North Platte crossing and headed for the Sweetwater country with 151 people in the camp and their teams in such good condition from the five-day rest and the good feed that some of the men claimed they hardly recognized their fattened animals. During the day they traveled 21½ miles—the longest distance covered in one day since they had left Winter Quarters. They passed another sentinel of the desert, the Red Buttes, during the day. On Sunday, June 20, because of very poor camping conditions, the camp moved on, traveling twenty miles before stopping. Actually they would have camped at a spot where they stopped for breakfast, but one of the Missouri companies did not want the pioneers to camp there and use the good grass for their animals; so six of their men disguised themselves as Indians and acted strangely to frighten them away. Therefore, the Mormons decided to push on and get ahead of the Missourians so that they could have a free choice of the best feed and camping places. John Brown and Wilford Woodruff, who had gone ahead looking over the country, had stopped to wait for the pioneers when Captain Smith and another hunter from one of the Missouri companies rode up, carrying buffalo meat to their camp near Independence Rock. Captain Smith invited the two men to spend the night with them. The invitation was accepted. Wilford Woodruff later wrote:

> I found that there was a great difference between the Missouri emigrants and our own, where there was no such thing as cursing, swearing, quarreling, contending with other companies, etc., allowed or practiced.[12]

The next day the pioneers stopped long enough at Independence Rock to look it over before going on. About one mile below it they forded the Sweetwater River, which the melting snow had made nearly three feet deep in the channel.[13] They continued another 4½ miles to Devil's Gate, which they found to be about 400 feet high, 120 feet wide, and 50 rods long "and the water rushing through it with a roar." They camped one mile west of Devil's Gate on the banks of the Sweetwater. They had now traveled 175¼ miles from Fort Laramie and 50¼ miles from the North Platte.

SOUTH PASS

The Saints traveled along the Sweetwater in a southwesterly direction for the next few days, crossing the river two or three times, camping on its north bank for the last time on June 25. They were now just a few miles ahead of a number of Missouri companies, having passed three of them lately. Each night they had been gradually climbing to a higher elevation, until they passed drifts of snow and "large bodies of ice near the small

The Sweetwater River where the Saints crossed in 1847. Devil's Gate in
background. *Courtesy of Church Historical Department.*

streams." During the night of June 25, their milk and water
"froze as if it were winter." They forded the Sweetwater for the
last time just before noon on June 26 and camped on the south
bank that night. After resuming travel on June 27, the pioneers
met eight men from Oregon on their way to the states; they had
twenty horses and mules laden with robes and skins. A number
of the brethren sent letters back with these men. After traveling
less than three miles since that morning, they arrived at the
continental divide, which, at this point, was known to travelers
as the South Pass of the Rocky Mountains. William Clayton said
it was supposed to divide the Oregon country from the Indian
territory. Orson Pratt found that it was 7,085 feet above sea
level. It was 278½ miles from Fort Laramie. Two miles farther
the pioneers arrived at Pacific Springs, where they "had the
satisfaction of seeing the water run west instead of east." While
here they met a party from Oregon on its way to the states. One
of the men, Major Moses Harris, was leaving the others at this
point, hoping to get employment as a pilot for one or more
companies traveling to Oregon. He had with him some copies of
a newspaper printed in Oregon and also a number of copies of
the *California Star* printed by Sam Brannan in Yerba Buena,
San Francisco. He was well acquainted with country around
Salt Lake and talked very discouragingly about settling there,

describing it as sandy and destitute of timber and vegetation
except sage brush. He spoke much more favorably of a valley to
the north under the Bear River Mountains known as Cache
Valley or Willow Valley, saying that it was a fine place to winter
cattle. He also spoke favorably of a valley known as Bear River
Valley which he said was forty miles above the mouth of Bear
River. He was obviously referring to what we know today as
Bear Lake Valley, a large part of which is in Idaho. Orson Pratt
said of Major Harris:

> We obtained much information from him in relation to
> the great interior basin of the Salt Lake. His report, like
> that of Captain Fremont's, is rather unfavorable to the
> formation of a colony in this basin, principally on account
> of the scarcity of timber.[14]

William Clayton remarked that the day, Sunday, June 27,
marked three years since Joseph and Hyrum Smith were killed;
they would like to have spent the day in fasting and prayer, but
the "gentile companies" were so close behind them and feed
was so scarce they felt it necessary to keep ahead of them for
the benefit of the teams.

JIM BRIDGER

On Monday, June 28, after traveling nineteen miles from
South Pass they came to a junction in the road, one road continuing in a westerly course—a shortcut road to Oregon—and the
other taking a southwest course. They took the southwest road
which led to California. Shortly after 5:00 p.m. they met Jim
Bridger and two of his men from whom they desired information about the country. William Clayton said it was difficult to
form a correct idea from the "imperfect and irregular way he
gave his descriptions."[15] Perhaps this can be explained by
Howard Egan's journal where it is written that Bridger was
drunk at the time. Among other things Bridger told them was
that nearly 100 wagons had gone on the Hastings' route through
Weber's Fork. According to Hastings, the distance from Fort
Bridger to Salt Lake was about one hundred miles. Bridger had
himself been over the route fifty times, but had no correct idea
of the distance. The Hastings' route left the Oregon Trail at
Fort Bridger. (Lansford Hastings had persuaded three parties to
take shortcuts through the Salt Lake valley in 1846. These were

the Harlan-Young party, the Bryant party and the Reed-Donner party.) The Utah tribe of Indians in the area around Salt Lake were belligerent, but there was no need to fear them because the "whole of them" could be driven out in twenty-four hours. He would not kill these Indians but would make slaves of them. Thomas L. (Peg Leg) Smith had a farm in the Bear River Valley in the Bear Lake region of Idaho. The soil was good and would have produced corn if it hadn't been for the cold nights. Bridger doubted that crops would mature in the Salt Lake valley because of early frosts. Utah Lake was the best country in the vicinity of Salt Lake with plenty of timber in the mountains and fish in the streams. The Indians south of Utah Lake raised corn, wheat, and other grains. Their grain and pumpkins were as good as any in old Kentucky.[16]

EVENTS ON THE GREEN RIVER

On Tuesday, June 29, the pioneers made the longest day's march on the trip because of lack of good feed along the way for their animals. They traveled 23¾ miles. For the past three days many of the men had been stricken with sickness. As some began recovering, others fell ill. The sickness usually began with a headache, succeeded by violent fever and delirium. Some people believed this sickness was caused by using mineral saleratus for baking bread. On June 30 several more became ill. The pioneers traveled 51 miles from South Pass and arrived at Green River about 11:30 a.m. It was about 17 rods wide and 12 to 15 feet deep. President Young gave orders to Tarlton Lewis to build a raft upon which to ferry over the first division. A little later Heber C. Kimball told the second division to build a raft. In the afternoon Samuel Brannan and two companions, who had traveled over 800 miles from California, came into the camp. They had come by way of Fort Hall in southern Idaho and had with them some copies of the *California Star* which Brannan had published. Elder Brannan gave them a report of his trip on the ship *Brooklyn* and stated that eleven people had died. He told of the settlement that had been established in the San Joaquin Valley and of meeting the last living straggler from the Reed-Donner Party making his way to the settlements of California, living upon human flesh for many weeks. [17] Elder Brannan told the pioneers their Green River camp was in upper California. Brannan's purpose seems to have been to convince the pioneers to go on to California.

From the experience gained at the crossing of the North

Platte River the pioneers were able to finish ferrying the wagons across the Green River before noon of Saturday, July 3. They traveled three miles that afternoon and set up camp for the weekend. In the evening five men were chosen to return to meet the next company of Saints: Phineas Young, George Woodard, Aaron Farr, Eric Glines—the tenth man who had stayed at the ferry against advice of the leaders, but who had left and caught up with the company on June 22—and Rodney Badger. Because the leaders could not spare horses, the men were to drive the wagon with the Revenue Cutter on it. They left camp on the morning of July 4; President Young and Heber C. Kimball rode back to the ferry with them. Here they met thirteen of the battalion men who had ridden hard to overtake them. Twelve of them came into camp, and William Walker went back with the five men to meet his wife.[18]

FORT BRIDGER

On Wednesday, July 7, the pioneers reached Fort Bridger and camped one-half mile beyond. It was 397 miles from Fort Laramie. Orson Pratt found the fort to be 6,665 feet above sea level. They decided to lay over for a day to set wagon wheels and make other repairs. Jim Bridger had told them there was no blacksmith on duty at the fort but Burr Frost, assisted by Thomas Tanner, had been doing blacksmithing for the pioneers throughout the journey and had done repair work for the Missouri companies who had camped near by. They spent July 8 making these repairs, while some members of the camp traded at Fort Bridger. Sergeant Thomas Williams and Sam Brannan were sent to meet Captain Brown and the rest of the sick detachment who were on their way from Pueblo; Elder Brannan would offer his services to pilot some of them through to California so that they could collect the rest of their pay.

On Saturday, July 10, about thirty-one miles from Fort Bridger the members of the camp saw smoke two miles away and went to investigate. They found a Mr. Craig and party from San Francisco on their way to the states. Miles Goodyear was with them. He was the first white farmer in Utah; at that time, he had a farm and a garden with many kinds of vegetables in it on the Weber River in Weber Valley, and could assure the pioneers that crops would mature in these mountain valleys. He said his farm was about seventy-five miles from where they were camped.

Goodyear's report of the Salt Lake valley was much more favorable than that of Major Moses Harris or that of Jim Bridger. He showed the brethren a northern road which he said was a shorter way to the Salt Lake valley. Although the Twelve did not consider the road safe, the majority voted to take it; therefore on Monday, July 12, the pioneers took the right-hand road. Each day new cases of sickness developed in the camp, but each sickness usually lasted only two or three days. After traveling less than two miles, the camp reached Bear River which was a rapid stream about six rods wide and two feet deep. During the day President Young became ill with mountain fever and stopped to rest a short time. A few of the men with their wagons stayed with him while the rest of the company moved forward, making 16½ miles for the day before camping.

Illness Causes the Camp to Divide

The next morning, July 13, word was brought to the main camp that President Young was not well enough to move forward that day. After a consultation, the leaders decided to send Orson Pratt ahead with twenty-three wagons and forty-two men in addition to the Crow party; their intention was to locate the route of the Reed-Donner party over the mountains; the pioneers had been informed that it would be impracticable to pass through Weber Canyon because of the depth and swiftness of the water in the Weber River. At about 3:00 p.m. Orson Pratt left the pioneer encampment near Cache Cave with his selected party; the main camp remained at the head of Echo Canyon, and President Young and those with him remained at Pudding Rocks near Coyote Creek where the whole company had stopped on July 12. That evening Willard Richards, Wilford Woodruff and George A. Smith went into the hills and "prayed before the Lord for the recovery of President Young; they received a testimony that he would recover from that very hour."[19]

TREK THROUGH THE MOUNTAINS

On July 14 Orson Pratt's company traveled 13¼ miles and camped at the junction of Red Fork (Echo Creek) and the Weber River. At this point the elevation was 5,301 feet. On this day Albert P. Rockwood, in President Young's camp, was the

sickest of all who had suffered illness in the pioneer company.
In the evening Howard Egan, Heber C. Kimball, Ezra T. Benson, and Lorenzo D. Young, also in Brigham Young's camp, ascended to the top of a high mountain and offered up prayers "in behalf of the sick." The next day, July 15, Wilford Woodruff brought his carriage back for Brigham Young and Elder Rockwood to ride in, for "it was the easiest riding vehicle in the pioneer camp." Orson Pratt's company renewed their journey down Echo Canyon after following the Weber River and crossing "from its right to its left bank" near the present site of Henefer, now in Summit County, Utah. They camped for the night on the meadow near present-day Henefer. A number of people ventured out on horseback to search for the Reed-Donner trail. Orson Pratt and John Brown finally located it, although it was nearly obliterated. By noon of this day, July 15, Wilford Woodruff with his carriage and the eight wagons with Brigham Young joined the main encampment at the head of Echo Canyon. They traveled together a little less than five miles and camped at the foot of some high red bluffs near a good stream of clear water. On July 16 the advance company went up a canyon west of Henefer, now Main Canyon. After traveling 3½ miles they passed Lone Tree where they built a bridge across the creek, soon reaching a divide called Hog's Back; but the pioneers called it Pratt's Pass or Reed's Pass. After traveling down hill for 2½ miles, they camped for the night.

The main company resumed travel about 8:45 a.m., July 16, crawling through a "narrow ravine [Echo Canyon] between very high mountains." They traveled for 16¼ miles through Echo Canyon, about which William Clayton wrote:

> There is a very singular echo in this ravine [Echo Canyon], the rattling of the wagons resembles carpenters hammering at boards inside the highest rocks. The report of a rifle resembles a sharp crack of thunder and echoes from rock to rock for sometime. The lowing of cattle and braying of mules seem to be answered beyond the mountains. Music, especially brass instruments, have a very pleasing effect and resemble a person standing inside the rock imitating every note. The echo, the high rocks on the north, high mountains on the south, with the narrow ravine for a road, form a scenery at once more romantic and more interesting than I have ever witnessed. Soon after we camped, I walked up the highest mountain on the south.[20]

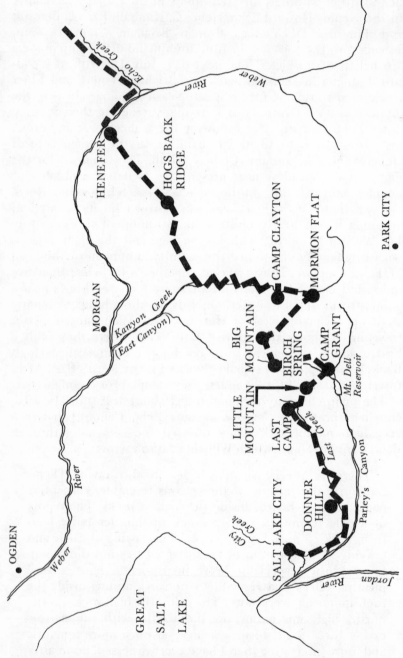

Fig. 7. Map of the last forty miles before entering the Salt Lake valley.
Courtesy of LaMar C. Berrett.

The long day's ride on July 16 made Brigham Young and A.
P. Rockwood worse. It was William Clayton's thirty-third birthday, and he commented that the distance they had traveled
"through this narrow pass" was thirty-three miles. Because of
the serious illness of Brigham Young, the main camp traveled
only 2½ miles on July 17 to a better camping ground and
stopped at 10:00 a.m. At about 2:00 p.m. many camp members
ascended a high hill about two miles from camp where they
engaged in prayer on behalf not only of the sick in camp but
also the Saints who were following and the wives and children
who had been left behind. Orson Pratt's advance company
worked for most of the day clearing rocks from the road they
had passed over and then traveled eight miles over rough road,
camping at last on the left bank of what is now East Canyon
Reservoir. During eight miles of travel they had crossed East
Canyon Creek thirteen times.

On Sunday, July 18, both companies remained in camp and
held religious services. Orson Pratt remarked that his company
was 85½ miles from Fort Bridger. Heber C. Kimball proposed in
a meeting that the main company move on the next day in
order to choose a suitable spot and plant potatoes before the
planting season ended. Many of the sick, including President
Young, were reported to be much better by afternoon, and all
were expected to recover.

On Monday, July 19, Orson Pratt and John Brown rode on
ahead of their camp for four miles up a gradual incline. Here
they tied their horses and climbed a high mountain which
became known as Big Mountain. As they gazed westward, they
received their first view of the Salt Lake valley. Between an
opening in the mountains they could see portions of a level
prairie to the southwest. It was the first time they had seen
anything but mountains westward since they had begun their
journey through the mountains. After further observations they
returned to their camp which had advanced 6½ miles during the
day.

While fifteen wagons stayed behind with President Young,
about forty, under the direction of Willard Richards and George
A. Smith, went ahead with instructions to follow the advance
company into the valley and plant potatoes, turnips, and other
vegetables at the first suitable place regardless of where the final
settlement might be made. When they arrived at the summit of
the dividing ridge, Hog's Back, they put up a guide board stating
that it was 80 miles to Fort Bridger. That night they camped on
East Canyon Creek five miles from Hog's Back.

On Tuesday, July 20, all companies moved forward. Brigham Young's sick group reached the middle group's camp ground of the night before, where three more wagons of sick people were camped; the middle group reached a large spring of cold water where Orson Pratt's company had spent the previous night. Orson Pratt's lead company traveled 2½ miles down Big Mountain Creek. There they turned to the right and traveled 1½ miles up a steep grade to the top of the ridge which became known as Little Mountain, descending then about one mile to Emigration Creek, which they called Last Creek. They traveled down the creek, or down Emigration Canyon, to within 1½ miles of the mouth of the canyon, where they made camp.

During the afternoon of July 21 Elders Orson Pratt and Erastus Snow, sent from the main camp, entered the valley with only one horse for both of them. One would ride a distance, then hitch the horse to a sage brush and hike on. When the other reached the horse, he would ride. But soon Elder Erastus Snow lost his coat and went back to look for it, while Orson Pratt continued. They had made a circuit of twelve miles by the time they returned to camp.

The main camp came to within one mile of Orson Pratt's lead camp, where they spent the night after traveling fourteen miles in thirteen hours. Both groups had done a considerable amount of work on the road during the day. President Young's rear company laid over on East Canyon Creek for the day. They had several new cases of sickness.

On Thursday morning, July 22, Orson Pratt went back to the main company and consulted with George A. Smith, Willard Richards and several others. They decided that Orson Pratt, George A. Smith, and a few others would ride ahead into the valley to look for a suitable place to plant seed, while Willard Richards would guide the pioneers down the canyon and into the valley. Accordingly George A. Smith, Orson Pratt, Erastus Snow, Joseph Matthews, John Brown, John Pack, Porter Rockwell, Jesse C. Little, and probably Lyman Curtis started on horseback for the valley. As they traveled forward they discovered that it would be better for the camp to cut out and dig the thick timber and underbrush at the entrance to the valley than it would be for them to go over a steep hill that the Reed-Donner party had ascended in 1846. They left a note for the camp to this effect and rode on. Orson Pratt describes their travels as follows:

After going down into the valley about five miles, we

turned our course to the north, down towards the Salt Lake. For 3 or 4 miles north we found the soil of most excellent quality. Streams from the mountains and springs were very abundant, the water excellent and generally with gravel bottoms. A great variety of green grass, and very luxuriant, covered the bottoms for miles where the soil was sufficiently damp, but in other places, although the soil was good, yet the grass had nearly dried up for want of moisture. We found the drier places swarming with very large crickets, about the size of a man's thumb. This valley is surrounded with mountains except on the north: the tops of some of the highest being covered with snow. Every 1 or 2 miles streams were emptying into it from the mountains on the east, many of which were sufficiently large to carry mills and other machinery. As we proceeded towards the Salt Lake the soil began to assume a more sterile appearance, being probably at some seasons of the year overflowed with water. We found as we proceeded on great numbers of hot springs issuing from near the base of the mountains. . . . We travelled for about fifteen miles down after coming into the valley, the latter parts of the distance the soil being unfit for agricultural purposes. We returned and found our wagons encamped in the valley, about 5¼ miles from where they left the kanyon.[21]

The main company, 2½ miles up the canyon from the entrance, broke camp at about 8:30 a.m. on July 22 and soon caught up with the advance company. They graded the hill on each side of Emigration Creek. As they traveled on, they found evidence that the Reed-Donner party had often spent much time cutting a road through the timber and heavy brushwood. In order to avoid going over a very steep hill that the Reed-Donner party had traveled over by hitching sixteen yoke of oxen to a wagon, the men spent four hours at the mouth of the canyon cutting a road through the underbrush for about fifteen rods. They made a fairly good road along the creek. They soon came in full view of the Salt Lake valley with the lake in the distance and made camp at 4:30 p.m. on a beautiful little stream, Mill Creek, the main camp having traveled 7¼ miles for the day.

Soon after camp was made, the explorers on horseback returned and said they had found a suitable place to plant seeds. There were two fine streams of water—the two branches of City Creek—about four miles north of camp. At a council meeting in

Plaque on This Is the Place Monument honoring the Reed-Donner Party who entered the Salt Lake valley in 1846 and whose trail the pioneers followed into the valley in 1847.

Dr. Willard Richards' wagon, they decided to move early the next morning to the place they had chosen and begin to plant.

President Young's rear company, which had spent the night on East Canyon Creek, began at 7:30 a.m. on July 22 and traveled eight miles up East Canyon Creek, crossing the creek itself eleven times. They camped in the evening where the road left Canyon Creek, and turned west toward the top of Big Mountain.

On Friday, July 23, the main camp on Mill Creek began to move at about 7:00 a.m. They backtracked one mile, then traveled northward two miles to a grove of cottonwood trees on the banks of a clear stream of water. This was the south branch of City Creek, the ground chosen as a permanent camp site as well as for farming purposes. This site is now the eighth ward in Salt Lake City and also includes the block upon which the city and county building now stands. William Clayton said the soil at this spot looked rich, and that the grass was about four feet high and mixed with rushes.[22]

Planting of the First Crops

At 9:30 a.m. on July 23 a meeting of prayer and thanksgiving

was held. Orson Pratt dedicated the land to the Lord.[23]
According to Thomas Bullock, the camp clerk, the camp was
1,073 miles from Winter Quarters via the travels of the Saints. A
committee consisting of Shadrach Roundy, Stephen Markham,
Seth Taft, Robert Crow and Albert Carrington was appointed to
select ground for planting of potatoes, corn, and beans. They
left the meeting at once to fill their assignment. Charles Harper,
Charles Shumway, and Elijah Newman were appointed to select
plows and drags and what men they would need to help them.
Hensan Walker, William Wardsworth and John Brown were
appointed a committee to "superintend the moving and rigging
of the sycthes." Stephen Markham was put in charge of teams
to see that fresh teams were exchanged on the plows for tired
ones. They also decided that each man could plant his own seed
as he pleased.

By 11:30 a.m. the committee on planting had selected a
piece of ground forty rods by ten rods for planting potatoes;
they also had selected a place for beans and corn. At noon
plowing was started a short distance northeast of the camp.

The first furrow was turned by Captain Taft's company, but
Taft's plow broke. William Carter, George W. Brown, and Shadrach Roundy took part in plowing the first furrows. It was
begun at a point where Main Street, now East Temple, inter-
sects First South Street. Because the soil was very dry, several
plows were broken during the day. At 2:00 p.m. some of the
men who had been appointed for that purpose began to build a
dam across City Creek and dig ditches to get the water onto the
land. After a soaking the ground was rather easy to plow. At
4:00 p.m. some of the brethren "began mowing grass preparing
for a turnip patch."[24]

During the day on July 23 the rear camp with Brigham
Young left East Canyon Creek, traveled over Big and Little
Mountains, and made camp on Last Creek, now Emigration
Creek, having traveled 11½ miles for the day. The sick were
gaining strength and seemed to be able to travel better than
previously.

On Saturday, July 24, the main camp, now on their permanent camp site, continued the plowing, digging, and general
preparation of the land for planting. Preparation of a five-acre
potato patch was completed about noon, and the brethren
began planting potatoes. This patch was apparently planted near
present-day Main Street from about First South to Third South.
The men also planted some early corn, and the plowers con-

146 tinued to plow south of the potato patch, preparing land for garden seed.

Orson Pratt, in his journal on July 24, stated: "This forenoon commenced planting our potatoes; after which we turned the water upon them and gave them quite a soaking."

Arrival of Brigham Young

Because of the loss of some of their animals, the rear company, camped at the foot of Little Mountain, got a late start on the morning of July 24. At the mouth of the canyon they turned to the right, went up a steep incline, and found Salt Lake valley before them. Brigham Young was riding in Wilford Woodruff's carriage, and it was at this point that the carriage stopped while he raised himself from his bed and after gazing out over the valley for some moments commented: "This is the right place. Drive on."[25]

They traveled on and arrived at the permanent camp site of the main camp at about the time the brethren started to plant potatoes at noon, having traveled 9¼ miles during the day.

Since July 14 the camp had generally been traveling in three separate groups, but with the arrival of the sick group on July 24, they were once again united, this time on the permanent camp site of the Saints.

Wilford Woodruff recounts impressions of that historical day:

This, the 24th day of July, 1847, was an important day in the history of my life, and in the history of the Church of Jesus Christ of Latter-day Saints. After traveling from our encampment six miles through the deep ravine valley ending with the canyon, we came in full view of the valley of the Great Salt Lake, or the Great Basin—the land of Promise, held in reserve by the hand of God as a resting place for the Saints.

We gazed with wonder and admiration upon the vast fertile valley spread out before us for about twenty-five miles in length and sixteen miles in width, clothed with a heavy garment of vegetation, and in the midst of which glistened the waters of the Great Salt Lake, with mountains all around towering to the skies, and streams, rivlets and creeks of pure water running through the beautiful valley.

After a hard journey from Winter Quarters of more than one thousand miles, through flats of the Platte River and

plateaus of the Black Hills and Rocky Mountains and over
the burning sands, and eternal sage regions, willow swails
and rocky regions, to gaze upon a valley of such vast extent surrounded with a perfect chain of everlasting mountains covered with eternal snow, with their innumerable
peaks like pyramids towering towards heaven, presented at
one view to us the grandest scenery and prospect that we
could have obtained on earth. Thoughts of pleasant medi-
tation ran in rapid succession through our minds at the
anticipation that not many years hence the House of God
would be established in the mountains and exalted above
the hills, while the valleys would be converted into
orchards, vineyards, fields, etc., planted with cities, and
the standard of Zion be unfurled into which the nations
would gather.[26]

Footnotes

[1]The North Platte River was running almost south-southeast at this point. (*See* map.)

[2]Matthias F. Cowley, *Wilford Woodruff* (Salt Lake City: Deseret News Press, 1909), p. 293.

[3]N. B. Lundwall, comp., *Exodus of Modern Israel* (Salt Lake City: N. B. Lundwall, n.d.), p. 51.

[4]The Crow company included the following people: Robert Crow, Elizabeth Crow, Walter H. Crow, William Parker Crow, Isa Vinda Exene Crow, Ira Minda Almarene Crow, George W. Therlkill, Matilda Jane Therlkill, Archibald Little, James Chesney, and Lewis B. Myers. The company had 5 wagons, 1 cart, 11 horses, 24 oxen, 22 cows, 3 bulls, and 7 calves.

[5]Cowley, p. 295.

[6]Prices at the store were: Moccasins $1.00 per pair; a lariat $1.00; a pound of tobacco $1.50; a gallon of whiskey $32.00; shirting, calico, and cotton goods $1.00 per yard; a buckskin knife $1.00; buffalo robes $3.00 to $5.00; buckskins $2.00 to $3.00 each; cows $15.00 to $20.00; horses and ponies on an average $40.00 each; flour $.25 per lb.; but they had no sugar, coffee, or spices, because their spring supplies had not yet come.

[7]Preston Nibley, *Brigham Young, the Man and His Works* (Salt Lake City: Deseret News Press, 1937), p. 94.

[8]Andrew Jenson, "Day by Day with the Utah Pioneers," *Salt Lake Tribune*, 4 June 1947.

[9]William Clayton, *William Clayton's Journal* (Salt Lake City. Deseret News, 1921), p. 215-16. Wilford Woodruff's count varies slightly from William Clayton's. He gave the following count: 79 wagons, 96 horses, 51 mules, 90 oxen, 43 cows, 3 bulls, 9 calves, 16 dogs and 16 chickens. *See also* Cowley, p. 295.

[10]Jenson, 11 June 1947.

[11]Jenson, 17 June 1947.

148   [12]Cowley, p. 303.

[13]Rumor has it that the Sweetwater River received its name because a mountaineer's mule with a load of sugar on its back drowned in the stream and the sugar dissolved into the water.

[14]Lundwall, p. 64.

[15]Clayton, p. 274.

[16]Clayton, p. 274.

[17]Paul Bailey, *The Gay Saint* (Hollywood: Murray and Gee, Inc., 1944), pp. 151-53, 158. A Mormon woman by the name of Mrs. Murphy, spelled Murray by Tyler, with her family, including two married children with their children—thirteen members in all—was with the Donner Party. Her daughter, Mrs. Johnson, was among some of those who left to get help. She said that when she left, her mother was in good health but when she returned her mother had disappeared. Mrs. Johnson was convinced that her mother had been murdered and eaten. *See* Daniel Tyler, "A Concise History of the Mormon Battalion in the Mexican War" (n.p., 1881), p. 313. Copies available in Brigham Young University Library, Provo, Utah.

[18]*HU*, 1:318.

[19]Jenson, 13 July 1947.

[20]Clayton, p. 296.

[21]Lundwall, pp. 77-78.

[22]Clayton, pp. 312-13.

[23]*HU*, 1:330.

[24]Jenson, 23 July 1947.

[25]This statement came from a sermon delivered by Wilford Woodruff on July 24, 1880, when he said: "On the twenty-fourth I drove my carriage, with President Young lying on a bed in it, into the open valley, the rest of the company following. When we came out of the canyon, into full view of the valley, I turned the side of my carriage around, open to the west, and President Young arose from his bed and took a survey of the country. While gazing on the scene before us he was enwrapped in vision for several minutes. He had seen the valley before in vision, and upon the occasion he saw the future glory of Zion and Israel, as they would be, planted in the valleys of the mountains. When the vision had passed, he said: 'It is enough. This is the right place. Drive on.' " (*See* Nibley, p. 98-99.)

[26]Cowley, p. 313.

8

Establishing Zion in the Mountains

Enlarge the place of thy tent, and let them
stretch forth the curtains of thine habita-
tions: spare not, lengthen thy cords, and
strengthen thy stakes. (Isaiah 54:2)

UTAH AND THE GREAT BASIN BEFORE
THE COMING OF THE MORMONS

The Spanish

The area of Utah was well known before the Mormons came;
however, knowledge of it was confined to a few hundred
people. In 1540, under Coronado, Captain Garcia Cardenas and
his men came close to the Four Corners area where Arizona,
Colorado, New Mexico, and Utah join at a common corner.
Two or three approaches to the Great Basin area were developed; one was from the direction of Santa Fe, New Mexico. The
New Mexico area had been settled in 1598, and the specific
settlement of Santa Fe was founded about 1609.

Between 1769 and 1776, the Spaniards planted missions
along the California coast from San Diego to San Francisco.
Contact between Santa Fe and these two colonial centers had
been made across Arizona before 1776, but in that year ten
Spaniards led by Fathers Francisco Antanasio (also Atanacio)
Dominguez and Silvestre Velez de Escalante were hunting a
more direct route.[1] They are the first white men of record to
enter Utah. Having been sent out to find another route, they
traveled along what became known as the old Spanish-Ute Trail
up across western Colorado and the Green River near Jensen,
Utah. They made their way up the Duchesne River and came

149

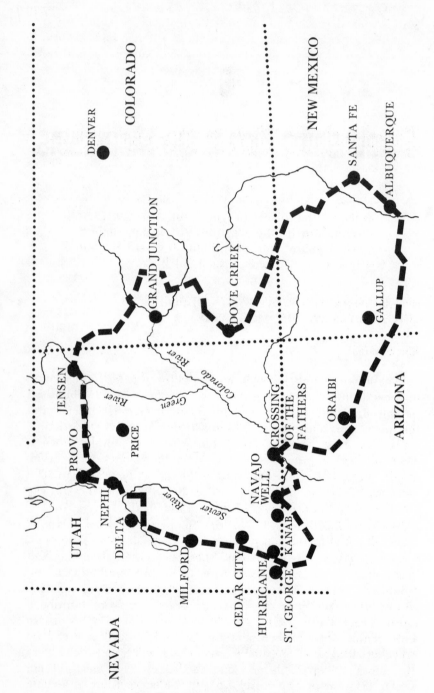

Fig. 8. Escalante's Route, 1776

down Spanish Fork Canyon into Utah Valley. Father Escalante
kept a diary of the journey. Throughout the trip he was looking
for sites upon which to establish villages, and he was thrilled
with Utah Valley. Four streams ran into the lake, and he said
each was capable of supporting two or three villages. He felt
that the valley would provide for as many pueblos of Indians as
there were in New Mexico.

These Spanish fathers met with the Indians in the valley and
found those situated around the lake living on fish, grass seeds,
and rabbits. The Spaniards traveled south along the base of the
Wasatch and Colorado Plateau until, on October 8, 1776, the
threat of winter forced them to give up their search of a route
to California; they returned to Santa Fe by crossing what is now
the Escalante Desert into Cedar Valley, down Ash Creek to the
Virgin River, and out toward Grand Canyon. Natives told them
they could not cross the Colorado River in that direction; so
they turned northeastward until they were about thirty miles
above the present Navajo Bridge where they crossed over the
Colorado River at what became the Crossing of the Fathers.

Rumor had it that in the northern Utah area a mythical
Buena Ventura River flowed into the Pacific Ocean; the Spanish
fathers never found it.

No record exists of how often the Spaniards returned to Utah
Lake, but evidence does exist of a few other visits. In 1805, for
example, a Spaniard named Manuel Mestas came over the old
Ute Trail from New Mexico, tracing stolen horses. And in 1813
Mauricio Arze and Lagos Garcia came to Utah, where they
traded for pelts and Indian slaves. One group of Spaniards who
came to the valley was brought to trial in New Mexico for
trading without a license. The Spaniards claimed they had had
to trade for Indian slaves in order to save the lives of their
horses. One other group came into Utah from Taos, New
Mexico.

The Fur Men

Etienne Provost, a fur trapper and trader, was in the Utah
Valley, perhaps in 1824. Whether he or Jim Bridger or someone
else was the first to see Salt Lake is debatable, but Jim Bridger
usually gets the credit. While smoking the pipe of peace with
Indians on the banks of the present Provo River, Provost and his
party were attacked and most of them were killed. Provo River
gets its name from this incident.

Escalante's crossing at Green River. *Courtesy of the National Park Service.*

In the 1820s beaver skins were worth from six to eight dollars per pelt. This lure brought many fur men into the Great Basin during that era—men such as Jedediah Smith, Peter Skene Ogden, William Wolfskill, Ewing Young, Thomas Fitzpatrick, Kit Carson, and many others, some of whom used the Spanish-Ute Trail to get there. [2]

Travel over this Spanish Trail—which led across Utah—between New Mexico and California became quite heavy after 1830. For nearly twenty years Spaniards and Americans drove thousands of California horses and mules over the trail eastward in exchange for Mexican goods coming west. One of the main activities along the trail was stealing Indian slaves who were to be sold in New Mexico or California.

Jedediah Smith, arriving at Utah Valley in 1826, played an important role in the settlement of the West. He named both the Adams River—now the Virgin River—and the Sulphur River at Escalante. And he was the first to open a route, much farther north than the Spanish Trail, from the Rockies to California.

Although Jedediah Smith and Joseph Smith were unknown to each other, they both helped to implement America's Manifest Destiny in the West. Jedediah grew to manhood in a village neighboring Joseph Smith's in western New York. Joseph Smith arrived in Independence, Missouri, in July 1831, about two months after Jedediah departed on his last journey to the West.

The Great Basin lies between the base of the Wasatch range of the Rocky Mountains on the east and the Sierra Nevada on the west. To the north is the Snake River drainage, and the Colorado River drainage is on the east and the south. This area includes nearly all of present-day Nevada; the western half of Utah; and parts of Idaho, Oregon, and California. The distance from north to south is about 900 miles and perhaps 400 to 500 miles east and west.

The British fur men came down as far as Bear Lake in 1818 and 1819. By 1823 the Rocky Mountain Fur Company was competing with the British for this territory. Peter Skene Ogden of Hudson's Bay Company, a British firm, established himself in what became known as Odgen's Hole. Jim Bridger and others of the Rocky Mountain Fur Company were in Cache Valley. To settle a bet as to whether Bear River emptied into the ocean, Bridger boated down the river in the spring of 1825 and is, therefore, said to be the first white man known to have seen Salt Lake. Jedediah Smith came upon it in 1826 when he made his journey from Weber Valley to California. In 1827 Smith returned to the Great Basin from California, having suffered a great deal on the journey. He wrote:

> We dug holes in the sand and laid down in them for the purpose of cooling our heated bodies. Our sleep was not reposed, but tormented nature made us dream of things we had not, and for the want of which it seemed possible or even probable that we would perish in the desert, unheard of and unpitied.[3]

After this he endured several more days of suffering before he and his companions arrived in the Salt Lake valley—a welcome sight to Jedediah—who wrote:

> Those who may chance to read this at a distance from the scene may perhaps be surprised that the sight of this lake surrounded by wilderness of more than 2,000 miles diameter excited in me those feelings known to the traveler who after a long and perilous journeying comes again in view of his home. But so it was with me for I had traveled so much in the vicinity of Salt Lake that it had become my home in the wilderness.[4]

In 1827 Jedediah Smith returned to the West Coast, where he

first went to southern California and then to Vancouver, where he arrived in a rather destitute condition. Dr. John McLaughlin, agent for the Hudson's Bay Company, treated him kindly; but he was severely censored by his company for his kindness because the company was now determined to "keep every damned Yankee east of the Rockies."

Jedediah Smith, "knight in buckskin," was killed on the Cimarron Trail May 27, 1831; but the Americans continued in the fur trade in the West until the silk top hat instead of fur came into style in Paris and London, and the price of pelts dropped from six to eight dollars per pelt to one dollar each. With the demand for furs gone, many of the fur men turned to guide service; Thomas Fitzpatrick, for example, became a guide for John C. Fremont. Jim Bridger built a fort in the Green River Country in 1843, where four years later he saw the Mormons pour through South Pass to settle in the Salt Lake valley.

Government Men, Missionaries, and Pioneers

As early as 1833 Captain Benjamin L. E. Bonneville, apparently on a secret mission for the government, brought wagons over the well-defined route the fur men had made up the North Platte River and through South Pass. In 1834 Nathaniel Wyeth, a Protestant missionary, established Fort Hall on the Snake River.

Also in the thirties the first Protestant missionaries moved over the trails. In their wake came the Oregon pioneers. The Bidwell-Bartelson party came in 1841, and by 1843 over a thousand people had come through South Pass on their way to California or over the Oregon Trail to the Northwest.

Thus, by the early 1840s the Great Basin was crossed on the south by the Spanish Trail and on the north by the Oregon Trail and the route to California.

Captain John C. Fremont, who became the official reporter of the region, followed the northern route around the Great Salt Lake to California in 1843 and returned over the Spanish Trail in 1844. Fremont prepared maps and charts, including surveys of the Great Salt Lake, which later proved to be of "great value to emigrants." It was he who noticed the change of stream direction, decided there was an area here with no outlet to the ocean, and called this interior region the Great Basin.

Fremont came again into the Salt Lake valley in 1845. This time he crossed the basin south of the lake on his way to

California. When he arrived at Sutter's Fort, now Sacramento,
he told of his short cut across the Salt Flats.

In 1846 Joseph Walker, who had come west with Bonneville in 1833, suggested to some emigrant companies at Fort Hall, Idaho, the possibility of settling in the Salt Lake valley. No one paid attention to him except members of the James R. McBride party, who left their families at Fort Hall and went into the Salt Lake valley to investigate. They probably entered only the region of desert country north of the Salt Lake located in present-day Box Elder County. One of them wrote in his diary, "Hell is not one mile from this place"; they went on to Oregon.

In 1846 Lansford Hastings, a western guide, had better luck in promoting the Great Basin. He persuaded three companies to leave the Oregon Trail at Fort Bridger and head through Echo Canyon for the Salt Lake country. This route became known as Hastings' Cut-off and was about 200 miles shorter than the Oregon Trail. His partner, James Hudspeth, led nine men—the Bryant Party—on mules through Echo Canyon down the Weber River to the Salt Lake, around its south end to the Salt Desert, and on to California. They made it on their mules but left word at Weber Canyon for a party behind them not to try it with their wagons. The message was not found, and the Harland-Young company struggled through, camping on the Jordan River in the same year. These were the first wagons to enter the Salt Lake valley; led by Hastings they finally made their way across the Salt Desert to California, suffering greatly on the way.

The third company to attempt to cross the Great Basin south of Salt Lake was the Reed-Donner Party. Having been warned by a letter wedged in a tree by Jim Hudspeth and left for Hastings, these people did not attempt the Weber Canyon Route. They turned into East Fork, went west over Big Mountain and Little Mountain and on down Emigration Canyon. They had to cut their way through much of this area; so they did not arrive in the Salt Lake valley until September, having taken 16 days on the Henefer-Salt Lake part of the journey of thirty-six miles. Without a guide, they continued on until they arrived in the Sierra Nevada on October 31, 1846, where part of them were trapped by early snows. Thirty-nine of eighty-seven members of the party died either of cold or of starvation. A Mormon woman—Mrs. Lavinia Murphy—was in the party. Of the thirteen members of her family, seven of them lost their lives, including Mrs. Murphy.

156　　The Reed-Donner party had hewn a road through the Wasatch Range—a road followed the next season by the Mormon pioneers and later by thousands of emigrants. It was later traveled by the gold-seeking forty-niners, by the Overland Stage, by Johnston's Army, and by the Pony Express.

Thus, the explorers, the trappers and traders, the missionaries, the government reconnaissance men, and the Oregon and California pioneers all preceded the Mormons into the Great Basin, but none had come to settle there. Unknowingly these men did the preparatory work for the Mormons to settle in the Great Basin and build God's kingdom.

SAINTS IN THE VALLEY

The First Sabbath in the Valley

The day after the arrival of Brigham Young in the valley on July 24, 1847, was the Sabbath, and religious services were held both in the forenoon and in the afternoon. As the settlers assembled in a circle amid their encampment, they gave thanks to God for their safe arrival in the valley. They administered the sacrament, using water and broken bread.[5] Not a soul had died and only a small number of their horses and cattle had been lost.

The speakers for the day were the seven apostles who were present. In the forenoon George A. Smith spoke, followed by Heber C. Kimball and Ezra T. Benson. In the afternoon Wilford Woodruff spoke first, followed by Orson Pratt and Willard Richards.[6] The principal discourse seems to have been given by Orson Pratt who took for his subject Isaiah 52:7, 8:

> How beautiful upon the mountains are the feet of him that bringeth good tidings, that publisheth peace; that bringeth good tidings of good, that publisheth salvation; that saith unto Zion, Thy God reigneth!
>
> Thy watchmen shall lift up the voice; with the voice together shall they sing: for they shall see eye to eye, when the Lord shall bring again Zion.

Elder Pratt said that these inspired words referred to the Latter-day Saints who were now beginning to establish themselves "in the midst of the Rocky Mountains" as the Prophet Joseph Smith had foretold.[7]

Although President Brigham Young was still too weak from his illness to preach a sermon, he gave them a few words of practical advice from his armchair. He told them they must not work on Sunday; they would lose five times as much as they would gain by it. No man should hunt and fish on that day, and no man should dwell among them who would not observe these rules. Also, there should be no buying and selling of land because every man was to have his land measured out to him both for city and for farming purposes. Each man could till the land as he pleased; nevertheless, he was to be industrious and take care of it.[8] This first land law was similar to what Brigham Young had said at Garden Grove, Iowa, when the Saints were camping there.[9]

The pioneers later determined that timber would be community property, and only dead timber should be used as fuel; furthermore, there was to be no private ownership of water. Up to this time use of the world's water seems to have been based on the doctrine of riparian right, which is the principle that the person who lives on or has property on the bank of a river or stream has access to and use of the water. Or if a person owns land upon which a spring originates he also owns the water from the spring and can control the use of it. Such a water policy did not suit the needs of the Saints in the Great Basin, where crops could be produced only with the help of irrigation. This policy would mean that a few people could gain control of the water available and others would have none. Consequently, the Saints established the policy of dividing up the water according to need and prior appropriation, and each piece of land was assigned an appropriate amount of water. The settlers, then, from the beginning of the colonies in the Great Basin, prevented land monopolies and established community ownership of water and timber.

Immediate Exploration

On Monday morning, July 26, 1847, while most of the members of the camp were engaged in the duties of providing temporary living quarters or of completing the planting of potatoes and a few vegetables, the seven members of the Twelve and a number of others began to explore the countryside in order to assess the fertility of the soil and other physical features of the valley. The Apostles sent John Brown and Joseph Matthews across the valley to the west range of moun-

Ensign Peak, named by Brigham Young on July 26, 1847. *Courtesy of David C. Rich.*

tains. Upon their return, they reported that the mountains were about fifteen or sixteen miles away from the camp, and the plain between was waterless and covered with wild sage.

They also reported that the land on the west was not as good as the land on the east.[10] Some of the men went into the canyons on the east in search of timber, where they found some of good quality, although it seemed to be quite a distance from the valley.

Brigham Young, along with most of the Twelve Apostles who were present, traveled northward. Still weak from his recent illness, he rode in Wilford Woodruff's carriage. They journeyed north a few miles, where they decided to climb to a peak part way up the mountain. From its summit they received a view of the whole valley, surveying the path of the Utah Outlet, later the Jordan River, from its entrance into the valley southward to its draining into the Salt Lake and emptying a little to the west of them. They also saw many other rivers and creeks running through the valley. While they were still on this moundlike mountain, someone suggested that it would be a good place upon which "to raise an ensign to the nations," and Brigham Young immediately named it Ensign Peak.[11] In later years it was claimed they unfurled the United States flag on the

peak that day, but this might not be so because there is no
evidence they had brought along an American flag on that exploring trip. Furthermore, the flag was to be an ensign to all
nations that they were welcome to come to Zion (Isaiah 11:12).
It was not the United States flag but rather a sign of the empire
of the Savior. It signified the gathering of Israel out of all
nations. About two miles north of their encampment, Brigham
Young and the others visited Warm Springs before ascending the
mountain, after which they returned from the peak and continued north until they reached some hot sulphur springs. Then
they returned to their camp for the night and continued their
explorations the next day. On July 27 the seven apostles—
Amasa Lyman having gone back from Fort Laramie to guide the
rest of the Mississippi Saints and the sick detachment of the
Mormon Battalion into the valley—and six others crossed the
Utah Outlet, traveling westward to the range that divides Salt
Lake and Tooele valleys. They stopped for lunch on the shore
of the Great Salt Lake at a place they named Black Rock, and
after eating they went for a swim in the buoyant waters. Orson
Pratt remarked about the occasion: "We cannot sink in this
water. We roll and float on the surface like a dry log. I think the
Salt Lake is one of the wonders of the world."[12] They next
went a few miles into Tooele Valley where they discovered that
the valley floor was quite level and the texture of the soil was
generally good, but there was not much water so vital for locating settlement sites. As night settled, they retired to the lake
shore at Black Rock and spent the night there. On July 28 they
traveled southward along the eastern base of the Oquirrh Mountains for approximately ten miles where they turned east and
recrossed the Salt Lake Valley, returning to their camp on City
Creek.

The Plan for the City

Late that afternoon, July 28, in company with the other
apostles and Thomas Bullock, Brigham designated the site for
the temple block to be between the forks of City Creek, and
upon motion of Orson Pratt the brethren unanimously voted
that the temple be built upon the site designated.[13] At that
time they also decided to lay out the city in ten-acre blocks
with streets eight rods wide. Sidewalks were to be twenty feet
wide on each side of the street. The blocks were to be divided
into lots of 1¼ acres each, making eight lots to a block. One

B. Young put his cane in the middle of temple Square

160 house was to be built in the center of each lot twenty feet back from the sidewalk.

> Upon every alternate block four houses were to be built on the east and four on the west sides of the square, but none on the north and south sides. But the blocks intervening were to have four houses on the north and four on the south, but none on the east and west sides. In this plan there would be no houses fronting each other on opposite sides of streets while those on the same side will be about eight rods apart, having gardens running back twenty rods to the center of the block. There were to be four public squares of ten acres each in addition to the temple block which was to be forty acres.[14]

Each man was to cultivate a garden on his large lot, growing all kinds of fruit and shade trees as well.[15] At a town meeting in the evening, all of the features for the city voted on earlier by the Apostles were submitted to the vote of the camp and were accepted unanimously.

ARRIVAL OF THE NEXT PIONEERS

On July 29 soldiers of the sick detachment, some of them with their wives and children, and the rest of the Mississippi Saints, all of whom had spent the winter at Pueblo, Colorado, arrived at the camp of the pioneers. This increased the population in the valley to a little over four hundred. The battalion boys built the first structure in the valley on July 30—a bowery as a shady place to hold meetings. It was about twenty-eight feet wide by forty feet long. Posts were set in the ground and long poles were laid across them, fastened with wooden pegs and rawhide thongs. Timbers and brush were placed upon the framework, providing shade but little other protection.

That evening, July 30, a "praise service for their safe arrival was held in the brush bowery."[16]

On July 31 Orson Pratt began to survey the city. He said he found by "meridian observations of the sun" that the latitude of the northern boundary of the temple block was 40 degrees 45 minutes and 44 seconds, and that

> the longitude, as obtained by lunar distances, taken by the sextant and circle, was 111 degrees 26 minutes 34

seconds. . . . Its altitude above the level of the sea was
4,300 feet, as ascertained by calculations deduced from
the mean of a number of barometrical observations taken
on successive days.[17]

The baseline of Orson Pratt's survey was on the southeast
corner of the temple block.

Later, land for farms and pastures was laid off in five, ten,
and twenty-acre plots, the smaller plots nearest the city and the
largest plots farthest away.

First Indian Contacts in the Valley

Three days after their arrival in the valley the pioneers were
visited by Indians, after which their visits became more frequent
and their numbers constantly increasing. These Indians were
from two different tribes, the Utes or Utahs to the south and
the Shoshones to the north. During the first week on one occasion
when members of both tribes were in the pioneer camp, a Ute
stole a horse from a Shoshone and rode off. The Shoshone
followed him, killed him, and returned to the pioneer camp
with the horse. Because of this incident and the inconvenience
to the work of the pioneers from such frequent visits by the
Indians to the pioneer camp, on the second Sunday in the
valley the Saints adopted a resolution "to trade no more with
the Indians except at their own encampment."[18]

Building the First Fort

The pioneers decided that they should build a series of
houses in the form of a fort on one of the blocks that had been
surveyed for protection from the Indians. The block selected
was four blocks south and three west of the temple block; work
upon this fort began on August 11. On August 21 Brigham
Young and Heber C. Kimball were the first to move into the
new houses built of logs and adobes, or sundried brick, with the
hearths made of clay. The east wall of the fort was made of
logs, while the north, south and west walls were of adobe. The
fort walls were the outside walls of the houses, which were built
on the inside with the roofs sloping inward. All openings were
on the inside of the fort except that each house had "a small
loop-hole looking out" so that the occupants could observe the
approach of an enemy.[19]

On August 2, the same day that Orson Pratt began his survey of the city, Ezra T. Benson left the settlement on a different kind of an assignment. Brigham Young had asked him to take three companions, one of them Porter Rockwell, and go eastward on horseback to meet the oncoming trains of immigrants. These men were to obtain the names of every individual in all the migrating Camps of Israel and make a list of the number of wagons, horses, oxen, and other animals and equipment. They were also to find out the needs of the immigrants as well as the condition of their health and then return as soon as possible to give a report "so that assistance might be rendered if necessary."[20] They took with them a letter from Brigham Young to "General Charles C. Rich and the Presidents and Officers of the Emigrating Company."[21]

Inasmuch as nearly all men of the pioneer company as well as many men of the sick detachment of the Mormon Battalion had left their families in Winter Quarters, Nebraska, or in Iowa, the leaders decided that, after establishing a permanent location for settlement of the Saints, these men could return east to their families.

On August 16 a number of men from both the pioneer company and the battalion held a rendezvous at the mouth of Emigration Canyon for the return journey. When the group pulled out on August 17 it consisted of 24 pioneers and 46 battalion men. They had 34 wagons, 92 yoke of oxen, 18 horses, and 14 mules. Since most of the wagons were drawn by ox-team, this group became known as the "ox train"; it was supposed that this group would need a week to ten days longer to arrive at Winter Quarters than would another group which was to come later. Although the ox-train waited for the later group for five days on the Platte River while they dried the meat from thirty buffalo cows, the later group never did catch up with them. In their travels, the members of the group discovered that in order for horses and mules to stand the daily grind, they must be fed grain every day; whereas the oxen with no other feed than grass were often able to gain strength from day to day. The ox-train was divided into two parts, with Shadrach Roundy and Tunis Rappleye as captains, although the battalion boys were also under the command of Lieutenant Wesley Willis.[22]

Ten days later a second company of pioneers and battalion

members left Salt Lake City under leadership of Brigham
Young, Heber C. Kimball, and the other five apostles who were
in the valley. This group consisted of 107 men, 36 wagons, 71
horses and 49 mules.[23] Like the ox train, this group also had
very meager provisions and depended on game and fish for their
subsistence. Although many of them had to walk, the return
journey was much faster than the westward trek.

On August 30 when Brigham Young's returning company was
four days out, they met Elder Benson and his three companions
returning from their visit to the oncoming companies. They
reported ten companies on their way to the Salt Lake valley
with 1,553 people. This seems to have been more than Brigham
Young had expected, and he and other leaders were much concerned about having so many people in the valley for the first
winter; it appeared that sufficient food was likely to be a
problem. They would need enough food not only to last them
through the winter but also until crops in the valley had
matured. The general migration westward from Winter Quarters
in the summer of 1847 was under the direction of Parley P.
Pratt and John Taylor, two of the apostles who had arrived
from England only a few days before the pioneer company had
left Winter Quarters in April. Perhaps they had had very little
time to find out the general plans of the majority of the Twelve
before they left for the west.

On September 4 Brigham Young's returning company met
the first of the oncoming pioneers on the Big Sandy River a few
miles west of South Pass. Parley P. Pratt's company was the first
they encountered. Brigham Young took Brother Pratt and
Brother Taylor to task for disarranging the plans projected by
the majority of the Apostles' quorum and for some disorder in
the companies. Elder Pratt was the ranking apostle of the two
and was the first to be met; therefore it was he who bore the
brunt of the chastisement.

The council sustained President Young's reproof and,
although Elder Pratt was at first not disposed to accept the
chastisement, he yielded by acknowledging his error. In his
autobiography Elder Pratt wrote of the incident:

> A council was called, in which I was highly censured and
> chastened by President Young and others. This arose in
> part from some defect in the organization under my super-
> intendence at the Elk Horn, and in part from other mis-
> understandings on the road. I was charged with neglecting

164   to observe the order of organization entered into under the superintendence of the President before he left the camps at Winter Quarters; and of variously interfering with previous arrangements. In short, I was severely reproved and chastened. I no doubt deserved this chastisement; and I humbled myself, acknowledged my faults and errors and asked forgiveness. I was frankly forgiven, and, bidding each other farewell, each company passed on their way. This school of experience made me more humble and careful in future, and I think it was the means of making me a wiser and better man ever after.[24]

The two companies camped together on the nights of September 4 and 5; then the returning pioneers continued on their eastern journey. After passing other companies on the westward trail, on September 7 they met the company of Joseph Horne and John Taylor on the Sweetwater River. At this time several inches of snow had fallen, and some of the people were quite concerned about the climate of the land into which they were moving. John Taylor attempted to cheer the group by joking about the matter and offering to insure the lives of the company at five dollars per head.[25]

The ladies of the westward company got out their dishes and linen and prepared a meal for their "guests." A fat heifer was killed to add to the game, fish, fruits, and jellies. This meal was prepared while the Twelve and other leaders were in a council meeting and was a pleasant surprise for them when they returned. After the meal was finished and everything cleared away, a dance was held to the merry tune of the violin mingled with the voice of the caller. Songs and recitations were interspersed between the dances. What had started out as a gloomy day of snow and clouds closed with pleasantness and praise to the Lord.[26]

On September 9 the returning pioneers met the last of the westward bound Saints for the year 1847. It was the company of Jedediah M. Grant, who brought the pioneers news from the East. During the following night, about fifty head of horses were stolen by the Indians, thirty from the pioneers' camp and twenty from Elder Grant's camp. Although efforts were made to recover them, only five were brought back. This reduction in the number of horses weakened both encampments.

On the morning of September 21 the pioneer camp was invaded by about two hundred Indians who attempted to throw confusion into the camp by riding in swiftly and scaring off all the horses. Some of the pioneers quickly jumped on a few horses and prevented this so that the Indians confiscated only about eight head. The Sioux Indian chief afterwards claimed they had mistaken the encampment of the white men for Crow or Snake Indians, with whom they were at war and later permitted the brethren to pick out their seven or eight horses from a band of about one thousand. Although the pioneers recognized a number of horses that had been stolen from the two companies on the night of September 9, the chief refused to let them have them but implied that he would return them to the men at Fort Laramie. But he did not.

At Fort Laramie Commodore Stockton, returning east by land with about forty people from the San Francisco Bay Area, overtook the eastbound pioneers, and Elders Young and Kimball had the privilege of dining with him. After the Saints left Fort Laramie, their teams grew steadily weaker, making the trip slow and monotonous. Also, food in the camp was scarce as the men killed game only intermittently. On October 16 the pioneers met a company of sixteen men from Winter Quarters with three wagons loaded with supplies. This group was made up of the old Nauvoo police—now the peace officers of Winter Quarters. They were led by Hosea Stout, George D. Grant, and James W. Cummings. A second company with twenty wagons, led by Bishop Newel K. Whitney and others, met the men at the Elkhorn River on October 30, bringing with them plenty of grain and food.

On October 31 just a mile out of Winter Quarters, Brigham Young called the group together and addressed them as follows:

Brethren, I will say to the pioneers, I wish you would receive my thanks for your kindness and willingness to obey orders. We are satisfied with you; you have done well. We have accomplished more than we expected. The one hundred and forty-three men who started, some of them sick, are all well. Not a man has died; and we have not lost a horse, mule or ox, except through carelessness. The blessings of the Lord have been with us. If the brethren are satisfied with me and the Twelve, please signify it with uplifted hands [all hands were raised]. I feel to bless you in the name of the Lord God of Israel. You are dismissed to go to your homes.[27]

As the men drove into the city of Winter Quarters the streets were lined with members of their families who had not seen them for more than six months; some of the battalion men had not seen their families for more than fifteen months.

The return journey had taken Brigham Young's group from August 26 to October 31—two months and five days.

THE FIRST WINTER IN THE SALT LAKE VALLEY

Arrival of Other Companies in 1847

Only a strong faith in God had caused more than 2,000 people to venture into a wilderness among savages. Thirteen different companies arrived in the valley during the summer of 1847.

The westward bound companies began arriving in the Salt Lake valley toward the latter part of September and continued to arrive until October 10, when Jedediah Grant's company came into the valley. These companies were as follows:[28]

Brigham Young's company	148
Mississippi Saints	47
Mormon Battalion	210
Daniel Spencer's company	204
Parley P. Pratt's company	198
A. O. Smoot's company	139
C. C. Rich's company	130
George B. Wallace's company	198
Edward Hunter's company	155
Joseph Horne's company	197
Joseph Bates Noble's company	171
Willard Snow's company	148
Jedediah M. Grant's company	150
Total	2,095

The first company—Daniel Spencer's, following Brigham Young's "Pioneer" company—had left Elkhorn River on June 18, and the last one, Jedediah Grant's, on or about the 4th of July.[29]

One company came in later from the west, however; this was a group of the battalion men from California. They had met Sam Brannan and James Brown west of the Sierra Nevada, who told them it was the wish of Brigham Young that those soldiers who were without means and whose families would not be in the valley should stay in California and obtain work through the winter, coming on into the valley the following spring. About half of them returned and the other half went on into the Salt Lake valley, arriving there on October 16. Two days later thirty-two of them, whose families were found not to be in the valley, left for Winter Quarters, braving the cold and blasts of winter in order to get to their families. After a great deal of hardship, hunger, and suffering, they arrived in Winter Quarters on December 18.

As other pioneers came into the valley, they added to the ten-acre fort that had been built by the pioneer company. Forts were added on both the north and the south, and later when another was added in the summer of 1848, the whole fort grounds occupied a space of approximately forty-seven acres.

Those Departing and Those Remaining

As previously reported, a number of the Saints who reached the Salt Lake valley in the summer of 1847 did not spend the first winter there. Seventy men had left with the ox-train. Counting Brigham Young, 108 had left on August 26. In addition, Ezra T. Benson and Porter Rockwell (probably with two others) had left on August 2. On August 9, Captain James Brown with Samuel Brannan and a few others left for San Francisco by way of Fort Hall. Captain Brown's objective was to draw the back pay due the men of the battalion from his detachment, the battalion having been discharged on July 16. Captain Brown took with him the muster roll plus power of attorney from each man to sign for and receive his pay. Seven battalion men accompanied him on this trip; they were Abner Blackburn, Gilbert Hunt, John Fowler, William Gribble, Henry Frank, Lysander Woodworth and Captain Brown's oldest son, Jesse S. Brown. On the way north through Weber Valley they called on Miles Goodyear whom they had met on their way west in July. This was probably the beginning of negotiations for the purchase of the Goodyear properties purchased after Captain Brown's return.

Later, Captain Jefferson Hunt and others left for California to purchase supplies, and a group of men went north to Fort Hall also for supplies. On November 16, O. P. Rockwell, E. K. Fuller, A. A. Lathrop, and fifteen others left for California to buy "cows, mules, mares, wheat, and seeds."[30] They bought 200 head of cows at six dollars each. On the return trip, which

168 took ninety days, they lost forty head in the Mojave Desert. Still others settled a few miles to the north, where they herded the cattle for the winter.

There appears to be a discrepancy as to the number of Saints who wintered in the valley that first year, but 1,671 is one estimate.[31] This means that somewhere an extra 150 men had emigrated back to Winter Quarters or that the figures given for the total of incoming pioneers in the various companies— amounting to 1,690—were more nearly like the figure of 1,553 reported by Ezra T. Benson to Brigham Young when they met on August 30. Elder Benson reported also 580 wagons, 2,213 oxen, 124 horses, 887 cows, 358 sheep, 716 chickens, and 35 hogs.[32]

Life in the Fort

Altogether the Saints planted 83 acres of corn, grain, potatoes, and garden stuff in the Salt Lake valley during the summer of 1847, but because the crops were planted so late many of them did not mature. The potatoes grew only to the size of marbles, sufficient for seed the following year.

According to arrangements previously made by the Apostles before they left the valley, a conference was held on October 3 under the direction of Elders Parley P. Pratt and John Taylor. President Young and the Apostles, with the exception of Lyman Wight who was in Texas, were sustained as those who would preside over the Church. Wight's case was held over until he could return and explain his actions. Father John Smith, who had been chosen earlier by the Twelve, was sustained as president of the Salt Lake Stake of Zion, with Charles C. Rich and John Young, oldest brother of Brigham Young, as his counselors. Next, the Saints voted in a high council: Henry G. Sherwood, Thomas Grover, Levi Jackman, John Murdock, Daniel Spencer, Lewis Abbott, Ira Eldridge, Edson Whipple, Shadrach Roundy, John Vance, Willard Snow, and Abraham O. Smoot. Tarlton Lewis was sustained as the bishop.

The pioneers built additional houses and forts with con- necting gates between them and to the outside. The fort added to the south was known as the south fort, that on the north as the north fort, and the center one was known as the "old fort." Some of the houses lining the inside walls of the forts and the walls between the forts were made of logs, but most of them were of adobe with shed-type roofs sloping inward. The roofs were made of poles covered with brush, in turn covered with dirt.

As the men completed their fall plowing and planting, and winter drew near, those who were able moved out of their tents and wagons into the houses in the fort. Before the winter was over 423 houses were built. Fortunately the winter was a mild one, for many of the Saints were without warm clothing and other conveniences. George Q. Cannon, a young man who came in with his uncle, John Taylor, later wrote:

> Neither their food nor their clothing was of such a character as to enable them to endure cold weather. Many were without shoes, and the best and only covering they could get for their feet was moccasins. Their clothing, too, was pretty well exhausted, and the goat, deer, and elk skins which they could procure were most acceptable for clothing, though far from pleasant to wear in the rain or snow.[33]

Parley P. Pratt wrote to his brother Orson:

> The winter was mild and pleasant, several light snows and severe frosts; but the days were warm, and the snows soon melted off. The cattle did well all winter in the pastures without being fed. Horses, sheep, and cattle were in better order in the spring than when we arrived, I mean those which were not kept up and worked or milked, but suffered to live where there was grass. Early in March the ground opened and we commenced plowing for spring crops.[34]

Since the Saints had received the impression the climate was very dry, they built the roofs of the houses nearly flat. But they were thankful to have even these crude houses after living in tents and wagon boxes for so long.

One of the more unpleasant incidents occurred in the early spring and was later described by Mary Isabella Horne, one of the pioneer women who spent the first winter in the valley:

> The weather continued fine until March, 1848, when a storm came on and we had rain, snow and sleet continually for ten days. Our house being covered only with poles,

Oldest house in Salt Lake City, built in 1847; now on Temple Square. *Courtesy of Historical Department, The Church of Jesus Christ of Latter-day Saints.*

grass and earth, it continued to rain in the house after it was fine outside. Wagon covers were fastened nearly to the roof over the head of the bed, sloping to the foot to shed the water and keep the bed dry. A large piece of table oil cloth was tacked up over the table while we ate our meals, and it was no uncommon thing to see a woman holding an umbrella over her while attending to her household duties. The Fort presented quite a ludicrous appearance when the weather cleared up. In whatever direction one looked, bedding and clothing of all descriptions were hanging out to dry.

One of the greatest sources of trouble and inconvenience were the mice. The ground was full of them. They ran over us in our beds, ate into our boxes, and destroyed much valuable clothing. Various kinds of mouse-traps were devised, but relief was obtained only after securing a kitten from the only family of cats in the camp.[35]

Schools were held in the fort and were taught by Julian Moses and Mary Jane Dilworth, who later became Mrs. F. E. Hammond. A bowery similar to the original one built on July

30 by the battalion men was built in the center of the fort, and religious services were held regularly throughout the winter.

The first man to build a house outside the fort was Lorenzo Young, the youngest brother of Brigham Young, who built a log cabin on City Creek northeast of the fort on a site now occupied by the Beehive House; he and his wife moved into it in December. Their friends were much against their moving there, fearing Indians might kill them; but Lorenzo Young said, "I'll risk that and no one but myself shall be responsible."[36] During the winter an incident occurred substantiating his friends' fears. Harriet Young was home alone with her infant son one winter day when an Indian came to the door and asked for "biscuit."[37] Mrs. Young had only three small biscuits in the house, but she gave two of them to the savage who was known as a "bad Indian." He took them and asked for more; she gave him the last one, but angry at receiving so little, he demanded more and aimed an arrow at her heart. A quick sign that she would bring him more food gained her the reprieve she needed to untie her large watchdog in an adjoining room. The dog attacked the Indian, sank its teeth into his thigh, and fought him to the ground. Mrs. Young relieved the Indian of his bow and arrow before calling off the dog. "He was badly hurt and cried bitterly." Mrs. Young, her anger now subsided and replaced by pity, washed and dressed the wound before sending the fierce-looking savage on his way.[38]

The settlers purchased a number of Indian children during the winter in order to save the children's lives. Indians came to the fort from time to time bringing children who were prisoners of war, and if the Saints refused to purchase them, the Indians would torture the children to death. Charles Decker purchased one of these unfortunate children and gave her to his sister Clara Decker Young. Clara named her Sally and raised her to womanhood. She later married Chief Kanosh.

Because of the mild winter it was possible at intervals for the pioneers to perform many tasks such as plowing, planting, fence-building, logging, and exploring. By spring twelve miles of fence had been built, enclosing 5,133 acres of ground, soon sown into various crops. Eight hundred seventy-five acres of winter wheat began to sprout in the early spring. The crop greatly encouraged the settlers, whose foodstuffs were running low. We might recall that the pioneers not only had to bring with them sufficient food to last them throughout their journey, but in addition, enough to last them throughout the coming year until the crops could ripen and be harvested in the summer of 1848. They also had to save grain and potatoes from their meager supplies to use for planting crops; otherwise there would be no further harvest.

As the spring of 1848 merged into summer, fall grain was beginning to mature and the spring grain was beginning to prosper, although frost and drought had already hindered crop growth to some extent. The supplies of the settlers were becoming scanty, and many of the Saints were almost constantly hungry.

Community Placed on Rations

Because the leaders had foreseen the imminent scarcity of food, they called a public meeting and placed the community on rations. Bishops Edward Hunter and Tarlton Lewis had been appointed to act in behalf of the destitute and see that they did not suffer. Beef was scarce since so many cattle had to be kept for work teams, and the cows had to be saved for milk. The few head of beef that were killed were so poor and the meat so tough that John Taylor jokingly remarked to brother Joseph Horne, assisting him to cut up a carcass, that it looked as if they would have to "grease the saw to make it work!"[39] Flour had been rationed and everyone was hungry; at the earliest signs of vegetation they were in search of supplemental rations. They cooked and ate thistle roots and used the tops for greens, and they ate sego roots, following the customs of the Indians.

Let us turn to the pages of one of the pioneers for some first-hand experiences of that summer. Priddy Meeks wrote:

My family went several months without a satisfying meal of victuals. I went sometimes a mile up Jordan to a patch of wild roses to get the berries to eat which I would eat . . . stems and all. I shot hawks and crows and they ate well. I would go and search the mire holes and find cattle dead and fleece off what meat I could and eat it. We used wolf meat, which I thought was good. I made some wooden spades to dig seagoes with but we could not supply our wants.

We had to exert ourselves to get something to eat. I would take a grubbing-hoe and a sack and start by sunrise in the morning and go, I thought six miles before coming to where the thistle roots grew, and in time to get home I would have a bushel and sometimes more thistle roots, and

Joseph Smiths Uncle
Pres. John Smith Led them
in Prayer because B.Y. was in winter
quarters

we would eat them raw. I would dig until I grew weak and
faint and sit down and eat a root, and then begin again. I
continued this until the roots began to fail; I then turned
my attention to making horn combs out of horns. I got
two five gallon kegs and a sack and threw it across the
saddle and away I went peddling combs for buttermilk and
clabber among those who were out with their stock for the
milk. I continued this until I heard Capt. James Brown
bought out a mountaineer of a large herd of cattle some
sixty miles [forty miles] north of the city.[40] I went there
and bought a horse load of cheese which we ate without
bread or meat.

Now everything did look gloomy, our provisions giving
out and the crickets eating that little we had growing,
and we a thousand [miles] away from supplies. When
Sunday came we had [a meeting.] Apostle Rich [he was not
then an apostle] stood in an open wagon and preached
out-of-doors. It was a beautiful day and a very solemn one
too. While preaching [he said,] Brethren, we do not want
you to part with your wagons and teams for we might
need them, (intimating that he did not know but we might
have to leave). That increased my solemnity. At that
instant I heard the [noise of] fowls flying overhead that I
was not acquainted [with. I] looked up and saw a flock of
seven gulls. In a few [minutes] there was another larger flock
passed over. They [came thicke]r and more of them until the
heavens were dark[ened wit]h them and lit down in the
valley till the earth was black with them and they would
eat crickets and throw them up again and fill themselves
again and right away throw them up again. A little before
sundown they left for Salt Lake, for they roosted on a
sandbar; a little after sunrise in the morning they came
back again and continued that course until they had
devoured the crickets . . . I guess this circumstance
changed our feelings considerable for the better.[41]

The crickets had come during the month of May when the
crops looked promising. They had swarmed in from the foot-
hills where the Saints, entering the valley the previous year, had
seen them in large numbers. They could not fly but hopped
about by the millions. The Saints tried to bury them; they
plowed ditches around their fields, filled them with water, and
drove the crickets into the water where they were drowned by
the thousands. Still they came on. The Saints tried fire, but the

174 crickets still came on. Failure to destroy them would mean famine. The supposedly insignificant foe became unbeatable through sheer numbers. The Saints were baffled. All they could do was continue to pray. And so at the point, after three weeks of invasion, when all seemed lost, the seagulls came. At first the Saints thought a new foe had come, but they soon discovered the gulls were devouring only the crickets. They withdrew from the fields and left the gulls at work; at the end of another three weeks the gulls had consumed the crickets and left the fields.

EXPANSION OF COLONIES

It was the intention of the leaders to have all the people live in the stockade the first winter as a matter of protection from the Indians, but because cattle had to be fed this could not apply to everyone. Jordan Valley was inadequate for all the cattle of the immigrants; consequently some of them had to move farther away. This was, then, the main reason that other settlements were established as early as the fall of 1847.[42]

On September 28, a few days after his arrival in the valley, Peregrine Sessions moved northward from the pioneer encampment about ten miles and camped that night on what became known as Sessions' Settlement, now called Bountiful. Hector C. Haight soon went six or seven miles north of Sessions' Settlement and camped on what became known as Haight's Creek, a little southwest of present-day Kaysville.

In December of 1847 Captain James Brown and four other men returned from California—the others who had gone to California with him stayed until the spring of 1848. By January 1848 he had purchased the twenty-mile square Miles Goodyear tract in the Weber Valley for the price of $3,000.[43] This amount was in all probability part of the battalion's money he had collected in California. Some of his sons and a few others went to the Weber Valley with him.

In the spring Brother Sessions ploughed the first land in Davis County, and Captain Brown and his boys did the same in present-day Weber County. Thus, as early as 1848, the first full crop year, some crops were grown in what became three different counties—Salt Lake, Davis, and Weber.

Also, many of the colonists left the forts in the spring of 1848 and began to spread out a few miles to establish other neighboring colonies such as Big Cottonwood to the southeast; East Mill Creek; Sugar House, closer to the southeast; Centerville, two miles north of Bountiful; Bingham to the southwest; South Cottonwood, south of Big Cottonwood; North Jordan; and West Jordan.

Colonists continued to pour into the valley during the summer of 1848. When Brigham Young arrived at the head of a group on September 20, he had with him 1,229 people with 397 wagons, 74 horses, 19 mules, 1,275 oxen, 699 cows, 184 loose cattle, 411 sheep, 141 pigs, 605 chickens, 37 cats, 82 dogs, 3 goats, 10 geese, 2 hives of bees, and 8 doves.

A few days later Heber C. Kimball arrived with 662 people and 226 wagons, 57 horses, 25 mules, 737 oxen, 284 cows, 150 loose cattle, 243 sheep, 96 pigs, 299 chickens, 17 cats, 52 dogs, 3 hives of bees, 3 doves, 5 ducks, and 1 squirrel. Following Heber C. Kimball came Willard Richards and Amasa Lyman with a company of 526 souls (502 whites and 24 negroes) with 169 wagons, 50 horses, 20 mules, 515 oxen, 426 cows and loose cattle, 369 sheep, 63 pigs, 44 dogs, 170 chickens, 4 turkeys, 7 ducks, 5 doves, and 3 goats. This company was a combination of Amasa Lyman's which left Winter Quarters for the Elkhorn River on June 29 and Willard Richards' which left Winter Quarters on July 3. This joint company arrived in the Salt Lake valley on October 19, 1848.

The population of the valley was increased more than 2,500 souls, and the second winter saw about 4,500 souls living in the valley. It was fortunate that some of the pioneers had left the fort, for it made room for many of the newcomers to obtain houses within the four stockades or forts that were now there.

By the spring of 1849 those in the fort were anxious to establish themselves in a permanent location, and they began settlements at Kaysville to the north; Provo, about 40 miles south; and a number of "closer in" places such as Genoa; Union; Little Cottonwood; Brighton to the east and south; Granger to the southwest but closer than Bingham; and Draper, about twenty miles to the south and two miles east.

They also expanded to the west about twenty-five miles and south a few miles, where they established Tooele and Grantsville. Before the year ended, they had gone south 125 miles, where, under the supervision of father Morley, the settlement of Manti was established. During the year 1850 approximately twenty new settlements were established, half of which were in Utah County, ranging from Lehi on the north to Payson on the south.

In 1851 at least fifteen more new colonies were established.

176 These included such settlements in southern Utah as Parowan, established on January 13, 1851; Fillmore, October 28, 1851; and Cedar City, November 11, 1851. Even San Bernardino in present-day southern California was one of the new colonies. The purpose of establishing a colony fairly close to the Pacific Ocean was to make possible for colonists—who might come by sea the year round—access to a series of colonies leading into the Salt Lake valley that would provide them help.

By the end of 1852, the first five years in the Great Basin, the Mormons had founded over seventy colonies ranging as far south as San Bernardino in California to Paragonah in southern Utah to Ogden in the north. The second five years (1853-1857) saw the Saints expand on the west to what was then Carson Valley in Carson County, Utah, to Fort Lemhi in Idaho 318 miles north of Salt Lake, to Fort Bridger and Fort Supply in the Greenriver Valley in Greenriver County, Utah, about 120 miles northeast of Salt Lake City. The number of colonies had increased to over 100.

The period of 1858 to 1867 saw the addition of another 130 colonies, some of which stretched into Nevada, Idaho, and Arizona.

By the time Brigham Young died in 1877, thirty years after the arrival of the Saints in the west, more than 350 colonies had been established under his direction.

In the decade following the death of Brigham Young the Church expanded its colonies as far north as the province of Alberta in Canada and as far south as the states of Chihauhua and Sonora in Old Mexico. These colonies were established because of the persecution of polygamists in the United States.

Footnotes

[1] For a most interesting account of the Spanish Fathers' visit into the Great Basin, read Herbert S. Auerbach, trans., "Father Escalante's Journal 1776-77," *Utah Historical Quarterly* 11:1-132.
[2] For more information on the Great Basin before the coming of the Mormons, read: LeRoy R. Hafen, *Old Spanish Trail: Santa Fe to Los Angeles* (Glendale, Calif.: Arthur H. Clarke Co., 1954); LeRoy R. Hafen, *The Mountain Men and the Fur Trade of the Far West* (Glendale, Calif.: Arthur H. Clarke Co., 1965); Donald Jackson and Mary Lee Spence, *The Expeditions of John Charles Fremont* (Urbana: University of Illinois Press, 1970); David E. Miller, "Peter Skene Ogden's Journal of His Expedition to Utah, 1825," *Utah Historical Quarterly* 20:159-86; Dale L. Morgan and Carl I. Wheat, *Jedediah Smith and his Maps of the American West* (San Francisco, California Historical Society, 1954).

[3]Maurice S. Sullivan, *The Travels of Jedediah Smith* (Santa Ana, Calif.: Fine Arts Press, 1934), p. 20.

[4]Sullivan, p. 23.

[5]*CHC*, 3:268.

[6]Hubert Howe Bancroft, *History of Utah* (1890; reprint ed., Salt Lake City: Bookcraft, 1964), p. 263.

[7]Orson F. Whitney, *Popular History of Utah* (Salt Lake City: Deseret News Press, 1916), p. 40.

[8]Whitney, pp. 40-41. *See also* Journal of Wilford Woodruff, 25 July 1847, Church Historical Department.

[9]*CHC*, 3:269.

[10]Joseph Fielding Smith, *Essentials in Church History* (22d ed., enlarged, Salt Lake City: Deseret Book Co., 1967), p. 372.

[11]Manuscript History of Brigham Young, Book 3, 26 July 1847. *See also CHC*, 3:271.

[12]Milton R. Hunter, *Utah in Her Western Setting* (Salt Lake City: Deseret News Press, 1943), p. 131.

[13]*CHC*, 3:280.

[14]*CHC*, 3:280-81. The temple block was later reduced to ten acres.

[15]*CHC*, 3:281.

[16]Bancroft, p. 264.

[17]*CHC*, 3:281.

[18]*CHC*, 3:286.

[19]Whitney, p. 45.

[20]Hunter, pp. 174-75.

[21]*HU*, 1:347-48. *See* Appendix VI for the complete letter.

[22]Later, when Shadrach Roundy met his family with one of the pioneer companies, Shadrach's oldest son took his father's place with the ox-train and Shadrach returned to the Salt Lake valley with his family.

[23]Bancroft, p. 266, footnote 35.

[24]Parley P. Pratt, *Autobiography of Parley Parker Pratt* (Salt Lake City: Deseret Book Co., 1964), pp. 359-60.

[25]*CHC*, 3:297.

[26]*CHC*, 3:297-98.

[27]Susa Young Gates, *The Life Story of Brigham Young* (London: Jarrolds Publishers, 34 Paternoster Row E.C. 4, 1930), p. 65.

[28]*CHC*, 3:301.

[29]*HU*, 1:359.

[30]Bancroft, p. 273.

[31]*HU*, 1:377, first footnote.

[32]Bancroft, p. 267, including footnote 38.

[33]George Q. Cannon, "History of the Church," *Juvenile Instructor*, 19 (15 February 1884)4:60. *See also CHC*, 3:304, footnote 35.

[34]Parley P. Pratt, "Letter to Orson Pratt," *Millennial Star* 11:22. *See also CHC*, 3:304, footnote 35.

[35]Isabella Horne, "Pioneer Reminiscences," *Young Woman's Journal* 13 (July 1902):294.

[36]*HU*, 1:367.

[37]This was Lorenzo D. Young, Jr., born on September 20, 1847, the first white male child born in Utah.

[38]*HU*, 1:367-68.

[39]*CHC*, 3:330, footnote 4.

178   [40]The "mountaineer" was Miles Goodyear.

[41]Priddy Meeks, "Journal of Priddy Meeks," *Utah Historical Quarterly* 10:163-64.

[42]*HU*, 1:372-73.

[43]*HU*, 1:375. Whitney states the amount of $3,000, but some historians claim the figure to be $1,950.00.

9

Civil Government in the Great Basin

ECCLESIASTICAL AUTHORITIES AS TEMPORARY CIVIL LEADERS

When the Latter-day Saints migrated into the Great Basin, they had no charter from any existing government. The job of civil government and good order in the community was left entirely up to them. They did not see the need of an immediate civil government separate from the ecclesiastical authorities; consequently, for the first years a theocracy or theo-democratic society was their form of government. On October 3, 1847, at a conference in the valley, father John Smith, previously selected by the departing apostles, was sustained as president of the Salt Lake Stake with Charles C. Rich and John Young as counselors. They selected a high council of twelve men consisting of Henry G. Sherwood, Thomas Grover, Levi Jackman, John Murdock, Daniel Spencer, Lewis Abbott, Ira Eldridge, Edson Whipple, Shadrach Roundy, John Vance, Willard Snow, and Abraham O. Smoot.[1] To these fifteen men the community voted "to entrust complete jurisdiction over municipal affairs."[2] Tarlton Lewis was appointed the first functioning bishop in the valley. Two apostles, Parley P. Pratt and John Taylor, out of the Saints' deference to their ecclesiastical positions, took charge, but they interfered neither with the religious nor the civil control held by the stake presidency and

180 the high council. Rather, they acted in the capacity of advisors functioning through the stake officials.

Charles C. Rich was selected as chief military commander under the direction of the stake authorities. Albert Carrington was selected to act as postmaster, clerk, and historian of the city, and John Van Cott as marshal, with John Nebeker as his assistant and as public complainer. A watermaster and a surveyor were also appointed.

Shortly after its organization on October 3 the high council named committees "to handle governmental functions." On October 9, 1847, Henry G. Sherwood, Albert Carrington, and Charles C. Rich were appointed a committee to draft laws for the government of the people in the valley.[3] On October 17 Henry G. Sherwood, Shadrach Roundy, and Albert Carrington were appointed "to hear and adjust claims in the Old Fort." On October 18 the council appointed John Young, Charles C. Rich, and Daniel Spencer to receive the claims on the plowed land and adjust them.

The high council continued to pass ordinances and perform other governmental functions until relieved of this duty by the First Presidency after the arrival of Brigham Young on September 20, 1848.

The Saints had no jail for confining offenders; consequently they substituted the whipping post. According to John Nebeker, public complainer, it was used only two or three times:

> Having no jails we instituted the whipping post. One or two were whipped. On one occasion, I had to prosecute a case before the High Council and execute a judgment. The case was for stealing, the judgment was ten dollars or ten lashes. The stolen article was a lariat and [the culprit] was caught at it. I volunteered to help him pay the fine but he would not, so he was whipped.[4]

George Q. Cannon commented on this form of punishment:

> President Young was decidedly opposed to whipping, but matters arose that we considered required punishment at the time. For instance, one of our best men now, who was then young, was accused of riding on horseback with a girl in front of him. This was looked upon as indecorous. He and others guilty of the same thing were severely reprimanded.[5]

Within fifteen months the ecclesiastical duties of the high council became so heavy that the First Presidency decided to relieve them of civil duties. On December 9, 1848, these duties were taken over by the Council of Fifty, otherwise known as the general council.[6] As a result, in February 1849 the city was divided into nineteen separate wards with a bishop over each who also became the magistrate over his particular ward, making Salt Lake City "in essence nineteen separate municipalities with the ward congregations as legislative agencies."[7] It was "under this temporal administration, [that] all over Utah as well as in Salt Lake, cities were built, lands divided off to the people, roads and bridges made, water ditches cut, the land irrigated, and society governed."[8]

Along with the sustaining of nineteen bishops in February, 1849, the stake itself was reorganized. John Smith was ordained to be patriarch to the Church and Charles C. Rich was sustained as one of the Twelve Apostles. Daniel Spencer became the stake president of the Salt Lake Stake, with David Fullmer and Willard Snow as counselors.

"This theo-democracy was a complete fusion of church and state." It functioned well "for the first years until after territorial status had been obtained and then the close relationship brought friction and conflict with federal officials."

THE STATE OF DESERET

For nearly two years the Church leaders handled all civil responsibilities; then in March, 1849, when the federal government still had not made any move to provide the Saints with any form of government, the leaders took it upon themselves to form a provisional government. In February they sent out a notice:

> . . . to all the citizens of that portion of Upper California lying east of the Sierra Nevada Mountains, that a convention will be held at Great Salt Lake in said Territory, on Monday the fifth day of March next, for the purpose of taking into consideration the propriety of organizing a territorial or state government.[9]

This—March 5—was the day that General Zachary Taylor succeeded James K. Polk as president of the United States.

When the citizens of the Great Basin gathered in convention

Pecking Prophet 14
2 least seniority drop out
most seniority becomes Prophet.

182 on that day, they elected Daniel Spencer, president of the Salt Lake Stake, to be convention chairman. William Clayton was elected secretary; Thomas Bullock, assistant secretary; and Horace S. Eldridge as marshal. A committee was commissioned to draft a constitution under which the people "might organize and govern themselves, until the Congress of the United States should otherwise provide by law." This statement makes clear that the people intended they should always be identified with the government of the United States. The committee consisted of ten members, four of whom were apostles and the rest prominent men in the Church. The assembly then adjourned until Thursday, March 8, at 10:00 a.m., when the committee presented a constitution to them. There were many suggested amendments and alterations. The work of the convention continued until March 10, when the constitution of the state of Deseret was unanimously adopted. Two days later, March 12, it was unanimously ratified by the people who were assembled in the bowery, and the officers for the state of Deseret were elected; 674 votes were counted in favor of the following ticket:

Brigham Young, governor — *Prophet*
Willard Richards, secretary — *Counselor*
Newel K. Whitney, treasurer
Heber C. Kimball, chief justice — *Counselor*
John Taylor and Newel K. Whitney, associate justices
Daniel H. Wells, attorney general
Horace S. Eldridge, marshal
Albert Carrington, assessor and collector
Joseph L. Heywood, surveyor of highways

These officers were elected in the same manner as those under the theo-democratic government. That is, a group of Church leaders was selected by the high council to choose the best man for each position, and they selected only one list of nominees. This list was submitted to the people without any campaigning.[10] Although no lieutenant governor was elected at the time, the constitution provided for one (Article III Section 1) who was also to be president of the senate. Heber C. Kimball was later elected to this office.

The constitution of the state of Deseret proposed that the state boundaries include:

All the territory of the United States within the following boundaries, to wit: commencing at the 33rd degree

Lord picks Prophet
we pick President of Church.

of north latitude, where it crosses the 108 degree of longi- 183
tude west of Greenwich, thence running south and west to
the boundary of Mexico; thence west to and down the
main channel of the Gila River and on the northern
boundary of lower California to the Pacific Ocean; thence
along the coast northwesterly to 118 degrees, 30 minutes
of west longitude; thence north to where said line inter-
sects the dividing ridge of the Sierra Nevada Mountains;
thence north along the summit of the Sierra Nevada Mountains to the dividing range of mountains that separates the
waters flowing into the Columbia River on the north from
the waters flowing into the Great Basin on the south to the
summit of the Wind River chain of mountains that separates the waters flowing into the Gulf of Mexico, from
the waters flowing into the Gulf of California; to the place
of beginning, as set forth in a map drawn by Charles Preuss
and published by order of the Senate of the United
States.[11]

As shown on the map of the state of Deseret, this description
included a tremendous amount of land including all of present-
day Nevada and Utah, all of Arizona to the Gila River except
the Gadsden Purchase, and parts of California, New Mexico,
Colorado, Wyoming, Idaho, and Oregon. By including a section
of the coastline of California, the Saints would have the seaport
of San Diego, giving them an outlet to the sea and a port
through which immigrants coming by the way of the Isthmus of
Panama could take a southern route into the interior of the
country in weather that would permit year-round migration.

The official name of the state was to be Deseret, a word from
the Book of Mormon, meaning honeybee. (Ether 2:3.) It was
meant to be a symbol of thrift and industry.

The leaders of the Church never intended the state of Deseret
to be a permanent arrangement; rather they had formed it to
serve the needs of the Saints as a "provisional government until
the Congress of the United States shall otherwise provide for
the government of the territory hereinafter named and described by admitting us into the Union."

The constitution followed in principle the pattern of other
state constitutions in the United States and divided the government into the three different branches: the executive, the legislative, and the judicial. The executive power was vested in the
governor, the lieutenant governor, the secretary of state, the

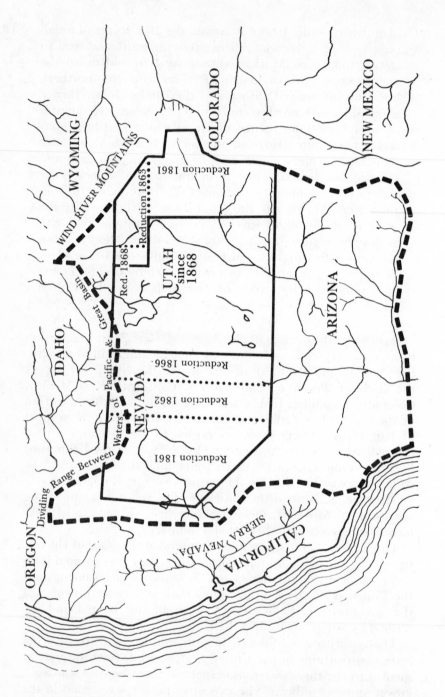

Fig. 9. The state of Deseret and Utah past and present.

auditor, and the treasurer, each holding office for four years.
The legislative branch was divided into a senate and a house of representatives, whose members were to be elected by the people for four years. The judicial branch of government was vested in a supreme court, which was to consist of a chief justice and two associate justices to be elected by the people—and such other inferior courts as the legislature might establish. No qualifications of legal training were set up for those who were to serve on the supreme court.

A state militia was provided for in which all able-bodied white male citizens between the ages of eighteen and forty-five were to serve. At its first session, the assembly was to provide for a census of all white inhabitants in the state. The constitution also provided that each member of the assembly (senator or representative) was to take an oath to support the federal constitution as well as that of the state of Deseret. The right of trial by jury was held inviolate by the constitution. No need for a jury trial arose until January 3, 1851, when some transients were arraigned and convicted for stealing.[12] Of unusual interest is that the constitution did not provide for the remuneration of any office holder, whether elective or appointive, with the exception of the governor who should receive compensation as provided by law. Orson F. Whitney states that "all officers . . . served without pay."[13] An unusually strong section guaranteeing perfect toleration of religion was another feature of the constitution. This is a note of unusual interest because of the many accusations of intolerance that had been charged to the people.

Accomplishments of the Legislature

During the two years of its existence, the legislature of Deseret passed a number of important and notable bills. One measure created a state university. Other measures fixed the boundaries of Salt Lake, Davis, Weber, Tooele, Utah, Sanpete, and Iron counties. Certain bills regulated the control of streams, timber, and industries. A measure prohibited the sale of liquor and ammunition to the Indians. The following cities were incorporated and granted municipal charters: Salt Lake City, Odgen, Manti, Provo, and Parowan. Certainly not the least of the acts of the legislature was its incorporation of The Church of Jesus Christ of Latter-day Saints.

When Brigham Young gave his message to the legislature on December 2, 1850—this was the second meeting of the legisla-

186 ture; the first was in July, 1849—he mentioned that no expense had been incurred by any of the departments of government for services rendered. This would mean that not even he, the governor, had been remunerated for his services. He also mentioned that not one case had been reported for trial before the county or supreme courts during the past year and "no offense beyond the control of a justice of the peace seems to have been committed."[14]

But the judiciary of Deseret did become of valuable service to the non-Mormon emigrants passing through the country who were participating in the gold rush. Captain Howard Stansbury, a government topographical engineer who spent a year or more among the Saints, described the justice of the courts of Deseret:

> Their courts were constantly appealed to by companies of passing emigrants, who, having fallen out by the way, could not agree upon the division of their property. The decisions were remarkable for fairness and impartiality, and if not submitted to, were sternly enforced by the whole power of the community. Appeals for protection from oppression, by those passing through their midst were not made in vain; and I know at least one instance in which the marshal of the state was dispatched, with an adequate force, nearly two hundred miles into the western desert, in pursuit of some miscreants who had stolen off with nearly the whole outfit of a party of emigrants. He pursued and brought them back to the city, and the plundered property was restored to its rightful owner.[15]

Petition for Statehood

Upon organizing the provisional state of Deseret, the leaders drew up a petition to the U.S. Congress for statehood, elected Almon W. Babbitt as their delegate and representative, and dispatched him to Washington, D.C. This petition was introduced into the senate by Senator Stephen A. Douglas, who declared it an application for admission as a territory. In reality, the petition requested "that the state of Deseret be admitted into the Union on an equal footing with the other states, or such other form of civil government as your wisdom and magnanimity may award to the people of Deseret." [16]

That the Saints gave Congress a choice considerably weakened their chances for statehood, especially in view of the political situation of the country with its delicate balance of

slave states in the south and its free states in the north. California and New Mexico also had petitioned congress for governments, California specifically requesting statehood as a free
state. By giving California statehood, the government would
offset the recent entrance of Texas into the Union as a slave
state. But the southern states did not wish at that time to make
more states out of that land ceded to the United States by
Mexico; they were not willing to give more than territorial
status to New Mexico and Utah. Prior to this time, the leaders
and many of the people of the Great Basin were themselves
doubtful about being granted statehood; consequently, a petition signed by 2,270 citizens was drafted in April, 1849, asking
Congress for a territorial government, and Dr. John M. Bernhisel
was selected to present this memorial to Congress. [17] He was
given a letter of introduction to Stephen A. Douglas, whom the
Saints hoped would help them. Dr. Bernhisel was accompanied
on his mission to Washington by Wilford Woodruff. They went
first to Philadelphia to confer with a friend of the Mormons,
Thomas L. Kane, who, upon learning the purpose of their mission, advised against it, concerned that a territorial government
would be oppressive to the Saints.

According to Wilford Woodruff Kane said:

> You are better off without any government from the
> hands of Congress than with a territorial government. The
> political intrigues of government officers will be against
> you. You can govern yourselves better than they can
> govern you. I would prefer to see you withdraw the bill
> rather than to have a territorial government, for if you are
> defeated in the state government, you can fall back on it
> again at another session, if you have not a territorial
> government; but if you have, you cannot apply for a state
> government for a number of years. I insist upon it; you do
> not want corrupt political men from Washington strutting
> around you, with military epaulettes and dress, who will
> speculate out of you all they can. . . . If you have a state
> governor, men may come along and say, "I am a judge," "I
> am a Colonel," "I am a governor," (and) you can whistle
> and ask no odds of them. But while you have territorial
> government you cannot do it. And then there are always
> so many intrigues to make political parties among you, the
> first thing you know a strong political party is rising up in
> your midst, and against your interests.[18]

188   This advice from Colonel Kane apparently prevented Dr. Bernhisel from presenting his memorial to Congress. Nevertheless, within less than a year Congress created a territorial government for Utah, and "the tragic history of Utah under territorial rule" for nearly half a century was to demonstrate how correct Colonel Kane's opinion had been.[19]

On July 7, 1850, Almon Babbitt wrote to Brigham Young that President Taylor was opposed to any kind of government for Deseret. He wrote:

> You will learn from President Taylor's message that he is not our friend; this I know for myself beyond a doubt. He did say before twenty members of Congress that he would veto any bill passed, state or territorial, for the Mormons;—that they were a pack of outlaws, and had been driven out of two states and were not fit for self-government. I went to him in person with Colonel Warren and charged these sayings upon him and he owned that he had said [them] ; and tried to reason with me in relation to the absurdity of the Mormons asking for a state or territorial government.[20]

Two days after Babbitt wrote this message to Brigham Young, President Zachary Taylor died and was succeeded in the presidency by Millard Fillmore who had become friendly to the Mormons through the efforts of Dr. Bernhisel.

It was perhaps this message from Babbitt that later caused Brigham Young some difficulty with the newly arrived officers of the territory of Utah. Brigham Young had said that Zachary Taylor was dead and gone to hell and he was glad of it, and they accused him of disloyalty to the government. Brigham Young's reply was that he was not disloyal to the government, but he did not like some of the rascals that were running it.

A TERRITORIAL GOVERNMENT GRANTED

During the months preceding the granting of a territorial government, a number of propositions were put forth by the enemies of the Church in order to prevent Deseret from receiving a government.[21] However in the end these propositions appear to have had no effect on the legislation.

Eventually it was the slavery issue that determined the political status of the state of Deseret. Dr. Leland H. Creer elaborates:

The question of religion never entered into the proposed compromise. It was the only feasible solution (that is, because of the political situation of the whole country). Yet the decision was unfortunate for the people of Utah. For if ever a people could profit by autonomy, it was the unfortunate Mormon emigres who had purposely fled to the barren wastes of the Salt Lake Desert in order to be left alone, free from further persecution by determined enemies. Under territorial tutelage, however, for forty-six years, these hopeless people were forced in the main to submit to the rule of unsympathetic foreign officials, who could not be expected as non-members of the faith, to appreciate their religious peculiarities and eccentricities. All this could have been avoided by statehood.[22]

The bill creating the territory was passed in the House of Representatives by a vote of 97 to 85 and in the Senate by a vote of 31 to 10 and was signed by President Millard Fillmore on September 9, 1850. The Saints did not have a choice in a name for the territory, nor did they get all the land they had originally requested; nevertheless, they did get a vast amount. They were given the land from the 37th parallel of north latitude—the present Utah-Arizona line—north to the 42nd parallel of north latitude—the present Utah-Idaho line—as the north line and from the Sierra Nevada on the west to the summit of the Rockies on the east. This still left a territory of 225,000 square miles, nearly three times the size of present-day Utah, which covers 84,916 square miles.

Territorial Officials

Creer writes concerning civil government of early Utah:

By the terms of the Organic Act, the executive power was vested in a governor, holding office for four years, who was also commander-in-chief of the Militia and ex-officio Superintendent of Indian Affairs. The legislative power was vested in a Legislative Assembly, consisting of a Council and a House of Representatives, the former comprising thirteen members holding office for two years and the latter, twenty-six members elected for one year. The Judicial power was vested in a supreme court, consisting of a chief justice and two associate justices; three district courts, each provided over by a justice of the supreme court; probate courts and justices of the peace. All territorial officers were appointed by the President of the United States with the advice and consent of the Senate.[23]

The Saints were disappointed that half of the first set of appointees were not members of the Mormon Church. On September 16 Dr. Bernhisel had suggested to President Fillmore the following people to be officials of the new territory:

Brigham Young, governor
Willard Richards, secretary of the territory
Zerubbabel Snow of Ohio, chief justice
Heber C. Kimball and Newel K. Whitney, associate justices
Seth M. Blair, U.S. attorney for the territory
Joseph L. Heywood, marshal

On September 20, President Fillmore named the following:

Brigham Young, governor and superintendent of Indians
Broughton D. Harris of Vermont, secretary
Lemuel J. Brandebury of Pennsylvania, chief justice
Perry E. Brocchus of Alabama, associate justice
Zerubbabel Snow of Ohio, associate justice
Seth M. Blair of Utah, U.S. attorney
Joseph L. Heywood of Utah, U.S. marshal
Jacob Holman, Henry R. Day, and Stephen B. Rose, Indian
    agents under Brigham Young

Later, on the first Monday in August, Dr. John Bernhisel was elected delegate to Congress. As a delegate from a territory he would take his seat in the House of Representatives where he would be permitted to speak but not to vote; territories had no representation in the senate. All of the officers named were members of the Church except Harris, Brandebury, Brocchus, Holman and Day. All of these men but Holman would later become embroiled in controversy with Mormon leaders and were therefore the instigators of forty-six years of controversy between the Saints in Utah and federally appointed officials. One must not get the impression, however, that all so-called foreign appointees (out-of-state non-Mormons) were necessarily anti-Mormon or unjust in their dealings with Mormons. Although it was usual to have the majority of territorial officials allayed against the Church, there were usually one or two who

endeavored to fulfill the responsibilities of their office in a fair
and impartial manner without interfering in the lives of the
Saints.

Listed in Appendix 9 are those territorial officials, designated
as either anti-Mormon, neutral, or friendly, who held the more
prominent offices in the territory from the time of its creation
until statehood. This listing is my judgment; other historians
may differ.

The Territorial Government Begins to Function

The first news of the passage of the bill which created the
territory of Utah is said to have reached Salt Lake City on
October 15, "but a copy of the act was not received until after
November 20."[24] It was printed in the *Deseret News* on
November 30, 1850, but this report did not name the newly
appointed officials. On January 27, 1851, Elder Henry E.
Gibson, a missionary returning to Salt Lake City by way of
California, brought with him a copy of the *New York Tribune*,
October 11, 1850, which contained a list of President Fillmore's
appointees to office for the territory of Utah.[25] Governor
Young was on a tour of the northern settlements when news of
his appointment reached Salt Lake City; the next day, January
28, Elder Gibson met him near Farmington and gave him the
news. Although Brigham Young had not yet received official
notice of his appointment, he nevertheless took the oath of
office as Governor on February 3, 1851, before Daniel H. Wells,
chief justice of the state of Deseret.

Although the Saints were disappointed they had not been
granted statehood and that not all of the appointees to office
were members of the Mormon Church or natives of the area,
they decided to make the best of the situation. In their favor,
Brigham Young was now governor by presidential appointment,
and three other Latter-day Saints had been commissioned to
represent the United States in the territory of Utah. The
governor, the U.S. attorney, and the marshal were residents of
Salt Lake City; and Zerubbabel Snow, although not living in the
territory, was a Mormon and already had relatives living there.

The General Assembly (senators and representatives) of
Deseret met on March 26 and on March 28; upon the recommendation of Governor Young, they resolved "that they cheerfully and cordially accepted the legislation of Congress for Utah
and that they welcomed the extension of the United States

192 government over the territory."[26] Governor Young also suggested arranging for a convenient transition from the provisional state of Deseret to the territorial government. Upon Governor Young's suggestion, the assembly passed a resolution which set April 5, 1851, as the time for the change to go into effect; thus, Deseret was superseded by the territory of Utah. In reality, however, the provisional government continued to operate until the "machinery of the Territorial Government got into full operation later in the year."[27]

First Clash with the Federal Appointees

The so-called foreign appointees as territorial officials did not arrive in Utah until the summer of 1851. Chief Justice Lemuel G. Brandebury, the first to arrive, came on June 7, 1851. Zerubbabel Snow, associate justice, Henry R. Day and Mormon Stephen B. Rose, two sub-Indian agents, along with Dr. John M. Bernhisel and Almon W. Babbitt arrived in the same party on July 19, 1851. They had been detained by high water at the crossing of the Elkhorn River. Associate Justice Perry E. Brocchus came with Albert Carrington and was the last to arrive on August 17.

Almon Babbitt brought with him $20,000 which had been appropriated by Congress for the construction of suitable public buildings. Congress had also appropriated $5,000 for the purchase of a library, and President Fillmore had appointed Dr. Bernhisel to take care of this matter.[28] Secretary Harris had with him the $24,000 which Congress had appropriated to pay the expenses of the legislature.

Discord between the appointed government officials became evident shortly after their arrival. Without waiting for them, Brigham Young had had a census taken and had ordered an election held. The executive documents ordering these actions did not bear the signature of the secretary of the territory. Neff says: "Evidently he expected the territorial government to remain dormant until his arrival."[29] Brigham Young pointed out that it was important a delegate to Congress be elected sufficiently early for his departure to Washington or he would suffer the consequences of cold weather on the journey. He also called to the attention of President Fillmore that although the delegates had been appointed in the fall of 1850 they had not arrived until the summer of 1851.

Secretary Harris, nevertheless, claimed that the Governor's

actions were illegal and refused to release the $24,000 he had
brought with him to pay the expenses of the legislature. Moreover, Secretary Harris informed Governor Young that he had
"private instructions designed for no eye but his own, to watch
every movement and not pay out any funds unless the same
should be strictly legal according to his own judgment." [30] In
regard to this, Governor Young wrote to President Fillmore:

> Is it true that officers coming here by virtue of an
> appointment by the President, have private instructions
> that so far control their actions as to induce the belief that
> their main object is not the strict and legal performance of
> their respective duties, but rather to watch for iniquity, to
> catch at shadows, and make a man an 'offender for a
> word'; to spy out our liberties, and, by manifold misrep-
> resentations, seek to prejudice the minds of the people
> against us? If such is the case better, far better, would it be
> for us, to live under the organization of our provisional
> government, and entirely depending upon our own re-
> sources, as we have hitherto done, until such time as we
> can be admitted as a state.[31]

The Saints probably would not have paid much attention to
this Vermont "stripling" if it had not been for the funds he
refused to release. Secretary Harris's complaint was nothing
more than a legal technicality which could have been settled
between men of good will.

Far more serious to the Saints was the difficulty that arose
with Associate Justice Perry E. Brocchus. Albert Carrington,
who traveled to Utah with Brocchus, called him a man of
mediocre ability whose real purpose was to get the people to
elect him their delegate to Congress. Judge Brocchus had let it
be known as early as his arrival in Kanesville, Iowa, that he
expected the Saints to elect him their delegate and that in
return he would be able to do them much good. Carrington felt
he was unworthy and in his diary beseeched "God the Eternal
Father to prevent the tragedy of having such a poor, corrupt
and venomous curse from representing Utah as a delegate." [32]
But before his arrival in Utah, Brocchus heard that the elections
had been held and that the Mormons had elected Dr. John
Bernhisel. The judge was bitterly disappointed and was in no
mood to cooperate with the people of Utah. On August 8
Governor Young assigned the three judges to their respective

districts. Chief Justice Brandebury was given the first district, which was comprised of Salt Lake and Tooele counties and the adjacent country east and west of the boundaries of the territory; Associate Justice Snow was assigned to the second district which comprised Davis and Weber counties, with adjacent country east, west, and north; and Associate Justice Brocchus was given the third district which included Utah, Sanpete, and Iron counties, with adjacent parts east, west and south.

Judge Brocchus, during his short stay in Utah, never visited his judicial district.[33] The historian Bancroft states that "Judge Brocchus . . . was a vain and ambitious man, full of self-importance, fond of intrigue, corrupt, revengeful, hypocritical."[34]

In the meantime, in order to establish good relations and "promote harmony and good will between the territorial officers and their constituents," all of the official appointees, both Mormon and gentile, were invited to sit on the stand at the September general conference of the Church. After receiving this invitation, Judge Brocchus requested the privilege of speaking at the conference.

His supposed purpose for speaking was to present a request of the government for a block of marble to go into the Washington Monument, under construction at the time. The government wanted a stone from each state and territory inscribed with its name. Actually, the state of Deseret had already made provision for this stone in a joint resolution of the Assembly on February 12, 1851. But Judge Brocchus' request was granted, and his official report to Washington said that the Saints listened to him attentively and respectfully for two hours.[35]

If he had kept to his subject, matters would have been all right, but he took to task the church leaders for what he termed speaking disrespectfully of the Government.[36] However, his greatest offense was his insult to the women:

I have a commission from the Washington Monument Association, to ask of you a block of marble as a test of your loyalty to the Government of the United States. But in order for you to do it acceptably you must become virtuous, and teach your daughters to become virtuous, or your offering had better remain in the bosom of your native mountains.[37]

After Judge Brocchus sat down President Young arose and told the judge that he was either "profoundly ignorant or

wilfully wicked." He went on to affirm his loyalty to the government and the constitution of the United States but said that
he detested corrupt office holders. Of Zachary Taylor he
repeated his insinuation: "I know Zachary Taylor. He is dead
and damned and I cannot help it."[38] He told the judge he had
insulted not only the women but also the men in charging them
with a "spirit of defection toward the government." The judge
was also informed he had never spoken to a more pure and
virtuous audience. President Young went on to say:

> I am indignant at such corrupt fellows as Judge
> Brocchus coming here to lecture us on morality and vir-
> tue . . . Ladies and gentlemen here we learn principle and
> good manners. It is an insult to this congregation to throw
> out such insinuations. I say it is an insult and I will say no
> more.[39]

The people were indignant and Brigham Young later said, "If
I had but crooked my little finger, he would have been used up,
but I did not bend it. If I had, the sisters alone felt indignant
enough to have chopped him to pieces."[40]

During the ensuing week Brigham Young corresponded with
Judge Brocchus and offered him the opportunity to attend a
later meeting. Said President Young:

> . . . if your honor shall then and there explain, satisfy, or
> apologize to the satisfaction of the ladies who heard your
> address on the 8th . . . I shall esteem it a duty and a
> pleasure to make every apology and satisfaction for my
> observations which you as a gentleman can claim or desire
> at my hands.[41]

Judge Brocchus refused the invitation and answered that he
did not intend any insult especially to the women, but that "my
speech in all its parts was the result of deliberation and care—
not proceeding from a heated imagination, or a sudden impulse,
as seems to be the general impression. I intended to say what I
did say."[42]

His speech was evidently given "with a view to its effect in
the East" and with an eye toward his political ambitions, for he
had already decided to abandon his judgeship in Utah.[43] This
occasion clearly demonstrated his temperamental unfitness for
the delicate position to which he had been assigned. Meddling

with the social and religious peculiarities of the inhabitants did not appertain to his office and had brought him contempt and social ostracism. Having estranged himself from the people, Brocchus demanded revenge for his wounded feelings. Toward this end he possessed unrivaled opportunities.[44]

Judge Brandebury and Secretary Harris, who had also been seated on the stand at the conference, were shortly afterwards persuaded by Brocchus to abandon their posts in Utah and return to the East with him. And Brocchus also persuaded Indian Agent Day to return with them. When Governor Young heard about this, he went to visit them to determine if it were true they were leaving, and they replied that was their intention—that Secretary Harris would take with him the $24,000 in government money he still had in his possession along with the territorial seal, the records and the documents pertaining to his office.[45] On September 28 after only 3 1/3 months' residence for Judge Brandebury, two months and nine days for Harris and Indian Agent Day, and one month and eleven days for Judge Brocchus, the four of them left the territory.[46]

Secretary Harris deposited the funds and property with the assistant treasurer of the United States in St. Louis, Missouri, with the exception of the territorial seal which he "forgot" to leave. The account of conditions in Utah by these four men received a tremendous amount of publicity. They declared that they had been forced to leave Utah because of the lawless acts and seditious feelings of Brigham Young and the great body of residents. On December 24, 1851, Delegate Bernhisel wrote to Willard Richards from Washington, D.C. that the excitement was intense, and it was considered a settled matter that Governor Young was to be removed from office.

In the House of Representatives Dr. Bernhisel demanded an investigation into the charges of the runaway officials. And Jedediah Grant, mayor of Salt Lake City, soon arrived in the East with documents to challenge the accusations. In addition, Dr. Bernhisel had the friendship and confidence of President Fillmore. Although the tremendous publicity caused a great deal of sentiment against the Mormons at first, the people still did not seem to be sympathetic toward the truant officials. The general feeling seemed to be that if their charges were true, it was all the more reason they should have remained at their posts. As the Mormon side became known, inflamed public opinion subsided "and the 'run-away' officials became objects of discomfiture and ridicule."[47]

With other friends in Washington such as former Vice-President George M. Dallas, Colonel Thomas L. Kane, Stephen A. Douglas, and Secretary of State Daniel Webster, the tide was turned in favor of the Saints; and Daniel Webster wrote a letter in June, 1852, to Brandebury, Harris, Day, and Brocchus, ordering each to return to his post or resign. They all resigned, and President Fillmore nominated Orson Hyde as chief justice and Heber C. Kimball as associate justice, along with Willard Richards as secretary of state; but the senate refused to approve the two men as justices on the grounds that they were not sufficiently versed in the law. The reasons for their rejecting Willard Richards are as yet generally unknown.

Second Group of Foreign Appointees

The President's consideration for the Saints was further manifested in his nomination and appointment, on August 31, 1852, of two men who proved to be friendly to the Mormons—Lazarus H. Reed of New York as chief justice and Leonidas Shaver of Virginia as associate justice. Benjamin G. Ferris of New York became secretary. H. H. Bancroft stated that the new officials enjoyed but a brief tenure in office, but this depends upon what he meant by "brief."[48] Secretary Ferris and Associate Justice Shaver arrived in October, 1852, and Chief Justice Reed arrived in June of 1853. Secretary Ferris did indeed stay only six months—long enough to gather material to write a book, *Utah and the Mormons*. In the meantime, the legislature had authorized Judge Snow to hold district court in each of the three districts. Whitney, however, states that "Chief Justice Reed and Associate Justice Shaver remained several years in the Territory, and were held in high esteem by all the citizens."[49]

Chief Justice Reed wrote in a letter:

> I waited on his excellency, Governor Young, exhibited to him my commission, and by him was duly sworn and installed as Chief Justice of Utah. I was received by Governor Young with marked courtesy and respect. He has taken pains to make my stay here agreeable.[50]

In another communication, he wrote:

> I have made up my mind that no man has been more

grossly misrepresented than Governor Young, and that he is a man that will reciprocate kindness and good intentions as heartily and freely as anyone, but if abused or crowded hard, I think he may be found exceedingly hard to handle.[51]

Judge Shaver was equally well liked by the Mormon people. He was in Utah for nearly three years before he suddenly died in the night of June 29, 1855. The suddenness of his death gave rise to an unfounded rumor he had been poisoned on account of a supposed difficulty with the governor.[52] But there is no evidence of any such difficulty. The governor called Judge Shaver "a straight-forward, judicious upright man." [53] And George A. Smith in a public speech said of him that he was

> . . . a worthy man and profound jurist, who by his upright course has honored his profession. His studious attention to his duty, his fine intellect, polished education, and gentlemanly bearing won for him the universal admiration and respect of this community.[54]

Judge John F. Kinney, the third chief justice, presiding at the time of Judge Shaver's death, spoke at Shaver's funeral services. Kinney paid tribute to Shaver's ability, integrity, firmness, and moral courage, commenting that even though Shaver had given decisions adverse to the wishes of the Church and community, prominent members of the Church were among his most ardent admirers.[55]

On October 31, 1853, Brigham Young wrote to Dr. Bernhisel:

> Judges Reed and Shaver conduct themselves very gentlemanly thus far, appear frank and friendly in their Department and are universally liked and respected in their Offices by the people and I would prefer to have them remain if possible.[56]

By this date, October 31, 1853, President Franklin Pierce, a Democrat, had succeeded President Fillmore, a Whig, in office; but Governor Young hoped that President Pierce would nevertheless reappoint the two judges.

In another letter written about June, 1854, to Bernhisel, Governor Young wrote,

If the Government officials are so badly off to get some 199
person to come here as judge, suppose they get the honorable Leo Shaver. He is still here and would like to remain
and if they cared anything about our preferences they
would let him.[57]

Apparently the Mormon efforts were successful and Shaver
was reappointed, only to die in office—much to the regret of
the Saints.

Rumors of Brigham Young's Release

After the public announcement at fall conference in 1852 to
the effect that the Saints were practicing plural marriage,
rumors began to spread that Brigham Young would be released
as governor, especially after Franklin Pierce became president in
March, 1853. The rumors created a furor throughout the
country, causing many anti-Mormons and others to believe that
Young was defying the authority of the federal government and
that he was guilty of blasphemy and treason. Consequently,
they became still more clamorous for his release. Governor
Young said: "I am and will be Governor, and no power can
hinder it, until the Lord Almighty says, 'Brigham, You need not
be governor any longer'."[58]

The historian, Dr. Andrew L. Neff states: "This was simply
the reaffirmation of the Church doctrine that Divinity rules the
world. It was a thoroughly orthodox Mormon statement, a re-
assurance to his communicants that all would be well, since God
would continue to rule and over-rule to the ultimate advantage
of the Saints."[59]

Governor Young, in an effort to correct misinterpretations
of the publicity, apparently decided to clarify the matter:

The newspapers are teeming with statements that I said
"President Pierce and all hell could not remove me from
office." I will tell you what I did say, and what I now
say: the Lord reigns and rules in the armies of the
heavens, and does his pleasure among the inhabitants of
the earth. He sets up a kingdom here, and pulls down
another there, at his pleasure. He walks in the midst of the
people, and they know it not. He makes kings, presidents
and governors at his pleasure. Hence I conclude that I shall
be Governor of Utah Territory just as long as He wants me

to be; and for that time, neither the President of the United States nor any other power can prevent it. Then, brothers and sisters, be not worried about my being dismissed from office; for when the President appoints another man to be Governor of Utah Territory, you may acknowledge that the Lord has done it, for we shall acknowledge his hand in all things.[60]

B. G. Ferris, secretary of the territory at that time, seems to be one gentile who, albeit ironically, at least correctly understood the governor's explanation:

> We have therefore the comfortable assurance that, when Judge Kinney presents his parchment [Ferris had the erroneous idea that Kinney was to replace Brigham Young] with the great seal and the sign manual of the President, Brigham will consider it the act of the Lord and yield.[61]

Ferris emphasized that the "present policy" of Brigham Young was to mollify the government, hinting that Young sought to hide his rebellion against the federal authorities. But Ferris' contention that Brigham Young had rebelled against the government during the period of the first federal appointees was in error. Brigham's policy had not changed; rather, the type of men he now dealt with and the circumstances had changed. Never at any time in the life and administration of Brigham Young had he any desire to rebel against the government. But he did want the appointment of upright, honorable men to the territorial offices of Utah, men who would fulfill their assignments in justice without the threat that they had come with a special commission to destroy or reform Mormonism.

Third Set of Foreign Appointees

After Chief Justice Lazarus H. Reed had been in Utah approximately one and one-half years, he visited his home town of Bath in Steuben County, New York, fully intending to return to Utah, but he died suddenly at the age of forty.[62] His death was a great loss to the Mormons; Justice Reed and the Saints had developed a mutual respect for one another. In August, 1854, President Pierce appointed John F. Kinney as chief justice. Judge Kinney was from Iowa, where he had served on the Iowa supreme court. His appointment proved fortunate for the Saints; Judge Kinney was not prejudiced against them and therefore had no intention of attempting to reform them. He did bring with him a load of goods from the States and opened a store for them—an act bringing a great deal of criticism from the anti-Mormons. The real reason for the criticism, however, was that he did not persecute the Mormons or discriminate against them in any way in his court. Catharine Waite, wife of Charles B. Waite—later serving as a judge in Utah—who was bitterly anti-Mormon, said of Judge Kinney: "The uniform course of Judge Kinney has been to aid and abet Brigham Young. . . ."[63]

At the expiration of Associate Justice Zerubbabel Snow's term of office in the fall of 1854, President Pierce chose not to reappoint him. In his stead, he appointed George P. Stiles. Stiles had previously been a member of the Church and had been a member of the city council in Nauvoo. He came west with the Saints but sometime after his arrival was excommunicated from the Church on grounds of adultery. Thus he did not receive the respect of Church leaders or the people; they were not pleased with his appointment as judge over them.

Upon expiration of the term of Seth M. Blair in 1854, President Pierce appointed Joseph Hollman of Iowa as attorney general for Utah Territory. Almon Babbitt was appointed secretary of the territory to replace Willard Richards, who had been acting secretary twice, the second time following the resignation of Benjamin G. Ferris.

After the death of Judge Shaver on June 29, 1855, William W. Drummond was appointed to replace him. Drummond became more responsible than any other person for the expedition of an army to Utah on grounds that the Mormons were rebelling against the federal government. Dr. Andrew L. Neff wrote the following of him:

> That the appointment of Drummond was a disgrace to the administration at Washington is universally admitted by both Mormon and non-Mormon writers. Linn refers to his career in Utah as scandalous; Bancroft calls him a "gambler and a bully." Remy, the French traveler, describes Drummond as a man of not very estimable character, being notorious for the immorality of his private life. The non-Mormon Stenhouse remarks: "Plurality of wives was to the Mormons a part of their religion, openly

acknowledged to all the world. Drummond's plurality was the outrage of a respectable wife of excellent reputation for the indulgence of a common prostitute and the whole of his conduct was a gross insult to the government which he represented and the people among whom he was sent to administer the law. For any contempt the Mormons exhibited toward such a man, there is no need of apology." Remy says further: "Drummond had made his position still worse by insulting or hostile remarks directed against the Mormons, their laws and institutions. He was constantly saying to whomever would listen to him that these laws were founded in ignorance, and that he—an open adulterer, mark—would never let slip an opportunity of protesting against the polygamy practiced in Utah." He declared further . . . that he would set aside all judgments rendered by probate judges and annul all their proceedings except such as pertained strictly to the usual business of probate courts.[64]

Such were the men appointed by the federal government at the time of Utah's territorial status—a succession of personalities reflecting either neutrality, friendliness, or hostility toward the Saints, affecting for good or ill the efforts of the Saints to live in civil and religious peace.

Footnotes

[1]Orson F. Whitney, *Popular History of Utah* (Salt Lake City: Deseret News Press, 1916), p. 53, footnote.

[2]Leland Hargrave Creer, *The Founding of an Empire* (Salt Lake City; Bookcraft, 1947), p. 310.

[3]Dale L. Morgan, "State of Deseret," *Utah Historical Quarterly* 8:74-75.

[4]Creer, p. 311. *See also* John Nebeker, "Early Justice in Utah," *Utah Historical Quarterly* 18:87-89.

[5]Hubert Howe Bancroft, *History of Utah* (1890; reprint ed., Salt Lake City: Bookcraft, 1964), p. 272, including footnote 51.

[6]Gustive O. Larson, *Outline History of Utah and the Mormons* (Salt Lake City: Deseret Book Co., 1961), p. 79.

[7]Creer, p. 311.

[8]Edward W. Tullidge, *History of Salt Lake City* (Salt Lake City: Star Publishing Co., 1886), pp. 57-58. *See also* Creer, p. 311.

[9]Andrew Love Neff, *History of Utah* (Salt Lake City: Deseret News Press, 1940), p. 114.

[10]Creer, p. 316. Chapter 12 of this book, the "State of Deseret," is excellent for a more detailed understanding of civil government in Utah

and the efforts of the people to obtain statehood. It particularly deals with
the political issue of slavery and how this problem affected statehood for
Utah.

[11]JH, 8 March 1849. *See also* Creer, p. 314.

[12]JH, 3 January 1851.

[13]Whitney, p. 55.

[14]Creer, p. 317.

[15]Creer, p. 318.

[16]Creer, p. 320. *See also Millennial Star*, 12:23-25.

[17]Creer, p. 320. *See also* Manuscript History of Brigham Young, 1849, pp. 73-74.

[18]Creer, p. 321. *See also* Journal of Wilford Woodruff, 26 November 1849; and Manuscript History of Brigham Young, 1849, pp. 161-64.

[19]Creer, 1. 321.

[20]Creer, p. 326. *See also* Manuscript History of Brigham Young, 1849, pp. 74-75.

[21]For example, on December 31, 1849, a Mr. Underwood of Kentucky introduced a counter memorial signed by William Smith and Isaac Sheen which stated that before the Mormons left Nauvoo fifteen hundred of them had taken an oath to avenge the blood of Joseph Smith on the nation. In a second memorial from Sheen and Smith, presented on March 14, 1850, the Mormons around Council Bluffs were accused of controlling the post office and obstructing the free circulation of newspapers. On February 22, 1850, a Mr. Wentworth introduced a memorial which stated that the Mormons were robbers and murderers and were in favor of polygamy and the bill prayed Congress to protect the lives of the American citizens while passing through the valley of the Great Salt Lake.

[22]Creer, p. 333.

[23]Creer, p. 333.

[24]Dale L. Morgan, "The State of Deseret," *Utah Historical Quarterly* 8:65-239.

[25]Whitney, p. 72, including footnote. This same paper contained the announcement of statehood for California.

[26]Creer, p. 334. *See also* Manuscript History of Brigham Young, 1851, pp. 14-15. For the whole resolution, see Appendix 7.

[27]Whitney, p. 75.

[28]*CHC*, 3:503.

[29]Neff, p. 170.

[30]*CHC*, 3:517. *See also* U.S., Congress, *Congressional Globe*, 32nd Cong., 1st sess., Appendix:92.

[31]*CHC*, 3:517.

[32]Neff, p. 171. Judge Brocchus "denied that he came [to Utah] with the idea of being elected a delegate to congress, but had expressed a willingness to accept the office, if elected. . . . In a letter to the judge under date of Sept. 20th, 1851, Governor Young represented that it was 'reported, and on pretty good authority,' that Brocchus had said that, 'if the citizens of Utah do not send me as their delegate to Washington, by G-d, I'll use all my influence against them, and will crush them. I have the influence and the power to do it, and I will accomplish it if they do not make me their delegate.' " (*CHC*, 3:517, including footnote 38).

[33]Whitney, p. 79.

[34]Bancroft, p. 456.

204 [35]Neff, p. 171.

[36]Brigham Young had previously said that Zachary Taylor was in hell; and in a speech on July 24, Daniel H. Wells had taken the federal government to task for standing idly by while the Mormons were persecuted in Missouri and Illinois. These statements were published in the *Deseret News.*

[37]William A. Linn, *The Story of the Mormons* (New York: Macmillan Co., 1902), p. 462. *See also* Whitney, p. 80, footnote.

[38]Manuscript History of Brigham Young, 8 September 1851, pp. 61-64.

[39]*CHC,* 3:523.

[40]Neff, p. 172.

[41]*CHC,* 3:523-24.

[42]*Deseret News,* 16 October 1852. The whole correspondence between Brigham Young and Brocchus was published, it having been copied from the *New York Herald.* cf. *CHC,* 3:521.

[43]Whitney, p. 80; *CHC,* 3:544.

[44]Neff, p. 172.

[45]Neff, p. 173. *See also* Bancroft, p. 458.

[46]Bancroft, p. 460. *See also CHC,* 3:531-34.

[47]Neff, p. 176.

[48]Bancroft, p. 461.

[49]Whitney, pp. 85-86. Chief Justice Reid's name is spelled Reid by historians Bancroft and Roberts, whereas it is spelled Reed by historians Neff, Creer, and Whitney.

[50]Whitney, pp. 85-86.

[51]Neff, p. 177.

[52]Bancroft, p. 461. *See also CHC,* 3:518.

[53]Bancroft, p. 461.

[54]*CHC,* 3:518, footnote 45.

[55]*CHC,* 3:519, footnote 45.

[56]Neff, pp. 178-79.

[57]Neff, p. 179.

[58]Neff, p. 179.

[59]Neff, p. 179.

[60]B. G. Ferris, *The Mormons, Their Government, Customs, and Prospects* (New York: Harper and Brothers, 1856), pp. 354-55.

[61]Ferris, pp. 354-55.

[62]Catherine V. Waite, *The Mormon Prophet and his Harem* (Cambridge, Mass.: Riverside Press, 1866), p. 25.

[63]Waite, p. 29.

[64]Neff, pp. 447-48.

10

Preliminaries to the Utah War

THE RUNAWAY OFFICIALS

The Utah war has been called various names, such as the Utah Expedition, The Echo Canyon War, The Mormon War, Buchanan's Blunder, and Buchanan's Crusade. Perhaps the groundwork for such a conflict began with the "runaway" officials in 1851. Even though the Saints were vindicated in the eyes of the administration in Washington, who had ordered the runaways to return or resign, Dr. Bernhisel had written to Governor Young "that although the returned officers had been beaten at every point, and their libelous report was not noticed by Congress; Utah did not stand as well in the eyes of the nation as before the explosion." [1]

DOCTRINE OF PLURAL MARRIAGE

When the doctrine of plural marriage—one of the charges against the Saints by the runaway officials—was announced to the world at the fall conference on August 29, 1852, many of the people throughout the country began to give credence to other charges against the Saints, so that not only were they now looked down upon because of what was considered the unchristian practice of polygamy, but they were also considered to be guilty of previous charges.

205

In other locations, such as Jackson County, Missouri, northern Missouri, and Illinois, the people in the states became suspicious of the Mormons because they were "too friendly" to the Indians. During the eastern period of the Church as well as during the early western period, the gentiles did not seem to understand the Mormon interest in the Indians. The explanation is a perfectly natural and simple one, but one not understood by an outsider. One must have an understanding of the Book of Mormon with its doctrine that the American Indian is a descendant of the house of Israel, that one major purpose of its coming forth in the last days was to convert the Indian to the gospel of Jesus Christ, that the responsibility of accomplishing this task lies with those to whom the gospel and the Book of Mormon have been revealed, and that these modern uncivilized descendants of ancient Israel were destined through the blessings of God to become in the last days a God-fearing people.

On May 2, 1855, Dr. Garland Hurt, Indian agent in Utah, sent a report directly to Washington, D.C., bypassing his superior, Governor Brigham Young, who was also Superintendent of Indian Affairs in Utah. This secret letter mentioned that the Mormons at their April Conference in 1855 had called many missionaries to the "Lamanites," and Dr. Hurt did not feel "altogether at liberty to remain silent" upon this matter. He wrote that these missionaries "embrace a class of rude, lawless young men, such as might be regarded as a curse to any civilized community."[2] He wanted to know if these emissaries should not be subjected to the "closest scrutiny."

Because of the eagerness of the Saints to help the Indians, the Indians themselves soon began to divide the white men into two separate categories, the Mormons and the "Americats." Dr. Hurt said this division was to the detriment of the non-Mormon whites, and was intentional on the part of the Mormons. He had the idea the Mormons would teach the Indians "they had been wrongfully divested of their lands," and he doubted the loyalty of the Mormon leaders.[3]

Acting Commissioner Charles E. Mix sent a copy of Hurt's report to Secretary of the Interior R. McClelland on July 10, 1855.

On November 22, 1856, the new United States Indian Commissioner Manypenny in his report said that the Indians of Utah

had, with but few exceptions, continued quiet and peaceable
and had manifested "an aptitude and disposition for agricultural labor beyond the general expectation."[4] Nevertheless he still believed that the Mormons and their missionaries had been detrimental to the Indians. This was a paradox almost without equal, all of it within the framework of the commissioner's own report.[5]

On September 12, 1857, three days before Brigham Young declared martial law in Utah, he wrote to Mr. Manypenny to find out "why appropriations made for the benefit of the Indians of the Territory should be retained in the treasury and individuals left unpaid?"[6]

Commissioner Manypenny answered on November 11, 1857, charging that Brigham Young had overdrawn appropriations to the amount of $31,380.60. He made some very serious and unwarranted charges against Brigham Young and the Mormons, claiming that the department had information from "reliable sources" that rather than encouraging amiable relations between the Indians and the people of the United States, they had endeavored to impress upon the Indians that a difference existed between the Mormons and the other citizens of the United States; that the Mormons were friends and that the United States government and its citizens were their enemies.[7] Of course, the army was already on its way to Utah when these charges were written.

REPORT OF SURVEYOR GENERAL DAVID BURR

B. H. Roberts, prominent Mormon historian, does not appear to believe that David H. Burr, the surveyor general for Utah, had anything to do with the coming of federal soldiers to Utah in 1857 and 1858, but other authors feel differently about the matter. Andrew L. Neff states that Burr was an "inveterate enemy of the Mormons. His enmity was in part due to Mormon disclosures with reference to his grafting propensities in connection with surveying contracts which were ultimately confirmed by federal examiners."[8]

Jules Remy and Julius Brenchley, who came to Utah in the fall of 1855 from Sacramento, visited with Burr a few days after their arrival. Both from him and from Dr. Garland Hurt they received adverse reports about the Mormons. After they had made their own investigation, they wrote "we could not quite coincide with the opinions of the surveyor and the doctor."[9]

> General Burr . . . never missed an opportunity of railing
> against the Mormons, while they in return accused him of
> malversation in his capacity of Surveyor-General. It will be
> seen . . . that it was on account of the malevolent and slan-
> derous deposition of Messrs. Drummond and Burr, that the
> federal government decided, in 1857, on adopting rigorous
> measures against the Mormons.
> The public and private life of these high functionaries
> was loudly censored by the Saints at the period of our
> visit. It was easy to foresee that matters could not thus
> continue, notwithstanding the Mormons were careful not
> to make the least complaint against them.[10]

David Burr had been appointed surveyor general of Utah for
a survey of the territory on February 21, 1855, by the federal
government. Like some of the other appointees, he did not take
long after his arrival to begin meddling in the affairs of the
people.

Remy and Brenchley went on to say that "newspapers in
Washington had published anonymous letters written from
Great Salt Lake City which represented the association of the
Mormons as fundamentally immoral and refractory to the
laws of the Union," and they knew from "unquestionable au-
thority" that these letters were written by one of the sons of
General Burr.[11]

DISAPPOINTED MAIL CONTRACTORS

To the civilized man, mail is a very important factor of life.
Lack of opportunity for communication between the original
Apostles of Christ who became widely separated and scattered
probably had much to do with their not being able to per-
petuate themselves in office with replacements. Mankind has an
inner desire to commune with his loved ones. As the pioneers
journeyed west, they took advantage of every opportunity to
send letters back and forth along the trail.

The first mail couriers to carry letters out of the Salt Lake
valley were Ezra T. Benson and his companions (including
Porter Rockwell), who carried letters eastward on August 2,
1847, under instructions to contact all of the oncoming Saints,
deliver letters to them, and make an inventory of each com-

pany. Thereafter, by common consent and courtesy, every oncoming and outgoing caravan of emigrants, and "every ox-
freight-train plying the road functioned as ex officio mail
carriers."[12] This, of course, made the mail a matter of chance.

Albert Carrington was appointed to be the first postmaster
for Salt Lake City in the fall of 1847 by the Church authorities
who were also the civil authorities; but this was not an official
appointment, for it was not until 1849 that the first official
post office was established in the Salt Lake valley. During the
first three years the mail, brought in by immigrants, was distributed to the Saints at the various places of worship at the
conclusion of worship services on Sundays.

Almon W. Babbitt is credited with being the first man to
establish any regularity in bringing mail into the valley when he
voluntarily offered to conduct a bimonthly mail delivery into
the valley at his own expense. Sometimes private letters or
government documents were brought in by special messenger.

In 1848 there were attempts to establish a private mail
service from the West to Missouri. On January 18, 1848, an
advertisement appeared in the *California Star,* published by Sam
Brannan, offering to carry letters to Independence, Missouri, for
50 cents each and copies of the California paper for 12 cents
each.

Military authorities in California offered to send mail East
free of charge, and on April 17, 1848, Lieutenant Christopher
Carson was sent with the first overland United States mail
carried from the Pacific;[13] however, this did not become a
regular occurrence.

In 1849 a group of St. Louis men attempted to establish a
mail and passenger line to California. They made one trip with
mail and 120 men as passengers but ran into unexpected difficulties and never attempted a second trip.

Toward the close of 1849 a group of Latter-day Saint men—
Shadrach Roundy, Jedediah M. Grant, John S. Fullmer, George
D. Grant, and Russell Homer—organized what became known as
the Great Salt Lake Carrying Company. Their object was to
freight goods from the Missouri River, including any mail, and
convey passengers to the gold regions of California. They were
to convey passengers to Sutter's Fort for $300 each and freight
at $250 per ton or 12½ cents a pound; however, they were
forced to suspend operations within a year because of lack of
finances.[14]

Still another private attempt was made in 1850 when Colonel

Estill of Missouri tried to organize a company. His idea was to have the Mormons buy half the stock and manage the western end of the business, but nothing came of this effort either.[15]

In March 1849 the government officially established a post office in Salt Lake City, with Joseph L. Heywood as the first official postmaster. But they did not establish an official mail route, and mail continued to come in by chance. In the spring of 1850 because of the increased demand caused by the gold rush, the government established the Great Salt Lake mail route from the Missouri River to Salt Lake City. A line was also established from Salt Lake City to Sacramento, California.

The first contract for carrying the mail from Salt Lake City to St. Joseph, Missouri, was awarded to Samuel H. Woodson for a monthly service for $19,500 per year. He was to begin July 1, 1850, and deliver mail until June 30, 1854. One of the rejected bids was that of Phineas Young, Brigham Young's older brother who bid $19,000, but this was for only eight trips per year because of the possibility that winter delivery was too uncertain.[16] It is regrettable that his honesty and foresight cost him the bid, because, as it turned out, it was only rarely and under insurmountable difficulties that the mail ever got through during the winter months.

By an act approved by Congress on September 27, 1850, Congress established postal routes in Utah from Salt Lake City to San Pete Valley through Utah Valley, from Salt Lake City to Brownsville (Ogden), and from Salt Lake City to Utah Lake and thence to Sand Pitch Valley.

In 1852 a route was established from Salt Lake City to American Fork, Provo, Springville, Payson, Summit Creek (Santaquin), Salt Creek (Nephi), Fillmore, Red Creek, Parowan, Johnson's Springs, and Cold Creek to Santa Clara and then via San Bernardino to San Diego. The report of the Postmaster General for June 30, 1853, showed this route to have taken in a total of $955.66 and expended $3,269.70 for a total loss to the government of $2,314.04.[17]

On January 27, 1851, a bid-request was advertised to carry the mail once each month between California and Utah. George Chorpenning was awarded a four-year contract at $14,000 a year, and the first mail left Sacramento for the Great Basin in May 1851. Finding the journey between Sacramento and Salt Lake City very difficult during the winter, Mr. Chorpenning began sending the mail by way of San Diego to Salt Lake City. He followed this policy during the following few winters.

On July 18, 1851, Samuel Woodson subcontracted with Feramorz Little, a Mormon and later a mayor of Salt Lake City, to handle the mail between Salt Lake City and Fort Laramie for $8,000 a year for the next two years and eleven months, the length of Mr. Woodson's contract. Little hired as associates Ephraim Hanks and Charles Decker. The carriers on each end of the line were to meet at Fort Laramie on the fifteenth of each month. At first, the only station between Fort Laramie and Salt Lake City was at Fort Bridger, 110 miles east of Salt Lake City. A service station was later set up at Devil's Gate.

Perhaps the most difficult trip ever made in bringing the mail west was on an occasion when Little arrived at Fort Laramie on November 15, 1852, only to find the eastern mail had not arrived. He had to wait for twenty days before it came. Starting back with a sprained ankle in early December, he took ten days to get to Devil's Gate, where he was told by the manager of the trading post that the snow was too deep to go on. However, Little and his party finally made it into Fort Bridger on December 22. Again he was warned not to go on, but he purchased some good horses and continued to the Weber River, where, because of snow and ice he had to leave the horses and one mail bag of seventy-two pounds, containing mostly newspapers. A bag containing letters, also weighing seventy-two pounds, was dragged by hand "nearly forty miles over snow in the Wasatch from ten to twenty feet in depth in many places."[18] Feramorz Little arrived in Salt Lake City on January 20, 1853.

On April 13, 1853, Brigham Young wrote:

> No mail has been received from the East since last November, and a part of that is still cached in the mountains; while the remainder was drawn over snowdrifts by hand. . . . During this long silence from the East we have received two mails from California by the south route containing very little news.[19]

On January 21, 1853, the governor and Legislative Assembly of Utah had petitioned Congress to remedy the mail situation by urging that a weekly mail be established between Salt Lake City and San Diego. They said the Salt Lake valley was inaccessible from Missouri for four months of the year and from Sacramento via Fort Hall for six months. They also pointed out that the southern route from California was accessible every month of the year and was protected by Mormon settlements over much of the route. Another factor that made the Southern California mail route look so promising was that since 1849 the Panama Railroad had been under construction and would soon be completed.[20] This would make it possible to get mail from the East not only much more regularly, but also much faster than overland from Missouri, especially in the winter months.

The U.S. Congress ignored the January 1853 petition of the governor and legislature of Utah for a weekly mail service over the southern route from San Diego; but in 1854 Mr. Chorpenning was the successful bidder for a monthly mail over the southern route for the low figure of $12,500 per year.[21]

At the expiration of Samuel Woodson's contract for the overland route from Missouri, the gentile firm of Hockaday and Magraw became the successful bidders for a four-year contract at $14,400 per year. W. M. F. Magraw was the manager of this venture. The mail was to be delivered in four-horse coaches once each month. After a time, because of difficulties and losses caused by hostile Indians, Congress raised the compensation to $36,000 for the year ending August 7, 1855.

Actually, there was general dissatisfaction in Utah with the mail service of Hockaday and Magraw, not only among the Mormons but also among many gentiles. On September 12, 1855, the *Deseret News* published an official list of the mail arrivals from the East and noted that only three times out of fourteen months had the mail arrived on time:

> The miserable manner in which 50,000 isolated citizens of the United States are supplied with mail facilities is a disgrace to the government, and a matter of inconvenience, disappointment and loss that none can fully appreciate except those who have experienced it as have the inhabitants of Utah. There is a gross injustice, miserable mismanagement, and the dead weight of foul corruption and fogyism somewhere, or such long standing and well-known evils would be removed.
>
> Utah is only allowed a monthly mail from the east, and that at the best is not required to arrive until the end of the month, and must leave early on the first of the next month, thus, when it even arrives by the allotted time, (which it has not done for nearly a year) compelling correspondents and business men to omit all, or nearly all, of their answers until another month. Hence, instead of a mail even once a month, it is vertually a mail once in two

YX Company

Because the mails were so irregular, the situation eventually brought about the organization of the Brigham Young Express and Carrying Company, which began to formulate in Fillmore during the winter of 1855-56 when the legislature and supreme court were in session there. This meeting adjourned to Salt Lake City, where they met on January 26, 1856. Brigham Young was chosen president with the following organization: vice-presidents Chief Justice John F. Kinney (non-Mormon), Heber C. Kimball, J. M. Grant, Honorable Almon W. Babbitt; Associate Justice George P. Stiles (excommunicated Mormon); Surveyor General David H. Burr (non-Mormon); secretaries W. Bell and W. Gerish (non-Mormons), Parley P. Pratt, Wilford Woodruff, Orson Pratt, and W. H. Hooper (a recent Mormon convert); reporter George D. Watt.[23]

Another meeting was held on February 2 when "One thousand miles [i.e., with stations and stock] was subscribed for, and the large number present unanimously voted to sustain the chartered company in carrying a daily express from the Missouri River to California. . . ."[24]

In 1856 Magraw requested of Congress and was granted an additional $17,750 to cover his losses on the mail contract; but Congress also directed the postmaster general to cancel his contract after August 18, 1856, and call for new bids. The contract was finally annulled in October, 1856.

Postmaster General James Campbell's request for new bids for the route appeared in the *Deseret News* of August 6, 1856, and the contract was to run from December 1, 1856, to November 30, 1860, with severe penalties imposed for partial or total failure to fulfill the contract, or for failure to meet the schedule.[25]

This gave Brigham Young and his company the opportunity they needed. Hiram Kimball, because of the backing of the Brigham Young Express Company (now shortened to the YX Company) was the low bidder at $23,600 per year. They expected to engage in the passenger and freighting business to help pay expenses, using the same stations, employees, animals, and equipment as were used for carrying the mail.

The contract called for a monthly mail between Independence and Salt Lake and was awarded to Kimball on

October 9, 1856, but unofficial reports did not arrive in Utah until the first part of February, 1857. Upon hearing these unofficial reports, the YX Company immediately went into action and the first mail carried by the company left Salt Lake City for the East on February 8, 1857, arriving in Independence twenty-six days later.[26] The Independence mail was picked up on May 1 and delivered twenty-eight days later. Regular mail was carried thereafter. Mail service between Independence and Fort Laramie was put under the direction of John Murdock and Wm. A. Hickman. O. P. Rockwell was put in charge of the mail between Fort Laramie and Salt Lake City. The idea of the YX Company was to begin immediately carrying the mail by pony express, preparing a wagon line for hauling freight at 12½ cents per pound by the summer of 1857, and having a stagecoach line to carry passengers by the fall of the year. Service was to be planned for winter as well as summer, for stations were to be established all along the trail. To begin with, stations were to be set up at the head of Sweetwater River, Rocky Ridge, Devil's Gate, La Bonte, Deer Creek in the Black Hills, Horseshoe Creek thirty miles west of Fort Laramie, and Beaver Creek (Genoa, which was 100 miles west of Florence, Nebraska). A village was to be set up at each of these stations, one mile square, where grain and vegetables were to be planted, and mills, shops, storehouses, and corrals were to be built.

The objective was to have a station eventually every fifty miles, because that distance could be made each day by mule teams. Also, in consideration of Church emigration, the poorer converts would be able to walk from station to station and purchase their supplies on the way.

Church leaders called upon members to donate animals or other materials needed, not necessarily with the idea of profit in mind but partially as a donation. Nevertheless, a record was to be kept so that if there were a profit the donors could be properly rewarded.

While organization of the YX Company moved rapidly ahead, sinister events were taking place that would bring a sudden halt to their ambitious plans. W. M. F. Magraw, who blamed the Mormons for cancellation of his mail contract, was determined to seek revenge. As early as October 3, 1856, he wrote a letter from Independence, Missouri, to Franklin Pierce. Pierce was a lame-duck president at the time inasmuch as his party had not renominated him for president and James Buchanan was the Democratic candidate in the forthcoming election. Magraw's

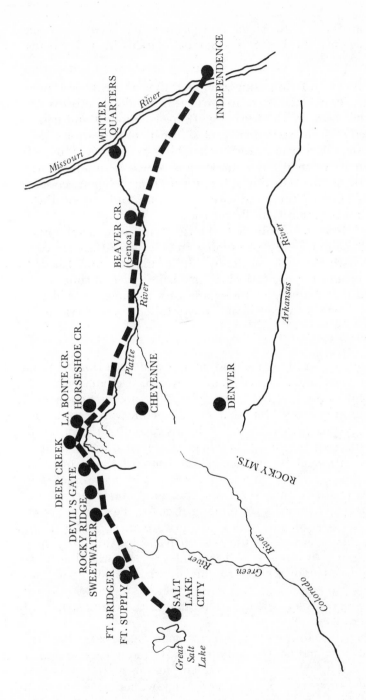

Fig. 10. Stations of the Brigham Young Express and Carrying Company.

letter was filled with bitter and vituperative accusations and charges against the Latter-day Saints. Part of his letter reads:

> There is no disguising the fact that there is left no vestige of law and order, no protection for life or property; the civil laws of the territory are overshadowed and neutralized by a so-styled ecclesiastical organization, as despotic, dangerous, and damnable, as has ever been known to exist in any country, and which is ruining, not only those who do not subscribe to their religious code, but is driving the moderate and more orderly of the Mormon community to desperation.
>
> . . . I have no doubt that the time is near at hand, and the elements rapidly combining to bring about a state of affairs which will result in indiscriminate bloodshed, robbery and rapine, and which in a brief space of time will reduce that country to the condition of a howling wilderness, . . . unless speedy and powerful preventatives are applied.[27]

Apparently Mr. Magraw had military intervention in mind when he mentioned "speedy and powerful preventatives. . . ."

He went on to say that he suffered "personal annoyances in the Mormon country" but that he had "endeavored to discard all feelings arising therefrom."[28] In his recital of the misdeeds of the Mormons he speaks only in general terms, stating that he does not cite specific incidents "for want of time" but that there is not want for naming of cases, parties and places. Historian Neff states that Magraw's "personal annoyances" consisted of: (1) Kimball's outbidding him for the mail contract, (2) the seizure of his mules for private debt, and (3) the scathing denunciations in the *Deseret News* by Editor Carrington for failure to observe mail schedules.[29] Historian Bancroft, referring to Magraw's letter to the president, said: "This dispatch was probably the actual reason that led to the withdrawal of the mail contract, and certainly among the reasons that led to the Utah War."[30]

The official contract for carrying mail that Hiram Kimball was to have signed by December 1, 1856, did not arrive in Salt Lake City until March 24, 1857. The reason for this was that the old contractors, Hockaday and Magraw, had not brought in any mail since the previous October, and the Post Office De-

Railroad and California.

Nevertheless, as we have seen, the brethren had not waited for the official signing of the papers but had begun to carry the mail as soon as unofficial word had arrived during the forepart of February, and the YX Company began to establish settlements at the selected station outposts. William A. Hickman and Lewis Robison were authorized to buy animals from the previous contractors, Magraw and Hockaday. Feramorz Little was designated to go east to purchase harnesses and carriages in connection with agent J. M. Groesbeck.[32] Mr. Horace Eldridge, the Church's financial agent in St. Louis, Missouri, was advised to keep in touch with agent Groesbeck and to watch for good buys in sugar and other products, which would be stored in a warehouse the Church would build in Independence, Missouri, until they would be moved to the various stations. On March 30, 1857, Brigham Young wrote to Horace Eldridge:

> The mail will be carried in the name of Hyrum Kimball. This was considered the best course to secure the contract. He has filed his bonds and enclosed is a power of Atty. from him to you, and a copy of the same, which you will forward to the second assistant Postmaster General, when you apply for the first quarter or contract.[33]

This was the first time the government had given such a contract to a Mormon, and President Brigham Young was especially anxious to keep faith with the government by seeing that every aspect of the mail contract was complied with.

Complaints of Thomas Twiss

By April 6, 1857, three companies of up to one hundred men had been sent from the Salt Lake valley to build the stations along the western route.[34] These stations were to be actual settlements and were to be built along the Mormon plan with ten-acre blocks and wide streets. They were to have sufficient housing and food on hand so that emigrants who might be caught like the handcart emigrants of 1856 could winter over if necessary.

Within a few weeks, one company had established a station at Genoa on the Beaver River, one hundred miles west of Omaha, Nebraska (Winter Quarters). They had fenced in two farms—one of 750 acres and another of 100 acres—and had planted corn, buckwheat, potatoes, and "garden greens." A small mill was working and also a brick yard. By July 1 the colony numbered 162 people, mostly men. [35]

A settlement was also made at Deer Creek, one hundred miles west of Fort Laramie, where a stockade with forty-two houses was nearly complete. A large stockyard had been built, fifteen acres of land had been fenced, broken, and planted, irrigation facilities had been constructed, and enough hay had been put up to last all winter.

Other settlements such as Horseshoe Creek, La Bonte, Devil's Gate, and Rocky Ridge were in various stages of completion by July 1857.

These settlements had been made, without anyone's approval, upon lands still claimed by the Indians, but Brigham Young could see no reason why they should wait. Also, he seemed to feel that the necessity of way stations to guarantee the success of mail delivery rather gave an implied approval, at least from the government. In writing to Horace Eldridge in St. Louis on May 29, 1857, he said:

> I learn from Dr. Bernhisel and others, that the Hon Manypenny and other functionaries are very much opposed to the settling of any portion of the Indian lands, because the Indian lands are not yet bartered for and they cannot give away even by mail contract what they have neither bo't nor paid for! If we should defer our wayside settlements till they had arranged these matters "righteously" with the "natives," how long should we wait? We do not mean to put it into the power of Gov't to refuse our making settlements, neither do we design to make much noise in our ceaseless labors to benefit the human family, and ourselves. How long should we have waited here for a home, had we waited until U.S. extinguished the Indian claim here? [36]

A man by the name of Thomas S. Twiss was the Indian Agent in the Upper Platte area of Nebraska in 1857. The settlement begun by the Saints at Deer Creek one hundred miles west of Fort Laramie was within the area of his jurisdiction. He wrote a letter in April apprising the commissioner of Indian Affairs that the Mormons were making a settlement at Deer Creek and perhaps at other places within his area. On July 13, 1857, Twiss wrote another letter to J. W. Denver who had apparently succeeded Manypenny as commissioner of Indian Affairs. The purpose of the letter was to speak out further against the Mormon settlements at Deer Creek and elsewhere. He claimed to believe the Mormons intended to monopolize all the trade with the Indians as well as the whites passing through Indian country; he also claimed that in some instances the Mormons had forcibly ejected Indians from their own lands.[37]

Dr. Leland H. Creer states that there is no record in the sources that indicates the Mormons ever intended to occupy "this country permanently. Twiss seems to have been unduly alarmed and feared the Mormon activities in his agency would limit his own trading operations among the Indians."[38] At April Conference in 1856 it was explained that the purpose of these settlements was "more particularly to facilitate immigration by establishing temporary settlements."[39]

Twiss' letter is filled with untruths, exaggerations, and contradictions. How could the Mormons monopolize "all the trade with the Indians" if they had been guilty of driving them away? Such treatment of the Indians would have been in direct opposition to Mormon Indian policy, and the Indians would have been more likely to have ambushed them than to have traded with them. It was obvious that Twiss had not been to Deer Creek himself; he said there were three hundred settlers, when they had had only seventy-six workers at the population peak. Twiss also failed to prove the reliability of his source of information by avoiding his name, which shows that his source did not wish to assume responsibility for his own statements.

CHARGES BY JUDGE W. W. DRUMMOND

When Judge Leonidas Shaver died suddenly on June 29, 1855, W. W. Drummond was publicly appointed to replace him. It may have been that President Pierce had privately appointed Drummond to succeed Shaver but had not yet notified Judge Shaver he would not be reappointed.[40]

Judge Drummond arrived in the fall of 1855 and went to Fillmore with the other two judges of the supreme court, Judge George P. Stiles, an excommunicated Mormon who had replaced Judge Zerubbabel Snow, and Chief Justice John F. Kinney, who had replaced Chief Justice Reed, to hold court during the winter of 1855-56. Drummond became antagonistic almost immediately, declaring that the laws of Utah were founded in ignorance and he would set aside all judgments rendered by probate judges that were not strictly in accord with the usual business of probate courts.[41] He further stated that he would never let slip an opportunity of protesting against the practice of polygamy in Utah. Yet as time passed it came to light that the judge was himself an open adulterer. Sometime after his arrival in Utah Mrs. Silas Richards, a sister of Mrs. Drummond, called on the Drummonds in company with her husband. Much to their astonishment, the woman the judge had brought with him and was introducing as his wife turned out to be a stranger to Mrs. Richards. Judge Drummond claimed he had been divorced from his first wife. In time, the Richards were able to contact her through the mail. They received from her the following letter:

Oquawka, Hendricks Co., Ill.
Sept. 14, 1856

Dear Brother and Sister:—

I received your letter last night, and am now seated to answer you.

Mr. Drummond left here in April to start for Utah. We heard from him twice in April, and then we heard no more until August, and that was after he reached Utah.

We read once in the paper that he had a woman with him; he got her in Washington City, District of Columbia; her name is Ada Caroll. He never was married to her, while he was in the States. As to living in Chicago, I do not, nor never did. We were living in Oquawka when he went away, and instead of leaving us plenty, he left us but little.

He sent me a draft a few days ago from California. He was in Sacramento city, but said that he was going to Utah to hold courts in September. . . .

Jemima Drummond[42]

Jules Remy stated that while he was in Utah he had an interview with Judge Drummond in the presence of Chief Justice John Kinney in which Judge Drummond stated: "Money is my God, and you may put this down in your journals if you like."[43]

While Judge Drummond was in Fillmore holding court in
January, 1856, he sent his Negro servant Cato to whip Levi
Abrams, a Jew who had been converted to Mormonism, because
Abrams had made some remarks about Ada Carroll, the
mistress he had brought with him from Washington, D.C.[44]
Drummond and Cato were arrested for "assault and battery
with intent to murder,"[45] but through some agreement that the
judge would leave Fillmore and not return, the case was
dropped. Drummond soon afterwards moved from Fillmore to
Utah county. He resided there until he left for Carson Valley in
the fall of 1856, where he presumably expected to hold court
for Judge Stiles (who had gone to Washington, D.C.), but it
appears either that he continued on to California without holding court or he left after only a brief term of court.

Drummond and his courtesan became socially ostracized in
Utah and the pressure became so great he deemed it better to
resign and leave, but not without seeking revenge upon the
Mormons and making an effort to throw the entire blame for
his failure squarely upon the shoulders of the Mormon leaders.

In California he created much bitterness against the Saints
through slanders published in the various papers of the state,
such as the *San Francisco Bulletin, Alta,* and the *Sacramento
Daily Union.* [46] At this time George Q. Cannon was in California publishing a paper for the Mormon Church called the
Western Standard. In it he refuted the false charges of Judge
Drummond, who, after stopping for a time in California, went
east by way of the Panama Railroad. When he arrived in New
Orleans, he mailed a letter of resignation to the United States
Attorney General Jeremiah S. Black. The letter was a long one
and was dated March 30, 1857. In it Drummond gave certain
reasons for his resignation which are here stated in briefer
form: (1) The Mormons looked to Brigham Young, the head of
the Church, and to him alone for the law by which they were to
be governed; (2) there was a secret oathbound organization
among male members of the Church sworn to resist the laws of
the country and obey only the law of the Holy Priesthood given
through Brigham Young; (3) there was a set of men set apart by
order of the Church to take both lives and property of persons
who questioned the authority of the Church; (4) records of the
supreme court had been destroyed; (5) federal officers were
constantly insulted, harassed and annoyed by the Mormons, and
(6) the federal officers were daily compelled to hear the form of
American government "traduced," and the leaders of the

nation, both living and dead, slandered in a vulgar and loathsome manner. [47]

In addition to the reasons given for his resignation, Drummond charged the Mormons with many other crimes. He said that Captain John W. Gunnison and his party were murdered by Indians but they were "under the order, advice and direction of the Mormons"; that the Mormons had poisoned his predecessor, Judge Leonidas Shaver; and Almon W. Babbitt, secretary of the territory, was killed by a band of Mormon marauders who had been sent from Salt Lake City for that purpose, and that purpose only. He also accused Brigham Young of interfering with the federal courts, telling grand juries whom they were to indict and whom not to indict. [48]

Charging these three deaths to the Mormons was ridiculous to anyone knowing the circumstances; the slightest motive for the Mormons to have killed any one of them has never been revealed. Captain Gunnison and Judge Shaver were, in fact, both favorites of the Mormon people. Gunnison had written many favorable articles about them and had made many personal friends among them. His guide and cook, who was also killed in the attack, was a Mormon. As to the murder of Secretary Babbitt, although he and Brigham Young did not always agree, he was still a loyal member of the Church even though addicted to drinking.

Drummond immediately made his letter of resignation public and justified himself in so doing by saying that the Democratic party with which he had always strictly acted was now the party in power and was therefore the party that should be held responsible "for the treasonable and disgraceful state of affairs that now exists in Utah Territory." [49]

Historian Neff states:

Drummond's sensational letter reveals his astuteness as a politician. This is evidenced not only by his concluding suggestions of what should be done but also by clever reference as to why his scheme should be adopted. Political expediency, party responsibility and the strong likelihood that his program would redound to the advantage and glory of the Democratic Party were cleverly drawn political motives for the writing of his vindictive document. [50]

Drummond recommended that a non-Mormon be appointed to the office of governor of Utah and that he be supported with "sufficient military aid," expressing the view that much good would result from such a course.[51] He pointed out that Governor Young had been appointed by President Millard Fillmore (a Whig) so that the public would blame the opposite political party for the supposedly tragic state of affairs in Utah.[52]

The first denial of Drummond's charges was made by Feramorz Little, one of the men who was then active in the mail service and was in New York at the time Drummond's charges were published in the press. He wrote a letter to the *New York Herald* in which he vigorously denied the charges of Judge Drummond stating that "the treasonable acts alleged against the Mormons in Utah are false from beginning to end" but the *Herald* did not print it. On April 18 it was printed in the *Mormon* (a New York paper being published by John Taylor), where the editor mentioned it had been sent to the *Herald*. Finally on April 25 the *Herald* published a 14½ line summary of the letter and then said: ". . . we have done our part by giving both sides of the story." On May 2 in the *Mormon* the editor remarked:

> The *Herald* seems to have a very easy conscience: . . . after publishing week after week the most outrageous attacks upon Utah, he published fourteen and a half lines from a friend in Utah, and says he has given both sides of the story!"[53]

Thomas Bullock, former territorial clerk of the House of Representatives, also wrote an emphatic denial, as did Mr. Curtis E. Bolton, Deputy Clerk of the United States for Utah, who addressed his letter to Attorney General Jeremiah Black. In it he denied the destruction of the court records, stating that they were all safe in his custody, refuted certain other charges, and then said if it were in his province he could refute all of Judge Drummond's charges with records, dates, and facts.[54]

But with no telegraph and no railroad, communication from Utah was still slow; and by the time Mr. Bolton's letter reached Attorney General Black, President Buchanan had already ordered an army to march to Utah. Judge Drummond's letter had created a mountain of prejudice against the Mormons throughout the land, and without any investigation whatever to ascertain the truth or falsity of the matter, and in spite of the immoral personal character of the writer, the president had

224 acted, believing it would be politically expedient to follow the recommendations of Drummond.

The Mormons had been a political football between the Democrats and the new Republican party in the election of 1856; and although the Democrats had won the presidential election, the Republicans had embarrassed them by tacking on to their principle of popular sovereignty in regard to the question of slavery the same principle regarding marriage, declaring if the people of a territory should have slavery, they should also have the right to determine whether they should have polygamy. In view of the unpopularity of the Mormons and polygamy, the Democrats did not dare to follow through on their principle of popular sovereignty and so were thoroughly embarrassed by the Republicans who had tied the two together and called them the "twin relics of barbarism."

Drummond's recommendations fitted well into the pattern by giving the Democrats an opportunity to separate slavery from polygamy and to show the nation they were as thoroughly anti-Mormon and anti-polygamy as were the Republicans. Although the president had also received the complaint of W. M. F. Magraw (the letter of Thomas Twiss had not arrived by the time the army was ordered to Utah), there is no doubt it was the letter of Drummond that was accepted as evidence that there was a rebellion against the country in Utah. The judge whose moral character had caused his social ostracism in Utah had succeeded in a coup d'etat. For the moment, at least, his revenge was complete.

Footnotes

[1]Manuscript History of Brigham Young, July 1852, p. 62.
[2]Andrew Love Neff, *History of Utah* (Salt Lake City: Deseret News Press, 1940), p. 438.
[3]Neff, p. 439.
[4]Neff, p. 440.
[5]Neff, p. 440.
[6]Neff, p. 440.
[7]Neff, p. 441.
[8]Neff, pp. 442-43.
[9]Jules Remy and Julius Brenchley, "A Journey to Salt Lake City" (London: n.p., 1861), 1:192.
[10]Remy and Brenchley, 1:209-10.
[11]Remy and Brenchley, 1:471, including footnote.
[12]Neff, p. 322.
[13]Leland Hargrave Creer, *Utah and the Nation* (Seattle: University of Washington Press, 1929), p. 226.

[14]Neff, pp. 326-27.

[15]Creer, p. 227.

[16]Neff, p. 323.

[17]Creer, pp. 227-28.

[18]Creer, p. 230. *See also* Neff, p. 323.

[19]Creer, p. 228.

[20]This railroad was 47.5 miles long and was completed in 1855. It was "the first transcontinental railroad of the Americas." It ran close to the line of the future canal. *See Encyclopedia Britannica*, 1966 ed., s.v. "Panama Canal."

[21]In 1858, because of pressure from commercial interests in San Francisco, the southern route was dropped until later growth in Los Angeles made it more practical. *See* Neff, p. 325.

[22]*CHC*, 4:207-8.

[23]*CHC*, 4:209. *See also Deseret News*, 30 January 1856.

[24]*CHC*, 4:209.

[25]Neff, p. 328.

[26]Leonard J. Arrington, *Great Basin Kingdom* (Cambridge, Mass.: Harvard University Press, 1958), p. 164.

[27]*CHC*, 4:210-11; Neff, p. 442. *See also* U.S., Congress, *House Executive Documents*, 35th Cong., 1st sess., vol. 10, no. 71, pp. 2-3.

[28]Neff, p. 442.

[29]Neff, p. 442.

[30]Hubert Howe Bancroft, *History of Utah* (1890; reprint ed., Salt Lake City: Bookcraft, 1964), p. 502.

[31]Arrington, p. 166.

[32]Neff, p. 329.

[33]Neff, p. 331.

[34]Arrington, p. 168.

[35]Arrington, p. 168.

[36]Arrington, P. 169.

[37]Creer, p. 124.

[38]Creer, p. 125.

[39]*CHC*, 4:212.

[40]Catherine V. Waite, *The Mormon Prophet and his Harem* (Cambridge, Mass.: Riverside Press, 1866), pp. 25-28. Waite states that he was appointed in the spring of 1855. *See also* Creer, p. 106, where he mentions that Kinney, Stiles, and Drummond were appointed during the years of 1853-54; but this is an error insofar as Drummond is concerned; he was appointed publicly to succeed Judge Shaver after Shaver's death.

[41]Neff, p. 448.

[42]*Deseret News Weekly*, 20 May 1857. Roberts states that the woman went by the name of Ada Caroll in Washington, D.C.; her true name was Mary Fletcher, and her husband, Charles Fletcher, and her mother, a Mrs. Ridgley, were living in Baltimore, Maryland. *See CHC*, 4:210, footnote. *See also* Remy and Brenchly, 1:208-9.

[43]Remy and Brenchley, 1:469.

[44]W. I. Appleby, "Judge Drummond Used Up," *Millennial Star* 19:401.

[45]Appleby, 19:401.

[46]*CHC*, 4:202, footnote 16.

[47]*House Executive Documents*, 35th Cong., 1st sess., vol. 10, no. 71, pp. 212-14; Edward W. Tullidge, *History of Salt Lake City* (Salt Lake

226　City: Star Publishing Co., 1886), pp. 131-34; *HU*, 1:580-82; Neff, pp. 449-51; *CHC*, 4:203-4; Creer, pp. 119-20.

[48]*CHC*, 4:203-4.

[49]Neff, p. 449.

[50]Neff, p. 449.

[51]*HU*, 1:582.

[52]In the 1856 national elections the Whigs had become the Republican party.

[53]*CHC*, 4:207, footnote 23.

[54]*HU*, 1:582-84. *See also CHC*, 4:206.

11
Utah War: Part 1

From the actions of President Buchanan it appears that he was afraid to wait for an investigation of the charges against the Mormons because if there were no rebellion in Utah it would upset the political opportunity that had suddenly been thrust upon the administration. He also violated the rules of common courtesy by ordering an army to Utah and appointing a successor to Brigham Young without notifying the governor either that an army was on its way or that the governor was to be released from his position. In short, Utah was treated as an enemy country would have been had war been declared upon her.

ANNULMENT OF THE MAIL CONTRACT

Steps were also taken to prevent news of the president's actions from reaching Utah; delivery of all mail to the territory was suddenly stopped.

Because of the failure of Hockaday and Magraw to properly close their mail contract, Ephraim Hanks and Feramorz Little had left Utah with the mail on December 11, 1856, under special contract with the postmaster in Salt Lake City to carry the mail east. Having arrived in Independence on February 27, 1857, and having delivered the mail, Little went on to Washington, D.C. to collect the pay for this special service. While in the East, he visited New York; there he wrote his letter declaring Drummond's charges to be false. He also met James Livingstone, a non-Mormon merchant from Utah, who told him that Hiram Kimball had been awarded the mail contract and the YX Company had begun to operate. Because he was also told they expected him to take charge of some of the returning mail, he immediately hastened towards Independence, Missouri, where he met John R. Murdock who had brought the latest mail from Utah, arriving in Independence early in March. On about May 1 Murdock started west with a large part of the mail that had accumulated. Little spent the next month purchasing an outfit, in which he started west in the first part of June with three wagons loaded with mail. During his stay in Independence, various contractors told him they were collecting supplies for a military expedition to Utah although nothing official concerning such an expedition had come from Washington. It was difficult for Little to conceive of such action on the part of the government.[1]

Near Fort Laramie, Little met Mayor A. O. Smoot and a young man named Emery; they had left Salt Lake City on June 2 and were taking the Utah mail to Independence. Little told Mayor Smoot of the rumors of a military expedition to Utah. Between Fort Laramie and New Fort Kearney, Nebraska, Mayor Smoot met two or three hundred United States troops, who said they were reconnoitering the country for hostile Indians who had been troublesome.[2] The officer in command had treated Smoot with courtesy and offered him a military escort as far as Fort Kearney; but Smoot declined the offer with thanks because he was traveling sixty miles a day and did not think the military would care to keep up with him. As Smoot and his companion continued eastward, they met several heavy freight trains whose drivers were reluctant to say where they were going except that they were headed west and that the train belonged to William H. Russell. Arriving two days later in Kansas City, twelve miles west of Independence, Smoot met Nicholas Groesbeck, who was in charge of the YX Company's business; together they visited the office of William H. Russell who told them that the government had ordered an army to Utah and that the freight trains on the plains contained supplies for the troops. Russell also said that Brigham Young had been superseded as governor and that a new governor and full set of officials would accompany the troops.[3]

When the Utah mail was delivered to the postmaster at Inde-

pendence, he accepted it but refused to give up the mail for
Utah, stating that he had received instructions from Washington, D.C. to deliver no more mail for Salt Lake City for the
present. He stated that it was because of "the unsettled state of
things at Salt Lake, rendering the mails unsafe. . . ."[4]

The Post Office Department had written the following letter
to Hiram Kimball giving an additional reason, however:[5]

> Post Office Department
> Contract Office,
> June 10, 1857.

Sir: The Indentures of Contract for the conveyance of the
mails on route No. 8911—Independence, Mo., to Salt Lake City,
Utah sent for execution to the care of the P.M. Salt Lake City
on the 16th October, last, do not appear to have been executed
by you until the 24th March following. The delay in executing
and the unsettled state of things at Salt Lake rendering the
mails unsafe, under present circumstances, the postmaster-
general declines extending the time for execution beyond the
period mentioned in the advertisement; and, therefore declines
to accept the contract executed by you. Hence your service on
the route will cease.

> Very Respectfully,

> Yr. Obt. St.
> Wm. H. Dundas
> 2d asst. P.M. general

Mr. Hiram Kimball
Salt Lake City
Utah Territory

The contract mailed from Washington, D.C., on October 16
had specified that December first was the time limit for executing acceptance. Under the best conditions it could not have
reached Salt Lake City before December 1; but as it was, the
mail for October and November which left Independence on
November 8, 1856, was held through the winter at the Platte
Bridge in Nebraska by the old contractors and did not reach
Salt Lake City until March 24. Thus it was impossible for the
new contractors to have signed the contract within the time
limit. Word had come to Salt Lake City in February by the

230 California mail, via the Panama Railroad, that Kimball had been awarded the contract; and, although it was impossible to sign it at that time, he and the Utah leaders had acted in good faith and had proceeded to fulfill the terms of the contract.

Neither Magraw nor Drummond had complained that the postal service had been interfered with. Perhaps the administration was using this means as an excuse to prevent word of the forthcoming military invasion of Utah from reaching Salt Lake.

NEWS OF THE COMING ARMY

If Mayor Smoot had needed confirmation of the information received from Russell, the refusal to deliver the mails was sufficient. Realizing that the stoppage of the mail service had put the YX Company out of business, Smoot and his mail agents proceeded to disband its stations and move its stock and moveable properties westward.

About 120 miles east of Fort Laramie, the party met Porter Rockwell on his way east with the Utah July mail. Rockwell returned with the men to Fort Laramie where they arrived on July 17. Here they decided that someone should return as fast as possible to convey the news to Utah. Leaving the other men to bring the YX property west, A. O. Smoot, Judson Stoddard, and Porter Rockwell hitched two span of their best animals to a light spring wagon and on the evening of July 18 left for the 513-mile journey to Salt Lake City. They arrived on the evening of July 23, having made the journey in five days plus a few hours; but Governor Young and other dignitaries were at Big Cottonwood Canyon near Silver Lake where they were celebrating the tenth anniversary of the arrival of the Saints in the Salt Lake valley.

This place was twenty-five miles from Salt Lake City and twelve miles east of Salt Lake valley in the heart of the mountains, about eight thousand feet above sea level. There were 2,587 people on hand, including six bands, consisting of the Nauvoo Brass Band, Springville Brass Band, Ogden City Brass Band, Great Salt Lake City Martial Band, Captain Balloo's Band (also spelled Ballou), and the Ogden City Martial Band. They had built three boweries whose floors were covered with lumber from saw mills nearby. The Stars and Stripes were flying from two of the tallest trees on the top of two of the highest peaks near the place of encampment. The Saints were spending the evening dancing.

According to George D. Watt (whose report was printed in
the *Deseret News* of July 29, 1857) it was about noon on July
24 that Smoot, Stoddard, and Rockwell rode into camp, accompanied by Judge Elias Smith from Salt Lake City.[6] They
reported quietly to Brigham Young and other leaders, who said
nothing about their message until about sunset when "the camp
assembled for prayers," at which time "General Wells made a
few remarks in relation to the latest tidings from the
states. . . ." That is, he told them about the encroaching army.
The meeting was then concluded with prayer and an evening of
song and dancing continued "until a late hour." On the morning
of July 25, they began to break camp, "every one apparently
highly gratified with the privileges they had been so blessed in
enjoying."[7]

On August 1, Lieutenant General Wells, commander of the
Nauvoo Legion, sent word to the district commanders that an
invading army from the eastern states was reported approaching, and they should be in readiness to march when called.[8] The
communication was as follows:[9]

> Headquarters Nauvoo Legion
> Adjt. General's Office
> G.S.L. City, Aug. 1, 1857

Sir: Reports, tolerably well authenticated, have reached this
office that an army from the Eastern States is now en route to
invade this Territory.

The people of this Territory have lived in strict obedience to
the laws of the parent and home governments, and are ever
zealous for the supremacy of the Constitution and the rights
guaranteed thereby.

In such time, when anarchy takes the place of orderly government and mobocratic tyranny usurps the power of rulers, they
have left the inalienable rights to defend themselves against all
aggression upon their constitutional privileges [*sic*]. It is
enough that for successive years they have witnessed the desolation of their homes; the barbarous wrath of mobs poured upon
their unoffending brethren and sisters; their leaders arrested,
incarcerated and slain, and themselves driven to cull life from
the hospitality of the desert and the savage. They are not willing
to endure longer these unceasing outrages; but if an extermina-
ting war be purposed against them and blood alone can cleanse
pollution from the Nation's bulwarks, to the God of our fathers
let the appeal be made.

You are instructed to hold your command in readiness to march at the shortest possible notice to any part of the Territory. See that the law is strictly enforced in regard to arms and ammunition, as as far as practicable that each Ten be provided with a good wagon and four horses or mules, as well as the necessary clothing, etc., for a winter campaign. Particularly let your influence be used for preservation of the grain. Avoid all excitement, but be ready.

Daniel H. Wells,

Lieut. General Commanding
By James Ferguson, Adt. Gen.

Scattered Saints Called to Utah

Since the Mormons had had to discover for themselves that an army was on its way to Utah, that none of the common courtesies of government had been observed, and that the general cloak of secrecy had been invoked by the federal government, the Saints had to put their own interpretation upon the actions of the administration. They thereby read into the procedures a far more menacing attitude on the part of the government than was actually intended. They felt the necessity of being at full strength and decided to not only call home all of the apostles who were on missions as well as nearly all of the Utah missionaries, but also to abandon most of the outlying settlements. Elder John Taylor in New York and Erastus Snow in St. Louis were soon on their way home. Samuel W. Richards was sent to England to replace Orson Pratt as European Mission President so that he could return home with Elder Ezra T. Benson who had also been in Europe. Elder Richards was requested to carry a message to President Buchanan on his way to England, informing him that his army could not enter Utah until satisfactory arrangements had been made. He also carried with him copies of the *Deseret News* of August 12, 1857, which contained an editorial of the views of the Presidency of the Church and the Twelve Apostles pertaining to the crisis. The editorial, though carefully prepared, was caustic. The message and papers were delivered to Thomas L. Kane, a stalwart friend of the Saints, who was requested to take them to President Buchanan, which he did.[10] After delivering these items to Kane, Elder Richards went on to New York City where he was interviewed by someone for the *New York Times,* which printed the Mormon side of the story as it was told to them. Elder Richards gave the story in much more moderate language than that in the *Deseret News* editorial. From New York he continued on to Great Britain where he reported to Orson Pratt, the European Mission President, that he and Elder Ezra T. Benson, as well as all Utah elders were to return to Utah. With four other elders the two apostles returned by the Isthmus of Panama railroad, up the coast to San Bernardino and on into Salt Lake City. In the spring of 1858 Elder Richards, with twenty-three other elders, landed in New York on March 10, 1858, arriving in Salt Lake City in May.

Similar instructions to return were forwarded to other elders in the United States, in Canada, and on the islands of the Pacific Ocean. Messengers were also sent to the Saints in Carson Valley and San Bernardino. Elder Peter Conover and ten or twelve men went to Carson Valley, arriving September 5, and in three weeks the settlers had disposed of their property as best they could and had started on their journey to Salt Lake City where they arrived on November 2. There were 450 people in the group traveling in 123 wagons. They brought with them 2,700 pounds of community ammunition purchased in San Francisco. This was in addition to large amounts in the possession of individuals. They also brought a large number of guns with them.[11]

Approximately one thousand Saints in San Bernardino returned in several different companies in the fall of 1857 and the spring of 1858. In November of 1857, the *Los Angeles Star* had this to say about the departing Saints:

> From our acquaintance with the people of San Bernardino, we must say that we know them to be a peaceable, industrious, law-abiding community. Under great disadvantage they have cultivated their farms, and caused the ranch [San Bernardino], which was, before their occupation almost unproductive, to teem with the choicest products of the field, and the garden. With their peculiarities of religion or church we have nothing to do; we know them to be good citizens, and cheerfully testify to the fact. Besides the people of San Bernardino, our state will lose three or four hundred other Mormon citizens, many of whom are now on the way to join the departing saints.[12]

The lack of an official announcement that troops were on the way to Utah only added to the curiosity and the interest of the public as the news gradually spread. The secrecy also made it plain that President Buchanan expected opposition and was hoping to achieve occupation of Utah before the Saints were able to organize, but since the Mormons had learned of the approaching army and had read into the movement more sinister plans than the government intended, open warfare became a distinct possibility.

The government began its military expedition from Fort Leavenworth on the banks of the Missouri River. Supply trains, under contract with Russell, Majors, and Waddell, had been sent out well in advance of the troops, however, on the basis that the oxen would travel much more slowly than the troops. Colonel Burton and his men could have destroyed those first unprotected supply trains which they met at South Pass on August 22, but his orders not to interfere with life or property prevented him from doing so.

Small contingents of the army were sent out from Fort Leavenworth as rapidly as they could be organized, depending upon the recruiting in various locations. Nearly all of the army for Utah (except the commissioned and part of the non-commissioned officers) was to consist of volunteer enlistments, many of whom turned out to be foreigners who were newly arrived in the United States and had enlisted because they were in need. Naturally, under such circumstances when hardship came and these men had become somewhat adjusted to conditions in the United States, many of them deserted.

Diary of Captain John W. Phelps

The diary of Captain John Wolcott Phelps gives us an insight into the westward journey of the army, including Phelps' opinion of the Mormons. Captain Phelps received his orders in Chicago on June 7, 1857, to join his battery at Fort Leavenworth. He did not underestimate the Mormons as some of the other soldiers and officers did; he said that their fanaticism in effect was equal to military organization and discipline—that they were generally foreigners and were taught to consider the army as persecutors.

Their opposition to government cannot be overcome

without the destruction of its cause, which involves the 235
complete destruction of their life as a public body, and to
effect this a large physical force—at least man to man—and
all the force of martial law is necessary. They number from
10 to 20,000 men who are capable of bearing arms; and
many of whom have born arms in actual service, and have
been disciplined.

Our government reckons upon their division, but with
greater reason they could reckon upon divisions among
us.[13]

On June 13, 1857, Captain Phelps reached Fort Leavenworth
in Kansas Territory where the army for Utah which was to be
2,500 strong was being outfitted and prepared for departure.
During the next five weeks men recruited for the army continued to arrive from various places such as Florida, New York,
Missouri, and Minnesota. In addition, horses from Missouri and
other places as well as mules from New Orleans continued to
arrive.

By July 18th the leading units of the army for Utah began
leaving Fort Leavenworth. The first to leave was the Tenth
Infantry under Colonel E. B. Alexander with a battery of the
Fourth Artillery leaving the following day under Captain
Phelps. The Fifth Infantry left on July 20, followed at a later
date by another battery of the Fourth Artillery under Captain
Jesse Lee Reno. These were the leading units of the army. The
last to leave in 1857 were six companies of the Second
Dragoons under Colonel Philip St. George Cooke, which did not
leave Fort Leavenworth until September 17. They were accompanied by Alfred Cumming, newly appointed governor of
Utah, and certain other newly appointed Utah officials. Colonel
Albert Sidney Johnston, who had been appointed commanding
officer of the expedition—replacing General William S. Harney,
the first appointee—also left on September 17 accompanied by
an escort of forty men who had been detached from the Second
Dragoons. This group traveled in light spring wagons, enabling
them to travel with much greater dispatch than the regular army
units.

As Captain Phelps and his men traveled westward, he commented in his journal about army deserters, strangers who came
into their camp from time to time whom he suspected to be
Mormon spies, conditions of travel, and occasional remarks
about the Mormons, including those who passed by occasionally.

236   On August 24 he commented that many of his soldiers were exceedingly stupid and would not have been enlisted in the military service of the countries in Europe from which they came. They would sell their best article of clothing for liquor, he claimed, despite their awareness that they would suffer from bitter cold as a consequence.

> . . . as the Mormons are chiefly foreigners, we exhibit to the sun the ridiculous spectacle of an army of foreigners led by American officers going to attack a set of foreigners on American soil.
> The few American soldiers who are found among these foreigners are generally the lowest of all Americans, and are frequently more worthless than the foreigners themselves.[14]

At Fort Laramie on September 3 he wrote about W. M. F. Magraw, the former mail contractor, now the head of an expedition of about one hundred men exploring a roadway from Fort Leavenworth via Fort Laramie and Salt Lake to California.

> They [i.e. the officers under Magraw] say that Magraw is an ignorant blackguard, totally unfit for the head of such an expedition, while the chief engineer of the party is. It appears that Magraw's brother was a delegate to the convention that nominated Buchanan for the presidency, and hence, in the political logic of the present day, must be a party chief for a scientific exploring expedition![15]

On September 14 Captain Phelps wrote that they had found a copy of the *Deseret News* of August 12 containing speeches of Heber C. Kimball, Elias Smith, and George A. Smith and an editorial, all of which included an allusion to the force which was moving against Utah.

> The Saints evidently feel considerably honored by having become objects of importance enough to attract such notice from the United States. They are not very determined as to what they will do; tho' fighting is talked of considerably. Brigham says that his women bother him for new bonnets and such things.[16]

On September 18, Captain Phelps recorded that it had been two months since they had left Fort Leavenworth, and they had traveled about 800 miles. Three days later he met Captain Van Vliet with Dr. Bernhisel. Van Vliet told them they would not be able to enter Salt Lake City "this winter" and that Brigham had said if they ever did, they would find it a desolation.

On September 30 Captain Phelp's battery arrived at Ham's Fork, thirty-five miles from Fort Bridger where the Tenth Infantry was already camped. His advance troops were all to rendezvous in this area. The Fifth Infantry and Captain Reno's artillery battery arrived on October 4, the day before Colonel Alexander received word that three supply trains had been burned.

MOUNTAIN MEADOWS MASSACRE

While the United States Army was supposedly secretly on its way to Utah in 1857, one of the greatest tragedies ever enacted in the history of the West occurred. It was the Mountain Meadows Massacre, in which approximately 120 men, women, and children were murdered by Indians and white men in the southern part of Utah. The white men who participated were members in good standing of the Mormon Church; and although they were in fear of their own destruction from 2,500 soldiers of the United States Army and from the threatened cooperation of those in the Fancher-Missouri Party, they should have exercised more Christian judgment and restraint. The principles of the gospel are based upon the premise that "it is better to suffer wrong than to do wrong." Yet in this instance we find otherwise intelligent members of the Church participating in the murder of many people. The results were twofold: the loss of many lives—most of whom were innocent—and a guilty burden for the participants for the rest of their lives—a burden carried also by their descendants and other loyal members of the Church.

How could anyone professing to believe and practice the gospel of Jesus Christ participate in such a tragedy? Although it does not justify the act, the answer is simply that the Saints feared for their lives. They had been driven from their homes five different times and had themselves suffered through the tragedy of the Haun's Mill Massacre. The last time they had left their homes they had traveled more than fourteen hundred miles under trying conditions to find a place in the valleys of the mountains where they would be out of the reach of their enemies and could worship God and raise their families in peace. Now an army was on its way to Utah, for what purpose these people did not know; they supposed that it was to crush them and force them to give up their religion.

The Saints had learned of the coming of the army on July 24; and on August 1 Daniel H. Wells sent instructions to the various units of the military to be ready to march on the shortest possible notice to any part of the territory.

The Emigrant Train

The people slaughtered at Mountain Meadows were partially from a larger group from Arkansas and partially from Missouri. A much larger party from Arkansas had quarreled and split into different groups after arriving in Utah. A portion of the larger Arkansas group, led by Captain Fancher and consisting of twenty-three men, twelve women, and thirty-four children, traveled through Utah with the Missouri group, a party of sixty-eight or seventy men who called themselves the "Missouri Wildcats".[17] Apparently the only reason the Arkansas party attached themselves to the Missourians was for protection from the Indians; the Arkansas people were circumspect, whereas the Missourians were rough and boisterous. The Latter-day Saints in Southern Utah were not aware that there were two parties until after the massacre.

No friction occurred between this group and the Mormons until the Francher-Missouri group arrived at Buttermilk Fort (Holden), where the actions of some of its men angered the local people. But the real difficulty began at Corn Creek about fifteen miles south of Fillmore where some members of the Fancher-Missouri Party poisoned a dead ox and put poison in a small pond of water. Some Piede Indians, who had come on a visit to their Pahvant friends, ate the poisoned ox and a number of them died from it. The cattle of some of the white people also died from drinking the poisoned water, and at least one young white boy, Proctor Robinson, died from handling the poisoned meat; a woman, Mrs. John Ray, became seriously ill from it.

The Indians were exceedingly angry but the strength of the emigrant party prevented them from attacking at this time; however, by the time they reached Beaver some of the angry Indians had caught up with them and had begun to harass them.[18] Friction between the whites and the emigrant train increased until they arrived in Cedar City where William R. Palmer states they "shot up the town, killed dogs and chickens

on the street and resisted arrest."[19] They tore down the field
fence and turned their animals into the field and burned fences
for firewood.[20]

Two men tried to buy whiskey, and when they could get
none one of them said they had the gun that killed Old Joe
Smith, and that his company would go to California and get an
army and come back and "wipe out every G — — d — — —
Mormon."[21]

The local police, powerless to do anything alone, insisted that
the Mormon military go out with them and bring back the
culprits to account for their crimes.

The local Mormon leaders held a meeting and decided to send
a messenger to Brigham Young for advice as to what to do
about the emigrants.

The Fancher-Missouri party left Cedar City and moved about
thirty miles west southwest to Mountain Meadows where they
intended to stay for a number of days to rest their animals and
fatten them before crossing the long desert stretch to California.
In the meantime, Indians who had followed the train had "sent
out runners to other bands for reinforcements. . . ."[22]

Attacking Indians

On Tuesday morning, September 8, 1857, the Indians
attacked the emigrants, and although they killed seven men and
wounded sixteen others they were repulsed. They now appealed
to John D. Lee, the government Indian farmer to the Piedes, to
lead them, but Lee claimed he felt the emigrants had been
punished enough and tried to get them to let the emigrants go.
Lee claimed the Indians threatened to kill him if he did not help
them kill the emigrants, that they also said they would declare
war against the Mormons and kill everyone in the settlements.
Lee, aware that the Indians in southern Utah outnumbered the
Mormons four to one, said, "I was the only white man there,
with a wild and excited band of Indians."[23] Tuesday afternoon
more Indians joined them. By Wednesday about fourteen other
white men had arrived. That evening the Indians made a second
attack upon the emigrants, but Lee said that with the help of
William Young, John Mangum, and Oscar Hamblin he finally
persuaded them to stop.[24] Thursday morning at about daylight,
the Indians made another attack upon the emigrant party, not
keeping their word, according to Lee.

On Wednesday two of the men from the emigrant train who

had escaped and were seeking help met three white men in Leaches Canyon about fifteen miles from Cedar City. The emigrants began to tell their story to the three, who had heard stories about the wickedness of the emigrants; the three men shot the two emigrants. One, Mr. William Aiden, was killed while the other, who was only wounded, managed to escape and return to the wagon train, reporting there that white men were apparently "in with" the Indians.

The death of Mr. Aiden was very possibly the real cause of the massacre. Word of his death and the escape of the other man came to Lee and the men camped near the springs at Mountain Meadows, and Lee sent a messenger to Lieutenant Colonel Isaac Haight. The Mormon Iron Militia from Cedar City was called out and arrived on the scene on Thursday with their major, John Higbee. It is only fair to these young men responding to a call to military duty to say that most of them thought the Indians had already massacred the emigrant train and that the militia were going on a mission of mercy to bury the dead. In all, fifty-four Saints were now at Mountain Meadows. They realized that the emigrants knew they were now involved and that soldiers from California would have a "real cause" for coming against them. They also realized that the Indians, angered over the loss of their braves who had been killed, might turn upon the Mormons if the Indians were denied revenge upon the emigrants. Consequently, members of the Saints along with the Indians decided that all emigrants who were "old enough to talk" must be "put out of the way."

A Treacherous Plan

They decided to decoy the Missourians out of their stronghold by promising them protection if they gave up their arms and then at a given signal to shoot all except the little children. This plan was carried out on Friday, September 11, 1857, shortly after noon; the Indians lying in ambush killed women and older children—seventeen younger children were saved—and the remainder of the men who had not been killed by the militia. It was arranged this way because a number of the militia objected to killing and were allowed to shoot in the air. It was all over in about five minutes. The massacre had been conceived as a part of the military campaign, but after it was over the men involved were immediately embarrassed and each took an oath never to tell anyone that white men were involved, not even

their wives and families.[25] Years later every man who told the 241
story placed the blame on others.

The messenger who had been sent to Brigham Young, James
Haslam, returned on Sunday afternoon, September 13, with a
message from Brigham Young that "the emigrants must be
protected if it takes all the men in southern Utah."[26] He was
too late.

Regrets

Those who committed the Mountain Meadows atrocity were
not heartless, cold-blooded killers. They were ordinarily good
men who committed a tragic crime in the name of safeguarding
their homes. It was a tragedy that weighed them down with
sorrow for the rest of their lives.

Responsibility for the Massacre

Perhaps the most important point to remember is that no
matter whom we might think guilty of the crime in this tragic
affair, their descendants had nothing to do with it. For,
according to the prophet Ezekiel,

> The word of the Lord came unto me again, saying,
> What mean ye, that ye use this proverb concerning the
> land of Israel, saying, The fathers have eaten sour grapes,
> and the children's teeth are set on edge?
> As I live, saith the Lord God, ye shall not have occasion
> any more to use this proverb in Israel.
> Behold, all souls are mine; as the soul of the father, so
> also the soul of the son is mine: the soul that sinneth, it
> shall die. (Ezekiel 18:1-4.)

These words are reinforced by the prophet Jeremiah:

> In those days they shall say no more, The fathers have
> eaten a sour grape, and the children's teeth are set on edge.
> But everyone shall die for his own iniquity: every man
> that eateth the sour grape, his teeth shall be set on edge.
> (Jeremiah 31:29-30.)

Thus, not a single descendant of any man who participated in
the massacre bears a shred of guilt, nor does any other living

Latter-day Saint. And neither Brigham Young nor any other general authority of the Church was guilty of perpetrating the deed.

Footnotes

[1] *HU*, 1:596-97.

[2] *HU*, 1:597.

[3] *HU*, 1:598.

[4] *Deseret News*, 5 August 1857. *See also CHC*, 4:217.

[5] *CHC*, 4:218.

[6] Judge Elias Smith was a son of a brother of Joseph Smith, Sr. (Asael Smith, Jr.) and was therefore a cousin of the Prophet.

[7] *CHC*, 4:237. *See also Deseret News*, 29 July 1857.

[8] The District Commanders were Colonel W. H. Dame, Parowan; Major L. W. McCollough, Fillmore; Major C. W. Bradley, Nephi; Major Warren S. Snow, Sanpete; General Aaron Johnson, Peteetneet (Payson); Colonel Wm. B. Pace, Provo; Major Samuel Smith, Box Elder; Colonel C. W. West, Weber; Colonel P. C. Merrill, Davis; Major David Evans, Lehi; Major Allen Weeks, Cedar; Major John Rowberry, Tooele.

[9] Vaux, "The Echo Canyon War," *The Contributor*, 3(March 1882)6:177.

[10] *CHC*, 4:241. *See also HU*, 1:665-66.

[11] *CHC*, 4:245.

[12] *CHC*, 4:246, footnote 11.

[13] LeRoy R. Hafen and Ann W. Hafen, *Documentary Account of the Utah Expedition*, The Far West and the Rockies Historical Series, vol. 8 (Glendale, Calif.: Arthur H. Clarke Co., 1958), p. 90, footnote. This volume is an excellent review of viewpoints from men on both sides of the Utah issues, and could be read with great profit by the serious student.

[14] Hafen and Hafen, p. 115.

[15] Hafen and Hafen, p. 122.

[16] Hafen and Hafen, p. 128.

[17] Juanita Brooks, *The Mountain Meadow Massacre* (Norman: University of Oklahoma Press, 1962), pp. 45-46.

[18] Brooks, p. 50.

[19] Letter of William R. Palmer to Dabney Otis Collins of Denver, Colorado, 16 December 1958. Palmer carried on a regular correspondence with Collins. He presented the writer with a copy of this correspondence.

[20] Palmer to Collins.

[21] Palmer to Collins.

[22] Brooks, p. 57.

[23] John D. Lee, *Mormonism Unveiled* (St. Louis: Bryan, Brand, and Co., 1877), p. 227.

[24] Lee, p. 229.

[25] Brooks, p. 150.

[26] Brooks, p. 113.

12

Utah War: Part 2

ACTIONS TO PREVENT THE ARMY FROM
ENTERING SALT LAKE VALLEY

While the army was on its way to Utah the Saints did not
stand idly by. As stated, as soon as word of the coming of the
army reached Utah, Lieutenant General Daniel H. Wells of the
Nauvoo Legion—the territorial militia—sent a note to his district
commanders informing them of the coming of the army and
instructing them to hold their respective divisions in readiness at
a moment's notice to march to any part of the territory.

The military in Utah had been reorganized early in 1857 for
the sole purpose of being more proficient in protecting the
outlying settlements from Indians, and this now made it
possible to react more quickly to the unexpected threat from
the federal government. In the letter, in addition to military
instructions, the leaders were requested to "use their influence
for the preservation of the grain."

The first movements in the field were on August 15. Colonel
Robert F. Burton left two days after receiving orders with the
seventy-five men who were ready. He was later joined by a
company from Provo under the command of Joshua Clark. By
August 21 he reached Fort Bridger and five days later met the
first Mormon immigrant companies at Pacific Springs, a few
miles west of South Pass. The next day, August 27, they met

243

several large government supply trains hauling provisions for the army. Entirely unprotected, the trains could have been easily destroyed had it not been for Burton's orders not to interfere with person or property. Upon arrival at the Sweetwater River a few miles east and north of the South Pass, Colonel Burton left half of his command and proceeded to Devil's Gate, arriving there on August 30 after having passed more Mormon immigrant trains. Near Devil's Gate he cached a large amount of supplies for future use. On September 8 he sent an advance party to the Platte River; they returned on September 12 with news that the advance companies of the United States forces were approaching. Colonel E. B. Alexander's division (eight companies of the 10th Infantry) reached Devil's Gate on September 22 where they camped. Only a day or two behind him were Captain Phelp's Artillery Battery, the Fifth Infantry, and Captain Reno's Artillery Battery, in that order. Colonel Burton and three companies camped within a half mile of the soldiers until Colonel Alexander's division arrived at Ham's Fork, a tributary to the Green River, on September 28. They stayed nearby and sent frequent reports of their every movement by express riders to General Wells or President Young.

About a month after Colonel Burton moved into the field, a volunteer company of forty-three men under Captain Andrew Cunningham was sent to make a settlement on the Snake River near Fort Hall in Idaho, but their real purpose was to be on the northern route in case the United States Army should try to make a detour by way of Soda Springs and Fort Hall and come into the Great Basin from the north.

Another still smaller detachment of twelve men—with Marcellus Monroe as leader, under the direction of Colonel C. W. West of the Weber County Militia—was sent through Ogden Canyon on horseback into the Bear Lake country where they were to become familiar with mountain passes, rallying points, and places of retreat in case any of the expeditionary forces tried to break through from that direction. After reaching the Bear Lake region they followed up Bear River, crossed the mountains by way of Lost Creek to the Weber River, and returned to Ogden.

Until nearly the end of August the settlers thought that General W. S. Harney was in charge of the expedition; but reports soon came in that General Harney had been detained in Kansas and that Colonel Albert Sidney Johnston had replaced him. On August 26 Brigham Young said: "I have sent word to General

Harney that I wish for peace, and do not want to fight anybody; but he must not come here with a hostile army, and if he undertakes it, we shall prepare to defend ourselves." [1]

Captain Stewart Van Vliet Sent to Utah

Before General Harney was relieved of his command he ordered Captain Stewart Van Vliet to proceed to Utah. There he was to obtain a suitable location for the troops near Salt Lake City, where they would be sufficiently near to be effective in supporting the civil authority yet far enough away to prevent "an improper association of the troops with the citizens."

> You will impress upon the officers in charge of your escort the imperious necessity for a very careful circumspection of conduct in his command. The men should not only be carefully selected for this service, but they should be repeatedly admonished never to comment upon or ridicule anything they may either see or hear, and to treat the inhabitants of Utah with kindness and consideration. [2]

From these instructions it appears that the army was not to be an army of invasion but merely an aid to the civil authorities. B. H. Roberts describes the misunderstanding existing on both sides.

> The great misfortune in the whole matter of this "Utah Expedition" was, that the purpose of the administration in sending it to Utah was not known by the Latter-day Saint Church leaders. . . . Neither did the "Expedition" have any clear understanding of its mission. Even Colonel Alexander, leading the advance division . . . knew nothing of its purpose; he knew only of its destination. [3]

On September 9 Captain Van Vliet met in the Social Hall in Salt Lake City with leading Church authorities. Although he could not give a satisfactory or definite explanation as to the purpose of the coming of the army, he did deny the rumors in Utah—that is, that it was for the conquest and destruction of the Mormon people; he said that no instructions had been given to violate the laws and rights of the people, and he felt the orders to the troops would be to support the government and the laws in case they were violated.

On the other hand the Church leaders had received no official communication and knew only that there was an uproar in the states against the Mormons because of the false reports of Judge Drummond and others and that all kinds of extravagant suggestions had been made as to how to solve the "Utah problem." They were also aware of what the talk of the soldiers was; Elder John Taylor later wrote of the fears of the Saints:

> We had men in all the camps, and knew what was intended. There was a continued boast among the men and officers, even before they left the Missouri river, of what they intended to do with the 'Mormons.' The houses were picked out that certain persons were to inhabit; farms, property, and women were to be distributed. 'Beauty and Booty' were their watchword. We were to have another grand 'Mormon' conquest, and our houses, gardens, orchards, vineyards, fields, wives and daughters were to be the spoils. [4]

Such reports were accompanied by bitter memories of what had happened in Missouri when the state militia had imprisoned their leaders, robbed the Saints of their property, ravished their women, and driven nearly 15,000 people from the state. Their memories also included the misconduct of Colonel Steptoes' troops while they were in Salt Lake valley in 1854 and 1855; therefore, in view of all these things, the leaders found Captain Van Vliet's explanations hardly reassuring. In light of their own past experiences and of Captain Van Vliet's meager knowledge of the purpose of the expedition and not knowing of the excellent personal leadership of the army, the Church leaders could hardly be expected to feel assured of the peaceful intentions of President Buchanan.

Captain Van Vliet had left his own escort at Ham's Fork, 143 miles from Salt Lake City, and had accepted as guides Bryant Stringham and Colonel N. V. Jones from General Burton's command. Van Vliet and his guides arrived in Salt Lake City on September 8. In a meeting on September 9 they read a letter from General Harney addressed to President Brigham Young of the Society of the Mormons, discussing the purpose of the coming of the army, the purpose for Captain Van Vliet's visit, the place for camping the army, and the ability of the community to furnish timber, beef, hay, and other supplies for the army.

Captain Van Vliet stayed in Utah for six days, during which time he visited Rush Valley approximately forty miles away because Colonel Steptoe had thought that would be a good location for a military reservation; but Van Vliet did not think so. President Young and the other Church leaders liked very much the gentlemanly manner and depth of character displayed by Captain Van Vliet; yet before he left Brigham Young told him there was an abundance of everything the army would need but that the army would not be allowed to buy anything. The captain did his best to convince them that the troops were not coming to make war on them, but they were not completely convinced. President Young said:

> We do not want to fight the United States, but if they drive us to it, we shall do the best we can; and I will tell you, as the Lord lives, we shall come off conquerors, for we trust in God.[5]

The captain later reported that President Young had said he had no objection to the army's coming but that they would bring with them a rabble from the frontiers who would persecute and annoy the Saints as had been done in former locations.

On Sunday, September 13, Captain Van Vliet attended both the morning and afternoon sessions of church, where he heard George A. Smith, John Taylor, and President Young speak; the President spoke in both services. It was on this day that George A. Smith gave a report of his trip to southern Utah, telling of the preparations of the military there. John Taylor asked that all those who would be willing, if necessary, to burn their buildings rather than submit to military rule and oppression to manifest it by raising their hands. All hands were raised simultaneously. President Young responded:

> We have transgressed no law, and we have no occasion to do so, neither do we intend to; but as for any nations coming to destroy this people, God Almighty being my helper, they cannot come here, [The congregation responded by a loud Amen]. That is my feeling upon that point.[6]

President Young also asked all American citizens to raise their hands, then all foreigners not yet naturalized. More than two-thirds of the audience were American citizens. He did this so that Captain Van Vliet could report to Senator Stephen A. Douglas that he had been wrong when he told his constituents that nine-tenths of the Mormons were aliens.[7]

Many ill-advised remarks were made in these talks and also in the interviews with Van Vliet that both preceded and followed the meetings; but from past experiences and from anxiety created by the present situation, temperate language could hardly be expected. Brigham Young commented on Congress's sending an investigating committee to Kansas in 1856 "or any other place but to Utah, but upon the mere rumor of liars they send out 2,000 armed soldiers to Utah to destroy the people without investigating the subject at all." Van Vliet said they might yet send one, and Brigham Young replied: "I do think that God has sent you out here, and that much good will grow out of it. I was glad when I learned that you were coming." Captain Van Vliet said he would try to stop the government trains at Ham's Fork, and President Young replied that if they could keep the peace for the winter something would turn up that might save the shedding of so much blood.

On his return East Captain Van Vliet was accompanied by Dr. John Bernhisel, Utah's delegate to congress. Colonel N. V. Jones also accompanied them until they reached South Pass where they met the United States troops. The captain advised them not to try to enter Salt Lake valley before winter because no arrangements could be made for supplies; they would have to fight their way through if they made the attempt.

Captain Van Vliet gave an accurate report of his Utah visit to Captain A. Pleasonton, the adjutant general of the "army for Utah" at Fort Leavenworth and later to Secretary of War John B. Floyd in Washington. B. H. Roberts is of the opinion that Van Vliet's reports had much to do with bringing about a final bloodless settlement of the difficulties.[8]

Defense Forces Move into the Field

The day after Captain Van Vliet left Utah Governor Young declared martial law, forbidding all armed forces from entering the territory and notifying the armed Nauvoo Legion to hold themselves in readiness to march at a moment's notice to repel any invasion; no person was to be allowed to pass into or through or from the territory without a permit from the proper officer. Following the proclamation, 1,250 men of the legion were ordered to report to Echo Canyon. On September 27, Lieutenant General Wells, with part of his staff and with Elders John Taylor and George A. Smith as counselors, left Salt Lake City for the defense area. Forty miles from Salt Lake City, General Wells ordered the militia who were already there under the direction of Colonels N. V. Jones and J. D. T. McAllister to construct fortifications at the Narrows in Echo Canyon and along the heights of the mountains. General Wells went on to Fort Bridger with a small group where he received reports from Colonel R. T. Burton and General Lewis Robison concerning the location and intentions of the United States Army units which had reached Ham's Fork.

From Fort Bridger General Wells forwarded to Colonel Alexander by General Lewis Robison and Major Lot Smith two copies of the laws of Utah, a letter from Brigham Young, and a letter from himself stating that he was in the field to help in carrying out the orders of Governor Young.

When Robison and Lot Smith were within a short distance of Camp Winfield—the name given to the camp by Colonel Alexander in honor of Lieutenant General Winfield Scott—they sent the papers to Colonel Alexander by a Mexican mountaineer named Marrianne.

Governor Young's letter quoted the Utah law in regard to the office of governor and stated: "I am still the governor and superintendent of Indian affairs for this territory, no successor having been appointed and qualified, as provided by law; nor have I been removed by the president of the United States."[9] He then mentioned he was sending them a copy of his proclamation forbidding entrance of armed forces into the territory and told them to retire forthwith, but if they found that impracticable they could stay in the vicinity of their present encampment at Black's Fork or Green River until spring on condition they would deposit their arms and ammunition with Lewis Robison, the quartermaster general of the territory. He also told them that if they were short of any particular provisions, these could be furnished to them on proper application.[10]

Of course Brigham Young did not expect Colonel Alexander to conform to his requests. Colonel Alexander's reply was that he was there by orders of the president of the United States, and their (the United States Army's) future movements would depend upon orders from competent authority. All later letters written by Colonel Alexander to General Wells or Brigham

Young were equally as respectful, but they neither complied with the Governor's requests nor changed the plans of the Saints.

Aggressive Action Begins

On October 3 a counsel of war was held at Fort Bridger, where the Saints decided to begin active operations. Those present were General Wells and his counselors Elders John Taylor and George A. Smith; Generals Ferguson, H. B. Clawson, and Lewis Robison; Colonels R. T. Burton, and Bryant Stringham; Captain Stoddard and Orrin P. Rockwell.[11]

Major J. D. T. McAllister had already been sent out along the Oregon Road to watch for troop movements. O. P. Rockwell was now sent to help by burning the grass on all roads beginning with the road through Soda Springs. Colonel Burton was to harass the United States troops in every way possible without risking his men. If the Mormon army allowed it, Fort Bridger and Fort Supply, the two Mormon settlements in Bridger Valley, would fall into the hands of the enemy and if left intact could furnish winter quarters for them. Therefore on October 3, the quartermaster general of the territory, Lewis Robison, applied the torch to Fort Bridger. "It burned very rapidly and made a great fire." On October 5 Fort Supply was burned to the ground including mills, houses, and other buildings, amounting to a value of $50,000.

The Burning of Supply Trains

Also, on October 3 while at Fort Bridger, General Wells ordered Major Lot Smith to take a small command of men and intercept the supply trains coming from South Pass. He was either to turn them back or to burn them.

He was also told that no provisions would be supplied to him and his men; they would be expected to board at the expense of Uncle Sam. [12]

Leaving with a total of forty-four men at 4:00 p.m. on October 3, 1857, Major Smith and his men rode all night. Early on October 4 they met an ox train loaded with supplies. Major Smith informed Captain Rankin and his men they must turn their supply train around and head eastward. Captain Rankin followed orders, but after Smith and his men were gone they again turned the supply train around and headed westward. During the day United States Army troops met them and took all the freight out of the wagons to prevent its capture.

When Major Smith discovered he had not been successful with the supply train he decided more stringent measures were necessary. He sent twenty men to try to capture the mules of the Tenth Regiment and with the rest he hunted for more supply trains. His scouts soon reported a large train of twenty-six wagons in two lines on the old Mormon road near the Sandy Fork. After supper they started at dark for the train, but upon arriving they discovered the teamsters were drunk and, said Lot Smith, "knowing that drunken men were easily excited and always ready to fight, and remembering my positive orders not to hurt anyone except in self-defense we remained in ambush until after midnight."[13]

Upon nearing the wagons Major Smith discovered there were two trains with twenty-six wagons in each train. This meant that the twenty men were badly outnumbered; nevertheless Smith decided to proceed. He lined his men up single file, and they rode into the light of the teamsters bonfire. With his men strung out, they still had the advantage in that the enemy could not see the end of the line of his troops.

Major Smith inquired for the captain, and Captain Dawson stepped forward. Smith told him they had some business to conduct which consisted of setting fire to the wagons. Dawson replied: "For G — — sake don't burn the train," and Lot Smith replied that it was for his sake they were going to. The teamsters were forced to stack their arms which a few of Smith's men guarded. Smith then took Captain Dawson with him and went to see the captain of the second train where a similar procedure followed. After searching for overcoats and other needed supplies, Major Smith and a big Irish Gentile whom he had with him, Big James, prepared torches and set fire to the wagons with the exception of two loads that were saved for the use of the teamsters. Major Smith and his men rode away leaving all the wagons ablaze.

That night they camped on the banks of the Sandy River. The next morning they met another train at a place since known as Simpson's Hollow. Captain Simpson was at that moment a distance from the train; Major Smith's men disarmed the teamsters, and Major Smith rode out to meet the captain. When they met, Smith told him he was there on business and demanded Simpson's pistols. Simpson replied: "By G — —, sir, no man ever took them yet, and if you think you can, without killing me, try it."

Smith told him that he admired a brave man but he didn't

like blood and didn't want to kill him. By this time they were in sight of the wagon train and Simpson could see that his men were under guard; he surrendered. Again, Smith's men supplied themselves with provisions, let Captain Simpson and his men choose two wagonloads of provisions for themselves, then set the others on fire and rode off.

The amount of property burned by Major Smith and his men is given in the House Documents of the 35th Congress. This list includes the property destroyed in supply trains numbers five, nine, and ten:[14]

	No. of Rations
2,720 pounds ham	
92,700 pounds bacon	115,875
167,900 pounds flour	149,244
270 bushels of beans	108,000
8,570 pounds Rio Coffee	143,000
330 pounds Java Coffee	
1,400 pounds crushed sugar	
2,970 gallons vinegar	297,000
800 pounds sperm candles	80,000
13,333 pounds soap	333,325
84 gallons molasses	
134 bushels dried peaches	
68,832 ration dessicated vegetables	
705 pounds tea	52,875
7,781 pounds hard bread	7,781

Stealing the Army's Animals

A day or two later after again meeting Captain Haight and his twenty men, the major and his men rounded up about 150 head of livestock they had found near Mountaineer Fort where they had burned the first trains; W. A. Hickman took them into the Salt Lake valley. Many of the bullwhackers (drivers) from the burned out trains accompanied him, commenting that they had had enough bullwhacking to last a lifetime.

Finding no more trains to burn, Major Smith finally started toward the main camp of the army on Black's Fork (Ham's Fork). Early the next morning Lot Smith and his sleeping companion climbed a high peak to look over the situation. There they met Orrin Porter Rockwell and Thomas Rich with about thirty men. With these additional men Smith's command now consisted of about eighty men, and he felt that they were strong

enough to reconnoiter the situation of the army. When they
arrived within sight of the camp they saw a large herd of cattle,
consisting of about fourteen hundred head in the bottom lands
below. By the time they reached the cattle, the guards had
started them towards the army camp. But the men intercepted
them, turned them in the opposite direction, and gave a yell
such as imported steers had never heard before; they started off
on the run. Major Smith describes the event.

> The guards were frightened as badly as the cattle and
> looked as pale as death. They came to me and asked me if
> we were going to take the stock. I replied that it looked a
> little as if we would. . . . The guards then started for camp.
> They were the worst frightened men I ever saw.[15]

The cattle were then divided into "suitable herds" and were
driven all night with Rockwell and Major Smith leading the
way. Rockwell and a few of the men took the cattle on into the
Salt Lake valley while Major Smith and the rest of the men,
including most of those who had been previously with Rockwell, turned to the vicinity of the last camp of the army on
Ham's Fork with the intention of convincing the army they had
better stop for the winter and go no nearer the Salt Lake valley.

After a near battle with Captain Marcy's troops who were out
looking for Smith, Lot and his men returned to Fort Bridger.
They soon received orders not to molest the troops any further
if they wished to go into quarters for the winter.

Juanita Brooks states that the Mormons did not have any
more effect in trying to stop the United States Army than a
swarm of mosquitoes would have trying to stop a buffalo.[16]
However, burning the grass, running off the animals, and
hampering the army did have a great effect. A modern military
textbook substantiates this effect.

> But before the column could enter the Great Salt Lake
> Valley, the alarmed Mormons skillfully separated the
> wagon train from the troops, burned the wagons, and
> captured many horses. Johnston's isolated force was com-
> pelled to spend the winter in the Rockies on short
> rations.[17]

Colonel Alexander's Problems

On September 28, 1857, Colonel Alexander found himself at

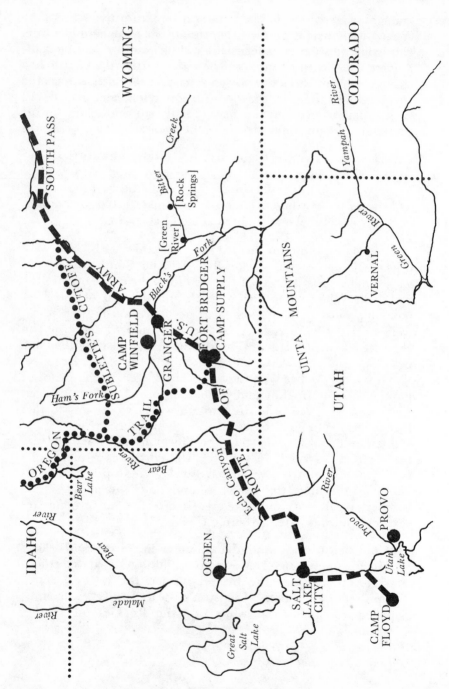

Fig. 11. The Utah Expedition, 1857-58.

Ham's Fork with no definite instructions from the war department as to the purpose of the expedition and no orders from
the new commander still on his way. The range had been destroyed by the burning of the grass, and the strength of an
evasive foe hindering them was unknown. Winter was already
threatening, and there were no suitable quarters at hand. As the
senior officer he called a council of officers to determine future
locations. Three places for winter quarters were suggested: the
east side of the Wind River Mountains to the northeast about
110 miles, where there was supposedly plenty of pasture; the
vicinity of Fort Hall 140 miles to the northwest; and Henry's
Fork of Green River and Brown's Hole about 90 miles to the
southeast. At first they decided on Fort Hall. On October 11
the expeditionary forces began moving to the northwest up
Ham's Fork. Snowstorms had begun and the weather was cold.
The animals were so weak they were making only three miles a
day. After a week a second council was held, and it was evident
the officers varied in their opinions as to what should be done.
Some wanted to make a forced march into Salt Lake City, but
they finally decided to return down Ham's Fork to the point
where the stream joined with Black's Fork.

THE UNITED STATES ARMY MOVES
INTO WINTER QUARTERS

At this point Colonel Johnston, the new commander, had
reached South Pass and had sent orders to march to Fontenelle
Creek (a tributary of the Green River) thirty miles north; but
before a start was made, a second order came for them to return
down Ham's Fork to its junction with Black's Fork, where
Colonel Johnston would meet them. Because of cold and snow,
the return trip was slower than the advance had been.

When it appeared the army would not try to make it into the
Salt Lake valley, General Wells with his staff and most of the
1,250 soldiers returned to the valley, leaving squads of men to
report the movement of the troops on Ham's Fork. But on
October 28 when word was received in Salt Lake City that
Colonel Johnston would soon arrive at Ham's Fork, General
Wells and his staff returned to Echo Canyon. General Charles C.
Rich had replaced George A. Smith as an advisor. From the
militia units which had been left to observe the army move-
ments General Wells learned that Colonel Johnston had joined
Colonel Alexander on Black's Fork on November 3.

With Colonel Johnston came more supply trains and cavalry troops. The arrival of Johnston boosted the morale of the troops, and General Wells, feeling the situation was serious, sent word to Governor Young to send more troops. Thirteen hundred more were called out, some of whom were on their way within two days. On November 11 word came that the enemy had decided to force their way into Salt Lake City by pack animals, expecting to make it to the city in twelve days. However, if this report were true, they apparently changed their minds, for Colonel Johnston soon decided to move to the area of Fort Bridger to establish a winter camp. The move was 35 miles, and it took two weeks in weather ranging from ten degrees above zero to sixteen degrees below. If shelter from the snowstorms could have been found, the army would have stopped, but there was none.

Colonel Philip St. George Cooke, with the six companies of the Second Dragoons, supply trains, and the new officers of the territory arrived at Camp Scott near Fort Bridger on November 19. This marked the arrival of the last of the United States troops on their way to Utah in the fall of 1857. Their loss of animals from starvation and freezing had been tremendous. Colonel Cooke's forces arrived with only 144 horses, having lost 134, or nearly half. The burning of the grass by the Mormon forces had reaped its toll.

Most Mormon Forces Withdrawn for the Winter

As soon as General Wells was sure the United States Army was settled down for the winter, he released all but approximately fifty of his defensive forces. Those fifty were stationed at the mouth of Echo Canyon under Captain John R. Winder who was to keep ten of them stationed at Yellow Creek near Fort Bridger to watch the enemy. During the winter the *London Punch* printed a cartoon showing ten Mormons herding the "Flower of the American Army."

HAPPENINGS DURING THE WINTER

Before the arrival of Colonel Johnston, there was an exchange of letters between Colonel Alexander and Governor Young, who invited him or any of the other officers to visit Salt Lake City "unaccompanied by troops" and learn for themselves the condition and feelings of the people. They were assured safe escort to and from the city.

On November 26 Governor Young sent 800 pounds of salt to the army because he had heard they were in short supply. He offered it to them as a gift but told them they could pay for it if they did not wish to receive it as such. Colonel Johnston refused to accept the salt on any terms, stating that he could accept no favors from traitors.

The salt was later given to Ben Simon, an eastern Indian, who took it into the camp where he sold it for $2.50 a pound. In the case of Colonel Johnston, who called the Mormons "Confederates" and a "traitorous people," it is rather ironic that later, April 6, 1862, he was killed while leading Confederate forces in the Civil War in the Battle of Pittsburgh Landing (Shiloh).

Utah Memorials Sent to President Buchanan and the United States Congress

During the winter of 1857-58, there were two capitals of the territory of Utah—one in Salt Lake City where Governor Young had never been officially notified of his dismissal, and one near Camp Scott two miles above Fort Bridger, where the newly appointed governor, the chief justice of the Supreme Court, and other territorial appointees were located. These civil officers made their headquarters above the military camp in a nook in the woods which they called "Ecklesville" in honor of the new chief justice, Delano R. Eckles. Governor Cumming issued a proclamation to the people of the Utah Territory, denouncing acts of the Mormons and stating that proceedings would be instituted against them; but the organization of a district court became a necessity to regulate the affairs of a thousand released teamsters and of civilian camp followers. Three hundred twenty-five of them were enlisted in the army for nine months in order to put them under military discipline.

In Salt Lake City the legislature met on December 14 and the next day listened to Governor Young's message in which he reviewed the proceedings of the federal government and justified Mormon resistance. On December 21 the legislature approved the message. On January 6, 1858, the legislature drew up a memorial to President Buchanan and the United States Congress in which they said all they wanted was truth and fair play. They also stated that the administration had been imposed upon by designing men, and that their actions had been hasty. They asked what the administration wanted from them and requested they be told "before you prepare your halters to hang, or apply the knife 'to cut out the loathesome, disgusting ulcer'." [18] A mass meeting was held in Salt Lake City on January 12, 1858, with Mayor A. O. Smoot as chairman. The people addressed a memorial to the United States Congress and asked them to reconsider their acts.

The Utah legislature appropriated one million dollars to pay the cost of a standing army of ten battalions of mounted riflemen.

Gunpowder was being manufactured at Cedar City, and during the winter manufacturing was begun in Provo.

The Coming of Colonel Thomas L. Kane

In the meantime, Colonel Kane visited President Buchanan to see if he might be of assistance in settling the difficulties. Buchanan refused to send him to Utah as an official representative of the administration or the government but made it clear that he was free to go at his own expense if he so desired. Although his health was poor, Colonel Kane felt the need to help his friends, the Mormons. Early in January 1858, he left his home in the East and journeyed to Utah via the Panama Railroad, traveling under the pseudonym of "Doctor Osborne." His purpose for coming under an assumed name was to see if the Mormons would treat a stranger as well as Colonel Kane had been treated at Council Bluffs. He arrived in Salt Lake City on February 25, meeting that evening with a group of leaders and having a private interview with President Young. Colonel Kane came with a definite plan in mind which Brigham Young did not feel disposed to accept, but he told Colonel Kane that he should go to the army and "do as the Spirit of the Lord led him." [19]

Colonel Kane stayed in Salt Lake City from February 25 until March 8, at which time he left for Camp Scott as an official representative of the Latter-day Saints. He was accompanied by a Mormon escort as far as Muddy Fork, about twelve miles from Camp Scott, and arrived at Camp Scott on March 12, spending the day with Governor Cumming. He had with him a letter to General Johnston, who had been promoted during the winter, from Brigham Young, offering beef and other supplies, which Johnston peremptorily refused.

Colonel Kane spent three weeks at Camp Scott. He could make no headway with General Johnston, Chief Justice Eckles, or any of the other territorial appointees except Governor

Alfred Cumming, whom he persuaded to go to Salt Lake City 259 without the army. On April 3 Governor Cumming announced to General Johnston his intention of going to Salt Lake City with Colonel Kane and requested certain traveling equipment. On April 5—Colonel Kane having sent word of their coming by messenger—they left Camp Scott and arrived in Salt Lake City on April 12, where Cumming was cordially received as governor.

A CHANGE IN PLANS

During Kane's absence from Salt Lake City the leaders of the people had met in council where they changed their plans and invoked a plan which had been hinted at to Captain Van Vliet. On March 18 they decided to abandon defending their homes through resistance to the army and the possible shedding of blood and to retreat southward, leaving behind enough men to burn all buildings and destroy everything else if necessary. As Governor Cumming approached Salt Lake City from Davis County he saw the vanguard of the people from north of Salt Lake City wending their way to the south. This disturbed him and later he strongly requested Brigham Young to stop them.

By April 15 Governor Cumming wrote General Johnston that he had been everywhere recognized as governor and had been treated respectfully.

During his stay in Utah Governor Cumming made many trips south to Provo and beyond. On one return trip from Provo to Salt Lake City he and Colonel Kane counted 600 wagons of families moving south. On another trip—May 6—between Springville and Salt Lake City they encountered 800 wagons moving south.

Colonel Kane received word of the death of his father and felt the necessity of returning East. Governor Cumming wanted to return to Camp Scott to get Mrs. Cumming and to request the army not to march into the valley until he received answers to the dispatches he was sending to Washington. If anything were to be done to stop the army from coming into the valley before a settlement was made it had to be done soon because the canyons would soon be clear of snow. Cattle sufficient to move 200 wagons on Henry's Fork of Green River and guarded by Colonel Cooke's soldiers were in good condition; supply trains parked at Fort Laramie for the winter were now on their way west; Captain Marcy would soon arrive with 1,500 horses and mules from New Mexico; over 3,000 soldiers for reinforce-

the army wanted "Booty & Beauty" but the people would be gone —

260 ments were at Fort Leavenworth, and General Johnston had informed Governor Cumming he would arrive in Salt Lake City on June 1 where he would station one army post with another on the Provo Bench.

Governor Cumming and Colonel Kane left Salt Lake City on May 13 with a special escort of six men under command of Major Howard Egan.

GENTILES MODIFY THEIR ATTITUDE
TOWARD THE SAINTS

When scandals over government contracts for army supplies to the expedition began to develop, the administration was criticized. People began to ask why an army was sent to put down a rebellion before it was determined if there was one. The *New York Times,* the *New York Tribune,* and the *New York Herald* all joined in the criticism which became still sharper when people learned that 40,000 Mormons were deserting their homes and farms rather than submit to the tyranny of the army.

On January 27, 1858, the United States House of Representatives sent a request to the administration to submit to the House the information which gave rise to the military expedition to Utah "together with the orders and correspondence." This material was sent to the House on February 26; and, although the administration strained every effort, it could not come up with anything except the letters from the adulterous judge (W. W. Drummond), the disappointed mail contractor (W. M. F. Magraw), and those from Thomas Twiss (the Indian agent) which were not written until the army had already been called out. Their publication did not enhance the position of the administration. Debate in the Senate showed there were many senators opposed to the actions of the administration. Senator Sam Houston was among the many who felt that a blunder had been made and called for a peaceful settlement of the difficulty.

Peace Commissioners

Although the President had previously felt he could not send an official representative to the Mormons (e.g. Thomas L. Kane) because of their resistance, pressure from the newspapers, the people, and from Congress forced him to do something. He still did not send an investigating commission to determine the reality of a rebellion but he appointed a "peace commission" consisting of Senator-elect Lazarus W. Powell of Kentucky and Major Ben McCulloch of Texas. He entrusted them with a "proclamation of pardon" dated April 6, 1858. It recited all of the accusations against the Saints and then declared "a free pardon to all who will submit themselves to the authority of the federal government."

By April 25 the peace commissioners were leaving Fort Leavenworth for Salt Lake City, traveling in five ambulances with three saddle horses and a staff of thirteen men. They arrived at Camp Scott on May 29 where they stayed for three days learning all they could about the situation.

They arrived in Salt Lake City on June 7, where they found a city practically deserted; the leaders and most of the people had already moved south. Word was sent to the leaders in Provo who returned to Salt Lake City. Arrangements were made for a meeting in the "old council house" on June 11 at 9:00 a.m. Because the windows had been removed in preparation for the destruction of the building, these had to be put back in place.

Attending the session with the peace commissioners was Governor Cumming. On the Mormons' side were President Young, Heber C. Kimball, George A. Smith, General Daniel H. Wells, and a host of others. However, the peace conference was almost disrupted before it began; on the way to the meeting Brigham Young received word from O. P. Rockwell that General Johnston had given orders to his army to march on June 14. The Governor and peace commissioners had assured Brigham Young he would not move until he heard from them. Such a breach caused some spirited correspondence between Governor Cumming and General Johnston, who admitted that he had said he would not start until he heard from them but claimed that it did not have the "binding force of a pledge."

After two days of meeting, June 11 and June 12, they reached an agreement. The Saints agreed to recognize and submit to the national authority, to admit the army into the territory without resistance, and to obey the laws and constitution of the United States. The administration agreed not to interfere with the religion of the people, and it was understood that the President's "proclamation of pardon" would apply.

The peace commission not only sent a report to Washington declaring the difficulties between the Mormons and the federal government settled but they also wrote to General Johnston pertaining to the march of the army through Salt Lake City, stating that the fields and gardens were insecure and the army's animals could cause much destruction if great care were not taken. They suggested to General Johnston that he issue a proclamation, which he did:

> I . . . assure those citizens of the Territory who, I learn, apprehend from the army ill treatment, that no person whatever will be in anywise interfered with or molested in his person or rights, or in the peaceful pursuit of his avocations; and, should protection be needed, that they will find the army (always faithful to the obligations of duty) as ready now to assist and protect them as it was to oppose them while it was believed they were resisting the laws of the government.[20]

General Johnston told the Commissioners, "I desire to encamp beyond the Jordan on the day of arrival in the valley."[21]

On June 14 Governor Cumming issued his proclamation of the acceptance of the President's pardon. It was signed by him and John Hartnett, the new secretary of the territory.

THE ARMY'S ENTRANCE INTO THE VALLEY

Although the people did not know of it, the instructions to the army from the beginning were that they not camp in or even near any of the larger settlements of the territory. It is possible that General Johnston, who had been appointed commander in August, was not aware of these original instructions when he expressed a desire to establish one army post in Salt Lake City and another on the Provo Bench (Orem). Whether the people knew it or not, neither they nor their leaders were taking any chances until they found out what the army was going to do. They would wait until the army was located before returning to their homes.

The army broke winter camp on June 13 and began moving forward in three columns with a "sufficient garrison being left at Fort Bridger." On the top of the butte to the southwest nearly 800 feet above the valley floor where Mormon soldiers had kept an eye on the army throughout the winter, parties of horsemen could be seen watching the army's departure. By June 14 they were encamped on Bear River where they received a message from the peace commissioners.

By the evening of June 25, the army was encamped at the mouth of Emigration Canyon, poised for its entrance into the valley. General Johnston had laid plans for an early morning entrance so that he could pass through Salt Lake City and cross to the west side of the Jordan River before making camp.

The morning of June 26 found the first units of the army arriving at the limits of the city at about 10:00 a.m. The peace commissioners rode through the city with the general staff. Brevet Colonel Charles F. Smith's battalion, constituting the advance guard, was the first to enter the almost deserted city. The Mormons had left behind only sufficient men to burn the buildings should the army stop in the city. There were a few gentiles standing on South Temple Street watching the army pass through. Following Colonel Smith's battalion were the Tenth Infantry, Phelp's artillery battery, Colonel Lording's battalion of mounted riflemen, and volunteers (released teamsters who had been recruited); Colonel Cooke's Second Dragoons constituted the rear guard. "Each command was followed by its train and a portion of the supply train."

By 5:00 p.m. the last of the army units were leaving the city. Colonel P. St. George Cooke, former commander of the Mormon battalion, uncovered his head as a token of respect for the Mormon men he had officered as his rear guard entered the city.

General Johnston, a strict disciplinarian, kept his promise as to the good order of the march, although after crossing the Jordan River there was some damage done to the fence of a field belonging to Joseph Young, and a few tons of hay were consumed; the army would accept responsibility for neither of these things, apparently blaming it on the camp followers.[22]

After camping west of the Jordan for three days, the camp moved on into Cedar Valley where they located permanently about thirty-six miles from Salt Lake City and the same distance from Provo.

THE SAINTS RETURN HOME

President Young had announced on Sunday morning, June 27, in a meeting at Provo, that General Johnston had passed peacefully through the city the day before, and as soon as they knew what he was going to do with his troops they would all go home.

When the camp was settled in a permanent location, Presi-

264 dent Brigham Young, in Provo, announced: "All who want to return to their homes in Great Salt Lake City are at liberty to do so." Then, with an escort of thirty men from Provo under Captain William Wall, Brigham Young and others left there at 6:00 p.m. on June 30 and arrived in Salt Lake City at 3:00 a.m. on the morning of July 1.

Following behind President Young, thirty thousand people made the trek back to Salt Lake City and other settlements northward.

The settlement of the difficulties with the government was hardly satisfactory to the Saints because it did not provide for an investigating commission which could have vindicated them from the false charges mentioned in the "pardon," but it did bring peace between them and the government.

On July 3, the peace commissioners, having faithfully carried out their assignment, left for Washington.

Footnotes

[1]*CHC*, 4:249.

[2]*CHC*, 4:252.

[3]*CHC*, 4:252. On October 8, Colonel Alexander, in a communication to the officers of his command, stated: ". . . I am in utter ignorance of the object of the government in sending troops here, or the instructions given for their conduct, after reaching here." (U.S., Congress, *House Executive Documents*, 35th Cong., 1st sess., vol. 10, no. 71, pp. 38-40.) *See also* LeRoy R. Hafen and Ann W. Hafen, *Documentary Account of the Utah Expedition*, The Far West and the Rockies Series, vol. 8 (Glendale, Calif.: Arthur H. Clarke Co., 1958), pp. 66-67; and *CHC*, 4:257.

[4]*CHC*, 4:259.

[5]*CHC*, 4:264.

[6]*Journal of Discourses* (1854-1886; lithographic reprint, Salt Lake City, 1966), 5:226. Hereafter cited as *JD*.

[7]*JD*, 5:230.

[8]*CHC*, 4:271.

[9]*CHC*, 4:276.

[10]*CHC*, 4:276.

[11]*CHC*, 4:278, footnote 8.

[12]Hafen and Hafen, pp. 220-46. This reference gives an excellent narrative of the burning of the supply trains by Lot Smith himself.

[13]Hafen and Hafen, p. 221.

[14]*CHC*, 4:285.

[15]Hafen and Hafen, p. 237.

[16]Juanita Brooks, *Mountain Meadow Massacre* (Norman: University of Oklahoma Press, 1962), p. 144.

[17]Department of the Army, *ROTCM no. 145-20: American Military History 1607-1958* (Washington, D.C.: U.S. Government Printing Office, July 1959), p. 183.

[18]*CHC*, 4:330.
[19]*CHC*, 4:349.
[20]Hafen and Hafen, p. 346.
[21]Hafen and Hafen, p. 346.
[22]*CHC*, 4:446, footnote 9.

13

Aftermath of the Utah War

It had been suggested to General Johnston that the army lay out a military post in Cache Valley. Although there was plenty of water and grass there, the General felt it was too far away from Salt Lake City. As he crossed the Jordan and marched to the southwest, he had in mind settling either in Rush Valley, which Colonel Steptoe, who had earlier recommended Brigham Young for reappointment as governor, had selected as a good place for a military camp, or Cedar Valley, west of Utah Lake, about ten miles wide and thirty miles long with a row of mountains on the east side of the valley between it and Utah Lake.[1] General Johnston decided on Cedar Valley, settling first in the north end near the mouth of West Canyon. The army stayed here from July to September 7th at which time they moved ten miles south because their water supply was drying up as it always did in the late summer.

There were only two Mormon settlements in the valley, containing about 200 people in all. Most of them lived at Cedar Fort, but about ten families, including five Carson brothers, Williams Beardshall, John Clegg, and Amos Fielding, had settled five or six miles farther south at Fairfield, named partly after Amos Fielding who had laid out the town, including 200 acres of farm land which they irrigated from the large spring nearby. As the army came west into Cedar Valley they met the families from Fairfield on their way out, moving south to join the rest

267

of the Saints. Through promises not to injure them in any way, General Johnston induced these Fairfield settlers to return. When the army moved south in September, they established their post just across the main creek to the south and southwest of Fairfield; they named it Camp John B. Floyd in honor of the secretary of war. The creek became the dividing line between the military and civilian population.

Not long afterward General Johnston sent for John Carson, the presiding elder in Fairfield, to whom he said:

> Mr. Carson, I have felt since I have been here that you feel like me and my men may harm you and your people. I want to tell you we do not intend to molest you or your people at all, but I do want to say this—whether you know it or not there is always a rough element that follows an army and they are coming here now. I can handle them on my side of the creek. It may be with the few police you have you may not be able to keep order. That is why I asked you to come here. If that time ever comes and you need some help, let me know and I will be glad to help you Mr. Carson. Good Day.[2]

Not many days afterward a man came and began to build a shack above the settlement near the creek which ran through the town and supplied the culinary water. He also began to build a corral that extended across the creek so that the stock, including the pigs, could drink. And he began building a toilet near the creek. Elder Carson went to see him and after explaining the reason, asked him to move his buildings away from the creek. The man replied, "I am putting that there, that there, and that there, in spite of Brigham Young, General Johnston, or God almighty."[3]

Carson made a second unsuccessful trip to persuade the man to move his buildings, after which he wrote a note to General Johnston. The general went to see the man, taking an orderly with a gun on his shoulder. The man retorted the same thing he had told Carson except that he left out the general's name. The general gave him thirty-six hours to move, or he would move him at the point of a bayonet. The man obeyed within the allotted time.

General Johnston was a good disciplinarian and a strict leader. Yet from what happened during the Camp Floyd period, the Mormons were justified in their anxiety about letting the army into the Salt Lake valley. Although their troubles did not

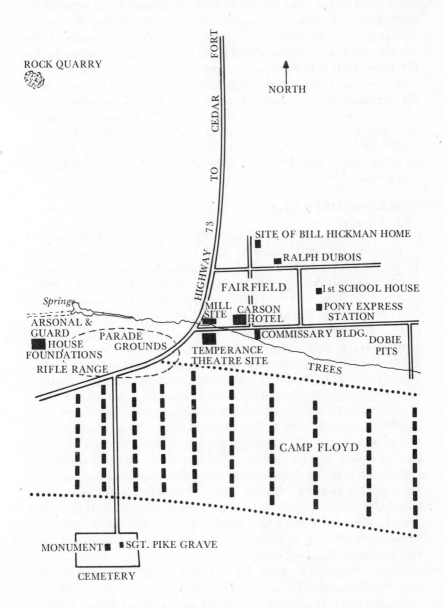

Fig. 12. Camp Floyd.

come mainly from the enlisted soldier, they did come from the presence of the army. The difficulties were mostly from three sources: 1) the camp followers such as gamblers and prostitutes who hang around a military camp to get money from the soldiers; 2) the discharged teamsters who were hired to drive the supply trains to the army and were released upon arrival; 3) the discharged soldiers who were sometimes released at Camp Floyd and were no longer under military discipline. It became necessary to increase the police force in Salt Lake City from forty-eight to two hundred, more than fourfold. Moreover, some of the gentile merchants in Salt Lake City were deliberately endeavoring to cause trouble so that soldiers would be brought in from Camp Floyd and thereby increase the spending in Salt Lake City.

NEW CIVIL OFFICERS

In addition to Governor Cumming, the new civil authorities were Chief Justice Delano R. Eckles; Associate Justices Charles E. Sinclair and John Cradlebaugh; Secretary of the Territory John Hartnett; Attorney General Alexander Wilson; Superintendent of Indian Affairs Jacob Forney; and territorial Marshal Peter K. Dotson, the only citizen of Utah (a non-Mormon).

It was assumed by the newspapers and many people of the United States that the new civil authorities and the army were going to be shining examples of morality and religious truth who would help to rid the Mormons of polygamy by rescuing their women and through precept and example would teach the Mormons to raise their standards to a higher Christian level.[4]

One of the associate justices turned out to be a drunkard who sometimes disgraced himself in public. A letter written by Chief Justice Eckles was picked up in the streets. It was addressed to a certain Lieutenant Bennett and the judge deplored the fact that he hadn't yet been able to find a mistress for Bennett. Yet, when the judge was about to depart for Washington, D.C. in the fall of 1858, he was given a dinner by certain civil and military authorities who envied him, joining his "family and friends in a moral and civilized society."[5]

Such things as this caused Brigham Young to say to Attorney General Alexander Wilson who had called on him before leaving early to return to the states because of his wife's health, "When you get back to the states, no doubt you will be asked many questions about me. I wish you would tell them that I am here, watching the progress of civilization."[6]

It is not from Mormon writers only that we have testimony of disturbance of community life because of the presence of the army. Albert G. Brown, Jr. wrote in the *Atlantic Monthly* of May 1859:

> The unruly crowd of camp followers which is the inseparable attendant of an army, has concentrated in Salt Lake City, and is in constant contact and conflict with the Mormon population. An apprehension prevails, day after day, that the presence of the army may be demanded there to prevent bloodshed. The governor [Cumming] is alien in his disposition to most of the federal officers; and the judges are probably on their way to the states to resign their commissions.[7]

The Divided Course of the Civil Authorities

After the new supreme court justices were sworn in, Chief Justice Eckles took up residence at Camp Floyd with Justice Sinclair assigned to be district judge in Salt Lake City district one and Justice John Cradlebaugh assigned to be district judge in Provo district two. It is well to keep in mind that supreme court justices in Utah acted in a dual role; that is, when the territorial supreme court was not in session, they acted in the capacity of district judges; thus the highest judge locally appointed or elected was the probate judge. After spending a few months in Utah, Chief Justice Eckles returned east for the winter, apparently in an effort to influence the administration in Washington to further restrict the rights of the Utah people.

One of the first acts of Judge Sinclair upon convening his court in November, 1858, was to request the grand jury to prosecute Brigham Young, Daniel H. Wells, and other leaders for treason, polygamy, and intimidation of the courts. Although the president of the United States had granted a pardon in all cases of treason and the pardon had been accepted by the people, Sinclair said that such a pardon must be judicially determined and personally accepted before it was effective, stating that although the pardon was "a public fact in the history of the country, this court cannot take judicial cognizance." [8] Stenhouse writes, "He wanted to bring before his court Brigham Young and the leading Mormons to make them admit that they had been guilty of treason, and make them humbly accept from him the President's clemency."[9] And Bancroft adds, "To ask a Mormon jury to indict the leading

272 dignitaries of the Church was, of course, little better than a farce."[10]

Territorial Attorney General Wilson, favoring the policy of peace as inaugurated from the beginning by Governor Cumming, instructed the grand jury that the peace commissioners had been invested with authority to put into effect the president's proclamation, that Governor Cumming had announced its acceptance, that the conditions upon which the pardon had been granted had been faithfully adhered to, and "that there are now no acts of sedition, treason, or rebellion against the government of the United States in this territory...."[11] This ended the matter of treason. As to the charge of intimidation, concerning Judge Stiles's court action in February, 1857, the charges were dropped against Hosea Stout and Jesse C. Little; but James Ferguson was tried before a jury partly Mormon and partly gentile. After many weeks of trial they brought in a unanimous decision of "not guilty."

Out of the "intimidation case" grew another case known as *Burr vs. Ferguson*. In this case David H. Burr was the plaintiff. He was also the gentile lawyer prosecuting the case in an effort to get Ferguson disbarred; he had a summons served on Brigham Young to appear as a witness. Brigham Young had not been appearing in public since the army had come, and he always had a guard at his house. His friends were somewhat disturbed over the summons but not so much as was Governor Cumming.

Eventually President Young appeared in court accompanied by Governor Cumming, Heber C. Kimball, D. H. Wells, Orson Hyde, George A. Smith, Orson Pratt, F. D. Richards, and John Taylor and others; but President Young was never put on the witness stand; the case was continued from time to time until it was finally dropped by Burr.

Judge Sinclair's career as a judge was rather a failure, and he became known in Utah as the judge who selected a Sunday for the first execution of a white man in the territory. The prisoner was Thomas Ferguson, a non-Mormon who had shot and killed his employer, Alexander Carpenter, also a non-Mormon. It caused such a commotion that the execution date was reset.

Judge Cradlebaugh came to Provo and organized his court on March 8, 1859, with the idea of investigating the Mountain Meadows Massacre and the Springville murders (explained later) which in itself was certainly a worthy endeavor and was fully within the judge's jurisdiction. But he seemed much more interested in trying to connect the Church leaders to these affairs than in discovering the actual killers. Thus, he brought in one hundred soldiers requisitioned from General Johnston at Fort Douglas. The judge and court officials established headquarters in the building in Provo used as the courthouse, and the soldiers were encamped nearby in the same block. Cradlebaugh's excuse for bringing in the troops was that he had heard there was no jail in Provo and that the soldiers were there to guard the prisoners and keep the peace. Twelve days later nine hundred more troops arrived under the command of Major Paul. They were also stationed near the courthouse building.

The citizens of Provo were indignant, and over five hundred of them signed a petition requesting the mayor and city council to have them removed. Governor Cumming was in Provo from March 14 to March 20, and the mayor appealed to him when Judge Cradlebaugh refused to comply. Governor Cumming appealed to General Johnston to withdraw the troops, stating that they were unnecessary. After the general refused to comply, Governor Cumming issued a proclamation stating the facts in the case and protesting the presence of the military in Provo. He said the soldiers were stationed near there without consultation with him and were in opposition to the spirit of instructions received from the government.

In Judge Cradlebaugh's original charge to the grand jury, he had virtually accused the Church authorities of directing the crimes of the Mountain Meadows Massacre and the Springville murders; and he added that the Utah legislature had enacted laws to prevent the judiciary from bringing such offenders to justice.[12]

At the end of two weeks when the grand jury had not brought in the indictments that Cradlebaugh desired, he summarily dismissed them as a useless appendage of the court, telling them they were dupes and tools of a tyrannical church despotism.

> The heads of your church order and direct you. You are taught to obey their orders and commit these horrid murders. Deprived of your liberty, you have lost your manhood, and become the willing instruments of bad men.
>
> I say to you, it will be my earnest effort, while with you, to knock off your ecclesiastical shackles and set you free.[13]

Cradlebaugh also told them that when the people manifested

a disposition to punish their own offenders, it would be time to enforce the law for their own protection—that if the court could not bring them to a sense of duty, it could at least turn the savages loose upon them. He was referring to two Indians named Moze and Looking Glass who had committed an assault upon a mother and her ten-year-old daughter at the Indian farm near Springville: he set them free without punishment.

Both the *New York Herald* and *Philadelphia Ledger* said that he was unfit for his position.[14] Attorney General Wilson, acting as the district attorney, was opposed to much of the action of Judge Cradlebaugh, who issued warrants and made a number of arrests without either Wilson's knowledge or that of the district clerk. It appears that the Springville murders were the result of a personal row between Abraham Durfee, G. G. (Duff) Potter and two of the Parrishes; they engaged in a gun battle in which Potter and the two Parrishes were killed.[15] Upon adjourning his court in Provo and having the prisoners removed to Camp Floyd, Judge Cradlebaugh accused Church leaders of being "in a conspiracy to obstruct the cause of public justice, and to cripple the earnest efforts of his court."[16]

Appeal to Washington Authorities

Not long afterward, Judge Cradlebaugh took three hundred soldiers to accompany him and went to Cedar City to investigate the Mountain Meadows Massacre. This was apparently shortly after he and Judge Sinclair had sent a joint letter to President Buchanan, dated April 7, 1859, in which they gave their side of the story concerning their court actions and recent events in Utah. United States Attorney Wilson wrote letters to Attorney General Jeremiah S. Black on March 28 and April 3, and finding that the two associate justices had written directly to President Buchanan, Attorney Wilson also wrote a letter directly to the president.

Governor Cumming wrote several letters (dated March 25, 27 and 31) to the Honorable Lewis Cass, secretary of state, with which he included copies of his correspondence with General Johnston and Judge Cradlebaugh, his own proclamation of protest, citizens petitions, and memorials. United States Attorney General Jeremiah S. Black addressed a communication to Judges Cradlebaugh and Sinclair on May 17 in which he told them that conditions in Utah made it extremely desirable that judges appointed to Utah territory confine themselves strictly to their own official sphere.

He further stated that it was the duty of the district attorney
to be the public accuser and the duty of the marshal to be
responsible for arrests and safe-keeping of the prisoners. He
summed up his findings by saying that the president was decidedly of the opinion:

1. that the governor of the territory alone has power to issue
   a requisition upon the commanding general for a whole or
   a part of the army;
2. that there was no apparent occasion for the presence of
   the troops at Provo;
3. that if a rescue of the prisoners in custody had been
   attempted, it was the duty of the marshal, and not of the
   judges, to summon the force which might be necessary to
   prevent it;
4. that the troops ought not to have been sent to Provo
   without the concurrence of the governor, or kept there
   against his remonstrance;
5. that the disregard of these principles and rules of action
   has been, in many ways, extremely unfortunate.[17]

When Attorney General Black's letter arrived, Judge Cradlebaugh was in southern Utah holding court and investigating the
Mountain Meadows Massacre. On the same date, May 17, Black
had written to attorney Wilson approving of his actions and
telling him to maintain his rights. Wilson was also told that his
refusal on an earlier occasion to violate the president's pardon
was also praiseworthy and correct. As early as May 2 Secretary
of State Cass had written to Governor Cumming that orders had
been issued from the war department which would remove any
discrepancy between the orders given to the civil and military
departments of the government. On May 6, John B. Floyd,
secretary of war, wrote to General Johnston instructing him
that he was only to use the troops under him "as a posse comitatus in the execution of the laws upon the written application
of the governor of the territory, and not otherwise."[18] When
Judge Cradlebaugh discovered that the three hundred troops
with him in southern Utah had been recalled to Fort Douglas,
he also left.

The instructions from Washington stopped the wild course of
Cradlebaugh, Sinclair, and Marshal Peter K. Dotson; and within
a few months the two judges were released from their offices by
President Buchanan. Cradlebaugh refused to recognize the right

of the president to remove him, so continued his office for a short time. But because government officials would not support him, he soon left Utah and moved to Nevada. After Nevada became a territory he was twice elected her delegate to congress.[19] Bancroft states that the actions of the judges "well nigh brought about a renewal of the Utah War, hostilities being prevented only by the timely interference of the government."[20]

Camp Floyd Incidents

Spencer-Pike Affair

There were two other incidents in 1859 that also nearly caused a conflict between the army and the citizens of Utah: the Spencer-Pike Affair and an effort to arrest Brigham Young. The first was an incident between Howard Spencer, a local young man seventeen years of age, and Sergeant Ralph Pike of the army. The army had requisitioned Rush Valley, west of Camp Floyd, as a reserve for pasture and hay. Near the line of the reserve in the north part of Rush Valley was a ranch owned by Spencer-Little & Co. Daniel Spencer, one of the owners, had received a demand from the army officers to remove his stock from the vicinity of his corrals. Mr. Spencer sent his nephew, Howard O. Spencer, with Al Clift to move them. They reached the ranch on the evening of March 22, 1859, just as the sun was setting. Howard was near the stockyard with a pitchfork in his hands putting hay in the horses' mangers when Sergeant Ralph Pike and several soldiers rode up. Sergeant Pike dismounted and came toward Howard with a gun in his hand, ordering him to move the stock. Because the young men were exhausted, having ridden from Salt Lake City, forty or fifty miles, arriving at sundown, young Spencer told him they were not going to move them that night. Spencer reported that

> ... with an oath he struck me with his gun. I held up the pitchfork to ward off the blow, the fork handle was of pine home-made, the blow broke it in three pieces, and came with such force, that I was felled to the ground with a crushed skull. Pike turned to mount his horse, when a soldier said, 'put his head down hill, so he can bleed free.' He caught me by the hair, and pulled me around, then they rode off laughing. A little ranch boy was with me; he ran and told Luke Johnson who came and took charge of

me. When President Young learned of it, he sent Allen
Hilton and Dr. Sprague, with a carriage for me. I was taken
to Salt Lake City and placed in the care of Dr. France and
Anderson. With their intelligent treatment, and careful
nursing, my life was saved.[21]

Historian Norman Furniss states:

Howard Spencer, a nephew of the man who owned the
controversial herds, had visited Rush Valley to inspect his
uncle's animals and property. While he was engaged in this
peaceful mission, a detachment of troops ordered him
away, and when the young man refused to leave, a soldier
struck him down with his rifle, fracturing his skull.

The army's version, as might have been expected, placed
the entire blame for the affair upon Spencer, asserting that
Pike had acted in self-defense. . . .[22]

Furniss mentions that Pike's encounter with Spencer reminded the Mormons that they had no legal title to their land
and property, "a situation easily exploited by the soldiers who
were not kindly disposed to them."

The breakdown of relations between Cumming and
Johnston prevented them from serving as mediators between the army and the Church. The governor accepted
the Mormons' version of the event and demanded prompt
investigation. Johnston's reply, in addition to rejecting all
accusations against his men, contained sarcastic statements
indirectly accusing the governor of having become highly
prejudiced in favor of the Church.[23]

John R. Young wrote that Spencer's love for law and order
prevented him from taking revenge on Sergeant Pike until he
saw the farce played when Pike came to Salt Lake City for
court in August of that year. He had been indicted by the grand
jury for "assault with intent to kill."[24] Young added:

Pike was brought into the Provost Court, with his gun
buckled on his side, escorted by his armed comrades, heard
the colored pleadings of Pikes counsel, and the prompt
decision of the judge, evidencing to unbiased men, that in
that court, there was no justice for a Mormon.[25]

In disgust Howard Spencer quietly left the courtroom and after Sergeant Pike came out with his friends, Spencer walked up to him, shot him, and walked away. It was such a surprise that neither the soldiers nor the civilians on the street recovered from the shock in time to take Spencer into custody. Pike died three or four days later. It was not until many years later that Howard O. Spencer voluntarily returned to Salt Lake City from the Sevier River country to stand trial, where he was eventually acquitted by the verdict of a jury.[26]

As unjust as the court decision had been in setting Pike free, his murder could not be condoned. The best to be said for Spencer's action is that it was done by an otherwise upstanding young man in a moment of youthful brashness and impulsiveness. In a civilized country every citizen gives up the right to take personal revenge upon a wrongdoer in return for protection from the law. Spencer's action impaired his own future usefulness to both society and the Church. The *Deseret News* said of the deed, "We do not approve of the act" and went on to say that it was far better to let the law take its course than for an injured person to avenge the wrongs against him.

The killing was much resented at Camp Floyd. The night after Pike's death, about twenty soldiers went to Cedar Fort six miles north where they set fire to a stack of hay and fired upon the people who came to try to put it out. Stock sheds and corrals nearby were also burned. After lighting the fire the soldiers, "shot up the town," but fortunately no one was hurt. General Johnston was told about it the following day and said that he would send a guard to protect the town but that he could not control the soldiers while Spencer was at large. The government later paid for damages amounting to approximately ten thousand dollars.

Attempted Arrest of Brigham Young

The second incident nearly caused a direct clash between federal troops and the Nauvoo Legion. M. Brewer and J. M. Wallace, with others, conspired to engrave a counterfeit plate to be used by the quartermaster at Camp Floyd to draw funds from the assistant treasurers of the United States in St. Louis and New York City. They engaged "a clever artist" among the Mormons to make the engraving. Counterfeit bills were printed from it, apparently on paper that had been obtained from President Young's office. The engraver was the same person who

had engraved the plates for Brigham Young from which the
Deseret Currency had been printed.

Although the plates were cleverly made, the forgery was discovered and Brewer, the principal man involved, was arrested at
Camp Floyd. He confessed and volunteered to turn state's evidence against the engraver, blaming him for the crime. He also
named someone in Brigham Young's office as having furnished
the paper. This put the crime so close to Brigham Young that
Colonel Crossman, one of the officers, jumped with glee and
said "we will make this stick on Brigham Young this time."[27]

A few of the officers at Camp Floyd concocted a scheme to
arrest not only the engraver but also Brigham Young. The
officers assigned to the task went to the office of Governor
Cumming, where he received them courteously. They showed
him a writ for the arrest of the engraver, and he approved of it.
He then sent a note to a Mormon official, and within fifteen
minutes the man was placed in the hands of the officers.

Having obtained the fullest cooperation of the governor to
this point, the officers presented the remainder of their plan to
him: to also arrest Brigham Young; but, assuming that he
would resist, the army was to be ordered into Salt Lake City,
where the artillery would blow a hole in the rock wall surrounding his residence so that soldiers could rush through and take
him by force to Camp Floyd. Governor Cumming purportedly
replied with indignation:

> I listened to them, sir, as gravely as I could, and ex-
> amined their papers. They rubbed their hands and were
> jubilant they 'had got the dead wood on Brigham Young'.
> I was indignant, sir, and told them, 'By ＿＿＿＿ ＿＿＿＿,
> gentlemen, you can't do it! When you have a right to take
> Brigham Young, gentlemen, you shall have him without
> creeping through walls. You shall enter by his door with
> heads erect as becomes representatives of your govern-
> ment. But till that time, gentlemen, you can't touch
> Brigham Young while I live, by ＿＿＿ !'[28]

The officers returned to Camp Floyd disappointed; and soon
the Mormons heard rumors that General Johnston was going to
send two regiments and a battery of artillery to enforce the
arrest of Brigham Young. Governor Cumming immediately
notified General Wells to have the militia in readiness to act on
orders. By 2:00 a.m. Monday morning, five thousand troops

280 were under arms.[29] A group of men were stationed at the point of the mountain south of Salt Lake City, where they could overlook the road coming from Camp Floyd. If there was any movement from Camp Floyd they were to signal—by smoke in the daytime or by fire if during the night. Another group of watchers were on Ensign Peak, where they could respond to the watchers and signal the alarm to the city, where militia units were within easy call. Fortunately no movement toward the city came from Camp Floyd during these tense days. Then word from the administration arrived from Washington, D.C. to the effect that government troops were not to be used except upon written orders of the governor.

Deseret Currency Plates Confiscated

After the arrest of the young engraver, Marshal Peter K. Dotson confiscated the counterfeit plates along with all of his tools; but he did not stop there. He also confiscated the Deseret currency plates belonging to the Church. They were taken to Camp Floyd, where they were considerably damaged. Dotson later tried to return them to Brigham Young in this condition, but President Young refused to receive them and filed suit for damages against Dotson. After a rather long trial he received judgment against Dotson for $2,600 and Dotson's house was sold to pay the claim.[30] Dotson, who had been a resident of Utah since 1851 and a United States marshal since 1855, sent his resignation on August 1, 1859, and took occasion to tell the administration that its policy toward Utah would be fatal to federal supremacy.[31]

ACTIVITIES OF JUDGE ECKLES

Judge Eckles, who had gone to Washington in the fall of 1858, returned to Utah in June of 1859 and opened his court— the southern district—at Nephi in August. He finished there on September 4 then opened court at Camp Floyd for three days on September 13. When he had completed court there, he wrote a long letter to Secretary of State, Lewis Cass, in which he mentioned nearly all of the old charges against the Latter-day Saints, still striving to bring conflict between them and the government.

Secretary Cass sent the main parts of Eckles's communication to Governor Cumming, asking him for a report on the "causes, if any, which operate to retard the due administration of the

laws, and prevent the maintenance of peace and order." He
asked by what means, in Cumming's judgment, the causes could
be most advantageously removed. He also wanted to know to
what extent these troubles came because the territorial legislature failed to provide measures for prevention, and to what
extent they existed because the people refused to aid in executing the laws.

GOVERNOR CUMMING'S DEFENSE
OF THE PEOPLE

Governor Cumming was also asked to state the present population of the territory, the proportion of them who were
Mormons, the number of people arriving in and departing from
the territory, and the capacity of the available land to support
the present or a larger population. This last request was made
because Judge Eckles had said that the country was already
over populated.

In his report to Secretary Cass, Governor Cumming was
highly complimentary of the local people and blamed many of
the difficulties in law enforcement on the judges themselves,
such as their failure to recognize the right of the territorial
marshal to function before the district courts in territorial
matters and their failure to recognize right of the probate courts
to original jurisdiction in civil and criminal cases. He also stated
that the Mormons were so convinced of the prejudice of the
judges against them that they could not expect a fair decision in
any case. They believed that the judges tended to convict a
person of crime if he were a Mormon, and especially if he were
a person of influence in the community. The reasons, among
many, that he mentioned for this opinion were: the unnecessary assemblage of a military force at Provo during court in
March of 1859; the imprisonment of citizens in guard tents both
then and at other times; the fact that the chief justice had his
residence at Camp Floyd, showing a dislike and distrust of the
people; finally, the unjust and frequent expressions of several
judges that the entire community had forfeited their right to
self-government.[32]

Judge Eckles's letter also accused more than two-thirds of the
male population of Nephi, including all of the civil and ecclesiastical officers, of fleeing when he arrived to hold court
although he had no soldiers with him; and because of their
flight, he had to send to Cedar County where the army and

282 camp followers were located for talesmen to complete his juries.[33]

In answer to this, Governor Cumming stated that Eckles not only had with him the marshal and bailiffs but also all of the talesmen (fifteen grand jurors and ten petit jurors), all of them from Cedar County, where there was a large itinerant population all dependent on the army for support. Governor Cumming explained that Utah County was adjacent to Juab County (Nephi) and had a far greater population of citizens from whom Eckles could have drawn his talesmen.

Governor Cumming estimated the total population, not counting the army and adjacent itinerants, at 53,000 of whom 50,000 were Mormons, most of the non-Mormons residing on the extreme west side of the Territory (later Nevada).

The governor praised the general character of the people in the territory.

> Persons unbiased by prejudice who have visited this Territory will, I think, agree in the opinion that a community is seldom seen more marked by quiet and peaceable diligence than that of the Mormons.
>
> After the passage of the army, hundreds of adventurers were attracted to these valleys, and met here some congenial spirits. Banded together for rapine and acts of violence, they have stolen large herds of horses and mules. Many of these men, maddened by intemperance, or rendered desperate by losses at the gaming table, or by various other causes, have shed each other's blood in frequent conflicts, and secret asassinations. These lawless and bloody deeds are committed by them almost daily with impunity, and when their atrocity and frequency, shock the public mind, it has become the custom with a certain set of people to exclaim against the people of Utah; but it is an injustice to impute the acts of these desparadoes to the community in general. With an equal show of justice might they be attributed to the inhabitants of the states and territories whence these men have so recently emigrated.[34]

This report was a vindication of the people of Utah and the false charges against them. It also represented the courage of the governor in repudiating the judges who had tried to create antagonism between the Mormon people and the federal government.

The first newspaper in Utah was the *Deseret News,* which began its existence on June 15, 1850. It had no competition until the fall of 1858, when a rival newspaper came into existence. An anti-Mormon paper circulating chiefly at Camp Floyd, it was called the *Valley Tan.*[35] The principal owner was the secretary of the territory, John Hartnett. During the difficulties between the local people and the judges, the *Valley Tan* was the mouthpiece and spokesman for the judges. Its first editor was Kirk Anderson who had formerly assisted with the publication of the *Missouri Republican* and who had arrived in Salt Lake City in September, 1858. The first number came off the press on November 6; the paper lasted for about one and one-half years. Because it soon became evident that there was not sufficient non-Mormon patronage to keep it going, efforts were made to get a good circulation among the Saints. About this time General Wells said to Secretary Hartnett: "You know, Mr. Hartnett, it is the wish of the administration that the difficulty that has existed should remain settled; that is also our wish." Mr. Hartnett said he did not approve of the course of the paper, but some of the officers of the army had sent word to the editor that they would not patronize him if he did not "pitch in like hell." It died in the winter of 1860.

Another paper was begun on August 27, 1859. It was called the *Mountaineer* and was published as a secular paper by three Latter-day Saint lawyers: Seth M. Blair, James Ferguson, and Hosea Stout, and was a vigorous opponent of anti-Mormon activities of the federal judges. Its motto was: "Do what is right, let the consequence follow." But there did not seem to be sufficient population to support a second pro-Mormon newspaper; the *Deseret News* seemed to take care of the needs of most of the people. Thus the *Mountaineer* also passed out of existence.

TWO NOTABLE VISITORS TO
SALT LAKE CITY

Horace Greeley

On July 10, 1859, Mr. Horace Greeley, founder and editor of the *New York Tribune* and a noted anti-slavery leader, arrived in Salt Lake City where he stayed for ten days. On July 13 he had a two-hour interview with Brigham Young and other leaders, mainly concerning the doctrines of the Church. His questions ranged from infant baptism to belief in a personal devil to plural marriage and were frankly asked. B. H. Roberts states they failed to reach the really fundamental things of the new dispensation of the Christian religion. Mr. Greeley appreciated the frankness with which President Young answered his questions, and was very favorably impressed by the appearance and manners of President Young and the other leaders, stating they looked as little like crafty hypocrites as any body of men he had ever met.

On Sunday, July 17, the only Sunday he spent in Salt Lake City, he attended both the morning and afternoon services in the tabernacle, listening to sermons by Orson Pratt in the morning and John Taylor in the afternoon. He was critical of their extemporaneous sermons, stating they could have said what they did in much less time and thus a few hours preparation on their part would have made more economical use of listeners' time. Perhaps one reason he felt this way was that he also thought their sermons were adapted to needs different from his own. He did think that the prayers in the meetings were "pertinent and full of unction" and that the music was generally better than that heard in the average religious gathering in the states.

Mr. Greeley visited Camp Floyd where approximately three thousand troops were stationed at the time. He could see no useful purpose for the troops' being there and criticized very severely the army contract arrangement with supplies, stating that they had been paid 22 cents per pound to freight flour from the states during the past year, but they had been permitted to purchase it in Utah at prime Missouri rates. This, in addition to the freighting costs, had netted the contractors $170,000 in one year on this item alone, "without risking a dollar or lifting a finger."

He was quite disgusted because the mail contractors who had a contract to deliver the mail twice monthly could deliver it weekly to a better advantage inasmuch as they were running a weekly stage coach service, but the government had informed the postmasters in Salt Lake City and St. Joseph, Missouri, to refuse to accept it on a weekly basis even though the government only had to pay for a semimonthly delivery.

Mr. Greeley was forceful in commenting on the fact that the Mormons were not ignorant, superstitious, or brutal, as he had

been told, nor were they an organized banditti, or a horde of
robbers and assassins; he said they were, in the main, an industrious, frugal, hard-working people. Since the army had come, the Mormons' drinking had increased. The average life in Utah was a hard one, taking three hundred days of labor to produce those necessities of life that could be produced in Kansas for one hundred and fifty days. He was disappointed that the Saints did not show more enthusiasm for fighting slavery. Greeley expressed his views concerning his trip to Utah in a series of articles published in the *New York Tribune*.

Captain Richard F. Burton

In August, 1860, Captain Richard F. Burton, a much-traveled British army officer, arrived in Salt Lake City where he stayed—with visits to Camp Floyd—until September 20. His impressions were later published in a book which he called *The City of the Saints*. Eight of its thirteen chapters were on Mormon "life in Utah and the religion of the Latter-day Saints."[36] The other five chapters were about his journey "across the Rocky Mountains to California." The whole book is composed of nearly six hundred pages. The Captain's stay was much longer than Mr. Greeley's the previous year; this gave him more time for a better analysis of the Church and people, although this was also not a sufficient time for a thorough study of the Saints and their religion. Nevertheless, Burton's book, published in 1862, is said to be the best non-Mormon treatise up to 1930 on the Mormon religion and philosophy and also the fairest criticism of it although he did treat some aspects of the faith with flippancy.[37]

He also failed to grasp the true concept of the faith in some instances, as shown by his statement that it was a new dispensation although not claiming to be; that is exactly what Mormonism does claim to be. Mr. Burton commented on the general safety of a person in Salt Lake City on the streets even after dark, comparing it with the three days he was in "Christian Carson City" where there were three murders. During his whole stay in Salt Lake City, there was none. He commented on the general friendliness of the Mormons toward the Indians, the untrustworthiness of anti-Mormon literature, and Mormon toleration of it. He was complimentary in his description of Brigham Young. His visit was decidedly favorable to the Latter-day Saints.

Events were shaping up in the states that would shortly cause the closing of Camp Floyd. In February of 1860, General Johnston left Camp Floyd for Washington, D.C., traveling by way of Southern California and the Panama Railroad. It appears, however, that he became commander of the military district known as the Department of the Pacific which included the state and territories of California, Oregon, Washington, Nevada, and Utah with headquarters in San Francisco. General Winfield Scott, not sure of General Johnston's loyalty to the Union after the beginning of the Civil War, relieved him of his command and replaced him with General E. V. Sumner who assumed command on April 26, 1861. Johnston had submitted his resignation on April 9; it was accepted on May 3, 1861. He then joined the cause of the South. Brevet Colonel C. F. Smith had been in charge at Camp Floyd as Colonel P. St. George Cooke was in the East; but Colonel Cooke was recalled to take command. In May a number of companies left Camp Floyd for New Mexico. Many of the camp followers, including women and gamblers, left with them, a relief to the people of Utah. In February of 1861, Secretary of War John B. Floyd was in disrepute, and Colonel Cooke ordered the name of Camp Floyd changed to Fort Crittendon.

As rumors of war filtered in by way of the Pony Express, it was obvious Fort Crittendon would soon be abandoned. Soon Colonel Cooke received orders to move the remainder of his troops and close down the fort. He was told that everything he could not take with him was to be sold at public auction except the munitions of war, and these were not to be sold but were to be destroyed. On July 16, 1861, the auction began that saw $4,000,000 worth of property sold for about $100,000. Hiram B. Clawson, Brigham Young's agent, paid about $40,000 of this amount for purchases. He also invited the officers to call on Brigham Young before their departure. They did so; and while there, they presented to Brigham Young the ninety-foot flagstaff that had flown the flag over the military camp since November 8, 1858. Toward the end of July, 1861, the last remnants of the Army marched away from Fort Crittendon. The army that had come to show the power of Uncle Sam and had camped three years in the desert, accomplishing nothing worthwhile, had gone.

Camp Floyd —

Governor Cumming, who, like General Johnston, was a southerner whose sympathies were with the South, quietly left Utah on May 17, 1861, approximately two months before his term of office came to a close. He left at a time when Brigham Young was visiting settlements in the south, without telling any of the Latter-day Saints' leaders of his departure. He seemed to want to avoid a demonstration of appreciation which the Saints would have undoubtedly given him. He returned to his home in Georgia where he joined the southern cause and became an exchange prisoner of war on March 24, 1864.

In Utah he had left behind a grateful citizenry whose confidence and friendship he had won through an understanding nature and a straightforward course of action toward the people. He left the executive office in the care of the secretary of the territory, Frances H. Wooton, another southerner who also soon departed.

THE COST OF THE UTAH EXPEDITION

The cost to the government in dollars is variously estimated from twenty to forty million dollars, with 6,600 regular troops involved up through 1858 and 10,500 other employees and camp followers through the same period. It was at a time when the treasury was low and caused a further drain, so that when President Lincoln took office in March, 1861, there were no funds in the treasury. To the Latter-day Saints, the Camp Floyd period was a time of moral degradation. The soldiers were able to talk a few of the Mormon girls into going to the camp for immoral purposes. Some of the young men were influenced into drinking and committing other sins. Murder became rather commonplace on the streets of Salt Lake City, although it usually involved camp followers fighting and killing each other. On the brighter side, it did give a financial shot in the arm to the economy of Utah. Before the coming of the army, money was a very scarce item. Many a Mormon was aided financially either directly or indirectly by the presence of the army. Also, there were a few soldiers who became converts to the Church, such as James McLane and Henry Snyder who lived and died in Fairfield.[38] Another noted convert was Charles H. Wilcken, who became a devoted guard and coachman to the First Presidency of the Church.[39]

[1]Robert E. Stowers and John M. Ellis, eds. "Charles A. Scott's Diary of the Utah Expedition, 1857-1861." *Utah Historical Quarterly* 28 (April 1960):173.

[2]David H. Carson, *History of the Carson Family* (Lehi, Utah, 1952), p. 4. Copy is available in the Brigham Young University Library, Provo, Utah.

[3]Carson, p. 4.

[4]*CHC*, 4:456.

[5]*CHC*, 4:457.

[6]*CHC*, 4:468.

[7]*CHC*, 4:463.

[8]*CHC*, 4:475.

[9]T. B. H. Stenhouse, *The Rocky Mountain Saints* (New York: D. Appleton and Co., 1873), p. 402.

[10]Hubert Howe Bancroft, *History of Utah* (1890; reprint ed., Salt Lake City: Bookcraft, 1964), p. 539.

[11]*CHC*, 4:475-76.

[12]Orson F. Whitney, *Popular History of Utah* (Salt Lake City: Deseret News Press, 1916), p. 165.

[13]Stenhouse, p. 408.

[14]*CHC*, 4:492.

[15]*CHC*, 4:495.

[16]*CHC*, 4:495.

[17]*CHC*, 4:498.

[18]*CHC*, 4:499.

[19]Bancroft, p. 575, footnote 6.

[20]Bancroft, p. 540.

[21]John R. Young, *Memoirs of John R. Young, Utah Pioneer, 1847* (Salt Lake City: Deseret News Press, 1920), pp. 188-89.

[22]Norman F. Furniss, *The Mormon Conflict* (New Haven, Conn.: Yale University Press, 1960), p. 224.

[23]Furniss, pp. 224-25.

[24]*CHC*, 4:504.

[25]Young, p. 190.

[26]Young, p. 190.

[27]*CHC*, 4:506, including footnote 4.

[28]Stenhouse, p. 411.

[29]Stenhouse, p. 412, first footnote.

[30]Bancroft, p. 573, footnote 2. *See also* Stenhouse, p. 412.

[31]*Deseret News*, 9 November 1859, p. 285.

[32]*CHC*, 4:510-14.

[33]Talesmen are persons chosen on a jury to fill in when too few of the original jurors are present.

[34]*CHC*, 4:511-12.

[35]This name was originally applied to leather that was tanned locally. It soon began to represent any article made out of homemade leather and eventually expanded into meaning anything that was made locally; especially a sort of a bad, low-quality whiskey.

[36]*CHC*, 4:527. *See also* Richard F. Burton, *City of the Saints and Across the Rocky Mountains to California* (New York: Harper and Brothers, 1862).

[37]*CHC*, 4:528, including footnote 24.

[38]William H. Snyder, Family Record (n.p., 1938). Copy is available in the Brigham Young University Library, Provo, Utah.

[39]Gustive O. Larson, *The "Americanization" of Utah for Statehood* (San Marino, Calif.: Huntington Library, 1971), pp. 155-73.

the Quest = $3.00

D.&C. is a Book of Warning = we are now
in the warning & Punishment day   Sec 1: 11 - 18
Sec 1 given as a preface to the book - It
is really out of place there

Read
      Sec 87: 6
      Sec 5: 18

14

Civil War Period
(Because of Disobedience) Slaves

THE PONY EXPRESS AND THE TELEGRAPH LINE

On April 3, 1860, the Pony Express had begun as a method of getting news faster to and from the West. It was an elaborate business enterprise set up by Russell, Majors, and Waddell, the government freighters and owners of the stagecoach line, more as a fantastic advertising medium than as a successful business enterprise. From St. Joseph, Missouri, to Sacramento, California, nearly 2,000 miles, men were expected to carry the mail by pony express in ten days' time. This would be an average of about eight miles an hour day and night, summer and winter. Eighty riders with 320 stations and stationmasters and numerous ponies were involved. During one winter and two summers, 308 relays were made each way, with more than 34,000 pieces of mail, at an enormous cost including a loss of hundreds of thousands of dollars.[1]

The telegraph line that was completed to Salt Lake City on October 18, 1861, saved the Pony Express from folding for financial reasons.

Many young Mormon men had participated in this dangerous but romantic venture; but it was now over, and President Brigham Young was given the privilege of sending the first message over the telegraph wires. He sent a message to the

292 president of the telegraph company in which he congratulated him and his associates upon completion of such a beneficial work and reaffirmed the Saints' allegiance to the federal government:

> Utah has not seceded, but is firm for the Constitution and laws of our happy country, and is warmly interested in such useful enterprises as the one so far completed.[2]

President J. H. Wade of the Pacific Telegraph Co. replied the next morning that it was gratifying that the first message over the line "should express so unmistakably the patriotism of Union-loving sentiment" of Brigham Young and people. On the same day, acting Governor Frank Fuller sent a message to President Lincoln:

G.S.L. City, October 18, 1861

To the President of the United States:

> Utah, whose citizens strenuously resist all imputations of disloyalty, congratulates the President upon the completion of an enterprise which spans a continent, unites two oceans, and connects with nerve of iron the remote extremities of the body politic with the great governmental heart. May the whole system speedily thrill with the quickened pulsations of that heart, as the parricide hand is palsied, treason is punished, and the entire sisterhood of states join hands in glad re-union around the National fireside.

Frank Fuller
Acting Governor of Utah Territory

President Lincoln replied:

Washington, D.C., Oct. 20th, '61

Hon. Frank Fuller, Acting Gov. of Utah:

> Sir: The completion of the Telegraph to Great Salt Lake City, is auspicious of the stability and union of the Republic. The Government reciprocates your congratulations

Abraham Lincoln[3]

October 23, the telegraph line was completed between Salt
Lake City and San Francisco, so that it now spanned the entire
continent.

Lincoln's Call for Men to Guard the Mail and Telegraph Lines

About six months later President Young received a wire from
President Lincoln, requesting him to raise ninety men for three
months' service to guard the mail and telegraph line between
Fort Bridger and Fort Laramie. In all, ninety-three men were
called under Lot Smith, who was designated as captain. On May
1, four days after the message, the men were on their way. The
reason for this call was that during March and April the Indians
had made a number of attacks upon mail stations. The men
remained in the service until August 14, during which time no
further attacks were made.

This was the only government service the Saints were called
upon to perform during the Civil War period.

UTAH TERRITORY IS DIMINISHED

On March 2, 1861, President Buchanan, with only two days
left in office, signed the act organizing the territory of Nevada
out of the western part of Utah. The land along the Carson
River had been occupied for about ten years by both Mormons
and non-Mormons when in June, 1859, the Comstock mine was
discovered, which brought in a flood of gentiles who objected
to being governed from Salt Lake City. The new territory was
the result, and Utah's western boundary was fixed at the 39th
meridian from Washington.

In 1861 the territory of Colorado was created from parts of
other areas, and the Utah boundary was moved west to the
32nd meridian. When Nebraska was also organized in 1861 a
piece from the northeastern corner of Utah was given to
present-day Wyoming.

In 1862, the Nevada territorial boundary had been moved
east to the 38th meridian by an act of Congress and again in
1866 it was extended to the 37th meridian. By 1868, Utah had
become the size that it is today. The counties left in Utah
numbered eighteen, as follows: Salt Lake, Davis, Weber, Utah,
Tooele, Juab, San Pete, Millard, Iron, Beaver, Washington,
Kane, Morgan, Box Elder, Cache, Wasatch, Summit, and Green
River; but the last one went in 1868 with the organization of
Wyoming as a territory.

In 1860-61, while other states were trying to get out of the Union, Utah was making an earnest effort to get into it. On December 16, 1860, Utah's delegate to Congress wrote to George Q. Cannon:

> I think three-quarters of the Republicans of the house would vote for our admission; but I may be mistaken. Many say they would gladly 'swap' the Gulf states for Utah. I tell them that we show our loyalty by trying to get in, while others are trying to get out, notwithstanding our grievances, which are far greater than those of any of the seceding states; but that I consider we can redress our grievances better in the Union than out of it; . . . [4]

About a year later the Utah legislature drafted an act calling for a convention to form a state constitution. Utah's then Governor John W. Dawson vetoed the act, but the people went ahead anyhow. They drafted a constitution and a memorial to Congress requesting statehood. Then the people of Utah voted upon the constitution and elected their officers.

But again, nothing came of the people's efforts; Utah's case was dropped and she found herself unable to get statehood while at the same time a war was being fought to keep other states from leaving the Union.

Mormon Attitude Toward the War

Having been rebuffed in their efforts to get into the Union, the Saints were naturally disappointed. They also recalled the prophecy given through Joseph Smith in regard to war between the North and the South (D&C 87) and felt that it was a result of the disobedience of the people of the United States to the laws of God. Thus, they held themselves aloof from either side, having rejected the efforts of certain southern senators who endeavored to persuade Utah to join the south and sending no volunteers to fight on the side of the North who levied an annual war tax upon Utah but did not request the services of any men for military duty.

They were further estranged from the federal government when Secretary of War Stanton, mistrusting the Mormons,

ordered Civil War volunteers from Nevada and California to stop
in Utah as a safeguard against the people turning against the
Union. The reason they gave for this action, however, was that
they were guarding the mail and telegraph lines.

A few words from a speech of Elder John Taylor in July
1861 briefly sums up the attitude generally adopted by the
Saints during the war. "We know no north, no south, no east,
no west; we abide strictly and positively by the Constitution,
and cannot by the intrigues or sophism of either party, be
cajoled into any other attitude.[15]

ABRAHAM LINCOLN AND HIS APPOINTEES

Lincoln, upon whom the Mormons looked as a friend, had
run for president of the United States on an anti-polygamy
platform. When he was asked after his election in 1860 what he
proposed to do with the Mormons, he said he proposed to "let
them alone;" that he expected to treat them like a farmer
would a green hemlock log on a newly cleared frontier farm
that was "too heavy to move, too knotty to split and too wet to
burn." He said he would "plow around it."[6] Nevertheless he
signed the Anti-Bigamy Law on July 8, 1862, as he was
politically obligated to do.

The first Lincoln appointees to office in Utah were John W.
Dawson (Indiana) as governor; Frank Fuller (New Hampshire),
already acting secretary, as secretary of the territory; James
Duane Doty (Wisconsin) as Indian superintendent; John F.
Kinney, who had succeeded Delano Eckles in July of 1860, as
chief justice; Robert P. Flenniken and Henry R. Crosby as
associate justices.

Governor Dawson arrived on December 7, 1861, and three
days later he gave his message to the territorial legislature. In it
he implied that the Mormons were disloyal but by promptly
paying her war tax could be vindicated. His talk was not
pleasing to members of the legislature. A few days later he made
improper proposals to a respectable woman, who exposed him.
He thereafter stayed in his dwelling place until December 31
when he left Utah for the East. At Mountain Dell mail station
he was beaten and robbed by eight ruffians but he continued his
journey eastward. At Bear River station he wrote to the *Deseret
News* his version of the affair. The ruffians were later arrested
and three of them, Lot Huntington, Moroni Clawson, and John
Smith, were killed while trying to escape from the law.

About a month later justices R. P. Flenniken and H. R. Crosby left the territory, and on February 3 Thomas J. Drake (Michigan) and Charles B. Waite (Illinois) were appointed to succeed them. On March 21, 1862, Stephen Harding (Indiana) was appointed governor to succeed Dawson. He arrived in Salt Lake City July 7, 1862.

Arrival of the California Volunteers

Five companies of infantry and two companies of cavalry under the command of Colonel P. E. Connor arrived in Salt Lake City on October 20, 1862, "with loaded rifles, fixed bayonets, and shotted cannon," although the Mormons had offered no resistance. They marched directly to the residence of Governor Stephen S. Harding, whose attitude toward the Mormons changed considerably after their arrival. Colonel Connor had chosen a site of 2,560 acres on the east bench above Salt Lake City for their military reservation where they set up their artillery with their muzzles turned in the direction of Brigham Young's residence. Such ill treatment and assumption of disloyalty on the part of the Mormons was irritating to them, and it only served to make the federal appointees to office "arrogant and aggressive." President Young, in speaking of the Mormons' enlisting to fight for the North in the Civil War, stated that there was a camp of soldiers from abroad (out of the territory) located within the corporate limits of the city and he would not ask one man to go.[7]

When Governor Harding—who had known Joseph Smith in New York in 1830—first arrived, he was very friendly; but after the arrival of the California Volunteers, he became hostile. His message to the legislature on December 1862 openly accused the Saints of disloyalty and attacked the laws of the territory, calling for many changes. He had previously invited all of the government officials and the army officers to be present for the message.

The legislature considered it so insulting that they treated it with silence; but when word reached Washington, one thousand copies of it were printed there for the governor's distribution. This caused more publicity than ever throughout the country.

When Harding first arrived in Utah, he had offered to resign if at any time the Saints decided they did not want him as governor. He and the judges were now requested to resign, but they flatly refused.

The Saints petitioned Washington to remove them, while the military Connor and his officers wrote in favor of the judges and Harding. In May of 1863 President Lincoln released Governor Harding; but also, to appease the anti-Mormons, he released Chief Justice Kinney and Secretary of the Territory Frank Fuller, both friendly to the Saints. John Titus (Pennsylvania) became chief justice; James Duane Doty, who had become governor, served for two years as Utah's successful Indian superintendent and Amos Reed (Wisconsin), who had come to Utah with Doty, became secretary of the territory. An era of comparative peace ensued for the Saints, for these men filled their positions honorably without trying to interfere in the lives of the people. In fact, Chief Justice Titus stated: "To be left alone was all that the people asked and all that they had struggled for since Utah was first admitted to the territory."[8]

Justice Kinney Sent to Congress

In order to show their appreciation to Judge Kinney for his fairness to the Latter-day Saints during his two different periods as chief justice in Utah, the Utahns elected him to the United States Congress in the fall of 1863 to serve as Utah's delegate in the House of Representatives for two years. The delegates were as follows: Dr. John M. Bernhisel 1850-59; Captain W. H. Hooper 1859-61; Dr. Bernhisel 1861-63; Judge John F. Kinney 1863-65; Captain Hooper 1865-73; the Honorable George Q. Cannon 1873-82; and John T. Caine 1883.

At the end of Judge Kinney's term he moved from Utah, but in 1889 he returned and spent his last years in Salt Lake City where he died on August 16, 1902.

APOSTATE FACTIONS OF THE EARLY 1860s

The Gibson Church

Captain Walter M. Gibson arrived in Utah in the fall of 1859, intent upon persuading the Mormons to move to New Guinea in the East Indies. He was advised by President Young to investigate the gospel, join the Church, and along with others, go on a mission to the people of New Guinea, by which way he could do them more good than any other.[9] By the middle of January, 1860, he and his daughter Talulah (he also had with him two young sons) were baptized by Heber C. Kimball. During the

298 following April he went east as a missionary with mission headquarters in New York City, where he claimed to have preached
his new faith and to have interviewed the Japanese embassy
members in their own language, receiving an invitation to visit
Japan. Within six months he was back in Salt Lake City, where
he was "blessed by Brigham Young," and was called to go with
a commission to all nations on earth. In November of 1860 he
left for San Francisco, supposedly on his way to Japan. After
disclaiming any connection with the Church, he gave a series of
lectures in San Francisco on Malasia, finally arriving in Honolulu, Hawaii, on July 4, 1861. He did not immediately associate
himself with the Church but finally did so at the semiannual
conference on Wailuku in October 1861. As all Utah missionaries had been called home because of the Utah War, there had
not been any missionaries from headquarters in Hawaii for three
years, and the native leaders were holding conference. Gibson
presented his credentials, assumed the presidency of the
Hawaiian Mission, and proceeded to move many of the local
Saints to the island of Lanai, where the Church and a native
elder, Haalelea, owned a large tract of land.

With the native Saints under his domination, he had them
work for him and soon purchased a large part of the island of
Lanai in his own name. He also proceeded to organize a church
along Mormon lines but selling offices in the priesthood for
from $5.00 for a deacon to $150.00 for an apostle.

By December, 1863, eight of the native elders, realizing
things were very different from when previous missionaries were
there, wrote to Church headquarters at Salt Lake City for
advice. In March of 1864 President Young sent apostles Ezra T.
Benson and Lorenzo Snow, with Elders Joseph F. Smith, W. W.
Cluff, John R. Young, A. L. Smith, and one or two other former
missionaries to Hawaii to straighten out matters. Although it
took them a few weeks to win back the native Saints and they
had to excommunicate Gibson, they finally succeeded, breaking
the hold of Gibson upon the Saints, who soon moved to other
islands.

Gibson was a wealthy man who became a political power in
Hawaii, finally becoming prime minister. Through misdeeds he
was forced to leave Hawaii in July of 1887, arriving in San
Francisco on August 6, where he died of tuberculosis on January 21, 1888. Although he had been excommunicated from
the Church, he apparently always felt kindly toward the Saints,
for on one occasion he said, "It is my opinion that the system

of polity practiced by the Mormon Church is the best in the
world. . . . It is founded upon righteousness, and I shall always
love them."[10]

The Morrisites

Another apostate was Joseph Morris, a Welshman, who joined
the Church in Wales in 1849 and became the cause of a tragic
and misunderstood affair in Utah. Before arriving in Utah in
1853, he had been stricken with a severe accident in the coal
mines of Wales and a severe illness in St. Louis, Illinois. These
difficulties affected his mind.

During his first eight years in Utah he had a varied existence;
he was married and divorced from three different wives and
twice excommunicated from the Church for adultery; he wrote
President Brigham Young forty fantastic letters which were
filled with rash claims and many vagaries. He professed to be a
prophet of God, sometimes claiming to be the "seventh angel"
spoken of in Revelations, again claiming to be Moses reincar-
nated. He also told Brigham Young and the Twelve not to send
out missionaries and to prepare the way for him to take over as
head of the Church; also he said that he would give them anything their hearts desired in righteousness.

After living in Sanpete and Utah counties, Morris moved to
Weber County where he succeeded in convincing a number of
people in the South Weber Ward and a few from the Slaterville
Branch that he was the true prophet of God. On February 11,
1861, Elders John Taylor and Wilford Woodruff were sent to
the ward to straighten out matters. After a patient public hearing when Bishop Richard Cook and fifteen others denounced
Brigham Young and claimed to believe in Morris, they were
excommunicated, and the faithful ward members were told to
treat them with kindness.

On April 6, 1861, Morris and five followers were baptized
and proceeded to organize a church. Morris became their leader,
with Richard Cook and John Banks as counselors. They located
at a place near South Weber which they called Kington Fort.
Morris preached the immediate coming of Christ and soon his
converts numbered in the hundreds. He also preached that when
Christ came, their wants would be supplied without labor. His
alleged revelations came so fast it kept as many as six secretaries
busy working on them. These revelations were filled with denunciations against both the Mormon Church and the United

300 States government, and they declared that God would fight their battles against all their enemies.

The Morrisites were living with all things in common, but since they were neglecting their daily pursuits, having been told it was not necessary to plant crops because Christ would come soon, they found themselves becoming short of both shelter and food.

Several times Morris set the date for the coming of Christ; and as each date would pass by in disappointment, discontentment began to rise. Some followers tried to leave but wanted to take with them the property they had given to the common cause. Four of them were captured and prevented from leaving. Their relatives and friends were concerned about their safety because Morris claimed several revelations telling him to kill apostates.[11] An appeal was made to Judge Kinney in his capacity as judge of the third district court, who issued a writ of habeas corpus, demanding the men be brought before his court. When it was served by Marshal J. L. Stoddard, the order was refused, the writ was burned, the marshal was threatened and told no more writs would be served, and there were over 100 armed men to prevent service.

On June 10, 1862, Chief Justice Kinney issued a second writ for John Jensen and William Jones, the other two prisoners having escaped. The writs were put in the hands of deputy territorial Marshals Robert Burton and Theodore McKean. Acting Governor Frank Fuller (Governor Harding was out of the territory), upon being informed there would be resistance, called out 250 of the militia to aid Marshal Burton. When they arrived at Kington Fort, a message was sent in for Joseph Morris, John Banks, Richard Cook, Parsons, and Peter Klemgard to surrender themselves as prisoners. They were given thirty minutes to reply and were told if they disregarded the summons, they should remove their women and children to safety. In addition to the message, Major Egan and Wells Smith approached the fort under a flag of truce hoping to discuss the matters with a delegation from the fort, but none came forward.

In the fort the question was discussed as to what to do, and Morris retired to his dwelling to seek revelation. About two hours later he came out with one, forbidding the men to surrender and promising them their enemies would be destroyed while not one of them should be harmed. Morris read the revelation to the assembled people; after he had finished, a cannon

ball crashed into the fort killing two women and knocking off 301
the chin of a young girl. Ex-Bishop Cook told each to retire to
his house and defend his family. For three days they resisted
the posse, killing two of them; then a man emerged with a white
flag. He was told the terms were the unconditional surrender of
all arms. Observing that the arms were being stacked, Captain
Burton and about twenty men entered.

Someone asked that Morris be permitted to speak. This
privilege was granted if he would be brief and not incite the
people. Morris then cried out "All who are for me and my God
in life or in death follow me," and he and others rushed for the
arms. Captain Burton ordered a halt but they rushed on; so he
ordered his men to fire, and Burton shot Morris, who died
instantly. In the melee, Banks and two women were also shot.
This stopped the rush.

Ninety-four men were taken to Salt Lake City. Their trial was
set for March, 1863, and seven of them were found guilty of
second degree murder. Three days later, Governor Harding,
whose resignation had been requested along with those of
Judges Waite and Drake, granted a "full and perfect pardon" to
them. The governor also pardoned about sixty others who had
been fined.

Although the affair was between the Morrisites and their dissenters, and it was a non-Mormon judge and a non-Mormon
acting governor who had ordered the deputy marshal and a
posse to arrest them, the posse members were Mormons; therefore, in all of the newspapers in the country the Mormons were
blamed. The soldiers at Fort Douglas befriended the Morrisites
and blamed the Saints as much as the rest of the country did, in
spite of the fact that Morris's statements were actually as much
a defiance against the federal government as they were against
the Mormons or the territorial government.[12]

Many of the Morrisites eventually rejoined the Mormon
Church, but Colonel Connor took about 200 of them to Soda
Springs, Idaho, with him in May, 1863, when he went there to
establish a military post.

This Morrisite affair was the final action that brought about
the release of Governor Harding, Judge Kinney, and the secretary of the territory, Frank Fuller.

1860

Missionaries of the Reorganized Church of Jesus Christ of Latter Day Saints

The Reorganized Latter Day Saints Church sent missionaries

Strangite

302 to Utah in 1863, where they managed to gain a few converts. They had formed a group out of three branches of the Strangite Church in 1852; and on April 6, 1860, they were successful in getting the Prophet Joseph Smith's son, Joseph Smith III, to assume the presidency of their group.[13] In 1869 two sons of the Prophet, Alexander Hale Smith and David Hyrum Smith, came to Utah as missionaries. While here, they publicly debated with their cousin, Joseph F. Smith, Hyrum's son.

The Church of Zion

Another apostate movement known as the Church of Zion or the Godbeite movement was organized in Utah in December of 1869. They also invited the prophet's son, Joseph, to become head of their faction; but they were too late, and their church disintegrated within a few months.

This movement involved men who had been important in the Church and who are mentioned elsewhere in this work. Some of them were William S. Godbe, E. L. T. Harrison, T. B. H. Stenhouse, Eli Kelsey, and Henry W. Lawrence.

DEVELOPMENT OF MINING IN UTAH

There had been a beginning of mining in Utah, principally in southern Utah in Beaver County before the coming of the California Volunteers; but after their arrival Colonel P. E. Connor, who looked upon the Mormons as "disloyal and traitorous to the core," gave his soldiers days off whenever it would not interfere with their military duty—and there was very little for soldiers to do—to go prospecting. His purpose was to advertise widely all mineral discoveries so that gentiles would come in such large numbers they would soon be able to outvote the Mormons at the polls.

Brigham Young, realizing that the survival of the Saints depended upon an agricultural economy, had recommended they leave mining alone so that they could grow crops. This left the mining field wide open to the gentiles. In order to promote his desires, General Connor established a newspaper called the *Union Vedette,* which was at first published at Fort Douglas but later in the center of Salt Lake City. Its first number came off the press November 30, 1863, with Captain C. H. Hempstead as the editor. He had assumed a hostile attitude toward the Saints and announced that General Connor would provide protection to all miners who would come to Utah and that offenders against them "would be tried as public enemies and punished to the utmost extent of martial law," as if the Saints would do bodily harm to anyone who came to Utah for mining purposes. [14]

Although President Young preferred that mining in Utah be left alone, he took a philosophical attitude toward the situation and said that if precious metals were discovered, the Lord would make it to the advantage of the people and the Church.

In later years both Captain Hempstead and General Connor, who made their homes in Utah after the Civil War, changed their attitude toward the Mormons. In fact, by 1872 Captain Hempstead, now a practicing lawyer, was Brigham Young's counselor and advocate; and in 1874 when Brigham Young was on trial in Judge McKean's court, General Connor offered to go his bail up to $100,000.

A PROVOST GUARD IN SALT LAKE CITY

In July 1864 General Connor established a provost guard in the middle of Salt Lake City. It was located across the street to the south of the south gate of the temple grounds in a building owned by the Church which had been rented to Captain Stover as a military storehouse. Stover was ordered to move his goods to Fort Douglas. Captain Hempstead, editor of the *Union Vedette,* was appointed provost marshal.

Occupation of the guardhouse was effected Sunday afternoon at 2:00 p.m. just as the people were gathering for church in the tabernacle. The citizens felt that, like the establishment of Fort Douglas, the guardhouse was an insult to them. They petitioned Governor Doty and the mayor of the city for its removal, but it was a time of war and nothing could be done about it. It stayed, with nothing much for the soldiers to do except to arrest a young man now and then, who, in order to irritate the soldiers would shout as he passed by "Hurrah for Jeff Davis!" [15] Those arrested would have to walk back and forth in front of the guardhouse with heavy bags of sand on their shoulders.

HISTORIC BUILDINGS

Old Council House

The first public building, not counting the boweries which

were constructed as temporary meeting places, was the council house on the southwest corner of South Temple and Main Street, which is the site presently occupied by Walgreen Drug Store (the Kennecott Building).[16] It was built from tithing funds and was designed as a "general council house" for the Church.[17] Construction began on February 26, 1849, and the building was completed in December of 1850. It was built of red sandstone, forty-five feet square and two stories high. The interior consisted of one assembly hall and two offices on each floor.

In addition to an office for Brigham Young, rooms were set aside on July 7, 1852, for administration of endowment ordinances and were used for this purpose until the Endowment House was constructed in 1855.[18]

The building was also used by the provisional state of Deseret as a state house and was temporarily purchased from the Church by the territorial government for $20,000.[19] The territorial legislature met in it for a number of years; it also housed the territorial public library until the construction of a new and larger building in 1866, which became known as the council hall.

In 1858, the council house was used as the meeting place for the peace conference in settling the Utah War. Beginning in 1869 it was occupied by the University of Deseret for a number of years. It was destroyed by fire in 1883.

Social Hall

The next public building to be erected in Salt Lake City was the social hall, which was built on the east side of State Street between South Temple and First South Streets. It was constructed in 1852 and was opened for use on January 1, 1853. The building was made of adobe and was thirty-three feet by seventy-three feet, having two floors—a half-basement and a main floor. The building was used for social and semisocial functions: balls, feasts, amateur theatricals, and birthday anniversaries of prominent persons. Priesthood meetings were often held there, and even the legislature and district court are known to have held sessions there.[20]

Captain Richard F. Burton of Great Britain, visiting in the summer of 1860, regretted that he was not there when the social season was functioning; he described a social that was held on the previous February 7, 1860, and said that it was a very

elaborate affair, beginning at 4:00 p.m. and lasting until 5:00 305
a.m. He said the party began and ended with prayer.[21]

The building had a long life of service to the people, but in
May, 1922, it was torn down to make way for buildings of a
different age.

The Old and New Tabernacles

On April 6, 1852, the first tabernacle to be built by the
Saints was dedicated.[22] It had been built in 1851-52 and was
located in the southwest corner of the temple block where the
assembly hall is presently located, except that it ran lengthwise
north and south, whereas the assembly hall has its greatest
dimensions east and west. The building was 64 by 126 feet and
would comfortably seat 2,200 people, making it the largest hall
in any frontier town in western America.[23] The pulpit was
situated near the center of the west wall.

At the semiannual conference on October 6, 1852, it would
not hold the people who wanted to attend. The need for a
larger place was recognized, and a bowery 138 by 156 feet was
constructed to the north of it, providing seating space for 8,000
people. But this provided only shade, being covered with brush;
it did not protect from wind, cold, and rain, so that it could be
used only in the summertime.

One reason for the need of such a large gathering place was
that the wards did not yet have their own meeting houses, and
general church services were usually held twice each Sunday for
everyone to attend.

Because of this dire need, a "new" tabernacle was begun in
1864 and was completed without the balcony in 1867. In April
1870 the present balcony was completed, increasing the seating
capacity to over 8,000 people and breaking up the echoes that
had previously caused so much difficulty. Without its present
balcony with an air space behind it, the building would not have
the fine accoustical qualities that the people enjoy today.[24]

The building is 150 by 250 feet and has twenty large double
doors so that it can be completely evacuated in five minutes.

The west end of the building contains the choir seats and the
pulpits and seats for the General Authorities or other dignitaries
that might be presiding at various other meetings. Also in the
west end is the famous organ that adds so much to the regular
Sunday broadcasts which have been given for so many years.

Under the choir seats in the west end is a small auditorium

The old Tabernacle, built 1851-52. *Courtesy of Fred Auerbach.*

containing a baptismal font where the sacred ordinance of baptism can be performed.

In 1969 a full basement was constructed in order to accommodate the vast amount of televising equipment that is so necessary for the broadcasting of conferences and other programs to the various parts of the world.

Seventies' Hall

The Seventies' Hall was situated across the street and one block south of the Social Hall and was located between First and Second South Streets. It was an adobe building also and was thirty by fifty feet, inside measurement. It was begun on November 27, 1850, and was dedicated on December 25, 1854; construction was under the supervision of Joseph Young, senior president of the First Council of the Seventy. It cost $3,500 to build and was at first known as the Seventies' Hall of Science but was later shortened to Seventies' Hall. It was built as a meeting place and classrooms for the seventies, the foreign missionary force of the Church.[25] The building was torn down many years ago, but that it once existed represents the eagerness for learning on the part of the early seventies of the Church.

The new Tabernacle under construction, built 1864-67. *Courtesy of Church Historical Department.*

Endowment House

In the northwest corner of the temple block a "temporary temple" known as the Endowment House was completed on April 27, 1855, and dedicated on May 5. That same day ordinance work was begun; it was continued until the spring of 1889, when President Woodruff ordered the building torn down. It was an adobe two-story structure with two one-story wings, standing where the present-day visitors' center is located.

The Salt Lake Temple

On July 28, 1847, Brigham Young, in the presence of several pioneers, "designated the site for the temple block between the forks of City Creek."[26] At the April, 1851, general conference, the erection of the temple was officially authorized by the vote of the people.[27]

At conference on October 9, 1852, upon the motion of Heber C. Kimball, the Saints voted to build the temple out of the best materials that could be furnished in the mountains of North America and to give the Presidency choice of where the stone and other materials should be obtained.[28] The vote was unanimous. The material finally accepted for building purposes

308 was said to be "temple granite" but in reality it was syenite, found up Little Cottonwood Canyon at the point where the Church storage vaults are presently located.[29]

On February 14, 1853, the groundbreaking ceremonies took place in the presence of thousands of people, and the laying of the cornerstones on April 6, 1853. The stones had been hauled about twenty miles by horses and ox teams until 1873 when a spur of the railroad was completed to the quarry.

Three other temples—Logan, St. George, and Manti—were built in Utah before the Salt Lake Temple was finally completed. On April 6, 1892, 40,000 people watched the laying of the capstone of the temple; and on April 6, 1893, just forty years to the day after the laying of the cornerstones, the Salt Lake Temple was dedicated, having been completed toward evening the previous day.

The dimensions of the temple were 99 feet north and south and 186½ feet east and west through the center of the building; the height of the walls was 167 feet 6 inches, with the east center tower 210 feet high and the west center tower 204 feet high. It was constructed at a cost of $4,000,000 in materials and labor.

The State House

On October 4, 1851, the Utah legislature created the county of Millard and designated a city to be built therein by the name of Fillmore in honor of President Fillmore, to be the first official capital of the territory which the people hoped would soon be a state.[30] The actual site of the city was chosen by a group of fifteen men and three boys on October 29, 1851. Anson Call, then a citizen of Davis County, was authorized to effect a county organization.

The reason for moving the capital to that region was that it was far more central to the territory than Salt Lake City, and the Pauvan Valley would sustain a large and growing population. Also, locating the capital there would encourage settlers to move to that region.[31]

The capitol building as designed by Truman O. Angel was to be in the shape of a Greek cross having four wings joined with a rotunda sixty feet in diameter and covered by a Moorish dome.[32] The wings were to be forty-one by sixty-one feet, two stories high with basements; and the building was to be constructed of rough hammered sandstone which was found locally in abundance.[33]

The south wing of the building was completed in December of 1855 at a cost of $32,000 which was already $12,000 more than the federal government had appropriated for the whole building. The 1855-56 territorial legislature met there in session for forty days. But it was to be the only complete session ever held in the building because life in the new partially built town with its lack of accommodations was found to be unacceptable to the legislators, who preferred the comforts of Salt Lake City. The federal government failed to make any further appropriations for the completion of public buildings at Fillmore; therefore, on December 15, 1856, the seat of the government was removed from Fillmore City to Great Salt Lake City until otherwise provided by law. [34]

Thus the building as planned was never completed, and the south wing is used today as a museum by the Utah State Division of Parks and Recreation. [35]

Salt Lake Theatre

The Salt Lake Theatre was constructed in 1861 and 1862. It was a close duplicate both outside and inside of the Drury Lane Theatre in London, England. [36] Mr. William H. Folsom was the architect, and the interior design was the work of E. L. T. Harrison. [37] It was built on the northwest corner of State Street and First South Street facing south. The exterior of the building was Grecian doric, the stage sixty-two feet deep by twenty-eight feet high.

In his dedicatory prayer Daniel H. Wells offered up the wish that the building might be destroyed rather than used for ungodly purposes. [38] It soon became the center of much of the recreational and cultural activity in the valley. Brigham Young had his rocking chair installed in the center of the front row, but "the left box on the proscenium was also reserved for him." [39] He insisted that no tragedies be performed in it, for life held too much tragedy already; he wanted the people to be amused and entertained.

Most of the funds for building the theater came from the resale of goods (tents, stoves, sugar, and other groceries). Hiram B. Clawson, Brigham Young's agent, had purchased these items from the auction sale of army goods held at the time Camp Floyd was abandoned in 1861. Glass, nails, and other building materials purchased at the sale were used.

Most of the people who worked on the building were paid in

310

The old capitol building in Fillmore, Utah, built in 1855. *Courtesy of LaMar C. Berrett.*

tickets to the theater to be used after it opened. Most of the families in the community were represented on the workrolls.

The building had a capacity of 1,500. Tickets in the upper- most gallery were as low as 37½ cents,[40] but because of the scarcity of money the pay was often in the form of goods. According to Artemus Ward, in addition to money, the receipts at the theater box office for one day included:

> twenty bushels of wheat, five of corn, four of potatoes, two of oats, four of salt, two hams, one live pig, one wolf skin, five pounds of honey in the comb, sixteen strings of sausages, one catskin, one churn (two families came in on this; it was a most ingenious churn and fetched butter in five minutes by rapid grinding), one set of children's em- broidered undergarments, one keg of applesauce, a dog (a cross between a scotch terrier and a Welsh Rabbit), and a German silver coffin plate.[41]

The first year all of the plays presented were those put on by local amateurs, but later some of the finest actors in England and America performed there. Mr. Samuel Bowles, editor of the *Springfield Republican,* visited the theater in 1865 with

Salt Lake Theatre under construction in 1861. *Courtesy of Fred Auerbach.*

Schuyler Colfax, at that time Speaker of the House in the United States. Bowles wrote of it:

> The building is itself a rare triumph of art and enterprise. No eastern city of one hundred thousand inhabitants—remember Salt Lake City has less than twenty thousand—possesses so fine a theatrical structure. It ranks, alike in capacity and elegance of structure and finish, along with the opera-houses and academies of music of Boston, New York, Philadelphia, Chicago and Cincinnati.[42]

BATTLE OF BEAR RIVER

In addition to aiding somewhat the economy of Salt Lake City, there was one useful act the California Volunteers accomplished while they were stationed in Utah. This act occurred when Connor took three hundred of his soldiers north in pursuit of a band of renegade Indians from various tribes who had gathered together to prey off the whites. They did not bother the Mormons so much as they did other whites who were passing through the country. The incident that led to their defeat was the killing of some non-Mormon miners who had left

312 the gold field in the Dakotas and were passing through Cache Valley on their way west. The purpose of the killing was to take their tents, food, and other property.

Judge Kinney issued warrants for the arrest of three chiefs, and Isaac Gibbs applied to Colonel Connor at Camp Douglas for aid. Three days later they left Fort Douglas with three hundred soldiers and Porter Rockwell as their guide. They passed along the west side of Cache Valley in cold January weather with snow on the ground. The soldiers found the Indians camped in a ravine through which Battle Creek entered Bear River about twelve miles from the present town of Franklin, Idaho. They attacked from the front and the flank January 29, 1863, at about 6:00 a.m.; the battle lasted until 10:00 a.m. In the cross fire not only were most of the Indian men killed but, unfortunately, a number of women and children also. Chiefs Bear Hunter, Saguitch, and Lehi were killed and the band almost annihilated. It is believed, however, that Pocatello and Sanpitch were there but escaped with about fifty Indian men.[43] Accounts differ as to the number of Indians slain, ranging from 200 to 368 (the latter said to have been counted by an eye witness) besides many of the wounded who died later. About ninety of those killed were said to have been women and children.[44] The soldiers burned about seventy Indian lodges and burned a large amount of grain, implements, and other property that had been stolen from various white parties. About two hundred horses and many rifles were confiscated.

Fourteen soldiers were killed outright, and fifty-nine were wounded, eight of whom died within the next ten days. Colonel Connor requisitioned a number of sleighs from the bishop of Franklin to haul the wounded back to Camp Douglas. This defeat broke the power of the renegade Indians in the north. Now it was safe for travelers passing through northern Utah and southern Idaho, also for the people, flocks, and herds of the Mormon settlements in Cache Valley and points north. It also made possible the settlement of new and favorable sights in the north that had been previously considered unsafe.

EXPANSION OF SETTLEMENTS IN
THE EARLY 1860s

Two major colony extensions were made in the early 1860s, the first over the rim of the Great Basin in the southwest corner of Utah, the second in a rather semiarctic region in the north-

east corner of Utah and the southeast corner of Idaho where the
valley floor was nearly six thousand feet above sea level. There
were other major contrasts between these two areas.

The first to be settled was the southern region. The call was
made to settle the region after the outbreak of the Civil War,
principally to increase the number of settlements already in the
area for growing cotton because they would no longer be able
to obtain it from the southern states.

Cotton culture had been tried first in the southern Utah
settlements in 1855; since that time some cotton had been
grown, but these were only small amounts. The southern settlements needed strengthening in other areas besides cotton
growing, too. In May and June of 1861 President Brigham
Young led a large company of Saints into the southern country
to look over the situation. The group included Daniel H. Wells,
George A. Smith, John Taylor, Wilford Woodruff, Abraham O.
Smoot, Edward Hunter (Presiding Bishop), Albert Carrington,
and others. They decided to strengthen the settlement along the
Santa Clara Creek and the Rio Virgin in the Rio Virgin valley.
At the time there were only seventy-nine families in the whole
of Washington County—twenty in Washington; twenty in Santa
Clara Fort; eleven in Virgin City; ten in Toquerville; six in
Grafton; six in Adventure; four in Gunlock; and two in Harris-
burgh.

At the fall conference on October 7, 1861, President Brigham
Young called for volunteers to go to Washington County to
raise cotton, sugar, grapes, olives, and other warm-country
crops. Many of the people thought that only those who had had
experience with these crops were expected to volunteer. Others
had heard of the bleakness of the country and had no desire to
go. As a result, only one man volunteered.[45]

The following Sunday, October 13, President Young read
over two hundred names from the stand calling people to go.
About one hundred others were added later. These people were
from Salt Lake County, Utah, Sanpete, Davis, Weber, Tooele,
Juab, Millard, and Beaver counties. In the end, less than two
hundred out of three hundred families accepted the call. The
response of Wandle Mace was quite typical of those who did
accept:

> To my great surprise my name was among the number
> of 300. When on the previous Sunday volunteers were
> called for, I supposed only those who were familiar with

the cultivation and manufacture of those products were wanted. I had not the remotest idea that I would be needed, nor did I feel the least inclination to go. But as soon as I heard my name called, my feelings changed, and I not only felt willing, but anxious to respond to the call.[46]

In addition to those called, a Swiss company of emigrants consisting of fifty or sixty people who had arrived in Salt Lake City in October continued right on to the Rio Virgin valley and settled the Santa Clara of today. A ward was organized there on December 22, 1861.

More than four hundred wagons were used to convey the new colonists south in the fall of 1861. Some of the settlers went into the upper valley of the Rio Virgin, but the majority settled in the lower part of Rio Virgin valley. There, in January 1862, a site was selected and was later named by Brigham Young in honor of George A. Smith.

Although the sudden spring floods caused a great deal of trouble and the rainfall was often scarce, the Saints persisted through the years and won the battle of the elements. The building of Call's Landing on the Colorado led in 1865 to three settlements on the lower tributary of the Rio Virgin called Muddy Creek. These were St. Thomas (after Thomas S. Smith), Overton, and St. Joseph. Today, St. Thomas is known as Mayor and all three settlements are in Lincoln County, Nevada.

As early as 1862 a group of Latter-day Saints from Cache Valley explored the Bear Lake region. After Connor's battle with the renegade Indians at Battle Creek in January 1863, it appeared as if the Bear Lake region would be safe for settlement. On August 23, 1863, Brigham Young called a meeting at Logan, the purpose of which was to get a company together to take immediate possession of the Bear Lake valley.[47] Charles C. Rich was selected to lead a settlement into the valley. The first settlers arrived on September 26, 1863, having taken eight days to travel the last forty-six miles over the mountains from Cache Valley. They first made settlements on the west side of the valley where the parent settlement was made. North Twin Creek, the parent settlement, became known as Paris, a corruption of the name Perris, it having been named in honor of the surveyor, Fred T. Perris.

In all, about forty-eight men, forty women, and thirty children stayed in the valley the first winter. Not all who had come stayed because they discovered that even at the end of September the weather was extremely cold. It snowed on September 28, five days after the first wagons arrived. Within a few days after the first arrivals, Thomas Sleight recorded in his diary "several persons have arrived and gone back dissatisfied."[48] But he was among those who stayed. The settlers spent the first winter in thirty-four log cabins. Thomas Sleight and wife spent the winter in a cabin with another young couple, Charles Atkin and his wife. They drew a line down the center of the room from the middle of the front door, and each couple lived on their side of the line. It is said they lived in perfect harmony for the winter.

In 1864 the Utah legislature created Richland County out of the eastern part of Cache County. The people thought that Paris was in Utah, but in 1872 they learned that the northern settlements of Bear Lake valley and the northern half of the lake were in Idaho. These northern settlements became Bear Lake County, Idaho, whereas the southern settlements—Garden City, Laketown and Randolph—became officially Rich County, Utah.

The problems of the Bear Lakers were the opposite of those in Washington County, Utah. Although Bear Lake valley had good rainfall, many streams flowing from the mountains, a beautiful lake filled with trout and other fish, and lots of good grassland, the short growing season limited the valley to certain crops; often the wheat would freeze before it was completely ripe. But of necessity they harvested the frozen wheat and made bread out of it, saying "it beat nothin' all to pieces." Through the first few years many became discouraged and left, but others endured and more came until the valley had more than eighteen settlements.

Many stories are told about the Bear Lake winters. One of the original settlers said that they always had "nine months winter and three months d − − − late in the fall." Another who came later was asked by a visitor how long the Bear Lake winters were and he replied: "I don't know, you see I've only been here four years."

In later years, settlers were sent from the Bear Lake region into parts of Wyoming and into other parts of southeastern Idaho.

Footnotes

[1]Ilene Kingsbury, "Salute to the Pony Express," *Utah Historical Quarterly* 28:131-34.

316   [2]*CHC*, 4:548.

[3]*CHC*, 4:550.

[4]*CHC*, 5:2. *See also Millennial Star* 23:29-30.

[5]*CHC*, 5:11.

[6]Orson F. Whitney, *Popular History of Utah* (Salt Lake City: Deseret News Press, 1916), p. 180.

[7]*JD*, 10:107.

[8]*CHC*, 5:25.

[9]Frank W. McGhie, "The Life and Intrigues of Walter Murray Gibson," (Master's thesis, Brigham Young University, June 1958), p. 66. For a more detailed account read Chapter 7 of this thesis.

[10]Gwynn Barrett, "Walter Murray Gibson: The Shepherd Saint of Lanai Revisited," *Utah Historical Quarterly* 40:162.

[11]Joseph Morris, *The "Spirit Prevails"* (San Francisco: George S. Dove and Co., 1886), pp. 379, 491, 509, 549. The prisoners' friends and relatives had reason to be concerned about the safety of the prisoners, as attested to by some of the statements in Morris's purported revelations:

> 19 January 1862. "And behold, I give unto you a commandment,—you shall stop the wicked course of those apostates, even should you have to put them to death in order to do so." p. 379.

> 3 April 1862. "You wish to know what you are to do if the faithful of my people will not go forth at your command and put traitors to death. . . . If they refuse to obey your command, I will come and slay them instantly." p. 491.

[12]Morris. "You need not to fear any authority in this territory, nor yet in the United States. . . ." p. 379. "No earthly power can approach you; therefore, you have nothing to fear." p. 581.

[13]These were the Waukesha, Yellowstone, and Beloit branches of Strang's church in Wisconsin. At first they adopted the name the "New Organization," but it was later changed to the Reorganized Church of Jesus Christ of Latter Day Saints.

[14]Whitney, p. 196.

[15]Whitney, p. 197. *See also CHC*, 5:56.

[16]*CHC*, 4:13.

[17]James R. Clark, *Messages of the First Presidency* (Salt Lake City: Bookcraft, 1965), 1:352.

[18]*CHC*, 4:13.

[19]This building was moved to a place just south of the present state capitol building where it serves as a museum today (1972).

[20]Whitney, pp. 89-90.

[21]Richard F. Burton, *City of the Saints and Across the Rocky Mountains to California* (New York: Harper and Brothers, 1862), pp. 230-32.

[22]Clark, 2:92.

[23]*CHC*, 4:14-15.

[24]For a well-written history of the construction of the "new" tabernacle, see Stewart Grow, "A Historical Study of the Construction of the Salt Lake Tabernacle" (Master's thesis, Brigham Young University, 1947).

[25]*CHC*, 4:14.

[26]*CHC*, 3:280.

[27]James E. Talmage, *The House of the Lord* (Salt Lake City: Bookcraft, 1962), p. 137.

[28]*JD*, 1:162.

[29]Talmage, p. 143.

[30]*CHC*, 4:10-11.

[31]*CHC*, 4:11.

[32]Paul Goeldner, *Utah Catalog American Buildings Survey* (Salt Lake City: Utah Heritage Foundation, 1969), p. 24.

[33]*Atlantic Monthly* (May 1959), p. 573.

[34]*Deseret News*, 15 December 1856.

[35]Goeldner, p. 24.

[36]*CHC*, 5:132, footnote 1.

[37]Goeldner, p. 23.

[38]George D. Pyper, *The Romance of an Old Playhouse* (Salt Lake City: Deseret News Press, 1937), p. 92.

[39]Ila Fisher Maughan, *Pioneer Theatre in the Desert* (Salt Lake City: Deseret Book Co., 1961), p. 93.

[40]Pyper, p. 93.

[41]This information was taken from a loose picture of the Salt Lake Theatre. The writing was credited to Artemus Ward. The picture is in possession of Russell R. Rich.

[42]Samuel Bowles, *Across the Continent* (Springfield, Mass.: Samuel Bowles and Co.; New York: Hurd and Houghton, 1865), p. 103. *See also CHC*, 5:132, footnote 3.

[43]Whitney, p. 191, footnote.

[44]Hubert Howe Bancroft, *History of Utah* (1890; reprint ed., Salt Lake City: Bookcraft, 1964), p. 632, including footnote 76.

[45]Ivan J. Barrett, "History of the Cotton Mission and Cotton Culture" (Master's thesis, Brigham Young University, May 1947), p. 105. This is an excellent work for anyone who desires to read a more detailed history of the cotton mission.

[46]Journal of Wandle Mace, Church Historical Department, p. 223. *See also* Barrett, p. 107.

[47]Russell R. Rich, *Land of the Sky-Blue Water* (Provo, Utah: Brigham Young University Press, September 1963), p. 18.

[48]Rich, p. 22.

15

Impact of the Iron Horse

In 1865 the Speaker of the House of Representatives, Schuyler Colfax, and his party, including Samuel Bowles, visited Utah. Bowles, who believed the coming of the railroad would be the doom of the Mormon Church, suggested this to Brigham Young, who replied: "I wouldn't give much for a religion which could not withstand the coming of a railroad."[1]

The Latter-day Saints quickly recognized the value of a medium of communication and transportation, and in June, 1832, shortly after the organization of the Church, their first newspaper, the *Evening and Morning Star,* came off the press in Independence, Missouri. This was followed by other periodicals such as the *Messenger and Advocate* (Ohio), *Elder's Journal* (Ohio and Northern Missouri), *Times and Seasons* (Nauvoo, Illinois), *Millennial Star* (Great Britain), *Frontier Guardian* (Council Bluffs, Iowa), *Deseret News* (Utah), *Improvement Era* (Utah), and many others.

While the Saints were crossing the plains, they used various means to send mail and messages between camps and among the scattered Saints, such as leaving a message on a buffalo skull along the road. But soon more efficient methods were employed: letters and notes were left in mileposts and when practical, messengers were used. As the pioneers traveled west along the Platte River they marked out a future route for a transcontinental railroad and spoke of it almost daily.[2]

319

After the arrival of the Saints in Utah, the gentiles mistakenly believed that the Mormons wanted to remain in isolation. The Latter-day Saints had not forgotten, however, that they were entrusted with the gospel of Jesus Christ and with the responsibility to take its message throughout the world. To remain in isolation would make impossible their carrying out this duty. Before the first government mail arrived in the valley on September 9, 1850, the Saints had been carrying the mail on their own as best they could. After 1850 they were, for many years, constantly requesting better mail service.

On March 3, 1852, the legislature of Utah petitioned the United States Congress for the construction of (1) a telegraph line from the East via Salt Lake City "to San Diego, San Francisco, or Astoria";[3] (2) a national turnpike road "from the mouth of the Nebraska River via South Pass and Great Salt Lake City to Sacramento, California"; (3) a "national central railroad from some eligible point on the Mississippi or Missouri River to San Diego, San Francisco, Sacramento, Astoria," or other places on the Pacific Coast.[4] From time to time the Utah legislature continued to petition Congress for these things until they became a reality. But, of the three—the telegraph, a national highway, and the railroad—the last was destined to make the greatest difference in the lives of the Latter-day Saints.

The first to come was the telegraph, arriving in Salt Lake City in the fall of 1861. By 1865 Church members began building their own telegraph lines running north and south through the colonies. By 1867 they had built 500 miles of line at a cost of $160 a mile. By November 6, 1871, the Mormon line—Deseret Telegraph—was completed into the Bear Lake valley in Idaho.

CONGRESSIONAL APPROVAL OF A NATIONAL RAILROAD

Although it was never acted upon, Senator Benton of Missouri introduced a bill in Congress in 1850 calling for construction of a railroad to the Pacific. During 1853 and 1854 nine railroad routes were surveyed across the continent, one of which was through Utah. The national conventions of the Republican and Democratic parties of 1856 and 1860 mentioned a Pacific railroad in their platforms. On July 1, 1862, President Lincoln signed a congressional bill authorizing the construction of a railroad to the Pacific Coast from near

Omaha, Nebraska, "as a measure of military protection for the
preservation of the Union."

The railroad was to be built by private companies but with the encouragement and financial aid of the government. Under several acts between July 1862 and July 1864 the type of aid was specified. The government was to lend money to the companies for thirty years, payable in gold, bearing 6 percent interest. For each mile of railroad built from Missouri to the base of the Rocky Mountains a subsidy of $16,000 would be provided; for 300 miles through the Rockies $48,000 per mile; for the sections between the Rockies and the base of the Sierra Nevada and from the western base of the Sierra Nevada to the Sacramento River, $32,000 per mile; through the Sierra Nevada the same as the Rockies, i.e., $48,000 per mile.

In addition to these subsidies, Congress provided an outright gift of twenty sections of land (12,800 acres) per mile. Although this land was to be every other section for a distance of twenty miles on either side of the tracks, Congress allowed the companies considerable latitude in selecting the land. This subsidy amounted to approximately 25,000,000 acres.

Builders of the First Transcontinental Railroad

The act of Congress authorizing the railroad also provided for organization of the Union Pacific Railroad Company. This company was to begin construction of the railroad at Omaha, Nebraska, as designated by President Abraham Lincoln. In addition, the Central Pacific Railroad, which had been organized under the laws of California in 1861, was to build the western part. Although ground was broken at Sacramento on January 8, 1863, and at Omaha on December 2 of the same year, progress was slow. Finally the government raised the subsidies to the figures already stated, and in 1866 work gradually got under way again.

Anxious to obtain more government subsidies, the Central Pacific hired nearly 15,000 Chinese laborers, and as many as 10,000 laborers sometimes worked on constructing the Union Pacific. These men, who were a mixture of Irish, Scottish, German, and Scandinavian, included many veterans of the Civil War, plus hundreds of Mormons on certain sections of the road. President Brigham Young signed a contract with the Union Pacific in May, 1868, to build the road from the head of Echo Canyon to Salt Lake City (ninety miles) if the road came that way, or from Echo Canyon to the lake northwest of Ogden

322 (about forty miles) if the final decision were to bypass Salt Lake City by going around the north end of the lake. When the Saints learned that the railroad would be built around the north end of the lake, they held a mass meeting on June 10, 1868, in Salt Lake City to persuade the contractors and the nation to pass through the city, but they were unsuccessful in their efforts.

Three prominent Latter-day Saints, Ezra T. Benson, an apostle; Chauncey West, a bishop; and Lorin Farr, a stake president, signed a joint contract to build approximately 200 miles of the Central Pacific Railroad from Humbolt Wells, Nevada, eastward to Ogden. With their contract and that of Brigham Young's, hundreds of Mormons received gainful employment. With the Central Pacific extending eastward and the Union Pacific extending westward, and with Collis P. Huntington of the Central Pacific and General Dodge of the Union Pacific lobbying Congress to determine where the junction of the two railroads should be, they both rushed to build railroad beds side by side west of Ogden. The Union Pacific reached Ogden on March 8, 1869, where the citizens held a celebration at 5:00 p.m. Many banners were raised, one greeting affably, "Hail to the highway of nations, Utah bids you welcome."[5] Speeches were made by Lorin Farr, mayor of Ogden, Franklin D. Richards, one of the Twelve Apostles, and a probate judge of Weber County.

Rival Gentile Capital

Because some of the gentile merchants who enjoyed patronage from Church members were constantly fighting the Church and the community, President Brigham Young inaugurated a boycott of their businesses in 1865. He also advised Latter-day Saints to begin entering the merchandising field. Eventually the boycott began to tell: in December of 1866 twenty-three merchants had volunteered to sell their stock for 75 percent of the value and leave the territory, providing the Church would buy them out and collect the money owed them by Church members. President Young was too shrewd to be taken in by this maneuver. The markup on their goods was far higher than 25 percent. He told them that Mormon merchants would also like to sell out under such favorable circumstances, adding, "Your withdrawal from the territory is not a matter about which we feel any anxiety. So far as we are concerned, you are at liberty to stay or go, as you please."[6] He explained that the Saints

were not averse to doing business with gentiles simply because
they were gentiles; such was "in direct opposition to the genius
of our religion."

There is a class, however, who are doing business in the
Territory, who for years have been the avowed enemies of
this community. The disrupture and overthrow of the
community have been the objects which they have perti-
naciously sought to accomplish. They have, therefore, used
every energy and all the means at their command to put
into circulation the foulest slanders about the old citizens. . . . While soliciting the patronage of the people, and
deriving their support from them, they have, in the most
shameless and abandoned manner, used the means thus
obtained to destroy the very people whose favor they
found it to their interest to court. They have done all in
their power to encourage violations of law, to retard the
administration of justice, to foster vice and vicious institutions, to oppose the unanimously expressed will of the
people, to increase disorder, and to change our city from a
condition of peace and quietude to lawlessness and
anarchy. They have donated liberally to sustain a corrupt
and venal press, which has given publicity to the most
atrocious libels respecting the old citizens.

And have they not had their emissaries in Washington to
misrepresent and vilify the people of this Territory? Have
they not kept liquor and surreptitiously sold it in violation
of law, and endeavored to bias the minds of the Judiciary
to give decisions favorable to their own practices? Have
they not entered into secret combinations to resist the
laws and to thwart their healthy operation and refused to
pay their taxes and to give the support to schools required
by law?

What claims can such persons have upon the patronage
of this community? And what community on the earth
would be so besotled as to uphold and foster men whose
sin is to destroy them? Have we not the right to trade at
whatever store we please? Or does the Constitution of the
United States bind us to enter the stores of our deadliest
enemies and purchase of them? [7]

Two days later President Young further clarified his position
on the matter by stating again that he was not implicating the

324 gentiles and Jews who were honest and honorable, and that he still intended to do business with them.

He gave two other reasons for refusing to accept the offer of the gentile merchants: (1) By accepting it and bringing about a wholesale gentile exodus, it would look to the rest of the country as if the Saints were persecuting the gentiles, and another army would be sent to Utah; (2) The exodus would have been only temporary because with the coming of the railroad many more gentiles and gentile merchants would not have been bound by any previous agreement.

Wallace Stegner states that, as a last resort these merchants who were driven out of business by the boycott gravitated to the railroad. They persuaded the Union Pacific, for a consideration of an every-other-house lot, to survey a townsite at the north end of Great Salt Lake, on Bear River Bay. Here, they were determined to build a gentile capital that would not only become the junction city of the railroad, but would "outshine Salt Lake City."[8] Corinne was founded in March of 1869, and within two weeks there were fifteen hundred people and three hundred buildings on the site—before the railroad had reached there. The first Protestant church buildings in Utah were built there—a Methodist church, a Presbyterian church, and an Episcopalian church. It also contained twenty-nine saloons and two dance halls. Boats such as the Kate Connor, the City of Corinne, the Rosie Brown, and the Pluribustah were built to ply the Bear River and bring in ore for the smelter. By 1870 the first anti-Mormon political party, the Liberal party, was organized in Corinne. The law firm of Johnson and Underdunk developed a mail-order business for granting divorces at $2.50 each; "the petitioner didn't have to be present, and could even get alimony if he wanted it." For a short time it appeared that Corinne would soon monopolize all east-west freight service, plus additional business to Montana's mining centers.

Perhaps to counter this trend President Young donated 133 acres of land in the city of Ogden to the railroads. Congress soon decided the railroads would make their junction at Promontory Point, fifty-three miles northwest of Ogden, and Ogden, not Corinne, would be the terminal city.

Wedding of the Rails

On May 10, 1869, the line was completed. The two railroads had made parallel road beds side by side for fifty-three miles from Promontory to Ogden. Later the Central Pacific purchased the roadbed of the Union Pacific and abandoned their own. The last railroad tie was made of California laurel wood and had been French polished. On its face was a silver plate with the inscription—"The last tie laid on the completion of the Pacific Railroad, May 10, 1869". Presented by West Evans and manufactured by Strahle and Hughes of San Francisco, a spike of gold, silver, and iron was presented by Arizona to be driven into the last tie; Nevada presented a silver spike, and California presented a gold spike made of twenty-three twenty-dollar gold pieces. Approximately fifteen hundred people were present for the ceremonies, including the dignitaries of both railroads, Governor Stanford of California, Governor Safford of Arizona, and the Honorable F. A. Fryth of Nevada. Unfortunately neither Brigham Young nor Governor Charles Durkee of Utah was present, although many other Utah dignitaries were there. Governor Durkee had spent the previous six months in the East and returned to Utah on May 10, the very day of the celebration. President Brigham Young, after the close of the April conference meeting, had left on a tour of the southern settlements and did not return to Salt Lake City until May 11. Brigham Young sent Bishop John Sharp to represent both the Church and the contracting firm of Young and Sharp. Ezra T. Benson, Lorin Farr, and Chauncey West represented the contracting firm of Benson, Farr, and West.[10]

The people of Salt Lake City held a celebration in the city simultaneously with the one held at Promontory. Although Governor Durkee was fatigued from his trip, he attended and made a brief speech. At the Promontory celebration the telegraph wires of the Union Pacific were attached to a sledgehammer, and the wires of the Central Pacific were attached to a spike. At 12:47 p.m. using the wired sledge, both Leland Stanford of the Central Pacific and Mr. Thomas C. Durant of the Union Pacific swung at the wired spike but each in turn missed. Nevertheless the telegrapher signaled three dots which triggered a celebration in every major city in the country.[11] After the last spike was driven, the telegraph wires sent the message that the work had been completed. To President Grant at Washington, D.C. went this telegram:

Promontory Summit, Utah,
May 10, 1869,

The last rail is laid, the last spike driven. The Pacific Railroad is completed. The point of junction is 1086 miles west of the Missouri River, and 690 miles east of Sacramento City.[12]

Immediately from the guns in San Francisco a salvo of 220 shots were fired in celebration. The valuable spikes driven into the last rail were not left there, but were replaced by ordinary iron spikes.[13] Not even the silver-plated laurel tie was left.

Both railroads failed to pay their Mormon contractors on time. This put them and their subcontractors in an embarrassing position. The contract with the Union Pacific had been signed by President Young, representing the Church, for approximately $2,125,000. A contract for the Saints to build the Central Pacific line from Humboldt Wells, Nevada, to Ogden was for approximately $4,000,000. By the time the Saints had completed the lines in the spring of 1869 they had been paid approximately $1,000,000 on each contract.[14] By August 1869 Central Pacific still owed them a million dollars and the Union Pacific probably a little more. Arrington writes that the failure of the railroads to meet their payments caused a near panic in Salt Lake City because laborers were destitute and contractors were heavily in debt to merchants and other creditors. Some people claim that worry over these finances was the direct cause of the death of Apostle Ezra T. Benson.[15]

Eventually some of the workers were paid in various ways, such as being given tithing credit, stocks and bonds in the Utah Central Railroad Co., and in some cases cash, credit, or produce obtained from the sale of company stocks. In order for Brigham Young to meet his obligations he was forced to issue $1,000,000 in first mortgage bonds, with the Utah Central Railroad as security because much of the settlement with the Union Pacific had to be taken in surplus railroad supplies. The Union Pacific had an unsavory reason for not being able to pay its obligations. They had organized a financial association called "Credit Mobilier of America" which supposedly handled building contracts. A congressional investigating committee discovered that the amount the railroad had paid to Credit Mobilier contractors was only $50,700,000, leaving a profit of about $43,900,000. The Credit Mobilier owners were so greedy they did not even make adequate provision for the unpaid bills of the railroad before draining off their huge profits. Through these tactics of greed, the promoter-contractors actually forced their own company into bankruptcy although the bankruptcy came years later in 1893.

Representatives, and later vice-president of the United
States—in 1865 and again in 1869 he had made visits to Utah—
was one of those who was caught up in the Credit Mobilier
scandal.

The Branch Line from Ogden to Salt Lake City

A few days after the completion of the railroad a number of
prominent men in Utah organized the Utah Railroad Company
in order to build a branch line from Ogden to Salt Lake City.
On May 17 near the Weber River just below Ogden, ground was
broken by President Brigham Young. There were thirty-seven
miles of line, and it was completely built by Utah capital and
Utah labor. By January 10, 1870, Brigham Young had driven
the last spike, completing the railroad in less than eight months.

The line had been built by many different wards, each taking
a small contract, usually near their location. Much of the work
was done by volunteer labor. The actual completion of the road
would have been much sooner, but the last of $530,000 worth
of supplies from the Union Pacific were not delivered until
December, 1869.

This road became known as the Utah Central Railroad and
was the first of four branch lines built by the Saints; the other
railroads were the Utah Southern, the Utah Northern, and the
Utah Eastern.[16] They were later sold partly to private interests,
but mostly they were merged into the Union Pacific where the
Church probably obtained Union Pacific stock in exchange.

CHANGES WROUGHT BY THE COMING
OF THE RAILROAD

The Latter-day Saint leaders were not unmindful of the many
changes that would be wrought by the coming of the railroad;
and although some of them were somewhat fearful of the influence that a great number of gentiles would have upon the
Utah communities individually, they had a deep conviction that
their church was the true Christian faith genuinely restored to
earth under the direction of the Savior, Jesus Christ, and would
therefore endure the crisis. When Brigham Young had told
Samuel Bowles that he would not give much for a religion that
could not withstand the advent of a railroad, he was in earnest.
Yet he learned that Mr. Bowles continued to be of the opinion

328 that the coming of the railroad would destroy the Church. Mr. Bowles was not alone in this opinion. Stone states that the forces fighting Mormonism were convinced that the railway would put an end to this peculiar faith. [17] The Church leaders attempted to prepare the people for the inevitable changes. They told them to expect an influx of gentiles which would add to the power of the anti-Mormons threatening to destroy them.

Arrington states that the coming of the railroad posed three major threats: (1) by offering entrepreneurs from the Midwest and the East opportunities to exploit new mines and markets, the Church leaders' theocratic control of the region would be threatened; (2) the economic autonomy of the Mormon Commonwealth would be threatened; (3) by involving the Saints more deeply in "worldly" trade, the "Kingdom of the Saints" would be broken into segments that were in conflict, and economic relationships would become more secularized. [18] Arrington feels that a well-directed program by Church leaders did much to offset these tendencies, although many adjustments had to be made by the people.

Now that it was necessary to raise cash to pay railroad fares for immigrants, the Perpetual Emigrating Fund Company was not able to assist so many people; as a result immigration dropped. But those who did come could do so in relative safety. Between 1847 and the coming of the railroad, over 6,000 Saints had lost their lives trying to reach Zion. After 1869 death among the immigrants was rare.

Before the arrival of the railroad in 1867 the Church leaders organized the School of the Prophets in order to aid them to secure the loyalty of the Church members during crises. They issued a number of economic policies and programs, one of which was an austerity program, wherein the individual church members sacrificed and donated to the Perpetual Emigrating Fund the money they had saved. The leaders helped minimize the number of undesirable workers coming into the country by assisting the Church to pay her railroad contract by getting Mormon labor on the job.

The School of the Prophets next sought to reduce the number of undesirables coming into the country by deflating the reports of mineral discoveries in Utah and encouraging Mormon laborers to take mining jobs. They also helped settlements establish local cooperative enterprises. Zion's Cooperative Mercantile Institution (ZCMI)—which had been organized in October 1868 in order to provide goods at lower prices than the gentile stores and to make it unnecessary for the people to patronize anti-Mormon merchants—became the wholesale supplier for a string of locally owned cooperative stores from one end of Zion to the other. Within ten years after the coming of the railroad at least 150 local cooperative stores had been established. Zion's Mercantile claimed to have saved the Latter-day Saints $3,000,000 during its first four years of operation.

A number of new industries became established which helped offset those that failed because they could not meet eastern competition. Some of these were: the cooperative Utah Manufacturing Company which was organized to manufacture wagons, carriages, and agricultural machinery; a furniture manufacturing enterprise; associations to further develop the silk industry; the gigantic Provo Woolen Mills; a wooden bucket factory; ink and match factories, and a number of other small factories.[19]

UNITY OF MORMON COMMUNITY

Through the persuasions of Brigham Young and the School of the Prophets, a trade committee was organized with a representative from each craft. Through this committee, an effort was made to persuade each craft to reduce wages from one-third to one-half "in order that Utah might be able to compete with the manufactures of the states."[20] Because of this wage reduction Brigham Young was highly criticized as being anti-labor, whereas his only purpose had been to help keep the craftsmen employed.

The establishment of a series of interior branch railroads helped bring unity and solidarity to the Mormon community. They provided the transportation that made it possible for farmers to expand their markets. With the coming of the Deseret Telegraph, President Young now had communication with most settlements at his fingertips. Transportation solidified the unity, maneuverability, and flexibility of the larger community life, maintaining Mormon cohesiveness.

Legal Property Rights in Utah

Until 1869 the Saints actually had no legal property rights in Utah. Knowing that these rights were coming to Utah, claim jumpers during the two or three years prior to the coming of the railroad had tried to squat in the public parks and on other

330 municipal properties. But under the watchful eye of a committee of the School of the Prophets which helped settlers in various areas with their land title applications, very few injustices occurred.

Reactivation of the Relief Society

The reactivation of the Female Relief Society late in 1867 aided greatly in keeping unity in the Church. The Relief Society helped to guard against the evils that came with the railroad. Eliza R. Snow helped to organize a branch of the society in each ward of the Church. Their goal was to teach the ladies to refrain from extravagance and from being tempted by the many goods the railroad would bring that might be beyond their means. The teachings were for the rich and poor alike.

Organization of the Retrenchment Society

Another aid in this respect was the Retrenchment Society, founded first in December of 1869 by President Young for his daughters. Its purpose was to prevent the young ladies of the Church from imitating the pride, folly, and fashions of the world—to encourage them to wear homemade articles and make them fashionable. The Retrenchment Society soon spread throughout the Church and is known today as the Young Women's Mutual Improvement Association. "The girls were taught to glean wheat, piece quilts, crochet, make hats, knit stockings, and to engage in many cultural activities."[21]

By 1872 when the Saints appeared to be weathering the influence of the railroad well enough, the School of the Prophets was deemed to be no longer necessary. This was not true, however, of the reactivated Relief Society or the Retrenchment Society. Their value to the Church was so great that they have continued to be a very integral part of it ever since.

Even in economics, the Saints were becoming successful; and as the years passed, the cooperatives were gradually replaced by private Mormon businesses in many fields.

Footnotes

[1]Irving Stone, *Men to Match My Mountains* (Garden City, N.Y.: Doubleday and Co., 1956), p. 289. *See also CHC*, 5:245.

[2] Orson F. Whitney, *Popular History of Utah* (Salt Lake City: Deseret News Press, 1916), pp. 216-17, footnote. *See also HU*, 1:487.

[3] *CHC*, 5:245.

[4] *CHC*, 4:31. *See also Utah Legislature Enactments*, Session of 1851-52, pp. 224-27; and *HU*, 1:488.

[5] *Salt Lake Telegraph*, 8 March 1869.

[6] *Deseret News Weekly*, 2 January 1867.

[7] *Deseret News Weekly*, 2 January 1867.

[8] Wallace Stegner, *Mormon Country* (New York: Bonanza Books, 1942), pp. 251-58.

[9] Stegner, p. 255.

[10] Robert M. Utley, *Special Report on Promontory Summit, Utah* (Santa Fe, N.M.: U.S. Department of the Interior, National Park Service Region Three, February 1960), p. 64. *See also* Bernice Gibbs Anderson, "The Pacific Roadways and the Golden Spike 1869-1969" (n.p., n.d.) p. 6.

[11] Robert M. Utley, "Golden Spike" (U.S. Department of the Interior, National Park Service, n.p., n.d.), p. 1.

[12] LeRoy R. Hafen, W. Eugene Hollon, and Carl Coke Rister, *Western America* (Englewood Cliffs, N.J.: Prentice-Hall, Inc., 1970), pp. 405-6.

[13] Stanford University is today the proud possessor of the golden spike.

[14] Leonard J. Arrington, *Great Basin Kingdom* (Cambridge, Mass.: Harvard University Press, 1958), p. 265.

[15] Arrington, p. 265.

[16] *See* Arrington, Chapter 10, for an excellent treatise on "Mormon Railroads."

[17] Stone, p. 289.

[18] Arrington, p. 234.

[19] Arrington, p. 247.

[20] Arrington, p. 248. *See also* Sermon of Brigham Young, 6 April 1869, *JD*, 12:374-75.

[21] Arrington, p. 253.

331

Seek for wisdom then Power will follow.

16

America's Greatest Colonizer

BRIGHAM YOUNG'S EARLY LIFE

Brigham Young did not live to experience the pleasure of seeing Utah attain statehood or to experience the setback of having the United States Supreme Court declare the anti-bigamy laws constitutional. He died after a six-day illness on August 29, 1877. Thus passed the life of one of the greatest men of the age, despised by many who had heard only of his notoriety which was spread principally by his enemies, but beloved by the Latter-day Saints who knew him best.

He had led a remarkable and noteworthy life, having presided over the Church for a total of thirty-three years, three as president of the Twelve Apostles and thirty as president of the Church.

Brigham Young was born in humble circumstances in the little village of Whitingham, Vermont, where his parents lived for only three years. His grandfather was Dr. Joseph Young, a medical doctor in the army during the French and Indian War. After Dr. Young's discharge he married a young widow, Elizabeth (Betany) Hayden Treadway, in 1758; during the next fifteen or so years, they were blessed with six children including their son John, born March 7, 1763.

Unfortunately, Dr. Young was killed in an accident in 1769. Because his widow, after four years, was unable to support her

333

children, John and his younger brother, Joseph, were "bound out" to a man named Jones, for whom they worked for their keep. In the spring of 1784, John turned twenty-one and was released from his indenture to Mr. Jones. In the meantime he had served three short terms in the continental army.

On October 31, 1785, John married Abigail Howe at Hopkinton, Massachusetts. They lived in Hopkinton until 1789, during which time two daughters, Nancy and Fanny, were born to them. After they moved to Durham, New York, a third daughter, Rhoda, was born. When they had moved back to Hopkinton, John Jr., Abigail (Nabby), Suzanna, Joseph, and Phinehas (sometimes spelled Phineas) were born to them.

During January of 1801 they moved to Whitingham, Vermont, four miles north of the Massachusetts state line. Here, their ninth child and fourth son, Brigham, was born. In 1804 they moved to Sherburne, New York, where the tenth and eleventh children, Louisa and Lorenzo, were born. In 1813 the Young family moved further west to the township of Aurelius and settled on a farm near Auburn.

On June 11, 1815, after thirty years of married life and the birth of eleven children, Abigail Howe Young died of tuberculosis at the age of forty-nine. Brigham was fourteen years old at the time. One child, Nabby, had died, five had married, and five were living at home; in addition, Fanny was now at home, having left her husband and returned to the household in time to take care of the children during the last few months of her mother's life.

His Religious Upbringing

Although Brigham's mother passed away when he was a youth, she had had a profound and lasting effect upon him. She is said to have been "a woman of quiet culture" with a deep abiding faith which helped to temper her husband's strict discipline. She and her husband were members of the Reformed Methodist Church, and they taught their children principles of righteousness from the Bible as they understood them. Brigham Young in later years said, "My parents were devoted to the Methodist religion, and their precepts of morality were sustained by their good example. . . . I was taught by my parents to live a strictly moral life." [1] His friends were later to profit by his good example, and many of his enemies were to learn that they had wrongly maligned him.

After his wife's death John Young moved southwest to the area of Tyrone near his daughter, Rhoda, and her husband, John P. Greene. The girls, Fanny and Louisa, did not go with them. The boys and their father cleared a farm, and for a time their only cash crop was maple sugar. The boys learned to work hard at an early age.

In 1817 Father John Young married a widowed neighbor woman, Mrs. Hannah Brown. Six years later, Brigham's half brother Edward was born. But Brigham was no longer living at home. After his father's second marriage, he had gone to live with his sister Susanna, Mrs. James Little, in Auburn.[2] Here he became a carpenter, painter, and glazier and worked on a building at the site of the state prison. At Auburn he also painted wooden buckets for a furniture manufacturer where he invented a paint crusher to mix paint. He also secured work in Port Byron, about eight miles north of Auburn on the banks of the Erie Canal. There his membership in the Port Byron debating and oratorical society proved to be much more important to his future than was his work. Because his parents had moved so much and because of their meager finances, he had had only a total of eleven days of formal schooling. The society afforded him the opportunity to learn the art of speaking and to profit from the mental development gained by debating.[3]

In Port Byron he fell in love with Miriam Works, the daughter of Asa and Abigail Works, who had also formerly lived in Hopkinton, Massachusetts. They were married October 8, 1824, after which Brigham escorted her to the small rented three-story frame house in Port Byron on the banks of the Erie Canal.[4]

HIS MEMBERSHIP IN THE CHURCH

Contact with the Book of Mormon

After five years of married life in Port Byron, during which time their daughter Elizabeth was born, Brigham and Miriam moved approximately fifty-five miles west to Mendon, New York. Brigham's father and two of his brothers and four sisters, most of them with their companions, were already living in the area. The John Young family had strong family ties which kept most of them living rather closely together throughout their lives.

In the summer of 1830, Samuel Smith, the first formal

336 missionary of the Church, left a copy of the Book of Mormon with Rhoda and John P. Greene, Brigham's sister and brother-in-law. It was perhaps a few weeks later that he left another copy with Phinehas Young, Brigham's brother, whom he met at lunch hour at an inn on Tomlinson's Corner in Mendon. These two copies were passed around to the Young families and their friends. Along with the help of five missionaries—Elders Eleazer Miller, Elial Strong, Alpheus Gifford, Enos Curtis, and Daniel Bowen—who came into the area in the summer of 1831, these books helped a branch of the Church to be established in Mendon, although it was the spring of 1832 before most of the Young family and their friends joined. The little branch soon consisted of the following members: John and Hannah B. Young; Brigham and Miriam Works Young; Phinehas H. and Clarissa Young; Joseph Young, as yet unmarried; Lorenzo D. and Persis Young; John P. and Rhoda Young Greene and children; Joel and Louisa Young Sanford; Fanny Young Carr, a grass widow; Isaac Flummerfelt and his wife and children; Ira and Charlotte Bond; Heber C. and Vilate Murray Kimball; Rufus Parks; John and Betsy Morton; Nathan Tomlinson (at whose inn Samuel had sold a copy of the Book of Mormon to Phinehas); and Israel Barlow and his mother, his brothers, and his sisters.[5]

Brigham was baptized on April 14, 1832, after more than a year and a half of investigation. He said:

> I weighed the matter studiously for nearly two years . . . before I made up my mind to receive that book (the Book of Mormon). I looked at it on all sides. All other religions I could fathom . . . but this new one I reasoned on month after month, until I came to a certain knowledge of its truth.[6]

His wife, Miriam, was baptized three weeks later. But tragedy soon entered his home; his wife died of consumption (tuberculosis) on September 8, 1832, leaving two little girls, Elizabeth then seven, and Vilate (named after Heber C. Kimball's wife), only two years old. Brigham and his daughters continued to live in Heber C. Kimball's home so that Vilate could be mother to the two girls.

A Visit to Meet the Prophet

Having "joined the church, read the Book of Mormon, heard

tongues spoken and interpreted,"[7] and having spoken in tongues himself, Brigham now felt it was time to meet the Prophet Joseph Smith who was living at Kirtland, Ohio, a distance of 325 miles. Taking Heber C. Kimball's team and wagon, Joseph Young, Brigham, and Heber left late in September for Kirtland. They found the Prophet in the trees cutting wood with his brothers. Everyone was introduced to each other and shook hands. That evening they met in the Smith parlor, where Brigham Young, John P. Greene, and later, the Prophet Joseph Smith, all spoke in tongues—not with wild, uncontrolled shouting but with restraint and dignity.[8]

After six enjoyable days the visitors returned to New York. They had met the prophet of God and were not disappointed. He was a man to whom all three would remain steadfast and loyal, never wavering.

From the time of his visit to the Prophet until one year later Brigham had traveled 2,400 miles, preaching the gospel and organizing branches. This year began the training of him who was destined to become the powerful leader of his people.

Further Preparation for Leadership

In September 1833 when Brigham and Heber moved together to Kirtland, Ohio, they shipped their goods to nearby Fairport via the Erie Canal and Lake Erie.[9] In Kirtland again Brigham and his daughters lived with the Kimball family until February 18, 1834, when Brigham married a young lady, Miss Mary Ann Angel, who was looking for a loyal Latter-day Saint as a companion.

Zion's Camp

During the summer of 1834 Brigham was one of the 205 men who traveled in Zion's Camp to Missouri to take provisions to the Saints who had been dispossessed in Jackson County and to help them be reinstated upon their lands. Although the 2,000-mile trip did not result in a restoration of the Saints to their lands and some of those who went classified it as a failure, Brigham Young felt that much had been accomplished. Surely for Brigham, who was destined to be the principal leader of his people in not only one exodus but two, these experiences were invaluable. He had been elected the captain of his twelve men, and Heber C. Kimball was captain of another group, the first time either had been asked to preside over groups that large.[10]

Back in Kirtland the Prophet requested Brigham to complete the building that was to house the printing press. Brigham also helped to complete the new schoolhouse, and he attended the School of the Elders, also called the School of the Prophets, during the winter. On February 14, 1835, the Twelve Apostles were selected; Brigham Young was the second man chosen, and Heber C. Kimball third. A few weeks later when the quorum was rearranged according to chronological age, Thomas B. Marsh was first, David W. Patten second, Brigham Young third, and Heber C. Kimball fourth.

From this time forth much of the responsibility for their family fell on the shoulders of Brigham Young's wife; Brigham was constantly in the service of the Church. In the Kirtland debacle during the fall of 1837 when so many of the leading elders of the Church fell by the wayside, Brigham Young proved his loyalty to the Prophet and the Church by vigorously defending them. In a meeting called by dissenters to gain support against Joseph Smith, Brigham had demanded the floor to defend the Prophet. He told them that Joseph was a prophet and he knew it; they could slander him as much as they pleased, but they would only destroy themselves, never the Prophet.[11] Three months later, on December 22, 1837, because of his constant defense of Joseph, he was forced to leave Kirtland for his own safety. By the time of the northern Missouri troubles in the fall of 1838, Thomas B. Marsh had apostatized and David W. Patten was killed in the battle of Crooked River, leaving Brigham Young as the senior apostle.

Service in Northern Missouri

With the Prophet, Hyrum, and Sidney in jail, and Marsh and Elder Patten gone, Brigham Young suddenly found himself not only the senior apostle on the scene but also the highest Church authority present, faced with the responsibility of an exodus from northern Missouri. One of his first acts was to have the leading men of the Church and all others available pledge themselves to help the poor to the extent of their ability. As Brigham began to organize the Saints for the exodus, the anti-Mormons began to recognize his abilities; finally on February 1, 1839, he was forced to leave Missouri with his family and Heber C. Kimball's, leaving Elder Kimball behind in hiding in order that he might continue to help the Saints.

On March 17, 1839, a meeting of the Twelve Apostles and a conference of the Church were conducted under Brigham Young's direction in Quincy, Illinois. On April 26 Brigham Young and other members of the Twelve were back in Far West, holding a meeting on the temple lot in conformity with the revelation contained in D&C 118, after which the Apostles returned to Nauvoo, established their families in houses, and during the summer and fall left on missions to Great Britain. Brigham and Heber left Nauvoo on September 14, 1839; both were weak with illness. With other apostles, they arrived in England on April 3, 1840.

On April 14 at a conference in Preston, England, Brigham Young was ordained President of the Twelve Apostles. Under his direction the mission prospered. He was in England for one year and sixteen days, during which time they began publication of the *Millennial Star,* printing 2,000 copies monthly. They also printed 5,000 copies of the Book of Mormon, 3,000 hymn books, and 60,000 tracts; they established a permanent shipping agency, emigrated 1,000 souls to Zion, and baptized between 7,000 and 8,000 converts.[12]

Brigham Young returned to Nauvoo on July 1, 1841. Eight days later while the Prophet Joseph Smith was calling upon Brigham Young he received the following revelation:

Dear and well-beloved brother, Brigham Young, verily thus sayeth the Lord unto you: My servant Brigham, it is no more required at your hand to leave your family as in times past, for your offering is acceptable unto me.

I have seen your labor and toil in journeyings for my name.

I therefore command you to send my work abroad, and take special care of your family from this time henceforth and forever. Amen. (D&C 126.)

This was apparently interpreted to mean that Brigham was not to be assigned to any extended missions, but he did go on one or two brief assignments away from home afterward.

The Nauvoo Period

The days spent in Nauvoo were in a period when the Prophet

340 Joseph began to rely more and more on the Quorum of the Twelve, giving them increasing responsibility. As President of the quorum, never once did Brigham fail the Church or the Prophet in an assignment.

After the Prophet's death, Parley P. Pratt wrote:

> This great and good man was led, before his death, to call the Twelve together from time to time, and instruct them in all things pertaining to the Kingdom, ordinances, and government of God. He often observed that he was laying the foundation, but it would remain for the Twelve to complete the building. Said he, 'I know not why, but for some reason I am constrained to hasten my preparations, and to confer upon the Twelve all the ordinances, keys, covenants, endowments, and sealing ordinances of the Priesthood, . . .'
>
> Having done this he rejoiced exceedingly, for said he, 'the Lord is about to lay the burden on your shoulders and let me rest awhile; and if they kill me, continued he, the kingdom of God will roll on, as I have now finished the work which was laid upon me, by committing to you all things for the building of the Kingdom according to the heavenly vision, and the pattern shown me from Heaven. . . .'
>
> He proceeded to confer on Elder Young, the President of the Twelve, the keys of the sealing power, as conferred in the last days by the spirit and power of Elijah, in order to seal the hearts of the fathers to the children, and the hearts of the children to the fathers. . . .
>
> This last key is the most sacred of all, and pertains exclusively to the first presidency of the Church, without whose sanction and approval, or authority, no sealing blessing shall be administered pertaining to things of the resurrection and the life to come.
>
> After giving them [the Twelve Apostles] a very short charge to do all things according to the pattern, he quietly surrendered his liberty and his life into the hands of his blood thirsty enemies. . . .[13]

Brigham Young Presides

After assigning 344 elders to areas of the mission field, Brigham Young himself left for the East on May 21, 1844, with Heber C. Kimball and Lyman Wight, never to see Joseph Smith in mortality again. Just a little over one month later—on June 27, 1844, the day the Prophet and Hyrum were martyred—President Brigham Young recorded in his journal:

> Spent the day in Boston with Brother Woodruff, who accompanied me to the railway station as I was about to take cars for Salem. In the evening while sitting in the depot, waiting, I felt a heavy depression of spirit and so melancholy I could not converse with any degree of pleasure.... I could not assign any reasons for my peculiar feelings.[14]

On July 9, while at Salem, Massachusetts, he heard rumors of the death of the Prophet; he thought they were only rumors, so he and Orson Pratt went on to Petersborough, where a conference was scheduled. One week later Brigham recorded:

> July 16. While at Brother Bement's house in Petersboro, I heard a letter read which Brother Livingston had from Mr. Joseph Powers of Nauvoo giving particulars of the murder of Joseph and Hyrum. The first thing I thought of was, whether Joseph had taken the keys of the kingdom with him from the earth; Brother Pratt sat on my left; we were both leaning back in our chairs. Bringing my hand down on my knee I said 'the keys of the kingdom are right here with the Church.'[15]

That day they also received a letter from Wilford Woodruff confirming the tragedy; they immediately left for Boston, where they arrived the next day. Brigham Young went to bed, where, for the first time, he shed tears of uncontrollable grief. After waiting six days in Boston, Brigham and five other apostles left together for Nauvoo, arriving at 8:00 p.m. on August 6. On August 7 an all-day meeting was held at which Brigham said:

> Joseph conferred upon our heads [the apostles] all the keys and powers belonging to the apostleship which he himself held. . . . How often has Joseph said to the twelve, 'I have laid the foundation and you must build thereon, for upon your shoulders the kingdom rests.'[16]

At a meeting on August 8, 1844, Brigham stepped forth to preside and to present the case of the Twelve Apostles for leadership of the Church. It was upon this occasion that numerous private journals and diaries testify that for a moment the man in the pulpit looked like Joseph Smith and his voice was the Prophet's voice. The people voted unanimously for the Twelve Apostles to be their leaders. Brigham said, "All that want to draw a party from the Church after them, let them do it if they can; but they will not prosper."

For Brigham Young and the other apostles, now in charge of the Church, life would never be the same again. Entrenched in leadership of the Church, the Twelve sent a circular to the Saints throughout the world stating their position and signifying that the work would continue to roll forth.

Exodus from the States

After 1½ years, President Young found himself responsible for the exodus of thousands of people seeking a new home in the West. His experiences in the Zion's Camp march and in the exodus from northern Missouri served to help him save many lives. But to leave a civilized country for the wilderness in the middle of the winter with the responsibility for the welfare of thousands of people was sufficient to test the mettle of the best of men. It is no wonder God had chosen a practical man with an iron will, yet one with humility and a deep conviction in the truthfulness of his mission. Another year and a half was to pass before President Young would gaze upon the Salt Lake valley, enraptured with vision, to pronounce the immortal words, "This is the right place! Drive on!"

SUSTAINED AS PRESIDENT OF THE CHURCH

After locating a spot for the city and getting the building of a fort underway, President Young, with seven other apostles and about 180 of the pioneers and battalion men, returned to their families at Winter Quarters and Council Bluffs. There they found that the summer of 1847 had been successful for the Saints who were growing crops on their temporary farms. An abundant grain crop was harvested, which gave the Saints in Iowa and Nebraska assurance that there would be enough to eat for the winter.

On December 5 nine of the Twelve Apostles met in the home of Orson Hyde at Council Bluffs, where a new First Presidency was selected; Brigham Young was chosen as President, Heber C. Kimball as first counselor and Willard Richards as second counselor. Three weeks later a conference was held in Kanes-

especially built for the occasion. On the final day the Saints
sustained by vote the reorganization of the First Presidency.
This action was confirmed by the Church at the annual conference in Kanesville on April 6, 1848, at a conference in Manchester, England, on August 14, 1848, and at the semiannual
conference of the Church in the Salt Lake valley on October 8,
1848, where about 5,000 people were present.

On June 1, 1848, Brigham Young started west for the last
time from the Elkhorn River, leading a company of 1,229
people with 397 wagons, arriving in the Salt Lake valley on
September 20 of the same year. President Young never left the
intermountain country again.

Water, Timber, and Land Policy of President Young

With water needed for irrigation, with timber not too plentiful for buildings, and with land available for the taking,
policies needed to be established to properly regulate the use of
these resources. As previously mentioned, through the establishment of the doctrine of use, Brigham Young inaugurated a new
water policy in the western world. Timber lands were declared
to belong to the public and rules were initiated regulating their
use. For example, at first only dead timber could be used.
Ruling out the sale of land and parceling it out assured those
Saints who came later of justice. Among other things, they were
not left to the mercy of land sharks or real estate dealers who
might raise prices beyond any possibility of purchase by the
poorer immigrants. The poor had equal opportunity with the
rich, and Mormon land law stated that no man should have
more than he could cultivate. These policies President Young
endeavored to have carried out in all of the settlements founded
under him.

Utah was unique in its farming. The average farm in the
United States in 1850 was 203 acres;[17] and in the areas with
which the Saints were acquainted, the average farm ranged from
113 acres in New York to 185 acres in Iowa. Because of the
need for irrigation, because of a constant flow of immigrants
who needed land with available water, and because the Church
leaders recognized the advantages of community living, large
farms were out of the question. The first farms given out under
strict control of Church leadership were generally limited to ten
acres. In fact, in February, 1849, no provision was made for any
farms larger than this.[18] Later, some twenty and forty-acre

Brigham Young, second president of The Church of Jesus Christ of Latter-day Saints. *Courtesy of Church Historical Department.*

farms were given out, but the average farm remained very small until after 1869 when the Homestead Law and Desert Lands Act became applicable to Utah. The irrigated farms remained small, however.

Another land feature was that each settlement would fence in a community field so that only an outside fence was necessary to protect the crops of everyone. Often a community pasture would also be fenced in.

Colonization under President Young

The settlement of the Great Basin was achieved under the immediate direction of Brigham Young, who was the dominating force in its settlement throughout his lifetime in the basin. What he achieved in colonizing could not have been done without the voluntary love and loyalty of the members of the Church, but most of them were willing to do whatever was asked of them by the man whom they staunchly believed to be inspired of God. President Young made it a point to receive information from every source available as to possible sites for settlement. He often sent out exploring parties whose leaders would report directly to him. He was ably supported by his two counselors, Heber C. Kimball and Willard Richards, and also by the Twelve Apostles who at this period were Orson Hyde, Parley P. Pratt, Orson Pratt, John Taylor, Wilford Woodruff, George A. Smith, Amasa Lyman, Ezra T. Benson, Charles C. Rich, Lorenzo Snow, Erastus Snow, and Franklin D. Richards.

Brigham Young was often able to do a little exploring himself as he traveled during the summer to distant colonies already established. Because of his love for people he always took a large entourage with him as he went throughout the settlements. Usually there would be a number of prominent leaders of the Church; and then, if there were not one or two hundred other people who started with him, they would pick up more as they went from settlement to settlement.

Another characteristic of Brother Brigham's, as he was admiringly called, was to take along a few young people of marriageable age so that they could not only get acquainted with each other but might fall in love. Often some of his own children and Heber C. Kimball's or those of other leaders would go along. With land easily obtainable, the president believed in rather young marriages, feeling that people would be less likely to get into trouble after marriage. Hard work was about all that was necessary to start a family. With an axe and a few other tools, a young man could soon build a log house for his bride.

A Typical Visit to the Colonies

A visit to the Bear Lake area in the spring of 1864 is descriptive and typical of the usual visits made by President Young. His purpose in going to the Bear Lake country was to comply with the wishes of Elder Charles C. Rich, who was in charge of the settlement that had been made in September, 1863. He wanted President Young to come early in the spring to aid in the selection of townsites so that the settlers could get busy making their permanent homes.[19] With Brigham Young were Heber C. Kimball, George A. Smith, John Taylor, Wilford Woodruff, Joseph Young, Jesse W. Fox (Utah's surveyor), Professor Thomas Ellerbeck, George D. Watt (a reporter), and seven teamsters. They left Salt Lake on May 16, 1864, in six light vehicles and a baggage wagon. On the afternoon of the third day they arrived at Franklin, Idaho; by that time their party included 153 people, sixty-seven on horseback and eighty-six in vehicles, including a number of women.

They left Franklin at 6:00 a.m. on the fourth day and arrived in Paris at 3:00 a.m. the next morning. Paris consisted of thirty-four log huts with dirt roofs. After resting a day, they drove south as far as present-day Fish Haven. On Sunday they held an outdoor meeting in the forenoon, at which Brigham Young, President Kimball, and Elders John Taylor and George A. Smith spoke. President Young's talk was a mixture of spiritual instruction and practical advice. Reading his sermon as recorded by George D. Watt gives one some insight as to why he was such a successful leader.[20]

> We cannot live without law. . . . Every good person wants to live under law and order. . . . Be sure to say your prayers morning and evening. If you forget your prayers this morning, you will forget them tonight, very likely, and if you cease to pray you will be very apt to forget God! When you build your permanent dwellings, build nice, commodious habitations . . . have the brethren build upon the block until every lot is occupied. Then if you should be attacked by Indians one scream will arouse the whole block. . . . Make your fences high at once . . . for to commence a fence with three poles it teaches your cows to be

breachy. . . . Be sure you do not let your little children go
away from this settlement to herd cattle or sheep. . . .
Send them to school. . . . When the brethren go into the
mountains, better a few go together . . . let every father
and mother make their [*sic*] homes so interesting that
their children will never want to leave it . . . make your
homes pleasant with foliage and beautiful gardens . . .
above all, teach them [the children] to remember that
God must be in all our thoughts. [21]

Settlements founded in 1864 were Ovid, Liberty, Montpelier,
and Bennington to the north of Paris and Bloomington and St.
Charles, Fish Haven, Garden City, and Laketown to the south;
others such as Dingle, Wardboro, Georgetown, Bern, and
Randolph were settled later. By the time they arrived home, the
trip had taken the leaders eleven days; Solomon Kimball, seven-
teen-year-old son of Heber C. Kimball, said they had held meetings at all the principal settlements along the route, both going
and coming. [22] It is obvious the leaders put in long hours in
order to serve the people.

Apostles Appointed Over Areas

Dr. Milton R. Hunter states that "during the early and most
active" period of colonization, President Young divided the
areas selected for settlement into large divisions and placed certain of the apostles directly over some of these areas. For example, in 1851 Charles C. Rich and Amasa Lyman were sent to
found a colony in southern California (which became known as
San Bernardino) where they were to preside and establish a
stronghold for the Saints. [23] George A. Smith was sent to the
little Salt Lake valley (Iron County) in 1851, after which he was
active in helping to settle colonies in the south. In 1853
Lorenzo Snow was assigned to the Brigham City area. Ezra T.
Benson was assigned to the Tooele area and later to the Oneida
County area in Idaho. In 1853 Orson Hyde was assigned to the
Bridger Valley (Fort Bridger and Fort Supply), then to Utah
territory, and in 1855 he was sent to Carson Valley on the
extreme western side of the territory. After returning from
there in 1858 he was assigned to the settlements in Sanpete and
Sevier counties. He made his home in the settlement of Spring
City in Sanpete County where he lived until the time of his
death on November 28, 1878. In 1863 Charles C. Rich was

assigned to the Bear Lake area, where he lived most of the time until his death on November 17, 1883, although he also maintained a home in Centerville in Salt Lake County.

In 1861 Erastus Snow and George A. Smith were appointed to make a settlement in Dixie. Brigham Young gave it the name of St. George, purportedly in honor of Elder Smith, but Erastus Snow became responsible for the Mormon settlements in southern Utah, Nevada, and northern Arizona, where he made annual trips throughout the region. Next to Brigham Young he was perhaps the greatest Mormon colonizer. [24]

During the last months of his life in 1877, President Young released all of the Twelve from presiding over local areas. This included Charles C. Rich, Brigham Young, Jr., Lorenzo Snow, and Franklin D. Richards in the north, and Orson Hyde and Erastus Snow in the south. The president felt their services in districts were no longer necessary and told them that their mission had a larger field. [25]

Bishops and Stake Presidents

Other important leaders in colonization were the bishops and stake presidents who would often be chosen prior to leading the new colonists into the area. Without the faith, loyalty, and integrity of these men on the actual scene, President Young could not have attained his great success. Faithfully and unselfishly these leaders looked after both the spiritual needs and the material welfare of the people.

Edward W. Tullidge said of the bishops:

> In Utah, they [the bishops] soon became the veritable founders of our settlements and cities; and having founded them, they have also governed them and directed the people in the social organization and material growth. . . .
>
> Under the government of the bishops, Utah grew up. . . . Brigham Young was their director, for he formulated and constructed everything in those days. . . . Under their temporal administration all over Utah, as well as in Salt Lake, cities were built, lands divided off to the people, roads and bridges made, water ditches cut, the land irrigated, and society governed. [26]

This was true of the bishops whether in Utah, Idaho, Arizona, or elsewhere.

Mormon colonization was carried on with a mixture of many nationalities and peoples; but they had a common tie in their religion, which was sufficiently strong to overcome the variety of customs, nationalities, and languages. About two-thirds of the colonists were born in the United States; of these, most were from the New England states. Nevertheless, there were also many from Missouri, Kentucky, Tennessee, and other states. Those of foreign birth were usually from England, but many came from Canada; others came from Germany, Holland, Scandinavia, Switzerland, and elsewhere. If a national group came together, they would often be sent in a body to organize a colony with others added to supply the needed tradesmen for balance.

Usually "when a new colony was to be founded, its membership was selected by Brigham Young." [27] He often called families and groups of families as missionaries to settle new towns. Occasionally it was a real test of their faith, when they had already been located long enough to have a comfortable house, a fine garden, and fruit trees ready to bear; as a rule, their religious faith brought a willing obedience.

Occasionally, volunteers would be called for; again Brigham Young might name each family, achieving a proper balance of trades for the colony. Now and then a man might be called to lead a group and be told he could select his own colonists. This was so with Isaac Morley, who settled Manti. Often new immigrants from England or elsewhere who had been factory workers or miners or who had no particular skill would be mixed with experienced pioneers who could assist them in learning the art of farming or some other skill.

But the greatest advantage of Mormon colonization over other efforts in the western United States was the common religious bond of the settlers. B. H. Roberts says there were two main reasons for the success of Mormon colonization: the loyalty of the people to their leaders and the unselfish and devoted personal sacrifice of these leaders in serving the people. For a list of the colonies founded under Brigham Young, see Appendix 8.

Immigration

After establishing a place of settlement in the West for the

Saints, Brigham Young realized the necessity of gaining more converts in order to become sufficiently strong to withstand further onslaughts of the enemy if such should occur. In fact, the problem was twofold: first, getting to the Great Basin those members of the Church who were still on the plains of Iowa, in other areas of the United States, or in Great Britain; and second, converting others to come and help occupy the land available. In a conference held in the Nauvoo Temple on October 6, 1845, the following covenant proposed by Brigham Young was unanimously carried: "That we take all the Saints with us to the extent of our ability, that is, our influence and property." [28]

In order to help fill this pledge, President Young organized the Perpetual Emigrating Fund Company (PEF). The first Saints to be aided by it were those still in Iowa. In 1850 there were still 7,823 Mormons temporarily scattered, while the Utah population showed 11,380. With the help of the fund the Utah population had risen to between 25,000 and 30,000 by the end of 1852. The last of the Saints exiled from Nauvoo arrived that summer at the same time as the first emigrants from Europe, who were also aided by the PEF. That year European emigration consisted of 250 members who had been aided by the fund and 726 others who had paid their own way. Among the latter were twenty-eight Saints from Scandinavia, the first from a non-English speaking country.

By 1853 more Saints wanted to emigrate than the fund could take care of, so a new plan called the ten-pound plan was adopted. Under it each adult paid ten pounds in advance and the Perpetual Emigrating Fund Company paid the rest. The Church now had three classes of emigrants: those who paid their own way, those who came under the ten-pound plan, and those whose friends at Salt Lake financed them. Church emigration from Europe from 1848 to 1855 was as follows:

1848, 4 companies with 754 souls
1849, 9 companies with 2078 souls
1850, 6 companies with 1612 souls
1851, 4 companies with 1370 souls
1852, 4 companies with 760 souls
1853, 9 companies with 2626 souls
1854, 10 companies with 3167 souls
1855, 13 companies with 4225 souls
Miscellaneous in 1848-1855, 319 souls

Because of rising costs and still more requests for PEF aid,
the handcart system was inaugurated in 1856. Because they left
too late in the season, two of the five companies which headed
west that year ran into difficulty. But the plan proved to be
feasible, and five more handcart companies came between 1857
and 1860. During 1860 Brigham Young inaugurated the Church
train system on an experimental basis. It proved successful and
was used exclusively for bringing in PEF immigrants between
1861 and 1868. During these years approximately 2,000
wagons were sent east, involving 2,400 men and about 17,500
oxen to pick up the immigrants at the railroad terminal and
bring them to Utah. By 1869 the railroad had arrived in the
territory, and between 1850 and 1887 (when the fund was confiscated by the government) through the aid of the Perpetual
Emigrating Fund Company, more than 80,000 souls had come
to help build Zion. [29]

Proselyting

But without an active missionary force there would have
been very few converts to come to Zion. When the first European Saints left for Zion in 1840, 6,614 converts had been
made in Great Britain. Ten years later in 1850 although 10,319
had migrated, the mission membership in Great Britain had
reached 32,747 souls.

When the new home for Zion had been securely established,
President Young began in 1849 to establish missions in various
parts of the world. At the fall conference that year, missionaries
were called to go to the Society Islands. These missionaries were
Addison Pratt, James Brown, and Hiram H. Blackwell. Lorenzo
Snow, Joseph Toronto, T. B. H. Stenhouse, and Jabez Woodward were called to Switzerland and Italy; John Taylor, Curtis
E. Bolton, and John Pack were called to France and Germany;
Erastus Snow and others were called to Scandinavia and Iceland; and Amasa Lyman, Charles C. Rich, and others were
called to islands in the Pacific. In 1850 Parley P. Pratt and
companions went to South America, and George Q. Cannon
with nine companions reached Hawaii. In 1851 John Murdock
and Charles Wendell went to Australia. Later they were joined
by nine other missionaries, some of whom went to New Zealand
and Tasmania. In 1853 Jesse Haven, William Walker and
Leonard I. Smith established a mission in South Africa.

Not all these missions were successful. Those in China, India,

352 South America (Parley P. Pratt), Gibralter, Spain, the West Indies, and British Guiana failed. In some instances authorities of the country refused entrance to the missionaries. President Young, however, continued a vigorous missionary program throughout the rest of his life.

Brigham Young and the Material Welfare of the Saints

To Brigham Young there was no separation of the spiritual and the material. The daily problems of food, clothing, and shelter were interwoven with the spiritual life of the individual. Since the Saints were a thousand miles from civilization, they had to depend largely on their own industry to supply themselves with the necessities of life. Their leaders had a responsibility to them for their material welfare as well as for their spiritual welfare. This was especially true when the people had been brought into an arid region where only long hours of difficult toil could wrest a living from the soil. Recognizing also that it would take the combined efforts of all the Saints to produce sufficient food and clothing, President Young discouraged mining from the very beginning. He was convinced that an agricultural economy was much more sound and durable than a mining economy.

Before returning to Winter Quarters after their arrival in the basin in 1847, President Young sent out his first general epistle to the Saints giving them detailed instructions pertaining to almost every aspect of life, from how, when, and what to plant to instructions as to what to do with their time in winter such as ditching and fencing. Hunter stated that some people felt that President Young's instructions were "high-handed; but they were practical, and, as a rule, the saints obeyed them to the letter if they were able." [30]

President Young encouraged the Saints to keep an accurate record of sowing, cultivating, and of the daily weather so that they could learn the best method of surviving in an "untried country."

The Mormon missionary system made it possible for the missionaries to pick up from many lands seeds, tools, plants of all kinds, books, ideas for industries and for any type of new business; and Brigham Young's general letters instructed them, as well as all Saints migrating to Zion, to bring anything that might be of use to the people:

. . . .and to all the Saints . . . we would say, come immediately and prepare to go West—bringing with you all kinds of choice seeds, of grains, of vegetables, fruits, shrubbery, trees, and vines; . . . also, the best stock of beasts, bird and fowl of every kind; also, the best tools of every description, and machinery for spinning, or weaving, dressing cotton, wool and flax, and silk, etc., or models and descriptions of the same, by which they can construct them; and the same in relation to all kinds of farming utensils and husbandry, such as corn shellers, grain threshers, and cleaners, smut machines, mills, and every implement and article within their knowledge that shall tend to promote the comfort, health, happiness, or prosperity of the people. [31]

President Young also told them that the situation of people was deplorable when their sons were not trained in the practice of every useful avocation and when their daughters did not "mingle in the hum of industry." He went on to tell them to produce what they consumed and to draw from the "native element the necessities of life," and for "home industry to produce every article of home consumption." [32]

President Young's own family, in order to encourage home industry, made more than 500 yards of cloth during the winter of 1851 and 1852. [33] Encouragement of domestic manufacture was Brigham Young's policy. [34] In 1856 the Deseret Agricultural and Manufacturing Society was organized in order to encourage greater production of articles within the territory. In 1869 Zion's Cooperative Mercantile Institution was organized not only so that Church members could trade more economically with each other but also to help keep home industry thriving.

Early Industries in Utah

Many of the early industries in Utah failed while others achieved great success. There were two main reasons for this: (1) Brigham encouraged the Saints to try many things, such as the manufacturing of paper, iron, silk, chinaware, pottery, and beet sugar; the raising of flax; the production of woolen products, cotton and cotton goods, leather and leather goods; and (2) the proper combination of management, labor, finance, and natural resources was not always present. Yet, in some cases, this could only be ascertained by effort. Sometimes

354 the proper piece of machinery would be unattainable. At other times the workers lacked sufficient skill. In agriculture the soil might lack the proper ingredients, or perhaps rainfall was insufficient, or other needed elements from nature were lacking. Nevertheless, the persistent efforts of President Young generally produced enough successes to keep the Saints fed, clothed, and housed. In 1875, two years before President Young's death, the government census listed Utah's industries as producing $5,000,000 worth of merchandise annually.[35]

BRIGHAM YOUNG'S LAST YEARS

During his later years, President Young was plagued by health problems, controversy with government officials, with a divorce suit urged on by gentile lawyers, and with being arrested. But there was also a brighter side. He was visited by John Wood, old friend and former mayor of Quincy, Illinois, by Alexander Doniphan, whose courage had once saved the life of Joseph Smith and others, and by Thomas L. Kane, whose service to Utah and her people had been invaluable in settling the Utah War.

In October, 1875, President Ulysses S. Grant came to Utah. As Brigham Young was being introduced to him on the train between Ogden and Salt Lake City by Elder George Q. Cannon—Utah's delegate to Congress—President Young said: "President Grant, this is the first time I have ever seen a president of my country." After he was introduced to Mrs. Grant, he spent a pleasant thirty minutes visiting with her. Perhaps the greatest consolation of President Grant's visit was that he modified his previously hostile attitude towards the Saints and, although he was never friendly toward them, he was not as aggressive as he previously had been in pushing for anti-Mormon legislation.

Completion of the St. George Temple

When the Church leaders had to stop giving endowments in the Nauvoo Temple, President Young told those who had not received theirs that they need not worry because temples would be built in the West. The President had the privilege of getting temples underway at Salt Lake City, St. George, Manti, and Logan. He had the privilege of presiding at general conference

Temple at St. George, Utah, under construction, 1873-77. *Courtesy of Church Historical Department.*

held at St. George on April 6, 1877, when the first temple completed in Utah was dedicated, a source of great satisfaction to him.

President Young's Last Visit to the Stakes of Zion

During the summer of 1877 President Young

> set the priesthood in order as it had never been since the first organization of the church upon the earth. He defined the duties of the apostles, he defined the duties of the seventies, he defined the duties of the high priests, the duties of the elders and those of the lesser priesthood, with plainness and distinctness and power—the power of God— in a way that it is left on record in such unmistakable language that no one need err who has the Spirit of God resting down upon him.[36]

President Young began the work of setting in order the stakes of Zion at the general conference in St. George and continued to do the same in other stakes as the President and Apostles moved northward. The dates and the route of these conferences

Temple at St. George, Utah, as it looks today. *Permission of Church Information Service.*

can be traced in the following record:

April 7	St. George Stake (organized)
April 17 and 18	Kanab Stake
April 23	Panguitch Stake
April or May ?	Utah Stake
May 12 and 13	Salt Lake Stake
May 21	Cache Stake
May 25 and 26	Weber Stake (reorganized)
June 17	Davis Stake
June 24 and 25	Tooele Stake
July 1	Juab Stake (reorganized)
July 1	Morgan Stake
July 4	Sanpete Stake
July 8 and 9	Summit Stake
July 14 and 15	Wasatch Stake
July 15	Sevier Stake (reorganized)
July 21 and 22	Millard Stake (reorganized)
July 25 and 26	Beaver Stake (reorganized)
July 29	Parowan Stake
August 19	Box Elder Stake
August 25 and 26	Bear Lake Stake

These twenty stakes were all that had been organized at the time of the death of Brigham Young. The last one he visited was at Box Elder on August 19.

DEATH OF BRIGHAM YOUNG

After visiting the Church conference in Brigham City the President returned to Salt Lake City, where he became ill on August 23. Six days later, August 29, 1877, surrounded by his family and friends, he died of cholera morbus. Shortly before passing away, he expressed gratitude for having his family near him and for being so well cared for. His last audible words were "Joseph, Joseph, Joseph." [37]

THE CHARACTER OF BRIGHAM YOUNG

From the day that Brigham Young, as president of the Twelve Apostles, officially assumed the leadership of the Church on August 8, 1844, he became a national figure and inherited, to a great extent, both the love and the antagonism that had been shown to Joseph the Prophet. If it were necessary for a man to earn the right of leadership through faith, loyalty, integrity, ability, and service, then Brother Brigham had earned that right. Although it took him many months of study and prayer to become convinced of the truthfulness of the Church, after he had "set his hand to the plow," never once did he turn back; never once did he weaken; never once did he doubt the genuineness of Joseph's claim to heavenly authority; and never once had he failed to give personal sacrifice for the benefit of the Church. For twelve years his conviction had been evidenced by performance. When others had wavered, his courage had bolstered them. In 1837 on a certain occasion several of the Twelve, the Three Witnesses, and a number of other authorities had been holding a meeting when the question was put before them as to how the Prophet Joseph could be deposed and David Whitmer made president of the Church. There were many others present who were opposed to such a measure. Brigham Young said:

> I rose up, and in a plain and forcible manner told them that Joseph was a Prophet, and I knew it, and that they might rail and slander him as much as they pleased, they could not destroy the appointment of the Prophet of God,

they could only destroy their own authority, cut the thread that bound them to the Prophet and to God, and sink themselves to hell. [38]

Captain Richard F. Burton of the British army who visited Salt Lake City for a few weeks in 1860, wrote a sketch of Brigham Young which is one of the most objective and fair treatments among all of the non-Mormon writers who attempted to portray him. [39]

Mark Twain's Visit to Brigham Young

Mark Twain has left us an interesting sidelight into the character of Brother Brigham. He went to see the president with his brother (secretary of the territory of Nevada) and some other Nevada dignitaries:

The second day, we made the acquaintance of Mr. Street (since deceased) and put on white shirts and went and paid a state visit to the king (Brigham Young). He seemed a quiet, kindly, easy-mannered, dignified, self-possessed old gentleman of fifty-five or sixty, and had a gentle craft in his eye that probably belonged there. He was very simply dressed and was just taking off a straw hat as we entered. He talked about Utah, and the Indians, and Nevada, and general American matters and questions, with our secretary and certain government officials who came with us. But he never paid any attention to me, notwithstanding I made several attempts to "draw him out" on federal politics and his high-handed attitude toward Congress. I thought some of the things I said were rather fine. But he merely looked around at me, at distant intervals, something as I have seen a benignant old cat look around to see which kitten was meddling with her tail. By and by I subsided into an indignant silence, and sat until the end, hot and flushed, and execrating him in my heart for an ignorant savage. But he was calm. His conversation with those gentlemen flowed on as sweetly and peacefully and musically as any summer brook. When the audience was ended and we were retiring from the presence, he put his hand on my head, beamed down on me in an admiring way and said to my brother:

"Ah—your child, I presume? Boy or girl?" [40]

At his funeral Daniel H. Wells, Wilford Woodruff, Erastus Snow, George Q. Cannon, and John Taylor all spoke genuine words of praise and gratitude for Brigham Young's life and accomplishments. Among the words of Wilford Woodruff are the following:

> I do not suppose there was ever a man breathed the breath of life who, in the short space of forty-five years, has done so much towards the establishment of the government and kingdom of God, as our beloved president [Brigham Young]. His life has been before many of you for several years, and to some from the commencement of his labors in this church. He felt the weight of this dispensation resting upon him; he certainly has been true and faithful unto death, and he is prepared to receive a crown of life. . . . It is said that 'blessings brighten as they take their flight.' I have often felt in listening to the glorious principles of President Young, that the people here heard him so much that they hardly prized the beauty and the extent of the results and virtues of his teachings. . . . He has been true and faithful to the end and therefore all is well with him. [41]

ESTIMATE OF BRIGHAM YOUNG BY A DAUGHTER

Let us read the words of one who knew a different and more intimate side of Brigham Young, his daughter, Susa Young Gates:

> The world knows Brigham Young as a statesman and colonizer; but to his children he was an ideal father. Kind to a fault, tender, thoughtful, just and firm. He spoke but once and none were so daring as to disobey. But that his memory is almost worshipped by all who bear his name is an eloquent tribute to his character. None of us feared him; all of us adored him. If the measure of a man's greatness is truly given by Carlyle, as bounded by the number of those who loved him and who were loved by him, then few men are as great as was my father, Brigham Young. [42]

ESTIMATE OF BRIGHAM YOUNG AS A PROPHET

To the Latter-day Saints, Brigham Young was loved best for

his calling as a prophet of God and for his love and devotion to that calling. Brigham Young—carpenter, painter, and glazier—brought up in a household where the love of Jesus Christ was taught, brought that love with him into the Church. Upon that foundation his knowledge of the gospel built a solid character which prepared him to serve at the head of the restored church and to serve the entire membership—the meek, the humble, the rich and the poor—to serve all who needed and wanted his service. And the membership loved him for his service and honored and revered him as a mighty prophet of God to the Saints of the latter days.

Footnotes

[1]S. Dilworth Young, *"Here is Brigham. . ."* (Salt Lake City: Bookcraft, 1964), p. 27.

[2]Young, p. 37.

[3]Young, p. 42.

[4]Young, p. 43. This little home is still standing, though it is not so near the banks of the canal, for the bed of the canal was later changed. In the summer of 1967 Mr. and Mrs. Matthew Uglialaro, present owners of the home, renovated it and installed a sewer system for the first time.

[5]Young, p. 61.

[6]Susa Young Gates, *The Life Story of Brigham Young* (London: Jarrolds Publishers, 34 Paternoster Row E. C. 4, 1930), p. 22.

[7]Young, p. 65.

[8]Young, pp. 65-70.

[9]Young, p. 75.

[10]Young, p. 93.

[11]Russell R. Rich, *Those Who Would Be Leaders* (Provo, Utah: Brigham Young University Extension Publications, May 1967), p. 3. *See also* Edward W. Tullidge, *Life of Brigham Young* (New York: n.p., 1877), pp. 82-83; and William E. Berrett and Alma P. Burton, *Readings in L.D.S. Church History* (Salt Lake City: Deseret Book Co., 1955), 1:238-39.

[12]Preston Nibley, *Brigham Young, the Man and His Works* (Salt Lake City: Deseret News Press, 1937), pp. 35-36.

[13]Young, pp. 346-47.

[14]Young, p. 351.

[15]Young, p. 352.

[16]*CHC*, 2:415.

[17]Milton R. Hunter, *Brigham Young, the Colonizer* (Salt Lake City: Deseret News Press, 1940), p. 141. This book will be used considerably through much of the remainder of this chapter. It is a must for someone who desires a further knowledge of Brigham Young's colonizing efforts.

[18]Hunter, p. 141.

[19]Solomon F. Kimball, "President Brigham Young's First Trip to Bear Lake Valley," *Improvement Era* 10 (February 1907):296.

[20]Kimball, pp. 301-4.

²¹Russell R. Rich, *Land of the Sky-Blue Water* (Provo, Utah: Brigham 361
Young University Press, September 1963), p. 41.

²²Kimball, pp. 301-4.

²³Hunter, p. 57.

²⁴Hunter, p. 58.

²⁵*CHC*, 5:507-8.

²⁶Hunter, p. 59. *See also* Edward W. Tullidge, *History of Salt Lake City* (Salt Lake City: Star Publishing Co., 1886), p. 75.

²⁷Hunter, p. 61.

²⁸*CHC*, 2:538.

²⁹For an excellent treatise on the Perpetual Emigration Fund and its accomplishments, read Gustive O. Larson, *Prelude to the Kingdom* (Francestown, N. H.: Marshall Jones Co., 1947).

³⁰Hunter, p. 159.

³¹Hunter, pp. 160-61. *See also* Brigham Young, "First General Epistle . . . to the Saints," JH, 8 September 1847. This letter was addressed not only to the Saints in the valley, but to Latter-day Saints everywhere.

³²Hunter, p. 162.

³³Hunter, p. 162.

³⁴*CHC*, 4:24-26.

³⁵Hunter, p. 166.

³⁶*CHC*, 5:508.

³⁷*CHC*, 5:509.

³⁸*Millennial Star* 25:487. *See also* Tullidge, *Life of Brigham Young*, p. 82; and Nibley, p. 18.

³⁹Hunter, p. 16. For a detailed description, see Richard F. Burton, *City of the Saints and Across the Rocky Mountains to California* (New York: Harper and Brothers, 1862), pp. 238-40.

⁴⁰Samuel L. Clemens [Mark Twain], *Roughing It.* 2 vol. (New York and London: Harper and Brothers, 1899), 1:116-17. *See also* Hunter, p. 56.

⁴¹*CHC*, 5:516.

⁴²Gates, p. 265.

Anti Bigamy Law 1862 - a Lincol[n]
B Young dies   9 Aug 1827

?: that never aimed at all
against Joseph Smith — B. Young
& Kimble

Shaffer & McKean.
(1870 Gov) (Chief Justice of Court)

Aug 29 - 1877 Pres. Young dies

Grant - pretty much Anti mormon
because of his Vice Pres. Colfax
and Reverend Newman (Chaplain of
Congress) Influenced ~~them~~ Grant
against mormons -
Case. Eliza Webb Young — B.Y. didn't
       favor her enough wanted a divorce
         Government recognize plural marriage
if she is awarded any alimony - finally
dismissed.
                    Dr.
Pratt - Newman Debate = Polygamy
(Scholar) (the darling of Political Set)
           papers said Dr. Newman should show
         Polygamy wrong by scripture
      picked Orson Pratt to debate with him
Aug 12 - 1870 first day of debate
 " Does the bible sanction Polygamy "
           at the tabernacle
 < Pratt corrected Newmans Hebrew
    " shall not take a wife into her
      sister."

17

Statehood for Utah

THE DOCTRINE OF PLURAL MARRIAGE

When the Latter-day Saints came to the Great Basin, there
was no federal law against the practice of plural marriage. Although the revelation was not committed to writing until July
12, 1843, Joseph Smith had received his first information about
it in 1831 upon inquiry as to why Abraham, Jacob, and other
prophets were permitted to have more than one wife. The revelation of the new and everlasting covenant of marriage which
the Lord gave embraced much more than that pertaining to the
prophet's question. He gave a whole new law of marriage, of
which the primary principle was marriage for time and all eternity. He also indicated that under certain circumstances a man
might have more than one wife sealed to him for the purpose of
multiplying and replenishing the earth. (D&C 132:63.) The
power to perform such sealings was given to Joseph Smith—
whom the Lord had appointed—and He explained there was
never to be but one man on earth at a time upon whom this
power and the keys of the priesthood were to be bestowed, and
any contract not made by this power would be of no efficacy or
force when men were dead. (D&C 132:7.)

The Prophet was told that those to whom this law of the new
and everlasting covenant of marriage was revealed would have to
obey it. (D&C 132:7.) This referred to the total law, including

364   the principles of eternal marriage as well as the aspect of plural marriage which was to be permitted only under certain conditions. Thus, the Prophet knew that he would be expected to enter into plural marriage upon the same principle and under the same conditions that the Bible patriarchs and prophets received their wives, that is, under sanction and approval of divine law.[1]

He was told the time had not yet come for him to start living the law.[2] Later, when he was instructed that the time had come, it was a difficult matter for him to enter the practice. Eliza R. Snow, who became one of the Prophet's wives, stated he hesitated to do so until an angel of God stood by him with a drawn sword and informed him that unless he established plural marriage, his priesthood would be taken from him and he would be destroyed.[3] Joseph Bates Noble married him to Louisa Beaman on April 5, 1841.

After the Apostles returned from Great Britain during the summer of that year, 1841, Joseph began to officially instruct selected Church authorities pertaining to its practice. This was done privately, because aware of the natural repugnance of the Christian ethic toward so-called polygamy, the anti-Mormons would gain a great advantage. Certain Church authorities were called to practice the new doctrine, and certain others who were otherwise good men took it upon themselves to teach and practice it without authorization.

A third group of men took advantage of the element of mystery in the Prophet's private teachings to spread the falsehood that the Prophet approved of promiscuous intercourse between the sexes—that there was no harm in it if it were kept secret. These men—John C. Bennett, William and Wilson Law, Charles and Francis Higbee, Charles Foster, and a small number of others—deceived a few women into committing sin with them. But when their wickedness was discovered the Prophet boldly denounced it, though it brought the wrath of many upon him and eventually led to his death.[4]

It was the second group, however—those otherwise good men who began teaching and practicing plural marriage without authorization—that caused the Prophet on October 5, 1843 to record in his journal:

Gave instructions to try those persons who were preaching, teaching, or practicing the doctrine of plurality of wives; for according to the law, I hold the keys of this power in the last days; for there is never but one on earth at a time on whom the power and its keys are conferred; and I have constantly said no man shall have but one wife at a time, unless the Lord directs otherwise.[5]

Through the remainder of the Nauvoo period there was an ever increasing number of Latter-day Saints who entered into the secret practice of plurality of wives, although it had been a most difficult principle for most of them to accept; this was especially so with Brigham Young, Heber C. Kimball, and Orson Pratt. But when they received a conviction in their hearts that under certain conditions it was a divine principle, they moved forward.

Testimony of Women

The same is true of the women who entered the practice. According to Lucy Walker:

When the Prophet Joseph Smith first mentioned the principle of plural marriage to me I felt indignant and so expressed myself to him, because my feelings and education were averse to anything of that nature. But he assured me the doctrine had been revealed to him of the Lord, that I was entitled to receive a testimony of its divine origin myself. He counseled me to pray to the Lord which I did, and thereupon I received from Him a powerful and irresistible testimony of the truthfulness and divinity of plural marriage, which testimony has abided with me ever since.[6]

Eliza R. Snow related her experiences and feelings in regard to plural marriage and said that the thought was repugnant to her feelings and education but when she reflected that this was the dispensation of the fulness of times embracing all other dispensations, it was plain that plural marriage must be included. She went on to say that she was sealed to the Prophet Joseph Smith and had never had cause to regret it.[7]

Bathsheba W. Smith, the wife of George A. Smith, revealed her conviction that the doctrine was from God and that she had given to her husband five wives who were good, virtuous, honorable young women, that she loved her husband very much and had joy in knowing that what she had done was acceptable to God.[8]

366   In Utah on August 29, 1852, President Brigham Young called upon Orson Pratt to publicly announce to the world that the Latter-day Saints were practicing plural marriage. This practice was immediately labeled with the term polygamy, although, in a technical sense what the Latter-day Saints practiced never was polygamy; it was polygyny. *The Americana Encyclopedia* states that polygamy "is the plurality of wives or husbands at the same time."[9] In the United States it is often confused with polygyny, one husband and more than one wife. This probably is because Mormon polygynous marriages were wrongly called polygamy.

The epithet polygamy was hurled at the Mormon practice by the enemies of the Church in order to make it sound as repulsive as possible. Even many devout Christians who revered the Old Testament prophets still looked upon it as unchristian and sinful.

By the time of the national political election of 1856 the newly formed Republican party had branded polygamy and slavery as the twin relics of barbarism.[10] Although John C. Fremont, the Republican candidate for president in 1856, was defeated, the Democrats were still smarting under the twin relics slogan. They therefore accepted without investigation the false charges of Judges W. W. Drummond and George Stiles, the disappointed mail contractor W. M. F. Magraw, and Indian Agent Thomas Twiss. In the Presidential election of 1860 the Republicans again had an anti-polygamy plank in their platform. This time the party was successful, and Abraham Lincoln was bound by the party platform.

ANTI-MORMON LEGISLATION AND UNFRIENDLY APPOINTEES

The First Anti-Bigamy Law

Justin Morrill of Vermont had introduced an anti-bigamy law in the House of Representatives in the spring of 1860, where it passed the House and was received by the Senate but was left untouched when the thirty-sixth Congress adjourned on March 3, 1861.

When the thirty-seventh Congress convened, the southern states were not represented, and the Republicans had a clear majority. On April 8, 1862, Representative Morrill again introduced his bill to punish and prevent so-called polygamy.[11]

In the Senate Bayard explained that the bill of the House was "intended to punish the crimes of polygamy, or bigamy properly speaking . . . but that it also punished cohabitation without marriage," and that it would be of "no utility to carry the act beyond the evil intended to be remedied," so this part was amended.[12] Although Senator James A. McDougall of California opposed it, the Senate passed the bill by a vote of thirty-seven to two, and President Lincoln signed it on July 1, 1862.

The essential elements in this first anti-bigamy, anti-Mormon bill were these. Section one defines the Act of Bigamy as that of a person having a husband or wife living and marrying another person; that the penalty for conviction shall be a fine not exceeding five hundred dollars, and by imprisonment not exceeding five years.[13]

Section two appears to contradict itself, claiming to revoke and annul the charter of the Church as granted under certain laws of the territory of Utah, but provides that the "act shall be so limited and construed as not to affect or interfere with the right of property legally acquired under the ordinances heretofore mentioned, nor with the right 'to worship God according to the dictates of conscience. . . .' but only intends to annul all acts pertaining to polygamy or spiritual marriage."[14]

Section three sets a limit of $50,000 on the value of real property that a religious or charitable organization can hold in a territory of the United States and provides that all property held contrary to the provisions of the act shall be forfeited and escheat to the United States but provides that existing vested rights in real estate should not be impaired by the provisions of this section.

The Latter-day Saints who believed wholeheartedly in the support of orderly government and its laws were now placed in somewhat of a dilemma.[15] They took the position that the law was an infringement upon their religious liberties, however, and was therefore unconstitutional. No officers were appointed to enforce the law and no funds for enforcement were allotted. Although Lincoln had signed the measure, he adopted the policy of leaving the Mormons alone, even to the appointment of much more acceptable territorial officials than his first appointees had been. His first appointments had been to mostly arrogant anti-Mormons. However, Chief Justice John F. Kinney, Governors Duane Doty and Charles Durkee, Chief Justice John Titus, and a few others were well liked by the Saints.

368   Some of the anti-Mormon officials in Utah tried to take immediate action against the Saints. Judges Waite and Drake threatened to arrest Brigham Young—using military force if necessary—on charges of marrying another wife. He appeared voluntarily in the court of Judge Kinney, however, and gave bond to appear when wanted. This put him beyond the reach of either Judge Waite or Judge Drake; later the grand jury refused to indict him on grounds of insufficient evidence.[16]

In 1865 when Speaker of the House Schuyler Colfax visited Utah with Samuel Bowles and other friends, he suggested to Brigham Young that he have a revelation to do away with "polygamy."[17] About two weeks after the Colfax party departed from Utah, James M. Ashley of Ohio, chairman of the committee on territories of the House of Representatives, came to Utah. President Young asked him, "Well, Mr. Ashley, are you also going to recommend us to get a new revelation on polygamy. . . ?"[18]

Attempts to Pass Further Anti-Mormon Legislation

Wade Bill

The purpose of the Wade bill, introduced in 1866, seemed to be to destroy local self-government in Utah. It called for the militia to be put directly under the control of the governor of the territory with all of the officers to be selected, appointed, and commissioned by him; the United States marshal was to select members of both grand and petit juries; probate judges in all of the counties were to be appointed by the governor. In addition, the bill provided that officers in the Mormon Church could not solemnize marriages; Utah laws exempting church property from taxation were to be annulled, except that $20,000 worth of property was to be exempted; the law giving the Church the right to regulate its own membership was to be repealed; and the trustee-in-trust of the Church was required to make a full report, on oath, every year to the governor of the territory accounting for "all church properties, moneys in bank, notes, deposits with the church, etc."[19] It died on the Senate calendar.

Cragin Bill

Introduced December 13, 1867, the Cragin bill retained all

the bad features of the Wade bill with a few others added,
including the abolishment of trial by jury for those accused of
violation of the Anti-Bigamy Act of 1862. The bill was not
considered until December, 1869, at which time it was received
favorably, but it did not come up for a vote.

Cullom Bill

This bill, introduced in 1870, was not so severe as the Cragin
bill, for it did not abolish trial by juries, prohibit "ministers" of
the Church from performing marriages, or require the trustee-
in-trust of the Church to make an annual financial report to the
governor of the territory. Nevertheless the bill was still excessively oppressive. It was strenuously opposed by Representative Thomas Fitch of Nevada and Aaron A. Sargent of California. For various reasons, including opposition from the *New
York Herald,* the *New York World* and the *Omaha Herald,* along
with the help of William S. Godbe, an apostate, who visited
President Ulysses S. Grant and convinced him the Mormons
were not disloyal to the government, the Cullom bill was
allowed to die on the Senate calendar.

Mormon Women Oppose Legislation

In the meantime, the Mormon women in Utah were aroused
against the efforts of the country to pass anti-polygamy legislation. In January, 1870, many Relief Societies met and protested
passage of the Cragin or Cullom bills. Finally on January 19, a
mass meeting was held in the tabernacle which included nearly
all of the leading women of the Church. Sarah M. Kimball,
president of the Fifteenth Ward Relief Society, was chosen
president of the meeting. Speeches were given by Mrs. Levi
Riter; Mrs. Phoebe Woodruff; Eliza R. Snow, general president
of the Relief Society of the Church; Harriet Cook Young; and
others. The ladies made it plain that they were not slaves; they
were in Utah by choice; they considered themselves co-workers
with their husbands; they would not stand idly by and see the
rights of their sons and husbands trampled on; and they
intended to honor, teach and practice the law of celestial
marriage.

Among the resolutions passed by the women were these:

Resolved: That we, the ladies of Salt Lake City in mass

meeting assembled, do manifest our indignation and protest against the bill before Congress, known as the Cullom bill, also the one known as the Cragin bill, and all similar bills, expressions and manifestos.

Resolved: That we acknowledge the institutions of the Church of Jesus Christ of Latter-day Saints as the only reliable safeguard of female virtue and innocence . . . we are and shall be united with our brethren in sustaining them against each and every encroachment.[20]

Ashley Bill

Between the first and second introductions of the Cragin bill—December 1867 and December 1869—another bill was introduced which called for the nearly total dismemberment of the territory of Utah. The bill proposed to give a strip of Utah on the west about two degrees wide (118 miles) to Nevada, which had already received two previous strips after having been originally carved out of Utah from the 1850 boundaries. This would have included Cedar City, Washington, St. George, and other Utah Dixie settlements. The strip on the east was to be given to Colorado and a piece on the northeast to Wyoming. This would have included northern Davis County, Morgan, Weber, Cache, and Rich counties.

That left to Utah would have been from Farmington southward, as far as Levan in Juab County about two degrees wide (118 miles); from thence to the present southern boundary of the state would have been one degree (59 miles) wide. This would have included Scipio, Fillmore, Beaver, and Parowan.[21] About 25,000 of Utah's population would have gone to Wyoming, and 10,000 would have gone to Nevada.

Originally the purpose of Ashley's bill was to blot out Utah completely, but when he learned that the Mormons would politically control the other territories, he redesigned it to leave the largest part of the population within a separate small unit until the other territories would be able to absorb them without the Mormons getting political control. He further learned, however, that it might still result in giving the Mormons control of Nevada and Wyoming and possibly Colorado, as well as the reduced territory of Utah. So the idea was abandoned. Mr. Bowles, editor of the Springfield *Republican* stated:

The idea of dividing the territory up among the adjoining territories is not practicable now [1869]; under it, the divide and conquer; for with their number and discipline, they could out-vote and out-manage three territories.[22]

PRESIDENT ULYSSES S. GRANT'S APPOINTEES TO UTAH

After the release of Governor Stephen Harding in 1863 and the resignations of Judges Charles B. Waite and Thomas J. Drake, Utah enjoyed a period of tranquility. Governors Doty and Durkee and acting Governors Edwin Higgins of Michigan and S. A. Mann of New York, were all well liked in Utah, as were Chief Justices John Titus of Pennsylvania, Charles Wilson of Illinois, associate Justices Enos Hoge of Illinois and Solomon P. McCurdy of Missouri (except for his part in the Brassfield wedding). United States Marshals Josiah Hosmer and Joseph M. Orr and District Attorneys Hosea Stout (a Mormon) and C. H. Hempstead were all satisfactory.

But with the election of President Ulysses S. Grant, whose vice-president, Schuyler Colfax, and other anti-Mormons had influenced him against the Mormons, a new breed of appointee came to Utah. Governor J. Wilson Shaffer, boasted that "Never after me, by G — — shall it be said that Brigham Young is Governor of Utah." [23] Because Chief Justice Wilson would not discriminate against Mormons, Governor Shaffer had him released; and James B. McKean, a forty-nine-year-old New York resident, was appointed chief justice. Mr. McKean said to a brother-in-law of President Grant:

> Judge Dent, the mission which God has called upon me to perform in Utah is as much above the duties of other courts and judges as the heavens are above the earth, and wherever and whenever I may find the local or federal laws obstructing or interfering therewith, by God's blessing I shall trample them under my feet. [24]

Other appointees of Grant were Vernon Vaughan of Alabama, secretary, who became acceptable to the Mormons; Obed F. Strickland of Michigan and Cyrus M. Hawley of Illinois, associate justices appointed in April, 1869, bitter anti-Mormons; M. T. Patricks, United States marshal; and George C. Bates, United States district attorney.

Governor Shaffer was a military man who came to Utah with the idea of crushing the Mormons. After staying in Washington for the winter of 1869 and 1870 to lobby for passage of the

Cullom bill, he arrived in Utah on March 20, 1870, still hopeful of the privilege of being able to hand out to cronies who had come to Utah many appointive jobs that the bill would make available to the governor. He was disappointed and died seven months later of consumption with which he was ill when he first came to Utah. He had managed to keep the Church members and even some of the government people in an uproar during his few months as governor.

Vernon Vaughan, secretary of the territory, was appointed governor by President Grant, but the anti-Mormons found him insufficiently, anti-Mormon and pressured the president for another man. He appointed Governor George Woods of Oregon, a former Missourian, whose Oregon term of Governor had just been completed. He arrived in Salt Lake City the latter part of April, 1871, and continued the anti-Mormon policies of former Governor Shaffer. Between him and Chief Justice McKean, the Saints were in for trying times.

WOMAN SUFFRAGE FOR UTAH

With the impression that polygamy in Utah existed only because the women were degraded, the suggestion was made to Representatives Ashley of Ohio and Hotchkiss of Connecticut to "elevate" them by giving them the vote. In this way polygamy would be destroyed because the women would supposedly vote it out. During the latter part of March Representative Julian introduced into the House "A Bill to Discourage Polygamy in Utah." It was a one-section bill giving the women of Utah the right to vote. Julian was somewhat surprised to find that W. H. Hooper, delegate from Utah, was in favor of it. That day Senator Pomeroy of Kansas introduced a similar bill into the Senate.

Three editorials in favor of the bill appeared in quick succession in the *Deseret News,* which dampened the ardor of the anti-Mormons, and the bill never came to a vote. But the idea had caught on in Utah and the territorial legislature soon passed an enfranchisement bill for women. It was next presented to acting Governor S. A. Mann (Governor Shaffer was still in Washington, D.C.), who was skeptical but signed it because it had been passed unanimously by both houses of the legislature. Two days later some of the Mormon women voted at a municipal election; Seraph Young, Brigham Young's niece, was the first woman to vote.

Although the Mormon women were the first to vote in the
nation, they were not the first to receive the franchise; two
months previously, on December 10, 1869, after Governor John
Campbell of Wyoming had vetoed the Wyoming bill enfranchis-
ing Wyoming's women, the legislature passed it over his veto.
Acting Governor Mann of Utah was the first executive in the
United States to sign a woman suffrage bill.

THE UTAH RING PRESSES FORWARD

With the coming to Utah of President Grant's appointees, the
anti-Mormon clique became known as the Utah Ring, often
spoken of as the "Ring." They organized the Liberal Political
Party in 1870 at Corinne, and began to engage in all types of
anti-Mormon activity, looking always toward the officials in
Washington for help. The Ring kept a constant lobby in Washington between 1872 and 1874. What the Cullom bill had failed
to give to the anti-Mormons by law, Judge McKean and the
other judges endeavored to take by decree. They endeavored to
take control of the selection of juries and ruled that probate
courts had no original jurisdiction in civil and criminal cases.
The Englebrecht Liquor Case came up in Judge McKean's court
shortly after his arrival on August 30, 1870; it went on through
court appeals for the next eighteen months until the United
States Supreme Court ruled in 1872 that the juries had been
illegally drawn. Thus, the reckless course of Judge McKean was
partially halted. This decision voided all of the criminal proceedings that had taken place in the territorial courts for the
past year and a half and discharged 138 prisoners. It threw a
bad light on the Grant administration in Washington, D.C., but
President Grant still continued to back Judge McKean, his other
appointed judges, and Governor Woods.

The Frelinghuysen and Voorhees Bills

The Frelinghuysen and Voorhees bills were introduced into
Congress in 1872 to get control of elections and the local courts
in Utah, but they did not pass. [25] The ideas in the Voorhees bill
had come from "Ringite" R. N. Baskin.

Blair Bill

Another bill of 1872 was one introduced in February by
James G. Blair of Missouri, who had the courage to propose that

374 all marriages in Utah be legalized and all prosecutions pending
of any polygynous marriages be dismissed. Blair did not receive
any support for such a measure, although he did receive the
gratitude of the Utah people.

The Logan Bill

In his December, 1872, message to Congress, President Grant
called for passage of legislation recommending a careful revision
of the laws of Utah by Congress and for the "ultimate extin-
guishment of polygamy." In a special message on February 14,
1873, he made further recommendations for laws against Utah's
people, the ideas presented being those of the Utah "Ring." He
said if no laws were forthcoming, military interference would be
necessary.

At this time the Logan bill was before the United States
Senate. It was a rehash of the Voorhees bill. If it had passed it
would have literally taken local self-government away from the
Utah people. Also in 1873 S. A. Merritt introduced into the
House a very drastic bill, similar to the Cullom bill of 1870, but
it also failed.

The Poland Law

With the encouragement of President Ulysses S. Grant and
the Utah "Ring," opposition continued into the next Congress.
On December 1, 1873, President Grant again asked Congress to
act. On April 25, 1874, the Poland bill was reported as House
Bill 3097. It was passed on June 23, and the next day President
Grant signed it, making it the first law against the Mormon
people to be enacted since 1862.

The bill, as it was finally enacted, made no reference to polygamy. It did take from the probate courts of Utah all
criminal, civil, and chancery jurisdiction which these courts had
had by Utah legislative enactment since 1852. The people had
had confidence in these courts because their judges were elected
from among them and they had the interests of the community
at heart. The lawless transient population that drifted into the
community was under their jurisdiction. Now, local authority
was gone. The offices of territorial marshal and attorney general
were abolished and their functions assigned to the United States
marshal and his deputies and the United States district attorney
and his assistants. Costs and expenses of all prosecutions against

any law of the territorial legislature were to be paid out of the
treasury of the territory.

Making up jury lists was to be done jointly by the clerks of the respective district courts and the probate judge of the county in which the court was to be next held. Although this method made it possible to have at least 50 percent gentile representation on grand and petit juries in the territory, Poll states that it actually "meant nothing so far as polygamy was concerned, for a hung jury trial could just as effectively break down the court processes as a 'no bill' grand jury." [26] Because of this, the Ring was very much disappointed in the Poland Law, which was far more moderate than many of its predecessors which had failed to pass.

DISMISSAL OF MCKEAN AND OTHERS

When the Grant-appointed United States District Attorney George C. Bates really got into the heart of matters in Utah, he was appalled at the lack of quality in the federal appointees and the corruption among them. He discovered that associate justice Obed F. Strickland had actually purchased his office from his predecessor Thomas Drake, who resigned a year before his term was up and recommended Strickland for the office upon his signing a note to pay him the year's salary of $2,800 in four equal installments. He found that associate Justice Cyrus M. Hawley was guilty of bigamy. Chief Justice McKean had been permitted by Oscar Sawyer, manager of the *Salt Lake Tribune* to write editorials for the paper supporting his own decisions in court. Since Sawyer was also correspondent for the *New York Herald*, McKean's anti-Mormon editorials did much to mold public opinion against the Saints.

Because Bates violently opposed Judge McKean's tactics, there was friction between them. After dismissal of cases in McKean's court, brought about by the reversal of the Englebrecht case in the United States Supreme Court, President Grant still refused to dismiss McKean. Instead in December of 1872 he removed Bates from office. This gave Bates more freedom to speak out against corrupt politicians. Although expressing a high personal regard for President Grant, he stated in an open letter to him:

> Your entire administration of affairs in Utah, your special message to congress, and many of the most im-

portant appointments made by you here, have all been the result of misrepresentation, falsehood, and misunderstanding on your part of the real condition of affairs in this territory. . . .

In other communications, soon to be made, in every instance accompanied by the evidence, I will demonstrate how other distinguished officers have bought their offices, how you were made a mere catspaw by corrupt senators and representatives, to send officers here whom you would not have trusted among your horse blankets in the executive stable.[27]

Although Bates made other serious charges against Judge McKean, McKean managed to stay in office until 1875. Both Hawley and Strickland resigned in the winter of 1873 and were succeeded in office by Philip H. Emerson of Michigan on March 10 and Jacob S. Boreman of West Virginia on March 20. Bates was succeeded as United States district attorney in Utah by William Carey of Illinois.

Judge McKean, who was a judge "with a mission," continued to pursue his anti-Mormon tactics. In 1873 Ann Eliza Webb Young, who claimed to be the 19th wife of Brigham Young, brought suit for divorce alleging neglect, cruel treatment, and desertion. She requested $1,000 per month support money during the trial, $6,000 preliminary counsel fees, $14,000 more on final decree with a final award of $200,000 for maintenance. She justified such large sums on the ridiculous basis that Brigham Young was worth $8,000,000 and had an income of $40,000 per month. Her attorney was George R. Maxwell of the Ring, who also held the office of Land Registrar in Utah. Judge McKean was in a dilemma. He could hardly award support money without actually admitting that a legal marriage had taken place, and to do that would be to admit that Mormon plural marriage was legal. Still, he was anxious to award Ann Eliza her requests.

On February 25, 1874, the judge ordered Brigham Young to pay $3,000 toward expenses of the prosecution and $500 per month maintenance from the day of filing in 1873. The law fee was to be paid in ten days and the back alimony in twenty days. Upon advice of his counsel that he was entitled to an appeal, President Young did not pay the law fee. He was brought into court on March 11, where he gave as his reason for not paying that he was entitled to an appeal; and according to law, pending an appeal (which had been made) the order of the court was stayed. Although Brigham Young's secretary, James Jack, paid the $3,000 fee, Judge McKean found Brigham Young guilty of contempt of court, fined him $25, and sentenced him to one day in the penitentiary. He spent the night there and was released the following day.

The newspapers throughout the country were indignant over such tactics. President Grant finally reached the end of his patience with Judge McKean; five days later, on March 16, 1875, both Chief Justice McKean and Land Registrar George Maxwell were notified of their release from office. The judge was replaced by Daniel B. Lowe of Kansas.

Governor George L. Woods, whose term of office had expired on December 28, 1874, had been refused reappointment and had been replaced by Governor Samuel B. Axtell. Axtell was not anti-Mormon, and the Ring made such a fuss that President Grant transferred him to the governorship of New Mexico, replacing him with George Emery, who became strictly a neutral and therefore acceptable to the Saints, although he was denounced by the anti-Mormon press.

PRESIDENT ULYSSES S. GRANT VISITS UTAH

In October, 1875, President Grant and a party of friends made a personal visit to Utah where he somewhat modified his views toward the Latter-day Saint people. Tullidge states that upon seeing the Sunday School children all dressed in white to greet him he turned to Governor Emery and said: "Whose children are these?" "Mormon children," answered the governor, and President Grant after a pause replied: "I have been deceived."[28]

With the departure of Judges Cyrus M. Hawley, Obed F. Strickland, James B. McKean, Land Registrar Maxwell, and Governor George Woods, Utah had relative peace until after the arrival in 1880 of Eli H. Murray as governor and the passage of the Edmunds Law in 1882. In the meantime, however, there was an attempt to test the constitutionality of the Anti-Bigamy Law of 1862.

The Reynolds Polygamy Test Case

Inasmuch as the Church leaders and the government officials were anxious to test the constitutionality of the Anti-Bigamy

378 Law, the United States Attorney, Bates, arranged with Church leaders to have a test case. George Reynolds, President Young's secretary, was indicted in October, 1874. He appeared in court, where he provided evidence of plural marriage; he was found guilty and was sentenced to pay a $500 fine and spend one year in prison. The case was appealed to the territorial supreme court, where it was dismissed on June 19, 1875, on grounds that the jury had been illegally drawn. On October 30, 1875, he was indicted a second time, found guilty and sentenced to a fine of $500 and two years in prison at hard labor. On July 6, 1876, the supreme court of the territory affirmed the decision of the lower court. It was then appealed to the United States Supreme Court, which decided on January 6, 1879, that every civil government had the right to determine whether monogamy or polygamy should be the law of social life under its jurisdiction, and therefore the law of 1862 was valid.

    B. H. Roberts states that the action of Congress and the Supreme Court "was violative of the community right of local self-government" and cites Judge Jeremiah S. Black's argument before the judiciary committee of the House of Representatives on February 1, 1883, as evidence.[29] He further argues that no account of Mormon plural marriages as a religious issue was taken, the court having made no distinction between "common law bigamy" and the Mormon plural marriage system.[30] Nevertheless, the Supreme Court is the national authority. President Young did not live to know of the decision of the Supreme Court; he died on August 29, 1877.

    When the Anti-Bigamy Law of 1862 was first passed, it was recognized as a rather inoperative bill, since no provisions were ever made for enforcement.

    The Poland Law of 1874 took some aspects of local self-government away from the people, but it did not accomplish much toward the enforcement of the Anti-Bigamy Law; the only conviction that had been achieved was in the George Reynolds case which was mutually agreed upon as a test case. After the decision by the Supreme Court in 1879, the anti-Mormons clamored for more and stricter legislation. Poll states that "to the saints it meant that a new position had to be taken; either the law must be obeyed or a new basis for continuing to ignore it must be found."[31] The Saints took a "wait and see" attitude and went on "minding their own business" as Brigham Young had counseled years before. The Edmunds Act was passed in 1882, making it law.

The Edmunds law defined polygamy as a crime and substituted the word *polygamy* for the word *bigamy* used in the 1862 bill. Any person who had a living husband or wife and married another was guilty and was to be fined no more than $500 and not more than five years in jail or both—the same as the 1862 law. Polygamous living was defined as "unlawful cohabitation" and was a misdemeanor punishable by a fine not to exceed $300 or by imprisonment not to exceed six months, or by both fine and imprisonment. Anyone living in bigamy, or polygamy, or in unlawful cohabitation, or who believed it right for a man to have more than one wife was excluded from jury duty. The right to vote or hold any office of public trust was taken from both men and women living in plural marriage.

All registration and election offices in Utah were declared vacated, and the supervision of elections was to be placed in a commission composed of five people appointed by the president of the United States. The president was authorized to grant amnesty for offenses committed prior to passage of the Edmunds Act, based upon future observance of the law; and children born to Mormon polygynous marriages prior to January 1, 1883, were legitimated. [32]

After the Hoar Amendment was passed, giving the governor the right to appoint all offices left vacant in Utah because the commission would not be able to conduct the election on August 8, 1882, as required by law, Governor Murray attempted to fill the offices by appointment. In September and October of that year he appointed 174 such officers, but the "office grab" did not succeed, because the officers elected by the people refused to vacate on the grounds that when they were elected to the office they were to hold it for a certain number of years, or until a duly qualified successor had been elected. On February 3, 1883, a test case was taken to the territorial supreme court and won by the "office grab" clique; but an appeal was made to the United States Supreme Court, where, before the case could come up, election time (August 1883) had come again, and the Mormons still had sufficient votes to control the elections.

The Idaho Test Oath

The anti-Mormon fever spread to the territories bordering

380 Utah, and in Idaho Harvey W. "Kentucky" Smith and his
friends drew up a bill and had it presented to the thirteenth
territorial legislature in January, 1885. This bill, if passed,
would disfranchise not only every Mormon who practiced plural
marriage, but also every Latter-day Saint in the territory of
Idaho. The test oath that was to be taken before voting required
a person to say that he was not a bigamist or a polygamist and
that he did not belong to any organization that taught,
counseled, or advised its members to practice such. Just before
the vote was taken in the Idaho Council (the territorial senate),
James E. Hart, the council's youngest member and the delegate
from Bear Lake County, received permission to speak. He
proposed an amendment to the bill, which, if accepted, would
disfranchise only those Church members who were actually
practicing plural marriage. However, it would have also disfranchised any gentile or Mormon who was immoral. The substitute oath was to state, "You do solemnly swear that you are
not a bigamist or a polygamist or that you do not cohabit with
any other woman who is not your wife." [33]

Upon hearing this motion, Judge Brierley of Alturas County
jumped to the floor and shouted: "My G — — Gentlemen. We
can't accept Hart's proposal. That would disfranchise all of
us." [34]

Hart replied: "No. It wouldn't disfranchise all of us. I
married a good pure Mormon girl in a place that I consider
sacred, where we promised to be true to each other and, so help
me God, I intend to do just that."

Although Judge Brierley's remark indicated that lawmakers
were at least as sinful as they considered the Mormons to be,
the amendment was rejected and the test oath passed as it was
originally drawn. [35] It kept all members of the Church from
voting or holding office in Idaho for nearly ten years, dis-
franchising about one-fourth of the population of the territory
(25,000). It was ruled constitutional by the United States
Supreme Court on February 3, 1890. [36]

The Edmunds-Tucker Law

B. H. Roberts claims that the real cause of the anti-Mormon
crusade was a fight for the political control of Utah on the part
of the crusaders. They not only wanted control of the offices in
Utah that federal officers could give them, but control of the
legislature and the treasury of Utah as well. Even with the Utah

Sept ata 58 Children

1849
B. Young: Prophecy about
Utah in last day - S.L.
would be empire.

Commission in political control and with the other aspects of   381
the Edmunds Law as weapons, the Ring was not satisfied with
the general progress made against the Saints, as they still could
not wrest political control from the Mormons. In spite of the
reduction in the Mormon vote, John T. Caine, the People's
Party candidate, won election in the fall of 1882 as delegate to
Congress over Philip T. Van Zile, the Liberal Party candidate,
by a vote of 23,639 to 4,844. In the test oath for voting designed by the Utah Commission, they installed the phrase "in
the marriage relationship" so that it would not apply to those
who were morally corrupt outside of wedlock.

After Edmunds Law enforcement began in November, 1883,
the Ringites were continually pressing for more stringent legislation. At first the Utah Commission remained neutral, but they
also were soon making demands for more legislation. Governor
Murray kept vetoing the election rules which had been drawn
up by an all-Mormon—but totally monogamous—legislature
according to the guidelines provided in Section 9 of the
Edmunds bill. He did this in order to keep the Utah Commission in control of the voting machinery. This continued until
March, 1886, when the secretary of the interior requested
Murray's resignation for "vetoing appropriation bills for arbi-
trary reasons, and otherwise impeding the government of
Utah."[37] Other anti-Mormon officials released shortly afterwards were Judge Orlando W. Powers and United States Marshal
Ireland.

Associate Justice Powers and Chief Justice Charles Zane were
the inventors of the "segregation" doctrine, an interpretation of
the cohabitation aspect of the Edmunds Law that permitted a
judge to divide illegal cohabitation into periods of time (such as
each three months, or every three weeks, or even living with a
plural wife every third day) and then sentencing the offender to
six months in jail and a fine of $300 for each offense. In this
way the judge could skirt the maximum sentence feature of the
Edmunds Law and keep a man in jail indefinitely. Lorenzo
Snow, president of the Church from 1898 to 1901, was indicted
in December 1885 on three counts of illegal cohabitation and
was sentenced to serve three consecutive sentences of six
months in jail. Later, the United States Supreme Court termed
this interpretation of the law unconstitutional, and any
prisoners who had already served over six months were released,
including Lorenzo Snow.

Governor Murray was succeeded by Caleb W. West who ar-

382 rived in Salt Lake City on May 5, 1886. His intentions were good, but he soon became convinced the Saints were adamant in their attitude and practice of polygamy. With the new governor, other territorial officials, the Utah anti-Mormons, and the *Salt Lake Tribune* crying for more stringent legislation by Congress, the Edmunds-Tucker bill was sent to President Grover Cleveland for his signature. He neither approved it nor vetoed it; consequently, after ten days, on March 3, 1887, it became law without his signature. There were twenty-seven sections to the bill. Some of the more outstanding were the following: [38]

1. For prosecutions of polygamy or unlawful cohabitation, the lawful husband or wife was considered to be a competent witness.

2. It became the duty of the attorney-general to institute and subpoena witnesses, compelling them to attend.

3. All marriages were to be of public record, giving all information pertaining thereto, including the name of the person performing the same.

4. Sexual offenses were made punishable and local laws providing prosecution for adultery need not be initiated by the husband or wife, but could be initiated the same as other crimes.

5. The probate judges in Utah were to be appointed by the president of the United States.

6. Territorial commissioners and marshals could exercise the powers of justices of the peace and sheriffs respectively.

7. The laws of Utah which recognized the right of "illegitimate" children to inherit were voided and no illegitimate child [principally referring to children from plural wives] born more than twelve months after passage of this act, was entitled to inherit or share in his or her father's estate.

8. It was made the duty of the attorney-general to institute proceedings whereby the property of the Church and the Perpetual Emigrating Fund held in violation of the Anti-Bigamy Law of 1862 was to be turned over to the secretary of the interior to be disposed of for the benefit of the territory in which it was located. Places of worship, parsonages, or cemeteries were to be exempted.

9. The Church of Jesus Christ of Latter-day Saints was disincorporated and the attorney general was empowered to take such proceedings as would complete the affairs of the late corporation.

10. It was made unlawful for any female to vote in any election held in Utah for any purpose.

11. The Nauvoo Legion and the local militia laws were abolished; and the new territorial militia was to be officered by appointees of the governor, rather than the legislature.

12. Elections and election proceedings were to remain the power of the federal government until Congress should rectify a new election law by the territorial legislature.

13. The office of territorial superintendent of district schools and the duties of his office were placed upon a commissioner of schools, appointed by the supreme court of Utah. Sectarian instruction in common schools was forbidden.

14. All persons convicted of polygamy or unlawful cohabitation were disfranchised. As a condition for voting, holding office or serving on juries, a man was required to pledge obedience to the anti-polygamy laws, and to promise not to preach, aid, or advise anything contrary thereto.

The years to the end of 1887 had brought 327 convictions; the year of 1888 brought 334 more; and 1889 brought another 346. By the time of the Manifesto, there were approximately 1,300 men who had been convicted in Utah, with a few others in Idaho and Arizona.

On June 30, 1887, the government began to take over Church property in accordance with the Edmunds-Tucker Law.

Idaho Test Oath and Edmunds-Tucker Law

On May 18, 1890, the United States Supreme Court affirmed the points of the Edmunds-Tucker Law pertaining to the confiscation of Church property by a six to three decision.[39] In the meantime, on February 3, 1890, the Idaho Test Oath was declared by the United States Supreme Court to be "not open to any constitutional or legal objection."[40] On November 30, 1889, nine Mormon converts who had applied for United States citizenship were told by Associate Justice Thomas J. Anderson of the territorial supreme court of Utah that an alien who was a member of the Church was not a fit person to be a United States citizen.[41] Other judges had previously refused to grant citizenship on the same grounds.

In 1889 in their report to the secretary of the interior, the Utah Commission (those five men in charge of Utah's election machinery) suggested not only that the Idaho Test Oath be applied to Utah but also that women who entered the polygamous relationship should be punished. The commission's reports had already become so extreme in 1887 and 1888 that

384 two members, John A. McClernand and Ambrose B. Carlton, prepared a minority report denying many of the statements of the majority. After Carlton resigned in 1889, Commissioner McClernand continued to oppose the reports and actions of the majority of the commission members.

Cullom-Struble Bill

The Republican Platform of 1888 pledged still more stringent legislation for Utah, however; and with the election of President Benjamin Harrison, he reappointed Charles Zane as chief justice in Utah and made Arthur Thomas (a member of the Utah Commission and former territorial secretary who had been constantly active against the Mormons) governor of Utah.

Shelby M. Cullom, now a senator, and Representative Isaac R. Struble drew up a bill that would not only apply the Idaho Test Oath to Utah but would also disfranchise all Latter-day Saints in all of the territories. This literally meant that no member of the Church in Utah or any other territory could be a citizen. Thus, even where the Saints were in the great majority, they would have absolutely nothing to say about their government. This bill was jointly introduced into the House and Senate on April 11, 1890, but died on the calendar of each branch of Congress. Nevertheless, it was a warning to the Latter-day Saints as to what was in the legislative hopper against them. About this time, James G. Blaine, the secretary of state in the President's cabinet, urged the Saints to do something to relieve the anti-Mormon pressure upon the government.

THE ISSUANCE OF THE MANIFESTO

After passage of the Edmunds Law, President Chester A. Arthur pushed enforcement, and prosecution of polygynists went forward with vigor. Sentences were so severe that most polygynists went into hiding; thus, until the end of Arthur's administration, only a few cases were handled in the courts.

After election of Grover Cleveland, a Democrat who took office on March 4, 1885, sentences were not so severe and many men gave themselves up. The anti-Mormon Ring in Utah kept up the tirade for stronger laws. Many of the General Authorities were forced into hiding. On February 1, 1885, President John Taylor gave his last public discourse, after which he and his first counselor George Q. Cannon went into hiding. Joseph F. Smith had previously gone into hiding and eventually went to Hawaii

where he spent a number of years. He arrived home about two
weeks before the death of President Taylor on July 25, 1887, at
the home of Thomas Rouche of Kaysville. President Cannon
was eventually arrested and let out on $45,000 bail. After
passage of the Edmunds-Tucker Law, the courts assumed the
nonexistence of the Church and proceeded to confiscate Church
properties; all expenses incurred in the process were taken out
of former Church funds.

The Idaho legislature had taken away from Church members
in Idaho the right of citizenship—the governor of the state
having been forced to sign the bill at the point of a gun—and
United States Marshal Fred T. DuBois was relentlessly hunting
down all Idaho polygynists.[42] He stated that none would go
unconvicted because he had selected a "jury that would convict
Jesus Christ."[43] The flimsiest evidence would often convict a
man of illegal cohabitation, such as finding that a man had
provided any type of support for other than his first family.

On January 19, 1841, the Prophet Joseph Smith had received
a revelation containing much information pertaining to the
doctrines and practices of the Church. Verse 49 of this revelation reads as follows:

> Verily, verily, I say unto you, that when I give a com-
> mandment to any of the sons of men to do a work unto
> my name, and those sons of man go with all their might
> and with all they have to perform that work, and cease not
> their diligence, and their enemies come upon them and
> hinder them from performing that work, behold, it be-
> hooveth me to require that work no more at the hands of
> those sons of men, but to accept of their offerings. (D&C
> 124:49.)

With nearly 1,300 men and women having been sentenced,
with all Latter-day Saints in Idaho having been disfranchised;
with the Church having been disincorporated and her real and
personal property confiscated; with all polygynists and all
women in Utah having been disfranchised; with the rights of
local self-government in Utah suspended (even to the privilege
of operating their schools); with pressure arising for the government to disfranchise all Mormons in territories; with prospects
for the future that the personal property of every Latter-day
Saint might be confiscated; with the United States Supreme
Court having declared the Anti-Bigamy Law of 1862, the Idaho
Test Oath, and the main parts of the Edmunds-Tucker Law as

constitutional, President Wilford Woodruff felt the time had come when it could be said that the members of the Church had gone forth with all diligence to perform the commands of the Lord, and the Lord would no longer require them to practice plural marriage. He therefore approached the Lord in prayer, and received an answer that the Saints were relieved of any further responsibility in this respect.

Under the power of inspiration he issued a statement declaring he intended to abide by the law of the land and publicly advised all Latter-day Saints to refrain from contracting any marriage forbidden by that law. (D&C: "Official Declaration," p. 257.) This statement issued by him has become known as the Manifesto, and is found at the end of the Doctrine and Covenants. On the day he issued it President Woodruff recorded in his journal:

> The United States government has taken a stand and passed laws to destroy the Latter-day Saints on the subject of polygamy, or patriarchal order of marriage; and after praying to the Lord and feeling inspired, I have issued the following proclamation which is sustained by my counselors and the twelve apostles.[44]

President Woodruff's proclamation was presented to the Saints at the semiannual conference on October 6, 1890. After it was read to the audience, Lorenzo Snow, President of the Quorum of the Twelve Apostles, presented the following resolution to the assembled audience:

> I move that, recognizing Wilford Woodruff as the President of the Church of Jesus Christ of Latter-day Saints, and the only man on the earth at the present time who holds the keys of the sealing ordinances, we consider him fully authorized by virtue of his position to issue the Manifesto which has been read in our hearing and which is dated September 24, 1890, and that as a Church in General Conference assembled, we accept his declaration concerning plural marriage as authoritative and binding.[45]

The vote was overwhelmingly in favor, although there were probably a few who did not vote for it.[46] President Snow, President Woodruff, and President George Q. Cannon, first counselor to President Woodruff, all spoke upon the subject in

the conference meeting. In his remarks President Cannon
said: "God gave the command, and it required the command of
God to change our attitude." He also read Doctrine and Covenants 124:49-50. President Woodruff's declaration was not a
denunciation of the rightfulness of plural marriage under certain
circumstances, but it was difficult for a few diehard Saints to
accept; and, over the years, there have been those who have
entered into the practice and therefore have been excommunicated from the Church. Apparently these people do not
accept the statement in the Doctrine and Covenants that unless
these General Authorities are overruled by a general assembly of
the Priesthood Quorums of the Church "there can be no appeal
from their decision." (D&C 107:32.)

STATEHOOD FOR UTAH

In 1891 hearings were held to determine whether the
Church's escheated property should be returned, and Charles
Varian, United States district attorney for Utah who was conducting the hearings, stated in anger:

> They [the Latter-day Saints] are not obeying the law of
> the land at all, but the counsel of the head of the church.
> The law of the land, with all its mighty power, and all the
> terrible pressure it was enabled to bring with its iron heel
> upon this people crushing them to powder, was unable to
> bring about what this man did in an hour in the assembled
> conference of the people. They were willing to go to
> prison; I doubt not some of them were willing to go to the
> gallows to the tomb of the martyr, before they would have
> yielded one single iota.[47]

The Utah Commission, which still controlled the election
procedures in the territory, refused to accept the sincerity of
President Woodruff's manifesto—as did many of the anti-
Mormons in Utah—but John McClernand, one member of the
commission, denied the report of the other four commission
members. Chief Justice Charles Zane, and United States District
Attorney Varian, who had previously used unconstitutional
methods to suppress the Mormons, and Governor Arthur
Thomas were among those few who accepted President Woodruff's manifesto as sincere.[48] Judge Zane did so immediately
and Governor Thomas and Varian not long afterward. Many of

388 the diehards in the anti-Mormon Ring in Utah who saw their chances for minority political control slipping away with Mormon conformity, yelled loud and long about its being a trick. They held on to their Liberal Party long after the dissolution of the People's Party and the division of the Utah people along national party lines. They did all they could to suppress statehood for Utah, but sentiment among many gentiles in the territory and the nation gradually changed in favor of the Saints.

On December 19, 1891, the leaders of the Church petitioned the government for amnesty. President Benjamin Harrison, who was skeptical of the Saints' sincerity, gradually changed. By January 4, 1893, he issued a full pardon to those who had been guilty of unlawful cohabitation prior to November 1, 1890, and had obeyed the law since that time and pledged to do so in the future.

On September 6, 1893, Joseph Rawlins—Utah's delegate to Congress from 1893 to statehood in 1896—introduced an enabling act into the House of Representatives in another effort to gain statehood for Utah. The committee on territories submitted a favorable report, and the measure was approved by the House of Representatives. It was passed by the Senate and signed by President Grover Cleveland on July 16, 1894.

In the meantime on October 28, 1893, what was left of the personal property of the Church was returned. The real property was returned after statehood in 1896.

From March 4 to May 8, 1895, a constitutional convention was held in Utah. Woman suffrage was restored in the constitution. The enabling act of Congress had contained a requirement that the Utah constitution prohibit polygamous or plural marriages forever unless revoked by the United States; consequently, the convention put the exact wording of the act into the constitution:

> Article III. The following ordinance shall be irrevocable without the consent of the United States and the people of this state: *First.* Perfect toleration of religious sentiment is guaranteed. No inhabitant of this state shall ever be molested in person or property on account of his or her mode of religious worship; but polygamous or plural marriages are forever prohibited.[49]

Charles Varian had a clause inserted, the purpose of which was

to provide against future polygynous marriages but would leave   389
"undisturbed those relationships that had been formed in the
past under the sanction of the Church of the Latter-day
Saints." [50] This meant that those plural marriages officially
sanctioned by the Church previous to the Manifesto would
remain undisturbed, and polygyny would gradually fade away
as those who had entered it with the sanction of the Church
passed from this life.[51]

The Election of 1895

After the constitution for the new state-to-be had been
formed, elections were held to fill the state offices. Much to the
disappointment of the democratic regime in Washington, D.C.,
Utah elected a full slate of Republicans. Heber M. Wells, son of
Daniel H. Wells, was elected governor over Democrat John T.
Caine. Some people were concerned that the disappointment of
the elections might lead the administration in Washington to
reject statehood for Utah. Thus John T. Caine, Governor Caleb
West, and other prominent Democrats went to Washington,
D.C. to use their influence. They were assured that, although
the Democratic administration was disappointed in the outcome
of the election, Utah had qualified for statehood and it would
be granted.

On January 4, 1896, President Grover Cleveland signed the
proclamation stating that the requirements of the enabling act
had been complied with, the constitution had been accepted by
the vote of the people, an election of state officials had been
held, and the winning candidates certified; and therefore, by
authority vested in him, the admission of Utah "into the Union
on an equal footing with the original states is now an accomplished fact." [52]

Utah received the news with great enthusiasm. In Salt Lake
City the Saints fired guns, rang bells, blew whistles, and general
jubilation was everywhere in evidence. Two days later the state
officers were installed. After waiting forty-seven years from the
time of their first request for statehood the Saints had attained
their goal, and Utah became the forty-fifth state in the nation.

Footnotes

[1]*CHC*, 2:97.
[2]Sermon of Orson Pratt, 7 October 1869, *JD*, 13:193.

390   [3]Eliza R. Snow Smith, *Biography and Family Record of Lorenzo Snow* (Salt Lake City: Deseret News Co., Printers, 1884), pp. 69-70.

[4]*CHC*, 2:105.

[5]*HC*, 6:46.

[6]This quotation is taken from a testimony by Lucy Walker Smith Kimball signed before James Jack, a Notary Public, on December 17, 1902; a copy is in the files of Russell R. Rich. It has also been inserted in JH, under date of May 1, 1843.

[7]Edward W. Tullidge, *Women of Mormondom* (1877; lithographed in Salt Lake City: 1957), pp. 294-96.

[8]Tullidge, pp. 320-21.

[9]*Encyclopedia Americana*, 25th ed., s.v. "Polygamy."

[10]It was adopted into their platform at Philadelphia on June 17, 1856.

[11]For a most able treatment of the conflict between the Mormons and the federal government over polygamy, read Richard D. Poll, "The Twin Relics" (Master's thesis, Texas Christian University, Fort Worth, May 1939). Copy available in Brigham Young University Library, Provo, Utah.

[12]Poll, p. 112.

[13]Poll, pp. 113-14. *See also* pp. 355-56, which quotes the Morrill Act in full.

[14]Poll, pp. 355-56.

[15]*See* D&C; and Articles of Faith, Number 12.

[16]Hubert Howe Bancroft, *History of Utah* (1890; reprint ed., Salt Lake City: Bookcraft, 1964), pp. 614-15.

[17]Poll, p. 124. *See also CHC*, 5:178.

[18]Poll, p. 125.

[19]*CHC*, 5:226. *See also* Edward W. Tullidge, *History of Salt Lake City* (Salt Lake City: Star Publishing Co., 1886), Chapter 42, for a much more complete listing of the contents of the bill.

[20]*CHC*, 5:232.

[21]*CHC*, 5:229-30.

[22]Samuel Bowles, *Our New West* (Hartford, Conn.: Hartford Publishing Co., 1869), p. 264. *See also CHC*, 2:230.

[23]*CHC*, 5:327.

[24]*CHC*, 5:448. *See also* Edward W. Tullidge, *Life of Brigham Young* (New York: n.p., 1877), pp. 420-21.

[25]*CHC*, 5:435-38.

[26]Poll, p. 161.

[27]*CHC*, 5:421.

[28]Tullidge, *Salt Lake City*, p. 623. *See also* Poll, p. 161.

[29]*CHC*, 5:471.

[30]*CHC*, 5:472.

[31]Poll, p. 163.

[32]*See* Poll, Appendix F, for the contents of the Edmunds Act.

[33]Russell R. Rich, *Land of the Sky-Blue Water* (Provo, Utah: Brigham Young University Press, September 1963), p. 146.

[34]This county was later divided into seven different counties, and none of them took the original name.

[35]Hart received only three votes for his amendment.

[36]*CHC*, 6:214.

[37]Poll, p. 226; *CHC*, 6:174.

[38]William E. Berrett and Alma P. Burton, *Readings in L.D.S. Church*

History (Salt Lake City: Deseret Book Co., 1955), 3:40-41. *See also* Poll, 391 pp. 254-55.

[39]Poll, pp. 261-62.

[40]Poll, p. 222.

[41]Poll, p. 264.

[42]Berrett and Burton, 3:81. *See also Idaho Daily Statesman*, 25 January 1931.

[43]M. D. Beal, *A History of Southeastern Idaho* (Caldwell, Idaho: Caxton Printers, Ltd., 1942), p. 311.

[44]*CHC*, 6:220. President Woodruff apparently means it was sustained by all of the apostles with whom he was able to discuss the matter, as some of them were in southern Utah at the time.

[45]The latter part of this statement is in accord with the statement of Joseph Smith on October 5, 1843, when he said, ". . . according to the law, I hold the keys of this power in the last days; for there is never but one on earth at a time on whom the power and its keys are conferred; and I have constantly said no man shall have but one wife at a time, unless the Lord directs otherwise." *See HC*, 6:46.

[46]*Deseret News*, 11 October 1890, p. 526.

[47]*CHC*, 6:229. *See also* Poll, p. 287.

[48]Gustive O. Larson, *The "Americanization" of Utah for Statehood* (San Marino, Calif.: Huntington Library, 1971), pp. 106, 109, 110, 128-32, 149-54. For those who wish a deeper understanding of the Mormon-federal government conflict, Gustive Larson's book is a must.

[49]Poll, p. 294.

[50]*CHC*, 6:326.

[51]*CHC*, 6:326.

[52]*CHC*, 6:337.

18

The Church after the Death of Brigham Young

Much to the astonishment and chagrin of the anti-Mormons the Church did not disintegrate after the passing of Brigham Young. Although the Saints mourned the loss of their beloved leader, they had complete confidence that God would raise up an equally capable prophet to replace him.

THE APOSTOLIC PRESIDENCY

When Brigham Young died, John Taylor was president of the Quorum of Twelve Apostles, although there were still two of the original Twelve active in the Quorum. These were Orson Hyde and Orson Pratt, who had each lost his seniority through having been dropped from the Quorum for a few months. Elder Hyde had been dropped in the fall of 1838 and Elder Pratt in the summer of 1842. These Quorum positions were not adjusted when each of the brethren first returned to the Quorum. The adjustments were made in later years in Utah when George A. Smith called the matter to the attention of Brigham Young. Also, for many years Wilford Woodruff was considered to outrank John Taylor, who had assisted in ordaining him to the apostleship. This was because Wilford Woodruff was chronologically older. When the first Quorum of the Apostles was called, the brethren were ranked, not according to which was chosen first—they were all chosen on the same day in the same

393

394 meeting—but according to age. Thus, Thomas B. Marsh, who was the next to the last man chosen, became the president of the Quorum. Roberts states that this "was held to be proper in the formation of the Quorum; but after that the principle of precedence in the Quorum was held to rest upon seniority of ordination."[1] John Taylor and Wilford Woodruff were called to the Quorum of the Twelve by revelation, along with John E. Page and Willard Richards on July 8, 1838. (D&C 118:6.) John E. Page and John Taylor were ordained to the apostleship on December 19, 1838, and Wilford Woodruff was ordained on April 26, 1839. Willard Richards was on a mission to England and was ordained on April 14, 1840. Apparently no difficulty or dissatisfaction arose from the rearrangement of seniority in the Quorum in 1875.

At the meeting of the Quorum of the Twelve on September 4, 1877, Brigham Young's former counselors, John W. Young and Daniel H. Wells, were selected to be counselors to the Twelve. Word was sent to Orson Pratt and Joseph F. Smith, both on a mission to England, to return to Salt Lake City; and a committee, consisting of John Taylor, John W. Young, Daniel H. Wells, and George Q. Cannon, was named to handle financial matters of the Church, including the building of temples and public works.[2]

At the general conference in October, 1877, the general membership unanimously approved the Quorum of the Twelve as the presiding Quorum of the Church. They also approved all the administrative acts they had taken since the death of President Young.

The Twelve Apostles continued to be the presiding Quorum of the Church until the October conference of 1880, when the First Presidency was reorganized.

SETTLEMENT OF THE BRIGHAM YOUNG ESTATE

One of the more unpleasant aspects of the administration of the Quorum of the Twelve was the conflict that developed over the settlement of Brigham Young's estate.[3] When President Young passed away he left a will he had signed on November 14, 1873. He had attempted to draw up a document that would be sufficiently clear and completely legal so that it would not cause complications and costly delays in the court. The Anti-Bigamy Law of 1862, false rumors as to the value of the estate, and a bitter anti-Mormon judge were each to have an effect on the settlement of the will as well as to cause embarrassment to

members of the Church and to most members of the family
over the contention that arose among certain heirs.

The Effect of the Anti-Bigamy Law on Brigham Young's Estate

The Anti-Bigamy Law of July 1, 1862, was perhaps more responsible than any other factor for the confusion involving ownership of certain properties that were listed in the name of Brigham Young. This law actually disincorporated the Church and limited the amount of real estate it could hold (other than houses of worship) to a value of $50,000; but it did specify that "existing vested rights in real estate shall not be impaired."[4] Otherwise, all real estate acquired or held in excess of $50,000 was to be forfeited or escheated to the United States. Arrington points out that technically the Church held no vested rights in real estate in 1862 because Utah was Mexican territory when they came, and after acquiring title, the United States government did not grant land titles in Utah until 1869.[5]

After passage of the Anti-Bigamy Law the federal government did not really begin to enforce it—particularly that portion pertaining to ownership of real estate—until after passage of the Edmunds-Tucker Law in 1887, after the death of Brigham Young. Nevertheless, the Church could never be sure when the government would begin to enforce it, and it began to use various methods to reduce the risk of having the property escheated and turned over to the federal government.

When laws made it possible for Utahns to enter tracts in the federal land office in 1869, it would have been unlawful to enter more than a total of $50,000 in the name of the Church because of the provisions of the Anti-Bigamy Act. Thus, much Church property was entered in the name of Brigham Young, the trustee-in-trust for the Church. Later some Church properties were also entered in the names of other trustworthy individuals. None of these transactions troubled the membership of the Church. They had full faith in their leaders because the Church had dealt much in the past with land holdings and the founding of business and property enterprises, always in an effort to further the economic welfare of the members, blending together temporal and spiritual salvation.

Under these circumstances, President Young entered into many business and economic enterprises financed by the Church; it became impossible to know which enterprises he had entered for the Church and which ones were his own personal business dealings. No doubt this confusion was partly intentional in order to prevent "carpet-bag crusaders" from destroying the power of the Church through use of the governmental judicial system.

President Young began an effort to straighten out these financial affairs in 1873 when he made out his will and also appointed his counselor George A. Smith to be trustee-in-trust for the Church, but because of the law of 1862 only certain known properties of the Church were transferred to President Smith. Then, before further clarification could be made, George A. Smith died in 1875.

President George Q. Cannon, who was private secretary to Brigham Young for most of the last twenty years of his life, said that President Young proposed changing his will, giving each heir $10,000 and leaving everything else to the Church; but reasons arose which prevented his doing this, although Elder Cannon felt there was a clause in the will which gave "ample powers" to the executors to settle everything of a trust character in a way that would fully protect the interests of the Church. [6]

The Men Involved in Settling His Estate

After the death of Brigham Young his will was read in the presence of his family and a few friends on September 3, 1877. It named George Q. Cannon, Brigham Young, Jr., and Albert Carrington, all three members of the Quorum of the Twelve Apostles, as executors. The will attempted an equitable division of his personal property among his wives and children, specifying what each one would receive. It appeared at the time that the stipulations of the will were satisfactory to those concerned, but more than a year later certain family members registered objections.

The will specified that the executors were to turn over to the Church the properties Brigham Young held as trustee-in-trust. John Taylor, as president of the Twelve Apostles, in order to protect Church interests appointed a committee to audit the accounts of President Young as trustee-in-trust and all other accounts of the Church. This committee consisted of Wilford Woodruff, chairman, Erastus Snow and Joseph F. Smith; Franklin D. Richards was added later.

Three Classes of Property

The auditing committee, the trustee-in-trust of the Church,

John Taylor, and his counselors and the executors of the estate
held many joint conferences and conducted joint investigations
in an effort to reach an equitable settlement for all.[7] They
discovered that the properties in Brigham Young's name would
have to be divided into three categories or classes. Class 1 property consisted of those properties definitely known to belong to
the Church but were in the name of Brigham Young. These
were of two types: those that had been deeded to George A.
Smith in 1873 while he was trustee-in-trust but had since re-
verted to Brigham Young—the temple block, the tithing office,
and others—and properties in the estate which had not been
conveyed to George A. Smith but were known, through the
history of their acquisition and use—the Church stock farm and
others—to belong definitely to the Church.[8]

Class 2 property included that which Brigham Young claimed
as his own, and in which the Church agreed it had no interest.

Class 3 property consisted of property that had once belonged to the Church but had been transferred to Brigham
Young by Brigham Young, trustee-in-trust, before his death, and
ownership was uncertain. This included the Salt Lake Theatre
and grounds, some property in the block where Brigham Young
lived, the Social Hall and lot, the Gardo House and grounds, and
others. Some of these properties had been in Brigham Young's
name since 1862.

In addition to these classes of property, decisions were also
necessary on the division of personal property, including stocks,
bonds, and notes (ZCMI and Utah Southern Railroad). Investigation showed that many of these enterprises were financed
partly or completely by the Church and the stock was held by
him in part or entirely in trust for the Church; consequently the
Church made a claim for certain of these properties.

An Audit of the Books

An audit of the books of Brigham Young and the Church
revealed that at the time of his death Brigham Young had kept
his records very carefully and was in debt to the Church the
sum of $999,632.90; but it was difficult to tell how much of
this sum was "unreimbursed drawings," how much had been
spent on property held in trust for the Church, or on Church-
sponsored enterprises.

No considerations had been allowed to Brigham for his services to the Church; therefore the executors decided to allow

398 him a credit of $300,000 which reduced the debt to $699,632.53.

Disposition of Properties

All class 1 property was to be turned over to the Church. Class 2 property was to be given to the family, as were also the class 3 properties except that the class 3 properties, along with certain stocks and bonds, up to the value of the total net indebtedness owed to the Church were to be deeded to the Church for the cancellation of the debt.[9]

By April 10, 1878, after six months of intensive meetings between the aforementioned executors and Church committees, they reached an agreement. Wilford Woodruff recorded the event in his journal:

> This is a very important day in the history of my life and the Church. . . . After six months of hard labor we have effected a settlement with the executors of the estate, George Q. Cannon, Brigham Young [Jr.] and Albert Carrington, who have done all in their power to settle the business in equity and righteousness."[10]

The settlement was presented to the probate court on April 15, and the heirs, petitioning the court for a quick settlement, "selected a committee to appraise and divide the property, and signed documents agreeing to accept the settlement."[11]

The day after the agreement was reached, however, two sons of Brigham Young, Alfales and Ernest, applied to the third district court in Salt Lake City, preventing a transfer to the Church of any properties that were in the name of their father. Six days later another complaint was filed against the executors by five family members against transferring certain stocks to John W. Young until his claim was legally established. The Twelve Apostles met with the family and gave a complete explanation so that they agreed to drop the suit. By November, 1878, when George Q. Cannon left for Washington, D.C., he wrote:

> In leaving home I had the satisfaction of knowing that all the legatees excepting one (Nabbie Young Clawson) had been settled with and they have signed releases; all the debts, excepting one or two trifling amounts, have been paid and everything closed up as far as possible.[12]

In the spring of 1879, however, Elizabeth A. Young, a
daughter of Brigham Young who had married and gone to California, along with six other heirs, all of whom had received
shares of the estate and had signed releases, took the case to the
third district court, where Judge Jacob S. Boreman, a bitter
anti-Mormon, was temporarily sitting on the bench. Arrington
states that "there is indirect evidence the judge may have encouraged the presentation of their complaint." [13] This encouragement, along with their disappointment in receiving a
smaller sum than they had expected may have been the reason
they took the case to court.

When Brigham Young died, rumor had it that his estate was
worth between $2,000,000 and $2,500,000. The executors had
discovered that the estate was worth only $1,626,000 before
the debts owed to the Church and others were subtracted. After
the properties held for and in behalf of the Church were taken
away, the value of his estate was reduced to $361,170. When
debts, executors' fees and other deductions had been made, it
was further reduced to $224,242.42.

The disappointment of these heirs in addition to the desire of
certain federal officials and anti-Mormons to harm the Church
now forced the executors of the estate and John Taylor,
trustee-in-trust for the Church, into court.

The plaintiffs asked for an injunction against the executors to
keep them from proceeding with their plans and against the
trustee-in-trust of the Church to prevent him from disposing of
the properties received by him. Since apparently everything had
been fairly well settled, most of the plans of the executors had
already been carried out and much of the property received by
the Church had been disposed of.

The Executors in Jail

Since conditions could not revert to what they had been,
Judge Boreman found the executors and the trustee-in-trust
guilty of contempt of court. President Taylor posted bonds of
$200,000 to prevent his going to jail, but the executors felt it
was an outrage and refused to post any more bonds than those
they were already under. On August 4, 1879, they were incarcerated in the Utah penitentiary where they remained until
August 28, 1879, when the territorial supreme court reversed
the decision of the third district court, with Judge Boreman
dissenting. It was said that Governor George Emery was "astonished" at the decision of Judge Boreman and thought it was

400 an outrage, a feeling which many other non-Mormons shared.[14]
Before the case was finally settled, non-Mormon receivers had been appointed to take charge of the estate properties, and the Church had entered a suit against the executors and heirs for recovery of its property and to quiet title.

Out of Court Settlement

On October 4, 1879, the suit was settled out of court when the Church agreed to pay the seven plaintiffs a combined total of $75,000, and they agreed to drop the suit. The Church also dropped its counter-suit.

B. H. Roberts said of the case:

> This suit was a very vexatious affair, founded on no just claims, and evidently began by agitators who hoped to profit by the litigation. On the part of the other heirs, the trustee-in-trust, and the executors, the $75,000 granted to the dissatisfied heirs was allowed in the interest of the estate, since the cost of the litigation threatened to far exceed that sum if the case was continued in the courts; and also the compromise was made in the interests of the peace of the large number of heirs, and all other parties immediately concerned, and of the public, which was agitated by these suits and counter suits; and naturally so, since the whole Latter-day Saint community had an interest in the church properties that would be affected by the decisions and orders of the court.[15]

President Taylor presented the agreement to the Church members at the semiannual conference on October 6, 1879, for their sanction, which was unanimously given.

Arrington, after his study of the case, summarized it this way.
1. The settlement had been favorable to the heirs of President Young because the Church leaders had no inclination to build up the Church at the expense of its members.
2. The reports of Brigham Young's wealth and income, which were intended to show his personal gain at the expense of a poverty stricken community, arose because of the failure to distinguish between his personal activities and those conducted in behalf of the Church.

3. The freedom of the trustee-in-trust of the Church to deal financially for the Church was curtailed by the Anti-Bigamy Law of 1862 and the activities of federally appointed officials.

4. Some people blamed Brigham Young for confusing his private accounts with those of the trustee-in-trust and for the ensuing difficulties, but the confusion in part was purposive because of the Anti-Bigamy Act of 1862.

5. Many enterprises for which historians have credited Brigham Young as an individual were made possible by the Church and its tithing funds. President Young's chief contributions to development of the intermountain west were as trustee-in-trust and not as a private business man.[16]

The Church membership, as well as the majority of the members of Brigham Young's family, suffered humiliation over the court battle, a humiliation relished by the anti-Mormons. The Church leaders, feeling that the matter had brought reproach upon the Church and that those who had filed suit had been inconsiderate and unchristian in "going to the law with a brother," excommunicated the offenders from the Church in May, 1880.

THE ANTI-MORMON CRUSADE, 1877-1880

When Brigham Young died and the Church did not, many anti-Mormon newspapers became more vehement than ever against it, so that during this period of the Apostolic Presidency there were some particularly vicious attacks. The September 5, 1878, Apostolic Presidency outlined what was called the new anti-Mormon campaign against them as follows:

The first proposed point in the new campaign is to prevent the admission of Utah as a state until polygamy is abandoned.

The second is to induce congress to repeal the law making women in Utah voters.

The third is to induce congress to disfranchise every man and woman living in polygamous marriage. And if this is not sufficient 'to defeat the political views' of the Mormons, 'to disfranchise the offspring of all unlawful wives.'

The fourth is to rescue the public schools from the control of the Mormons, and to insist upon the establishment of free schools and prohibit the teaching of denominational sentiments in them.[17]

The Petition of the Non-Mormon Women

On November 7, 1878, the non-Mormon women of Salt Lake City held a mass meeting in the Congregational church with about two hundred in attendance. They drew up an address to Mrs. Rutherford B. Hayes—wife of the president of the United States—and the women of the United States in which they deplored the evils of polygamy and the fact that George Q. Cannon, a man with four wives, was permitted to serve in Congress. They requested that statehood for Utah be delayed until these evils were abolished. They also sent a circular to ministers throughout the country asking that their address to Mrs. Hayes and the women of the United States be read to their congregations, after which the ladies were to sign protests and send them to the congressmen of their district.

Counter-Petition of Latter-day Saint Women

On November 16 the Latter-day Saint women in Salt Lake City held a counter demonstration in the Salt Lake Theatre. Two thousand were present. Many of their speeches were received wholeheartedly, and the women drew up a preamble in which they claimed that the Latter-day Saint women had been misjudged and misrepresented by other women in regard to their sacred rights of wifehood and motherhood. They then proceeded to formulate a series of resolutions, beginning by declaring themselves loyal American citizens and claiming the rights guaranteed by the first amendment to the constitution in regard to religion, a right they claimed to be exercising not to the injury of others but within the pale of peace and justice.[18] Mormon women in other parts of the territory also held meetings.

Murder of Joseph Standing

Prior to the outbreak of the Civil War, most of the Saints in the southern states and the missionaries in the area migrated to Utah. There was no organized missionary work there after the Civil War until 1875, when Henry G. Boyle from Pima, Arizona, reopened the missions. Work then progressed very well and

many branches of the Church were opened in many states. In
January, 1878, Elder John Morgan succeeded President Boyle as mission president, and mission activity was intensified. Many converts from the South migrated to Arizona and to the San Luis Valley of Colorado.

The newspapers throughout the nation began to comment on the success of the Mormons in the South. This annoyed many of the sectarian ministers and brought forth much anti-Mormon literature which tried to give the impression that the Church itself had actually been outlawed by the United States government and therefore her representatives were "legitimate objects of mob violence." [19] One person said to Elder Joseph Standing, president of the Georgia conference, "The government of the United States is against you, and there is no law in Georgia for Mormons." [20]

President Standing wrote a letter to Governor Alfred H. Colquitt on June 12, 1879, in which he called Colquitt's attention to the threat against the elders and members of the Church, particularly in the area of Varnell Station, Whitfield County, where elders had had to flee and Church members' houses had been entered and searched. He called the attention of the governor to the laws of Georgia which opposed lawlessness and extended to citizens the right to worship God according to the dictates of their consciences, suggesting that a word from the governor would make possible safe travel for the missionaries and assurance on the part of the Saints that they would not be stoned and shot and their houses entered in defiance of law and order. He said that the governor's attention to the matter would be appreciated. [21] Governor Colquitt directed the secretary of the executive department of Georgia to answer that Mr. Standing's position regarding the laws of Georgia was correct, that he regretted to hear of the reports from Whitfield County and would instruct the state prosecuting attorney for that district to look into the matter; if the reports were true, he would prosecute the offenders. [22] There is no evidence that he took any action, however.

On July 20, 1879, Elder Standing and his companion, Elder Rudger Clawson, were on their way to a conference to be held in Rome, Georgia. They stopped near Varnell Station at about 9:00 p.m., where they found Church members in such a state of fear they were not willing to give the elders lodging for the night. Consequently, the elders went about a mile and a half farther and stayed with Henry Holston, a non-Mormon friend, who told them much about the threats in the neighborhood to whip and even kill the elders.

The next morning after a brief visit to some of the Saints, the elders were met by a mob of twelve men who took them into the woods off the highway. Elder Standing asked them by what authority they were being molested and requested to see the warrant for their arrest if they had one. They replied, "We'll show you by what authority we act." As they walked through the woods, Elder Standing made an effort to persuade them from violence, but his persuasion seemed to have no effect on the mob members except to make them angry. Elder Clawson was knocked to his knees by Ben Clark, a Baptist deacon, and was prevented from being further assaulted with a club by one of the kinder members of the mob.

As they reached a spring, Elder Standing, who had been affected with a burning thirst, took a drink, although he was somewhat afraid he would be shot while drinking. A conversation between the elders and their assailants followed, lasting nearly an hour, in which the "vilest accusations" were made against the Mormons. At this point, three members of the mob who had been reconnoitering on horseback rode up; one of them said, "Follow us." Elder Standing, over-wrought, suddenly jumped up, clapped his hands together, and shouted, "Surrender!" One of the mob who had been on the left of Standing fired into Elder Standing's face; he immediately fell to the ground. The bullet had entered below one eye and had come out of his forehead. One mobster said, "This is terrible that he should have killed himself in such a manner."

Another of the mobsters pointed at Elder Clawson and said, "Shoot that man." The elder turned around to face the mob, folded his arms, and said, "Shoot!" His calmness gained respect for him, and they lowered their guns. Permission to go for help was granted to Elder Clawson. He went to Holston's and asked him to take care of the body while he went for the coroner. Holston found that Elder Standing was still alive, though unconscious, and created shade for him with boughs. Elder Clawson returned with the coroner, and the three of them, accompanied by others, returned to Elder Standing, where they found that after Holston had left, the mob had returned and fired twenty bullets or more into Elder Standing's face and neck, at such close range that there were powder burns on his body. This could have been done to show that all the men were unified in accepting blame for the murder.

The coroner's jury came to a decision that the deceased had
met his death by pistol and gun shots inflicted upon him by the
twelve men whom they named; they recommended that the
coroner issue a warrant for their arrest. Two people, a man
named Jonathan Owensby, and a young Mormon girl named
Mary Hamlin, offered to identify the mobsters. Elder Clawson
brought the body home to Salt Lake City where a special service was held in the Salt Lake tabernacle. Then he returned to
Dalton, Georgia, the county seat of Whitfield County, where
the trial was held. President John Morgan was also in attendance
at the trial. One man was tried for murder and found not guilty,
and two others were tried for riot and found not guilty, in
spite of the fact that two people who knew the men in the mob
had seen them and identified them. President Morgan wired to
the *Deseret News* "The old, old story. Verdict, not guilty."[23]

Elder Clawson, who had faced the murderers with such calmness, was ordained an apostle on October 10, 1898, and became
president of the Council of the Twelve. He died at the age of
eighty-six on June 21, 1943.

ELDER THATCHER'S MISSION TO MEXICO

The first missionaries of the Church to go into Mexico arrived
there in 1876. Elder Meliton G. Trejo had first published in
Spanish a few tracts containing material taken from the Book of
Mormon. One of these tracts later came into the hands of Dr.
Platino C. Rhodacanaty of Mexico City, who became interested
and corresponded with President John Taylor. Rhodacanaty
was Greek on his father's side and Mexican on his mother's side.
He was a teacher in a Presbyterian college and spoke several
languages. President Taylor sent him a number of Church
books. He became convinced of the truthfulness of the gospel
and soon began to get others interested.

At the October conference in 1879, Elder Moses Thatcher of
the Council of the Twelve from Logan, Utah, was called on a
mission along with Elders James Z. Stewart of Draper, Utah,
and Meliton G. Trejo, who was living at San Pedro, California.
They arrived in Mexico City on November 16 and found that
Rhodacanaty had been publishing a monthly periodical called
Voz del Desierto, in which he was teaching the principles of the
gospel. Rhodacanaty was baptized soon along with Silviano
Arteaga, who was said to be a pure Aztec. On November 23, six
others having been baptized, a branch was organized with

Rhodacanaty as branch president. By the close of 1879, sixteen persons had been baptized. [24]

While the elders were in Mexico, much publicity—both favorable and unfavorable—was given to the Church in the newspapers. With patience the elders were able to make it mostly favorable. They met many high government officials, among them the minister of public works and colonization, Fernandez Leal, who had previously visited Utah and now said that Mexico would gladly welcome any of the Mormons who would care to settle there. [25] Elder Thatcher met Emelio Biebuyck, a Belgian who had been in Utah in 1854 and 1855 and who had a large colonization contract with the government. Biebuyck pressed the elder, attempting to persuade him to bring members of the Church to settle in Mexico, offering them special inducements. Elder Thatcher considered the offer important enough to present it to the First Presidency and the Apostles' Quorum; he therefore left Mexico City on February 4, 1880, and arrived in Salt Lake City on February 22, ten days ahead of Biebuyck. The First Presidency and the Council of the Twelve, after mature consideration decided that settling in Mexico was premature and rejected Biebuyck's kind offer. Before leaving Mexico, Elder Thatcher with Elders Stewart and Trejo dedicated the land of Mexico that the gospel might be spread among her people. [26]

When Elder Thatcher left in February (1880), Elder Stewart was left in charge of the mission. By December of the same year, Elder Thatcher, along with others, returned to Mexico, where he supervised the publication of a great amount of literature. He stayed until September 15, 1881, at which time he sustained Elder August H. F. Welcken as mission president and returned to Utah. On the way home Elder Feramorz L. Young, one of the elders returning with him, died of typhoid fever and was buried at sea. By June of 1889, all Utah elders were withdrawn from Mexico and the mission was not reopened again until June of 1901. The experiences of the Saints during this mission provided the principal reasons for establishing colonies in northern Mexico in the 1880s.

EXPANSION OF SETTLEMENTS

During the Apostolic Presidency (1877-80), Mormon settlements continued to expand throughout the intermountain west, many of them beyond the rim of the Great Basin, especially into Arizona. A few settlements had been established there as early as the 1860s. These were Pipe Springs, 1863; Call's Landing, 1864; Moccasin Springs, 1864; Littlefield (Beaverdam), 1864; and Lee's Ferry, 1872. In addition, Brigham Young had sent colonists to Navajo County along the Little Colorado River in 1876 where three colonies had been established. He had also laid plans for further expansion in Arizona, which took place after his death.

In 1877 three more colonies were established on the Little Colorado River: Snowflake, Taylor, and Showlow, with others coming later. To the southwest, in Maricopa County, Lehi and Papago were settled in the same year, with Mesa following in 1878. These settlements were about fifteen miles east-southeast of Phoenix, the capital of the territory. Many of the Mesa settlers were from the Bear Lake area, where Frances Pomeroy had suffered with rheumatism and desired a warmer climate. A group of these early Bear Lake settlers met with a group from Salt Lake City, and together they traveled to Arizona where they founded Mesa.

In November, 1877, Mormon colonists arrived in the San Pedro Valley along the San Pedro River in Cochise County, which lies in the very southeast corner of Arizona. Three colonies were established that year—St. David, Benson, and Almo. St. David was named after David P. Kimball, a son of Heber C. Kimball, who had presided as president of the Bear Lake Stake from 1869 to 1874.

It was in this valley along the San Pedro River on December 9, 1846, that the Mormon Battalion had had a battle with wild bulls. A day or two later they had marched into the Pima and Maricopa Indian country. Noting what superior and intelligent people they were as well as peaceful, Colonel Cooke, the commanding officer, had suggested to Captain Hunt of Company A that it might be a good place for the Mormons to settle. Captain Hunt requested the privilege of discussing the matter with the Indians, who were favorable to the proposition. It may be that knowledge gained of the area at this time was one reason the Saints later colonized there.

In 1879 settlers were sent into Graham County, north of Cochise County, to settle along the Gila River. The first settlement, formally organized into a ward on September 26, 1880, was called Smithfield.

On January 27, 1878, the first stake to be formally organized in Arizona became the Little Colorado Stake, with wards at

Brigham City (formerly Ballinger), Sunset, St. Joseph (formerly Allen), and Taylor.[27] Lot Smith was installed as stake president, with Jacob Hamblin and Lorenzo H. Hatch as his counselors. On June 29, 1879, the Eastern Arizona Stake was organized. It included the settlements on Silver Creek in the southeast corner of Navajo County, such as Snowflake, Taylor, and Showlow and the Mormon settlements along the Little Colorado River in Apache County, such as St. John's, Springerville, and Eager. Chosen as stake president was Jesse N. Smith, a cousin of the Prophet Joseph Smith, who selected Lorenzo H. Hatch, formerly in the Little Colorado stake presidency, and Oscar Man as counselors.

On December 10, 1882, the Maricopa Stake, which included Lehi, Papago, and other settlements in Maricopa County, was organized, with Alex F. McDonald as president.[28]

It was not until June 10, 1883, that the settlements in the San Pedro Valley (Cochise County) were organized into the St. Joseph Stake with Christopher Layton, formerly of Layton, Utah, as president and David P. Kimball and James H. Martineau as counselors.

In May, 1878, eighty Saints from Alabama and Georgia reached the San Luis Valley in Colorado, where they were joined by settlers from southern Utah—particularly from San Pete County—and established the colonies of Manassah and Sanford. Other Saints from the south, including those in Whitfield County where Elder Standing was shot, joined them. On June 10, 1883, the San Luis Stake was organized with Silas S. Smith, another cousin of the Prophet Joseph, as the stake president.

In 1879 more settlements were made along the Bear River in Oneida County, Idaho, at which time Preston and Riverdale were established.

On August 29, 1878, Star Valley in Wyoming was dedicated for settlement, and later many of the settlers from the Bear Lake valley moved there. The chief settlement was named Afton. The Star Valley settlements were attached to the Bear Lake Stake for a number of years.

In 1879 and 1880, two settlements were established in Lincoln County, Nevada. These were Bunkerville Ward with Edward Bunker as bishop and Mesquite Ward with William Branch as bishop.[29]

During the Apostolic Presidency a few new settlements were also established in Utah. These were in eastern Utah along the eastern part of the territory, San Juan Valley, where Bluff, established in 1880, became the principal settlement. Also in 1879 Ashley and Mountain Dell were settled on the Green River in the northeastern part of Utah.

The Jubilee Conference

For the Israelites of the Old Testament, every seventh year was a sabbatical when special blessings were to be visited upon the poor, certain debts were to be forgiven, Hebrew slaves were to be liberated, and the Israelites were commanded to let their lands rest without tillage. Inasmuch as these laws proved impractical, they were moved to the fiftieth year (the year following seven sabbaticals) which was called the Jubilee Year. Although the Jubilee Year was recognized, it was not fully observed. [30]

The Latter-day Saints decided to observe the fiftieth year of the organization of the Church with a celebration, during which they would emulate to a certain extent the old Israelite Jubilee. Said President John Taylor:

> It occurred to me, that we ought to do something, as they did in former times, to relieve those that are oppressed with debt, to assist those that are needy, to break off the yoke of those that may feel themselves crowded upon, and to make it a time of general rejoicing. [31]

At the Jubilee conference on April 6, 1880, it was announced that half the debt owed to the Perpetual Emigrating Fund Company was to be forgiven. The total amount owing was $1,604,000; thus $802,000 of the debt was to be cancelled; but this did not mean that each person owing money was to have half of his debt cancelled. Rather, the full amount owed by the poor was to be blotted out of the books; whereas those who were able to pay but had not done so were still expected to meet their obligations. "For in former times," said President Taylor, "they did not release the rich [from debt], it was the poor." [32] This cancellation of debt for the poor was carried into effect by the wards and stakes, although some of the cows and sheep that were distributed were contributed from the general Church finances. Inasmuch as the Relief Society had 34,761 bushels of grain in storage and many farmers were in sore need

410 of seed because of the drouth, it was proposed at the conference that this grain be loaned without interest to those needing it; said President Taylor, "It is the time of Jubilee."[33]

Thus the Church set the example and recommended to individual members that they be lenient to those people who owed them and were in distress. Said President Taylor:

> . . . . if you will go to work and try to relieve them as much as you can, under the circumstances, God will relieve you when you get into difficulties. I will tell you that, in the name of the Lord. Let us act on a kind, generous, brotherly principle, doing good one to another and carrying out the principles of the everlasting gospel in our lives.[34]

In a pamphlet which contained a full report of the Jubilee conference, the Apostles said: "Free the worthy debt-bound brother if you can. Let there be no rich among us from whose tables fall only crumbs to feed a wounded Lazarus."[35]

All of the Twelve Apostles had been in attendance at the Jubilee conference, except George Q. Cannon, who was in Washington, D.C., as Utah's delegate to Congress. The Apostles at this time were John Taylor, Wilford Woodruff, Orson Pratt, Charles C. Rich, Lorenzo Snow, Erastus Snow, Franklin D. Richards, George Q. Cannon, Joseph F. Smith, Brigham Young, Jr., Albert Carrington, and Moses Thatcher, who replaced Orson Hyde who had died on November 28, 1878. Orson Pratt was the only member of the original Twelve Apostles present for the Jubilee year.[36] He took a very active part, speaking twice; the Saints enjoyed very much his reminiscences of past Church history.

Pioneer Day Celebration

The Jubilee spirit was carried on throughout the year, particularly so during the July 24th celebration, at which time people from twenty-five different countries rode on three floats in the parade as representatives of the different nationalities that had been gathered together through the preaching of the gospel. On a banner was written: "I will gather you out from all nations." At this time Utah had a population of 143,690, showing an increase of nearly 60,000 people during the past decade.[37]

During the October conference in 1880, reports were made pertaining to the distribution of the cattle and sheep that had been announced at the April conference; on the last day of conference, October 10, the First Presidency was reorganized with John Taylor as president, George Q. Cannon as first counselor, and Joseph F. Smith (the son of Hyrum) as the second counselor. Elders Francis M. Lyman and John Henry Smith were called to serve in the Quorum of the Twelve, with one vacancy left unfilled.

A Brief Sketch of President Taylor's Life

John Taylor was born in Milnethorpe, Westmoreland County, England, November 1, 1808. John, the eldest living son of James Taylor and Agnes Taylor (whose maiden name was also Taylor), was left behind to settle family affairs and sell his father's property when the family moved to Toronto, Canada, in 1830. He finally arrived in Toronto in 1832. Having learned the trade of cooper (barrel-maker) and also that of wood turner, he set himself up in the business of wood turner; but he spent much of his spare time in the service of the Methodist Church, where he became a class leader and itinerant preacher. It was not long before he met and fell in love with Leonora Cannon, a woman of refinement and education with a deep religious nature.

As time passed, John and a few friends began to question certain dogmas of the Methodists until they became known as dissenters.[38] They were holding study classes with John Taylor as their teacher. At this time, 1836, Elder Parley P. Pratt came among them as an apostle and missionary of the Church of Jesus Christ of Latter-day Saints. For three weeks John Taylor studied the sermons and teachings of Elder Pratt, along with the contents of the Book of Mormon and Doctrine and Covenants, after which he concluded that the Elder's doctrine was a message of truth. Taylor and his wife were baptized on May 9, 1836, along with several others of their group. When Elder Pratt left Canada in the fall, he put Elder John Taylor "in charge of all the saints and branches in Upper Canada."[39]

Request to Join the Saints in Northern Missouri

In March, 1837, Elder Taylor made a trip to Kirtland, Ohio,

John Taylor, third president of The Church of Jesus Christ of Latter-day Saints. *Permission of Church Information Service.*

to meet the Prophet Joseph Smith. The Prophet returned Elder Taylor's visit in August, 1837, traveling to Toronto with Sidney Rigdon and Thomas B. Marsh. He requested Elder Taylor to join the main body of Saints in northern Missouri. Elder Taylor left Canada in the fall of 1837, but inasmuch as he had to stop in Indiana to earn funds before traveling farther, it was October 1, 1838, before he and Elder Mills arrived in Far West.

Ordained to the Apostleship

In the meantime he had been called to the apostleship along with John E. Page, Wilford Woodruff, and Willard Richards, through a revelation given July 8, 1838. (D&C 118.) He was ordained under the hands of Brigham Young and Heber C. Kimball on December 19, 1838, while the Prophet and his fellow prisoners were languishing in the Liberty and Richmond jails.

Mission to England

In the fall of 1839, after the designation of Nauvoo as the new gathering place, John Taylor, with the other apostles and elders, went back to his native land as a missionary. He arrived in Liverpool, England, with Wilford Woodruff and Theodore Turley on January 11, 1840. Among his important converts was his wife's father, George Cannon and his family, including his teen-age son George Q. Cannon, who later became a member of the Quorum of the Twelve and a counselor to three presidents of the Church, the first of whom was John Taylor himself.

John Taylor left England with the majority of the Twelve in April, 1841, and arrived back in Nauvoo on July 1, where he became publisher of both the *Nauvoo Neighbor* and the *Times and Seasons*. This period was a pleasant and enjoyable one for him because of his many associations with the Prophet.

The Westward Trek

On June 27, 1844, John Taylor was one of the two men—the other was Willard Richards—who were in jail with Joseph and Hyrum when a mob of approximately 150 men attacked them, killing the Prophet and Hyrum and wounding Elder Taylor in four places. It was many weeks before he was restored to normal health.

On February 16, 1846, he crossed the Mississippi River with his family for the westward migration into a wilderness beyond the borders of civilization. Five months later, he arrived at Council Bluffs on the Missouri River. Within a week, leaving their families in wagons, John Taylor, Parley P. Pratt, and Orson Hyde left for a mission to England to straighten out affairs in the British mission; they arrived in England on October 3, 1846.

In the spring of 1847 none of these three apostles returned to Winter Quarters in time to go with the pioneer company to the Great Basin. When they did come, John Taylor brought with him a number of scientific instruments, which included two sextants, one circle of reflection, two artificial horizons, several thermometers, and telescopes.[40] These instruments were given to Brigham Young, who returned from getting the pioneers underway when he heard that Elder Taylor was coming with the instruments. While the pioneer company rolled on to the Great Basin, Parley P. Pratt and John Taylor helped organize other companies that left for the west during the summer. John Taylor's group arrived in the Salt Lake valley on October 5, 1847. He and Parley P. Pratt were the only apostles who spent that first winter in the Salt Lake valley, the eight who were in the pioneer company having returned to Winter Quarters.

The First Winter in the Valley and Further Missionary Work

John Taylor buoyed up the spirits of those who weakened during that first winter. His presence proved to be a blessing to the people. After two years in the valley he was again called to Europe on a mission, leaving on October 19, 1849, and arriving in England on May 27, 1850. After a few weeks he went to France to introduce the gospel to that nation. While there he arranged to have the Book of Mormon published in French. In August, 1851, he went to Hamburg, Germany, where he was able to get the Book of Mormon translated into German. Before returning to America, he supervised the introduction of the gospel into Italy and Scandinavia, as well as other parts of Europe. After an absence of almost three years, he returned to Salt Lake City on August 20, 1852.

Editor of *The Mormon*

He was not permitted to stay at home long because in the

summer of 1854 he was sent east to "preside over the churches in the eastern states, supervise emigration and publish a paper in the interests of the Church." [41] Elder Taylor proceeded to New York, where he rented a building on the corner of Nassau and Ann Streets with the offices of the *New York Herald* on one side and the *New York Tribune* on the other. [42] The first issue of a paper called *The Mormon* came off the press February 17, 1855. In one of the early numbers, Elder Taylor wrote:

> We have said before, and we say now, that we defy all the editors and writers in the United States to prove that 'mormonism' is less moral, scriptural, philosophical; or that there is less patriotism in Utah than in any other part of the United States. We call for proof; bring on your reasons, gentlemen, if you have any; we shrink not from the investigation, and dare you to the encounter. [43]

Elder Taylor published *The Mormon* for more than two and one-half years, defending the Church against attacks made by the *New York Mirror,* the *New York Herald,* and the *New York Sun.* When it became known in 1857 that President Buchanan had ordered an army to Utah, Elder Taylor returned, arriving home in August. He became involved in all of the activities of the conflict, participating in the peace talks on June 11 and 12, 1858.

Duties in the Great Basin

From the end of the Utah War to the death of Brigham Young in August, 1877, John Taylor kept busy not only with his church responsibilities but also with civic duties. During the entire time, he was a member of the Utah legislature and served five successive terms as speaker of the House of Representatives. Among his church activities were annual visits, in company with Brigham Young, to the stakes both north and south of Salt Lake City.

B. H. Roberts comments on Taylor's leadership of the Church:

> Great energy characterized President Taylor's administration of affairs in the Church, both in Zion and abroad. He pushed forward with increased zeal the work on the temples, of which three were in course of erection, at the

Temple at Logan, Utah, built in 1877-84.

time of his taking control of affairs. He required bishops to hold weekly priesthood meetings in their wards; presidents of stakes to hold general priesthood meetings monthly in their respective stakes; and appointed quarterly conferences in all the stakes of Zion, publishing the dates of holding them for half a year in advance, a custom which has continued until the present. [44]

President Taylor increased missionary activity by sending out more missionaries and expanding their fields of labor into more nations. He received a revelation on October 13, 1882, calling George Teasdale and Heber J. Grant to the apostleship and Seymour B. Young to the First Council of the Seventy. [45] Elder Teasdale filled the vacancy from the reorganization of the First Presidency on October 10, 1880; Elder Heber J. Grant filled the vacancy created by the death of the venerable Orson Pratt.

DEATH OF PRESIDENT TAYLOR

By 1885 the government was pressing vigorously for enforcement of the Edmunds Law; and President Taylor felt it would be wise for him, his counselors, and many of the Twelve to go into retirement. He gave his last public discourse in the taber-

Temple at Manti, Utah, built in 1877-88. *Permission of Church Information Service.*

nacle on February 1, 1885, wherein he warned the Saints of trouble to come. Although he remained within a few miles of Salt Lake City, he was never located by the officers seeking his arrest.

He continued to direct the policies of the Church and to issue letters to the Saints until he passed away peacefully at the home of Thomas F. Rouche in Kaysville, Utah, on July 25, 1887, at the age of 78 years, 8 months, and 25 days.[46] The Edmunds-Tucker Law, which had gone into effect on March 3, 1887, increased the already heavy persecution and had its effect upon President Taylor's death. In a long announcement by his counselors, printed in the *Deseret News* the day after his death, they stated that President Taylor had never condescended to speak evil even of those who persecuted him.[47]

Footnotes

[1]*CHC*, 5:520.
[2]*CHC*, 5:522.
[3]For a very capable discussion of this complicated litigation, see Leonard J. Arrington, "The Settlement of the Brigham Young Estate," *Pacific Historical Review* 21(February 1952). I have drawn heavily upon

418   this article, although I am also indebted to B. H. Roberts, in *CHC*, 5:524-31.

⁴Arrington, p. 2.

⁵Arrington, p. 3.

⁶Arrington, p. 9.

⁷By action of John Taylor and with approval of the Saints at General Conference, the Twelve Apostles and their counselors John W. Young and Daniel H. Wells and the Presiding Bishops had been appointed "counselors to the trustee-in-trust." Arrington, p. 11, footnote 34.

⁸Arrington, pp. 11-12.

⁹For a more detailed clarification, see Arrington, p. 15.

¹⁰Arrington, p. 11.

¹¹Arrington states that the receipts were signed by all the heirs except "three or four." Arrington, p. 11, footnote 39.

¹²Arrington, p. 17.

¹³Arrington, p. 17.

¹⁴Arrington, p. 18, footnote 56.

¹⁵*CHC*, 5:531.

¹⁶Arrington, pp. 19-20.

¹⁷*CHC*, 5:539.

¹⁸*CHC*, 5:540-41. *See also Deseret News*, 20 November 1878.

¹⁹*CHC*, 5:560. Material on the murder of Standing is taken from Chapter 149 of this book, and from John Nicholson, *The Martyrdom of Joseph Standing* (Salt Lake City: Deseret News Co., 1886), where a much more detailed account is given.

²⁰*CHC*, 5:560.

²¹*CHC*, 5:561.

²²*CHC*, 5:561.

²³*CHC*, 5:567.

²⁴Andrew Jenson, *Latter-day Saint Biographical Encyclopedia*, 4 vols. (Salt Lake City: Deseret News Press, 1901), 1:131.

²⁵Jenson, 1:132.

²⁶Jenson, 1:133.

²⁷*CHC*, 5:581.

²⁸Joseph Fielding Smith, *Essentials in Church History* (22d ed., enlarged, Salt Lake City: Deseret Book Co., 1967), p. 601.

²⁹*CHC*, 5:585.

³⁰*Encyclopaedia Britannica*, 1957 ed., s.v. "Jubilee or Jubile, Year of."

³¹Preston Nibley, *The Presidents of the Church* (Salt Lake City: Deseret Book Co., 1941), pp. 111-12.

³²*CHC*, 5:592.

³³*CHC*, 5:593.

³⁴*CHC*, 5:593.

³⁵*CHC*, 5:593-94.

³⁶The Prophet Joseph's brother, William B. Smith, was still alive; but he had been excommunicated from the Church, October 19, 1845. He died at Osterdock, Iowa, November 18, 1893.

³⁷Smith, p. 479.

³⁸Nibley, p. 92. I am indebted primarily to Preston Nibley and B. H. Roberts for this brief sketch of the life of John Taylor. *See* B. H. Roberts, *Life of John Taylor* (Salt Lake City: Bookcraft, 1963).

[39] Nibley, p. 93.

[40] *CHC*, 3:161.

[41] Nibley, p. 106.

[42] *CHC*, 4:62.

[43] *CHC*, 4:63.

[44] Roberts, p. 329.

[45] Roberts, p. 349. This revelation contains much valuable instruction pertaining to Church policy and purity of priesthood officers. It was added to the Doctrine and Covenants for a time as Section 138, but when it was decided to confine the D&C to the formative period of the Church (for the present) it was taken out.

[46] Roberts, pp. 413-14. *See also Deseret News*, 26 July 1887.

[47] *Deseret News*, 26 July 1887.

19

Administration of Wilford Woodruff

A BRIEF SKETCH OF THE LIFE
OF WILFORD WOODRUFF

Wilford Woodruff was born March 1, 1807, in Farmington (now Avon), Hartford County, Connecticut; his father was Aphek Woodruff and his mother was Beulah Thompson Woodruff. His ancestors on both sides of the family had lived in Farmington for three or four generations.

Wilford's father had three sons by his first wife and six children by his second wife. Aphek worked both in a flour mill and in a saw mill for over fifty years; Wilford worked with his father until he was twenty years of age, after which he followed the occupation of a miller until he was thirty-one.

Although a devout Christian, Wilford reached the age of twenty-six years without having formally joined a church. Of this he wrote:

> At an early age my mind began to be exercised upon religious subjects, but I never made a profession of religion until 1830 when I was twenty-three years of age. I did not then join any church for the reason that I could not find a body of people, denomination, or church that had for its doctrine, faith, and practices those principles, ordinances, and gifts which constituted the gospel of Jesus Christ as taught by Him and His apostles.[1]

Wilford was taught by a man named Robert Mason who lived in Sainsbury, Connecticut that:

> .... the day was near when the Lord would establish His Church and Kingdom upon the earth with all its gifts and blessings. He said that such a work would commence upon the earth before he died, but that he would not live to partake of its blessings. He said that I should live to do so, and that I should become a conspicuous actor in that kingdom. [2]

Joins the Church

When he was baptized into the Church three years afterward, the first person he thought of was Robert Mason. When he arrived in Missouri with Zion's Camp in 1834 he wrote a long letter to father Mason:

> I informed him that I had found the true gospel with all its blessings; that the authority of the Church of Christ had been restored to the earth as he had told me it would be; that I had received the ordinances of baptism and the laying on of hands; that I knew for myself that God had established through Joseph Smith, the Prophet, the Church of Christ upon the earth.
>
> He received my letter with great joy and had it read over to him many times . . . He was very aged and soon died without having the privilege of receiving the ordinances of the gospel at the hands of an elder of the Church.
>
> The first opportunity I had after the truth of baptism for the dead was revealed, I went forth and was baptized for him in the temple font at Nauvoo. [3]

After being dismissed from Zion's Camp, Wilford, having neither wife nor children, stayed in northern Missouri. In the fall of 1834 he was ordained to the office of a priest and was called on a mission. He spent the fall of 1834 and the year of 1835 doing missionary work in southern Missouri, Arkansas, Tennessee, and Kentucky. By the end of 1835 he had traveled 3,248 miles, held 170 meetings, baptized 43 persons, assisted Elder Warren Parrish with the baptism of 20 more, confirmed 35, organized 3 branches of the Church, ordained 2 teachers and 1 deacon, procured 30 subscribers to the *Messenger and*

Advocate, and had three mobs rise against him and leave him unharmed.[4]

For the next eight or nine months he did missionary work in Kentucky and Tennessee, traveling at various times with Elders Warren Parrish, Abraham O. Smoot, and David W. Patten, one of the Twelve Apostles. He also assisted Elder Thomas B. Marsh in raising $1,500 from the southern brethren to buy land in Missouri for the Church, returning to Kirtland with A. O. Smoot and Jesse Turpen in the fall of 1836.

His Marriage and Further Missionary Work

On April 13, 1837, Wilford was married to Phoebe Whitmore Carter. A month later he left on a mission with Jonathan Hale to the Fox Islands off the coast of Maine. While enroute, he visited his father and other relatives in Farmington and Avon, Connecticut, preaching the gospel to them and baptizing his uncle Ozem Woodruff, Ozem's wife Hannah, and their son, John. On July 15 his wife, Phoebe, met him here among his relatives and on July 20 they left to visit her family, the Carters, in Scarboro, Maine. They did not arrive in Scarboro until August 8 because of the amount of preaching Wilford did along the way.

On August 13 Elders Woodruff and Jonathan Hale, leaving Sister Woodruff with her relatives, left for the Fox Islands. They arrived on August 20 and began a most successful mission, converting many people on both the north and south islands, establishing a branch of the Church at each place.

From time to time Elder Woodruff left these islands to preach the gospel elsewhere, returning intermittently. On one such trip he returned to Connecticut, where he baptized his father, his stepmother, and other members of their family. He was again on the Fox Islands on August 9, 1838, when he received a letter from Elder Thomas B. Marsh, president of the Twelve Apostles, stating that Elder Woodruff had been called by revelation on July 8, 1838 (D&C 118), to become a member of the Quorum of the Twelve.[5] He was requested to return to Far West, Missouri, because the revelation had stated that the Apostles should depart on a mission from that place on April 26, 1839, to go across the sea. As he had previously encouraged the Saints on the islands to move to Zion, he now desired to take them with him to Missouri. With the financial help of Nathaniel Thomas, who had sold his property, they went to the mainland and purchased ten wagons, ten sets of harnesses, and twenty horses at a cost of about $2,000. Elder Woodruff then left for Scarboro, Maine, to get his wife and his daughter—born at Scarboro on July 14—while Nathaniel Thomas gathered up the Fox Island Saints.

A Two-Thousand Mile Journey

Woodruff and the Fox Island Saints left Scarboro together on October 9, 1838, to begin a 2,000 mile journey by wagon. Hearing of the terrible persecution of the Saints in northern Missouri, they stopped at Rochester, Illinois, where they had arrived after many hardships on December 19. In the spring of 1839 Elder Woodruff arrived in Quincy, Illinois, in time to make the journey to Far West for the meeting at the temple site on April 26, where he and George A. Smith were ordained apostles. He returned to Quincy on May 2 with the other apostles. The next day six of them visited Joseph Smith, who had arrived from northern Missouri after spending nearly six months in prison. Brother Woodruff said it was the first time he had seen the Prophet in two years.[6] On May 18, 1839, Elder Woodruff arrived in the future city of Nauvoo with Brigham Young to provide shelter for their families before leaving on their missions abroad. After settling their families in Montrose, Iowa, on July 22, 1839, Elder Woodruff with others experienced the miraculous healing through the Prophet Joseph Smith of Elijah Fordham, Joseph Bates Noble, and others.[7]

His Mission Abroad

Ill on August 8 with what was called the ague, Elder Woodruff left for his mission abroad with Elder John Taylor. After many trials and hardships, all the while preaching the gospel on their way to New York City, they sailed from New York Harbor on December 19 in company with Elder Theodore Turley of the Seventies Quorum, arriving in Liverpool, England, on January 11, 1840.

England proved to be another highly successful missionary venture for Brother Woodruff. Through revelation he was directed to go south to Herefordshire, where he stopped at the residence of Mr. and Mrs. John Benbow. He soon learned of an organization known as the United Brethren who had broken away from the Methodist Church and were looking for more

light. He converted six hundred of them and baptized them all
in a pool of water at the Benbow residence. Over a period of
eight months Elder Woodruff baptized 1,800 people in Herefordshire, Gloucestershire, and Worcestershire.[8] The Twelve
left England in April, 1841, arriving in New York at the end of
May, where Wilford left the others and went to Scarboro,
Maine, to meet his wife at the home of her parents. Before
returning to Nauvoo in October, they again visited his relatives
in Connecticut. In Nauvoo he assisted in locating immigrants,
worked on the Nauvoo Temple, assisted John Taylor in publishing the *Times and Seasons,* built a comfortable house for his
family, and "was continually active in all his Church duties."[9]

He was in Portland, Maine, on July 9, 1844, when he received
the sorrowful news of the death of Joseph and Hyrum. He left
immediately for Boston, where he met Brigham Young. Under
date of July 17 his journal states:

> Elder Brigham Young arrived and we called upon Sister
> Vose. Brother Young took to the bed and I the arm chair,
> and then we veiled our faces and gave vent to our grief.
> Until now I had not shed a tear since the death of the
> Prophet. My soul had been nerved up like steel. After
> giving vent to our grief in tears we felt more composed.[10]

The Twelve gathered at Boston and went by train, boat, and
stage to Nauvoo, where, on August 8, the people sustained them
as the leaders of the Church. On August 12, Elder Woodruff was
appointed to preside over the European mission. With his wife
and two children he left Nauvoo on August 28. After visiting
their parents in Connecticut and Maine, they sailed from New
York City on December 8.

With more than 11,000 members in the British mission,
Wilford was kept busy. Receiving word from Brigham Young
that the Saints were moving to "somewhere west of the Rocky
Mountains," Wilford was released to return to Nauvoo. When he
arrived with his family on April 23, 1846, most of the General
Authorities were already on their way west.

The Westward Trek

By May 26 Wilford Woodruff had completed his preparations
for the western move. He left Nauvoo with his family and
arrived at Council Bluffs, Iowa, on July 7. In August he moved

across the river to Winter Quarters. On October 15 while cutting trees to build his cabin, he was crushed by a falling tree, sustaining numerous bruises and breaking his breastbone and three ribs.

After a difficult winter at Winter Quarters, Nebraska, Wilford left with the pioneer company in April, making the journey of 1,035 miles into the Salt Lake valley in three months and seventeen days.

After one month and two days in the valley, Elder Woodruff left with 106 others on horseback to return to Winter Quarters, arriving on October 31. He found that his wife had given birth to a daughter a few days earlier.

Another Mission

During the ensuing winter two of Wilford Woodruff's sons, Joseph and Ezra, died. In the spring of 1848 Elder Woodruff expected to journey into the Salt Lake valley with his family and others, but President Young requested him to go on another mission to the eastern states. He left Winter Quarters on June 21 with his family and others, eleven in all. They went through Mt. Pisgah and back to Nauvoo. Selling his mules, carriage, and outfit at Nauvoo, he took a steamer down the Mississippi to St. Louis. He then went on to Louisville, where he visited his brother-in-law and sister, Mr. and Mrs. Luther Scammon. While they were in Louisville the Woodruffs' nine-month-old daughter died. They finally arrived in Boston on August 12, having traveled 2,595 miles from Winter Quarters.

While he was on this mission Elder Woodruff traveled a great deal, leaving his wife and family with her folks in Scarboro, Maine, where he had had the privilege of baptizing her father, Ezra Carter, Sr., whose wife had previously joined the Church. He also visited the Fox Islands, where he had converted 100 people twelve years before. And he had the privilege of visiting Thomas L. Kane in Pennsylvania a number of times. He also visited many branches of the Church in New England and did missionary work in Canada. While on this mission to the eastern states he baptized around 200 people.[11]

Early in 1850 he received a letter from the First Presidency instructing him to return west and bring with him all the Saints he could gather. He went to Maine on March 2 and made arrangements to take with him many of his wife's family as well as other Church members. Alexander Badlam, a nephew of Sam

Brannan, had gone to California on business earlier, and while he was there he had gathered up a little bag of gold dust from the Saints who were digging gold there and sent it to Wilford Woodruff to assist him. With the money from this dust Elder Woodruff was able to pay the expenses of his family and a number of others to Zion. He felt this was the fulfillment of a statement in his patriarchal blessing, given him by Joseph Smith, Sr., in which he said that Wilford should have access to the treasures hidden in the ground to assist him in getting himself and others to Zion.[12]

With about 100 Saints he left for New York on April 9 where they gathered more than a hundred more members, making a total of 209. After a wearisome journey they arrived in Salt Lake City on October 14, 1850.

His Life in the Valley

In Salt Lake City Wilford Woodruff participated in all of the activities of the Saints, faithfully carried out every assignment, became a member of the legislature in 1851, helped build the old tabernacle in 1852, attended the dedication of the Salt Lake temple site on February 14, 1853, helped lead a colony of Saints into Tooele Valley in 1853, and organized a horticultural society in 1855 to sponsor the growing of fruit.

During these years he received no salary from the Church; so he found it necessary, at times, to labor with his hands to support his family. He had a twenty-acre farm just south of Salt Lake City. After returning from an extensive trip through the southern settlements in 1854 with other general authorities, he recorded that he had harvested 369 bushels of wheat, 400 bushels of potatoes, and 200 bushels of corn.[13]

During his first seventeen years in the Church, his life was nomadic; of the first ten years he spent only one summer at home because he was involved in missionary work during the remaining summers. After returning from his mission in 1850 he was not requested to travel abroad any more, although he did travel extensively throughout the Mormon settlements and made a couple of trips to the East, one in 1893 when he was past 85 years of age.

In 1868 at the request of President Young, Elder Woodruff moved to Provo along with John Taylor and Joseph F. Smith, where he was very active in civic and church affairs. He worked with his hands to earn his living,

... Grubbing willows, breaking land, building bridges, digging ditches, constructing roads, erecting fences, barns, and houses. He was, indeed, a model of industry. . . . All honorable work was God's work, whether he dug a ditch, preached a sermon, or wrote history. . . .[14]

After October Conference in 1868 Brother Woodruff wrote:

It was the first time for thirty-two years that all the Quorum of the Twelve had been together. The last time before this was at the home of Elder Heber C. Kimball in Kirtland.[15]

The Quorum at this time—1868—consisted of Orson Hyde, Orson Pratt, John Taylor, Wilford Woodruff, George A. Smith, Ezra T. Benson, Charles C. Rich, Lorenzo Snow, Erastus Snow, Franklin D. Richards, George Q. Cannon, and Joseph F. Smith. At this conference George A. Smith was sustained as a counselor in the First Presidency and Brigham Young, Jr., was called to fill the vacancy in the Quorum of the Twelve.

In 1871 at sixty-four, Elder Woodruff purchased a ranch in Randolph, Rich County, Utah, where he spent many pleasant summers harvesting hay and gathering wood from the canyons.[16]

In 1876 he spent the fall and winter in St. George with President Young. The general conference of the Church was convened there in April, 1877, and the St. George Temple was dedicated. Brother Woodruff was called to be president of the temple and was presiding in that position on August 29, 1877, when President Young died. Woodruff was then released to move back to Salt Lake City, where the Twelve presided as the Presidency of the Church for the next three years. When John Taylor became President of the Church at the October Conference in 1880, Elder Woodruff was sustained President of the Quorum of the Twelve.

After passage of the Edmunds Law, President Woodruff was forced to evade the United States deputy marshals. While doing so he visited stakes in Southern Utah, Eastern Utah, Arizona, and Nevada. He was in Fayette, Utah, when he heard of President John Taylor's death and returned to Salt Lake City. Although subject to arrest, he managed to keep in touch with other members of the Twelve.

Wilford Woodruff, fourth president of The Church of Jesus Christ of Latter-day Saints. *Courtesy of Church Historical Department.*

Wilford Woodruff Succeeds to Leadership of the Church

With Wilford Woodruff as their president, the Twelve Apostles again assumed the leadership of the Church. The two counselors in the former First Presidency resumed their positions in the Quorum, which were the fifth and sixth places. This arrangement continued for the next twenty-one months until. the April Conference when President Woodruff was sustained as President of the Church on April 7, 1889, with George Q. Cannon and Joseph F. Smith again sustained as counselors.

SOME NOTABLE EVENTS DURING WILFORD WOODRUFF'S PRESIDENCY

The Issuance of the Manifesto

Perhaps the most important event during the time President Woodruff presided over the Church was his issuance of the Manifesto, which has already been dealt with in chapter eighteen. Although a few members of the Church refused to accept the right of President Woodruff to issue such a document, they should have remembered that he and only he had the keys to

430 perform such marriages, and when any one or all of the three presiding quorums of the Church—i.e., the First Presidency, the Twelve Apostles, the First Quorum of the Seventy—make a decision, it can be overridden only by the several priesthood quorums of the Church. If the priesthood quorums do not override such a decision, it is the duty and obligation of every member of the Church to abide by it, for according to the Doctrine and Covenants:

> In case that any decision of these Quorums is made in unrighteousness, it may be brought before a general assembly of the several quorums, which constitute the spiritual authorities of the church; otherwise there can be no appeal from their decision. (D&C 107:32.)

Relief to Members of the Church

The issuance of the Manifesto brought relief to the Latter-day Saints and chagrin to the bitter anti-Mormons who would no longer have an excuse to get political control of the territory or to persecute the Saints further. On November 1, 1891, in a sermon given in Logan, President Woodruff said:

> The Lord showed me by vision and revelation exactly what would take place if we did not stop this practice . . . He has told me exactly what to do, and what the result would be if we did not do it. . . . I want to say this; I should have let all the temples go out of our hands, I should have gone to prison myself, and let every other man go there, had not the God of heaven commanded me to do what I did do. . . . [17]

Granting of Amnesty

On December 19, 1891, the First Presidency and the Twelve Apostles petitioned the federal government for amnesty in regard to their so-called polygamous offenses.[18] This petition was endorsed by Governor Arthur L. Thomas, Chief Justice Charles S. Zane (now serving his second term) and many leading gentiles. In the spring of 1893 President Benjamin Harrison, who had visited Utah on January 4 of that year, issued a proclamation of amnesty to polygynists for past offenses, limiting it to those who had entered into the polygynist relationship before November 1, 1890. This limitation was included, apparently, in case some of the Saints had entered into a polygynous relationship after the issuance of the Manifesto. In accordance with this action, the Utah Commission ruled that the restrictions against voters in Utah should be removed.[19]

THE POLITICAL MANIFESTO

In 1895 the general authorities formulated what was known as the Political Manifesto. Moses Thatcher of the Council of the Twelve had accepted the nomination for senator on the Democratic ticket and B. H. Roberts of the First Council of the Seventy had accepted the nomination for United States representative. They had done this without consulting the other general authorities, and the First Presidency felt they should not have done this if they expected to maintain their positions in their quorums. Eventually, the General Authorities formulated a manifesto as a guideline to govern political participation by those who are called to high church positions.[20] The manifesto reads as follows:

THE POLITICAL RULE OF THE CHURCH

To the Officers and Members of the Church of Jesus Christ of Latter-day Saints, in General Conference Assembled

We unanimously agree to, and promulgate as a rule, that should always be observed in the church and by every leading official thereof, that before accepting any position, political or otherwise, which would interfere with the proper and complete discharge of his ecclesiastical duties, and before accepting a nomination or entering into engagements to perform new duties, said official should apply to the proper authorities and learn from them whether he can, consistently with the obligations already entered into with the church upon assuming his office, take upon himself the added duties and labors and responsibilities of the new position. To maintain proper discipline and order in the church, we deem this absolutely necessary; and in asserting this rule, we do not consider that we are infringing in the least degree upon the individual rights of the citizen.

We declare that in making these requirements of ourselves and our brethren in the ministry, we do not in the least desire to dictate to them concerning their duties as American citizens, or to interfere with the affairs of the state; neither do we consider that in the remotest degree we are seeking the union of church and state.[21]

Elder Moses Thatcher was the only general authority who refused to sign this manifesto. Because of his refusal, he was dropped from the Quorum of the Twelve. This political rule is still in effect, and it is most appropriate and necessary for the benefit of orderly church administration.

DEDICATION OF THE SALT LAKE TEMPLE

On February 14, 1853, ground was broken for the building of the Salt Lake temple; on April 6, 1853, the cornerstones for the footings of the temple were laid. On April 6, 1892, the capstone of the temple was set in place by President Woodruff in the presence of 40,000 people. As he stepped forward, President Woodruff stated: "Attention, all the House of Israel, and all ye nations of the earth. We will now lay the top stone of the temple of our God, the foundation of which was laid and dedicated by the prophet, seer, and revelator, Brigham Young." [22] He then pressed an electric button and the stone dropped in place. Then the Hosanna shout led by President Snow was given three times: "Hosanna! Hosanna! Hosanna! to God and the Lamb! Amen! Amen! Amen!"

One year later—on April 6, 1893—the temple (having been completed only the evening before) was dedicated to the work of the Lord. President Woodruff had the pleasure of offering the dedicatory prayer. This was the culmination of forty years of sacrifice and effort on the part of the Latter-day Saints. The services were held in the assembly hall on the top floor of the temple; and because of the limited space available, the services were repeated twice daily from April 6 to May 18 in order to accommodate all members of the Church who desired to attend. Approximately 2,600 persons attended each session, and a conservative estimate is that in all 75,000 persons attended.[23]

In the fall of 1892, although he was past 86 years of age, President Woodruff took a trip east, accompanied by other Church authorities. At Independence, Missouri, he was very pleased to be welcomed by the mayor of the city and other officials.

Laying the capstone of the Temple at Salt Lake City, Utah, April 6, 1892.
Courtesy of Church Historical Department.

THE FIRST WORLD'S PARLIAMENT OF RELIGIONS

In the summer of 1889 Charles Carroll Bonney conceived the
idea of holding a World's Parliament of Religions in connection
with the World's Columbian Exposition (a World Fair), to be
held in Chicago in 1893. At the appropriate time, invitations
were sent out to the various religions of the world and a special
effort was made to induce oriental religions to participate, including those that practiced "polygamy." When the Church of
Jesus Christ of Latter-day Saints received no invitation, they
decided to request the opportunity of being represented. They
wrote to Bonney, who had become president of the World's
Congress Auxiliary. After waiting ten days without a reply,
Church leaders sent Elder B. H. Roberts as the representative of
the Church to seek representation. Elder Roberts, in talking
with Bonney, discovered that it was the opinion of the general
committee of the parliament that the Church ought not to be
represented. Elder Roberts reminded Bonney that the Church
had been accused of preaching only among the ignorant and of
not daring to come into contact with the enlightened world;
now, when it proposed to place a statement of its doctrines side
by side with the creeds of all other religions, the parliament was

434 inconsistent in objecting to its admission and such an objection would be inconsistent to the character of the gathering. [24]

After one or two other interviews and much correspondence between Bonney and Reverend John Henry Barrows, the chairman of the parliamentary meetings, Barrows granted permission to the Church to be represented. Elder Roberts submitted his address to the parliament leaders in writing, and they said it was a "good paper." As the time for the parliament drew near, Elder Roberts was notified that he was to deliver his paper in a small side hall. Inasmuch as he had expected to deliver his address before the main parliament in the Hall of Columbus where the other religions were represented, he told the officers that the Church would be content with the distinction of "being the one voice in all the world that could not be heard in such an assembly, and would seek other means of declaring her views and announcing her mission." [25]

Elder Roberts then made a statement to the press revealing the treatment he had received; he did so in the form of an open letter to Bonney and Reverend Barrows. The Associated Press sent out a synopsis of the letter, and many leading newspapers printed editorial comments on it which were generally critical of the parliament officials and favorable to the Church.

Forty years later in 1933 when the World's Fair was again held in Chicago, another parliament of religions was held. This time the Church received the same courteous invitation as the other religions; and again B. H. Roberts was appointed to represent the Church. He was the only one present who had attended the 1893 parliament. I was in Chicago at the time and heard the address given by Elder Roberts, along with three other addresses presented that evening. So many members of the Church attended on that particular evening that it was by far the largest audience ever in attendance.

The sponsors of the World's Parliament of Religions, desiring another large audience, invited Elder Roberts to speak again about a week after his first address. Again, the Latter-day Saints of the Chicago area attended, and I with them. Again three other speakers had the pleasure of having a large audience. At the end of the services the presiding officer made a special plea to the Mormons to attend the remainder of the services which were to be held each evening.

CHANGE IN FAST DAY

In 1855 when poor crops were harvested because of drouth

and grasshoppers, the Church inaugurated its first regular fast day, the first Thursday of each month. It was to be a day when people would donate in kind the food they did not eat which would then be distributed among the poor.

Since many of the Saints were, in 1896, employed by gentile merchants, and others were in pursuits which made difficult their regular weekday attendance at fast meetings, the First Presidency sent out a letter of instruction, designating the first Sunday of every month as fast day. They also included instructions pertaining to the observance of the fast:

> In some places the custom has arisen to consider it a fast to omit eating breakfast. This is not in accordance with the views and practice of the past. When fasts were observed in the early days, it was a rule to not partake of the food from the previous day until after the meeting in the afternoon of the fast day. In making donations to the poor also it has been the understanding that the food that would be necessary for the two meals should be donated to the poor, and as much more as those who are liberally inclined, and have the means, may feel disposed to give.[26]

Today these instructions are still valid except that donations are made in money instead of in food.

STATEHOOD

On September 6, 1893, Utah's Delegate to Congress who was a friendly non-Mormon, introduced a bill in the House of Representatives entitled "An Act to Enable the people of Utah to Form a Constitution and State Government and be Admitted into the Union on an Equal Footing with the Original States." [27] It was passed by the House on December 13 and by the Senate in July, 1894, after which President Grover Cleveland signed it.

The state constitutional convention was held beginning March 4, 1895, and continuing for sixty-six days. John Henry Smith (a son of George A. Smith) was the convention president. The constitution that was created was overwhelmingly ratified by the people, and Utah entered the Union as the forty-fifth state. On that day President Woodruff said: "I feel thankful to God that I have lived to see Utah admitted into the family of states. It is an event that we have looked forward to for a generation."[28]

It was Governor Heber M. Wells (the first governor of the state of Utah) who recommended in one of his messages to the legislature that Utah celebrate a jubilee during the month of July, 1897, inasmuch as it had been fifty years since the pioneers had entered the Salt Lake valley. The recommendation was approved and a committee called the "Jubilee Commission" was appointed to make preparations for the celebration. Spencer Clawson was the chairman of the commission. All of the surviving members of the pioneers of 1847 were to be special guests. Those whose residences could be located outside the Salt Lake valley were sent an invitation and a railroad ticket. Brother Green Flake, the only surviving Negro pioneer, living with his son in Gray's Lake, Idaho, wrote the following letter of acceptance:

Gray's Lake, Idaho

Mr. Clawson,

Dear friend, I received your most kind and welcome letter and ticket, and was glad to receive it, and I will be down to the Jubilee.

Yours truly,

Friend Green Flake [29]

The celebration began on July 20 and ran through July 24. On the first day the Brigham Young monument, which stands in the center of South Temple and Main Streets, was unveiled and dedicated. The ceremonies were preceded by a parade of the pioneers, and each pioneer was given a solid gold medal upon which was engraved a picture of Brigham Young with a pioneer wagon on the left, an 1897 model locomotive on the right, a beehive on the top, and a pony express rider on the bottom. [30] Six hundred fifty of these medals were distributed.

Each succeeding day featured a different parade; on July 21 the parade showed Utah's advancement during fifty years. July 22 featured the Sunday School children with an evening parade which was said to be "gorgeously illuminated with electrical decorations featuring Great Salt Lake, real and fanciful." July

featured the parade of the counties with a float from each
county displaying its resources. Saturday, July 24, was the
parade of parades when all previous parades, including that of
the pioneers, entered into one gigantic spectacle. On Sunday,
July 25, a memorial service in honor of all deceased pioneers
was held in the tabernacle as a conclusion of the celebration.

DEATH OF PRESIDENT WOODRUFF

On March 1, 1897, President Woodruff enjoyed his ninetieth
birthday, and during the week of July 24 he rode in the first
carriage of the parade. One year later (July 24, 1898), President
Wilford Woodruff delivered his last public address in Salt Lake
City when Pioneer Square, where the stockade had been built in
1847, was dedicated as a public park.

On August 13 he went to California with his wife Emma,
George Q. Cannon, and Bishop Clawson, hoping that a change
of climate would benefit his health. He expired at the home of
Colonel Isaac Trumbo at 6:40 a.m. on September 2, 1898, in
the presence of his first counselor, George Q. Cannon. President
Woodruff was in his ninety-second year when he died. His body
was brought to Salt Lake City, and a public funeral was held on
September 8 in the tabernacle, where the deceased received well
deserved praise and respect.

Near the end of his life President Woodruff made a summary
of the miles he had traveled for the Church, and the discourses
he had given. Beginning in 1834 until the end of 1895 he had
traveled 172,369 miles; he had held 7,655 meetings and
preached 3,562 discourses; he had organized 51 branches of the
Church, and obtained 77 preaching places. He had traveled in
England, Scotland, and Wales, and in twenty-three states and
five territories in the United States.[31] For sixty-three years
Wilford Woodruff kept a journal in which he recorded his experiences; these journals are now a valuable record, preserved in
the Church Historian's Office.

President Woodruff had hoped to live long enough to see the
Church free of debt, but this was one of his desires that did not
materialize.

Footnotes

[1]Matthias F. Cowley, *Wilford Woodruff* (Salt Lake City: Deseret
News Press, 1909), p. 14.

[2]Cowley, p. 16.

438   [3]Cowley, pp. 17-18.

[4]Wilford Woodruff, *Leaves From My Journal* (Salt Lake City: Juvenile Instructor Office, 1882), p. 21.

[5]Woodruff, p. 51.

[6]Woodruff, p. 60.

[7]Woodruff, pp. 62-65.

[8]Woodruff, p. 81.

[9]Preston Nibley, *The Presidents of the Church* (Salt Lake City: Deseret Book Co., 1941), p. 144.

[10]Nibley, p. 145.

[11]Cowley, p. 341.

[12]Woodruff, p. 94.

[13]Nibley, p. 155.

[14]Cowley, p. 451.

[15]Cowley, p. 454.

[16]Nibley, p. 159.

[17]Nibley, pp. 164-65.

[18]Polygynous is the proper term: a man married to more than one wife. Amnesty is a general pardon of an offense usually given by a government to a group of people often before trial or conviction.

[19]Joseph Fielding Smith, *Essentials in Church History* (22d ed., enlarged, Salt Lake City: Deseret Book Co., 1967), p. 496.

[20]This included the First Presidency, the Twelve Apostles, the First Council of the Seventy, the Presiding Patriarch, and the Presiding Bishopric.

[21]*CHC*, 6:334.

[22]Smith, pp. 497-98.

[23]*CHC*, 6:236.

[24]*CHC*, 6:239.

[25]*CHC*, 6:240.

[26]*CHC*, 6:348-49. *See also Deseret News*, 14 November 1896.

[27]Smith, p. 499.

[28]Nibley, p. 166.

[29]Kate B. Carter, *The Story of the Negro Pioneer* (Salt Lake City: Daughters of the Utah Pioneers, 1965), p. 6.

[30]*CHC*, 6:349-50.

[31]*CHC*, 6:354.

20

Administration of Lorenzo Snow

A BRIEF SKETCH OF THE LIFE
OF LORENZO SNOW

Mantua, Ohio, was a wilderness area when Lorenzo Snow was born on April 3, 1814, to Oliver and Rosetta L. Pettibone Snow. He was the fifth child and first son in the family that had moved into the Ohio township when there were only ten other families present. The nearest market for their farm produce was New Orleans, and it took six months to make the round trip. Later, two younger brothers were born into the family. Lorenzo, the oldest boy, had many responsibilities in his youth when his father was away on public business.

Although his school days were few, he read a great deal, finally completing one term in high school at Ravenna, Ohio, and having a special "term of tuition" under a Hebrew professor.[1] He afterwards attended Oberlin College, a Presbyterian institution. While on his way there in September, 1835, he met Elder David W. Patten, one of the original Twelve Apostles of the Church who was doing missionary work at the time. Their conversation turned toward religion, and Elder Patten's message made a lasting impression on the young Lorenzo Snow.

This was not the first time Lorenzo Snow had heard of Joseph Smith and Mormonism, for in 1831 when he was seventeen years old he had gone to Hiram, Ohio, about four miles from his home, with other members of his family to hear the Prophet Joseph Smith speak at a meeting held in a bowery at the John Johnson farm. Although he was favorably impressed with the Prophet, Lorenzo was a youth of seventeen and had other interests; he was bent on a military career. His mother and his sister, Leonora, had already joined the Church, however. He was receptive when his sister Eliza, who had joined the Church on April 5, 1835, and had moved to Kirtland, wrote inviting him to visit her and attend the Hebrew school which was being opened by the leaders of the Church. He was soon in Kirtland, where he began to mingle with Joseph Smith and other Church leaders. In June, 1836, he was baptized, but he was disappointed because he received no manifestation of the Holy Ghost. The manifestation followed his baptism, however, in a singular experience about two or three weeks afterward and was so powerful that Lorenzo Snow testified, ". . . . its realization was more perfect, tangible and miraculous than even my strongest hopes had led me to anticipate." [2] Thereafter he devoted more than sixty years to the service of the Lord.

His Early Missions

During the winter of 1836-37, while attending the School of the Elders, he was ordained an elder; and in the spring of the year, he left on a mission to travel through the state of Ohio "without purse or scrip," which was rather a trial to a young man who had always had sufficient means to pay his way. [3] He returned to Kirtland in the spring of 1838 to find a great deal of disaffection in the Church. This was the major reason why the Snow family decided to leave for Far West, Missouri, the other headquarters of the Church, where most of the leaders had already gone; so, with his father, mother, two sisters, and two brothers, he left on the thousand-mile journey in their horse and ox-drawn vehicles. They arrived in Far West in July, 1838.

On about October 1, he set out on a second missionary journey. While laboring in Kentucky in February, 1839, Lorenzo received word that the Saints had been driven out of Missouri. He decided to visit his former state of Ohio and finish up some business there; so, he left on the 500 mile journey with $1.25 and faith in the Lord. He finally reached the place of a Brother Smith in Ohio, where a year earlier he had stayed while he did missionary work. His health was so poor that the Smith family did not recognize him at first, but soon he was the

recipient of their kindness as they cared for him while he was
confined to bed for a number of days.

After doing missionary work in Ohio until the fall of 1839, he accepted a position as a schoolteacher in Shalersville, Ohio, for the winter of 1839 and 1840. In the spring of 1840, he joined his father's family in Nauvoo, Illinois, where the Saints were gathering. Shortly after his arrival he was engaged in religious conversation with Elder Henry G. Sherwood when the Spirit of the Lord rested upon him. He said:

> ... The eyes of my understanding were opened, and I saw as clear as the sun at noon-day, with wonder and astonishment, the pathway of God and man. I formed the following couplet which expresses the revelation as it was shown to me:
> 'As man now is, God once was, As God now is, man may become.'[4]

At that time, he revealed this statement to no one but his sister, Eliza; but after arriving in the mission field on his third mission—to Great Britain in the summer of 1840—he told his experience and the couplet to Brigham Young, who replied:

> Brother Snow, that is a new doctrine; if true, it has been revealed to you for your own private information, and will be taught in due time by the Prophet to the Church; till then I advise you to lay it upon the shelf and say no more about it.[5]

Lorenzo followed this advice. After returning home from his mission to England on April 12, 1843, Brigham Young came to him and told him it was true doctrine, for the Prophet had just been teaching it to the people.

Lorenzo spent the summer of 1843 visiting relatives in Illinois and Ohio; in the fall he accepted a position as schoolteacher at Lima, Illinois, a settlement of the Saints in Adams County, about thirty miles south of Nauvoo.

In the spring of 1844 he was called on another mission, this time to Ohio to preach the gospel and distribute among the people the Prophet's "Views of the Powers and Policy of the Government of the United States." He was in Cincinnati when he heard the news of the martyrdom of the Prophet Joseph Smith and his brother Hyrum. He secured a horse and buggy to return to Nauvoo. While on the last stretch of the trip between Carthage and Nauvoo, he saw a mob of men coming toward him on horseback, eyeing him suspiciously. As he met them, one of the buggy wheels struck a rock and jolted the wagon. Lorenzo turned to them and in an angry voice said: "Boys! Why in hell don't you repair this road?" One of the men said: "He is one of us. He is all right, let him pass." [6] His uncouth manner not only served to protect him but it also protected several hundred dollars he was carrying to Nauvoo to be given to various people.

Marriage

Lorenzo spent the year of 1845 working on the Nauvoo Temple and preparing to move westward. Until the Prophet had taught him the law of celestial marriage, Elder Snow had been content to remain single and would have probably remained so, his interest in preaching the "restored gospel" absorbing his full interest. But with the Prophet's teachings about marriage bearing upon his mind, in the fall of 1845 at the age of 31 he became sealed for time and eternity to Charlotte Squires and Mary Adeline Goddard in the same ceremony in the Nauvoo Temple. Later, he also married Harriet Amelia Squires and Sarah Ann Richards. During the fall and winter of 1845 and 1846 Lorenzo was called to be an officiator in the temple, a pleasure to him because of his spiritual nature. He was also asked to be superintendent of the grammar schools of the city, a position for which he was well suited.

The Westward Trek

By February 15, 1846, Lorenzo Snow started on the westward trek by crossing the Mississippi River with his family in the company of some of the apostles. The following summer he reached Mt. Pisgah, Iowa, where he spent the winter of 1846 and 1847. In the early spring when Charles C. Rich went west— he had been called to join the main body of Saints at Winter Quarters—Lorenzo was called to preside over the Saints at Pisgah.

In the spring of 1848 Lorenzo left Mt. Pisgah and journeyed into the Salt Lake valley as a captain in Brigham Young's large company. Lorenzo's company of a hundred families consisted of 321 people, 99 wagons, 20 horses, 3 mules, 388 oxen, 188 cows, 38 loose cattle, 139 sheep, 25 pigs, 158 chickens, 10 cats, 26 dogs, and 2 doves.

They arrived on September 22 and made their first home in the old fort, where they stayed for a year until they could procure a home of their own. Lorenzo and his families occupied cabins similar to the one he had lived in at Mt. Pisgah.[7]

A Call to the Apostleship

On February 12, 1849, Lorenzo was invited to attend a meeting of the Twelve Apostles. He was greatly surprised when he was informed that he had been selected to fill one of the vacancies in the Quorum of the Twelve.

Mission to Europe

In the fall of 1849 Lorenzo was called to assist in gathering funds for bringing the poor Saints to Zion. This movement resulted in the founding of the Perpetual Emigrating Fund Company at the October Conference. At this time Elder Snow was called to take the gospel message to Italy, but he was also authorized to take the gospel wherever he desired.[8] He traveled east with the first company of missionaries sent from the Rocky Mountain region. They left Salt Lake valley on October 19. While traveling across the plains, they were under the direction of Shadrach Roundy. At one time they were miraculously saved from 200 onrushing Indian warriors.[9]

Elder Snow arrived in England on April 18, 1850, in company with his fellow apostles, Erastus Snow and Franklin D. Richards. He stayed in Great Britain for a few months where he helped raise funds for the PEF and had the pleasure of seeing many old friends and converts he had brought into the Church on his previous mission to Britain.

He left England on June 15, 1850, for Italy in company with Elders Joseph Toronto and T. B. H. Stenhouse. They had very little success in Italy except in the piedmont country at the foot of the Alps, where they converted a number of families who had been members of the Waldensians, or Vadois, said to be the oldest Protestants in Europe. These convert families came to the United States mostly during the 1850's; today they have thousands of descendants. While in Europe, Lorenzo Snow sent missionaries to Switzerland, Malta, Gibraltar, Calcutta, and Bombay. He went to England where he had the Book of Mormon translated and published in the Italian language. He also traveled a great deal, visiting Switzerland, Sicily, Gibraltar, and Malta; he intended to visit India before returning home, but he received a letter (as did the other apostles in the mission field) asking that they all be on hand for the general conference of the Church on April 6, 1853.

A Call to Box Elder

At conference in October, 1853, Lorenzo was called to take fifty families and move to Box Elder to strengthen Zion in that area. The first settlers had arrived there on March 11, 1851; at the time of Lorenzo Snow's call, the population was 204. He arrived there with part of his family on May 11, 1855, and spent more than forty years there, although he fulfilled other missions and traveled in the meantime. He changed the name of the settlement from Box Elder to Brigham City in honor of his beloved friend, Brigham Young. After his return from a short mission to Hawaii in 1864 he began to develop the many cooperative enterprises that made the Saints in Box Elder County so prosperous for a time. In connection with the parent company—the Brigham City Mercantile and Manufacturing Association—the Saints organized a tannery, a boot and shoe shop, a saddle and harness shop, a woolen factory, a cooperative sheep herd of 5,000 sheep, a cooperative dairy that began with sixty cows and grew to 500, a horned-stock herd of beef cattle that grew to 1,000 head, a meat market, a hat factory, a pottery factory, a broom factory, a brush factory, a molasses factory, a shingle mill, two saw mills, a blacksmith business, a furniture business, a tailor business, and a unit for the manufacture and repair of wagons and carriages. They also manufactured a miscellany of other items such as artificial flowers and hat and shoe binders. They even founded a cotton farm of 125 acres in southern Utah to provide the cotton needed for the manufacture of cloth. These businesses provided employment for many of the young men and women, teaching each of them a useful trade.

A Visit to the Holy Land

In a letter dated October 15, 1872, from President Young and Daniel H. Wells, George A. Smith, first counselor to President Young, was instructed to take a small, select group with him on a contemplated journey through Europe and Asia Minor to the Holy Land. Lorenzo Snow and his sister Eliza with Presi-

dent Smith and four others made up the party. President
Young's letter in part had said:

> ... We desire that you observe closely what openings
> now exist, or where they may be effected, for the intro-
> duction of the Gospel into the various countries you shall
> visit. When you get to the land of Palestine, we wish you
> to dedicate and consecrate that land, that it may be
> blessed with fruitfulness, preparatory to the return of the
> Jews, in fulfillment of prophecy and the accomplishment
> of the purposes of our Heavenly Father.[10]

On the way to Palestine they visited England, Holland,
Belgium, France, Italy, and Egypt. From Egypt they went by
ship to Jaffa. A few days later they rode up to the summit of
the Mount of Olives on horseback, where a tent, table, seats,
and carpet had been prepared for them. Here on March 2, 1873,
President George A. Smith rededicated the Holy Land—it had
been previously dedicated by Orson Hyde on October 24,
1841—for the gathering of the Jews and the rebuilding of Jerusalem. President Smith's dedication was followed by prayers
from each of the brethren.

Visiting the Stakes of Zion and the Lamanites

President Snow returned to Brigham City on July 7, 1873,
after more than an eight-month absence. The dignitaries of
Brigham City and the people gave him a heartwarming welcome.[11] Apostle Snow continued to make his home in Brigham
City, but he often visited the settlements of the Saints with
other General Authorities.

On Sunday, August 19, 1877, at a quarterly conference in
Brigham City, President Brigham Young released Elder Snow
from his duties as president of the Box Elder Stake and installed
his son, Oliver Snow, in that position. During the following
week Lorenzo went with John Taylor and others to Paris, Bear
Lake County, Idaho, where they released Charles C. Rich from
his duties as president of the Bear Lake Stake and installed
William Budge in that position.

On April 14, 1879, when the cornerstones of the Manti
Temple were laid, Lorenzo Snow gave the dedicatory prayer. He
also offered the prayer of dedication upon the completion of
the temple nine years later, on May 21, 1888.

On July 2, 1885, Lorenzo Snow received an assignment from President John Taylor to go among various Indian tribes to make a survey of conditions in order to determine whether to establish missions among them. He left on August 8, going first to the Umatella Indians near Pendleton, Oregon, then two hundred miles northeast to the Nez Perce tribe near Lewiston, Idaho. After completing his visit there, he went nearly five hundred miles southeast to Neeleyville, near the Bannock River, where he found 150 to 200 Indians, part of whom were members of the Church. On September 24, 1885, after a short visit in Brigham City, Elder Snow left with many other men to visit the Wind River reservation in the west central part of Wyoming, arriving on October 3. Over three hundred of these Shoshone Indians, including Chief Washakie, had been previously baptized by Bishop Amos Wright, who was one of the men accompanying Elder Snow at this time.

Upon completion of this visit, Elder Snow returned to Brigham City, where in the early morning hours of November 20, 1885, his home was surrounded by seven United States deputy marshals who arrested him on the charge of "unlawful cohabitation." He was later tried on three different counts for this offense under the segregation interpretation of the Edmunds Law and was given the maximum sentence of six months in jail and a fine of $300 on each count. He entered the penitentiary to begin serving these sentences on March 12, 1886.[12] In writing to his family he often took a humorous point of view toward the situation. Upon one occasion he wrote:

> In a general sense we are here as the invited guests of the Nation, boarded and lodged all at Government expense, a remarkable instance illustrating in a striking manner that spirit of philanthropy pervading the bosom of our mighty republic.[13]

His case was appealed to the United States Supreme Court on a writ of habeas corpus, and the judgment handed down was that there was but one offense committed and the trial court had no jurisdiction to inflict punishment in regard to more than one conviction. Thus the segregation interpretation was declared illegal; inasmuch as Lorenzo Snow had already served nearly eleven months, he was released from prison on February 8, 1887. He immediately went on a visiting tour, speaking at a conference in Manti on February 21, 1887, then in meetings at Spring City, Mt. Pleasant, Moroni, and Deseret and attending conference at Fillmore the following Sunday. He returned to Brigham City after almost a year's absence on March 6, when he spoke to a capacity crowd in the Brigham City Tabernacle.

With most of the First Presidency and the Apostles either away on missions or in exile, he was assigned to conduct the general conference of the Church in the new tabernacle in Provo on April 6, 1887. Only four other apostles (Franklin D. Richards, John Henry Smith, Heber J. Grant, and John W. Taylor) were in attendance. Following the conference, Elder Snow again visited the settlements of the Saints in the south.

At the general conference of the Church in April, 1889, when Wilford Woodruff was sustained President of the Church, Lorenzo Snow was sustained as President of the Quorum of the Twelve Apostles. [14]

Raising of the Dead

At the age of twenty-two, Lorenzo Snow had received a patriarchal blessing from Joseph Smith, Sr., in which he was told:

> Thou shalt become a mighty man. Thy faith shall increase and grow stronger until it shall become like Peter's—thou shalt restore the sick; the diseased shall send to thee their aprons and handkerchiefs and by thy touch their owners shall be made whole. The dead shall rise and come forth at thy bidding. [15]

On Sunday, March 9, 1891, in Brigham City Lorenzo Snow, through his faith and the power of the priesthood, actually called a young lady back from the dead, an event similar to the raising of Lazarus by the Savior. The young lady was Ella Jensen, who had been ill with scarlet fever for several days. In order to relieve the parents of part of the burden, neighbors had been taking turns staying overnight with Ella to help look after her. One of these neighbors recalled:

> About three or four o'clock in the morning I was suddenly awakened by Ella calling me. I hurried to her bed. She was all excited and asked to get the comb, brush, and scissors, explaining that she wanted to brush her hair and

trim her finger nails and get all ready, 'for,' she said, 'they are coming to get me at ten o'clock in the morning.' I asked who was coming to get her. 'Uncle Hans Jensen,' she replied, 'and the messengers. I am going to die and they are coming at ten o'clock to get me and take me away.'[16]

Leah tried to comfort her and told her she would feel better if she would try to sleep, but Ella insisted she was going to die and wanted to get ready. She requested Leah to call her parents.

The parents were called and as they entered the room the daughter told them that her Uncle Hans, who was dead, had suddenly appeared in the room, while she was awake, with her eyes open, and told her that messengers would be there at ten o'clock to conduct her into the spirit world.[17]

Her parents told her they thought she must have been dreaming, but she insisted she was going to die at ten o'clock and wanted to see all of her relatives to tell them goodbye.

At 10:00 a.m., while her father, Jacob Jensen, was holding her hand he said he felt her pulse stop. He turned to his wife and said: "Althea, she is dead, her pulse has stopped." He decided to hitch up his team and go to town to get Elder Snow and make arrangements for the funeral. When he arrived at the Tabernacle, Lorenzo was speaking from the pulpit. He immediately read the note sent to him and excused himself by saying he must go visit some people who were in deep sorrow. He requested Elder Rudger Clawson, the Box Elder stake president, to go with him.

After their arrival at the Jensen home, while he was standing at Ella's bedside, Elder Snow asked for some consecrated oil. Ella's father later described what happened.

I was greatly surprised, but told him yes and got it for him. He handed the bottle of oil to Brother Clawson and asked him to anoint Ella. Your father [he is here speaking to LeRoi C. Snow] was then mouth in confirming the anointing.

During the administration I was particularly impressed with some of the words which he used . . . He said: 'Dear Ella, I command you in the name of the Lord, Jesus

Christ, to come back and live, your mission is not ended.
You shall yet live to perform a great mission.' He said she would yet live to rear a large family and be a comfort to her parents and friends.[18]

After the administration, Elder Snow told her parents not to mourn any longer because everything would be all right, but that he and President Clawson would have to leave because of their busy schedule.

Ella remained in the same condition for over an hour after Elder Snow and Clawson had left, altogether more than three hours since her spirit had left her body. In the meantime, word of her death had spread throughout Brigham City, and many people had called at the Jensen home to extend their condolences. While her parents were sitting at her bedside, Ella suddenly opened her eyes and said: "Where is he?" When asked who, she replied: "Why Brother Snow. He called me back."[19]

Ella Jensen said that after opening her eyes on the morning of her death, she could see some of her relatives from the spirit world, and after they had departed, for six hours until the time of her death, she had heard the most beautiful singing.[20]

Her parents thought she was delirious and Ella said: "Father you think that I am out of my mind don't you? I will very soon prove to you that I am rational." She then told her mother about two of her aunts she had met in the spirit world, Aunt Mary who told Ella she had died while Ella was a baby, and her Aunt Sarah who said she had died just before Ella was born. Her mother said she had described her aunts perfectly. Ella then turned to her father and said: "Do you now think I am out of mind?" He replied: "No, I guess you have had a very wonderful experience."[21]

Ella subsequently became the mother of eight children.

An Instance of Healing

A little over two years after the restoration to life of Ella Jensen, a twenty-three year old man by the name of Andrew May who lived at Calls Fort north of Brigham City, was stacking hay when a tine of the Jackson fork struck him in the back and went through his body, breaking his ribs and pushing the bones through his breast. Dr. Carrington from Brigham City came and examined him, taking some blood from his lungs through the breast. He then said: ". . . there is no use doing anything for a dead man; all he needs is a wooden overcoat [a coffin]". [22] Andrew was administered to and was still alive the next morning when Elder Snow called. He blessed Andrew and told him that he would live as long as life was desirable to him and that if he were faithful to the Church he would fill a mission and would hold responsible positions in the Church. Elder Snow also told him that he would always be active and take pleasure in work.

Andrew May filled a mission to the eastern states from 1899 to 1901; he later served as bishop of the ward at Rockland, Idaho, for seventeen years. In political life he became a representative in the Idaho Legislature.

President of the Salt Lake Temple

Prior to the remarkable healing of Andrew May, President Snow was appointed to preside over the Salt Lake Temple. This was shortly after its dedication on April 6, 1893. He was set apart for the work on May 19. The great spirituality of the man, along with his love of people, and his administrative ability qualified him well for this position. He thoroughly enjoyed his few years of service in presiding over the temple, as did the people working under his supervision.

A Remarkable Visitation

On September 2, 1898, while he was walking the streets of Brigham City, Elder Snow received a telegram from President Joseph F. Smith telling of the death of President Woodruff. That evening at 5:30 p.m. he left by train for Salt Lake City, where he arrived at about 7:15 p.m. After putting on his temple robes he retired to the sacred altar, where it was his habit to pray. Here in supplication he reminded the Lord how he had pleaded that President Woodruff should outlive him that he might not have to bear the heavy burdens and financial responsibilities of the Church. [23]

Nevertheless, Thy will be done. I have not sought this responsibility but if it be Thy will, I now present myself before Thee for Thy guidance and instruction. I ask that Thou show me what Thou wouldst have me do. [24]

After finishing his prayer, he expected a special manifestation.

He waited for some time. There was no reply, no voice, no visitation. He left the altar and the room in great disappointment and passed through the celestial room into the large corridor where a glorious manifestation was given to him. While later relating his visitation to his granddaughter who was in the temple with him he said:

It was right here that the Lord Jesus Christ appeared to me at the time of the death of President Woodruff. He instructed me to go right ahead and reorganize the First Presidency of the Church at once and not wait as had been done after the death of the previous presidents, and that I was to succeed President Woodruff. . . .

He stood right here about three feet above the floor.[25]

At MIA June Conference in 1919 LeRoi C. Snow related this experience of his father's after which President Heber J. Grant arose and verified the experience. He told of the meeting of the Apostles in the temple on September 13, 1898. After each of the Apostles had favorably expressed himself on the reorganization of the First Presidency, President Snow arose and said that he was "instructed of the Lord in the temple the night after President Woodruff died to organize the Presidency of the Church at once." Then President Grant said: "President Anthon H. Lund and myself are the only men now living who were present at that meeting."[26]

A few days after the MIA conference, LeRoi Snow visited Anthon H. Lund in his office and retold the incident described by President Grant; he added that he had heard President Snow tell a number of times of the Savior's appearance to him. And Elder Arthur Winter testified that he had heard President Snow tell of the Savior's visit in the temple—that the Savior had not only told him to reorganize the First Presidency immediately, "but also to select the same counselors that President Woodruff had."[27]

THE PRESIDENCY OF LORENZO SNOW

Thus, at the age of eighty-four, on September 13, 1898, at a meeting of the Twelve Apostles Lorenzo Snow was ordained President of the Church. President Snow told the Apostles that he would do the very best he could and would depend upon the Lord for assistance. He then selected George Q. Cannon and

Joseph F. Smith as his counselors; they had served the two previous presidents in the same capacity. On October 9, the last day of the semiannual general conference of the Church in 1898, these three men were unanimously sustained by the vote of all the priesthood quorums, followed by a vote of all the people. Franklin D. Richards was sustained as the President of the Quorum of the Twelve.

Financial Difficulties of the Church

President Snow inherited a bad financial situation in the Church, caused by the escheatment and maladministration of Church properties by the federal government. Although both real and personal properties had been returned to the Church, they had been considerably depleted while in government hands; many businesses, known as "revenue-producers" had been sold. The United States district attorney in Utah admitted that "this entire proceeding has been and is a scandal upon the administration of justice, and I shall use my best endeavors to arrest further raids upon this Trust Fund, and to put its administration into more competent hands."[28]
Arrington states:

> The church which at its inception had had to ask a poor farmer to mortgage his farm to print the first edition of its sacred book, and which by 1887 had reached the point where it was able to carry out missionary, educational, charitable, and economic activity on a wide scale, now found that financial wherewithal with which to continue this activity imperiled by processes which were declared by a majority of the court to be perfectly legal and proper."[29]

It was at this point that President Woodruff "wrestled mightily with the Lord" and issued the Manifesto, which eventually stopped further escheatment of church property; nevertheless, by then the Church was left in a crippled financial condition.

Even the Church's ability to assist emigrants to come to the Great Basin was taken away when the Edmunds-Tucker Law dissolved the Perpetual Emigrating Fund Company and confiscated its funds. During the 1880s the Church had collected more than $500,000 per year in tithing, but by 1890 this figure

Lorenzo Snow, fifth president of The Church of Jesus Christ of Latter-day Saints. *Permission of Church Information Service.*

had dropped to just over $300,000, principally because the members did not care to pay tithing to the Church only to have it confiscated by the government.[30] Arrington explained that the long-run effect of the Edmunds-Tucker Law was to put the Church into debt at least a half-million dollars. Certain obligations and commitments made during the 1890s, such as the completion of the Salt Lake Temple, increased expenditure for education and welfare during the depression of the 1890s, and large sums invested in the "sugar, salt, and hydroelectric power industries" increased the Church's debt to more than $1,250,000 by 1898, with its creditors pressing hard for payment of the debt.[31]

Such was the situation when Lorenzo Snow was sustained as President of the Church; and although the annual tithing receipts were up to $600,000 in 1898 this was hardly sufficient to operate the Church program. An effort was made to pay the debts and restore the credit of the Church through the issuance of $1,500,000 in bonds to eastern financial interests; but when negotiations for the sale of the bonds failed, President Snow decided to ask the Latter-day Saints to buy the bonds rather than again "go into the world for the means."[32] Church authorities decided to issue three series of bonds of $500,000, each bearing interest at the rate of 6% per annum. The first issue was offered for sale on January 1, 1899, and was sold within a few weeks. The second issue was sold during the year, and the improved financial condition of the Church made a third issue unnecessary. Half of the total issue was redeemed by 1903 and the other half was redeemed in 1907. A total of $200,000 interest was paid on the two bond issues.

The improved financial condition of the Church was made possible through the vigorous efforts of President Snow in urging the Saints to practice the law of tithing again as it had been revealed in 1838. (D&C 119.) In the spring of 1899 while praying to the Lord over the financial situation of the Church, President Snow received a revelation that he and other leading brethren should make a trip to St. George to hold a conference with the Saints.[33] Although he did not know the purpose of the trip as yet, President Snow formed a company and they left Salt Lake City on May 15, 1899. At the opening session of conference on May 17 President Snow said:

> My brethren and sisters, we are in your midst because the Lord directed me to come; but the purpose of our

coming is not clearly known at the present, but this will be made known to me during our sojourn among you.[34]

It was in a later meeting of the conference during President Snow's speech that the Lord revealed to him in vision the purpose of the visit. President Snow suddenly paused in his discourse as he contemplated the revelation before him. When he continued with a voice strengthened by the inspiration of God, he told the Saints the purpose of the Lord's call for him to visit the southland. It was to persuade the people to obey the law of tithing which would be a blessing both to the Church and to the people. He promised the people that if they would faithfully obey this law, the eighteen month drouth would end.[35]

After leaving St. George President Snow and his party held a series of meetings in the various settlements as they traveled northward, preaching the theme of tithing and the blessings promised through obedience to this law. These meetings were continued until they arrived in Salt Lake City, where the Young Men's and Young Women's Mutual Improvement Associations were holding their annual conference. Here President Snow found the opportunity to present the subject of tithing before the young people of the Church. While he was speaking to the young men's meeting, a visiting member of the MIA general board wrote the following resolution which was presented to the audience at the conclusion of his address:

> Resolved: That we accept the doctrine of tithing, as now presented by President Snow, as the present word and will of the Lord unto us, and we do accept it with all our hearts; we will ourselves observe it, and we will do all in our power to get the Latter-day Saints to do likewise.[36]

The resolution was unanimously accepted when everyone present rose to his feet and shouted "aye."

On July 2 a solemn assembly of the priesthood was held in the Salt Lake Temple, where all twenty-six of the General Authorities were present, with representatives from all forty stakes, 478 wards, and all of the auxiliary organizations of the Church. Altogether, there were present 623 priesthood bearers who unanimously accepted the same resolution that had been presented to the Young Men's Mutual Improvement Association.

President Snow's emphasis on the law of tithing increased the

456 interest of Church members in observing this law; and, although he did not live long enough to see the Church completely free of debt, during the three years of his presidency the Church had moved from a precarious financial position with unstable credit to a solid and stable financial position with excellent credit.

The Political Case of B. H. Roberts

In November, 1898, B. H. Roberts, a member of the First Council of the Seventy, again became a candidate for the United States House of Representatives on the Democratic ticket—this time with the full consent of his colleagues, the General Authorities of the Church. During the campaign, sectarian ministers and the Republican press made much of the fact that he had served a term of imprisonment under the Edmunds Law in 1889 for unlawful cohabitation. This was in spite of the fact that he had been elected to the Constitutional Convention in 1894, and in 1895 he had run as the Democratic nominee for representative. Each time he had run with no complaint from any politician.

In spite of the complaints of ministers and Republicans, in 1898 he was elected by a plurality of 5,665 votes out of a total of 67,805, and it was generally conceded that his election was due to non-Mormon votes.[37] It was thought that after a decisive election, the opposition would concede; but this was not to be the case. Some people claimed that his election was a violation of an unwritten agreement between the Mormons of Utah and the federal government when Utah was admitted to the Union. There had been no agreement that Mormon polygynists should be barred from future political activity. In fact, the United States Congress had personally restored the franchise to those polygynists whose marriages had preceded the issuance of the Manifesto, prior to the constitutional convention in 1894.

President Snow denied that the Church had participated in the nomination, election, or seating of Roberts, stating that it was a secular affair; non-Mormons had participated in his nomination in the regular convention of his party, and non-Mormons had aided in his election. "He was not a Church candidate in any sense of the word ... He was elected as an American citizen by American citizens. ..."[38]

Nevertheless, between the time of election and the opening of Congress, a petition sponsored by the Salt Lake Ministerial

Association and containing more than 7,000,000 signatures
(many of them were duplications) requesting his exclusion had
reached Congress. The House of Representatives appointed a
committee of nine to determine whether B. H. Roberts should
be seated. The results of the study were that seven members of
the committee voted against seating Elder Roberts, while the
minority of two favored seating him first and then taking a vote
for exclusion, which would then require a two-thirds vote.

The majority based its argument on the assumption that
there had been a violation of an alleged compact between the
United States and Utah when Utah became a state, when in
reality the only requirement for statehood of Utah in regard to
polygamy was that written in the Enabling Act:

> And said convention [i.e., constitutional convention]
> shall provide, by ordinance irrevocable without the con-
> sent of the United States and the people of said state—
> First—To what extent polygamy is practiced or polyg-
> amous secured, and that no inhabitant of said state shall
> ever be molested in person or property on account of his
> or her mode of religious worship; provided, That polyg-
> amous or plural marriages are forever prohibited. [39]

The Utah constitutional convention, in order to make sure
that this requirement was followed, adopted the exact wording
into the constitution. There was nothing said in regard to polygamous living by those whose relationships were formed prior
to the Manifesto of 1890, nor was anything said requiring that a
polygynist should never be elected or appointed to office. [40]
Yet the sudden upsurge of objection to the seating of B. H.
Roberts in the House of Representatives caused the members of
that body to vote 244 for his exclusion and only 50 against it,
with 36 abstaining; thus, the members of the House acted in
harmony with the demands of the people. [41] One reason for the
negative reaction to the seating of B. H. Roberts was that he
was still living with his plural wives. Another reason was the
recurrence of charges that "Mormons were reverting to the
practice of polygamy." These charges were made in a series of
articles written by Theodore Schroeder and published in Salt
Lake City in a sectarian magazine called *The Kinsman*. These
articles started a discussion across the nation about Mormon
deception.

President Snow was no longer weighed down so heavily with the burden of the political rights and material welfare of the people as the Presidents of the Church had been prior to statehood; and now that the financial burdens of the Church had been successfully lightened, he turned to thoughts of the greater responsibility of the Twelve in continuing to take the gospel message to the world until all people had had an opportunity to hear of the gospel of Jesus Christ. He felt that the Apostles and their assistants, the Seventies, were spending too much of their time in the stakes of Zion working in the MIA when the leaders of the stakes were capable of building up Zion.

He thus decided to expand missionary work into Asia, and on February 14, 1901, he called Elder Heber J. Grant to head a mission to Japan. In company with others called to that mission Elder Grant left on July 24, 1901, and arrived in Japan on August 12. Progress in the mission was slow; but after the publication of articles in periodicals telling of the purpose of the mission and tracts explaining the restoration of the gospel, the first convert was baptized on March 8, 1902. He was Hajimi Kakazaha, a former Shinto priest. As many as eleven missionaries at one time labored in the mission, but because of the centuries of traditional and pagan teachings, only a few converts were made. Elder Alma Taylor stayed there for nine years. But because the missionaries could more profitably spend their time elsewhere, they were eventually withdrawn from Japan and did not officially return until after World War II.

THE WORLDWIDE VISION OF PRESIDENT SNOW

President Snow regarded the opening of the Japanese mission as just the beginning. He desired also to have the gospel message taken into Russia, Austria, and the countries of South America. He said, in regard to Elder Grant:

Things seem to be going on favorably with him; but whether he will accomplish much or not matters not in one sense; it is for the apostles to show to the Lord that they are his witnesses to all the nations, and that they are doing the best they can.[42]

At what was to be his last conference of the Church in

tion and responsibility of stake presidents and bishops, remind-
ing them that they were to look upon the Church members
under their jurisdiction as if they were members of their own
families.

> It is not for the apostles to look after them. The
> apostles have a work that is in another direction alto-
> gether. I want the presidents of the stakes hereafter to
> realize that it is their business, not the business of the
> apostles; it is the business of the high priests, the elders,
> the bishops, priests, teachers, and deacons, to look after
> these things [i.e., of a local character]. Do not lay this
> duty upon the shoulder's of the apostles. It is not in their
> line, at least only occasionally.[43]

This policy was in perfect harmony with responsibilities of the
Twelve Apostles as given through the Prophet Joseph Smith
who said:

> The twelve are . . . to bear the keys of the kingdom to
> all nations, and unlock the door of the gospel to them, and
> call upon the seventies to follow after them, and assist
> them.[44]

President Snow felt the time was approaching when more of the
time and attention of the Twelve should be turned toward their
worldwide mission.

At the dawn of a new century, with Church membership at
approximately 268,000, in an address given in the Tabernacle
on January 1, 1901, President Snow said:

> I hope and look for grand events to occur in the Twen-
> tieth Century. At its auspicious dawn, I lift my hands and
> invoke the blessings of heaven upon the inhabitants of the
> earth. May the sunshine from above smile upon you. May
> the treasures of the ground and the fruits of the soil be
> brought forth freely for your good. May the light of truth
> chase darkness from your souls. May righteousness increase
> and iniquity dimish as the years roll on. May justice
> triumph and corruption be stamped out. And may virtue
> and chastity and honor prevail, until evil shall be overcome
> and the earth shall be cleansed from wickedness. Let these

sentiments, as the voice of the Mormons in the mountains of Utah, go forth to the whole world, and let all people know that our wish and our Mission are for the blessing and salvation of the entire human race. May the twentieth century prove the happiest as it will be the grandest of all the ages of time, and may God be glorified in the victory that is coming over sin and sorrow, misery and death. Peace be unto all! [45]

After a highly successful period of a few weeks more than three years as President of the Church, Lorenzo Snow died of pneumonia in his 88th year on October 10, 1901. His funeral services were held in the Tabernacle on October 13 and his remains were taken to Brigham City cemetery immediately afterwards.

Footnotes

[1]Preston Nibley, *The Presidents of the Church* (Salt Lake City: Deseret Book Co., 1941), p. 172.

[2]Nibley, p. 174.

[3]Nibley, p. 176.

[4]Nibley, p. 179.

[5]Thomas C. Romney, *The Life of Lorenzo Snow* (Salt Lake City: Deseret News Press, 1955), p. 47.

[6]Romney, p. 71.

[7]Romney, p. 86.

[8]Romney, pp. 92-96.

[9]Nibley, p. 183. *See also* Romney, pp. 98-99.

[10]Nibley, p. 195.

[11]Romney, pp. 293-94.

[12]Romney, p. 379.

[13]Romney, p. 380.

[14]Nibley, p. 201.

[15]LeRoi C. Snow, "Raised from the Dead," *Improvement Era* 32(September 1929):881.

[16]Snow, p. 882.

[17]Snow, p. 882.

[18]Snow, pp. 884-85.

[19]Snow, pp. 885-86.

[20]Romney, p. 405; Snow, p. 973.

[21]Snow, p. 980. *See also* Romney, p. 412.

[22]Romney, p. 417.

[23]LeRoi C. Snow, "An Experience of My Father's," *Improvement Era* 36(September 1933):677.

[24]Snow, "An Experience," p. 677.

[25]Snow, "An Experience," p. 677.

[26]Snow, "An Experience," p. 677.

[27]Snow, "An Experience," p. 679.

[28]Leonard J. Arrington, *Great Basin Kingdom* (Cambridge, Mass.: Harvard University Press, 1958), p. 376. In chapters 12 and 13 of this book, Arrington presents a vivid picture of the handling of these funds and the resulting financial difficulty of the Church.

[29]Arrington, p. 377.

[30]Arrington, p. 400.

[31]Arrington, pp. 401-2.

[32]Arrington, p. 402.

[33]Romney, p. 451.

[34]Romney, p. 456.

[35]Romney, p. 457. The inspiring events of this occasion have been pleasingly portrayed by the Church in a movie called "Windows of Heaven."

[36]*Improvement Era* 10(August 1899):795. *See also CHC,* 6:359.

[37]*CHC,* 6:363-64.

[38]*CHC,* 6:365.

[39]*CHC,* 6:369.

[40]*CHC,* 6:369.

[41]This vote was taken in the House on January 25, 1900.

[42]*CHC,* 6:377.

[43]*CHC,* 7:379.

[44]*CHC,* 6:380.

[45]James B. Allen and Richard O. Cowan, *Mormonism in the Twentieth Century* (Provo, Utah: Brigham Young University Press, 1967), p. 3. *See also Deseret News,* 1 January 1901, p. 5.

21

Administration of Joseph F. Smith

A BRIEF SKETCH OF THE LIFE
OF JOSEPH F. SMITH

Joseph F. Smith was born to Hyrum and Mary Fielding Smith at Far West, Missouri, on November 13, 1838. His father had been arrested on November 1 along with some of the other leaders of the Church. After Joseph's birth, Mary was ill for many months. With her husband in jail, she and her baby and five step-children—the children of Hyrum's first wife, Jerusha Barden—were taken care of by her sister, Mercy Fielding Thompson. In the spring of 1839, still confined to her bed, Mary was carried out of Missouri to Quincy, Illinois, where she was reunited with Hyrum. He and Joseph had arrived there from jail in Missouri on April 27, 1839.

The Westward Journey

After the martyrdom of Hyrum the family remained in Nauvoo until the summer of 1846, when Mary, anxious to be with the body of the Church, left Nauvoo just a few days before it was attacked by the mob.[1] She left her family camped on the Iowa side of the river while she went to Keokuk, where she traded her Nauvoo property for wagons, horses, and oxen sufficient to travel westward with the Saints.

Mary moved her family across Iowa in company with her brother, Joseph Fielding, and other relatives. They stayed at Winter Quarters, where Joseph was herd boy until the spring of 1848, when it became possible for them to continue the journey west. Joseph was a teamster, driving a yoke of oxen all the way and performing all the duties of a man except that of standing guard at night. On Saturday, September 23, 1848, they arrived at the old fort in Salt Lake City at 10:00 p.m., after having had many profitable experiences—some sad, some joyful.

His Mother's Death

Widow Smith settled on Mill Creek, south of Salt Lake City, where she built a comfortable house within two years and obtained some valuable farming property.[2] But she was not to enjoy her house for long; she became ill during the summer of 1852 and died on September 21 in the presence of her family and friends. Her long hours of laboring as both father and mother for her children had weakened her resistance to the rigors of a pioneer life. It was a severe blow to Joseph and the other children, who continued to hold the household and farm together for a time. Joseph continued to have the principal care of the livestock, a job that he had from 1846 to 1854, and he never lost an animal through carelessness.[3]

Called on a Mission

At general conference in April, 1854, his name was among those read from the stand to go on a mission to the Hawaiian Islands. He was just over 15½ years old when they left on May 27, 1854, under the direction of Elder Parley P. Pratt, who had set him apart for his mission and had promised him that he would learn the language of the Hawaiians "by the gift of God as well as by study."[4]

Joseph F. Smith was the youngest of the twenty-one missionaries; so it was a comfort to him to have two of his father's cousins among the group.[5] They arrived at San Bernardino, California, on June 9. By early September Joseph F. Smith and eight other missionaries of the group had earned sufficient funds to pay their passage to Hawaii. They arrived in Honolulu on September 27.

After a mission filled with both rewarding and trying experiences, Joseph sailed from Honolulu with six other returning

missionaries on October 6, 1857. He had learned the native
tongue well and had also become well versed in the principles of
the gospel; both were to serve him well in later life. He returned
to Salt Lake City on February 24, 1858, after an absence of
three years and nine months.

Two Years at Home and Another Mission

The day after his arrival in Salt Lake City, Joseph presented
himself to President Brigham Young and immediately enlisted
in the Nauvoo Legion to help protect the Saints from Johnston's Army which was camped near Fort Bridger at the time.
Joseph testifies to the grimness of the experience.

> From that time until the proclamation of peace, and a
> 'free and full pardon' by President Buchanan came, I was
> constantly in my saddle, prospecting and exploring the
> country between Salt Lake City and Fort Bridger, under
> the command of Col. Thomas Callister and others. I was
> on picket guard with a party of men under Orrin P. Rock-
> well when commissioners Powell and McCollough met us
> near the Weber River with the Presidents' proclamation.[6]

On March 20, 1858, Joseph F. Smith was ordained a seventy
and assigned to the 32nd Quorum; on October 16, 1859, he was
ordained a high priest and sustained a member of the Salt Lake
Stake high council. In the meantime, on April 5, 1859, he had
married his cousin Levira, the daughter of Samuel Smith, his
father's brother.

Joseph expected to have a little time for himself, but at the
April Conference in 1860 he was called on a mission to Great
Britain. Joseph left on April 27, 1860, with a company of
missionaries that included his cousin-brother-in-law, Elder
Samuel H. B. Smith.

As in the Sandwich Islands (Hawaii), Joseph soon became a
conference president. Joseph, along with many other missionaries, was released on April 25, 1863. He returned to Salt Lake
City on September 27, 1863.

A Third Mission

On March 1, 1864, Joseph F. Smith left Salt Lake City on his
third mission. It was another mission to Hawaii to help

straighten out the strange doings of Walter Gibson. During the Civil War Gibson had been the only missionary from Utah in the islands, and as described earlier in this work, he had built his own organization in which he sold offices in the priesthood for from $5.00 to $150. Ezra T. Benson and Lorenzo Snow were in charge of the matter, but neither could speak the Hawaiian tongue; so a few former missionaries accompanied them.

After a confrontation with Gibson and after his excommunication from the Church in April, 1864, Joseph F. Smith was appointed mission president, and the apostles returned to America. With the other missionaries to assist him, Joseph F. gradually won back the loyalty to the Church of the native Saints, and he was soon released to return to his home, arriving in December, 1864.

A Call to the Apostleship

After his return from Hawaii, Joseph F. Smith secured employment in the Church Historian's Office under his father's cousin, George A. Smith, who was historian for the Church from 1854 to 1870. On July 1, 1866, after a prayer meeting President Brigham Young felt impressed to ordain Joseph F. to the apostleship and to be a counselor to the First Presidency, although nothing was made public about it at the time. On Tuesday, October 8, 1867, at a conference he was sustained as a member of the Council of the Twelve, replacing Amasa M. Lyman, who had been removed.[7]

Plural Marriage

While he was working in the Historian's Office, Joseph F. was instructed by President Young to enter the practice of plural marriage. On May 5, 1866, with the consent of his first wife and with her present as a witness, he was married to Julina Lambson, the niece of George A. Smith.

On March 1, 1868, he married Sarah Ellen Richards, daughter of Willard Richards, former counselor to President Young. On January 1, 1870, he married Edna Lambson, youngest sister of his wife, Julina. He later married Alice Ann Kimball and Mary Taylor Schwartz. His first wife was childless, but the other wives bore him forty-three children and adopted five others, making a total of forty-eight children.[8]

In addition to his usual duties at home, he and others, among them Wilford Woodruff and Abraham O. Smoot, were called in 1868 to move to Provo, where he lived for a little less than two years. The purpose of this move was to give strength to the city government in combating a disorderly group who were stealing stock and committing other trespasses of the law. From 1873 to 1875 he presided over the European missions. Upon the death of George A. Smith, Joseph was released to return home, where he was immediately appointed to preside over the Saints in Davis County. But at the April Conference in 1877, which was held in St. George, he was again called to preside over the European missions. His wife, Sarah, accompanied him on this assignment. Because of the death of President Young, it was cut short. For the next three years the Apostles presided at the head of the Church.

Joseph F. Smith and Orson Pratt went east in 1878 on an assignment "to gather up records and data relative to the early history of the Church." They went first to Independence, Missouri, where they visited the temple lot. They then visited the widow of John E. Page, a Mrs. Eaton. Learning that William E. McLellin lived there, they had three or four meetings with him before leaving for Richmond, Missouri, where they made numerous visits and had many valuable conversations with David Whitmer, the only one of the Three Witnesses still living. Next they went to Far West, where Joseph F. had been born forty years before. Jacob Whitmer, son of John Whitmer (one of the Eight Witnesses to the Book of Mormon), received them discourteously.

After leaving Far West, they visited the Prophet Joseph Smith's sister, Lucy Smith Millikan, at Colchester, Illinois, who received them graciously. After a pleasant visit with her, they went to Plano, Illinois, where they hoped to visit the Prophet's son, Joseph; but he was away at a conference of the Reorganized Church. They next visited Kirtland, Ohio; and from there they journeyed to Palmyra, New York, where they visited the Hill Cumorah. From there they went to New York, where they met Elders John Sharp and William Staines and conducted a great deal of Church business in regard to immigration and missionary work. Elder Joseph F. Smith sent a telegram to his cousin Joseph, son of the Prophet Joseph Smith, asking if he could see the manuscript of the Inspired Version of the Bible if he should call on his way home. The answer was: "cannot tell you 'til I see you." When they returned to Chicago Joseph F. left Elder Pratt and went to Plano alone; but his cousin Joseph was much more hostile than he had been when Joseph F. had visited him in Nauvoo in 1860, and he refused to show him the manuscript. But he gave him a printed copy that the Reorganized Church had published in 1867.[9] Elders Pratt and Smith arrived home on September 28, 1878, having taken less than a month for the tour; such were the wonders of "modern" transportation.

The Endowment House and Historian's Office

After their return from the East, Joseph F. was appointed to preside over the Endowment House and was again assigned to labor in the historian's office. With his assignments to attend stake conferences, although there were only twenty-two stakes at the time, Elder Smith was constantly busy.

Counselor in the First Presidency

On October 10, 1880, when the First Presidency was reorganized, Elder George Q. Cannon became first counselor and Elder Joseph F. Smith second counselor to President John Taylor. With the passage of the Edmunds Law and Edmunds-Tucker Law, Joseph F. Smith was in exile from September 1884 to September 1891. During this time President Smith visited various stakes and branches of the Church, including the new ones in Colorado, New Mexico, and Arizona, as well as the stakes throughout southern Utah. He also went on a third mission to the Hawaiian Islands. His party arrived there February 9, 1885.

While in the Hawaiian Islands, President Smith found that the Spaulding Manuscript that had been lost for so many years was in the possession of an L. L. Rice. Rice donated the original manuscript to Oberlin College in Ohio and eventually permitted President Smith to borrow a copy of it for printing purposes. President Smith sent this copy to Salt Lake City on June 21, 1885.[10] He presided over the Hawaiian Mission until he received word of the illness of President John Taylor at which time he sailed from Honolulu on July 1, 1887, and arrived in Kaysville, Utah on July 18, where President Taylor was in seclusion. President Cannon was already there. President Taylor died on July 25. During the years of his exile, whenever President Smith was at home in Salt Lake City, he had secret places of retirement which he changed from time to time.

On February 2, 1888, he was assigned to a mission in Washington, D.C., to help manage the financial business of the Church there and to allay prejudice against the Saints. He went under the assumed name of Jason Mack, the name of his grandmother's oldest brother. Elder Charles Penrose, who was with him, was known as Charles Williams. Elder Smith returned to Utah on March 8, 1889. But it was still necessary for him to stay in exile. Since he probably knew more about the records of the Church than any other (especially the records in the Endowment House), it was not expedient for the Church to allow President Smith to be arrested. Even after the issuance of the Manifesto, he stayed in retirement until official word was received on September 7, 1891, that amnesty had been granted to him.

At general conference on Sunday, October 4, 1891, the members of the First Presidency were all seated on the stand together for the first time in seven and one-half years. From this time on, the First Presidency could transact business "without fear or hindrance."[11]

THE PRESIDENCY

On October 17, 1901, one week after the death of Lorenzo Snow, the Apostles met in session to select and sustain a new First Presidency of the Church. Patriarch John Smith met with them by invitation. Some question must have arisen as to who would become President. Brigham Young, Jr. had been ordained an apostle on February 4, 1864, by President Brigham Young; but he was not set apart as a member of the Twelve at that time. On July 1, 1866, Joseph F. Smith was ordained an apostle by President Brigham Young, but he was not set apart as a member of the Twelve at that time. On October 8, 1867, at the age of 28, Joseph F. Smith was set apart as a member of the Quorum of the Twelve. On October 9, 1868, at the age of 31, Brigham Young, Jr. was set apart as a member of the Twelve. Thus Brigham Young, Jr. had been ordained an apostle first, but Joseph F. was sustained as a member of the Twelve first. This matter was settled later at a meeting of the First Presidency and the Twelve Apostles on April 5, 1900.

The Apostles elected and set apart Joseph F. Smith as Presi-

Joseph F. Smith, sixth president of The Church of Jesus Christ of Latter-day Saints. *Permission of Church Information Service.*

dent of the Church; and he chose John R. Winder, second
counselor in the Presiding Bishopric, as his first counselor.
Anthon H. Lund, a member of the Quorum of the Twelve, was
chosen as second counselor. The selection of Elder Smith meant
that the membership of the Church now understood that seniority in the apostleship was to be determined by date of
entrance into the Quorum of the Twelve rather than by date of
ordination to the apostleship. A special conference of the
Church was set for November 10, 1901, so that the membership
could vote upon the chosen authorities.

President Smith and Finances

Some members of the Church were very much concerned
about Joseph F. Smith's being President of the Church, as they
felt he was neither experienced in business nor spiritual enough;
however, he became highly successful in handling the business
of the Church and was also a deeply spiritual president.
Actually, his prudent financial practices, learned of necessity
through raising a large family, and his financial experience as a
counselor to three previous presidents had given him abundant
experience in preparing for his responsibilities of running the
financial aspects of the Church. He continued the policy of
Lorenzo Snow in emphasizing the honest payment of tithing,
and he used the funds wisely in retiring the bonded indebtedness of the Church.

By 1906, the debt of the Church had been paid off, and in
his opening speech at the April Conference of the Church in
1907 President Smith said:

Today the Church of Jesus Christ of Latter-day Saints
owes not a dollar that it cannot pay at once. At last we are
in a position to pay as we go. We do not have to borrow
any more, and we won't have to if the Latter-day Saints
continue to live their religion and observe the law of tithing. It is the law of revenue of the Church.[12]

During the early years of his presidency, the Church had a
great increase in expenditures for church buildings, such as
stake houses, ward chapels, and mission headquarters throughout the world. The Authorities also greatly expanded the
missionary work which brought increased expenditures.

Under President Smith the policy of paying the homeward

fare of missionaries was begun and continues to the present time. Nevertheless, the continued faithful payment of tithing by the members of the Church enabled President Smith to keep the Church out of debt.

The Reed Smoot Case

On January 20, 1903, when President Smith had been in office a little more than a year, Reed Smoot was elected by the Republican legislature to be United States Senator from Utah. He had been chosen a member of the Quorum of the Twelve in April of 1900, and before his appointment as senator, he had conformed to the Church rule of obtaining a "leave of absence" in order to be a candidate for the office he sought.[13] However, there was a formal protest made against an apostle of the Mormon Church being a United States Senator. The principal question was whether Smoot as an apostle, having supposedly taken an oath to the Church, could also take an oath to support and defend the Constitution of the United States.

This protest was launched by eighteen men of different professions from Salt Lake City. The chief promoters, however, were William Paden, pastor of the First Presbyterian Church in Salt Lake City, and E. B. Critchlow, a prominent Salt Lake City lawyer. According to one writer, "The lawyer arranged the form of the protest and the minister gathered the material."[14] The protest contained many false charges. Reverend John L. Leilich, one of the protest signers, also entered a separate protest charging that Reed Smoot was a "polygamist"; but as this was entirely false, Reverend Leilich was thoroughly embarrassed when it came time to present his proof. The charge was thrown out.

A great deal of money was spent to arouse sentiment throughout the United States; and by the time Congress met, "petitions by the wagon loads from all parts of the United States were rolling into the Senate chamber."[15] When the Senate met on March 5, 1903, objection was made to seating him; but they decided that he should be seated and then his case should be referred to the Committee on Privileges and Elections for investigation. Julius C. Burrows of Michigan was chairman of this committee. His grandfather was a former member of the Church who had gone to Missouri with Zion's Camp in 1834, and was considered a real trouble maker. Later he had been excommunicated.[16] His grandfather's excom-

munication seemed to have prejudiced Senator Burrows, who
was bitterly anti-Mormon.

On January 4, 1904, before the beginning of hearings by the committee, Senator Smoot made a full and complete denial of the false charges against him. The committee hearings began on January 16, 1904, and continued until June, 1906. The press of the country "sensationally published the testimony as fast as it was given—especially the parts of it detrimental to the Latter-day Saint Church in Utah, with editorial comment in the main extremely bitter and prejudicial to the moral standing of the Church in public opinion."[17]

A great variety of witnesses with all shades of opinion took the stand. Much conflicting testimony was given. Many of the leading Church officials, including President Joseph F. Smith, testified. President Smith said that when he first took the stand on March 2, 1904, of the twelve committee members only one—Senator William P. Dillingham of Vermont—seemed not unfriendly. But the three days passed and President Smith continued to answer the questions courageously and honestly, including the fact that he was still living with his plural wives. As anti-Mormon committee members asked personal questions, prying into the private life of President Smith and the sacredness of his religion, other committee members began to show sympathy and even friendliness toward him.

Finally on June 11, 1906, the thirteen members of the Committee on Privileges and Elections presented their report. Senator J. C. Burrows signing for the eight members of the majority, ended his report with the following resolution: "Resolved: That Reed Smoot is not entitled to a seat as a senator of the United States from the State of Utah."[18]

A minority report which was signed by five members of the committee stated there was no just ground for expelling Senator Smoot or for finding him disqualified to retain his seat in the Senate.[19] It was another six months before the case was called up for debate in the Senate on December 13, 1906, when Senator Dubois of Idaho made a long speech supporting the proposition that Reed Smoot was not entitled to his seat in the Senate. From then until February 20, 1907, the matter was debated in the Senate. Senator Hopkin moved an amendment to the motion which was accepted. It read: "Two-thirds of the Senators present concurring therein," meaning that two-thirds of the votes would have to be against Senator Smoot before he could be excluded from the Senate. Before the vote was taken,

Boies Penrose, leader of the Senate, looked out over the Senate and remarked: "I don't see why we can't get along just as well with a polygamist who doesn't polyg as we do with a lot of monogamists who don't monog."[20] When the vote was taken there were 28 yeas, 42 nays, and 20 abstentions; thus, of those who voted, Senator Smoot received a 60 percent vote in his favor.

During the investigation the testimony, the arguments, and reports filled four large volumes with 3,429 pages of material, and although much of it was adverse to the Church, in the end the hearings turned out to be advantageous to the Church, as many people modified their attitude toward it. The hearings did bring out, however, that the Manifesto had not been strictly adhered to, since two of the apostles had been performing marriages outside of the United States, claiming that the statement in the Manifesto "law of the land" meant only the laws of the United States. This caused President Joseph F. Smith to issue another Manifesto at the annual conference of the Church in April, 1904. Again it was heartily approved by the vote of the people. The result of the activity of the two apostles in performing these plural marriages was that they resigned from their positions in the Quorum of the Twelve; Elder John W. Taylor submitted his resignation on October 6, 1905, and Elder Mathias F. Cowley resigned on October 28, 1905.[21]

The Kearns Attack, the American Party, and the Magazine Crusade

Three other events affecting the Church occurred at the same time as the Smoot case. The first of these was the attack on the Church of Senator Thomas Kearns, the other senator from Utah, a non-Mormon. Kearns had been elected to the Senate in January of 1901, and he very much wanted to be reelected. As he was a very wealthy man, he purchased the *Salt Lake Tribune* to help further his cause. He also solicited the support of President Joseph F. Smith, who refused to aid him. Actually he was a rather crude man who did not possess the qualifications of a senator, and his actions in the Senate had somewhat alienated both Utah Mormons and gentiles. When Kearns discovered that he would not be reelected, he began a tirade of the most bitter kind against the Church and particularly against President Joseph F. Smith. This attitude in his articles in the *Tribune* was to last for many years. On February 28, 1905, just six days

before his term as senator was up, he launched into a most
bitter attack on the Church on the Senate floor. The speech was
written much beyond Kearns's capabilities, and he faltered as he
read it. It had been prepared by Frank J. Cannon, a highly
intelligent man, himself a disappointed former senator who was
an unworthy member of a worthy family.

As another means of revenge, Kearns and Cannon, with other
anti-Mormons, affiliated themselves with the newly organized
American Party in 1904. By 1905 their party had captured the
municipal offices in Salt Lake City and managed to hold them
until 1911, when most of the better class of gentiles deserted
their cause and a citizens' ticket, composed of Mormons and
honorable gentiles, was elected.

Kearns had made Cannon editor of the *Tribune,* and he used
it almost daily to slander the Church, particularly Joseph F.
Smith. No other community would have stood for such slander
day by day. It has been said that the *Nauvoo Expositor* was
"Holy Writ" as compared to the *Salt Lake Tribune.* Perhaps
because of bitter attacks in the *Tribune* many magazines in the
United States took up the gauntlet. Among those that printed
particularly bitter articles about the Saints during 1910 and
1911 were *Pearsons, Everybody's Magazine, McClures,* and
Cosmopolitan; with the death of *Cosmopolitan* in the 1960s,
the Church has now outlived them all.

To all of the bitter attacks upon him personally President
Smith made no reply except to say:

> I feel in my heart to forgive all men in the broad sense
> that God requires me to forgive all men, and I desire to
> love my neighbor as myself; and to this extent I bear no
> malice towards any of the children of my Father. But
> there are enemies to the work of the Lord, as there were
> enemies of the son of God ... I forgive them for this. I
> leave them in the hand of the just Judge. [22]

In the midst of these series of anti-Mormon articles, *Colliers*
published a favorable letter about the Church written by ex-
President Theodore Roosevelt to Isaac Russell. It is only fair to
President Roosevelt to say that during his presidency he always
exhibited a friendliness toward the Church and its people, including the desire to have Senator Smoot retain his seat in the
Senate.

Salt Lake City had endured the wild stories of the hack drivers for many years. Hotel owners would send their employees to the depot in carriages to vie for guests. These drivers would fill the guests full of wild tales about the Mormons. By 1902 the First Council of the Seventy and the Young Men's Mutual Improvement Association became interested in making an effort to better portray the truth to the many Salt Lake visitors. On March 6 the First Presidency authorized the First Council of the Seventy to organize a Bureau of Information. With the aid of the Young Men's general board and others, they erected a small octagonal building twenty feet across inside the south gates of the temple block; and the Bureau of Information began its career in a $600 building on August 4, 1902.

About seventy-five members of the Church were called to act as guides. They distributed free literature, but most of all, they modified the opinion of the many tourists who now received a much more correct impression of the Latter-day Saint people. In the first year of its operation, 150,000 people visited Temple Square, and it has been a favorite tourist attraction ever since. This was the first of many visitors' centers throughout the world reaching millions of people each year. There is now a beautiful new visitors' center on Temple Square.

The First Purchases of Historic Landmarks

President Smith had perhaps two reasons for beginning the purchase of old landmarks in the history of the Church. As a member of the Smith family, he probably had more of a personal interest in them than previous presidents. Secondly, he was the first President of the Church who had funds to spend on such purchases. It is possible he also saw the future value in pleasure and spiritual uplift that would be afforded members of the Church in visiting these old landmarks. The first purchase made under President Smith's direction was the Carthage Jail, where his own father and his Uncle Joseph had been martyred, June 27, 1844. This purchase was made November 5, 1903, and included the old jail on two acres of ground for $4,000.

On May 21, 1905, Elder Junius F. Wells purchased 100 acres of the farm in Sharon, Vermont, where Joseph Smith, the Prophet, was born on December 23, 1805. Subsequent purchases were made, bringing the total land purchased to 283 acres. That summer and fall (1905) he supervised the erection of a tall granite monument and a cottage on the farm. The cottage was placed over the cellar of the house in which Joseph was born. By December 8, 1905, the tall granite monument was in place, and President Joseph F. Smith and twenty-nine other prominent men and women from Utah went to Vermont by train for the dedicatory services held on the one-hundredth anniversary of the Prophet's birth. The party left in a special railroad car for South Royalton, Vermont, on December 18, 1905; they arrived there Friday morning, December 22, where they were met by Elder Wells. Because of the inclement weather the kind people of the town of Royalton provided free of charge the use of Woodard's Hall in the village of South Royalton for President Smith and his party.[23]

On the morning of December 23, the visitors and a few hundred local residents gathered in rather mild weather at the Memorial Farm for the dedication of the monument. At 11:00 a.m. the services were begun. President Smith called on Elder Wells to give an overview of the erection of the monument. He revealed some interesting facts concerning the monument—that it was 50 feet, 10 inches high and the needle, which was 38½ feet high, weighed thirty-nine tons. The total weight of the monument was 100 tons. Other speakers of the day were President Smith, Elder Francis M. Lyman of the Quorum of the Twelve, Dr. Edgar J. Fish of South Royalton, and Elders John Henry Smith, Hyrum M. Smith, Jesse N. Smith, and Charles W. Penrose. President Smith gave the dedicatory prayer, after which the benediction was pronounced by Patriarch John Smith, the oldest son of Hyrum and half-brother of President Smith. Following the prayer Edith A. Smith, the oldest lady representative of the Smith family, unveiled the monument.

The success in removing prejudice through the establishment of a memorial at the Smith farm served to encourage Church leaders to purchase other landmarks. On June 10, 1907, Elder George Albert Smith purchased for the Church the old Smith farm of one hundred acres in Manchester Township, near Palmyra, New York, where Joseph received his first vision and where Moroni made many of his visits to the future Prophet.

On April 14, 1904, a purchase of twenty-five acres of the original temple lot at Independence, Jackson County, Missouri was made. This was a portion of 63.27 acres originally purchased for the Church in 1831 by Bishop Edward Partridge. Nine other land purchases in Independence were made during

478 President Smith's administration. The total cost of all ten purchases amounted to $64,450.[24] In 1909 the Church purchased a forty-acre tract of land in the heart of the former city of Far West, Missouri. It included the temple site that had been selected and dedicated during the Northern Missouri period (1836-1839). In 1914 a mission chapel was erected at Independence, and in 1917 a suitable mission home was built as a residence for the mission president.

A few months before the death of President Smith, Elder Junius F. Wells supervised the erection of a monument in the center of President Smith's lot in the Salt Lake City Cemetery in honor of the Patriarch Hyrum Smith. It was also made out of granite from Barre, Vermont.[25] The unveiling took place on the anniversary of the martyrdom of Hyrum and Joseph—June 27, 1918.

The beginning of the purchase of landmarks of the Church by President Smith was continued by other presidents, and visiting them today is a joy and a pleasure to members of the Church. They also serve in the present age as useful missionary tools. Other purchases will be discussed later.

A Visit to Europe

On July 21, 1906, President Joseph F. Smith, his wife, Edna, Charles W. Nibley (the Presiding Bishop of the Church), Nibley's wife, and members of Nibley's family left Salt Lake City for Europe. This was the first time that either a President of the Church or a Presiding Bishop had ever visited Europe during his office tenure. They visited first the Netherlands Mission, landing in Antwerp, Belgium, on August 5. On August 7, in Rotterdam, Holland, an eleven-year-old boy who was a faithful member of the Church said to his mother, "The prophet has the most power of any missionary on earth. If you will take me with you to meeting and he will look into my eyes, I believe they will be healed." He had suffered with an affliction in his eyes for many years and was slowly going blind. At the close of the meeting President Smith moved towards the door to shake hands with the people. John Roothoff's mother led him to President Smith, who shook hands with him and spoke to him. He then raised the bandage on the boy's inflamed eyes, saying something in English that the boy did not understand, but John was satisfied that the President had done what he desired. When he arrived home he joyfully said to his

mother: "Mamma, my eyes are well; I cannot feel any more
pain. I can see fine now, and far, too." [26] He was able to attend
school again; later, he moved to Salt Lake City, where he lived
for many years.

After visiting other missions in Germany, Switzerland,
France, and England, President Smith and his party returned to
Salt Lake City in time to prepare for the semiannual conference
of the Church which began October 5, 1906. President Smith
again visited Europe during the summer of 1910.

Buildings during President Smith's Era

Several notable buildings were erected during President
Smith's administration in addition to a large number of stake
buildings (tabernacles), ward meeting houses, and mission headquarters buildings. Perhaps the first of these was the Dr. Grove's
Latter-day Saints Hospital in Salt Lake, begun July 1, 1903, and
completed January 1, 1905. The Bishop's Building was begun
April 17, 1907, and dedicated January 27, 1910. At first it also
housed the Relief Society, the Young Ladies MIA, and the
Primary. Hotel Utah was commenced June 1, 1909, and com-
pleted June 6, 1911; although much criticism was voiced for
such a structure, President Smith justified it at the October
semiannual conference in 1911 and referred to Doctrine and
Covenants 124 pertaining to the building of the Nauvoo House.
Perhaps the most needed of all the buildings constructed under
President Smith was the Church Office Building at 47 East
South Temple, where nearly all of the General Authorities still
have their offices today (1972). Excavation was begun on
September 3, 1913, and the building was ready for use early in
1917. In addition to the General Authorities, the office of the
Church Historian and the Genealogical Library were housed
there. The first Deseret Gymnasium—used for many pur-
poses—was opened for use September 20, 1910.

President Smith also was responsible for beginning of construction of both the Alberta and Hawaiian Temples. On June
27, 1913, he dedicated a site for the construction of a temple in
Cardston, Canada. Construction was well along when he passed
away. On June 1, 1915, President Smith, in the presence of
Elder Reed Smoot of the Quorum of the Twelve and Presiding
Bishop Charles W. Nibley, dedicated a site in Hawaii for the
building of a temple which was more than half completed when
he died.

A remarkable event happened to President Joseph F. Smith toward the end of his life. On October 3, 1918, while he was pondering the atonement of Christ in his mind, the Lord blessed him with one of the choicest revelations of his lifetime. It was a vision of the redemption of the dead, and it dealt with the visitation of the Savior to the spirits of the dead while his body lay in the tomb. The revelation came to President Smith while he was in his room reflecting upon the atoning sacrifice by the Son of God. He opened the Bible and read the third and fourth chapters of First Peter and dwelt upon First Peter 3:18 and First Peter 4:6. At this point the spirit of the Lord rested upon him and he saw the hosts of the dead. He saw gathered together the spirits of the just who were waiting the entrance of the Son of God into the Spirit World. While the spirits were waiting, he saw the Son of God appear among them and declare liberty to those who had been faithful. The Savior preached the gospel to them, including the doctrine of the resurrection and the redemption of mankind from the Fall "and from individual sins as a condition of repentance."

The Savior did not go to those who had been wicked upon the earth or to those who had rejected the warning of the prophets. This ministry of Jesus among the dead was limited to that brief period of time between his crucifixion and resurrection. Yet President Smith wondered at the words of Peter, who said he preached to the spirits in prison who were disobedient. As he wondered, he perceived that the Lord had appointed messengers from among the righteous and commissioned them to carry the gospel to those in darkness; these messengers went forth to preach to those who had died in their sins or who had rejected the first principles and other necessary truths. In this way the dead, both righteous and wicked, knew that the redemption had been accomplished through the Son of God. Thus, the Savior's time in the spirit world was spent in preparing the faithful to carry the gospel message to the others in darkness.

Among those assembled in this immense congregation he saw Adam and Eve, many faithful women, Abel, Seth, Noah, Shem, Abraham, Isaac, Jacob, Moses, Isaiah, Ezekiel, Daniel, Elias, Malachi, and many more, including many Nephite prophets. The Savior taught them and gave them power to come forth after his resurrection. He also saw in the spirit world many of

the modern prophets who had died, including Joseph and
Hyrum Smith, Brigham Young, John Taylor, Wilford Woodruff,
and others. He saw that the faithful elders of the dispensation
would continue to preach the gospel among those in darkness
after their departure from mortality, and the dead who
repented were to be redeemed.

President Smith stated:

> Thus was the vision of the redemption of the dead
> revealed to me, and I bear record, and I know that this
> record is true, through the blessing of our Lord and Savior,
> Jesus Christ. . . . [27]

Growth of the Church

At the close of President Smith's administration, there were
75 stakes of Zion, an increase of 26 since he had taken office in
1901; there were 839 wards, an increase of 234; there were 22
missions, an increase of 6.[28]

The Great World War

A sorrowful event which occurred during the closing years of
President Smith's administration was the outbreak of World War
I. It began in 1914 between Austria and Serbia but soon included many other countries. Finally the United States was
forced to declare war against Germany on April 6, 1917. The
Church leaders devoted much time to prayer concerning their
attitude toward this great holocaust and felt inspired to accept
it as an obligation of the Latter-day Saints to defend their
country's freedom along with all other patriotic Americans. At
the time of the armistice on November 11, 1918, President
Smith himself had six sons in the armed services of his country.

PRESIDENT SMITH'S DEATH

On November 10, 1918, President Smith said to the members
of his family who were gathered around him:

> Without anything to start with in the world, except the
> example of my Mother, I struggled along with hard knocks
> in early life. . . .
> If there is anything on earth I have tried to do as much

as anything else, it is to keep my word, my promises, my integrity to do what it was my duty to do.[29]

Nine days after this meeting with his family, two days after his seventeenth year as President of the Church and six days after his eightieth birthday, President Smith passed away peacefully in the midst of a world epidemic of influenza which prevented a public funeral for him since Salt Lake City was under quarantine. A graveside service held for him in the open air was conducted by President Anthon H. Lund. President Heber J. Grant and Bishop Charles W. Nibley made brief remarks, and the grave was dedicated by President Charles W. Penrose, second counselor to President Smith.

HIS ENEMIES BECAME HIS FRIENDS

No leader of the Church since the days of the Prophet Joseph Smith had been more villified by the press than was President Joseph F. Smith. Yet, because of Joseph's integrity and his dignified life, Charles C. Goodwin, for such a long time editor of the *Salt Lake Tribune* and publisher of *Goodwin's Weekly,* who had been one of the worst villifiers of all, by April 8, 1916, had so completely changed his mind about President Smith that he could say:

A more kindly and benevolent man has seldom held an exalted ecclesiastical position in these latter days than President Joseph F. Smith of the Church of Jesus Christ of Latter-day Saints. Passing down the seventy-seventh year of the highway of life, and living with broad tolerance of the affairs of men, he stands a commanding influence in his state. To his people he is the great spiritual leader. To men at large he is a man of wide sympathies, great business acumen and a born leader of the great institution of which he is the head.

One who has known him for two generations, says of him: 'Once stern and unrelenting, he has mellowed as the years go on, until he sees but the good in humanity and forgives men their trespasses.'

His early life was of great hardship, surviving as he did many adventures and many soul-rending experiences that try the hearts of men. . . .

He came into the world at the beginning of the early

troubles of his people. His mother fled with him from Nauvoo, Illinois.

At the age of eight years he drove an ox team across the desert. He reached Salt Lake with his mother September 23, 1848. From that time until this his service to the Mormon Church has been a record of large achievements.

His life all these years has been lived with great simplicity, constant labor and great personal frugality.

He stands today a patriarch ruling with a gentle hand over a people blessed with such prosperity as few religious bodies have ever known. [30]

During his two more years of life Joseph F. Smith continued to receive the admiration of more and more of his former enemies and still greater devotion from his own people.

Footnotes

[1] Joseph Fielding Smith, *Life of Joseph F. Smith* (Salt Lake City: Deseret News Press, 1938), p. 131.

[2] Preston Nibley, *The Presidents of the Church* (Salt Lake City: Deseret Book Co., 1941), p. 235.

[3] Smith, pp. 160-63.

[4] Smith, p. 164.

[5] Silas S. Smith, son of Silas, and Silas Smith, son of Asael, Jr.

[6] Smith, p. 195.

[7] Smith, p. 228.

[8] Smith, pp. 226-490.

[9] Smith, p. 251.

[10] Smith, p. 269.

[11] Smith, p. 301.

[12] *CHC*, 6:421.

[13] *CHC*, 6:390.

[14] *CHC*, 6:390-91. The names of the rest of the group who made the protest were: Parley L. Williams, E. W. Wilson, Charles C. Goodwin, William A. Neldon, Rev. Clarence T. Brown, Ezra Thompson, J. J. Corum, George R. Hancock, W. Mont Ferry, Rev. John L. Leilich, Harry C. Hill, Clarence E. Allen, George M. Scott, S. H. Lewis, H. G. McMillan, and Rev. Abiel Leonard. (L. W. Colbath also signed, but he later withdrew his name.)

[15] Smith, p. 330.

[16] Smith, p. 331.

[17] *CHC*, 6:394.

[18] Smith, p. 337. The eight members of the majority report were: Julius C. Burrows, Michigan, chairman; Edmund C. Pettus, Alabama; James B. Frazer, (state of residence not given); Joseph W. Bailey, Texas; Lee S. Overman, North Carolina; Chauncey M. Depew, New York; Fred T. Dubois, Idaho; and Jonathan P. Dolliver.

484 [19]Smith, p. 346. The five members signing the minority report were: J. B. Foraker, Ohio; Albert J. Beveridge, Indiana; William P. Dillingham, Vermont; A. J. Hopkins, Illinois; and Philander C. Knox, Pennsylvania.

[20]*Reader's Digest* (June 1958), p. 142, quoting Francis T. Plimpton at Amherst College.

[21]Joseph Fielding Smith, *Essentials in Church History* (22d ed., enlarged, Salt Lake City: Deseret Book Co., 1967), p. 513.

[22]Smith, *Joseph F. Smith*, pp. 350-51.

[23]Smith, *Joseph F. Smith*, pp. 355-56.

[24]*CHC*, 6:430.

[25]When I visited the Barre quarries in the summer of 1967, I discovered that one company had nine wholesale outlets in Utah.

[26]Smith, *Joseph F. Smith*, p. 397.

[27]Smith, *Joseph F. Smith*, pp. 467-71.

[28]Smith, *Joseph F. Smith*, p. 431.

[29]Nibley, p. 259.

[30]*CHC*, 6:477-78.

22

Administration of Heber J. Grant

A BRIEF SKETCH OF THE LIFE OF HEBER J. GRANT

Heber Jedediah Grant was born November 22, 1856, to Rachel Ridgeway Ivins Grant and Jedediah Morgan Grant, married in 1855. Heber's father had achieved prominence as a Latter-day Saint because of his faithfulness and ability. When he came west at the age of thirty-one, he was one of the seven presidents of the First Council of the Seventy. On January 19, 1851, he was elected first mayor of Salt Lake City; and on April 7, 1854, he was chosen second counselor to President Brigham Young in the First Presidency of the Church. But Heber was not destined to enjoy the companionship of or profit from his father's counsel, for Jedediah passed away rather suddenly when he was only forty years old on December 1, 1856, nine days after Heber's birth. It was his talented and faithful mother who was to be the guiding light of this man of God during the years of his childhood and youth. She instilled in him a great love for the Lord Jesus Christ and a staunch faith in the mission of Joseph Smith. She supported herself and her son by taking in boarders and by sewing. Sometimes she would treadle her sewing machine for so many hours that her legs would give out and she would have Heber treadle the machine with his hands.

485

Heber was six years old in 1862 when he became personally acquainted with President Young. On a winter day he ran into the street to catch a ride on the back of Brigham Young's cutter sleigh, for it was the custom of boys then to "hang on behind" for a block or two and then jump off. When he tried to jump off, the sleigh was going so fast he did not dare to do so. He soon became very cold; about this time President Young noticed him. He had his driver stop and tuck Heber under the robes in the front seat. After Heber was warm, President Young asked him who he was and where he lived. President Young then told Heber what a wonderful man his father had been and expressed a hope that Heber would be as good as his father was. Heber was invited to call at Brigham Young's office to visit with him. His mother sent him to President Young's office soon afterwards and said that after that he always found a hearty welcome at President Young's office or at his home.[1]

His Determination to Succeed

Heber grew long and lanky "but was not very robust." When he played baseball he did not have the strength or stamina to play with boys of his own age so he soon found himself playing on a team with boys much younger. But this only gave him the resolve to play on a championship baseball team. With a dollar earned from shining the shoes of his mother's boarders, he bought a baseball and spent hours throwing it at the barn of their neighbor, Bishop Edwin D. Wooley, who mistakenly took his zeal for baseball as an escape from other work and concluded that he was the laziest boy in the Thirteenth Ward. Nevertheless, Heber kept practicing until he became the pitcher of the team that won the baseball championship of the territory.

His determination to succeed won many a battle for him and brought him many successes that he otherwise would never have had. Because he wanted to see the plays in the Salt Lake Theatre but had no funds for tickets, he became the water boy in the "third circle" (third gallery), often wishing that his patrons had filled up with water before reaching the theater, because when his five gallon can became empty he would have to walk across the road beyond the social hall to the nearest well to refill it. Years later, when he was President of the Salt Lake Theatre

Company, he would look up to the third gallery from his box seats and think of his earlier experiences.

When he was still a youth, someone pointed out to him a man who made $150 per month as a bookkeeper for Wells Fargo & Co. This seemed a vast sum of money; therefore he determined to become a bookkeeper and work for Wells Fargo. Immediately he joined the bookkeeping class at Deseret University. At fifteen years of age he secured a position as bookkeeper and policy clerk in an insurance office, which was in the front part of A. W. White & Company's bank. When he was not busy, he volunteered to assist with the bank work. Mr. Morf, the bookkeeper for the bank, was a fine penman and helped Heber with his own penmanship, which Heber practiced until, years later, he received a diploma at the Territorial Fair for the finest penmanship in Utah. He often earned more before and after office hours writing cards, invitations, and making maps than his regular salary.

At nineteen, he accepted employment from Henry Wadsworth, the agent of Wells Fargo & Co. Although he was working for the agent and not for the company, he volunteered to do extra work and was soon keeping the books for the Sandy Smelting Co., which Wadsworth had been doing personally. This so pleased Wadsworth that he hired Heber to do collecting for Wells Fargo & Co., for which he paid him extra; Heber thus realized another ambition of his youth—that of working for Wells Fargo & Co.

On New Year's Eve, Heber was working late at the office writing calling cards when Wadsworth came in and gave him a check for one hundred dollars for his extra labor in keeping the Sandy Smelting Co. books without compensation, complimenting him for his work and willing attitude. In regard to this experience Heber said: "The satisfaction enjoyed by me in feeling that I had won the good will and confidence of my employer was worth more than twice one hundred dollars."[2]

In later years President Grant wrote:

I have found nothing in the battle of life that has been of more value to me, than to perform the duty of today, to the best of my ability; and I know that where young men do this, they will be better prepared for the labors of tomorrow.[3]

At twenty, when Heber was offered the post of assistant

cashier in Zions Saving & Trust Co., he had to give a bond of $25,000; so he thought it would be good to have the president of the company, Brigham Young, sign his bond for him. When he asked President Young to do so, he smiled and replied: "Heber, I don't see how in the world I can get out of signing your bond. I said so many good things about you at the director's meeting that if I now refuse to sign your bond they will accuse me of not telling the truth!"[4]

Called to Be Stake President

Three weeks before he was twenty-one on November 1, 1877, Heber J. Grant was married to Lucy Stringham in the St. George Temple. She is said to have been a woman of excellent character with a sweet disposition and "considerable judgment in business affairs." In the fall of 1880, shortly before Heber's twenty-fourth birthday, President John Taylor informed him that he had been chosen to succeed Francis M. Lyman as president of the Tooele Stake. This meant quite a financial sacrifice for Heber, but he accepted the call wholeheartedly. He claims that he had never spoken in public for more than ten minutes at a time, and when he made his first talk as president of the Tooele Stake, he spoke for only seven and one-half minutes, telling everything he could think of and repeating some of it twice.[5] From his later experiences as President, he said he had learned that no man could touch the hearts of his hearers unless he possessed the spirit of God and was thus capable of bearing witness to the truth of the gospel.

Called to Be an Apostle

In October 1882 Heber J. Grant was called by a revelation to President John Taylor, along with George Teasdale, to the apostleship. When Heber was a child, Eliza R. Snow had prophesied in tongues that he would become an apostle of the Lord Jesus Christ, and Zina D. Young had given the interpretation. His mother made a record of it and often told him if he would behave himself he would be an apostle, to which Heber would reply: "Every mother believes that her son will become president of the United States, or hold some great office. You ought to get that out of your head, Mother."[6]

After his call to the apostleship, Elder Grant felt somewhat uneasy because he lacked experience, inspiration, and a testimony worthy of such a position; but all this was cleared up in February of 1883 when he was crossing some Navajo Indian land in Arizona with Lot Smith, Brigham Young, Jr., and others. He went off alone to pray, and it was manifested to him that because of his clean living and the desire of his father, Jedediah M. Grant, and the Prophet Joseph Smith, this honor was bestowed upon him; it now remained for him to make a success or failure of that calling. From that time on, he received great joy in testifying of the gospel both at home and abroad.[7]

During the next eighteen years, Elder Grant busied himself with visits to the various stakes of Zion and in taking care of his business interests. He claimed to have learned a lesson from going into debt too much in his anxiety to make money and from suffering the results of the depression that struck in 1893. He said, "If the Lord will only forgive me this once I will never be caught again." [8]

In 1897 he suffered a severe illness and had to have an operation. These setbacks were followed by an attack of pneumonia. By March 12, 1898, he was able to once more speak in the Tabernacle and gave credit to the Lord and the brethren of the priesthood for saving his life.

It was shortly after this that Horace Ensign convinced him that, although he was tone deaf, it was possible for him to learn to sing. Through persistence and thousands of hours of practice he finally learned to sing "Oh, My Father," "God Moves in a Mysterious Way," "Come, Come, Ye Saints," "The Flag Without a Stain," and two or three other hymns.[9]

Eventually Elder Grant developed a truism that each of us would do well to remember: "That which we persist in doing becomes easy to do, not that the nature of the thing changes, but that our ability to do it increases."

His Call to Mission Service

In 1901 Elder Grant went to Japan in charge of opening the Japanese Mission. It was the first full-time mission he had served for the Church. At the time of his call on February 4, 1901, his fellow apostle Elder John W. Taylor said to him: "You are not in a position to accept this call because of the debts you owe. The Lord has accepted your sacrifice, and I prophesy that you will go to Japan a free man financially." [10] Within four months he left for his mission having paid $4,600 in tithing and having paid off all his notes.

During the little more than two years in Japan, President Grant was not entirely happy because he could not learn the Japanese language very well.

On one occasion he went into the woods and prayed that when his work was finished in Japan he would appreciate it if he were called to the British Isles to succeed Francis M. Lyman as president of the European Mission. He arrived home in September, 1903 and by November 28 he had arrived in Liverpool, England, where he spent three pleasant and successful years, returning to Salt Lake City in December, 1906.

President of the Council of the Twelve

During the next ten years President Grant remained at home, occupying his time with his Church duties and managing his extensive business affairs. When President Francis M. Lyman died, Elder Grant succeeded him as President of the Council of the Twelve Apostles, having been set apart to that office on November 23, 1916. He had been an apostle for thirty-four years. In reporting to the Saints at the April Conference in 1917, President Grant paid a great compliment to his fellow General Authorities:

> I rejoice that in all my associations with the general authorities of the Church since I was six years of age I have never heard one word, in public or in private, fall from the lips of these men, but would be for the benefit, for the uplift, for the improvement morally and intellectually, physically and spiritually of the Latter-day Saints.[11]

THE PRESIDENCY OF HEBER J. GRANT

On November 23, 1918, only four days after the death of President Joseph F. Smith, Heber J. Grant was chosen and set apart at a meeting of the Twelve Apostles as the President of the Church. He chose as his counselors Anthon H. Lund and Charles W. Penrose, former counselors to President Joseph F. Smith. Because of an epidemic of influenza no general conference of the Church was held until June 1, 1919, when he was unanimously accepted by the members of the Church.

The new officers who were accepted unanimously included Melvin J. Ballard to fill the vacancy in the Apostles Quorum,

created when Elder Grant moved into the Presidency. President
Grant had planned on calling his close friend, Richard W. Young
to this vacancy but received revelation from the Lord that Elder
Melvin J. Ballard, president of the Southern States Mission, a
man whom he hardly knew, was to be the new apostle.[12] After
acceptance of the new officers, President Grant spoke at the
conference.

> I shall do the best I can to fulfill every obligation that
> shall rest upon me as president of the Church of Jesus
> Christ of Latter-day Saints, to the full extent of my
> ability.
>
> I will ask no man to be more liberal with his means than
> I am with mine in proportion to what he possesses, for the
> advancement of God's kingdom.
>
> I will ask no man to observe the Word of Wisdom any
> more closely than I observe it.
>
> I will ask no man to be more conscienteous and prompt
> in the payment of his tithes and his offerings than I will
>
> I will ask no man to be more ready and willing to come
> early and to go late and to labor with full power of mind
> and body than I will labor, always in humility.[13]

President Grant's message to his people was "Keep the Commandments," and this might be said to have been the theme of
his administration. He always admonished the Saints to be doers
of the word and not hearers only, telling the leaders if they
could not abide by the teachings of the gospel, they should step
aside and let others who could do so take their places. At the
dedication of the Hawaiian Temple and many times thereafter
he said:

> It is not the miraculous testimonies we may have, but it
> is keeping the commandments of God, and living lives of
> absolute purity, not only in act, but in thought, that will
> count with the Lord.[14]

One of the greatest contributions President Grant made to
the Church was his ability to meet prominent and influential
people of the nation and break down opposition, remove
prejudice, and win many friends for the Church. Under his
guidance the Church enjoyed an era of steady growth for nearly
twenty-seven years.

Heber J. Grant, seventh president of The Church of Jesus Christ of Latter-day Saints. *Permission of Church Information Service.*

Elder Grant became President of the Church just twelve days after the signing of the armistice which ended the fighting of World War I. It was a time when many changes would come about. During the war many Latter-day Saint men had been scattered throughout the United States receiving training in various military camps, where they became acquainted with new people and new opportunities for a livelihood. Many of them returned to these areas after the conclusion of the war to marry a local girl or establish themselves in some branch of industry or business. Thus, a new diffusion of membership began. Most of the Latter-day Saint servicemen remained loyal to their church, becoming active members wherever they settled, providing leadership in many communities. The area showing the greatest growth in Church membership after World War I was the West Coast of the United States, where the 1930 membership showed 39,000 as compared with the 1920 membership of 13,000.[15]

There were many other changes that would also add to the diffusion of Church membership. A new industrial age was on the horizon. The tractor would soon replace not only the horse but much hand labor, reducing the number of people needed for the production of food and fiber. This meant that many men who had been needed on the farm would have to seek a new kind of employment.

Church statistics show that at the end of 1918 Church membership was 495,962 which was an increase of 268,331 since the end of the nineteenth century.[16]

Temples in New Areas

A pleasant duty that President Grant performed was the dedication of the Hawaiian Temple. The Latter-day Saint temples are each dedicated as "a house of prayer, a house of fasting, a house of faith, a house of learning, a house of glory, a house of order, a house of God." (D&C 88:119.)[17] In the temples of the Lord ordinances are administered for the living and also by the living for and in behalf of the dead. (1 Cor. 15:29.) President David O. McKay said:

All ordinances performed by the priesthood of the Most High are as eternal as love, as comprehensive and enduring

494

Temple at Laie, Hawaii. *Permission of Church Information Service.*

as life, and through obedience to them, all mankind, living
and dead, may enter into and abide eternally in the kingdom of God.[18]

It is also only in the temples of the Lord that Latter-day Saints
perform marriages for time and all eternity. For the above
reasons the temple was a necessity and an advancement for the
Church that it might fulfill its responsibilities as the universal
church of Christ. It began to place holy temples in various areas
beyond Utah.

The Hawaiian Temple

President Joseph F. Smith dedicated a temple site at Laie,
Hawaii, on the island of Oahu, June 1, 1915, on ground that the
Church had purchased in 1865. The matter of building a temple
in Hawaii was presented to the Church at the general conference
on October 3, 1915, when the Saints decided by a unanimous
vote to build a temple for the benefit of the Polynesian
Saints.[19] President George Q. Cannon, who as a young man in
1850 was one of the missionaries to open Hawaii to the gospel
message, returned there on a visit in 1900 and told the Saints
both at Laie and Honolulu that the time would come soon

Temple at Cardston, Alberta, Canada—first temple built outside the United States. *Permission of Church Information Service.*

when the people of the islands would have a temple in which to perform ordinances for the living and the dead. Nineteen years later, on Thanksgiving Day, November 27, 1919, President Heber J. Grant offered the dedicatory prayer for the completed temple at appropriate exercises for the occasion.

The Alberta Temple

The next temple to be completed outside of the Utah area was in Cardston, Alberta, Canada, where President Joseph F. Smith had dedicated the ground on July 27, 1913, and David O. McKay had lain the cornerstone on September 19, 1915. He also laid the capstone September 23, 1917, but it was not until August 26, 1923, that President Grant dedicated the completed edifice. Eleven dedicatory sessions were held in order to accommodate all of the Saints who desired to attend.

The Arizona Temple

The third temple to be built away from the Utah area in the twentieth century was in Arizona, where the site was dedicated by President Grant on November 28, 1921; the temple dedica-

Temple at Mesa, Arizona. *Permission of Church Information Service.*

tion took place on October 23, 1927. Thirteen sessions in all were held through October 27. This temple has become known as the Lamanite temple because of the words uttered by President Grant in his dedicatory prayer:

> We beseech thee, O Lord, that thou wilt stay the hand of the destroyer among the descendants of Lehi who reside in this land . . . that all the great and glorious promises made concerning the descendants of Lehi may be fulfilled in them. . . .[20]

Anniversaries

The First Vision

President Grant's administration was marked with a number of important anniversaries, the first of which was the one-hundredth anniversary of the Prophet's first vision of the Father and the Son in the spring of 1820. It was made the feature of the general conference in April of 1920; and it was celebrated by services throughout the Church, where special topics were considered in the wards following the conference. At conference time, however, a cantata called "The Vision," which had been especially prepared for the occasion by Evan Stephens, was presented.

The Centennial Anniversary of Moroni's Appearance

The next anniversary was the centennial of the first appearance of the Angel Moroni on September 21, 1823. For three days—September 21, 22, and 23, 1923—the Eastern States Mission held a commemoration at the Joseph Smith farm and the Hill Cumorah in Manchester township, New York, attended by President Grant and other General Authorities. The exercises throughout the conference depicted epochs and events "which revealed the existence of the Book of Mormon".[21] Favorable publicity was given through the local papers including the *Rochester Herald* and the *New York Herald,* which told of the unfolding of the story of an ancient civilization which had existed in the area:

> The narrative is the very basis of Mormon theology and belief and leads directly up to the revelation given through Joseph Smith of the foundations of the Mormon Church. . . .
> The speakers at the conference told the story with the simplicity and directness of a Norse Saga. As point after point of the drama of the lost tribes, of their rise to a great civilization and of their final downfall in the bitterness of war was related, those not conversant with the tale were gripped and fascinated by the strangeness of the recital, and when a speaker dramatically pointed to the earth and mentioned that upon the very spot where he stood some of the epic events might have taken place there was a decided thrill to being there.[22]

During the conference, in addition to the authorities and approximately 160 missionaries, from two to three thousand people were in attendance.

Deliverance of the Plates

Four years later President Grant, with other leading men and women of the Church, attended the one-hundredth anniversary of the deliverance of the gold plates of the Book of Mormon to Joseph Smith for translation. Meetings were again held at Hill Cumorah and in the Sacred Grove.

One of the most notable events of President Grant's administration was the Centennial Conference which celebrated the
one-hundredth anniversary of the restoration of Christ's church
in this, the dispensation of the fullness of times. One year
earlier, a committee had been appointed which was headed by
Elder George Albert Smith to determine the nature of the celebration that should take place.

The plan they formulated and carried out was this:

1. The convening of the regular conference on Sunday, April 6,
   1930, with the morning meeting, a priesthood meeting with
   representatives of all quorums in attendance.
2. The illumination of the Salt Lake Temple and all other
   temples throughout the conference week, which was to indicate the joy of the people in having had the privilege of
   successfully carrying out the Lord's work for one hundred
   years.[23]
3. The publication of a *Comprehensive History of the Church*
   covering the first century of the organized existence of the
   Church.
4. The performing of a pageant featuring God's "Message of
   The Ages" which was to be given the night of April 6th and
   continued throughout the week or longer if the interest of
   the public desired it.[24]
5. The general Conference to be for four days instead of the
   usual three days.[25]

All of the committee's plans were successfully carried out.
One of the highlights of the conference was the universal blessing and benediction of President Grant upon the peoples and
nations of the earth as God's children, which he gave with
dignity and humility as God's vicegerent upon the earth.[26]

At the end of the first century of the gospel's restoration
there were 700,000 living members of the Church. See
Appendix 10 for further Centennial Statistics.

Further Acquisition of Landmarks

In connection with the celebrations held in the Sacred Grove,
at the Smith Farm, and at Hill Cumorah was the purchase of
several other landmarks of Church history. The first of these
was the purchase of the Inglis farm of ninety-six acres in 1923.

It straddled the Canandaigua Road and ran halfway up the Hill Cumorah on the west side. On February 17, 1928, what was known as the Mormon Hill Farm was purchased. This farm consisted of 187 acres and bordered the Inglis farm on the west side of Hill Cumorah, over the top of the hill and stretching out to the east. This gave the Church a total of 283 acres in the area and included the whole of the Hill Cumorah.

On September 26, 1926, the Church purchased what was known as the Peter Whitmer Farm in Fayette, Seneca County, New York. It consisted of approximately 100 acres and was the place where the Church had been organized on April 6, 1830. A colonial type farm house was on the property, and although it is not the house in which the Church was organized, it was built not too many years afterwards.

On May 13, 1937, eighty-eight acres of the original Martin Harris Farm were purchased. The farm had on it what is known as the Lakestone Home, built in 1850. Martin Harris had sold 150 acres of the farm on April 1, 1831. The original Martin Harris Home had burned in 1849. Today, the Lakestone Home is maintained by the Church as a tribute to Martin Harris, who sold part of it to pay off the printing debt for the first edition of the Book of Mormon and bore his testimony to its truthfulness for forty-six years.

On February 20, 1937, Wilford Wood of Bountiful, Utah, made the first purchase of land for the Church in the city of Nauvoo since before 1846. On the above date he and Jack Smith, a grandson of Hyrum Smith, purchased a portion of the original temple block. It was the lot with a well that furnished water for the temple, including the baptismal font. A second purchase of about one-fourth of the temple lot was made by Elder Wood from a Jewish gentleman. It had an opera house on it at the time which was being used as a theater. Approximately six months after the purchase the movie machine caught on fire and caused the building to burn down.

Elder Wood next purchased two Icarian houses built on two lots of the original temple block. His fifth purchase of temple-block property was a lot purchased from a Catholic priest. It was also during President Grant's administration that Elder Wood began the purchase of private homes in Nauvoo of leading members of the Church. Much credit is due to Wilford Wood, who purchased many landmarks of Church history in his own name and later turned them over to the Church without any profit whatsoever.

In 1918 the people of the United States amended the constitution so that it was illegal to manufacture, sell, possess, or consume alcoholic beverages. This was what was known as voting the country dry. Although far less alcohol was consumed under the new law and health conditions in the country were much improved, the liquor interests waged a constant battle for repeal of the amendment. Enforcement of the law was difficult and much illegal liquor was sold. It was nevertheless true that the United States was better off under prohibition, but the relentless hammering away by the liquor interests began to convince the average citizen that prohibition was a failure. In 1932 Franklin D. Roosevelt ran for President of the United States on a platform calling for repeal of the eighteenth amendment. His victory was the signal for the various states to begin voting procedures. President Grant and his counselors, with a deep moral issue involved, requested the Latter-day Saints to vote against repeal. The Saints in heavily populated Mormon counties of Idaho did so; but in Utah there were insufficient numbers of them who did so, and Utah became the thirty-sixth state in the nation (out of forty-eight) to vote for repeal. Thus, Utah was the state that brought about repeal of prohibition, much to the embarrassment of the General Authorities. Upon receipt of the vote in Utah, the liquor interests in New York put on a parade in which they carried a banner saying "Thank God for Utah"! May she never again become famous for supporting the false propaganda of money-mad interests who promised it would bring back prosperity. Crime, drunkenness, divorce and sickness, along with taxes to support the alcoholics and to build more jails and sanitariums rose rapidly, and the country has never been as sound in these areas since then as it was during the fifteen years of prohibition. The liquor interests had been aided by a terrible depression which had collapsed the stock market and left millions of people unemployed, including many thousands in the Mormon West.

The Welfare Plan

The years of depression brought about the inauguration of the present welfare plan of the Church. During April Conference in 1936 the First Presidency introduced it to the people. Although the plan did not solve all of the unemploy-

ment and financial problems of the Saints, it did become a great
plan of self-help. Today its influence is greater than ever, providing aid and employment in many ways, especially for those who desire to work and be self-sufficient but cannot get work in regular streams of industry because of partial physical impairment or for other reasons.

World War II

When B. H. Roberts wrote his *Comprehensive History of the Church of Jesus Christ of Latter-day Saints* for publication in 1930, he spoke of World War I and the revelations on wars that had been given through Joseph Smith, especially in Doctrine and Covenants 87, given December 25, 1832, in which the Lord revealed the wars to come. Roberts spoke of the "wars in their own lands" (war with Mexico—1846-48; the Civil War—1861-1865; the "war in foreign lands"—Franco-Prussian War—1870-1871; and World War I). And he said, "And the end may not even now have been reached, for the Son of Man, the resurrected Christ, has not yet come."[27]

Joseph Smith's prophecy of war (D&C 87) was certainly verified with the outbreak of World War II on September 1, 1939, when Hitler crossed the German border into Poland. Two days later, France and Great Britain declared war on Germany. Events soon occurred that brought all of the great powers into the conflict and nearly every nation on earth was affected, the United States becoming directly involved when Japan attacked Pearl Harbor on Sunday, December 7, 1941.

After five years of carnage, death, and starvation, the war was brought to a conclusion when Germany capitulated on May 8, 1945, and Japan surrendered September 2, 1945; but the world would never again be the same.

The Church was affected in many ways. On August 24, 1939, one week prior to Hitler's invasion of Poland, the Church ordered all American missionaries out of Germany. Shortly afterward, the neutral nations requested all foreigners to leave, and all missionaries in Europe were transferred. In 1940, with the war spreading, missionaries were withdrawn from South Africa and the Pacific (except Hawaii).[28] By the end of 1940, only North and South America and Hawaii had regular full-time missionaries.[29]

Many Latter-day Saints entered the armed forces to help defend their country; and a sad situation saw Latter-day Saint

502 pitted against Latter-day Saint, when the German Saints, duty-bound, fought for their country. Again the war brought a dispersion of the Saints which provided for leadership and the spreading of Church members into many new localities, just as persecution of the Christians in Jerusalem aided the dissemination of Christianity throughout the Western World in apostolic and postapostolic times.

Footnotes

[1] Preston Nibley, *The Presidents of the Church* (Salt Lake City: Deseret Book Co., 1941), p. 271. I am indebted to Preston Nibley for much of the material about President Grant.

[2] Nibley, p. 276.

[3] Nibley, p. 274.

[4] Nibley, p. 277.

[5] Nibley, p. 278.

[6] Nibley, p. 282.

[7] Nibley, p. 286.

[8] Nibley, p. 288.

[9] President Grant's learning to sing was only mechanical, however, and was due to great persistence. My father told me of an occasion when Elder Grant visited stake conference in Bear Lake Stake and the people requested him to sing. He said: "Which of my two songs would you like?" There were two groups of people, one group being back in a cove. The pianist who became his accompanist was in the group which had requested the opposite song from the main group. When the pianist concluded the introductory music, Elder Grant began to sing the other song. Of course the pianist quickly changed to the proper music.

In 1938 Elder Joseph F. Merrill of the Council of the Twelve told me: "I once asked President Grant if the few songs he had learned to sing were actually worth the thousands of hours he had spent on them and he evaded giving me an answer;" which is, perhaps, evidence that when a person's talents are too minimal along a certain line, his time might be better spent on something for which he has more natural ability.

[10] Nibley, p. 295.

[11] Nibley, p. 311.

[12] I personally heard President Grant make this statement.

[13] *CHC*, 6:491.

[14] *CHC*, 6:486. See also *Honolulu Star Bulletin*, 6 December 1919.

[15] Richard O. Cowan's chart showing Church membership by decades. Cowan is associate professor of religious instruction at Brigham Young University.

[16] Church Historian's compilation.

[17] See also David O. McKay, "The Los Angeles Temple," *Improvement Era* 59(March 1956):141.

[18] McKay, p. 142.

[19] "The Hawaiian Temple," *Improvement Era* 39(April 1936):227.

[20] "The Arizona Temple," *Improvement Era* 58(November 1955):824.

[21]*CHC*, 6:522.

[22]*CHC*, 6:524. *See also Rochester Herald,* 22 September 1923.

[23]This was the beginning of the illumination of temples, which has been carried on rather extensively since.

[24]It actually lasted for a full month, closing on May 5.

[25]*CHC*, 6:536-37.

[26]*CHC*, 6:541.

[27]*CHC*, 6:447.

[28]Joseph Fielding Smith, *Essentials in Church History* (22d ed., enlarged, Salt Lake City: Deseret Book Co., 1967), pp. 526-27.

[29]James B. Allen and Richard O. Cowan, *Mormonism in the Twentieth Century* (Provo, Utah: Brigham Young University Press, 1967), p. 41.

23

Administration of George Albert Smith

A BRIEF SKETCH OF THE LIFE
OF GEORGE ALBERT SMITH

George Albert Smith was born to John Henry and Sarah Farr Smith on April 4, 1870. John Henry Smith—former second counselor to President Joseph F. Smith—was the son of George A. Smith—former second counselor to President Brigham Young—who was the son of "Uncle" John Smith (the Prophet Joseph Smith's uncle and former stake president of Adam-ondi-Ahman, Zarahemla, Montrose, and Salt Lake Stakes and presiding Patriarch to the Church), who was the son of Asael Smith, Sr., the Prophet Joseph's paternal grandfather, who had predicted that a prophet would be raised up in his family who would revolutionize the religious faith of the world.

Eleven of George Albert Smith's forebears crossed the plains to Utah—his father, four grandparents, and six great-grandparents.[1] He was born in a very modest home across the street west from Temple Square[2] and was baptized in City Creek at eight and confirmed a member of the Church in fast meeting in the Seventeenth Ward. George Albert had a happy childhood.

The Beginning of a Lifetime of Missionary Work

At the age of twenty-one George was called on his first

505

mission, but it was not a foreign mission or a mission away from the body of the Saints. President Wilford Woodruff asked him to labor among the young people in the stakes of Juab, Millard, Beaver, and Parowan in building up the Young Men's Mutual Improvement Association.[3] He and his companion, William B. Dougall, Jr., held meetings throughout these stakes and organized Mutual Improvement Associations over a four-month period, after which they were released to return to their homes.

The following year Elder Smith was called on a mission to the southern states. Before leaving, he married his childhood sweetheart, Lucy Emily Woodruff, daughter of President Wilford Woodruff, on May 25, 1892. After he had been in the mission field for four months, he was made mission secretary. His wife was now called on a mission and joined him in Chattanooga, Tennessee, where they served together as missionaries until June, 1894. While on this mission Elder Smith made great progress in becoming a capable public speaker.[4]

His Call to the Apostleship

During the nine years after his return from the southern states, Elder Smith served as superintendent of the Sunday School in the Seventeenth Ward and as superintendent of the YMMIA (Young Men's Mutual Improvement Association) in the Salt Lake Stake until he was called to fill a vacancy in the Quorum of the Twelve and was sustained at the October Conference in 1903 at the age of thirty-three.[5]

European Mission President

George Albert Smith performed the regular duties of an apostle in the Church (and was also a member of the general board of the YMMIA) until he was called in the spring of 1919 to assume the duties of European Mission president. With his wife and two of their children he arrived in Liverpool in June. Since this was shortly after World War I and there was still a shortage of food in Great Britain, missionaries were not allowed to enter the country. After eleven months—May 31, 1920—of continuous effort to reverse that ruling, he received word that missionaries would now be allowed to enter Great Britain. He firmly established the work in England and also visited the missions in Germany and the Scandinavian countries. In June 1921 he was released to return to Salt Lake City.

In September, 1921, Elder Smith was called to be general superintendent of the YMMIA, in which capacity he served until January 23, 1935.

First Preaching of the Gospel by Radio

On May 6, 1922, Elder Smith participated in the first preaching of the gospel by radio, along with President Heber J. Grant and others. This was the ushering in of the preaching of the gospel from the housetops that was prophesied in the Old Testament pertaining to the last days. It was the beginning of a modern age in which science, through radio, television and other means, would make it possible to take the gospel message to the remote corners of the earth.

Missionary Visits

George Albert Smith made many visits to the various missions of the Church, but perhaps the most interesting was his tour of the missions of the South Pacific in 1938. In January of that year he sailed to Honolulu where he met Elder Rufus K. Hardy, who was to assist him on the tour. On February 7 they met the mission president, Thomas D. Rees, with whom they toured the Australian continent. Meetings were held in Melbourne, Tasmania, Adelaide, Brisbane, and Perth.

After a month in Australia, Elder Smith and his companion held a three-day conference in Auckland, New Zealand, where they enjoyed the association of the Maori people. They also visited Wellington and Perth. Because of illness, Elder Hardy remained in New Zealand while Elder Smith visited the Saints in the Tongan Islands with Alexander Wishart, a local elder.[6] Elder Hardy then joined Elder Smith for a month's tour of Samoa. On July 14 they returned to Salt Lake City.

Later Positions and Accomplishments

After the death of President Rudger Clawson, George Albert Smith was ordained President of the Quorum of the Twelve on July 8, 1943, in which capacity he functioned until he was ordained President of the Church on May 21, 1945. During his six years as the head of the Church he continued to be a joyous,

508 happy person with a positive outlook on life and was always expressing his gratitude to and love for his colleagues and the members of the Church as well as to outsiders, with whom he readily made friends.

Among other positions he held in life in addition to his busy schedule as a Church Authority was that of national vice-president general of the Sons of the American Revolution in 1926, and he continued as a national officer after that time. He also served as president of the Utah Society and as its director many times. He served as president of the International Irrigation Congress and also as president of the International Dry Farm Congress. He was organizer of the Utah Pioneer Trails and Landmarks Association in 1930, serving as its president until his death.[7] For many years President Smith was a member of the board of directors of the Oregon Trail Memorial Association and was one of the organizers of the American Pioneer Trails Association. Under his leadership more than a hundred monuments and markers were erected from Nauvoo, Illinois, westward along pioneer trails to Arizona, Idaho, Wyoming, Nevada and California.[8] The largest of all these was the This is the Place Monument.

In 1898 he was appointed by President William McKinley to the federal position of Receiver of Public Monies and Special Disbursing Agent in the United States Land Office in Salt Lake City. He was reappointed by President Theodore Roosevelt and held the position for nine years.[9]

As early as 1911 George Albert Smith became an active sponsor of scouting when the MIA scouts were organized. In 1913 the program of the Boy Scouts of America was adopted by the YMMIA General Board, and Elder Smith became a member of the executive board of the Salt Lake Council, a member of the region twelve executive committee, and a member of the executive board of the national council. For his services to scouting President Smith received both the Silver Beaver and Silver Buffalo awards.[10] During his guidance, Utah assumed a position ahead of all other states in the percentage of boys who were scouts.[11]

His Service to the Youth

John D. Giles has stated:

If President Smith had one hobby to which he was more devoted than to any other . . . it was young people. From

George Albert Smith, eighth president of The Church of Jesus Christ of Latter-day Saints. *Permission of Church Information Service.*

his earliest manhood to the time his strength began to fail, he embraced every opportunity to serve youth.[12]

As President of the Church, his interest in the youth continued, including those of college age. He was deeply devoted to providing facilities for an expanding seminary and institute program, providing funds whenever possible for improvements of physical facilities. He was also a particular friend of the Lamanite people, speaking in their behalf in Washington, D.C.

THE PRESIDENCY OF GEORGE ALBERT SMITH

On May 21, 1945, just one week after the death of President Grant, the Quorum of the Twelve Apostles and the presiding Patriarch sustained George Albert Smith as the eighth President of the Church. At the time he was seventy-five years old and had been an apostle for nearly forty-two years, the last two of which he had been President of the Quorum. He chose as his counselors the same brethren who were counselors to President Grant at the time of his death, J. Reuben Clark, Jr., first counselor, and David O. McKay, second counselor.

Although President Smith had the privilege of presiding over the Church for only six years, he not only had the love and respect of the Church members but also of many of the country's leaders. The Church continued to move forward under his capable direction. He particularly stressed the importance of providing for the young people of the Church.

Dedication of the Idaho Falls Temple

In March, 1937, the First Presidency announced that the Church would build a temple in Idaho, and on December 19, 1939, the work of excavation was begun. On August 19, 1941, the capstone was laid on the top of the tower; from the outward appearance of the temple it appeared to be completed, but because of a shortage of supplies during World War II completion was delayed until September, 1945.

On Sunday, September 23, President Smith officiated at the dedication. All of the General Authorities were present for the occasion. [13] The temple is situated at Idaho Falls near the Snake River in a beautiful setting. Inasmuch as so many of the Saints in the area wanted to attend the dedication, eight sessions were held. The temple was principally for the benefit of the stakes in

Temple at Idaho Falls, Idaho. *Permission of Church Information Service.*

Idaho and the Big Horn and Star Valley Stakes of Wyoming. It is fireproof, constructed of reinforced concrete. Marble used in its construction came from Utah, France, Italy, and Sweden.[14]

Elder Benson's Mission to Europe

Inasmuch as George Albert Smith became President of the Church about two weeks after the capitulation of Germany ended that phase of World War II, his thoughts turned to the suffering Church members in Germany and the other European countries. In November, 1945, he visited President Harry S. Truman in Washington, D.C., asking permission and transportation to send them food and clothing. President Truman replied that those people had no money to pay for such things, and President Smith informed him that the Saints did not want money for them. He said: "They are our brothers and sisters." President Truman gave permission and asked how soon the goods would be ready. President Smith replied, "They are ready now." As a result, thousands of boxes of provisions were sent to the Saints in Europe.

A sequel to this showed the true Christian spirit and genuine brotherly love in the action of the Saints in Holland. Although the supposedly neutral countries of Holland, Belgium,

512 Denmark, and Norway had been crushed and robbed by the hordes of the German army, the Saints in Holland sent many thousands of pounds of potatoes they had grown to the hungry Saints in Germany. In considering the plight of the European Saints, the First Presidency felt the necessity of sending someone to aid them both spiritually and temporally. Elder Ezra Taft Benson was assigned to this calling, and he departed on February 4, 1946, with credentials from the First Presidency and documents from government officials.

> He was instructed to visit all the countries in Europe which were accessible, seek out the members of the Church, administer to their wants, set in order the branches and give such encouragement as could be given to comfort and bless these stricken people.[15]

United States military officers received him with kindness and aided him immensely, especially with much-needed transportation. Elder Benson reported that the Latter-day Saint servicemen in Europe also rendered invaluable service.[16] He found thousands of members who had remained loyal to the Church through all their suffering.[17] After seven months in Europe, Elder Benson and his traveling companion had "traveled 15,035 miles by plane, 5,951 miles by train, 1,296 miles by ship and boat, 11,551 miles by private automobile and 2,940 miles by jeep, truck, station wagon, bus cable railway, streetcar, and horse and buggy, making a total of 36,773 miles of travel." He had directed the distribution of relief supplies, reopened missions, reorganized branches, and generally set the Church in order in England, Holland, Denmark, Norway, Sweden, Finland, Belgium, France, Switzerland, Czechoslovakia, Austria, Poland, and the occupied zones of Germany. In December, 1946, he was succeeded as European Mission president by Elder Alma Sonne.[18]

Resumption of Missionary Work

As previously noted, the Church had to halt nearly all missionary work during World War II except in North America, and then only a few missionaries were available because most young men of missionary age were in the service. Many of the burdens of labor at home were left to fathers and older men. With the surrender of the axis powers, the men in the service began to return home, where many of them immediately volunteered for missionary service so that when it was possible to get back into many foreign countries, the missionaries entered. By the end of 1946 the Church had over three thousand missionaries in various fields of labor throughout America, Europe, and the islands of the sea.[19]

The Centennial Celebration of 1947

Seventeen years before the 1947 centennial celebration was to take place, Elder George Albert Smith, member of the Twelve and also president of the Utah Trails and Landmarks Association, was appointed to be chairman of an executive committee whose duty it was to plan appropriate events for commemoration of the one-hundredth anniversary of the pioneers' entrance into the Salt Lake valley. Various other commissions and committees were appointed, with changes taking place in the personnel from time to time. By the time of the centennial year, 1947, George Albert Smith was President of the Church and Herbert B. Maw was governor of the state of Utah. President David O. McKay, second counselor in the First Presidency, had become chairman of the Centennial Commission.

Many and varied were the innovations planned for the year. At conference on April 4, 1947, President Smith spoke of the pioneers of July 24, 1847, and remarked about the accomplishments of the Church in the intervening years. He talked of the pioneers again on April 6, as did President David O. McKay. The speeches of nearly all the other conference speakers at the April Conference were related to the faith and devotion of the pioneers.

May 1 was the legal opening of the centennial celebration although some events had already preceded that date. Already at other Church conferences, the Utah Symphony Orchestra had given twenty-two performances in thirteen cities in honor of the pioneers.[20] The MIA sponsored contests to bring forth the "best of modern talent in this centennial year" in drama, story, speech, and song. A traveling art exhibit which visited every county in the state honored the pioneers in picture. From July 15 to August 30, an art exhibit of "One Hundred Years of American Painting," featuring the accomplishments and progress of the people, was on display in the State Capitol Building, where nearly 1,000,000 people attended. Brigham Young University held a historical cavalcade on July 4 and 5.[21] The

514 Mutual Improvement Association's June Conference was the greatest ever held to that time. The drama departments of the University of Utah, Brigham Young University, and Utah State Agricultural College each made a special effort to provide appropriate plays for the occasion by giving a combined total of 187 appearances in fifty-eight different localities.

Two Great Pageants

The pageant, "The Message of the Ages," was given in the Tabernacle beginning May 5 and continued each night except Sunday nights until June 5, making twenty-five performances in all—a total of 135,000 people attending. The *Deseret News* of June 7, 1947, stated that the cost to stage this pageant—for light, curtains, costumes, etc.—was more than $40,000.[22] It was free to the public. Another drama, "Promised Valley," was staged in the University of Utah Stadium from July 21 through August 10. Over 85,000 attended this excellent production. In addition, Ogden and Logan also produced centennial pageants.

The Governors' Conference

In the midst of the centennial activities forty-five governors from as many states and the two governors from Hawaii and Alaska honored Utah by holding their thirty-ninth annual governors' conference in Salt Lake City from July 12 to July 18. President George Albert Smith was host to the group at a buffet dinner served at his home in southeast Salt Lake City, where good will and friendliness prevailed to an extent leaders of one hundred years before could hardly have imagined.

Reenactment of the Pioneer Trek

Under the supervision of the Sons of the Utah Pioneers, the trek of the original pioneer company from Nauvoo to Salt Lake valley was reenacted with the exact number of personnel: 143 men, three women, two children, and seventy-two automobiles decorated with "wagon boxes," canvas covers, and plywood oxen to give them a resemblance of covered wagons.[23]

When they arrived in Nauvoo, Mayor Lowell F. Horton and the people gave them a royal welcome with "Welcome Pioneers" or "Welcome Mormons" signs posted all over the city. The only people who were disappointed were a few of the local merchants who had stocked up on numerous extra barrels of beer only to find they had no customers among the trekkers.[24] At 7:30 p.m. the night before leaving Nauvoo, the trekkers presented their first of many public programs which they gave along the way. About 2,000 spectators gathered around the stand which had been erected by the Nauvoo Chamber of Commerce. Senator Mac Downing of the Illinois Legislature—representing the governor (who was in Salt Lake City attending the governors' conference) and other law-making bodies—testified that civilization had come a long way in Illinois during the past hundred years, and whereas the people in Governor Ford's time had declared open war against the Saints, they were now happy as part of that state to welcome the sons and daughters of those people back to the land of their forebears.[25]

At the Nauvoo Program, as at others on the trek, mementos were presented by the Sons of the Utah Pioneers to state and city officials. On Tuesday morning, July 15, the trek got underway, and the participants endeavored to follow "as much as feasible the organization and routine of President Brigham Young's original pioneer group of a century ago."[26] They first made their way southward and crossed the Mississippi River at Hamilton, Illinois, to Keokuk, Iowa, where they were welcomed to the city and to the state of Iowa by the mayor. Then they drove northward to Montrose, across from Nauvoo, where a century before many Mormons had lived and where the first exiles from Nauvoo to the West had crossed on flatboats on February 4, 1846. They paused long enough to present another program and then continued on to Corydon (near Richardson's Point) for the next presentation. The first night's encampment was at Garden Grove—the first permanent campsite of the Saints—where "Mormon Day" was being held. The citizens gave them the best campground, the city park, where the trekkers planted a Utah Blue Spruce—the state tree of Utah—to commemorate the event.

And so it went throughout the trek. Every city welcomed them and each was a gracious host, often giving them free soft drinks and ice cream. But it fell to Gering, Nebraska, to provide the biggest crowd for the trekkers. They were celebrating Oregon Trail Days and had postponed their parade from morning until afternoon in order to link it with the appearance of the trekkers.[27] Forty thousand people were present.

After a final evening's program at Fort Bridger, Wyoming, the trekkers arrived at the This is the Place Monument—to be un-

516 veiled two days later—at midafternoon, then drove on to Sugar House for a service before continuing on to the Brigham Young Monument for an impressive greeting by the First Presidency, Mayor Earl J. Glade, and other dignitaries. "Where a persecuted people had trod a hundred years ago, their descendants had been hailed, not for what they had done, but for the deeds of those who had been persecuted." 28

This Is the Place Monument

The highlight of the centennial celebration was the erection and dedication of the massive This is the Place Monument. Cooperation of the Utah state officials and the Church brought its erection to fruition. It is truly one of the great monuments of the world and is said to be fifteen monuments in one, for it separately honors that many individuals and groups: the first entrance of the white man into the Great Basin (Fathers Dominguez and Escalante with their party); the early explorers and trappers; the Reed-Donner Party, who preceded the pioneers; the various incoming groups of Latter-day Saint pioneers with the first company; and the native Indian chief whose valuable friendship helped make possible the building of a great empire and church in the midst of the Rockies.

Mahonri M. Young, grandson of Brigham Young who had gained a worldwide reputation as a sculptor, was chosen to be the sculptor of the monument. He put in nearly six years of preliminary work on the models and a total of eight years' work before the monument was completed. The Monument Commission included Duane G. Hunt, Bishop of the Catholic diocese of Salt Lake City, as first vice chairman, the Reverend Arthur G. Moulten of the Episcopal Church, and Herbert Auerbach of the Jewish faith. The site selected was a plot near the mouth of Emigration Canyon near the spot where Brigham Young thoughtfully gazed upon the valley from the carriage of Wilford Woodruff and replied: "It is enough. This is the right place. Drive on."

In 1936 the site was declared by the state legislature as a state park. In addition to five hundred acres around the monument it included a strip one mile wide for thirty-six miles from Henefer to the monument, which was to be restored insofar as possible to its condition when the pioneers traveled over it in 1847.29

On July 24, 1947, the day of dedication, thousands of people

This Is the Place Monument erected for the centennial celebration of 1947.

518 gathered around the monument; as chairman of the Monument Commission by appointment of the governor, President Smith presided at the services. Each member of the First Presidency spoke, as did Bishop Hunt, the Reverend Mr. Moulton, and Rabbi Alvin Lucks. Each of the fifteen bronze plaques on the monument was unveiled separately; and insofar as possible, the unveiling was done by direct descendants of the heroes represented on each particular plaque. After the unveiling, President Smith uttered the dedicatory prayer. The monument is over sixty feet high with statues of Brigham Young, Heber C. Kimball, and Wilford Woodruff on the center pylon. It is eighty-four feet wide.

The best way to honor the pioneers is to emulate and make practical in our lives the ideals and virtues which animated their lives and strengthened them sufficiently to overcome the trials of pioneer life in order to help build God's kingdom.

EDUCATIONAL FRUITS OF THE FIRST CENTURY IN THE SALT LAKE VALLEY

From the time of the restoration of the gospel in this dispensation, learning has been a way of life for the faithful Latter-day Saint, who deems it his duty and obligation to learn as much as he can in this life first of all as pertaining to the principles of the gospel and secondly to secular education. "The Latter-day Saint student conceives his school work to be part of his purposeful preparation for eternal life and joy." [30] This philosophy of determined learning is derived from statements given in the Doctrine and Covenants in the early years of the Church, most of which have come through revelation from God. Some of these scriptures follow:

The glory of God is intelligence. (D&C 93:36.)

Teach ye diligently and my grace shall attend you, that you may be instructed more perfectly in theory, in principle, in doctrine, in the law of the gospel, in all things that pertain unto the kingdom of God, that are expedient for you to understand;

Of things both in heaven and in the earth, and under the earth; things which have been, things which are, things which must shortly come to pass; things which are at home, things which are abroad; . . . and a knowledge also of countries and of kingdoms. (D&C 88:78-79.)

... seek ye diligently and teach one another words of wisdom; yea, seek ye out of the best books words of wisdom; seek learning, even by study and also by faith. (D&C 88:118.)

Whatever principle of intelligence we attain unto in this life, it will rise with us in the resurrection.

And if a person gains more knowledge and intelligence in this life through his diligence and obedience than another, he will have so much the advantage in the world to come. (D&C 130:18-19.)

It is impossible for a man to be saved in ignorance. (D&C 131:6.)

Such statements had a powerful effect on the early leaders and membership of the Church so that they began to provide methods and ways to conform again, first to gospel knowledge and secondly to secular knowledge.

As early as 1831 provision was made in the Church for schools, teachers, and schoolbooks.[31] In 1833 a school for mature men, to study the gospel and related topics, one of the first schools for adult education in America, was begun. Wherever the Saints moved they founded schools until, at Nauvoo in 1842, they expanded to the level of higher education by founding a university. They were equally as diligent in founding schools in the West after their arrival in 1847, so that when the seventh census of the United States was taken in 1850, it showed the average illiteracy in the country to be 4.9%; whereas in Utah it was only 0.25%, the lowest of the states and territories cited.[32]

A century after the Saints arrived in the Great Basin, various studies made during the 1940s when membership of the Church in Utah was only 74%, showed her to lead the nation in educational achievement; and if the Saints had been treated as a separate group, the percentages in their favor would have been still larger. Listed below very briefly are the results of different studies pertaining to education in Utah in the 1940s.

Accomplishment in education:	Utah in 1st place
Ability to support education:	Utah in 32nd place
The degree in which accomplishment is commensurate with ability:	Utah in 4th place
Efficiency of educational effort:	Utah in 1st place[33]

The conclusion of this study: "Utah has first place
among the states by
a wide margin. . . ."[34]

Dr. Edward L. Thorndike, in a study of the origin by birth of
men of achievement in the United States, found that in proportion to the population, Utah led the second highest—Massachusetts—by more than 20%, whereas in the number of men of
science Utah led the second highest—Colorado—by about
30%.[35] These are the accomplishments of people who belonged
to a religion that for many years most people believed attracted
only the ignorant. Perhaps Brigham Young's statement about
education best typifies today the driving force for learning behind the Latter-day Saints. "Education is the power to think
clearly, the power to act well in the world's work, and the
power to appreciate life."

CHURCH STATISTICS AT THE END OF THE FIRST
CENTURY IN THE GREAT BASIN

The year 1947 was the year in which the Church reached a
membership of one million. There were 164 stakes, with 1,230
wards and branches in the stakes, and the work in all the
mission fields throughout the world had again been resumed
following World War II.

MONUMENTS TO BRIGHAM YOUNG

On May 20, 1950, a tour party composed of thirty-eight
members, including President George Albert Smith, left Salt
Lake City on what was called the Brigham Young Memorial
Tour, sponsored by *The Improvement Era*. On May 28 they
held a dedicatory service in Whitingham, Vermont, the little
village where Brigham Young was born. A massive granite
monument twelve feet high in honor of Brigham Young had
been erected on the town's memorial and recreational area two
miles above the village.[36] On this day more than a thousand
people witnessed the unveiling. Judge Harrik B. Chase of
Brattleboro, Vermont, who spoke, said: "The name of Brigham
Young has become accepted as a symbol of perseverance, courage
to bear difficulties, and capacity to surmount them. This monument is a fitting tribute to a great American, Whitingham's
famous son."[37]

Four days later the members of the Memorial Tour were in Washington, D.C., for the dedication services of a white Italian-marble statue of Brigham Young. Again, more than a thousand people gathered in the rotunda of the capital for the ceremonies.[38] Vice-president of the United States, Alben Barkeley, spoke and was lavish in his praise of Brigham Young. Among his comments were these. "I am proud that there will stand here forever in Statuary Hall, this man of God, who was instrumental in establishing the kind of civilization that exists in the vast territory in which his memory will be forever cherished."[39] And, "He was an advocate of justice and democracy—of the kind of democracy we must preserve."[40]

The praise given to Brigham Young during this memorial tour by prominent men of the nation typified the great change in attitude that the people in general had made toward the Latter-day Saints.

PRESIDENT SMITH'S LAST ACTS

On October 17, 1950, President Smith dedicated the Eyring Science Center at Brigham Young University. It was the last of his many dedications. On December 31, 1950, he spoke at the sacrament meeting in the Yale Ward of the Bonneville Stake. It was his own ward and was the last of a lifetime of many speeches. On January 9, 1951, President Smith went to his office for the last time. His health had worsened, and for the last three months of his life he could direct the Church only from his home. After a noble life in the constant service of mankind, particularly in the service of the Lamanites and the youth of the Church and any person in need, he passed away at 7:27 p.m. on the evening of his eighty-first birthday, April 4, 1951, with his three children present.[41]

Under his administration the missionary work of the Church had reached its highest peak, having expanded into a number of new areas. When he became president in 1945, there were only a few hundred missionaries in the field because of World War II. Within five years there were more than 5,000. Many new stakes and wards had been created and the building program had accelerated. Over 200 meeting houses were constructed during his presidency of six years.[42] Membership had passed the 1,100,000 mark; it had passed the 1,000,000 mark during the centennial year of 1947. The prestige of the Church in the United States and other nations had reached a new high. But

522 more important, the spirit of love and unity within the Church was gratifying evidence of the love and influence of President Smith for his fellow men. President Smith had traveled over a million miles in line of duty.

On January 16, 1884, when he was a boy not yet fourteen, Patriarch Zebedee Coltrin gave him a lengthy blessing in which he said:

> . . . thou art destined to become a mighty man before the Lord, for thou shalt become a mighty apostle in the Church and kingdom of God upon the earth. . . . [43]

No truer words were ever spoken.

President George Albert Smith passed away on April 4, two days before the beginning of the annual general conference of the Church in 1951. Conference was held on Thursday, Friday, and Sunday, April 6, 7, and 9, with President Smith's funeral on Saturday, April 8. Among the speakers was Miss Irene Jones, a blind woman representing the Society for the Aid of the Sightless. President Smith's relative and good friend, Israel A. Smith, president of the Reorganized Church, came to Salt Lake City to pay his last respects to the departed President.

Footnotes

[1] Archibald F. Bennett, "Born of Goodly Parents," *Improvement Era* 53(April 1950):269.

[2] George Albert Smith, "After Eight Years," *Improvement Era* 53(April 1950):263.

[3] Smith, p. 270.

[4] Smith, p. 270.

[5] Smith, p. 270.

[6] Preston Nibley, "Sharing the Gospel with Others," *Improvement Era* 53(April 1950):311.

[7] John D. Giles, "George Albert Smith—A Prophet Goes Home," *Improvement Era* 54(May 1951):321-22, 369.

[8] Giles, p. 321-22, 369.

[9] George Albert Smith, "From a Prophet to His People," *Improvement Era* 52(April 1949):301.

[10] Giles, p. 323.

[11] D. E. Hammond and Forace Green, "President George Albert Smith—Scouter," *Improvement Era* 53(April 1950):291.

[12] Giles, pp. 323, 368.

[13] Joseph Fielding Smith, *Essentials in Church History* (22nd ed., enlarged, Salt Lake City: Deseret Book Co., 1967):534.

[14] N. B. Lundwall, *Temples of the Most High* (Salt Lake City: Bookcraft, 1966), p. 195. *See also Improvement Era*, 48(October, 1945):565.

[15] Joseph Fielding Smith, p. 535.

[16] Ezra Taft Benson, "Letter," *Improvement Era* 49(May 1946):287.

[17] Joseph Fielding Smith, p. 535.

[18] Frederick W. Babbel, "Europe's Valiant Saints Forge Ahead," *Improvement Era* 49(October 1946):622. For more detail concerning Elder Benson's mission read this article.

[19] Joseph Fielding Smith, p. 536.

[20] David O. McKay, "Honoring the Pioneers," *Improvement Era* 50(May 1947):270.

[21] McKay, pp. 270-71.

[22] Carter E. Grant, *The Kingdom of God Restored* (Salt Lake City: Deseret Book Co., 1955), p. 567.

[23] Wendell J. Ashton, "The Centennial Trek," *Improvement Era* 50(September 1947):580, 618.

[24] Personal interview with my father who was one of the trekkers.

[25] Ashton, pp. 618, 619.

[26] Ashton, p. 618.

[27] Ashton, p. 682.

[28] Ashton, p. 686.

[29] "Centennial Days," *Improvement Era* 50 (September 1947):575.

[30] John A. Widtsoe and Richard L. Evans, "The Educational Level of the Latter-day Saints," *Improvement Era* 50(July 1947):447.

[31] Widtsoe and Evans, p. 444.

[32] Widtsoe and Evans, p. 444; *See also* J. D. B. DeBow, *Statistical View of the United States* (Washington, D.C.: A.O.P. Nicholson, Public Printer, 1854), p. 152.

[33] Widtsoe and Evans, p. 445. *See also* Raymond M. Hughes and William H. Lancelot, *Education—America's Magic* (Ames: Iowa State College Press, 1946).

[34] Widtsoe and Evans, p. 446.

[35] Widtsoe and Evans, p. 446. *See also* Edward L. Thorndike, "Origin of Superior Men," *Scientific Monthly* (May 1943).

[36] Clarence S. Barker, "From the Green Hills to Statuary Hall," *Improvement Era* 53(August 1950):631.

[37] Barker, p. 631.

[38] Barker, p. 630.

[39] Grant, p. 571.

[40] Barker, p. 630.

[41] Giles, p. 321. His devoted wife had died in 1937.

[42] Doyle L. Green and Albert L. Zobell, Jr., "A Period of Progress," *Improvement Era* 53(April 1950):273.

[43] Doyle L. Green, "Tributes Paid to George Albert Smith," *Improvement Era* 54(June 1951):404-5.

24

Administration of David O. McKay

A BRIEF SKETCH OF THE LIFE
OF DAVID O. MCKAY

David Oman McKay was born on September 8, 1873, in Huntsville, Utah, to David and Jeanette Evans McKay. His paternal grandparents were converts from Scotland, and his maternal grandparents were converts from Wales. He was the third of ten children and was the oldest boy. When he was seven years old his two older sisters died within one week, one from rheumatic fever and the other from pneumonia.[1] They were buried side by side in the same grave.

The next spring David McKay, David O.'s father, received a mission call to Great Britain. Feeling that running the farm and taking care of three children with another one on the way so shortly after the death of the two oldest girls would be too great a burden for his wife, David McKay, out of great love and consideration, announced that he would ask for a postponement of the call. His wife replied: "David, you go on that mission. You go now. The Lord wants you now, not a year from now, and he will take care of me."[2] He left for his mission on April 19, 1881, and ten days later a new daughter arrived in the McKay home.

In the absence of his father young David O. McKay, the oldest child, recognized his family responsibilities and rapidly matured beyond his years.

He learned how to work hard and how to enjoy the fruits of honest toil. As he grew into the responsibilities of the Aaronic Priesthood he learned how to keep busy with useful projects in the service of others. The Aaronic Priesthood boys were organized each winter, in addition to their regular meetings and Church duties, to go into the canyons and secure firewood.

The older boys would go into the canyons and bring the logs into town, and the younger boys assumed the responsibility of sawing, splitting, and piling the wood in the sheds until the supply was sufficient to carry the family through the coldest months. They also saw to it that plenty of wood was available for the widows and the wives of those away on missions. [3]

Work in the Sunday School, College, and Missionary Labors

In addition to his regular priesthood duties David O. McKay became secretary of the Sunday School in his ward at the age of fifteen. Four years later he became a teacher in the Sunday School, a position he liked so well that he continued at it until he enrolled as a senior at the University of Utah on October 4, 1896. [4]

During his years at the university he "played piano for a dance band, played on the university football team, became president of his senior class, and was chosen by his classmates to give the major student oration at graduation of 1897." [5] Shortly before his graduation he received a mission call to the British Isles. He was set apart as a missionary on August 1, 1897, and upon his arrival in Great Britain he was assigned to missionary duties in Scotland where he spent a successful two years.

While he was in Scotland, he had the opportunity of visiting both his father's birthplace in Thurso and his mother's birthplace in Merthyr Tydfil, Wales. Before his release he received a letter offering him an appointment to the faculty at Weber Stake Academy where he began his duties in September, 1899.

In September of 1900 he became second counselor in the Weber Stake Sunday School, where he was assigned the responsibility of class work. He worked out a system of graded departments with definite courses of study in each department—an innovation at that time—and helped build a competent staff of teachers in each ward with corresponding supervisors on the stake board.[6]

Marriage and a Call to the Apostleship

The first marriage of the twentieth century in the Salt Lake Temple was that of David O. McKay and Emma Ray Riggs on January 2, 1901. This was the beginning of more than sixty-nine years together in which seven children were born and raised in an atmosphere of love, harmony, discipline, and free agency with proper parental guidance.

After two and one-half years as a teacher at Weber Stake Academy, on April 17, 1902, David O. McKay was appointed principal. He was still serving in this capacity when he was called to be a member of the Quorum of the Twelve at general conference on April 8, 1906, and was ordained and set apart the following day. Because he was in the midst of raising $60,000 by donation for an additional building for the academy, he requested permission to remain as principal until the new building was completed.[7] It was dedicated in 1908 and Elder McKay was released, but he continued to make his home in Ogden and was sustained as president of the board of trustees of the academy, in which position he remained until his call to be president of the European Mission in 1922.[8]

Upon his becoming an apostle in 1906 he was released from his duties on the Weber Stake Sunday School board, but he was not long free from his connection with the Sunday School; he was called to be second assistant to President Joseph F. Smith in the General Sunday School superintendency at conference on October 6, 1906. He became the first assistant on April 14, 1909, and on November 27, 1918, he became general superintendent, a position he held until his call to the First Presidency in 1934.[9]

A World Tour

On December 2, 1920, Elder McKay was set apart to tour the missions and schools of the Church with Elder Hugh J. Cannon, editor of *The Improvement Era,* as his companion. They left

528 two days later and did not return until December 24, 1921, having traveled 24,277 miles by land and 32,819 miles by water.[10] They had visited all missions of the Church except South Africa.[11]

European Mission President

Late in 1922 when Elder McKay was called to succeed Elder Orson F. Whitney as president of the European Mission, his six living children were sorrowful to see the family home in Ogden sold where they had been born and where they had spent such a happy childhood.[12]

Perhaps his two most important accomplishments in the mission field were his encouraging British newspapers not to publish derogatory stories about the Church and his "extending the assignment of missionary work to members of the Church as well as the full-time missionaries."[13]

DAVID O. MCKAY BECOMES PRESIDENT

On October 6, 1934, Elder McKay became second counselor to President Heber J. Grant, a position he held until President Grant's death in 1945, after which he held the same position under President George Albert Smith until President Smith's death.

Forty-five years to the day from the time he was ordained to the apostleship David Oman McKay was sustained as the ninth President of the Church of Jesus Christ of Latter-day Saints on Sunday, April 9, 1951. He chose Elder Stephen L Richards as first counselor and J. Reuben Clark, Jr. as second counselor.

Administration of President McKay

President McKay took over leadership of the Church when the nations of the world as well as the Church were going through a period of tremendous change. Colonialism was losing its hold and new nations were being created. Although the Soviet Union and her allies had concluded World War II only a few years before, the Communists were relentlessly pushing their atheistic influence into new sections of the world, ever advancing their cause of eventual world domination. For a few years World War II caused many people to draw closer to God, including many Latter-day Saints. Memberships of churches in the United States increased in population 34% between 1940 and 1950 with a corresponding population increase in the world of only 15%. At the end of 1951 religious congregations in the United States had a total membership of 88,673,005 persons, which was 58% of the population as compared to 49% in 1940 and 47% in 1930. By 1960, 64% of the nation's population had become church members. This percentage remained constant through 1964 but has now, in 1972, dropped to 62%.[14] Although church membership had steadily increased throughout the nation's history it has never risen so rapidly as it did during the 1940s, at which time it grew by 22,000,000 as compared with only 5,000,000 during the 1930s. At the end of 1951 Protestant denominations had more than 52,000,000 members, Roman Catholics over 29,000,000, with Jewish congregations listing 5,000,000 members. The Protestants and Catholics had maintained "about the same relation to each other for more than fifty years."[15]

Of statistics gathered from 252 religious bodies in the United States, seventeen were listed with a membership of over 1,000,000. The Church of Jesus Christ of Latter-day Saints was listed as fifteenth in size with a membership of 1,111,314 at the end of 1951.[16] By 1970 the Mormon Church ranked thirteenth.[17]

Many members of the Church who had been uprooted throughout World War II were still on the move or were driving their roots ever deeper in new areas, and, like the early Christians who were scattered because of persecution in Jerusalem and Palestine, they took their religion with them wherever they went. This scattering of Church members created a need for organizing many branches of the Church in new areas and for providing more leadership in established branches, creating in turn new opportunities for missionaries in expanding and growing programs. President McKay was quick to grasp the significance of the situation and organized new missions, wards, and stakes throughout the world as fast as sufficiently worthy members with leadership qualities were available.

Overall, President McKay's administration was marked with growth, progress, change, expansion, and a rededication to the principles of the gospel by many of the members of the Church.

Primary Children's Hospital

One day in 1911 Louie B. Felt and May Anderson of the general presidency of the Primary were walking along a street in Salt Lake City when they saw a crippled little boy. The thought came to them: "Why can't we do something to help children

530 such as he?" [18] This was the beginning of the project for building the Primary Children's Hospital. Forty-one years later on Sunday, March 2, 1952, President McKay dedicated the new hospital building which had cost $1,256,193 and which had been raised under the auspices of president LaVern W. Parmley and vice-president Francis G. Bennett of the board of trustees of the hospital. Varied methods had been used to encourage members to contribute to the hospital fund, but over the years a major method of financial support for operating the hospital had come from encouraging each primary child to donate a penny for each year of his age on his birthday. This was expanded to include every member of the Church, who was encouraged to donate one cent for each year of his age. [19]

The purpose of the hospital is to help correct maladies and deformities of children. Parents of children who are able to pay make a contribution, but if they are unable to do so, all young children who need the assistance of the hospital are welcome.

Monument to Joseph Standing

On May 3, 1952, President McKay was at Varnell Station near Dalton, Georgia, where he dedicated a monument and park to the memory of Joseph Standing, who had been killed on that spot by a mob on July 21, 1879. That the old feelings of hatred for the Mormons were gone was evidenced by the widespread interest in the establishment of the park and monument to Elder Standing's memory and the fact that W. C. Puryear and the family of Dalton had donated the land to the Church. The park is 402 feet long and 78 feet wide and includes the monument with the spring near the center of the park from which Elder Standing had taken a drink shortly before he was shot. It is located at the side of a road with parking area in one end, a small seating capacity in the middle, and an open picnic area near the other end which has been beautified with a wooded area. The plaque on the monument states in part:

This memorial park and monument honor the memory of Elder Joseph Standing of Salt Lake City, Utah, a missionary of the Church of Jesus Christ of Latter-day Saints (Mormon), who was killed here by a mob July 21, 1879. His companion, Elder Rudger Clawson, who later became President of the Council of the Twelve Apostles of the Church, was unharmed. [20]

During the summer of 1952 President McKay made a memorable two-month trip to Europe. It was only the third time that a president of the Church had visited Europe. President Joseph F. Smith had visited in 1906 and President Heber J. Grant in 1937, although all presidents of the Church, except the Prophet Joseph Smith, had labored in Europe while they were members of the Council of the Twelve.[21] With his wife and party President McKay flew across the Atlantic Ocean on June 1 to Europe, where for the next fifty days he visited ten missions and nine countries, addressed forty-five meetings, dedicated five chapels, selected a temple site near Berne, Switzerland, "held numerous conferences with mission presidents; visited with Queen Juliana of the Netherlands, the President of Finland, and several American ambassadors; and attended a royal garden party given at Buckingham Palace by Queen Elizabeth II of Great Britain."[22]

While in Paris, France, President McKay had mentioned that "the main purpose of [my] trip [is] to investigate the possibility of setting up chapels throughout Europe—to encourage Church members to remain at home and not to emigrate to America."[23] His trip typified the growth and expansion of the Church that had begun after World War II and would continue throughout his administration. He brought great spiritual comfort and inspiration to the Saints who were living in a still troubled Europe.

President McKay found the Saints in Europe "yearning for something real and spiritually uplifting...."[24] They were growing in spirituality as evidenced by stronger leadership; the European Saints were assuming more and more responsibility. Growth and progress were evident in each mission, especially in Finland, the newest of the missions. He found a great need for more missionaries. He also found that Latter-day Saint servicemen in Europe were extremely active in the Church and often exhibited the same zeal as missionaries, attracting attention among their associates through their exemplary lives and being ever ready to explain the gospel message to them. The wall of prejudice against the Mormons was being broken down. Perhaps one reason for this was the vast improvement in meeting places over what they had been when President McKay had been the European Mission president twenty-nine years before. For example, in Great Britain the Church now had twenty-three

532   meeting houses of its own and had even acquired a number of chapels in Finland.[25]

Through the cooperation of the American radio station RIAS in Berlin President McKay sent greetings and blessings to the 8,500 members of the Church in the Soviet zone of Germany.[26] With his party, President McKay returned to Salt Lake City on July 26, 1952, where they were greeted by hundreds of friends and admirers. President McKay's trip to Europe was considered the top news story of the Church in 1952. Other top stories concerned President McKay's announcement that a temple would be built in Switzerland; actual work of building the Los Angeles temple which was commenced in August; the death of two apostles, Elder Joseph F. Merrill and Elder John A. Widtsoe; appointments of LeGrand Richards to the Quorum of the Twelve and Joseph L. Wirthlin as Presiding Bishop with Thorpe B. Isaacson and Carl W. Buehner as counselors; dedication of the monument and memorial park to Joseph Standing; dedication of the Primary Children's Hospital; creation of eleven new stakes and one mission (Central America); dedication of 135 new chapels during the year; appointment of Elder Ezra Taft Benson to President Eisenhower's cabinet; and the unusual growth of the Church due to the adoption of a newly introduced program of proselyting that had proven successful in California.[27]

A Much-Traveled President

Again in August, 1953, President McKay and his party began another tour that took them to Berne, Switzerland, and New Chapel, County Surrey, in England to dedicate temple sites. Then followed a 37,000-mile tour of Europe, South Africa—he was the first president to do so—and Latin America.[28] In early 1955 he toured all of the Pacific Islands including New Zealand and Australia, after which he recommended that a temple be built in Hamilton, New Zealand, near the site of the Church college, to serve the Saints in the South Pacific.[29] In August and September he made another trip to Europe at the time the Tabernacle Choir was also touring there. At this time the temple in Switzerland was officially dedicated and opened, and the ground-breaking ceremony for the temple in England was held.[30]

The traveling of the President and other General Authorities to the missions of the world and the beginning of temple build-

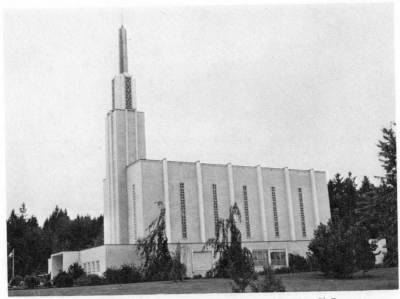

Temple near Berne, Switzerland. *Courtesy of LaMar C. Berrett.*

ing in distant lands did much toward encouraging the Saints to remain in their native lands where they could build up and strengthen the missions, wards, and branches of the kingdom of God. Thus the Church began to take on a world outlook and to assume its role of uniting the children of God into one great brotherhood in Christ.

Further Temple Dedications

On March 11, 1956, President David O. McKay dedicated the Los Angeles Temple. The land had been purchased in 1937 under President Grant, but ground-breaking ceremonies did not take place until September 22, 1951, when they were conducted by President McKay. This temple is the largest one yet built in this dispensation, containing ninety rooms. The spire, topped with the statue of the Angel Moroni, towers 257 feet. It is visible to ships twenty-five miles at sea. The assembly room on the third floor will accommodate 2,600 people. Prior to the dedication it had been open to the public for viewing for nearly two months from December 1955 to February 18, 1956, during which time 682,361 people, both Mormon and non-Mormon, went through the sacred structure. The dedicatory services, beginning on March 11, were conducted in the assembly room

Temple at Los Angeles, California. *Permission of Church Information Service.*

but with closed circuit television to other rooms; 6,700 people were privileged to view the presentation. Before the services were over, more than 50,000 people had attended the various sessions. At the opening session every General Authority of the Church except one—who was absent due to the illness of his wife—was in attendance. President McKay gave a beautiful dedicatory prayer.[31]

On April 20, 1958, a little more than two years later, the New Zealand Temple was also dedicated by President David O. McKay. On the same visit he dedicated the Church College of New Zealand. He followed this by dedicating the temple in Great Britain, twenty-six miles from London at Newchapel Farm, Lingfield, England, on Sunday, September 7, 1958, with services repeated on September 8 and 9. While he was in London for the dedication, President McKay observed his 85th birthday on September 8.

Within a span of five years President McKay had dedicated four temples in four different parts of the world: Switzerland, Los Angeles, New Zealand, and London. Surely the building of these temples to serve the membership of the Church was evidence that the Church was not just a small Christian sect in the western United States but a universal Church of Jesus Christ,

Temple at New Zealand. *Permission of Church Information Service.*

Temple at London, England. *Permission of Church Information Service.*

Temple at Oakland, California.

taking its message and service to all the children of God, fulfilling the responsibility of its mission as given by the Lord to take the message to every nation, kindred, tongue and people.

The Oakland Temple in Oakland, California, dedicated on November 17, 18, and 19 in 1964, was the last of five temples to be dedicated by President McKay. Although he had been ill a short time previously, he spoke and gave the dedicatory prayer at all six sessions. These sessions seemed to infuse him with new strength, and he continued for some time to improve in health as he exerted vigorous leadership of the Church.[32]

Ground-breaking ceremonies for the building of two more temples in Utah, one at Ogden—on September 8, 1969—and one at Provo—on September 15, 1969—had also taken place before the death of President McKay. In addition a fifty-seven acre site had been selected at Silver Spring, Maryland, near Washington, D.C., upon which to build a temple for the benefit of Church members in the eastern sector of the United States and Canada.

Priesthood and Church Correlation

President Brigham Young began to work on what might be termed Church correlation as early as 1877, although he did not use that term.[33] It has ever since been a subject of deep interest to the Church, especially since Church growth has been rather

constant and steady, and spontaneous innovations are sometimes added as needed but are not always completely correlated
into the existing structural setup of the Church. It is and will be
a continuous process to try to correlate Church activities from
time to time in order to get the greatest efficiency in finances,
in spiritual advancement, in church activity, and in every aspect
of life connected with God's plan of salvation.

At April Conference in 1908 the First Presidency gave instructions relating to correlation which resulted in the Presiding
Bishopric's writing them a letter recommending the appointment of a committee to look into the work and duties of the
lesser priesthood. They suggested the appointment of Joseph B.
Keeler, David O. McKay, Stephen L Richards, Nephi Anderson,
and David O. Willey, Jr. [34] The First Presidency added the name
of Rudger Clawson and made the suggested appointments,
assigning to the committee the additional duty of preparing
outlines for the high priests and elders quorums. [35] This committee was to assist the Presiding Bishopric in preparing study
materials. Elder Clawson became chairman of the committee,
and David A. Smith was elected secretary.

In 1914 the First Presidency appointed a committee known
as the Correlation Committee, whose principal duty was to consider courses of study for the auxiliaries and avoid duplications
with other organizations of the Church. [36] This was the first
time the word *correlation* was used to define the desires of the
General Authorities along the lines of unification and centraliza-
tion.

On March 24, 1960, the First Presidency wrote to the General Priesthood Committee that they had over the years felt the
need of a correlation between and among the courses of study
put out by the General Priesthood Committee and other committees of the Church. They also felt a "very urgent need of a
correlation of studies among the auxiliaries of the Church." [37]
The General Priesthood Committee began an exhaustive study,
cooperating with auxiliaries of the Church to determine results
of coordinating the programs of the priesthood and the auxiliaries so that duplication and overlapping could be minimized.

Priesthood correlation involves the carrying out of Church
activities by individual members of the families, who are
presided over by the parents, who are presided over by priesthood leaders, who in turn are presided over by stake presidents,
who are presided over by Regional Representatives and the
General Authorities.

On September 30, 1961, in the priesthood session of conference President McKay introduced Elder Harold B. Lee, chairman of the Melchizedek Priesthood Committee, and said that he would give a message on the correlation of studies by the two priesthoods and auxiliaries.[38] Elder Lee informed the priesthood members that each organization would have its specific function and that each subdivision was of equal importance and would function with its specific duties so that as each part of the human body was necessary to make the body function properly, so also would the Church function as a perfectly organized human body.[39]

Elder Lee also explained that correlation meant to place the priesthood of God at the center and core of the Church and kingdom of God and to see that Latter-day Saint homes have their place in the divine plan of saving souls, for no other instrumentality could take the place of the home or fulfill its essential functions. He further confided that it was the feeling of the First Presidency and Council of the Twelve that there should be more coordination and correlation between the activities and programs of the priesthood quorums, auxiliary organizations, and the educational system of the Church than presently existed—that the members could "hopefully look forward to the consolidation and simplification of Church curricula, Church publications, church buildings, church meetings, and many other important aspects of the Lord's work."[40]

The Organization

Elder Lee further stated that after 1½ years of study by the Educational Committee—a sub-committee of the General Priesthood Committee—the First Presidency and Council of the Twelve had decided to establish an all-Church coordinating council and three coordinating committees; one for the children, one for the youth, and one for adults. The council and committees would coordinate the total instructional and activity programs of all auxiliaries and priesthood quorums which should include missionary instructions and activities for the entire Church.[41]

The Church leaders later appointed the councils and committees as outlined by Elder Lee in his conference talk. Functioning under the direction of the First Presidency and the

Twelve, the coordinating council would have one of the apostles as chairman, and the three apostles who were to be chairmen of the various coordinating committees were also to be members of the council, along with the Presiding Bishop, executives of the auxiliaries and other Church organizations, and the four correlation secretaries. The four apostles—others were later added—were to act as the executive committee. The function of the all-Church coordinating council would be to "formulate policy which will govern the planning, the writing, coordination, and implementation of the entire Church curriculum."[42]

Elder Harold B. Lee became chairman of the coordinating council, with Elder Marion G. Romney chairman of the Adult Committee, Elder Richard L. Evans chairman of the Youth Committee, and Elder Gordon B. Hinckley chairman of the Children's Committee. The four persons who had assisted with the original study became executive secretaries of the various groups. Other members were called to serve with the executive planning groups. Next, twenty-five more individuals were called to form task committees, whose assignment was to review curricula and recommend new courses if needed.

The general boards and auxiliaries have the responsibility of carrying out the program developed by the correlation committees. In early 1970 the chairmen of the three age-group committees were made advisors to the auxiliaries serving their age-group levels.

Priesthood Committees

In 1963 four priesthood-centered committees were announced. These were: (1) the Home Teaching Committee, (2) the Missionary Committee, (3) the Priesthood Genealogy Committee, and (4) the Priesthood Welfare Committee. An apostle was appointed chairman of each of the first three committees and each was appointed a member of the Correlation Executive Committee. The Presiding Bishop of the Church was appointed chairman of the Welfare Committee.

On January 1, 1964, "home teaching" replaced "ward teaching." This had been preceded by a series of orientation lessons during the last three priesthood meetings in 1963. Home teaching gave to the "home teacher" more responsibility than simply presenting a lesson each month. It became the instrument by which the priesthood was to see that every program in the Church was "made available to parents and their children."[43] It

540 also emphasized that every family head was responsible for the spiritual welfare of his family. It was to be supervised by quorum or group leaders; that is, the leaders of the elders were responsible to see that the elders' families were properly looked after, and so on. Each month the home teachers reported directly to their quorum or group leaders, giving not only a written report but also an oral evaluation.

The ward home teaching committee was made up of the bishopric, the three Melchizedek Priesthood leaders and the priesthood executive secretary, and it soon became the priesthood executive committee. This group, along with leaders of the auxiliaries, became the ward council. Like the ward council, the stake executive committee and the heads of the auxiliaries formed the stake council which correlated all stake programs under the direction of the stake presidency. In the wards, responsibility for welfare was given to the elders, missionary work to the seventies, and genealogy and temple work to the high priests.[44]

A youth executive committee and a youth council have been formulated. The youth executive committee consists of the bishopric plus a priest as youth executive secretary and the president of the Laurel class as assistant. They prepare the agenda for the youth council which consists of the executive committee plus the presidencies of the Aaronic Priesthood quorums and of the officers of MIA classes of corresponding ages for girls.[45] One of the important activities of the youth council is that of helping the young people of the ward to interest their friends in the principles of the gospel. The young people often do this through the recreational, educational, and cultural programs of the Church.

Priesthood Regions and Appointment of Regional Representatives

The geographical regions of the Church known as Welfare Regions were made to serve an expanded purpose and a total of sixty Priesthood Regions came into being as of January 1, 1964. One of the stake presidents in the region was named chairman for each of the priesthood programs. Because of needs of the growing Church the First Presidency recommended the appointment of Regional Representatives at the October Conference of 1967. These men would not be General Authorities. The names of sixty-nine men were read and approved at the second session of the conference. The duties of these men would be whatever was assigned them by the General Authorities but they were immediately assigned the duty of conducting two regional conferences each year in which stake and ward leaders were to be instructed in the various programs of the Church. The general priesthood committees were to provide the instruction at these regional meetings. The new Regional Representatives began their assignments on January 1, 1968.

Additional Areas Correlated

In 1969 other Church areas were correlated under the direction of the Church Correlation Committee. A Church Library Coordinating Committee was organized with Earl E. Olsen, Assistant Church Historian, as chairman. Their duties were to correlate "all library activities and procedures of the Church." [46] The former Servicemen's Committee became the Military Relations Committee, with expanded duties bringing all activities concerning Church members in the military service under the priesthood with Elder Harold B. Lee as chairman and Elder Boyd K. Packer as Managing Director.

The Unified Social Services Committee was formulated and organized by bringing together three other Church programs performing social service functions. These were the Indian Placement Bureau, Youth Guidance, and the Relief Society Social Services. Elder Marion G. Romney became chairman of this new committee, and Elder Marvin J. Ashton, newly appointed Assistant to the Quorum of the Twelve, became managing director. The Music Committee was also reorganized and put directly under the priesthood with Elder Mark E. Petersen as chairman. The committee's purpose is to implement a unified Church music program, to provide technical help where necessary, and to encourage musical excellence.

Church Correlation a Permanent Part of Church Structure

The present outlook is that the Church will continue to grow at a rather constant rate which means that the leaders must ever be on the alert to see that the greatest efficiency possible is maintained in its structure. Thus from time to time it will be necessary to innovate further correlation procedures. These procedures may be given to the leaders either through inspiration or revelation as the Lord sees fit.

President McKay's emphasis upon the family as the basic organization of both church and country brought new strength into Latter-day Saint homes at a time in the United States when family unity was faltering because of divergent interests of family members with nothing in particular to draw them together, with working mothers losing their influence through absence from the home, and with the general attitude sweeping the country that young people should have the right to do as they please. He said that no other success can compensate for failure in the home. His innovation of a regular family home evening is a feature in placing the responsibility of properly instructing the children upon the heads of the parents. This was not entirely new, for the Church leaders had introduced such a program as early as 1915 when the First Presidency declared: "If the Saints obey this council, we promise that great blessings will result. Love at home and obedience to parents will increase. Faith will be developed in the hearts of the youth of Israel, and they will gain power to combat evil influences and temptations which beset them."[47]

A manual of study for home evenings was written to assist the parents in teaching their children, and family home evenings officially began again as of January 1, 1965. Each year since, the Church has provided a new manual. For those families who hold their regular home evenings, it is a great aid to the parents in carrying out their responsibilities as given in the Doctrine and Covenants:

> And again, inasmuch as parents have children in Zion, or in any of her stakes which are organized, that teach them not to understand the doctrine of repentance, faith in Christ the Son of the living God, and of baptism and the gift of the Holy Ghost by the laying on of hands, when eight years old, the sin be upon the heads of the parents.
>
> And they shall also teach their children to pray, and to walk uprightly before the Lord. (D&C 68:25, 28.)

Accelerated Increase in Membership

At the end of the year 1965 Church membership had increased from 1,111,314 in 1951 to 2,395,932. The number of stakes had increased from 175 to 414, and the number of full-time missions had grown from 43 to 74. During this same period 1,960 chapels and 5 temples had been constructed.[48] At the close of 1969 the Church reached 2,807,456 members. In 1950 the number of convert baptisms was 14,700 by 5,313 missionaries, while in 1969 it had risen to 70,010 with 12,689 missionaries in the field at the beginning of 1970.[49]

Much of the Church's growth had come about because of a great increase in the number of missionaries, innovations in methods of reaching people, and the introduction by President McKay in April, 1959, of the "every member a missionary" program. This was a program in which every member of the Church would assume the responsibility of spreading the gospel message to his friends, neighbors, associates and acquaintances through asking the "golden questions": "What do you know about the Mormons?" and "Would you like to know more?" The names of those who expressed an interest were given to missionaries who would present to them the gospel message; whereas those who were not interested were not to be annoyed, for it was not the intention of Church leaders to force the gospel upon anyone. Also to aid the missionary effort, families often assumed the responsibility of inviting small groups of their friends and neighbors into their homes where the elders could give them the message of the gospel in a brief but concise set of lessons (usually six) containing the basic fundamentals of the gospel. The effect of this every-member-a-missionary program took a few months, but by 1960 there were 48,586 convert baptisms as compared to 33,060 in 1959.[50]

In the fall quarter of 1951 Brigham Young University had 5,086 full-time daytime students; in the fall of 1969 it had 24,144 with eighty major buildings having been erected between those two dates. During those years Church colleges in Hawaii and New Zealand had been opened, five schools were opened in Santiago, Chile; thirty-six elementary and two high schools were opened in Mexico, and others were completed in Pago Pago, American Samoa, and Tahiti. Ricks College had an expanded enrollment in 1969 of 4,500 and had also erected many new buildings.[51]

The Church Continues to Create a More Favorable Attitude

Throughout the administration of President McKay his popular leadership continued to create favorable attitudes toward the Church from the gentile world in contrast to the

544 attitudes of people toward the Church during the latter part of the 19th and first part of the 20th centuries which were characterized by bitter anti-Mormon feelings. This change in attitude is illustrated in the fact that Protestant, Catholic, and Jewish business and professional men took the initiative in uniting with Latter-day Saint business and professional men in Utah to pay a community tribute of appreciation to President McKay on December 10, 1962, the beginning of his 90th year, by sponsoring a testimonial dinner in his honor at the Hotel Utah. More than 460 prominent men of Utah—mostly non-Mormon—met on that evening and paid great tribute to him for his Christlike service to his church, his country and his fellow men.[52]

Another interesting item illustrating the ever more favorable attitude toward the Latter-day Saints pertains to the increasing number of Church men and women in important governmental positions. Prior to 1930 this kind of participation would probably have been political suicide to any administration. More than 1,500 distinguished men and women from all over the world called on President McKay during his administration, including four presidents of the United States: Harry S. Truman, Dwight D. Eisenhower, John F. Kennedy, and Lyndon B. Johnson.[53]

Expansion of Chapel Construction

Church building construction during President McKay's administration was a continuously expanding process. Typical of the times was the announcement he made while he was in Great Britain in 1963 to dedicate a chapel at Merthyr Tidfil, Wales, his mother's birthplace. He declared that in the British Mission forty-six chapels were under construction, and thirty-six more would be started before the end of the year, with the local Saints raising 20% of the cost of construction.[54] At the time of his death more than 60% of all chapels and other buildings of the Church had been built during his administration.

World's Fair Exhibits

New York City was to sponsor a World's Fair in the years 1964 and 1965, and the Church, along with other religious denominations, was offered the opportunity of setting up an exhibit. The Church leaders decided to build a building in which a display explained by missionaries would give the visitors an

opportunity to hear the Gospel message. The theme of the exhibit was "man's search for happiness," and a fifteen-minute
film by this title was shown in each of the two small theaters.
As the visitors passed through they could sign one of the fifteen
or twenty registers and make comments. From these books the
missionaries received thousands of referrals. The effects were
immediate; people from all over the world were attracted by the
gospel message. Elder Bernard P. Brockbank, the supervisor of
the pavilion, was of the opinion the exhibit could eventually
result in as many as fifty thousand baptisms.[55]

On the whole the exhibit was so highly successful that the
Church has set up many other such exhibits, including one at
the Hemisfair in San Antonio, Texas, in 1968 and another at
the World's Fair in Osaka, Japan, in 1970. Each proved to be
highly successful, although the exhibit in Texas was on a much
smaller scale than the others. The Church also began to em-
phasize the gospel message more at a number of Church information centers, such as on Temple Square, the Joseph Smith
Memorial Farm, Liberty Jail, Independence, Missouri, and
Nauvoo, Illinois, where ground breaking for a new center was
held May 31, 1969.

DEATH OF PRESIDENT MCKAY

After more than sixty-three and one-half years as a General
Authority and eighteen and one-half years as President of the
Church, President McKay passed away on January 18, 1970, at
the age of ninety-six. He was beloved by both Mormon and
gentile. His body lay in state in the Church Office Building for
three days, where devoted friends and members of the Church
by the thousands paid their respects to him. His funeral was
conducted in the Tabernacle by his former first counselor Elder
Hugh B. Brown. Speakers included Elder Brown, President
Joseph Fielding Smith, Elder Nathan Eldon Tanner, and Elder
Harold B. Lee. The Tabernacle Choir sang four songs. President
McKay's body was laid to rest in the Salt Lake City
Cemetery.[56]

In his eulogy at the funeral of President McKay, President
Nathan Eldon Tanner summed up his accomplishments.

Under his leadership the Church has enjoyed unprec-
edented physical and spiritual growth. The missionary
program has made greater progress, and we have seen more

David O. McKay, ninth president of The Church of Jesus Christ of Latter-day Saints. *Courtesy of LaMar C. Berrett.*

temple building than ever before. Priesthood programs and activity have been greatly enlarged, a successful correlation program inaugurated, and Regional Representatives of the Twelve have been called to assist in furthering the Church's worldwide program. In response to a growing need for an answer to some of the social problems confronting us, there has been greater emphasis on the importance of the home and family relationships than at any other time.[57]

President Lee mentioned that as President McKay sensed the decline in family home life in the United States and other nations "he directed the establishment of a church-wide family home evening program" which was an activity designed to draw parents and children together.[58] Its purpose is also to unify the family in learning and living the gospel of Jesus Christ. As President McKay declared, "What you think of Christ will determine in large measure what you are."[59]

On the occasion of President McKay's ninetieth birthday celebration, held a few days prior to his birthday on Sunday, September 8, 1963, in the Church Office Building and sponsored by the General Authorities, Elder Harold B. Lee said: "If I were an artist and had to paint a picture of a prophet I could find no better example to stand for all those past and present than President David O. McKay."[60] This is also the sentiment of many nonmembers as well as many members of the Church.

Footnotes

[1]Llewellyn R. McKay, *Home Memories of President David O. McKay* (Salt Lake City: Deseret Book Co., 1956), p. 5.

[2]Thomas E. McKay, "An Important Decision," *Improvement Era* 55(June 1952):419.

[3]Jeanette McKay Morrell, *Highlights in the Life of President David O. McKay* (Salt Lake City: Deseret Book Co., 1966), p. 17.

[4]Llewellyn McKay, p. 7.

[5]Seminaries and Institutes of Religion, *Church History and Doctrine Student Supplement* (Provo, Utah: Brigham Young University Press, 1966), p. 88.

[6]Morrell, p. 39.

[7]Morrell, p. 54.

[8]Morrell, pp. 54-56.

[9]Morrell, pp. 62-63.

[10]Morrell, p. 66.

[11]Llewellyn McKay, p. 31.

[12]Llewellyn McKay, p. 32.

[13]Morrell, p. 74.

548   [14]Milton V. Backman, Jr., *American Religions and the Rise of Mormonism* (Salt Lake City: Deseret Book Co., 1965), p. 422.

[15]Dr. Benson Y. Landis, "Membership in Churches in U.S. Gains 34% in Ten Years," *Church News*, 27 September 1952, p. 7.

[16]Landis, p. 7.

[17]Milton V. Backman, Jr., personal interview April 11, 1972. Dr. Backman is an authority on American religions.

[18]David O. McKay, "Church Head Commends Many Contributors to New Primary Hospital," *Church News*, 5 March 1952, p. 3.

[19]In later years this has been raised to a suggestion of a minimum of two cents per year for each year of a person's age.

[20]Henry A. Smith, "Joseph Standing Memorial Park Will Honor Martyred Missionary," *Church News*, 30 April 1952, p. 8.

[21]Doyle L. Green and Albert L. Zobell, Jr., "President David O. McKay Visits Europe," *Improvement Era* 55(September 1952):632.

[22]Green and Zobell, p. 632.

[23]Morrell, p. 121.

[24]Green and Zobell, p. 633.

[25]Green and Zobell, pp. 633-34.

[26]Green and Zobell, p. 634.

[27]"Church in Review in '52" *Church News*, 27 December 1952, pp. 1, 8, 9.

[28]Llewellyn McKay, pp. 34-35.

[29]Morrell, p. 192.

[30]Llewellyn McKay, p. 35.

[31]Morrell, pp. 163-71.

[32]Morrell, pp. 273-78.

[33]Interview with Lauritz Peterson of the Church Historical Department, 14 September 1970. *See also* James R. Clark, *Messages of the First Presidency* (Salt Lake City: Bookcraft, 1965), 2:284.

[34]Letter of Presiding Bishopric to the First Presidency, 8 April 1908.

[35]Letter of First Presidency to Presiding Bishopric, 8 April 1908.

[36]Letter of David O. McKay to Rudger Clawson, 6 August 1914.

[37]Richard O. Cowan, "A Review of Priesthood Correlation in the 1960s" (n.p., n.d.), p. 1. Appreciation is expressed to Dr. Richard Cowan, professor of religion at Brigham Young University, for his collection of statements and thoughts of the General Authorities on priesthood correlation.

[38]*Conference Report of the Church of Jesus Christ of Latter-day Saints* (Salt Lake City: Church of Jesus Christ of Latter-day Saints, October 1961), p. 77. Hereafter cited as *CR*.

[39]*CR*, October 1961, p. 77.

[40]*CR*, October 1961, pp. 77-79.

[41]*CR*, October 1961, pp. 79-80.

[42]Cowan, p. 4.

[43]First Presidency Letter (27 April 1915), as cited in Cowan, p. 8, and *CR* (October 1964), pp. 83, 84.

[44]*General Handbook of Instruction*, (Salt Lake City: Church of Jesus Christ of Latter-day Saints) no. 20, 1968, p. 15.

[45]Stephen W. Gibson, "New Bishop's Youth Council," *Church News*, 3 May 1969, p. 4.

46*Church News*, 11 January 1969, p. 4.

47First Presidency Letter (26 April 1915), as cited in Cowan, p. 8. *See also CR*, (October 1964), pp. 83-84.

48Morrell, p. 296.

49*Church News*, 24 January 1970, p. 11, and 11 April 1970, p. 17.

50Church statistics in Church Historical Department.

51*Church News*, 24 January 1970, p. 11.

52Morrell, pp. 220-51.

53Morrell, p. 298.

54Morrell, p. 257.

55Personal interview, 25 July 1964.

56*Church News*, 24 January 1970, p. 4.

57Nathan Eldon Tanner, *Church News*, 24 January 1970, p. 14.

58Harold B. Lee, *Church News*, 24 January 1970, p. 15.

59Lee, p. 15.

60Morrell, p. 260.

25

Administration of Joseph Fielding Smith

A BRIEF SKETCH OF THE LIFE OF
JOSEPH FIELDING SMITH

Elder Joseph Fielding Smith became the tenth President of the Church on January 23, 1970, in his ninety-fourth year after having served nearly sixty years as a member of the Council of the Twelve. He was sustained by vote of the solemn assembly at the general conference of the Church on April 6, 1970. He is the son of Joseph F. Smith, the sixth President of the Church, who was the son of Mary Fielding and Hyrum Smith, the Patriarch, brother of Joseph the Prophet. He was born in the family home on Second West Street in Salt Lake City on July 19, 1876, to Julina Lambson and was the tenth child of his father and the fourth child and first son of his mother. Later thirty-three more children by natural birth and five more by adoption were added to the family. Although he was born into a large polygynous family where the necessities of life were difficult to obtain, there was plenty of love and harmony in the family, and Joseph Fielding's grandson was later to write: "He was to be amply blessed with all the things that money cannot buy, though with few that it can. He would not be encumbered with the distractions of ease and comfort."[1]

In order to bolster the family budget Joseph Fielding's mother became a midwife, delivering over a thousand babies

551

552 without losing a mother or a baby. Young Joseph often drove his mother to the home of the expectant mother where he would sit in the buggy and wait, wondering why babies were so often born in the middle of the night.[2] He grew up with plenty of work to do because his father had a family farm in Taylorsville near the Jordan River where the boys were expected to work. He also had his chores to do around the house, and when two of his older sisters went east to school he took over the job of making the bread, which he would mix at night and put in pans the next morning.[3]

Joseph Fielding was more studious than his brothers. Often when they would go fishing or hunting he would stay at home with his books. He would usually try to get his chores done quickly so that he could spend time studying in his father's library. Studying the standard works was one of his favorite ways of spending time.

A Patriarchal Blessing

When Joseph Fielding was twenty years old he received a patriarchal blessing from his uncle John Smith, the presiding Patriarch of the Church and the half brother of his father. This blessing was somewhat of a foreshadowing of Joseph Fielding's future.

It is thy privilege to live to a good old age and the will of the Lord that you should become a mighty man in Israel. . . . Thou shalt realize also that thou hast much to do in order to complete thy mission upon the earth. It shall be thy duty to sit in counsel with thy brethren and to preside among the people. It shall be thy duty also to travel much at home and abroad by land and water, laboring in the ministry, and I say unto thee, hold up thy head, lift up thy voice without fear or favor as the Spirit of the Lord shall direct, and the blessing of the Lord shall rest upon thee. His spirit shall direct thy mind and give thee word and sentiment that thou shalt confound the wisdom of the wicked and set at nought the councils of the unjust.[4]

The sermons of Joseph Fielding are evidence that he was mindful of the counsel given to him in this blessing.

Louie Shurtliff, the daughter of a close friend of President Joseph F. Smith—Louis W. Shurtliff, president of Weber Stake—moved in with the family of President Joseph F. Smith in order that she might attend the University of Utah (which was then a few minutes' walk from the Smith home on Second West Street). It was not long before young Joseph Fielding fell in love with her, and they were married on April 26, 1898.

One year later Joseph Fielding was called on a mission to Great Britain. After his return it was more than another year before their first child was born, a daughter, Josephine. More than three years later, a second daughter, Julina, blessed their home. Louie did not survive her third pregnancy; she died of "pernicious vomiting due to pregnancy" on March 30, 1908, after ten years of marriage.

President Joseph F. Smith counseled his son to find another wife who would be a mother to his little girls, and on November 2, 1908, Joseph Fielding and Ethel Reynolds were sealed in marriage. Ethel was not only a devoted mother to Joseph's two daughters but bore him four daughters and five sons of her own. Like his first marriage, Joseph Fielding's second was a successful and happy one, as he was always a devoted husband and father. Perhaps no greater tribute could be paid to a husband by his wife than was paid to Joseph Fielding by Ethel after nearly twenty-four years of marriage when, in addition to other praiseworthy statements, she wrote:

> The man I know is a kind, loving husband and father whose greatest ambition in life is to make his family happy, entirely forgetful of self in his efforts to do this. He is the man who lulls to sleep the fretful child, who tells bedtime stories to the little ones, who is never too tired or too busy to sit up late at night or to get up early in the morning to help the other children solve perplexing school problems. When illness comes the man I know watches tenderly over the afflicted one and waits upon him. . . .
>
> The man I know is most gentle. . . . He welcomes gladly the young people to his home. . . . He enjoys a good story and is quick to see the humor of a situation. . . .
>
> The man I know is unselfish, uncomplaining, considerate, thoughtful, sympathetic, doing everything within his power to make life a supreme joy for his loved ones.[5]

But Joseph Fielding was again not to escape sorrow as his wife Ethel passed away in 1937 after twenty-nine years of blissful marriage. The following year on April 12, 1938, Joseph married Jessie Ella Evans, who had a beautiful contralto voice and was a member of the Tabernacle Choir. She became lovingly known to Joseph Fielding's children as Aunt Jessie and was his constant companion for the next thirty-three years until her death of a heart ailment on August 3, 1971.[6]

Early Service in the Church

Joseph Fielding was ordained a seventy and set apart for a mission to Great Britain on May 12, 1899. With eighteen other elders he embarked from Philadelphia on May 21 and took two weeks to cross the ocean. At mission headquarters in Liverpool he was assigned to the Nottingham Conference. He arrived in Nottingham at 7:30 p.m. and went to the conference headquarters where the missionaries were living, but as the missionaries had not heard of his coming no one was home. He stood his trunk outside the door of the house and sat on it. Soon a few youngsters in the street gathered around and began to sing:

Chase me, girls, to Salt Lake City,
Where the Mormons have no pity.[7]

Joseph Fielding returned from two years of valuable mission experience in June, 1901. Declining a position elsewhere at a much higher salary he accepted a position in the Church Historian's Office.

He also functioned as a member of the 24th Quorum of Seventies where he became quorum instructor and a home missionary, functioning in the latter capacity until his call to the apostleship in 1910. In 1903 he became one of the presidents of the quorum, as well as being called to serve on the general board of the Mutual Improvement Association. In 1904 he was ordained a high priest and became a member of the Salt Lake Stake high council where he also continued to function until his call to the apostleship. With his duties as a home missionary, as a member of the MIA general board, as a member of the stake high council in addition to his duties in the Church Historian's Office, the greatest part of his life was given in service to the Church. They were years of happiness because he was busy in the work that he loved.

At the April Conference in 1910 Joseph Fielding was called to be a member of the Quorum of the Twelve and was ordained and set apart to that office on Thursday, April 7. He now assumed the regular duties of that office including the constant schedule of necessary travel, but he also remained a member of the MIA general board until 1919. He was very active in the Genealogical Society of Utah, serving as secretary from 1907 to 1922, as a member of the board of directors in 1908, and as librarian and treasurer in 1909. During the summer of 1909 he and a companion visited all the genealogical societies in large cities in the United States, bringing home many new ideas which were inaugurated into the Utah society.[8] One of these ideas resulted in the founding of the *Utah Genealogical and Historical Society Magazine,* begun in January, 1910, with Joseph Fielding as editor. Although he gave up the editorship of the magazine when appointed to the apostleship he actively supported the society in every way, becoming vice-president from 1925 to 1934, at which time, upon the death of the president, Anthony A. Ivins, he became the president and served until 1964. During these years of activity in the genealogical society Elder Joseph Fielding Smith wrote dozens of articles for the magazine, always donating the author's royalties directly to the magazine itself.

On January 6, 1919, Elder Smith was set apart as first counselor to the president of the Salt Lake Temple, in which capacity he served until January, 1935. In June of 1945 he was set apart as president of the Temple where he served until 1949. In 1906 he became assistant Church historian, a position he continued to hold as an apostle until 1921, when he was appointed Church Historian. He functioned in this capacity for the next forty-nine years until he was ordained President of the Church. During these years, in addition to the many articles he wrote, Elder Smith also authored twenty-five books, becoming, perhaps, the most prolific Church writer to date.

When one contemplates the varied and vast amount of work accomplished by each of the General Authorities one is amazed and can conclude that perhaps the influence of the Holy Ghost aids them in their positions. In 1950 Elder Joseph Fielding Smith became Acting President of the Quorum of the Twelve Apostles. On April 9, 1951, he was made President of the Quorum when David O. McKay became President of the

556 Church. On October 29, 1965, he assumed the added duty of counselor to President McKay.[9]

PRESIDENT SMITH'S ADMINISTRATION

During his years of service in the Church President Smith saw the world move from the horse-and-buggy age to the jet age and the "moon age." Fortunately the horse-and-buggy trips the General Authorities used to take are no longer necessary. Modern transportation has made it possible for a man in his middle nineties with a clear mind and a healthy body to keep a vigorous schedule at the office and still do much traveling. Few men the age of President Smith could follow such a rigorous schedule of work as he did. He could do it because he enjoyed his work. Prior to his death, on a lovely day when his sister came to visit him and found him hard at work, she chided him for not taking a day off. He replied, "All my days are off." She told him to go home and take a nap, that George Albert Smith, Stephen L Richards, and J. Reuben Clark always did. President Smith humorously replied: "Yes, and look where they are now."[10]

When President Smith was called to the apostleship in 1910 the Church had a membership of 393,000 and sixty-two stakes.[11] The week after he was ordained President of the Church the 501st stake was organized, and membership was just under 3,000,000, reaching that figure by July, 1970.[12]

President Smith presided over the Presidency meetings almost every day, the weekly joint meeting of the Presidency and Twelve Apostles held in the Salt Lake Temple every Thursday morning, the joint weekly meeting of the Presidency and the Presiding Bishopric, and a vast array of other meetings, including the annual and semi-annual general conferences of the Church.

In addition to speaking at many stake conferences in the Salt Lake valley and at many other special events in the valley, he traveled widely in fulfilling his calling as President of the Church. For example, during 1970 he traveled to Los Angeles on March 8 where he set apart a new temple presidency; he traveled to Mexico City where on July 12 he attended sessions of two different stake conferences and spoke to over 5,000 people; on August 31 he was in Mesa, Arizona, where he set apart a new president of the Mesa Temple; he spent September 11 through 19 in Hawaii visiting the Saints, the Church College

Joseph Fielding Smith, tenth president of The Church of Jesus Christ of Latter-day Saints. *Permission of Church Information Service.*

Temple at Provo, Utah. *Courtesy of David C. Rich.*

of Hawaii, and the Language Training Mission. In Ogden, Utah, on October 11 he was honored by the townspeople and Weber State College students; on October 18 he addressed 800 missionaries at the Language Training Mission in Provo, Utah; on October 20 he was in Idaho Falls, Idaho, to set apart a new temple presidency; on November 8 and 9 he was in St. George, Utah, to set apart a new temple president and to speak to 400 seminary and institute students. In 1971 he was in Logan, Utah, on January 10 to speak to students at the new Utah State University Assembly Center; on January 12 he was at BYU in Provo; on February 13 he addressed 2,000 students at a University of Utah stake fireside; on April 18 he addressed 13,000 young people from forty-six southern California stakes in Long Beach, California. He was back in California on April 25 to dedicate the Laguna Hills Ward chapel in El Toro; on May 4 he was in Provo where Dallin H. Oaks was announced as the forthcoming president of Brigham Young University. On May 7 he addressed the graduates at Ricks College in Rexburg, Idaho; on May 15 he was at Snow College in Ephraim, Utah, where he was given a plaque of thanks "for living a life worthy of receiving the Lord's revelations to the children of the world." The following week on May 21 he presided at the cornerstone laying ceremonies for the Provo Temple; on May 31 he was in Inde-

Temple at Ogden, Utah, architect's rendering. *Permission of Church Information Service.*

pendence, Missouri, presiding at the dedication of the new Latter-day Saints visitor's center on a portion of the original temple site. He spoke in Provo, Utah, on June 8 at the fiftieth anniversary of education weeks at Brigham Young University; on August 27 through 29 he was in Great Britain presiding over the first area general conference of the Church, where he spoke five times. After presiding over the October General Conference he spoke at the funeral of Elder Richard L. Evans. He returned to Provo on November 12 to preside over the installation of Dallin H. Oaks as the new president of Brigham Young University; on November 13 he presided at a solemn assembly in the St. George Temple.[13]

President Smith began his travels in 1972 by presiding at the dedication of the Ogden Temple running from January 18 through 20 and the Provo Temple on February 9.[14]

THE CHURCH MOVES FORWARD IN A YEAR OF PROGRESS

But traveling was just a part of President Joseph Fielding Smith's busy year. The Church continued to move forward in many areas. Twenty-five new stakes and four new missions were added during 1971, bringing the total number of stakes to 562 at the close of the year and the total number of missions to 98. New and better methods of teaching were added in the wards and stakes through a teacher development program.[15]

Correlation continued to be an ongoing process in the Church and will undoubtedly continue to be in a growing and dynamic organization that has passed the three-million-membership mark and continues to be interested in every phase of a person's life from the cradle to the grave. A unified admissions system for all Church schools of higher learning was announced. Also, during the year the bishops and branch presidents began the new bishop's training course which was "aimed at helping them to learn how to more effectively carry out their varied responsibilities."[16]

In February 1971 the Social Service Department was given the responsibility of carrying out the Lamanite programs of the Church. A new area called the Department of Central Purchasing and Materials Control was organized in order to streamline the purchasing of goods and supplies. This department will do most of the purchasing for the Church. In May contracts to construct the temple near Washington, D.C., were let, with a target date for completion set at May 1974. The temple presidencies for the Ogden and Provo temples were named. In January 1971 plans for the first regional area conference of the Church were announced and were later carried out in August at Manchester, England. On May 30 the Independence visitor's center, Independence, Missouri, was dedicated under the direction of President Smith, and on September 4 President N. Eldon Tanner presided over the dedication of the new Nauvoo visitor's center.

The First Presidency initiated a new medical missionaries program by calling Dr. Blair Lamar Bybee to serve in the Samoan Mission and Sister Marilyn Lyons, a registered nurse, to serve in the Tongan Mission. Plans for the building of a new Sevier Valley Church Hospital were announced by Dr. James O. Mason, commissioner of the Health Services Corporation. Typical of the Church's interest in development of the body and mind was the opening of the nearly 23,000-seat Marriott Activities Center at Brigham Young University on December 3, 1971.

A sad note for the Church was the stilling of the voice of Elder Richard L. Evans, who died on November 1 after having been announcer for the Tabernacle Choir broadcasts since 1930.

His messages as "The Spoken Word" were not only a joy to the
Latter-day Saints but had become a source of peace and consolation to millions of non-Mormon listeners throughout the continent who listened regularly to the Columbia Broadcasting System program.

Because of a strong central organization, the Church of Jesus Christ of Latter-day Saints, through authority and revelation from God, provides many services today for its members. Let us glance briefly at some of these.

Internal Communications

On February 5, 1972, the First Presidency announced the completion of a new internal communications organization, with a managing director over four separate departments:

1. Director of Instructional Materials. He will be concerned with curriculum planning, correlation, editing, and graphic materials.

    All materials intended to be used in the program, magazines, and curricula of the various organizations and departments of the Church go to the Director of Instructional Materials who will then assign these materials to one of the following correlation secretaries and task committees:

    a. Adult Curriculum Correlation Secretary and Task Committee

    b. Youth and Young Adult Curriculum Secretary and Task Committee

    c. Child Curriculum Correlation Secretary and Task Committee

    d. Priesthood Services and General Correlation Secretary and Task Committee

2. Director of Magazines. He directs the production and circulation of *The Ensign, The New Era, The Friend,* and the Unified Magazines (foreign language magazines of the Church).

3. Director of Administrative Services, which includes budgeting, production coordination, printing procurement, mailing, and internal printing.

4. Director of Distribution and Translation. He has charge of adaptation, translation, non-English printing and distribution. The Managing Director of Internal Communications serves

under the direction of the First Presidency and the Council of the Twelve. The three-member advisory committee of the Twelve serve as advisors to the auxiliary organizations (Relief Society, Sunday School, Young Men's and Young Women's Mutual Improvement Associations, and the Primary), all other advisors having been released.[17]

Church Information Service (CIS)

A small but vital organization within the Church is the Information Service which came into existence in 1957.[18] Its predecessor was the Radio, Publicity, and Mission Literature Committee. The principal duties of this committee were to prepare and distribute radio programs, tracts and brochures, filmstrips, records, and other aids, principally for the missions. As demands increased from the missions and then from the stakes and other Church departments, the work load made a division of responsibilities desirable. Thus the Church Information Committee was formed principally to handle nonmember contacts through the Church Information Service, information centers, fairs, and expositions. The Missionary Committee supervises all aspects of missionary activities.

Today (1972) the executive committee of the Church Information Committee consists of three members of the Quorum of the Twelve. John Q. Cannon, a lawyer and former corporate secretary of Radio Corporation of America, is coordinator of this activity and directs a small but competent staff. Henry A. Smith, Church press secretary, works closely with this office in correlating news releases and serving as liaison with the General Authorities.

The functions of CIS are varied. Its primary objective is to promote missionary work by projecting an accurate image of the principles and activities of the Church.

The Church Information Service ministers in twelve areas.

1. It publishes the monthly *CIS Information Bulletin* which serves as a public-relations-idea exchange for stake and mission leaders and some other Church officers. Each stake and mission is encouraged to appoint a competent person as public relations director to work under the direction and authority of his president. The bulletin suggests news and feature stories for newspapers, radio and television, and other public relations projects. The bulletin carries a sampling of newspaper and

magazine clippings about the Church from many parts of the
world.

2. It maintains a photo library for newspapers, magazines, other publications, television, and filmstrips for in-Church and out-of-Church use. In addition to its own library, CIS has access to the photo archives of the Church Historical Department. CIS has a staff of photographers and darkroom facilities.

3. It provides stakes and missions with requested information and materials for locally produced publicity.

4. It develops and distributes posters for open houses and displays.

5. It assists with publicity for the Tabernacle Choir, general conferences, MIA conferences, Hill Cumorah Pageant, Mormon Miracle Pageant, and Promised Valley.

6. It writes and distributes Church-related editorials and articles requested by stake and mission officers or by the media directly. Weekly editorials presently are being sent to some 100 locations in several languages.

7. It prepares and gives wide distribution to special Church feature stories such as description and use of temples, welfare program, Indian student placement, family home evening, seminary, and LDSSA.

8. It works closely with Bonneville International Corporation and other electronics media on special programs such as the yearly "Faith in Action" series over NBC stations.

9. It provides information to publishers, other business people, and individuals writing from around the world. A large number of requests, for example, are handled daily from students doing term papers and theses.

10. It provides a hosting service for special visitors. Thousands of persons are hosted annually, including heads of state, diplomats, educators, musicians, and officials of other churches.

11. It selects, prints, and distributes reprints of outstanding articles prepared by non-Church people.

12. It provides photo, writing, and promotional services to other Church departments as requested.

It is likely that the recent organization of the Department of Internal Communication will affect the Church Information Service in the near future. It may be that the duties of the CIS will be confined strictly to "external communications."

Communication has always been a vital factor in man's dealings with man, and successful communication has always been a vital factor to the success of any organization, be it a business, a church, a fraternal organization, or whatever. Perhaps the greatest reason for the loss of the original Christian faith was the lack of proper communication. The Apostles became widely separated and lost the opportunity to provide for perpetuation of their offices when they could not communicate with each other. For a Church that feels it has the responsibility of taking the gospel to the world, there is no other way to accomplish its goal except through communication. In order to accomplish this gigantic task it must employ the most up-to-date and modern methods available. It must also use a variety of methods in order to reach those people that ordinary methods do not.

The invention of the Gutenberg press at about the middle of the 15th century made possible reaching the masses with the printed word. The development of radio around the 1900s made possible reaching unlimited numbers of people with the spoken word. The invention of the dissector tube in 1928 by Philo T. Farnsworth (a Latter-day Saint) made ready the development of television, begun prior to World War II. But it developed with great rapidity immediately following the war so that by 1953 there were 27,000,000 television receiving sets in the United States and 3,000,000 in other parts of the world, and by 1972 this had reached over 100,000,000 sets in the United States and more than 50,000,000 in the rest of the world.[19]

The First Radio Station

The Church built the first commercial radio station in Utah in a small shack on top of the Union Pacific Building in Salt Lake City in May, 1922, with the call letters KZN, and sold it in June 1924.[20] In October 1924 the entire proceedings of general conference were broadcast for the first time. In 1925 Earl J. Glade convinced the Church leaders of the value of owning a radio station, and they repurchased controlling interest in the station previously sold, changing the call letters to KSL. By 1932 KSL had a 50,000 watt license, had moved into new facilities on the top floor of the Union Pacific Building, and had joined the Columbia Broadcasting System. Later KSL-FM and KSL Television were added.

The invention of the transistor made it possible for people with limited financial means in remote areas to own a radio. This innovation, along with the early bird satellites above the earth, found the Church, through its ownership of various types of stations, in a position to begin preaching the gospel from the "housetops" to "every nation, kindred, tongue, and people." In Europe, however, the government-owned or -controlled television stations are not available for the Church to use. But the greatest single deterrent to world coverage is Communism, which controls over one-third of the earth's people.

Acquisition and Operation of Facilities

In a revelation given August 31, 1831, the Lord states:

> For verily, the sound must go forth from this place into all the world, and unto the uttermost parts of the earth— the gospel must be preached unto every creature, with signs following them that believe. (D&C 58:64.)

In order that the gospel be sent to the uttermost parts of the earth, not only must there be scientific possibilities, but the Church must possess physical facilities. Realizing that more stations than KSL would be needed, Bonneville International Corporation was organized with Arch L. Madsen as president. Its purpose was to acquire radio and television stations as they became available and to operate these church-owned broadcasting properties. Two television stations, four AM radio stations, six FM and five shortwave transmitters have been acquired.[21] Through these facilities the Church broadcasts in five areas: Standard AM Radio, FM Radio, International Shortwave Radio, Television, and special transoceanic cable feeds. It is probable that the Church will sell the shortwave transmitters and replace them with satellite broadcasting.

The use of AM radio in the United States is highlighted by the Tabernacle Choir—formerly broadcast with Richard L. Evans' "Spoken Word," now replaced by Spencer Kinnard— which is the oldest continuous coast-to-coast network radio broadcast in American radio and is said to be a "missionary tool of immeasurable value." The choir broadcast is heard weekly over 194 CBS stations, over another 250 stations in the United

States and Canada by tape, and over 150 Spanish and 80 Portuguese stations in South America, with the narration translated into the appropriate language. It is also heard on the Armed Forces Radio. Also hundreds of other stations play the choir's music from recordings.

General conference is now heard over forty-seven United States radio stations, one United States shortwave station (to Europe, Mexico, and Central and South America, in English, German, Spanish and Portuguese), and 235 television stations in the United States and Canada. It is also heard on tapes over 6 Spanish stations in the United States, 73 Spanish stations in Mexico and Central and South America, and 6 Portuguese stations in Brazil. Certain sessions of conference (Saturday and Sunday mornings) are broadcast by closed circuit—using telephone and transoceanic cables—to locations, usually chapels, in the United Kingdom (56), Germany (21), Austria (7), Holland (4), and France (2), each translated into the appropriate language. The priesthood meeting is broadcast closed circuit by radio to 675 chapels in the United States and Canada, and by television to 9 stake centers in Salt Lake City and to locations at Brigham Young University in Provo, Utah.

For those who work nights the Church now rebroadcasts all sessions (except the priesthood session) of the conference over KSL Radio in Salt Lake City and KMBZ Radio in Kansas City and WNYW International Shortwave, beginning at midnight over a three-day period following conference. These rebroadcasts are heard in many parts of the United States and the world, including Canada, Alaska, Mexico, Europe, Central and South America and the islands of the Pacific. Letters expressing gratitude have come from the western United States, Canada, Mexico and other areas.

For international broadcasting (shortwave) there are over 3,000 stations around the world in more than 100 countries. The Church owns five of the seven international licenses given out by the Federal Communications Commission in the United States. These five transmitters are known as WNYW (Radio New York Worldwide). In one conference session broadcast over WNYW wherein a few choir albums were offered to those writing from the greatest distances, the mail response came from 61 foreign countries, 37 of the 50 states and 8 ships at sea. Television represents the "nearly-perfect device for mass communication," and in this country where every television set operates for an average of six hours and twenty-seven minutes each day, a wonderful opportunity is provided for preaching the gospel.

Because of respect gained for the Church through Tabernacle Choir broadcasts and for Latter-day Saint members in their areas, up to 240 television stations have donated air time for conference broadcasts. Surely the marvels of science are helping to make possible the taking of the gospel to every nation, kindred, tongue and people; and President Arch L. Madsen of Bonneville Corporation states that this is only the beginning, as unlimited horizons are now within the Church's grasp.

The Missions and Missionary Work

The earliest message of the restored gospel was spread by word of mouth as individuals who heard of it would tell their friends and relatives, some of whom took the message to others even before the organization of the Church.

The first formal missionary work of the Church in this dispensation was that done by Elder Samuel H. Smith in the summer of 1830; he took a few copies of the Book of Mormon with him and went into Manchester and Fayette, New York. Although Samuel seemed to believe his mission did not accomplish much, his placing two copies of the Book of Mormon (one with John P. Greene, Brigham Young's brother-in-law, and the other with Phineas Young, Brigham Young's brother) later led to the conversion of the Youngs, the Kimballs, the Murrays, the Tomlinsons, and a number of other families in and around Mendon, New York.

Between the call of Samuel H. Smith and the call of Heber C. Kimball in 1837 over four hundred missionaries were sent out. Heber C. Kimball was set apart in June, 1837, as the first formal mission president of the Church and was sent to preside over a mission in Great Britain. From that time to the present formal missions have functioned in the Church. Today (1972) there are one hundred one such missions functioning in fifty-seven different countries of the world, with slightly over 15,000 full-time missionaries in the field.[22] These are in addition to the part-time stake missionaries. Worthy young ladies as well as worthy young men are called, as are older people, to do missionary work. Mission presidents formerly had two main responsibilities, that of presiding over the missionaries and that of presiding over the members. As the number of stakes throughout the world has increased, however, in some missions the stakes are able to absorb all new converts into their own membership. This is the ideal the Church hopes to attain in all missions because the stakes are able to carry on the full Church program; whereas often the missions are not able to do so because of insufficient numbers and lack of leadership in some locations. Moreover, missions do not have patriarchs or welfare projects.

Although a fairly uniform pattern of spreading the gospel is followed in all missions, conditions must be somewhat flexible in order to meet the challenge presented in each of the various mission fields. For example, although the same message is taught, methods of approach must be entirely different among the Navajo Indians than among their white neighbors or among the Buddhists in the Orient. Furthermore, in most cases, missionaries going into foreign lands must have training in the language of the land. For this reason the Church has established language training missions, where missionaries spend the first few weeks of their missions getting acquainted with the language and learning techniques of presenting the gospel.

At Brigham Young University the Language Training Mission teaches different languages which include Spanish, Portuguese, German, Afrikaans, Navajo, French, and Italian.

At the Church College of Hawaii oriental languages are taught. These include Mandarin, Cantonese (these two are Chinese languages), Korean, Japanese, Thai, Samoan, and Tahitian. At Ricks College Dutch, Finnish, Norwegian, Danish, and Swedish are taught.

When missionaries first began taking the gospel to people of this dispensation, they would go into the mission field for a period of time anywhere from a few months to a few years, according to their circumstances. Gradually the length of a mission call became somewhat standardized although it is influenced by circumstances and is changed from time to time. Military obligations for young men in the Church have affected the length of time they are permitted to serve as missionaries. Within the past few years the length of missions has been shortened in certain categories. At present young men, whether going to an English speaking country or whether to a foreign country, serve two years from the time their missions officially begin. The term for young ladies and couples has been shortened to eighteen months. Future changes in the length of mission calls may come as the Prophet and Apostles act to make them fit the circumstances of the times.

Because missionary work is one of the three great responsibilities and services performed by the Church, many different
techniques are used in order to get the gospel of Jesus Christ
before the world. Tabernacle Choir broadcasts, the Church of
the Air, bureaus of information, Temple Square guide service,
publication of tracts and pamphlets, extension of genealogical
library services to nonmembers, and publication of Church
periodicals are some of the techniques used. But nothing takes
the place of the missionaries in the field who teach the principles of the gospel and perform the ordinances of the Church.
The missionaries themselves use various techniques such as
tracting, presenting lessons at firesides or wherever invited to do
so, and setting up exhibits. One of the most successful methods
of missionary work is the referral system where friends and
members interest their associates and relatives in the gospel and
then request the missionaries to call on them and teach them.

At present 70,000 to 85,000 converts are added to the rolls
of the Church each year, roughly averaging about five converts
per missionary.

Although a knowledge of the gospel and of the language in
which it is to be taught are vital tools for any missionary, no
missionary can be successful without faith, prayer, humility,
and diligence in laboring for the cause. With these qualities
every missionary is entitled to the influence of the Holy Ghost
to aid him in his endeavors. At present the Missionary Executive
Committee of the Church is composed of three apostles, three
members of the First Council of the Seventy, and a secretary
and another apostle as chairman of the committee.

America's Witness for Christ

The Hill Cumorah pageant has become one of the outstanding and unique missionary methods of presenting the
gospel. The inspiration for the annual pageant probably came
from previous pageants staged at the Joseph Smith Memorial
Farm or at the Hill Cumorah itself. A pageant was produced
each year from 1930 to 1936, beginning with John W. Stonley's
commission by the Palmyra branch presidency, who wrote a
dramatic pageant called "Footprints in the Sand of Time" for
the 100th anniversary of the Church. But the actual beginning
of the pageant *America's Witness for Christ* was in 1937 when
Dr. H. Wayne Driggs, a professor of English at New York University and a member of the "New York Committee," sub-

mitted a manuscript by that title which was adapted from the Book of Mormon and became the nucleus of the pageant, although the script has been greatly altered over the years.[23]

Although Elder Oliver Smith and others greatly assisted with the 1937 production, a new missionary, Elder Harold I. Hansen, who arrived in the Eastern States Mission on July 12 and who had had a considerable amount of experience in drama at Utah State University in Logan where he had received a bachelor's degree in dramatic arts, was eventually put in charge. He had also had considerable experience in pageantry under the tutorship of J. Karl Wood of Logan, Utah, who, over the years, staged a number of pageants for the Logan Pageant Society (which afterwards furnished costumes for many years for the Hill Cumorah pageant).[24]

At first Elder Hansen was put in charge of producing only scene one, with Joseph Williams and Oliver Smith producing scene two. But after Hansen blocked the first scene, the New York Committee held a meeting and appointed him to direct all three scenes, with Oliver Smith in charge of overall production and Joseph Williams in charge of the background music. With the pageant scheduled for July 23, Elder Hansen ran into many discouraging factors, and even declared to President Franklin Evans, the newly arrived mission president, that he wanted nothing more to do with pageants. He personally felt that he had gone into the mission field to do missionary work, and this did not appear to him to be missionary work.

But on the night of presentation, when during the performance many things happened which he felt were not originally a part of the production but were the intervention of a higher power, his attitude changed; and Dr. Hansen has been the director of the pageant ever since, although dozens of others have assisted. Because of the war it was necessary to suspend pageant performances from 1942 through 1947, after which time President Roy W. Doxey of the Eastern States Mission insisted on beginning production again. President David O. McKay, second counselor in the First Presidency of the Church in charge of missionary work, gave his full support to the project and approved expenditure of necessary funds.[25] After much effort, President Doxey was able to get Dr. Hansen released from his summer teaching duties at the State University of Iowa long enough to direct the pageant again.

The pageant proved its usefulness both as a proselyting medium and as a friendmaker. An estimated 30,000 people attended the performances on August 6 and 7, 1948. A survey of a part of those attending was made and 1,080 forms were compiled, of which 242 nonmembers desired missionaries to contact them. Cooperation of local lumberyards and other businesses in Palmyra, Canandaigua, and other surrounding towns was very good, showing their wholehearted desire to revive the pageant. Church leaders appreciated their kind support, and made public expressions of gratitude.

The passing of time has shown the wisdom of reviving the pageant which has continued to grow in every respect. It was increased to a six-night run, and attendance has averaged over 100,000 each year. Dr. Hansen, who has been assisted by various experts over the years, is still the director, staging an outstanding performance each year, altering and improving the script from time to time. Dr. Crawford Gates, famous Latter-day Saint composer, has written and recorded the background music. After 2,350 hours of work on the part of the composer between 1943 and 1957, with the services of the eighty-member Utah Symphony Orchestra and the 170 voices of the combined Brigham Young University choruses, the excellent composition was recorded in the acoustically appropriate Salt Lake Tabernacle. Dr. John Harvey Fletcher, nationally known as the father of stereophonic sound, has likewise designed a superior sound system so that all aspects of the pageant have reached a peak of excellence that is a marvel to the experts as well as the spectators. The First Presidency has given full support, and it appears that so long as it is possible to stage such an excellent performance which will declare the gospel to the spectators with such clarity, the Church leaders will continue to sponsor *America's Witness for Chirst.*

DEATH OF PRESIDENT SMITH

After enjoying good health throughout a long and durable life, President Joseph Fielding Smith passed away suddenly and quietly at 9:25 p.m. on Sunday evening, July 2, 1972, as he sat in a chair at the home of his daughter and son-in-law, Elder and Sister Bruce R. McConkie. He was seventeen days short of his ninety-sixth birthday. His final week had been a busy one. On Monday, June 26, he spent the day working in his office. On Tuesday he met with his counselors in the regular weekly meeting of the First Presidency. Wednesday was another full day at the office. Thursday he gave what became his final

572 address to the mission presidents' seminar. Friday was another full day ending with his attendance at a mission presidents' banquet in the evening. Sunday he attended fast meeting in his own ward and visited with his daughter Josephine before returning to the McConkie home where he had been staying.[26]

President Smith's funeral was held in the Tabernacle on Thursday, July 6, with interment in the Salt Lake Cemetery.

Footnotes

[1]Joseph F. McConkie, *True and Faithful* (Salt Lake City: Bookcraft, 1971), p. 11. This book is highly recommended for one who desires more information on President Smith's life. It is brief but concise.

[2]McConkie, pp. 15-18.

[3]McConkie, pp. 15-18.

[4]McConkie, pp. 20-21. *See also Improvement Era* 53(April 1950):315.

[5]McConkie, pp. 83-84. *See also Improvement Era* 35(June 1932):459.

[6]McConkie, pp. 50-51.

[7]McConkie, p. 24.

[8]McConkie, p. 38.

[9]J. M. Heslop and Dell R. Van Orden, *Joseph Fielding Smith, A Prophet Among the People* (Salt Lake City: Deseret Book Co., 1971), pp. 155-56.

[10]McConkie, p. 74.

[11]McConkie, p. 93.

[12]*Church News*, 31 January 1970, p. 15. This was a prognostication which materialized.

[13]Heslop and Van Orden, pp. 157-61. *See also Church News*, 25 December 1971, p. 3.

[14]*Church News*, 15 January 1972, p. 5, and 5 February 1972, p. 11.

[15]*Church News*, 25 December 1971, p. 5.

[16]*Church News*, 25 December 1971, p. 5.

[17]*Church News*, 5 February 1972, p. 3.

[18]Contents of this article were checked by Grant W. Heath of the Church Information Service on February 24, 1972.

[19]Personal interview with Paul Evans of Church Broadcasting Services, 2 March 1972.

[20]John L. Wells, "The Church Broadcasting System" (n.p., December 1969), p. 3.

[21]Arch L. Madsen, "The Sound Must Go Forth," *CR*, (October 1966), p. 92. Unless otherwise specified, the material from this point on pertaining to Church Broadcasting has been drawn from President Madsen's talk. However, the figures were brought up to date in a personal interview with Richard D. Alsop of the Special Affairs Services on September 9, 1970, and again on March 2, 1972, with Arch L. Madsen and Paul Evans.

[22]For an up-to-date list of these missions, write to Elder Ned Winder, Secretary Church Missionary Committee, 47 East South Temple, Salt Lake City, Utah.

[23]This was a committee of Latter-day Saints in New York appointed by two Eastern States Mission presidents to formulate a pageant for presenta-

tion at Hill Cumorah. *See* Charles W. Whitman, "A History of the Hill Cumorah Pageant (1937-1964) and an Examination of the Dramatic Development of the Text of America's Witness for Christ" (Ph.D. dissertation, University of Minnesota, 1967), p. 18. Unless otherwise noted the basic material used in this writing concerning the pageant has been drawn from Whitman's dissertation.

[24]It is rather ironic in light of what has since occurred that when Elder Hansen first received his mission call to the Eastern States Mission, he was very disappointed since he had always had a heartfelt desire to serve in Denmark, the native land of his parents and the home of many of his relatives. He had prepared himself for such a call by studying the Danish language and went to the Eastern States Mission feeling that someone had made a mistake.

[25]Interview with Roy W. Doxey, 31 August 1970. *See also* Whitman, pp. 72-73.

[26]*Church News,* 8 July 1972, p. 5.

26

The Church as an Ensign to the Nations

A BRIEF SKETCH OF THE LIFE OF HAROLD B. LEE

Harold B. Lee was born on the family farm in Clifton, Idaho, to Samuel M. and Louisa Bingham Lee on March 28, 1899. His great-grandparents, Francis Lee and his wife, joined the Church in Indiana in 1832, went through the tribulations in Liberty, Far West, and Nauvoo, and came to the Salt Lake valley in September 1850.

Elder Lee was a member of a family of six children. All of them had to work hard, for times were not easy. In one of Elder Lee's talks to the youth he said,

> We began to do chores shortly after daybreak so we could start with the days work by sunup. When the days work was finished we had yet to do our evening chores, usually by the aid of a lantern. Despite the fact that there were no wages and hours regulations or child labor laws we did not seem to be stunted from our exertions.[1]

Harold Lee started district school at the age of five and began at the Oneida Stake Academy at the age of thirteen, where he participated in basketball and debating and became adept at playing the slide trombone. High school was followed by attendance at Albion State Normal School for a year. His first teaching job was in a one-room schoolhouse south of Weston, Idaho. A little later he accepted a position as principal of the district school at Oxford, Idaho, when he was still only eighteen years old.

After three years he accepted a call to the Western States Mission, where he served as president of the Denver District. He was released in December, 1922, and in 1923 he changed his residence to Salt Lake City. He attended summer sessions at the University of Utah but completed his schooling by taking correspondence courses and extension classes.[2] He served as principal of two schools in the Granite District in Salt Lake County from 1923 to 1928.

Elder Lee next became a salesman, then intermountain manager of Foundation Press, "a library distributing organization." In 1932 he resigned this position to become Salt Lake City commissioner in charge of the department of streets and public properties.

Church Service

In Salt Lake City Elder Lee served as Pioneer Stake religion class superintendent, Sunday School superintendent, member of the high council, counselor in the stake presidency, and, at the age of thirty-one he became stake president, serving for seven years from 1930 to 1937.[3] This was at a time when the country was in the throes of a severe economic depression; many members of his stake were among those who were in need and became discouraged.[4]

In 1932 he and his counselors inaugurated a stake welfare plan whereby the members, by their own efforts and with the help of their brethren in the Church, could be supplied with the necessities of life. They "established a warehouse for storing and distributing food and other commodities." The stake presidency also inaugurated a stakewide budget system, resulting in a recreational program for the whole stake in which all members, regardless of their financial circumstances, could participate. A gymnasium was built in which recreational activities were centralized. A third major activity of the stake presidency was the launching of a program of leadership development and teacher training.

In 1936 the Church correlated its varied relief activities in various stakes into one churchwide welfare program, and President Lee became managing director on January 1, 1937, a position he held for the next twenty-two years.[5] In order to devote full time to his new church calling Harold B. Lee resigned his position as Salt Lake City commissioner and gave up a promising political career. Although powerful pressures were later put upon him to reenter politics, he refused to do so.[6]

At the general conference of the Church on April 6, 1941, Elder Lee was unanimously sustained a member of the Quorum of the Twelve Apostles. Under assignment of the First Presidency he toured the Church with Elder Melvin J. Ballard, introducing and organizing the welfare plan.

Elder Lee married Fern Lucinda Tanner on November 14, 1923. To them were born two daughters, Maurine (Mrs. Ernest J. Wilkins, who died in 1966) and Helen (Mrs. L. Brent Goates). There are ten grandchildren. Sister Lee died on September 24, 1962. On June 17, 1963, President Lee married Frieda Joan Jensen.[7]

As a General Authority, President Lee "directed or advised many of the general Church committees and auxiliaries. In recent years he has been most closely connected with the Correlation Executive Committee, overseeing the organization and development of the program that now correlates many of the teaching and administrative programs of the Church."[8] On January 23, 1970, he was set apart as first counselor in the First Presidency and ordained President of the Quorum of the Twelve.

Harold B. Lee Ordained

On Friday, July 7, 1972, the Council of the Twelve retired to the Temple where they reorganized the First Presidency. Elder Harold B. Lee was ordained and set apart as President of the Church with President Spencer W. Kimball serving as voice. President Lee then set apart N. Eldon Tanner as his first counselor, Marion G. Romney as second counselor, and Spencer W. Kimball as President of the Quorum of the Twelve.[9]

Within an hour after the meeting in the temple the First Presidency granted an interview to news reporters. When asked about a message to the membership of the Church, President Lee replied, "The safety of the Church lies in the members' keeping the commandments. There is nothing more important that I could say. As they keep the commandments blessings will come."[10]

Harold B. Lee, eleventh president of The Church of Jesus Christ of Latter-day Saints. *Permission of Church Information Service.*

President Lee went on to say:

> We approach the future like the prophets of old. Like
> Nephi when he said, 'I, Nephi, went forth not knowing
> beforehand the things that I should do,' we will lean on
> the spiritual guidance of the Lord; we will move as led by
> the Spirit of the Lord.[11]

In an attitude of humility, yet with resolute conviction, he
committed himself to the challenge before him:

> To keep pace with the growth and to see that the mem-
> bers everywhere are properly shepherded, taught, and led
> becomes now our greatest responsibility. Through the
> graces of the Almighty we have been directed to lay some
> cornerstones, and we hope to build on that foundation in
> the years that lie ahead.[12]

The Church Education Program

Education in the Church has deep significance, for one of the
Church's tenets is that no man can be saved in ignorance.
Brigham Young declared that "education is the power to think
clearly, the power to act well in the world's work, and the
power to appreciate life." One realizes that such goals are at-
tainable without a formal education; nevertheless, those who
have no opportunity for an education find it extremely difficult
to attain their goals without it. Thus, the Church has been an
advocate of formal learning, always taking steps to provide
members with opportunities to learn.

From the establishment of the first elementary school in
western Missouri in 1831 and the School of the Prophets in
Kirtland, Ohio, in 1833, said to be one of the first schools of
adult education in America, the Church has been in the fore-
front in providing secular and religious learning for its members.
In the United States as the various arms of civil government
began to offer more opportunities for education, the Church
began to withdraw from providing a full program of secular
education and now does so in the United States only on the
college level and in other countries where their governments do
not provide adequate opportunities for their citizens.

Under the administration of President McKay, a former
school teacher and administrator, Church education expanded
from a rather strong local intermountain system to a worldwide

organization endeavoring to provide opportunities for all Church groups wherever sufficient members are available.

Today, the board of education of the Church is the governing body of the entire Church education system, with the members of the board consisting of the First Presidency, the Quorum of the Twelve, five other General Authorities, and the president of the Relief Society. The President of the Church is president of the board and his counselors function as vice-presidents.

An executive committee consisting of a secretary and approximately seven board members considers all business presented by administrators of Church schools and approves or makes recommendations for changes before any item is presented to the full board.

From time to time the Church leaders have altered the administrative machinery of the Church's educational arms. In 1953 the Church unified its school system, and Ernest L. Wilkinson, president of Brigham Young University, became chancellor of all Church schools in addition to his presidency of Brigham Young University. In the fall of 1953 he appointed William E. Berrett, vice-president of Brigham Young University, as administrator of the Seminaries and Institutes.

In February 1965 the Unified Church School System was reorganized into two units with President Wilkinson remaining as president of Brigham Young University and Harvey L. Taylor, who had been serving both as vice-president of Brigham Young University and vice-chancellor of the unified schools, became administrator of all schools of the Church except Brigham Young University. In this capacity he became responsible for the functioning of all other Church educational programs throughout the world, acting as the agent of the Church Board of Education in carrying out their policies and directions pertaining to all parts of the system. William E. Berrett remained in charge of the Seminaries and Institutes. In 1966 Keith R. Oaks and Joseph T. Bentley became assistant administrators to Harvey L. Taylor, with Harold R. Johnson as assistant director of personnel in 1967. By 1968 all these men were responsible for programs operating in the United States and thirteen foreign countries employing approximately 3,200 personnel in eleven major administrative units. These units included:

1. Ricks College at Rexburg, Idaho
2. LDS Business College at Salt Lake City, Utah

3. The Church College of Hawaii at Laie
4. The Church schools in Northern Mexico, including elementary schools in Colonia Juarez, Colonia Dublan, Colonia Pacheco, and the Juarez Academy in Colonia Juarez; twenty-nine elementary schools in other areas of Mexico and the Benemerito de las Americas School in Mexico City, serving children in grades seven through twelve with plans to serve them through normal school (teacher training)—by 1968, a total of 5,120 children being educated in Church schools in the Republic of Mexico
5. Three elementary schools serving over 400 pupils in Santiago, Chile
6. The Church College of New Zealand (a secondary school) with an enrollment of 635 students
7. The Church College of Western Samoa (a secondary school) and three elementary schools serving altogether approximately 1,250 students in Western Samoa
8. The Mapusaga High School in American Samoa (the eastern islands) accommodating 365 students
9. The Liahona High School and nine side schools (grades 6, 7, and 8) in Tonga serving a total of about 1400 students
10. The Papeete Elementary School in Papeete, Tahiti, serving over 480 children
11. The vast system of seminaries, institutes and Deseret Clubs of the Church with William E. Berrett as administrator

On June 2, 1970, the First Presidency announced the reunification of the Church School System when they announced the appointment of Elder Neal Maxwell as commissioner of education over the total Church program, including Brigham Young University.[13] Commissioner Maxwell assumed his new duties on August 1, 1970, with Joe J. Christensen becoming associate commissioner responsible for the seminaries and institutes approximately three months later. Dee Anderson became associate commissioner in charge of finance, and Kenneth Beesley became associate commissioner in charge of colleges and schools. Since that time many other appointments have taken place including three new presidents over Brigham Young University, Ricks College, and Church College of Hawaii.

Seminaries and Institutes

The seminary program of the Church began in 1912 under the administration of President Joseph F. Smith when Joseph F.

582 Merrill, a stake president, initiated the opening of a seminary near the Granite High School. This is a program of weekday religious education provided for high school students so that during the school day they may have the opportunity of studying a religious course for one period of the day.

From the beginning the program proved to be a success, and it grew steadily in numbers during the administrations of Presidents Joseph F. Smith, Heber J. Grant, and George Albert Smith.

By the time President McKay was sustained in April 1951, there were 135 seminaries in the Church, all operating on a released-time basis (i.e., a student was excused from one high school class period to attend a seminary class) in Utah, Idaho, Wyoming, and Arizona, but in the fall of that year the Church Board of Education initiated nonreleased-time classes (usually held early in the morning) which made it possible to greatly expand the program and serve thousands of Latter-day Saint high school students who had not previously enjoyed the privilege of seminary courses. By 1968 the Church had 208 released-time seminaries and approximately 1,820 nonreleased-time seminary classes which were operating in 48 states of the Union and in Mexico and Canada.[14]

By 1972 seminaries were operating in all fifty states of the Union and in twenty-nine countries outside the United States. There were 230 released-time seminaries with 2,735 classes and 2,918 nonreleased-time seminaries; in addition there were fifteen special seminaries functioning for the deaf, the blind, and for other exceptional young people, making a total enrollment of 138,069 for the school year 1971-72.

In 1954 the seminary program was extended to the Indian members of the Church, and by 1959 over 2,000 Indian students were enrolled. At first the seminary buildings were for the most part located adjacent to federal boarding schools operated by the Federal Bureau of Indian Affairs, but later the program was made available to young Lamanite members living under various conditions, including living at home. By 1968 930 classes were being taught by full-time missionaries and local teachers, involving over 11,000 students in twenty-three states and Canada. These classes are supervised by fifty full-time seminary coordinators who provide assistance and guidance to teachers. This program, however, provides classes from kindergarten through high school in order to provide Indian children with a more complete background of the teachings of the Church.

By 1972 Indian seminaries were operating in only nineteen of the United States, also in Canada; but the enrollment had increased to 17,013.

In 1967 a seminary home study program was initiated, serving individual Church members and small groups of young people of high school age in areas only thinly populated with Church membership. In 1968 this program was expanded to include England and Australia, so that by the end of 1969 the home study program served in the United States, England, Australia, and Canada, with 2,500 students enrolled. By 1972 there were 1,774 home study classes with an equal number of voluntary (unpaid) teachers.

Institutes of religion were first begun in the fall of 1926, when an institute class was opened near the campus of the University of Idaho at Moscow, Idaho. Gustive O. Larson, seminary instructor, had previously taught classes in religion for college students at Cedar City, Utah. Institutes are to colleges what seminaries are to high schools, but they function as more than an organization for the formal instruction of religious courses; they provide a "home away from home" for Latter-day Saint students attending non-Church institutions of learning. By the time President McKay was sustained as President of the Church, there were sixteen full-time institutes and a handful of part-time institutes of the Church. By 1968 the Church had established seventy-three full-time institutes of religion and 136 part-time institutes adjacent to college and university campuses in thirty-three states of the Union and the province of Alberta, Canada.[15]

Four years later the number of institutes had increased to 337 in 46 states of the Union, Washington D.C., and Canada. In addition, institutes were functioning in sixteen countries outside the United States with a total enrollment of 53,395, making 208,477 the total enrollment of seminaries, Indian seminaries, and institutes for the school year of 1971-72.

Closely associated with the institute program of the Church is the Student Association which is presently under the direct supervision of Elder Marion D. Hanks, Assistant to the Twelve. It was initiated in 1966 with Elder Paul H. Dunn as its assigned General Authority and "is a priesthood correlation program designed to correlate all phases of Church activities as they relate to the college student."[16]

584

BRIGHAM YOUNG UNIVERSITY
25,000 Students

UNITED STATES
117,168 Seminary Students
45,969 Institute Students
31,042 College Students

LDS BUSINESS COLLEGE
800 Students

CANADA
2,418 Seminary Students
1,602 Indian Seminary Students
1,036 Institute Students

BRITISH ISLE
1,036 Seminary Stu
522 Institute Stua

ICELAND
15 Seminary Students

RICKS COLLEGE
5,245 Students

BRAZIL
902 Seminary Stude
101 Institute Stude

CHURCH COLLEGE OF HAWAII
1,300 Students

HAWAII
867 Seminary Students
86 Institute Students

ALASKA
242 Seminary Students

URUGUAY
131 Seminary Stua
100 Institute Stud

PERU
173 Elementary Students

MEXICO
4,716 Seminary Students
426 Institute Students
6,053 Elementary Students
2,006 Secondary Students

PANAMA
8 Seminary Students

CHILE
1,354 Elementary Students
340 Secondary Students

BOLIVIA
13 Seminary Students
173 Elementary Students

GUATEMALA
812 Seminary Students
63 Institute Students

ARGENTINA
270 Seminary Studen
303 Institute Studen

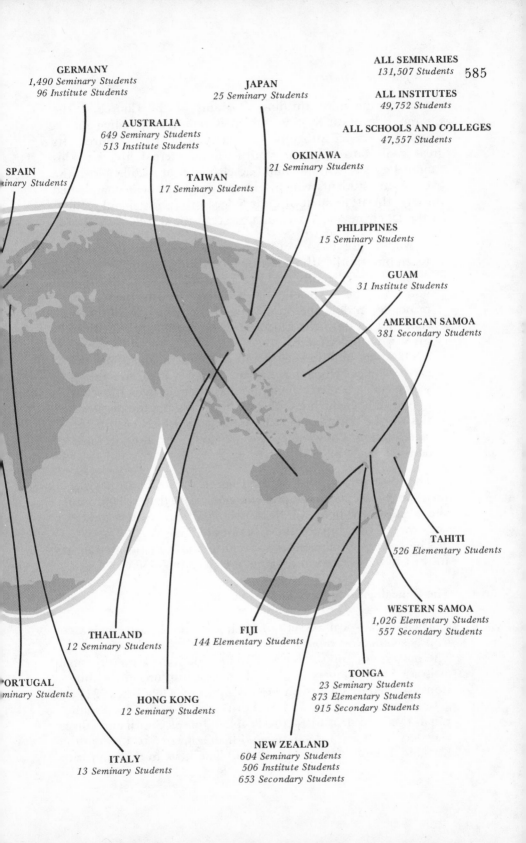

GERMANY
1,490 Seminary Students
96 Institute Students

JAPAN
25 Seminary Students

ALL SEMINARIES
131,507 Students 585

ALL INSTITUTES
49,752 Students

AUSTRALIA
649 Seminary Students
513 Institute Students

ALL SCHOOLS AND COLLEGES
47,557 Students

OKINAWA
21 Seminary Students

SPAIN
inary Students

TAIWAN
17 Seminary Students

PHILIPPINES
15 Seminary Students

GUAM
31 Institute Students

AMERICAN SAMOA
381 Secondary Students

TAHITI
526 Elementary Students

WESTERN SAMOA
1,026 Elementary Students
557 Secondary Students

THAILAND
12 Seminary Students

FIJI
144 Elementary Students

TONGA
23 Seminary Students
873 Elementary Students
915 Secondary Students

PORTUGAL
minary Students

HONG KONG
12 Seminary Students

ITALY
13 Seminary Students

NEW ZEALAND
604 Seminary Students
506 Institute Students
653 Secondary Students

One of the most thrilling programs of the Church is the Church Education System, which is rapidly expanding into a worldwide service program for the youth of the Church. Its great goal is to help the youth obtain eternal life, but this cannot be done without building character and ability into the lives of the students which, in turn, can only be accomplished through the attainment of knowledge both spiritual and secular. In the Doctrine and Covenants, we read the words of the Lord:

And I give unto you a commandment that you shall teach one another the doctrine of the kingdom.

Teach ye diligently and my grace shall attend you, that you may be instructed more perfectly in theory, in principle, in doctrine, in the law of the gospel, in all things that pertain unto the kingdom of God, that are expedient for you to understand;

Of things both in heaven and in the earth, and under the earth; things which have been, things which are, things which must shortly come to pass; things which are at home, things which are abroad; the wars and the perplexities of the nations, and the judgments which are on the land; and a knowledge also of countries and of kingdoms—(D&C 88:77-79.)

The ultimate purpose of the Church schools is to provide a program of secular and religious education that will promote the utmost well-being of those who participate, not only for their mortal lives but for the eternities.

The present administrative structure and statistics pertaining to the Church education program are given in Appendix 11.

The Genealogical Society and Its Services

The Genealogical Society of Utah was founded on a membership basis on November 13, 1894, by leaders of the Church. [17] The purpose of the society was to provide some kind of formal assistance to members of the Church in fulfilling their obligations to become saviors on Mount Zion (*see* Obadiah, v. 21) by acting under the keys and authority restored by the Prophet Elijah (Malachi 4:5, 6) to the Prophet Joseph Smith and Oliver Cowdery on April 3, 1836, when Elijah appeared to them in the Kirtland Temple. (D&C 110:14-16.) The keys to this authority gave the members of the Church the privilege and responsibility of searching out their dead ancestors and providing the ordinances for them vicariously so that when their ancestors hear and accept the gospel in the spirit world as spoken of by Peter (1 Peter 3:18-20, 4:6) they may accept this ordinance work and be ready to advance according to the plan of salvation.

Just as Jesus did a vicarious work for all mankind (1 Corinthians 15:20-22) so also does he permit us to do the necessary ordinance work for our dead who did not have the opportunity of accepting the gospel plan here on earth.

When Jesus was on earth as a mortal he taught that "except a man be born of water and of the Spirit, he cannot enter into the kingdom of God." (John 3:5.) Yet only a small percentage of God's children have ever had the opportunity of receiving baptism and the gift of the Holy Ghost. Only through such a vicarious plan, permitting the living to be saviors on Mount Zion for those unprivileged dead, is it possible for God to be both just and merciful. Thus it is not surprising that the Genealogical Society of the Church of Jesus Christ of Latter-day Saints is one of the most active and perhaps the largest genealogical society in the world today.

The Genealogical Society is under the direct supervision of the First Presidency and the Twelve Apostles, with Theodore M. Burton, Assistant to the Council of the Twelve Apostles, as president.

With headquarters in Salt Lake City the main genealogical library makes available, not only to members of the Church but to all others who are willing to abide by the rules set up for its use, regardless of race, creed, or color, a library of more than 114,000 volumes of the "world's printed and manuscript family genealogies, past and current periodicals, and published histories of towns, counties, states, and countries."[18] Approximately 5,000 new volumes are added each year.

But the heart of the library's record-gathering program is its collection of over 715,000 rolls of 100-foot microfilm, making the equivalent of over three million, four hundred thousand books of records available to library patrons. The society has eighty-five microfilm cameras that photographers are constantly operating in various parts of the world, adding about 5,000 one hundred foot rolls of microfilm each month. They are filming such documents as land grants, deeds, probate records, marriage records, parish registers, census returns, and other records of value for genealogical purposes.

The library also has on file a collection of over 7,500,000 genealogical records of individual families compiled by members of the Church. The genealogical information contained in this family-group record collection is known as the Church records archives and has been posted on convenient forms filed in loose-leaf binders available to the public in open shelving.[19]

Also on file are over 38 million index cards containing the names and genealogical data pertaining to both living and dead members of the Church and many of their relatives and deceased ancestors.[20]

Library patrons may have this vast information available to them by simply preparing a request slip, showing whether they want a copy of the temple index card or the archive record showing a person as either a parent or a child.

Today the library program has become a complex organization of over 450 employees who are working in twelve departments. Among these are the following: The Temple Records Index Bureau (known as the TIB), The Research Department, The Microfilm Department, The Examining Department, The Records Adjustment Department, The Typing and Proofreading Department, The Sealing Department, The Records Control Department, and The Records Tabulation Department.[21]

The Branch Genealogical Library Program

Many members of the Church are not aware that the Genealogical Society has a network of branch genealogical libraries. In March, 1972, there were 114 branch libraries in operation. They were located in thirty-four of the contiguous United States plus Alaska and Hawaii, Australia (2), Canada (4), Mexico (2), and New Zealand. These libraries are now controlled and standardized by the main library in Salt Lake City.

The facilities of these libraries are not elaborate nor are they intended to be; they are specialized interlibrary loan agencies through which microfilms from the main library in Salt Lake City are made available to patrons in the local areas for a nominal fee. Not all microfilms in the main library are available to branch libraries inasmuch as some archivists put restrictions on their use when permission to film certain records is given, but it is safe to say that at least 95% of the films are available.

The maintenance of these branch libraries is provided by the local members of the Church whose services are entirely voluntary. A small fee is charged the user of microfilm (presently 50¢ per roll of film) to cover mailing and handling costs.

Although all other people may use these branch libraries, they are naturally organized to fit the needs of the Church. Most of them are located in Latter-day Saint meeting houses, usually in connection with the Church's regular meeting-house library program. The standard facilities consist of (1) a minimum of four microfilm reading machines, (2) a standard basic book collection of about fifty volumes, (3) a microfilmed copy of the Salt Lake City library's main card catalog, and (4) a reading area.

Most of the basic book collection normally pertains to genealogical sources within the United States, but there are also well-selected books on research in Great Britain, Canada, Scandinavia, and continental Europe with emphasis centered on the local needs in each branch library. Microfilms are available at the main library in Salt Lake City pertaining to genealogy in more than twenty-six countries.[22]

When ordering films from the main library through the branch libraries, one must plan on about three weeks' time to obtain the films within the continental United States. All films (and books in the branch libraries) are to be used at the premises of the branch library. Films are retained at the branch library for a two-week period and are then returned to Salt Lake City. Neither the people in the branch libraries or the main library engage in extended searches or any kind of paid genealogical research. They are there to help the patrons do their work. The genealogical library system is not a commercial venture and was not designed to be self-supporting.

As the founders stated when the Genealogical Society was first organized in 1894, "the purposes . . . are benevolent, educational and religious, pecuniary profit not being its object."[23]

Granite Mountain Records Vault

In about 1935 Church leaders began to contemplate the need of a safe storage vault to house the growing mountain of Church records as well as the voluminous genealogical microfilms that were being obtained by the Genealogical Society of the Church. In 1956 the Genealogical Society and the Church Building Committee formulated the design for the vault which included the following:

(1) the vault must be within 25 miles of the Church Admin-

istration Building; (2) the storage area must be a minimum of 30,000 square feet (expandable to 58,000 square feet) with about 28,000 square feet for offices; (3) the air temperature must be 65 to 72 degrees and humidity must be within 40 to 50 percent; (4) the air must be filtered; (5) the storage vault must have an overburden of earth or rock at least 250 feet deep; (6) water, sewer, and electric power must be available.

After an exhaustive investigation the Church Building Committee decided on a location in Little Cottonwood Canyon. It is twenty miles from the Church Administration Building and is in the same area from which came the blocks for the Salt Lake Temple, the Church Office Building, the Utah State Capitol Building, and the This is the Place monument.[24]

Work was begun in 1960 with the drilling of a 500-foot test core into the mountain. As all tests proved highly satisfactory, an access road was then constructed. Next an exploratory tunnel ten feet wide and thirteen feet high was built 200 feet beyond the core drilling at the end of which a small flow of cool, clear water ran. A concrete reservoir with a storage capacity of about 33,000 gallons was built. The daily flow at the present time is approximately 37,000 gallons, currently more than ample for culinary and laboratory needs.

The completed structure includes a floor space of 65,111 square feet with six storage vaults, the three on the west being 25 feet x 190 feet and the three on the east being 25 feet x 200 feet. The natural temperature of the vault is approximately 57 degrees the year round, and the natural relative humidity of the air is about 50 percent. These storage vaults are ventilated with filtered air.

The office area, laboratory space, receiving area, and loading dock are all on the south end. The vault is at about 6,000 feet elevation with an overburden of rock more than 500 feet thick. Rock taken out of the tunnels was utilized to build a parking area on the south side for the employees.

With records being microfilmed today the vault has sufficient safe storage space to house all genealogical and church records for many years to come. Nevertheless, the Church owns sufficient property in the vicinity to build eight more vaults of comparable size.

The project turned out to be even more satisfactory than the building committee had anticipated and is ideal for storage of the Church's valuable records.

Most of the storage space in the vault is designated for use by

the Genealogical Society, but one compartment is used by the   591
Church Historical Department, and various other Church
departments also utilize space there. When microfilms are made
for the Genealogical Society, the positives are kept in the main
library for daily use and all negatives are stored in the vault. A
second set of positives is kept at the vault for circulation to the
branch libraries.

Auxiliaries to the Priesthood

The gospel of Jesus Christ is the plan of salvation for every
son and daughter of God. Its purpose is to provide a way of life
that will lead mankind back into the presence of God, provided
his children, in their free agency, choose to follow that plan.
The business of the Church is to teach the gospel plan to God's
children and to put into their hearts the desire to live in accordance with it. For this reason the Church is interested in every
aspect of man's life from the cradle to the grave.

In order to assist the priesthood in accomplishing these
objectives, auxiliary organizations have been created for every
age group within the Church. As soon as children are old
enough to comprehend, they enroll in the Primary Association
where they are instructed until they reach the ages of eleven
and twelve years, at which time they enroll in the Young
Women's and Young Men's Mutual Improvement Associations
where they receive socialization and instruction in various
aspects of life, such as wholesome recreation and physical
betterment, development of their various talents (musical,
dramatic, speaking), guidance in choosing a profession, and
instruction in spirituality. MIA is for the young and the young
at heart; there is no age restriction for anyone over eleven.

Sunday School is for all ages where members come to
worship and receive instruction in gospel principles.

Relief Society has become an international organization for
the women of the Church. All women are welcome. They
receive instruction in culture, homemaking, spiritual living,
social relations, and service to humanity, but they also make
practical application of the principles taught, for they provide
service to humanity in many ways. The Relief Society members
work closely with the bishop of the ward in providing care for
the sick or needy, comforting the weary and those in sorrow.

The organization for the men is the priesthood itself,
organized into quorums of deacons, teachers, and priests in the

Aaronic priesthood (beginning at the age of twelve) and elders, seventies, and high priests (with special callings of Bishop, Patriarch, and Apostle) in the Melchizedek Priesthood.

As the Church membership expanded, the report for 1970 gave the following enrollment or attendance:

Primary:	enrollment	459,355
YMMIA:	enrollment	351,591
YWMIA:	enrollment	383,916
Sunday School:	attendance	818,733

The membership in the various quorums of the priesthood as of Dec. 31, 1971, is as follows:

Aaronic Priesthood	
Deacons	136,969
Teachers	98,814
Priests	152,886
Total Aaronic	388,669
Melchizedek Priesthood	
Elders	252,051
Seventies	23,914
High Priests	88,416
Total Melchizedek:	364,381
Apostles	16
Patriarchs	735
Grand total priesthood holders in the Church:	753,050

The New Church General Office Building

In line with Church correlation, one of the badly needed improvements was to provide space for Church organizations and services where they could have efficient interaction and coordination with one another. At present (1972) fifty-six organizations are scattered in Salt Lake City and its outskirts in sixteen locations. In order to accomplish this needed improvement the General Authorities planned a new office building which would be sufficiently large to provide convenient space for these various branches of Church activity.

In 1960 they announced plans for the construction of an office building just north of the present Church headquarters which would be approximately 500 feet above ground level and would include 38 stories. Each story of the center structure would include approximately 30,000 feet of floor space, making over 1,000,000 square feet of office space. At that time as a part of the building the planners contemplated a mission home where all missionaries who had been called would live for a few days while receiving instruction. These plans were later changed and the Church has since purchased the Lafayette School, a large building across the street to the northeast, has refurnished it for a cost of approximately $600,000 and has made an excellent mission home which has been in use since August 14, 1971. The number of stories for the office building was later reduced to twenty-eight plus an elevator penthouse, and the floors of the center structure were reduced to 23,000 square feet. There are twenty-one elevators in the building, very efficient, moving from the first floor to the top without stopping in less than one-half minute.

The architect for the building is George Cannon Young. Bids were opened in July 1969 with three years allowed to complete the building. The low bid was submitted by a partnership of two firms, Christensen Brothers and W. W. Clyde and Company for $31,396,000. The contract was signed on July 29, 1969. The facing of the building is white quartzite. The slabs are twenty-eight to thirty-eight feet long, three feet wide, and twenty inches thick. The building has two emergency generators which operate some elevators in an emergency and provide emergency lighting for the halls and stairways. A 700-seat cafeteria is on the first level of the basement (three stories are below ground level). A three-level underground parking plaza contains 1,250 stalls. A 350-seat auditorium is on the main floor, and a board room and other committee rooms occupy the entire 22nd floor.

The Church Historical Department occupies the floors of the east wing, and the Genealogical Society occupies all floors of the west wing plus the second through the fifth floors of the tower (the center structure). The First Presidency, the Twelve Apostles, and most other General Authorities will remain in the Church Office Building in which they are presently located.

Church Welfare Plan

As stated earlier in the biographical sketch of President Lee, the present Church welfare plan was begun in 1936. After earnest prayer the First Presidency inaugurated a Church-wide program to try to relieve the needs of Church members in the United States and in many other countries through a combination of self-help and unified effort. It was an effort to alleviate

New Church General Office Building. *Courtesy David C. Rich.*

government dole and to restore dignity to the individual by making it possible for him to give service for the necessities of life he received. It was also an effort to provide for the widow and orphan who were not in a position to help themselves.

Elder Harold B. Lee as president of the Pioneer Stake in Salt Lake City had originated such a program in his stake. Its success led the authorities to inquire of the Lord as to whether something similar might not be beneficial for the entire Church. They received an affirmative answer, and the details were worked out; the plan was announced at general conference to the membership of the Church.

Although certain aspects of the plan have been changed from time to time to fit the needs and changing times, the basic ideas have remained the same. The plan not only furnishes appropriate goods to the needy but provides employment for the handicapped whose services may be sufficiently impaired to prevent them from being employed elsewhere. Here they can further develop their skills and feel the dignity which comes from providing for themselves with honest labor. Many able-bodied people have retired from other positions to work in the Church welfare system, finding a certain joy and pleasure in serving their fellowmen. It also provides opportunities for every able-bodied Church member to enjoy fellowship and brotherhood while performing volunteer services on welfare projects.

The Church welfare report reveals the following statistics: during the year 84,507 people were assisted; 9,226 were placed in remunerative employment; 190,921 man-days of work were donated to the welfare plan; 4,815 unit-days of equipment were donated.

Unified Social Services Department

The Church leaders, interested in every aspect of each member's life, have discovered much to do in dealing with God's children, in addition to providing the regular services through the auxiliary organizations and the regular worship services and providing for the spiritual needs of the members. There are always special segments of members and individuals who have exceptional problems in which the Church can be of service. Over the years, as the Church has increased in membership, leadership, and financial ability, various agencies have emerged to provide a variety of exceptional social services to members, as well as nonmembers, who might be desirous of Church aid.

In keeping with the correlation program, various social-service agencies were consolidated into one organization in October 1969 when the Unified Social Services Department was created under the direction of the First Presidency. These agencies included the Indian student placement program, the Relief Society social service program, and the youth guidance program.[25] An advisory committee was appointed consisting of two of the Apostles, the Presiding Bishop, and the president of the Relief Society. One of the other Apostles, Marvin J. Ashton, became chairman of the department and an Assistant to the Twelve, Robert L. Simpson, became managing director.

The department, working in correlation with the wards and stakes, offers a variety of services, of which the following are included:

1. Special services to ward and stake officers:
   a. The social service worker meets with the bishop or stake president to identify social-emotional problems and discusses methods of dealing with them.
   b. The person or family with problems counsels with the worker upon request of the bishop and with the approval of the stake president. The worker then makes recommendations to the bishop on how to proceed.
   c. At the request of the stake presidents the department provides training seminars of ward and stake leaders in such subjects as understanding human behavior, interviewing and counseling, and handling special needs of the people.
   d. The department assists in mobilizing and training volunteer social service workers called by the stake presidents who are qualified professionally or have special abilities to work with people who have social-emotional problems.

2. Youth guidance services:
   These include short-term counseling in crises to young people and their parents which cannot be provided by the wards and stakes; foster care services to youth until their home situation problems can be resolved so that they can return; summer day camps for children eight through fourteen, where the children meet from 9 a.m. to 4 p.m. and are helped to improve their "social and emotional functioning." Parent education groups are conducted in conjunction with the day camp.

3. Indian student placement:
   This is a program in which Indian youths between the ages

of eight and eighteen years are placed in Latter-day Saint
homes for the purpose of giving them educational, spiritual, social, and cultural opportunities that they otherwise would not have. They must be living the standards of the Church and must have the potential to achieve average grades in school; they must have a sincere desire with parental support to participate in the service. They must also be physically and emotionally healthy so that they can make a satisfactory adjustment in the foster home and community.

The foster parents must be active Church members who uphold the moral and spiritual standards of the Church. The foster parents pay the living expenses of the foster child.

A professional social worker of the Unified Social Services is responsible for the placement and supervision of the Indian child.

4. Adoption Service:

This provides counseling for young unwed parents

in a program to aid them in repentance and to offer marriage or adoption as alternatives to a mother's keeping a child or abortion. It also provides placement services for adoptive parents and adoptive children, through creating a family for barren couples and finding Latter-day Saint homes for children.

By law all agencies involved in providing services to unwed expectant mothers and arranging for adoption and foster care of children must have state licenses. By assignment of the First Presidency the Unified Social Services Department is the licensed agency of the Church for these services and now has licensed agencies located in Arizona, California, Colorado, Georgia, Idaho, Nevada, Oregon, Utah, Washington, and Alberta, Canada.

Because of licensing requirements and the need to provide services to all unwed mothers who desire help, it is not necessary for them to be referred by their bishop or any other Church authority. Services may be received "upon request by phone or personal appearance at the agency."

5. Services to youth away from home:

This includes youth and unmarried persons eighteen to twenty-five years of age leaving home for employment or reasons other than school, military or missions. When a young person moves from home the bishop or branch president fills out a Youth Away From Home Information Card and sends it to the Unified Social Services. A copy of the card is sent to the person's new bishop or branch president. The agency or area office of the social services department assists the new bishop in making employment and housing information available to the youth when needed.

6. Services to members of the Church in prison:

"Church programs including religious services, home teaching, and family home evenings, are used as part of the rehabilitation program for confined members and their families."

7. Educational Services:

These services are carried out under the supervision of an educational services supervisor. His specific functions are: to help clients obtain financial aid at high school and post-high school levels; to implement a tutoring program for those who need it among neglected youth, unwed mothers, and Indian students; to arrange for and provide testing where needed for those students having academic difficulties due to lack of ability, to emotional stress, or to inconsistent motivation; to assure that each social worker in the Indian Placement Program keeps track of, encourages, and fellowships the graduates from his district for a period of five years. The social services department works with the Indian committee of the Church in providing this service.

8. Services related to drug abuse and alcoholism:

"The Social Services Department coordinates with national, state, and local agencies in order to complement rather than duplicate services already being offered." A program of education for local Church leaders is being formulated to aid in preventing these problems.

9. Student training:

The Unified Social Services Department provides clinical training for graduate social work students in an accredited graduate school of social work. Both graduate and undergraduate students are accepted for training. Many staff members also have agency membership in national and local professional organizations.

The Health Services Corporation

During the summer of 1970 the First Presidency correlated under one corporate roof the health services of the Church through organizing the Health Services Corporation, with James

O. Mason as commissioner.[26] The corporation consists of a Board of Trustees with the Presiding Bishop and his counselors as chairman and vice-chairmen. Thus the commissioner is directly responsible to the Presiding Bishop's office.

The corporation is a separate entity but has a close working relationship with the Unified Social Services and the Church education system. This is exemplified by having on the board of trustees both Elder Marvin J. Ashton, the General Authority supervising the social services and Neal Maxwell, commissioner of Church education.

The Health Services Corporation has, at present, two major responsibilities, the first of which is to administer the fourteen hospitals of the Church located in Utah and Idaho. They are run as if they were one large hospital with two thousand beds, so that maximum efficiency is attained.

The corporation also gives instruction on nutrition and health care, emphasizing health education and disease prevention.

The second major responsibility is the new health missionary program which was begun in 1971. The goal of this program is to send out medically trained personnel to members in underdeveloped areas where "the missionaries will be a blessing to the members" through not only administering to their immediate medical needs but teaching them sanitation, health care, and disease prevention.

The corporation also works closely with such private organizations as Ayuda, Inc., which is a nondenominational organization bent on assisting people in underdeveloped areas (such as those in Guatemala and the Navajos of the American southwest). Although nondenominational it was organized by Harris Done and his friends. Dr. Done, a Latter-day Saint dentist, received his desire and inspiration for such an organization from principles of the gospel that were ingrained into his life. Ayuda, Inc. outfitted a dental trailer—literally a mobile hospital—and presented it to the Health Services Corporation.

The health missionary program is in its infancy, but it is destined to be a great blessing to the members of the Church and to its nonmember friends who desire its services and can profit greatly from its assistance.

Church Growth

Since the Church was organized on April 6, 1830, with six members, it has constantly grown larger, although the rate of

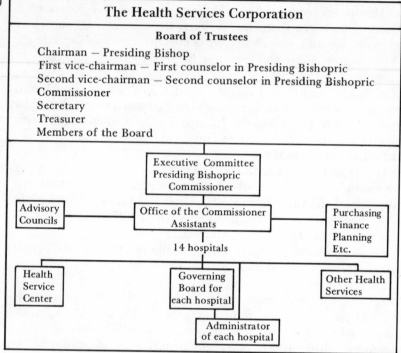

The Health Services Corporation

Board of Trustees

Chairman — Presiding Bishop
First vice-chairman — First counselor in Presiding Bishopric
Second vice-chairman — Second counselor in Presiding Bishopric
Commissioner
Secretary
Treasurer
Members of the Board

Executive Committee
Presiding Bishopric
Commissioner

Advisory
Councils

Office of the Commissioner
Assistants

Purchasing
Finance
Planning
Etc.

14 hospitals

Health
Service
Center

Governing
Board for
each hospital

Other Health
Services

Administrator
of each hospital

Fig. 14. Organization chart of the Health Services Corporation.

growth has changed somewhat from time to time because of various circumstances both external and internal.

From the chart it is obvious that the Church multiplied in membership many times over in the first few years after the restoration of the Church organization, growing from six members to 400 within the first nine months of its existence, and then showing 6,650% growth during the next ten years. During the second ten-year period the Church doubled its membership, an attainment that has not happened since. The greatest amount of growth since that time, numerically as well as in percentages, has been during the last decade (1960-70) when the Church showed 73 percent growth with an increase of 1,237,630 members during the decade. This may be the greatest growth that the Church will make for some time to come, although our decade of the 1970s will probably see more growth numerically.

It took 117 years, or exactly 100 years after the arrival of the Saints in the Salt Lake valley to acquire the first million members of the Church. The second million members were acquired in 16 years, or by 1963, whereas the third million members

CHURCH GROWTH CHART[27]

End of Year or Decade	Membership	% Growth During Decade	No. Stakes	Wards & Independent Branches in Stake	Missions	Missionaries Set Apart During Decade (Not Including Local Missionaries)	Converts Baptized During Decade
1830	400		0		0	16	
1840	30,000	6,650%	11		2	661	
1850	60,000	100%	1		9	1,425	
1860	80,000	33%	4		8	751	
1870	110,000	37.5%	9		8	709	
1880	160,000	45%	23		10	1,544	
1890	205,000	28%	32		12	2,389	
1900	268,331	31%	43	488	16	6,126	
1910	393,437	47%	62	694	21	8,254	
1920	526,032	34%	83	959	24	7,424	
1930	672,488	28%	104	1,000	30	10,140	66,942
1940	862,664	28%	134	1,191	35	8,811	76,736
1950	1,111,314	29%	180	1,541	43	14,942	95,041
1960	1,693,180	52%	319	2,882	58	21,280	261,952
1970	2,930,810	73%	537	4,922	94	64,490	830,069
1971	3,090,953				98	7,536	79,126

Fig. 15. Church growth by decades from 1830 to 1971.

602 were acquired by 1971, within an eight-year period. It appears that the next million members will be acquired in eight years or less because convert baptisms are again on the upswing, and although pressures in the United States are against large families, the birth rate in the Church seems to be at least holding its own.

In 1920 only one person out of 222 in the United States or .45% was a Latter-day Saint, whereas by the end of 1970 about one person out of every 100 was a member of the Church. Church growth as shown by organization of new stakes presents a vastly accelerating picture during the past twenty or so years. The first stake in the Church was organized February 17, 1834, nearly four years after the organization of the Church. Upon leaving the East in 1846, all stakes were dissolved and a new start was begun in the Salt Lake valley in 1847, with the organization of the Salt Lake Stake. By the death of Brigham Young in 1877 twenty stakes had been organized. By the end of the year 1900 the number of stakes had reached a total of forty-three, all of them in the intermountain west. In 1928 the 100th stake of the Church was organized, requiring ninety-eight years of Church organization to reach that number. The next 100 stakes required only twenty-four years; the 200th stake was organized in 1952. Eight years were required to reach the 300th stake in 1960, and only four years to reach the 400th stake organized in 1964. One reason for organizing stakes so much more rapidly during the 1950s and 1960s was the desire to have fewer numbers than previously in each stake, since smaller stakes and wards produce a higher rate of religious activity per person, and more efficiency in administration.

It required nearly six years after that to reach 500 stakes; this number was attained on January 18, 1970, the day of President McKay's death. During the year of 1970 a record 41 stakes were organized so that at the end of the year there were 537 stakes functioning in Zion.

Rate of Organization of New Stakes

No. of Stakes	Year	No. of Stakes	Year
1	1834	300	1960
50	1901	350	1962
100	1928	400	1964
150	1945	450	1968
200	1952	500	1970
250	1957	550	1971

An interesting facet of Church membership is the change in distribution which presents a vivid picture of the Church's beginning, as it were, from a nucleus in the midst of the Rocky Mountains and spreading until it engulfed the far corners of the world.

The spread of Church membership was much different in 1900 than it is today. In 1900 with 268,000 members of the Church, 87.7% or 235,000 lived in the intermountain area; by 1960 this had been reduced to 53.3%; by 1970 this had been further reduced to 40.5%. Only 1% lived on the Pacific Coast in 1900 as compared to 20.12% in 1960 and 20.94% in 1970. Comparing the total membership distribution of 1900 with 1960 and 1970, the percentage distribution of Church membership is as follows:

A Comparison of Church Membership
Distribution by Percent in 1900, 1960, and 1970

Area	1900	1960	1970
North America			
Pacific Coast	1.0%	20.2%	20.94%
Intermountain	87.7%	53.3%	40.50%
Midwest	1.4%	8.85%	9.35%
Mid-Atlantic	3.5%	7.68%	9.77%
Membership in			
North America	93.6%	89.95%	80.56%
Latin America	1.1%	2.10%	7.87%
Europe (and Africa)	2.8%	3.71%	5.27%
Pacific and Far East	2.5%	4.24%	6.30%
Total Members	100.0%	100.00%	100.00%

The 1971 membership population report of the Church gives an interesting breakdown by areas and states. See Appendix 12.

While the percentage of Church membership has shrunk considerably in the Intermountain West during the past half century or so, although making a constant growth numerically, the percentage of membership in the midwestern and eastern part of North America has increased considerably, having by the end of 1970 9.35% and 9.77% of the total Church membership.

Moreover, during the past twenty-five or thirty years the Church has made phenomenal growth in Latin America (7.87% of Church membership with 205,733 members) and the Pacific

604 and the Far East (6.3% of Church membership with 164,868 members).

Although Europe and Africa have not attained such a phenomenal increase, having at the end of 1970, 137,809 members or 5.26% of the total Church population, their membership has nevertheless increased quite rapidly since World War II; it had been slowed down considerably because of many immigrants to America after the end of hostilities.

Future growth of the Church looks bright in nearly all areas but especially so in the Far East, Central and South America, and on the Pacific Coast of the United States.

Footnotes

[1] Marion G. Romney, "Harold B. Lee, Apostle of the Lord," *Improvement Era* 56(July 1953):522.

[2] Richard L. Evans, "Harold B. Lee, of the Council of the Twelve," *Improvement Era* 44(April 1941):270.

[3] Evans, p. 271.

[4] Romney, p. 505.

[5] *Church News*, 8 July 1972, p. 3.

[6] Romney, p. 506.

[7] *Church News*, 8 July 1972, p. 3.

[8] "President Harold B. Lee Ordained Eleventh President of the Church," *Ensign* (August 1972), pp. 20-21.

[9] "Harold B. Lee," *Ensign*, pp. 19-20.

[10] Stephen W. Gibson, "Presidency Meets the Press," *Church News*, 15 July 1972, p. 3.

[11] Gibson, p. 3.

[12] "Harold B. Lee," *Ensign*, p. 20.

[13] *Church News*, 27 June 1970, p. 3.

[14] *Church Schools* (Provo, Utah: Church of Jesus Christ of Latter-day Saints, 1968), p. 1.

[15] *Church Schools*, p. 1.

[16] *Church Schools*, p. 37.

[17] For a well-written history of the Society see Merrill Lofthouse, "A History of the Genealogical Society of the Church of Jesus Christ of Latter-day Saints to 1970," (Master's thesis, Brigham Young University, May 1970).

[18] "Why Genealogy?" A pamphlet distributed by the Genealogical Society of the Church of Jesus Christ of Latter-day Saints, (n.p., n.d.), p. 2.

[19] "Why Genealogy?," p. 5.

[20] "Why Genealogy?," p. 6.

[21] Lofthouse, Chapter 6.

[22] These countries and their number of rolls of film at the library are as follows: Mexico (86,213 rolls), Denmark (67,274), Sweden (60,443), Great Britain (59,905), The Netherlands (51,732), Germany (42,768), France (40,267), Belgium (27,887), Finland (13,318), Canada (10,419),

Poland (7,222), Hungary (7,165), Norway (6,993), Austria (5,396),
Guatemala (2,640), Argentina (1,971), Switzerland (1,535), New Zealand
(1,458), Australia (1,418), Russia (834), Iceland (765), Bahamas (668),
Polynesia (310), Peru (78), Italy (72), Korea (40), miscellaneous other
countries (111).

[23]Lofthouse, p. 6.

[24]"Plan of Church Records Vault." (n.p., n.d.). The greater part of the
information about the vault has been taken from this article. A copy is in
the possession of Russell R. Rich.

[25]Marvin J. Ashton, "The Church Focuses on Social and Emotional
Problems," *Ensign* (January 1971), pp. 30-31.

In addition to the above, reference material on the social services was
taken from: (1) "Services of the Unified Social Services Department of
the Church of Jesus Christ of Latter-day Saints," a looseleaf handbook for
the professional personnel of the department prepared by the In-Service
Training Committee, 1970; (2) "Social and Health Services," a handbook
of administrative materials prepared for administrative personnel within
the department, 1971; (3) Personal interview with Elder Dallas Thompson
of the Unified Social Services.

[26]*Church News*, 3 October 1970, pp. 4, 15. All information about the
Health Services Corporation was taken from this article and from an interview with Dr. James O. Mason, August 27, 1972.

[27]The statistics for this article are based on conference reports as found
in the *Church News, Conference Reports,* and various charts worked out
by Dr. Richard O. Cowan and his students.

Temple at Washington, D.C., artist's concept; scheduled for completion in 1974. *Permission of Church Information Service.*

Appendix 1

COMMUNICATION TO THE GOVERNOR OF IOWA*

To His Excellency,
Governor of the Territory of Iowa,

    Honored Sir: The time is at hand, in which several thousand free citizens of this great Republic, are to be driven from their peaceful homes and firesides, their property and farms, and their dearest constitutional rights—to wander in the barren plains, and sterile mountains of western wilds, and linger out their lives in wretched exile far beyond the place of professed civilization; or else be exterminated upon their own lands by the people, and authorities of the state of Illinois. As life is sweet we have chosen *banishment* rather than death. But Sir, the terms of our banishment are so rigid that we have not sufficient time allotted us to make the necessary preparations to encounter the hardships and difficulties of those dreary and uninhabited regions. We have not time allowed us to dispose of our property, dwellings, and farms, consequently, many of us will have to leave them unsold, without the means of procuring the necessary provisions, clothing, teams, etc. to sustain us but a short distance beyond the settlements: hence our persecutors have placed us in very unpleasant circumstances.

*HC 7:601.

607

608   To stay, is death by 'fire and sword', to go into banishment unprepared, is death by starvation. But yet under these heart-rending circumstances, several hundreds of us have started upon our dreary journey, and are now encamped in Lee county, Iowa, suffering much from the intensity of the cold. Some of us are already without food, and others [have] barely sufficient to last a few weeks: hundreds of others must shortly follow us in the same unhappy condition.

Therefore, we, the Presiding Authorities of the Church of Jesus Christ of Latter-day Saints, as a committee in behalf of several thousand suffering exiles, humbly ask your Excellency to shield and protect us in our constitutional rights, while we are passing through the territory over which you have jurisdiction. And should any of the exiles be under the necessity of stopping in this territory for a time, either in the settled or unsettled parts, for the purpose of raising crops, by renting farms or upon the public lands, or to make the necessary preparations for their exile in any lawful way, we humbly petition your Excellency to use an influence and power in our behalf: and thus preserve thousands of American citizens, together with their wives and children from intense sufferings, starvation and death.

And your petitioners will ever pray.

Appendix 2

CONTRACT BETWEEN A. G. BENSON AND CO.
AND SAMUEL BRANNAN*

Whereas, the Latter-day Saints generally known under the name of Mormons, though devotedly attached to the principles on which the government of the United States and of the several states are founded, have become satisfied that owing to the prejudices against them which designing men have created in the minds of the great mass of the community, who do not appreciate their character, nor understand their designs, they cannot, under the jurisdiction of any of the present states, enjoy the privileges and security which their constitutions and laws promise to all sects and creeds.

And whereas, they have resolved to seek for liberty and security beyond the jurisdiction of the states, and under the fostering care of the United States, within their territories, not doubting that in becoming a nucleus on the shores of the Pacific, around which a new state shall grow up, constituted of a people, who, from their more intimate knowledge of them will be free from those prejudices, which now drive them into exile, thereby affording them peace and security, the only

*HC 7:589-91. The last paragraph, following the signatures, was written at the bottom of the copy of the contract by Brannan as an explanation to the Apostles.

boons they ask at the hands of man, and

Whereas, it is their earnest desire to depart in peace, and reach their future homes, without that molestation on their pilgrimage which the government of the United States might, under a misapprehension as to their designs, feel themselves called upon to offer; and *whereas,* A. G. Benson states that he has it in his power to correct any misrepresentations which may be made to the president of the United States, and prevent any authorized interference with them on their journey, and also to extend to them facilities for emigration, especially by sea, and afford them great commercial facilities and advantages at their new homes; *wherefore,*

It is covenanted and agreed between A. G. Benson aforesaid, on behalf of himself and such as he may hereafter associate with him on the one part, and Samuel Brannan, for and in behalf of the Latter-day Saints, by their principal men, duly authorized on the other part, that the said _____ shall take the necessary steps to guard the said Latter-day Saints against the effects of misapprehension, and prevent interference with them, by the officers or agents of the United States, on their journey westward, and shall, as far as in his power, facilitate trade with them in their new settlement, and promote emigration, to strengthen them there; and on the part of the said _____ for and on behalf of the Latter-day Saints aforesaid, it is covenanted and agreed that, in case the said saints shall be enabled to reach their new homes without molestation from the government of the United States, and they or any of them shall acquire lands from the said United States or from any other source, then one-half of the said lands shall belong and be conveyed to the said Benson, and those whom by written contract, he may have associated with him, his and their heirs and assigns, said lands if not surveyed to be held in common until a survey shall be made when they shall be *ipso facto* divided by alternate sections, the odd numbers belonging to the said Latter-day Saints, and the even numbers belonging to the said Benson and his associates; but if surveyed they shall be divided by sections, half sections, quarter sections, or otherwise, so as to carry into effect this agreement in its true nature and intent; and if the said saints or any of them, or the said Brannan or any of his associates, assigns or heirs shall within ten years, lay off and establish any city or cities, town or towns on the lands acquired by them or any of them, each alternate lot in said cities and towns, shall belong and be

conveyed to the said ＿＿＿＿＿＿ and his associates and
assigns as hereinbefore stipulated by the said Brannan, that the
said saints shall exert all their lawful authority and influence to
prevent the imposition of any tax on the vacant lands held by
said ＿＿＿＿＿＿, his associates and assigns, so long as they
use due diligence to settle the same, or any higher tax upon
vacant city and town lots held by him and them, than shall be
imposed on vacant lots held by resident citizens.

And it is further stipulated and agreed by the said Brannan in
behalf of said Latter-day Saints, that they shall not in any
manner on their journey, or after their arrival in the west,
violate the laws or Constitution of the United States, it being
hereby solemnly declared by him, that their dearest object, and
most earnest desire is to enjoy for themselves, their wives, children and neighbors, of whatever religion or political faith, the
protection which that Constitution and those laws promise to
all men of whatever creed.

Witness our hands and seals at the city of New York on the
＿＿＿＿＿＿ day of January, 1846.

[Signed] **Samuel Brannan, A. G. Benson.**
Witness: **W. I. Appleby**

This is only a copy of the original which I have filled out. It
is no gammon but will be carried through if you say, amen—it
was drawn up by Kendall's own hand—but no person must be
known but Mr. Benson.

BRANNAN'S LETTER THAT ACCOMPANIED
THE CONTRACT*

New York, Jan. 26, 1846.

Dear Brother Young: I haste to lay before your honorable
body the result of my movements since I wrote you last, which
was from this city, stating some of my discoveries in relation to
the contemplated movements of the general government, in
opposition to our removal.

I had an interview with Amos Kendall in company with Mr.
Benson, which resulted in a compromise, the conditions of
which you will learn by reading the contract, between them and
us, which I shall forward by this mail. I shall also leave a copy
of the same with Elder Appleby, who was present when it was
signed. Kendall is now our friend and will use his influence in
our behalf in connection with twenty-five of the most promi-

*HC 7:588-89.

612 nent demagogues of the country. You will be permitted to pass out of the states unmolested. Their counsel is to go well armed, but keep them well secreted from the rabble.

I shall select the most suitable spot on the Bay of San Francisco for the location of a commercial city.

When I sail, which will be next Saturday at 1 o'clock, I shall hoist a flag with Oregon on it. Immediately on the reception of this letter you must write to Messrs. A. G. Benson [and Co.] and let them know whether you are willing to coincide with the contract I have made for our deliverance. I am aware that it is a covenant with death, but we know that God is able to break it, and will do it, the children of Israel from Egypt had to make covenants for their safety and leave it for God to break them, and the Prophet has said 'as it was then so shall it be in the last days.' And I have been led by a remarkable train of circumstances to say, amen—and I feel and hope you will do the same. Mr. Benson thinks the Twelve should leave and get out of the country first and avoid being arrested if it is a possible thing, but if you are arrested you will find a staunch friend in him, and you will find friends, and that a host, to deliver you from their hands—if any of you are arrested, don't be tried west of the Allegheny Mountains. In the east you will find friends that you little think of. It is the prayer of the saints in the east night and day for your safety and it is mine first in the morning and last in the evening. I must now bring my letter to a close. Mr. Benson's address is No. 39 South Street—and the sooner you can give him an answer the better it will be for us. He will spend one month in Washington to sustain you—and he will do it, no mistake. But everything must be kept as silent as death on our part—names of the parties in particular. I now commit this sheet to the post praying that Israel's God may prevent it from falling into the hands of wicked men. You will hear from me again on the day of sailing if it is the Lord's will. Amen.

Yours truly,

A friend and brother in God's Kingdom,

[Signed] SAMUEL BRANNAN.

Appendix 3

THOMAS L. KANE'S DESCRIPTION OF THE
CITY OF NAUVOO AND THE EXILED MORMONS*

A few years ago, ascending the upper Mississippi in the autumn, when its waters were low, I was compelled to travel by land past the region of the rapids. My road lay through the Half Breed tract, a fine section of Iowa, which the unsettled state of its land titles had appropriated as a sanctuary for coiners, horse thieves and other outlaws. I had left my steamer at Keokuk at the foot of the lower falls, to hire a carriage and to contend for some fragments of a dirty meal with the swarming flies, the only scavengers of the locality.

From this place to where the deep water of the river returns my eye wearied to see everywhere sordid vagabond and idle settlers, and a country marred without being improved, by their careless hands. I was descending the last hillside upon my journey, when a landscape in delightful contrast broke upon my view. Half encircled by a bend of the river, a beautiful city lay glittering in the fresh morning sun. Its bright new dwellings, set in cool green gardens ranging up around a stately dome-shaped hill, which was crowned by a noble marble edifice, whose high tapering spire was radiant with white and gold. The city

*John R. Young, *Memoirs of John R. Young, Utah Pioneer, 1847* (Salt Lake City: Deseret News Press, 1920), pp. 31-38.

appeared to cover several miles, and beyond it, in the backgrounds, there rolled off a fair country chequered by the careful lines of fruitful husbandry. The unmistakable marks of industry, enterprise and educated wealth everywhere, made the scene one of singular and most striking beauty. It was a natural impulse to visit this inviting region. I procured a skiff, and rowing across the river, landed at the chief wharf of the city. No one met me there. I looked and saw no one. I could hear no one move, though the quiet everywhere was such that I heard the flies buzz and the water ripples break against the shallow beach. I walked through the solitary streets. The town lay as in a dream, under some deadening spell of loneliness, from which I almost feared to wake it, for plainly it had not slept long. There was no grass growing up in the paved ways, rains had not entirely washed away the prints of dusty footsteps, yet I went about unchecked. I went into empty workshops, rope walks and smithies. The spinner's wheel was idle, the carpenter had gone from his work bench and shavings, his unfinished sash and casings, fresh bark was in the tanner's vat, and fresh chopped light wood stood piled against the baker's oven. The blacksmith's shop was cold; but his coal heap and ladling pool and crooked water horn were all there, as if he had just gone for a holiday. No work people looked to know my errand. If I went into the garden clinking the wicket latch loudly after me, to pull the marigolds, heartease and lady-slippers and draw a drink with the water sodden well bucket and its noisy chain, or, knocking off with my stick the tall, heavyheaded dahlias and sunflowers, hunted over the beds for cucumbers and loveapples, no one called out to me from any opened window, or dog sprang forward to bark an alarm.

I could have supposed the people hidden in the houses, but the doors were unfastened, and when, at last, I timidly entered them I found dead ashes white upon the hearths, and had to tread a tip-toe as if walking down the aisle of a country church, to avoid arousing irreverent echoes from the naked floors.

On the outskirts of the town was the city graveyard, but there was no record of plague there, nor did it in any wise differ much from other Protestant American cemeteries. Some of the mounds were not long sodded: some of the stones were newly set. Their dates recent and their black inscriptions glossy in the mason's hardly dried lettering ink. Beyond the graveyard, out in the fields, I saw in one spot hard by where the fruited boughs of a young orchard had been roughly torn down, the still

smouldering embers of a barbecue fire that had been constructed of rails from the fencing around it. It was the latest
signs of life there. Fields upon fields of heavy headed yellow
grain lay rotting ungathered upon the ground. No one was at
hand to take in their rich harvest.

As far as the eye could reach they stretched away, they
sleeping too, in the hazy air of autumn. Only two portions of
the city seemed to suggest the import of this mysterious soli-
tude. On the eastern suburb the houses looking out upon the
country showed, by their splintered woodworks and walls
battered to the foundation, that they had lately been a mark of
destructive cannonade, and in and around the splendid temple,
which had been the chief object of my admiration, armed men
were barracked, surrounded by their stacks of musketry and
pieces of heavy ordnance. These challenged me to render an
account of myself and why I had the temerity to cross the
water without a written permit from the leader of their band.
Though these men were more or less under the influence of
ardent spirits, after I had explained myself as a passing stranger,
they seemed anxious to gain my good opinion. They told the
story of the dead city—that it had been a notable manufacturing
and commercial mart, sheltering over twenty thousand persons.
That they had waged war with its inhabitants for several years,
and had finally been successful only a few days before my visit,
in an action fought in front of the ruined suburb, after which
they had driven them at the point of the sword. The defense,
they said, had been obstinate, but gave way on the third day's
bombardment. They boasted greatly of their prowess, especially
in this battle, as they called it. But I discovered they were not
of one mind, as to certain of the exploits that had distinguished
it. One of which, as I remember was, that they had slain a father
and his son, a boy of fifteen, not long a resident of the fated
city, whom they admitted to have borne a character without
reproach.

They also conducted me inside the wall—of the curious
temple, in which they said, the banished inhabitants were
accustomed to celebrate the mystic rites of an unhallowed
worship. They particularly pointed out to me certain features of
the building, which having been the peculiar objects of a former
superstitious regard, they had as a matter of duty sedulously
defiled and defaced. The reputed site of certain shrines they had
thus particularly noticed, and various sheltered chambers, in
one of which was a deep well, constructed, they believed, with a

dreadful design. Besides these, they led me to see a large and deep chiseled marble vase or basin, supported upon twelve oxen, also of marble, and of the size of life, of which they told some romantic stories. They said the deluded persons, most of whom were emigrants from a great distance, believed their Deity countenanced their reception here for a baptism of regeneration, as proxies for whomsoever they held in warm affection in the countries from which they had come. That here parents "went into the water" for their lost children, children for their parents, widows for their spouses, and young persons for their lovers. That thus the great vase came to be for them associated with all dear and distant memories, and was therefore the object, of all others, in the building, to which they attached the greatest degree of idolatrous affection. On this account the victors had so diligently desecrated it as to render the apartment in which it was contained too noisome to abide in. They permitted me also to ascend into the steeple to see where it had been lightning struck on the Sabbath before, and to look out east and south on wasted farms like those I had seen near the city, extending till they were lost in the distance. Here in the face of pure day, close to the scar of divine wrath left by the thunderbolt, were fragments of food, cruses of liquor, and broken drinking vessels, with a bass drum and a steamboat signal bell, of which I afterwards learned the use with pain.

It was after nightfall when I was ready to cross the river on my return. The wind had freshened after sunset, and the water beating roughly into my little boat, I headed higher up the stream than the point I had left in the morning, and landed where a faint glimmering light invited me to steer. Here among the dock and rushes, sheltered only by the darkness, without roof between them and the sky, I came upon a crowd of several hundred creatures, whom my movements roused from uneasy slumber upon the ground. Passing these on my way to the light I found it came from a tallow candle in a paper funnel shade such as is used by street vendors of apples and peanuts, and which flaring and fluttering away in the bleak air off the water, shone flickeringly on the emaciated features of a man in the last stage of a bilious, remittent fever. They had done their best for him. Over his head was something like a tent made of a sheet or two, and he rested on a but partially ripped open old straw mattress, with a hair sofa cushion under his head for a pillow. His gaping jaw and glazing eye told how short a time he would enjoy these luxuries, though a seemingly bewildered and excited person, who might have been his wife, seemed to find hope in occasionally forcing him to swallow awkwardly a measured sip of the tepid river water from a burned and battered bitter smelling tin coffee pot. Those who knew better had furnished the apothecary he needed, a toothless old bald head, whose manner had the repulsive dullness of a man familiar with death-scenes. He, so long as I remained, mumbled in his patient's ear a monotonous and melancholy prayer, between the pauses of which I heard the hiccup and sobbing of two little girls who were sitting upon a piece of driftwood outside. Dreadful indeed, were the sufferings of those forsaken beings, bowed and cramped by cold and sun burn, alternating as each weary day and night dragged on. They were almost all of them, the crippled victims of disease. They were there because they had no homes, nor hospitals, nor poor house, nor friends to offer them any. They could not satisfy the feeble cravings of their sick. They had not bread to quiet the fractious hunger cries of their children. Mothers and babes, daughters and grandparents, all of them alike, were bivouacked in tatters, wanting even covering to comfort those whom the sick shiver of fever was searching to the marrow.

These were the Mormons, famishing in Lee county, Iowa, in the fourth week of the month of September, in the year of our Lord, 1846. The city, it was Nauvoo, Ills. The Mormons were the owners of that city, and the smiling country around, and those who stopped their plows, who had silenced their hammers, their axes, their shuttles and their workshop wheels, those who had put out their fires, who had eaten their food, spoiled their orchards and trampled under foot their thousands of acres of unharvested grain, these were the keepers of their dwellings, the carousers in their temple, whose drunken riot insulted the ears of their dying. They were, all told, not more than six hundred forty persons who were thus lying on the river flats, but the Mormons in Nauvoo had numbered the year before over twenty thousand. Where were they? They had last been seen, carrying in mournful trains their sick and wounded, halt and blind to disappear behind the western horizon, pursuing the phantom of another home. Hardly anything else was known of them and people asked with curiosity—what had been their fate, what their fortune!

Appendix 4

HIGH PRAISE FROM THE COMMANDING OFFICER*

Head Quarters Mormon Battalion,
Mission of San Diego,

January 30, 1847.

(Orders No. 1.)

The Lieutenant-Colonel commanding congratulates the Battalion on their safe arrival on the shore of the Pacific Ocean and the conclusion of their march of over two thousand miles. History may be searched in vain for an equal march of infantry. Half of it has been through a wilderness where nothing but savages and wild beasts are found, or deserts where, for want of water, there is no living creature. There, with hopeless labor we have dug deep wells, which the future traveler will enjoy. Without a guide who had traversed them, we have ventured into trackless table-lands where water was not found for several marches. With crowbar and pick and axe in hand, we have worked our way over mountains, which seemed to defy aught save the wild goat, and hewed a passage through a chasm of

*Cited in Daniel Tyler, "A Concise History of the Mormon Battalion in the Mexican War" (n.p., 1881), pp. 254-55. Copies available in the Brigham Young University Library, Provo, Utah.

620 living rock more narrow than our wagons. To bring these first wagons to the Pacific, we have preserved the strength of our mules by herding them over large tracts, which you have laboriously guarded without loss. The garrison of four presidios of Sonora concentrated within the walls of Tucson, gave us no pause. We drove them out, with their artillery, but our intercourse with the citizens was unmarked by a single act of injustice. Thus, marching half naked and half fed, and living upon wild animals, we have discovered and made a road of great value to our country.

Arrived at the first settlement of California, after a single day's rest, you cheerfully turned off from the route to this point of promised repose, to enter upon a campaign, and meet, as we supposed, the approach of an enemy; and this too, without even salt to season your sole subsistence of fresh meat.

Lieutenants A. J. Smith and George Stoneman, of the First Dragoons, have shared and given valuable aid in all these labors.

Thus, volunteers, you have exhibited some high and essential qualities of veterans. But much remains undone. Soon, you will turn your attention to the drill, to system and order, to forms also, which are all necessary to the soldier.

By order

Lieut. Colonel P. St. George Cooke.
P. C. Merrill, Adjutant.

Appendix 5

ORGANIZATION OF THE PIONEER CAMP

In general charge were the eight apostles who were present with Brigham Young as President. General Clerk of the camp was Thomas Bullock.

I. Israelitish Organization of the Camp

Directing Division I (The Tens #1-7)

   Brigham Young

Directing Division II (The Tens #8-14)

   Heber C. Kimball

Captains of Hundreds

   Stephen Markham
   Albert P. Rockwood

Captains of Fifties

   Addison Everett
   Tarlton Lewis
   James Case
   John Pack
   Shadrach Roundy

First Ten

Wilford Woodruff, Captain	John S. Fowler
Jacob D. Burnham	Orson Pratt
Joseph Egbert	John M. Freeman
Marcus B. Thorpe	George A. Smith
George Wardle	

Second Ten

Thomas Grover, Captain	Jesse C. Little
Barnabas L. Adams	Ezra T. Benson
Amasa M. Lyman	Roswell Stevens
Albert Carrington	Sterling Driggs
George W. Brown	Thomas Bullock
Willard Richards	

Third Ten

Phineas H. Young, Captain	John Y. Green
Thomas Tanner	Brigham Young
Addison Everett	Truman O. Angel
Lorenzo D. Young	Bryant Stringham
Joseph S. Schofield	Albert P. Rockwood

Fourth Ten

Luke S. Johnson, Captain	John Holman
Edmund Ellsworth	S. Alvarus Hanks
George R. Grant	Millen Atwood
Samuel Fox	Tunis Rappleye
Eli H. Peirce	Williams Dykes
Jacob Weiler	

Fifth Ten

Stephen H. Goddard, Captain	Tarlton Lewis
Henry G. Sherwood	Zebedee Coltrin
Sylvester H. Earl	John Dixon
Samuel H. Marble	George Scholes
William Henrie	William A. Empey

Sixth Ten

Charles Shumway, Captain	Andrew P. Shumway
Thomas Woolsey	Chauncey Loveland
Erastus Snow	James Craig
William S. Wardsworth	William P. Vance
Simeon Howd	Seeley Owen

Seventh Ten

James Case, Captain
William C. A. Smoot
William Carter
Burr Frost
Benjamin F. Stewart
Eric Glines

Artemas Johnson
B. Franklin Dewey
Franklin G. Losee
Datus Ensign
H. Monroe Frink
Ozro Eastman (nonmember)

Eighth Ten

Seth Taft, Captain
Stephen Kelsey
Charles D. Barnum
Rufus Allen
James W. Stewart
Levi N. Kendall
David Grant

Horace Thornton
John S. Eldredge
Almon S. Williams
Robert T. Thomas
Elijah Newman
Francis Boggs

Ninth Ten

Heber C. Kimball, Captain
William A. King
Hosea Cushing
George Billings
Philo Johnson

Howard Egan
Thomas P. Cloward
Robert E. Baird
Edson Whipple
William Clayton

Tenth Ten

Appleton M. Harmon, Captain
Horace K. Whitney
Orrin Porter Rockwell
R. Jackson Redden
Francis M. Pomeroy
Aaron F. Farr

Nathaniel Fairbanks
Carlos Murray
Orson K. Whitney
Nathaniel T. Brown
John Pack

Eleventh Ten

John S. Higbee, Captain
Solomon Chamberlain
Joseph Rooker
John H. Tippetts
Henson Walker

John Wheeler
Conrad Kleinman
Perry Fitzgerald
James Davenport
Benjamin W. Rolfe
(nonmember)

Twelfth Ten

Norton Jacobs, Captain
George Woodward
Lewis Barney
Andrew S. Gibbons
John W. Norton

Charles A. Harper
Stephen Markham
George Mills
Joseph Hancock

Shadrach Roundy, Captain
Levi Jackman
John Brown
David Powell
Oscar Crosby (colored)

Hans C. Hanson
Lyman Curtis
Matthew Ivory
Hark Lay (colored)
   or Hark Whales

Fourteenth Ten

Joseph Matthew
John S. Gleason
Alexander P. Chessley
Norman Taylor

Gilbard Summe
Charles A. Burke
Rodney Badger
Green Flake (colored)

Women and Children

Harriet Page Wheeler Young (wife of Lorenzo)
   Isaac Perry Decker
   Lorenzo Zabriskie Young

Clarissa Decker Young (wife of Brigham)

Ellen Saunders Kimball (wife of Heber)

II. Military Organization of the Camp

Lieutenant General

Brigham Young

Colonel

Stephen Markham

Majors

John Pack
Shadrach Roundy

Captains

Captains of Tens in Israelitish organization

III. Captain of the Night Guard

Stephen Markham

(Forty-eight men were regular members of the night. Ordinarily twelve were on duty half the night every other night.)

Appendix 6

LETTER OF BRIGHAM YOUNG TO
THE EMIGRATING COMPANIES *

Pioneer Camp, Valley of the Great Salt Lake, Aug. 2, 1847

To General Charles C. Rich and the Presidents and Officers of
the Emigrating Company.

Dear Brethren.——We have delegated our beloved brother,
Ezra T. Benson, and escort to communicate to you by express
the cheering intelligence that we have arrived in the most
beautiful valley of the Great Salt Lake; that every soul who left
Winter Quarters with us is alive, and almost every one enjoying
good health. That portion of the Battalion that was at Pueblo
are here with us, together with the Mississippi company that
accompanied them, and they are generally well. We number
about four hundred souls, and we know of no one but what is
pleased with our situation. We have commenced the survey of a
city this morning. We feel that the time is fast approaching
when those teams that are going to Winter Quarters this fall
should be on the way. Every individual here would be glad to
tarry if their friends were here, but as many of the Battalion as

*Orson F. Whitney, *History of Utah* (Salt Lake City: George Q. Cannon
and Sons Co., 1904), 1:347-48.

626 well as the Pioneers have not their families here, and do not
expect that they are in your camp, we wish to learn by express
from you the situation of your camp as speedily as possible,
that we may be prepared to counsel and act in the whole
matter. We want you to send us the name of every individual in
your camp, or, in other words, a copy of your whole camp roll,
including the names, number of wagons, horses, mules, oxen,
cows, etc., and the health of your camp; your location, prospects, etc. If your teams are worn out, if your camp is sick and
not able to take care of themselves, if you are short of
teamsters, or if any other circumstance impedes your progress,
we want to know it immediately, for we have help for you, and
if your teams are in good plight, and will be able to return to
Winter Quarters this season, or any portion of them, we want to
know it. We also want the mail, which will include all letters
and papers and packages belonging to our camp, general and
particular. Would circumstances permit, we would gladly meet
you some distance from this, but our time is very much
occupied, notwithstanding we think you will see us before you
see our valley. Let all the brethren and sisters cheer up their
hearts and know assuredly that God has heard and answered
their prayers and ours, and led us to a goodly land, and our
souls are satisfied therewith. Brother Benson can give you many
particulars that will be gratifying and cheering to you which I
have not time to write, and we feel to bless all the Saints.

In behalf of the council,

Brigham Young, President
Willard Richards, Clerk

Appendix 7

RESOLUTION OF THE GENERAL ASSEMBLY OF THE
STATE OF DESERET WELCOMING THE EXTENSION OF
THE U.S. GOVERNMENT OVER THE TERRITORY—PASSED
MARCH 28, 1851.*

Be it resolved by the General Assembly of the State of
Deseret

1. That we cheerfully and cordially accept the legislation of
Congress in the Act to establish a Territorial Government for
Utah.

2. That we welcome the Constitution of the United States—
the legacy of our fathers—over this Territory.

3. That all officers under the Provisional State Government
of Deseret are hereby requested to furnish unto their successors
in office every facility in their power, by returning and delivering unto them public documents, laws, ordinances, and
dockets, that may or can be of any use or benefit to their said
successors in office.

4. That Union Square, in Great Salt Lake City, be devoted
for the use of public buildings of said Territory.

5. That Governor B. Young be our agent to make drafts
upon the treasury of the United States for the amount

*Orson F. Whitney, *Popular History of Utah* (Salt Lake City: Deseret
News Press, 1916), p. 75.

628 appropriated for said buildings, and to take such other measures as he shall deem proper for their immediate erection.

6. That we appoint an architect to draft designs, and a committee of one to superintend the erection of said buildings.

7. That Truman O. Angell, of said city, be said architect, and Daniel H. Wells, of said city, the committee; and that they proceed immediately to the designing and erection of said buildings.

8. That, whereas, the State House in Great Salt Lake City having been originally designed for a "Council House," and erected by and at the expense of the Church of Jesus Christ of Latter-day Saints for the purpose, as well as to accommodate the Provisional Government; that we do now relinquish unto said Church the aforesaid building, tendering unto them our thanks for the free use thereof during the past session.

9. That we fix upon Saturday, the fifth day of April next, for the adjustment and final dissolving of the General Assembly of the State of Deseret.

H.C. Kimball, President of the Council
J.M. Grant, Speaker of the House

Appendix 8

MORMON COLONIES FOUNDED UNDER BRIGHAM YOUNG

Mormon Colonies, 1847-1857

1. Salt Lake City, July 24, 1847
2. Bountiful, September 29, 1847
3. Farmington, fall of 1847
4. Parley's Park, fall of 1847
5. Pleasant Green, fall of 1847
6. Ogden, January 1848
7. Big Cottonwood, spring of 1848
8. East Mill Creek, spring of 1848
9. Sugar House, spring of 1848
10. Centerville, spring of 1848
11. Bingham, August 1848
12. Mound Fort, fall of 1848
13. South Cottonwood, fall of 1848
14. North Jordan, December 1848
15. West Jordan, December 1848
16. Kaysville, spring of 1849
17. Provo, spring of 1849
18. Genoa (Mormon Station), June 1849
19. Union (Little Cottonwood), 1849
20. Lynne (Bingham's Fort), 1849
21. Brighton, fall of 1849
22. Granger, fall of 1849
23. Draper, November 1849
24. Manti, November 22, 1849
25. Tooele, fall of 1849
26. Grantsville, fall of 1849
27. Harrisville, spring of 1850
28. Uinta (Easton), 1850
29. Lehi, August 1850
30. Pleasant Grove, July 1850
31. Lake View, 1850
32. Springville, September 1850
33. Payson, October 20, 1850
34. Alpine, fall of 1850
35. Spanish Fork, fall of 1850
36. American Fork, fall of 1850
37. Layton, fall of 1850
38. Marriott, fall of 1850
39. Slaterville, fall of 1850
40. West Weber, fall of 1850
41. Wilson, 1850
42. North Ogden, fall of 1850
43. Lindon, 1850
44. Parowan, January 13, 1851
45. Salem, spring of 1851
46. Herriman, spring of 1851
47. Brigham City, March 4, 1851
48. Farr West, 1851
49. Willard, spring of 1851

50. Santaquin, summer of 1851
51. San Bernardino, 1851
52. Nephi, September 1851
53. Fillmore, October 28, 1851
53a. Cedar City, November 11, 1851
54. South Weber, November 1851
55. Midvale, fall of 1851
56. Mona, December 1851
57. Pleasant View, fall of 1851
58. Harper, spring of 1852
59. Paragonah, spring of 1852
60. Harmony, spring of 1852
61. Cedar Valley, October 1852
62. South Hooper, 1852
63. Batesville, 1852
64. Mt. Pleasant, spring of 1852
65. Spring City, 1852
66. Butterfield, before 1853
67. Ephraim, winter of 1852-53
68. Perry, April 1853
69. Fort Supply, November 15, 1853 to October 3, 1857
70. E. T. City, spring of 1854
71. Crescent, 1854
72. Wanship, 1854
73. Santa Clara, December 1854
74. Clover, fall of 1854
75. Peterson, 1855
76. Fairfield, spring of 1855
77. Las Vegas, 1855-1858
78. Fort Bridger, 1855-1857
79. Lake View, summer of 1855
80. Pine Valley, 1855
81. Holden, 1855
82. Morgan, 1855
83. Moab (Elk Mountain Mission), May 21, 1855
84. Lemhi (Salmon River Mission), 1855-1858
85. Beaver, February 6, 1856
86. Franktown, 1856
87. Wellsville, September 1856
88. Mapleton, 1856
89. Pinto, fall of 1856
90. Milton, 1856
91. Washington, May 15, 1856
92. Mendon, 1857
93. Meadow, spring of 1857
94. Peoa, 1857
95. Goshen, 1857
96. Gunlock, 1857

Mormon Colonies, 1858-1867

97. Heberville (Price), January 13, 1858
98. Toquerville, spring of 1858
99. Virgin City, December 7, 1858

100. Mountain Dell, 1858
101. Harrisville, spring of 1859
102. Charleston, spring of 1859
103. Coalville, May 17, 1859
104. Plain City, March 1859
105. Deseret, spring of 1859
106. Logan, April 1859
107. Providence, April 20, 1859
108. Minersville, May 17, 1859
109. Harrisburg, spring of 1859
110. Fountain Green, July 1859
111. Hoytsville, 1859
112. Eden, 1859
113. Henefer, 1859
114. Richmond, July 1859
115. Kanosh, 1859
116. Gunnison, 1859
117. Millville, fall of 1859
118. Moroni, 1859
119. Cheney's Ranch, 1859
120. Franklin, fall of 1859
121. Mountain Green, 1859
122. Smithfield, October 1859
123. Deep Creek, spring of 1859
124. Heber City, spring of 1859
125. Midway, spring of 1859
126. South Jordan, March 1, 1859
127. Fairview, 1859
128. Grafton, December 1859
129. Scipio, fall of 1859
130. Kamas, spring of 1860
131. Spring Lake, spring of 1860
132. Hyde Park, April 1860
133. Paradise, spring of 1860
134. Hyrum, April 1860
135. Juab, 1860
136. Richville, summer of 1860
137. Avon, 1860
138. Benjamin, 1860
139. Rockport, August 1860
140. Center, 1860
141. Adventure, 1860
142. Harrisville (Weber), 1860
143. East Porterville, fall of 1860
144. Morgan, fall of 1860
145. Huntsville, fall of 1860
146. Greenville, February 1861
147. Little Cottonwood, 1861
148. Porterville, spring of 1861
149. Fayette, spring of 1861
150. Enterprise, summer of 1861
151. Mountain Dell (Utah), 1861
152. Rockville, November 1861
153. Saint George, December 4, 1861
154. Duncan's Retreat, 1861
155. Echo, fall of 1861
156. Shonesburg, January 20, 1862.
157. Coveville, 1862

158. Croyden, 1862
159. Vernon, April 1862
160. Hebron, April 27, 1862
161. Wallsburg, 1862
162. Northop, spring of 1862
163. Adamsville, spring of 1862
164. Springdale, fall of 1862
165. Zion Park, 1862
166. Tonaquint, evacuated 1862
167. Mantua, spring of 1863
168. Pipe Springs, 1863
169. Belleview, spring of 1863
170. Middletown, spring of 1863
171. Spring Lake, 1863
172. Petersburg, 1863
173. Monroe, fall of 1863
174. Salina, fall of 1863
175. Paris, fall of 1863
176. Glenwood, January 1864
177. Portage, spring of 1864
178. Circleville, spring of 1864
179. Joseph, spring of 1864
180. Richfield, March 13, 1864
181. Indianola, 1864
182. Clinton, 1864
183. Panguitch, March 16, 1864
184. Woodland, April 15, 1864
185. Malad, April 1864
186. Marsh, 1864
187. Bloomington, April 22, 1864
188. Montpelier, spring of 1864
189. Fish Haven, spring of 1864
190. Garden City, 1864
191. Laketown, 1864
192. Liberty, spring of 1864
193. Ovid, 1864
194. Saint Charles, spring of 1864
195. Moccasin Springs, 1864
196. Clarkston, 1864
197. Glendale (Berryville), spring of 1864
198. Bennington, spring of 1864
199. Eagle Valley, July 7, 1864
200. Mount Carmel, fall of 1864
201. Easton, 1864-65
202. Call's Landing, 1864
203. Eden, 1864
204. Littlefield (Beaver Dam), 1864
205. Marysvale, October 1864
206. Oxford, fall of 1864
207. Saint Thomas, Jan. 8, 1865-1871. Resettled, 1881
208. Overton, 1865-1871. Resettled, 1881
209. Saint Joseph, 1865-1871. Resettled, 1881
210. Logandale (West Point), 1865-1871. Resettled, 1881

211. Simonville, 1865-1871
212. Millpoint, 1865-1871
213. Oak City, spring of 1865
214. Alton, spring of 1865
215. Pahreah, 1865
216. Cherry Creek, spring of 1865
217. Upton, 1865
218. Woodruff, October 1865
219. Spring Valley, 1865
220. Wardbaro, fall of 1865
221. Bluffdale, December 1865
222. Port Sanford, spring of 1866
223. Bear River City, January 1866
224. Panacca, 1866
225. Mountain Meadows, n.d.
226. Honeyville, 1866
227. West Point, March 1867
228. Leeds, fall of 1867
229. Petersboro, 1867
230. Saint Johns, fall of 1867
231. Berryville, 1867

Mormon Colonies, 1868-1877

232. Alta, 1868
233. Samaria, February 10, 1868
234. Oakley, 1868
235. Levan, spring of 1868
236. Dayton, summer of 1868
237. Treasureton, 1868
238. Kanarraville, by 1869
239. Newton, spring of 1869
240. Saint John, spring of 1869
241. Manila, 1869
242. Skull Valley Indian Mission, 1869
243. Eureka, 1869
244. Quincy, 1869
245. Meadowville, August 6, 1869
246. Clifton, fall of 1869
247. Fairview, fall of 1869
248. Randolph, March 14, 1870
249. Trenton, March 17, 1870
250. Kanab, March 1870
251. Chester, June 1870
252. Cambridge, 1870
253. Cannon, 1870
254. Freedom, 1870
255. Milford, 1870
256. Hillsdale, 1871
258. Georgetown, April 29, 1871
259. Sandy, 1871
260. Soda Springs, May 1871
261. Johnson, spring of 1871
262. Mound Valley, 1871
263. Annabella, spring of 1871
264. Moen Copie, 1871
265. Pioche, 1871

632

266. Mayfield, fall of 1871
267. Vermillion, fall of 1871
268. Leamington, fall of 1871
269. Murray, 1872
270. Lake Shore, 1872
271. Preston, spring of 1872
272. Central (Inverury), January 1872
273. Warrena, February 1852
274. Hatch, 1872
275. Lee's Ferry, 1872
276. Mink Creek, 1872
277. Riverdale, 1872
278. Sterling, 1872
279. Venice, 1873
280. Pettyville, 1873
281. Prattville, April 1873
282. Tuba, May 17, 1873
283. Burrville, June 23, 1873
284. Whitney, summer of 1873
285. Bern, August 1873
286. Fort Cameron, September 1873
287. Elba, 1873
288. Dingle, 1873
289. Daniel, March 1874
290. Mount Trumbull, February 8, 1874
291. Elsinore, spring of 1874
292. Grass Valley, 1874
293. Koosharon, August 1874
294. Cannonville, December 24, 1874
295. Cleveland, December 8, 1874
296. Woodland, fall of 1874
297. Greenwich (Grass Valley), 1874
298. Wales, n.d.
299. Deweyville, n.d.
300. Curley, n.d.
301. Aurora, March 25, 1875
302. Redmond, spring of 1875
303. Albin, May 1875
304. Snowville, n.d.
305. Escalante, June 1875
306. Orderville, spring of 1875
307. Washakie (Indian farm), spring of 1875
308. Nashville, 1875
309. Mapleton, 1875
310. Marion, 1875
311. Mount Sterling, 1875
312. Chesterfield, 1875
313. Nounan, 1875
314. Vineyard, 1875
315. Argyle, 1875
316. Fremont, spring of 1876
317. Grouse Creek, spring of 1876

318. Saint Joseph (Allen City), March 1876
319. Brigham City (Ballenger), March 1876
320. Thomas' Fort, 1876
321. Hunter, 1876
322. Sunset, March 1876
323. Obed, June 1876
324. Tonto Basin, July 17, 1876
325. Timpanogos, 1876
326. Mill Creek, 1876
327. Kingston, fall of 1876
328. Woodruff, December 1876
329. Ramah, winter of 1876-1877
330. Bunkerville, January 6, 1877
331. Garden Creek, March 21, 1877
332. Saint David, March 1877
333. Benson, 1877
334. Almo, 1877
335. Syracuse, 1877
336. Lanark, October 1877
337. Price, fall of 1877
338. Huntington, fall of 1877
339. Castle Dale, 1877
340. Ferron, fall of 1877
341. Lehi (in Arizona), 1877
342. Papago, 1877
343. Showlow, 1877
344. Snowflake, fall of 1877
345. Jenson, fall of 1877
346. Mill, winter of 1877-1878
347. Junction, before 1878
348. Almy, before 1877
349. Loa (Rabbit Valley), before 1877
350. Mesa, January 1878
351. Taylor, January 1878
352. Forest Dale, February 1878
353. Pine Ward, 1878
354. Conejos, 1878
355. Los Cerritos, 1878
356. Mountain Dell, February 1878
357. Merrill, 1878
358. Burnham, 1878

The colonies listed are those established in the Great West while President Brigham Young was directing Mormon land settlement. A few of them were settled after his death, which occurred on August 29, 1877, but those colonies were in Arizona and President Young had planned the project before his death.*

*Appreciation is given to Milton R. Hunter for permission to publish these lists. They are taken from *Brigham Young, the Colonizer* (Salt Lake City: Deseret News Press, 1940), pp. 361-67.

Appendix 9

UTAH TERRITORIAL OFFICIALS

Below are listed those territorial officials who held the more prominent offices in the territory from the time of its creation until statehood. They are categorized either as anti-Mormon (A), neutral (N), or friendly (F). Most of those listed as either neutral or friendly soon gained the respect and confidence of the Church leaders and the average Church member. The categorization is of the writer, from which others may differ.

Governors

Name	Date of Commission	Period	Appointed by	Attitude Toward Church
Brigham Young	9/28/50	1850-1857	Fillmore & Pierce	F
Alfred Cumming	7/11/57	1857-1861	Buchanan	F
Francis Wooton (Acting)		1861-1861		F
Frank Fuller (Acting)		1861-1861		F
John Dawson	10/3/61	1861-1861	Lincoln	A
Frank Fuller (Acting)		1861-1862		F
Stephen S. Harding	3/31/62	1862-1863	Lincoln	A
James Duane Doty	6/2/63	1863-1865	Lincoln	F
Charles Durkee	7/17/65	1865-1869	Johnson	F
Edwin Higgins (Acting)		1869-1869		N
S. A. Mann (Acting)		1869-1870		F
J. Wilson Shaffer	1/17/70	1870-1870	Grant	A
Vernon H. Vaughan	11/1/70	1870-1872	Grant	F

634
George L. Woods	2/2/72	1872-1875	Grant	A
Samuel B. Axtell	2/2/75	1875-1875	Grant	F
George Emery	7/1/75	1875-1879	Grant	N
Eli H. Murray	1/27/80	1880-1885	Hayes & Arthur	A
Caleb W. West	4/2/86	1886-1889	Cleveland	N
Arthur L. Thomas	5/6/89	1889-1893	Harrison	N
Caleb W. West	4/14/93	1893-1896	Cleveland	N

Supreme Court Justices in the Territory of Utah

Name	Position	Date of Commission	Period	Appointed by	Attitude
L. G. Brandebury	Chief Justice	3/12/51	1851-1851	Fillmore	A
Perry E. Brocchus	Assoc. Justice	9/2/50	1850-1851	Fillmore	A
Zerubbabel Snow	Assoc. Justice	9/28/50	1850-1854	Fillmore	F
Lazarus H. Reed	Chief Justice	8/31/52	1852-1854	Fillmore	F
Leonidas Shaver	Assoc. Justice	8/31/52	1852-1855	Fillmore	F
John F. Kinney	Chief Justice	8/24/54	1854-1856	Pierce	N
George P. Stiles	Assoc. Justice	8/1/54	1854-1857	Pierce	N
W. W. Drummond	Assoc. Justice	9/12/54	1854-1857	Pierce	A
E. D. Potter	Assoc. Justice	7/6/57	1857-1857	Buchanan	A
Delano Eckles	Chief Justice	7/13/57	1857-1860	Buchanan	A
Charles E. Sinclair	Assoc. Justice	8/27/57	1857	Buchanan	A
John Cradlebaugh	Assoc. Justice	6/4/58	1858	Buchanan	A
R. P. Flennikan	Assoc. Justice	5/11/60	1860-1861	Lincoln	A
John F. Kinney	Chief Justice	6/27/60	1860-1863	Lincoln	F
H. R. Crosbie	Assoc. Justice	8/1/60	1860-1861	Lincoln	A
Thomas J. Drake	Assoc. Justice	2/3/62	1862	Lincoln	A
Charles B. Waite	Assoc. Justice	2/3/62	1862	Lincoln	A
John Titus	Chief Justice	5/6/63	1863	Lincoln	F
Solomon P. McCurdy	Assoc. Justice	4/21/64	1864-1868	Lincoln	N
Charles C. Wilson	Chief Justice	7/25/68	1868-1870	Johnson	F
Enos D. Hoge	Assoc. Justice	7/27/68	1868-1869	Johnson	N
Obed F. Strickland	Assoc. Justice	4/5/69	1869-1873	Grant	A
Cyrus M. Hawley	Assoc. Justice	4/19/69	1869-1873	Grant	A
James B. McKean	Chief Justice	6/17/70	1870-1875	Grant	A
Philip H. Emerson	Assoc. Justice	3/10/73	1873	Grant	
Jacob S. Boreman	Assoc. Justice	3/20/73	1873-1880	Grant	A
David P. Lowe	Chief Justice	3/19/75	1875-1875	Grant	
Alexander White	Chief Justice	9/11/75	1875	Grant	
John M. Cogland	Assoc. Justice	3/28/76	1876		
Michael Shaeffer	Chief Justice	4/20/76	1876	Grant	
John A. Hunter		7/1/79	1879	Hayes	
Stephen P. Twiss	Assoc. Justice	12/3/80	1880	Hayes	
Philip H. Emerson	Assoc. Justice	5/16/81	1881	Garfield	
Charles S. Zane	Chief Justice	9/1/84	1884-1888	Arthur	A
Jacob S. Boreman	Assoc. Justice	1/7/85	1885	Arthur	A
Orlando W. Powers	Assoc. Justice	4/20/85	1885-1886	Cleveland	
Henry P. Henderson	Assoc. Justice	8/2/86	1886	Cleveland	
John W. Judd	Assoc. Justice	7/19/88	1888	Cleveland	
Elliot Sandford	Chief Justice	7/20/88	1888	Cleveland	N
Thomas J. Anderson	Assoc. Justice	2/11/89	1889	Cleveland	A
John W. Blackburn	Assoc. Justice	10/11/89	1889	Harrison	
Charles S. Zane	Chief Justice	1/7/90	1890	Harrison	A&F*

*Charles S. Zane was one of those few men who were antagonistic to the Saints because he sincerely wanted to do away with "polygamy." After the Manifesto he cooperated with the people and became the first chief justice of the State Supreme Court.

James A. Miner	Assoc. Justice	8/2/90		
George W. Bartch		1/3/93	1893-1896	Harrison
Harvey W. Smith		5/8/93	1893-1895	Cleveland
Samuel A. Merrit		1/17/94	1894-1896	Cleveland
William H. King		8/2/94	1894-1896	Cleveland
Henry H. Rolapp		11/30/95	1895-1896	Cleveland

Representatives in Congress During Territorial Status for Utah

These men were actually called Delegates. A delegate was a representative from a territory who had a seat in the U.S. House of Representatives, where he was allowed to speak but not allowed to vote.

These delegates were elected by the people or appointed by their legislature.

Name	Period Served
Dr. John M. Bernhisel	1850-1859
W. H. Hooper	1859-1861
Dr. John M. Bernhisel	1861-1863
John F. Kinney	1863-1865
W. H. Hooper	1865-1873
George Q. Cannon	1873-1882
John T. Caine	1883-1893
Frank J. Cannon	1893-1896

Presidents of the United States from Arrival of the Saints in the Great Basin Until Attainment of Statehood for Utah

Name	Political Party	Period of Service	Attitude
James K. Polk	Demo.	1845-1849	F
Zachary Taylor	Whig	1849-1850	A
Millard Fillmore	Whig	1850-1853	F
Franklin Pierce	Demo.	1853-1857	N
James Buchanan	Demo.	1857-1861	A&N*
Abraham Lincoln	Rep.	1861-1865	F
Andrew Johnson	Rep.	1865-1869	F
Ulysses S. Grant	Rep.	1869-1877	A
Rutherford B. Hayes	Rep.	1877-1881	A
James A. Garfield	Rep.	1881-1881	
Chester A. Arthur	Rep.	1881-1885	A
Grover Cleveland	Demo.	1885-1889	N
Benjamin Harrison	Rep.	1889-1893	A
Grover Cleveland	Demo.	1893-1897	N

*After the entrance of Johnston's Army into the Salt Lake valley President Buchanan became more conciliatory.

Appendix 10

SOME CENTENNIAL STATISTICS, 1930

**Living members of the Church at the end
of the First Century**   700,000

Temples erected—nine, of which eight were ordinance
temples, with seven in use.

Stakes of Zion   104

Total wards and branches in
stakes of Zion   1,032

Missions   29

Mission branches   800

**Statistics for 1929, the last full year of
the first century were:**

Children blessed   19,071

Children baptized in stakes
and missions   15,468

Converts baptized in stakes
and missions   6,511

Total baptisms   21,979

Total missionaries in foreign missions	2,226
Stake missionaries	903
Missionaries who received training in mission home during past year	942
Persons recommended to the temples	68,573
Birth rate	29 per 1,000
Marriage rate	14.5 per 1,000
Death rate	7.8 per 1,000
Families owning their own homes	70%
Money spent from tithes for education	918,000.00

The totals of Temple Ordinances performed from the beginning in 1842, to the end of the first century of the Church's existence (Dec. 31, 1929) were given as:

	Living	Dead
Baptisms		6,973,367
Endowments	239,022	4,449,670
Ordinations, Elders	3,310	1,822,119
Sealing, wives to husbands	119,263	640,977
Children sealed	98,899	1,009,038
Adoptions	2,507	14,693
Special Ordinances	14,771	6,205
	477,772	14,916,069

Appendix 11

STAFF OF CHURCH EDUCATIONAL SYSTEM

Neal A. Maxwell, Commissioner

Joe J. Christensen, Associate Commissioner for Seminaries and Institutes

Dee F. Andersen, Associate Commissioner for Colleges and Schools

Kenneth H. Beesley, Associate Commissioner for Colleges and Schools

Dallin H. Oaks, President, Brigham Young University

Henry B. Eyring, Jr., President, Ricks College

Stephen L. Brower, President, Church College of Hawaii

R. Ferris Kirkham, President, LDS Business College

Keith R. Oakes, Administrator, Elementary and Secondary Schools

Frank D. Day, Assistant Administrator, Seminaries and Institutes

Dan J. Workman, Assistant Administrator, Seminaries and Institutes

Frank M. Bradshaw, Assistant Administrator, Seminaries and Institutes

South America:

Chile	5 Elementary 1 Secondary
Bolivia	1 Elementary
Peru	1 Elementary
Paraguay	1 Elementary — opened February 1972
Mexico:	35 Elementary 3 Secondary
	1 Prep (University Prep) 1 Normal (Teacher Training)
American Samoa:	1 Secondary
New Zealand:	1 Secondary
Tahiti:	1 Elementary
Tonga:	1 Secondary 1 Elementary 9 Middle (Jr. High) grades 6-8
Fiji:	1 Elementary
Western Samoa:	1 Secondary 8 Elementary
Total Schools	72
Approximately	16,000 students
Approximately	1,200 employees

Seminaries and Institutes

Neal A. Maxwell, Commissioner of Education
Joe J. Christensen, Associate Commissioner
Frank D. Day, Assistant Administrator
Dan J. Workman, Assistant Administrator
Frank M. Bradshaw, Assistant Administrator

Appendix 12

STATISTICAL SUMMARY OF WORLD MEMBERSHIP
OF THE CHURCH OF JESUS CHRIST OF
LATTER-DAY SAINTS FOR 1971

Stakes	2,268,696
Missions	445,534
Sub-total	2,714,230
Lost and Unknown	344,266
In Transit	32,457
Grand Total	3,090,953

Church Growth During 1971

Children Blessed in Stakes	60,616
Children Blessed in Missions	8,043
Children Not Blessed in Stakes	5,886
Children Not Blessed in Missions	2,822
Children of Record Baptized in Stakes	48,458
Children of Record Baptized in Missions	5,066
Converts Baptized in Stakes	46,760
Converts Baptized in Missions	36,754

Social Statistics
(Based on 1971 data from the Stakes)

Birth Rate per 1,000	28.50
Number of Persons Married per 1,000	15.12
Death Rate per 1,000	4.92

State or Country	Stake	Mission	Total
Alabama	7,586		7,586
Alaska	4,496	2,134	6,630
Arizona	100,308	6,015	106,323
Arkansas	3,263	1,275	4,538
California	365,343	2,178	367,521
Colorado	38,076	180	38,256
Connecticut	3,533		3,533
Delaware	1,149		1,149
Florida	24,414		24,414
Georgia	11,728	2,228	13,956
Hawaii	21,419	3,795	25,214
Idaho	193,264	141	193,405
Illinois	13,785	2,514	16,299
Indiana	9,957	2,229	12,186
Iowa	5,471	184	5,655
Kansas	5,838	939	6,777
Kentucky	4,018	6,617	10,635
Louisiana	7,993		7,993
Maine	3,272	399	3,671
Maryland	8,350	115	8,465
Massachusetts	5,071		5,071
Michigan	13,064	370	13,434
Minnesota	4,484	2,793	7,277
Mississippi	6,079		6,079
Missouri	9,489	1,965	11,454
Montana	19,781	3,066	22,847
Nebraska	3,701	1,366	5,067
Nevada	47,269		47,269
New Hampshire	2,019		2,019
New Jersey	6,192		6,192
New Mexico	17,282	4,561	21,843
New York	15,225	747	15,972
North Carolina	12,009	3,038	15,047
North Dakota		2,026	2,026
Ohio	17,110	590	17,700
Oklahoma	8,429	359	8,788
Oregon	57,644	1,534	59,178
Pennsylvania	8,003	3,077	11,080
Rhode Island	904		904
South Carolina	9,888	1,265	11,153
South Dakota	3,282		3,282
Tennessee	3,970	3,355	7,325
Texas	39,959	2,555	42,514
Utah	789,419		789,419
Vermont		1,744	1,744
Virginia	17,036	2,720	19,756
Washington	65,458	651	66,109
Washington, D.C.	5,101		5,101
West Virginia	3,230	5,992	9,222
Wisconsin	3,633	1,407	5,040
Wyoming	28,561	393	28,954

Canada	37,350	21,333	58,683	643
Alberta	18,427	1,926	20,353	
British Columbia	3,919	7,234	11,153	
Manitoba		1,067	1,067	
New Brunswick		633	633	
Newfoundland		200	200	
Northwest Territory		12	12	
Nova Scotia		1,155	1,155	
Ontario	9,625	5,949	15,574	
Quebec		1,226	1,226	
Saskatchewan		1,847	1,847	
Yukon		84	84	
Cuba		26	26	
Bermuda		44	44	
Mexico	19,617	61,707	81,324	
Central America	4,894	27,590	32,484	
Costa Rica		2,680	2,680	
El Salvador		9,518	9,518	
Guatemala	4,894	8,346	13,240	
Honduras		4,031	4,031	
Nicaragua		1,407	1,407	
Panama		947	947	
Puerto Rico		661	661	
South America	32,686	85,688	118,374	
Argentina	4,594	19,035	23,629	
Bolivia		3,303	3,303	
Brazil	16,197	19,581	35,778	
Chile		19,692	19,692	
Colombia		3,394	3,394	
Equador		1,452	1,452	
Paraguay		763	763	
Peru	4,521	8,234	12,755	
Uruguay	7,374	8,975	16,349	
Venezuela		1,259	1,259	
Great Britain	31,076	40,339	71,415	
England	27,617	24,867	52,484	
Ireland		4,023	4,023	
Scotland	3,459	8,276	11,735	
Wales		3,173	3,173	
Europe	14,111	38,754	52,865	
Austria		2,666	2,666	
Belgium		3,357	3,357	
France		9,514	9,514	
Germany	8,389	14,659	23,048	
Greece		14	14	
Iceland		-	-	
Italy		1,788	1,788	
Luxemborg		-	-	
Netherlands	3,317	3,785	7,102	
Poland		-	-	
Portugal		-	-	
Spain		828	828	
Switzerland	2,405	2,143	4,548	

644 Scandinavia		15,155	15,155
Denmark		4,040	4,040
Finland		3,034	3,034
Norway		3,044	3,044
Sweden		5,037	5,037
Africa	3,128	3,256	6,384
Ethiopia		89	89
Kenya		104	104
Rhodesia		345	345
South Africa	3,128	2,718	5,846
Zambia		-	-
Asia	5,018	39,036	44,054
Afghanistan		27	27
Formosa (Taiwan)		5,080	5,080
Hong Kong		3,419	3,419
Iran		156	156
Japan	4,468	11,559	16,027
Korea		5,165	5,165
Lebanon		348	348
Malaya		395	395
Marinnas Island		-	-
Okinawa		1,449	1,449
Philippines	550	9,222	9,772
Thailand		560	560
Turkey		42	42
Burma		-	-
India		206	206
Indonesia		102	102
Pakistan		-	-
Vietnam		1,246	1,246
South Pacific	68,043	32,307	100,350
Australia	17,842	6,900	24,742
Cook Islands		1,029	1,029
French Polynesia		4,750	4,750
New Calidonia		-	-
New Zealand	26,262	6,207	32,469
Samoan Islands	13,987	8,275	22,262
Tongan Islands	7,419	5,146	12,565

Population Totals

United States	2,133,072
All Other Countries	581,158
Sub Total	2,714,230
Lost and Unknown	344,266
In Transit	32,457
Grand Total	3,090,953

Above information is from "Statistical Compilation of Form E for 1971" (Salt Lake City: Church Archives).

Bibliography

Allen, James B., and Cowan, Richard O. *Mormonism in the Twentieth Century*. 2d. ed. Provo, Utah: Brigham Young University Press, 1967.

Appleby, W. I. "Judge Drummond Used Up." *Millennial Star* 19:401.

Arrington, Leonard J. *Great Basin Kingdom*. Cambridge, Mass.: Harvard University Press, 1958.

Arrington, Leonard J. "The Settlement of the Brigham Young Estate." *Pacific Historical Review* 21:1-20.

Ashton, Wendell J. "The Centennial Trek." *Improvement Era* 50(September 1947):580.

Auerbach, Herbert S., trans. "Father Escalante's Journal 1776-77," *Utah Historical Quarterly* (Utah State Historical Society, Salt Lake City) 11:1-132.

Backman, Milton V., Jr. *American Religions and the Rise of Mormonism*. Salt Lake City: Deseret Book Co., 1965.

Bailey, Paul. *The Gay Saint: a novel*. Hollywood: Murray & Gee, Inc., 1944.

Bailey, Paul. *Sam Brannan and the California Mormons*. Los Angeles: Westernlore Press, 1959.

646 Bancroft, Hubert Howe. *History of California.* 7 vols. San Francisco: History Co., Publishers, 1886.

Bancroft, Hubert Howe. *History of Utah.* 1890. Reprint. Salt Lake City: Bookcraft, 1964.

Barker, Clarence S. "From the Green Hills to Statuary Hall." *Improvement Era* 53(August 1950):630.

Barrett, Gwynn. "Walter Murray Gibson: The Sheperd Saint of Lanai Revisited." *Utah Historical Quarterly* (Utah State Historical Society, Salt Lake City) 40.

Barrett, Ivan J. "History of the Cotton Mission and Cotton Culture." Master's thesis, Brigham Young University, May 1947.

Beal, M. D. *A History of Southeastern Idaho.* Caldwell, Idaho: Caxton Printers, Ltd., 1942.

Berrett, William E. *The Restored Church.* 13th ed. Salt Lake City: Deseret News Press, 1965.

Berrett, William E., and Burton, Alma P. *Readings in L.D.S. Church History from Original Manuscripts.* 3 vols. Salt Lake City: Deseret Book Co., 1955.

Bowles, Samuel. *Across the Continent.* Springfield, Mass.: Samuel Bowles & Co.; New York: Hurd & Houghton, 1865.

Bowles, Samuel. *Our New West.* Hartford, Conn.: Hartford Publishing Co., 1869.

Brooks, Juanita. *The Mountain Meadow Massacre.* Norman: University of Oklahoma Press, 1962.

Brooks, Juanita, ed. *On the Mormon Frontier: The Diary of Hosea Stout.* 2 vols. Salt Lake City: University of Utah Press, 1964.

Burton, Richard F. *City of the Saints and Across the Rocky Mountains to California.* New York: Harper & Brothers, 1862.

Carson, David. *History of the Carson Family.* Lehi, Utah, 1952.

Carter, Kate B. *The Story of the Negro Pioneer.* Salt Lake City: Daughters of the Utah Pioneers, 1965.

Church Schools. Provo, Utah: Church of Jesus Christ of Latter- 647
day Saints, 1968.

Clark, James R. *Messages of the First Presidency.* 5 vols. Salt
Lake City: Bookcraft, 1965.

Clayton, William. *William Clayton's Journal: A Daily Record of
the Journey of the Original Company of "Mormon"
Pioneers from Nauvoo, Illinois, to the Valley of the
Great Salt Lake.* Salt Lake City: Deseret News, 1921.

Clemens, Samuel L., [Mark Twain]. *Roughing It.* 2 vols. New
York and London: Harper & Brothers, 1899.

*Conference Reports of the Church of Jesus Christ of Latter-day
Saints.* Salt Lake City: Church of Jesus Christ of Latter-
day Saints.

Conyers, Josiah B. *A Brief History of the Leading Causes of the
Hancock Mob, in the Year 1846.* St. Louis: Cathcart &
Prescott, 1846.

Cooke, Philip St. George. *Conquest of New Mexico and California.* Chicago: Rio Grande Press, 1964.

Cowan, Richard O. "A Review of Priesthood in the 1960's"
(n.p., n.d.).

Cowley, Matthias F. *Wilford Woodruff, Fourth President of the
Church of Jesus Christ of Latter-day Saints: History of
His Life and Labors as Recorded in His Daily Journals.*
Salt Lake City: Deseret News Press, 1909.

Creer, Leland Hargrave. *The Founding of an Empire.* Salt Lake
City: Bookcraft, 1947.

Creer, Leland Hargrave. *Utah and the Nation.* Seattle: University of Washington Press, 1929.

DeBow, J. D. B. *Statistical View of the United States, . . . being
a Compendium of the Seventh Census, . . . based upon
the schedules and other official sources of information.*
Washington, D.C.: A. O. P. Nicholson, Public Printer,
1854.

Department of the Army. *ROTCM no. 145-20: American Military History 1607-1958.* Washington, D.C.: U.S. Government Printing Office, July 1959.

648 Ferris, B. G. *The Mormons, Their Government, Customs and Prospects.* New York: Harper & Brothers, 1856.

Flanders, Robert Bruce. *Nauvoo: Kingdom on the Mississippi.* Urbana: University of Illinois Press, 1965.

Ford, Thomas. *A History of Illinois from Its Commencement as a State in 1818 to 1847.* Chicago: S. C. Griggs & Co., 1854.

Furniss, Norman F. *The Mormon Conflict.* New Haven, Conn.: Yale University Press, 1960.

Gates, Susa Young. *The Life Story of Brigham Young.* London: Jarrolds Publishers, 34 Paternoster Row E.C. 4, 1930.

Goeldner, Paul. *Utah Catalog American Buildings Survey.* Salt Lake City: Utah Heritage Foundation, 1969.

Grant, Carter E. *The Kingdom of God Restored.* Salt Lake City: Deseret Book Co., 1960.

Green, Doyle L., and Zobell, Albert L. "President David O. McKay Visits Europe." *Improvement Era* 55(September 1952):632.

Gregg, Thomas. *History of Hancock County, Illinois.* Chicago: Charles C. Chapman & Co., 1880.

Grow, Stewart. "A Historical Study of the Construction of the Salt Lake Tabernacle." Master's thesis, Brigham Young University, 1947.

Hafen, LeRoy R. *The Mountain Men and the Fur Trade of the Far West.* Glendale, Calif.: Arthur H. Clarke Co., 1965.

Hafen, LeRoy R. *Old Spanish Trail: Santa Fe to Los Angeles.* Glendale, Calif.: Arthur H. Clarke Co., 1954.

Hafen, LeRoy R., and Hafen, Ann W. *Documentary Account of the Utah Expedition.* The Far West and the Rockies Historical Series, vol. 8. Glendale, Calif.: Arthur H. Clarke Co., 1958.

Hafen, LeRoy R.; Hollon, W. Eugene; and Rister, Carl Coke. *Western America: the Exploration, Settlement and Development of the Region Beyond the Mississippi.* Englewood Cliffs, N. J.: Prentice-Hall, Inc., 1970.

Heslop, J.M., and Van Orden, Dell R. *Joseph Fielding Smith, A* 649 *Prophet Among the People.* Salt Lake City: Deseret Book Co., 1971.

Hughes, Raymond M., and Lancelot, William H. *Education— America's Magic.* Ames: Iowa State College Press, 1946.

Hunter, Milton R. *Brigham Young, the Colonizer.* Salt Lake City: Deseret News Press, 1940.

Hunter, Milton R. *Utah in Her Western Setting.* Salt Lake City: Deseret News Press, 1943.

Jackson, Donald, and Spence, Mary Lee. *The Expeditions of John Charles Fremont.* Urbana: University of Illinois Press, 1970.

Jenson, Andrew. *Church Chronology: A Record of Important Events Pertaining to the History of the Church of Jesus Christ of Latter-day Saints.* Salt Lake City: Deseret News Press, 1914.

Jenson, Andrew. "Day by Day with the Utah Pioneers." *Salt Lake Tribune,* 5 April 1947-24 July 1947.

Jenson, Andrew. *Latter-day Saint Biographical Encyclopedia.* 4 vols. Salt Lake City: Deseret News Press, 1936.

Journal of Discourses. 26 vols. 1854-86. Lithographic reprint. Salt Lake City, 1966.

Kimball, Solomon F. "President Brigham Young's First Trip to Bear Lake Valley." *Improvement Era* 10(February 1907):296.

Kingsbury, Ilene. "Salute to the Pony Express." *Utah Historical Quarterly* (Utah State Historical Society, Salt Lake City)28:131-34.

Larson, Gustive O. *The "Americanization" of Utah for State-hood.* San Marino, Calif.: Huntington Library, 1971.

Larson, Gustive O. *Outline History of Utah and the Mormons.* Salt Lake City: Deseret Book Co., 1961.

Larson, Gustive O. *Prelude to the Kingdom.* Francestown, N.H.: Marshall Jones Co., 1947.

Lee, John D. *Mormonism Unveiled.* St. Louis: Bryan, Brand, & Co., 1877.

650 Linn, William A. *The Story of the Mormons.* New York: Macmillan Co., 1902.

Lofthouse, Merrill. "A History of the Genealogical Society of the Church of Jesus Christ of Latter-day Saints to 1970." Master's thesis, Brigham Young University, May 1971.

Lundwall, N. B., comp. *Exodus of Modern Israel.* Salt Lake City: N. B. Lundwall, n.d.

Lundwall, N. B. *Temples of the Most High.* Salt Lake City: Bookcraft, 1966.

McConkie, Joseph F. *True and Faithful.* Salt Lake City: Bookcraft, 1971.

McGhie, Frank W. "The Life and Intrigues of Walter Murray Gibson." Master's thesis, Brigham Young University, June 1958.

McKay, Llewellyn R. *Home Memories of President David O. McKay.* Salt Lake City: Deseret Book Co., 1956.

Maughan, Ila Fisher. *Pioneer Theatre in the Desert.* Salt Lake City: Deseret Book Co., 1961.

Meeks, Priddy. "Journal of Priddy Meeks." *Utah Historical Quarterly* (Utah State Historical Society, Salt Lake City)10:145-223.

Miller, David E. "Peter Skene Ogden's Journal of His Expedition to Utah, 1825." *Utah Historical Quarterly* (Utah State Historical Society, Salt Lake City)20:159-86.

The Mormon Battalion and Its Monument. Salt Lake City: The State of Utah Mormon Battalion Committee, 1916.

Morgan, Dale L. "The State of Deseret." *Utah Historical Quarterly* (Utah State Historical Society, Salt Lake City)8:65-239.

Morgan Dale L., and Wheat, Carl I. *Jedediah Smith and his Maps of the American West.* San Francisco: California Historical Society, 1954.

Morrell, Jeanette McKay. *Highlights in the Life of President David O. McKay.* Salt Lake City: Deseret Book Co., 1966.

Morris, Joseph. *The "Spirit Prevails"*. San Francisco: George S.
Dove & Co., 1886.

Nebeker, John. "Early Justice in Utah." *Utah Historical Quarterly* (Utah State Historical Society, Salt Lake City)18:87-89.

Neff, Andrew Love. *History of Utah*. Salt Lake City: Deseret News Press, 1940.

Newhall, John B. *A Glimpse of Iowa in 1846*. 1846. Reprint. Iowa City: State Historical Society of Iowa, 1957.

Nibley, Preston. *Brigham Young, the Man and His Works*. Salt Lake City: Deseret News Press, 1937.

Nibley, Preston. *The Presidents of the Church*. Salt Lake City: Deseret Book Co., 1941.

Nicholson, John. *The Martyrdom of Joseph Standing*. Salt Lake City: Deseret News Co., 1886.

Pratt, Parley P. *Autobiography of Parley Parker Pratt*. 6th ed. Salt Lake City: Deseret Book Co., 1964.

Provo, Utah. Brigham Young University Library. "A Concise History of the Mormon Battalion in the Mexican War" [by Daniel Tyler].

Provo, Utah. Brigham Young University Library. Family Record [by William H. Snyder].

Provo, Utah. Brigham Young University Library. The Life of Joseph Holbrook.

Pyper, George D. *The Romance of an Old Playhouse*. Salt Lake City: Deseret News Press, 1937.

Remy, Jules, and Brenchley, Julius. "A Journey to Salt Lake City." London: n.p., 1861.

Rich, Russell R. *Land of the Sky-Blue Water*. Provo, Utah: Brigham Young University Press, September 1963.

Rich, Russell R. *Those Who Would Be Leaders*. 2d. ed. Provo, Utah: Brigham Young University Extension Publications, May 1967.

Roberts, Brigham Henry. *A Comprehensive History of the*

Church of Jesus Christ of Latter-day Saints. 6 vols. Salt Lake City: Deseret News Press, 1930.

Roberts, Brigham Henry. *Life of John Taylor.* Salt Lake City: Bookcraft, 1963.

Roberts, Brigham Henry. *The Rise and Fall of Nauvoo.* Salt Lake City: Bookcraft, 1965.

Romney, Thomas C. *The Life of Lorenzo Snow.* Salt Lake City: Deseret News Press, 1955.

Salt Lake City. Church Historical Department. Journal [by Wandell Mace].

Salt Lake City. Church Historical Department. Journal History of the Church of Jesus Christ of Latter-day Saints.

Salt Lake City. Church Historical Department. Journal [by Wilford Woodruff].

Salt Lake City. Church Historical Department. Manuscript History of Brigham Young.

Scott, Reva. *Samuel Brannan and the Golden Fleece.* New York: Macmillan Co., 1944.

Smith, Eliza R. Snow. *Biography and Family Record of Lorenzo Snow.* Salt Lake City: Deseret News Co., Printers, 1884.

Smith, George Albert. "After Eighty Years." *Improvement Era* 53(April 1950):263.

Smith, Joseph. *History of the Church of Jesus Christ of Latter-day Saints.* Edited by Brigham Henry Roberts. 7 vols. Salt Lake City: Deseret News Press, 1964.

Smith, Joseph Fielding. *Essentials in Church History.* 22d ed., enlarged. Salt Lake City: Deseret Book Co., 1967.

Smith, Joseph Fielding. *Life of Joseph F. Smith.* Salt Lake City: Deseret News Press, 1938.

Snow, Le Roi C. "An Experience of My Father's." *Improvement Era* 36(September 1933):677.

Snow, Le Roi C. "Raised from the Dead." *Improvement Era* 32(September 1929):881.

Stegner, Wallace. *Mormon Country.* New York: Bonanza Books, 1942.

Stenhouse, T. B. H. *The Rocky Mountain Saints*. New York: D. 653
Appleton & Co., 1873.

Stone, Irving. *Men to Match My Mountains*. Garden City, New York: Doubleday & Co., 1956.

Stowers, Robert E., and Ellis, John M., eds. "Charles A. Scott's Diary of the Utah Expedition, 1857-1861." *Utah Historical Quarterly* (Utah State Historical Society, Salt Lake City)28:155-76.

Sullivan, Maurice S. *The Travels of Jedediah Smith, a Documentary Outline, including the Journal of the Great American Pathfinder*. Santa Ana, Calif.: Fine Arts Press, 1934.

Talmage, James E. *The House of the Lord*. Salt Lake City: Bookcraft, 1962.

Tullidge, Edward W. *History of Salt Lake City*. Salt Lake City: Star Publishing Co., 1886.

Tullidge, Edward W. "Life of Brigham Young: or, Utah and Her Founders." New York: n.p., 1876.

Tullidge, Edward W. *Women of Mormondom*. 1877. Lithographic reprint. Salt Lake City, 1957.

United States, Congress. *Congressional Globe*. 32d Cong., 1st sess., Appendix:92.

United States, Congress. *House Executive Documents*. 35th Cong., 1st sess., vol. 10.

Utley, Robert Marshall. *Special Report on Promontory Summit, Utah*. Santa Fe, N. Mex.: U.S. Department of the Interior, National Park Service Region Three, February 1960.

Vaux. "The Echo Canyon War." *The Contributor* 3(March 1882)6:177-79.

Waite, Catherine V. *The Mormon Prophet and his Harem: an authentic history of Brigham Young, his numerous wives and children*. Cambridge, Mass.: Riverside Press, 1866.

Whitman, Charles W. "A History of the Hill Cumorah Pageant (1937-1964) and an Examination of the Dramatic Development of the Text of America's Witness for Christ." Ph.D. dissertation, University of Minnesota, 1967.

654 Whitney, Orson F. *History of Utah.* 4 vols. Salt Lake City: George Q. Cannon & Sons Co., 1904.

Whitney, Orson F. *Popular History of Utah.* Salt Lake City: Deseret News Press, 1916.

Widtsoe, John A., and Evans, Richard L. "The Educational Level of the Latter-day Saints." *Improvement Era* 50(July 1947):444.

Woodruff, Wilford. *Leaves From My Journal.* Salt Lake City: Juvenile Instructor Office, 1882.

Young, John R. *Memoirs of John R. Young, Utah Pioneer, 1847.* Salt Lake City: Deseret News Press, 1920.

Young, S. Dilworth. *"Here is Brigham. . .": Brigham Young, the Years to 1844.* Salt Lake City: Bookcraft, 1964.

Index

A

Abrahms, Levi, 221
Adams, Barnabas L., 109
Agnew, Joseph, 47
Aiden, William, 240
Alberta Temple, 479, 495
Alexander, E. B., 235, 244, 249, 253-55, 256
Allen, James
   enlists Mormon Battalion, 57
   at Council Bluffs, 59
   death of, 66
Allen, Rufus, 102
Allred, James, 17
American Party, 475
"America's Witness for Christ," 569-71
Anderson, Capt., 43
Anderson, Dee, 581
Anderson, May, 529
Anderson, Nephi, 537.
Anderson, Thomas J., 383
Angel, Truman O., 308
Anti-Bigamy Law (1862)
   passage of, 366-68

and Brigham Young's estate, 395-96
Anti-Mormon crusade (1877), 401-5
Apostolic Presidency, 401
Appleby, W. I., 29, 611
Arizona Temple, 495-96
Artega, Silviano, 405
Arthur, Chester A., 384
Arze, Mauricio, 151
Ashley Bill, 370-71
Ashley, James M., 368
Ashton, Marvin J., 541, 596, 599
Atchison, David R., 100
Auerbach, Herbert, 516
Axtell, Samuel B., 377

B

Babbitt, Almon W., 3, 44
   elected delegate to Washington, 186
   arrives in Utah, 192
   delivers mail, 209

sent to South America, 351
preaches to John Taylor, 411
sent with John Taylor to
England, 414
sends Joseph F. Smith to
Hawaii, 464
Priesthood, auxiliaries to, 591-92
Priesthood correlation, 536-41
announcement of, 538
organization of, 538-41
expansion of in 1969, 541
Primary Children's Hospital, 529-30
Promised Valley, 514
Promontory Point, 324-25
Provo Temple, 536, 558-59
Provost, Etienne, 151
Puryear, W. C., 530

Q

Quail, 46
Quincy Committee
proposal of, at Nauvoo, 35-36
peace terms of, 43-44
Queen Elizabeth II, 531
Queen Juliana, 531

R

Railroad
and Mormon Church, 319
transcontinental approved,
320-21
Mormons employed by, 322
joined at Promontory Summit,
324-26
payment of contractors, 326-27
to Salt Lake City, 327
changes brought by, 327-29
Rankin, Capt., 250
Rappleye, Tunis, 162
Rawlins, Joseph, 388
Ray, Mrs. John, 238
Redding, Jackson, 109
Reed-Donner Party, 136, 155-56

Reed, Amos, 297
Reed, Lazarus H., 197-98, 200
Regional Representatives, 540-41
Relief Society, 330, 591
Remy, Jules, 207-8, 220
Reno, Jesse Lee, 235
Reorganized Church of Jesus Christ
of Latter Day Saints, 301-2
Republican Party (1856), 224
Retrenchment Society. See Young
Women's Mutual Improvement
Association
Revenue Cutter, 104-6, 131
Reynolds, Ethel, 553
Reynolds, George, 378
Reynolds Polygamy Test Case,
377-78
Rhodacanaty, Platino C., 405
Rice, L. L., 468
Rich, Charles C., 5, 14-15, 17
as counselor at Mt. Pisgah, 20
number in company of, 166
as counselor in Salt Lake Stake,
168, 179
leads settlement to Bear Lake
Valley, 314, 346
as apostle under Brigham Young,
345
sent to San Bernardino, 347-48
sent to Pacific Islands, 351
at Jubilee, 410
Rich, Thomas, 252
Richards, Franklin D., 322
appears in court, 272
as apostle under Brigham Young,
345, 348
on auditing committee, 396
at Jubilee, 410
with Lorenzo Snow on mission,
443
attends conference at new Tabernacle in Provo, 447
sustained as President of Twelve,
452
Richards, LeGrand, 532
Richards, Samuel W., 232
Richards, Sarah Ann, 442
Richards, Sarah Ellen, 466
Richards, Mrs. Silas, 220

676   fears of Saints, 246
       martial law declared, 248
       supply trains burned, 250-52
       salt sent to U.S. Army, 257
       memorials to Buchanan and
          Congress, 257-58
       and Thomas L. Kane, 258-59
       Saints move south, 259
       criticism of administration, 260
       peace commissioners, 260-62
       Saints return home, 263-64
       problems caused by soldiers,
          268-70
       peace commission upheld,
          272-73
       cost of Utah Expedition, 287
    *Utah Genealogical and Historical
       Society Magazine*, 555

V

Valparaiso, 30
Van Cott, John, 180
Van Vliet, Stewart, in Utah as an
   observer, 237, 245-48
Van Zile, Philip T., 381
Vance, John, 168, 179
Varian, Charles, 387
Voorhees Bill, 373
Voz del Desierto, 405

W

Wade Bill, 368
Wade, J. H., 292
Wadsworth, Henry, 487
Waite, Catharine, 201
Waite, Charles B., 201, 296, 301,
   368, 371
Walker, Hensan, 145
Walker, Joseph, 155
Walker, Lucy, 365
Walker, Major, 67
Walker, William, 351

Wall, William, 264
Wallace, George B., 166
Wardsworth, William, 145
Warren, William B., 36-39
Washakie, Chief, 446
Watt, George D., 346
Webster, Daniel, 197
Welcken, August H. F., 406
Welfare Plan
   beginning of, 500-501
   structure of, 593-95
Wells Fargo, 487
Wells, Junius F., 476-78
Wells, Daniel H.
   as defender of Nauvoo, 46
   as attorney general, 182
   as chief justice of Deseret, 191
   as commander of Nauvoo
      Legion, 231
   announces army, 231, 243
   as general in Utah War, 248-56
   appears in court, 272
   goes to southern Utah to over-
      see expansion, 313
   speaks at Brigham Young's
      funeral, 359
   as counselor to Twelve, 394
Wells, Heber M., 389, 436
Wendell, Charles, 351
West, Caleb W., 381
West, Chauncy, 322
Whipping post, 180
Whipple, Edson, 108
   on high council, 168, 179
Whitingham, Vermont, 520
Whitmer, David, visited by Joseph
   F. Smith, 467
Whitmer, Jacob, 467
Whitney, Newel K., 3, 15, 165
   as treasurer State of Deseret,
      182
Widtsoe, John A., 532
Wight, Lyman, 99-100
Wilcken, Charles H., 287
Willey, David O., Jr., 537
Williams, Joseph, 570
Williams, Thomas, 22
Willis, Wesley, 162